WEB DESIGN

IN A NUTSHELL

Third Edition

Jennifer Niederst Robbins

Beijing • Cambridge • Farnham • Köln • Paris • Sebastopol • Taipei • Tokyo

Web Design in a Nutshell, Third Edition
by Jennifer Niederst Robbins

Published by O'Reilly Media, Inc., 1005 Gravenstein Highway North, Sebastopol, CA 95472.

O'Reilly books may be purchased for educational, business, or sales promotional use. Online editions are also available for most titles (*safari.oreilly.com*). For more information, contact our corporate/institutional sales department: (800) 998-9938 or *corporate@oreilly.com*.

Editor: Steve Weiss
Developmental Editor: Linda Laflamme
Technical Editors: Tantek Çelik and
 Molly E. Holzschlag
Production Editor: Mary Brady
Copyeditor: Linley Dolby

Proofreader: Sada Preisch
Indexer: Lucie Haskins
Cover Designer: Edie Freedman
Interior Designer: David Futato
Cover Illustrator: Lorrie LeJeune
Illustrator: Christopher Reilley

Printing History:

January 1999:	First Edition.
September 2001:	Second Edition.
February 2006:	Third Edition.

 This book uses RepKover™, a durable and flexible lay-flat binding.

ISBN-10: 0-596-00987-9
ISBN-13: 978-0-596-00987-8
[M]   [03/07]

Table of Contents

Part II. The Structural Layer: XML and (X)HTML

Part III.   The Presentation Layer: Cascading Style Sheets

Part IV. The Behavioral Layer: JavaScript and the DOM

Part V. Web Graphics

Foreword

I recall sitting at my desk many years ago, struggling with a piece of HTML markup, when someone walked by and dropped off a floppy disk. Written in block letters across the label was "Netscape .9b"—a pre-release beta version of what would soon become the most widely used browser of that time. I installed it and clicked around my company's web site, and I remember thinking to myself, "Huh. My job just completely changed."

Up to that point in the nascent history of the World Wide Web, there had really been only one browser to worry about. Nearly everyone used Mosaic, and as long as my pages were also functional in a text-only browser like Lynx, I could safely forget about that aspect of web design. But suddenly there was competition. And with competition came new concerns about rendering, feature support, and bugs.

That would prove to be one of innumerable watershed events in more than a decade of growth and evolution of the Web as a world-changing technological platform. Soon after Netscape shipped its browser, my job would completely change over and over again. First came fonts and colors; then frames, JavaScript, database-driven dynamic web applications, XML, Cascading Style Sheets, Flash, semantic markup—and all of those innovations have iterated through countless new versions. If there's one thing that is certain in the life of a web designer, it's that every day something you thought you knew will change. And then change again.

Yet in any journey—whether literal or metaphorical—it pays to occasionally find a vantage point and take stock of where you've been and how far you have to go. We've come a long way on the Web, but we also have so much more to learn.

The earliest days of the Web were the domain of the webmaster. At that time, the Web was viewed as another service provided as technical infrastructure—much like the email server or firewall. The webmaster's duties included maintaining the HTTP server, keeping things secure, monitoring bandwidth usage, and—oh, yeah—creating the HTML pages for this new service. Web design back then was simply the output of a web server. And the IT department found itself in the position of building pages and even occasionally using Photoshop. Those were crazy times.

By the mid '90s, the Web had moved from IT to marketing. Every company needed a web site if they expected to survive, and there was a mad scramble to develop an "interactive strategy." This was the era of the transitional web designer—when people with experience in more traditional media design came to the Web and tried to bend it to fit. No control of typography? Build the whole page as an image. Page layout not up to our standards? We'll hack on tables and invisible GIFs until things look exactly like they should. The Web didn't respond very well to this onslaught. The cornerstones of digital design—usability, content reuse, accessibility—buckled under the hubris of graphic artists.

But today holds both tremendous opportunity and significant trepidation for those who call themselves web designers. The legacy of the so-called "Browser Wars" is behind us; we have a strong and stable platform for building with increasing sophistication. A foundation of accepted and well-implemented industry standards offers a constancy we once could only dream of. But at the same time, the Web has factions of innovation racing off in countless directions. Good designers now worry as much about semantics, device-agnosticism, and Ajax-style interactions as they do about color, typography, and layout. It is an understandably intimidating time.

The weight of this book in your hands is a testimony to that complexity. And if it seems daunting, at least take comfort in the fact that the author could not possibly be a more capable guide. Jennifer Robbins has been designing web sites longer than anyone else I know. For years she has been the one we've all turned to for reassurance and clarity as our industry propels itself into the future.

There is nobody I would trust more than Jennifer to show us where we've been, and where we're heading next. You should, too.

—Jeffrey Veen
December 2005, San Francisco

Contributors

Tantek Çelik

Tantek Çelik contributed Appendix E, *Microformats: Extending (X)HTML*. He is also a Lead Technical Editor for this book. His bio is listed on the Technical Reviewers page.

Derek Featherstone

Derek is a well-known instructor, speaker, and developer with expertise in web accessibility consulting and training. He advises many government agencies, educational institutions, and private sector companies, providing them with expert accessibility testing, and review and recommendations for improving the accessibility of their web sites to all people. As a member of the Web Standards Project (*webstandards.org*), Derek serves on two task forces: Accessibility/Assistive Devices and DOM Scripting. He is a dedicated advocate for standards that ensure simple, affordable access to web technologies for all. Derek wrote Chapter 5, *Accessibility*.

Aaron Gustafson

Aaron Gustafson has been working on the Web since 1996, plying his trade for many top companies including Delta Airlines, Gartner, IBM, Konica Minolta, and the U.S. EPA. He is an advocate for web standards and open source languages, often writing on those topics and more for A List Apart, Digital Web Magazine, and on his blog, *easy-reader.net*. When not behind a desk, he can sometimes be found publicly preaching the web standards gospel alongside Molly E. Holzschlag. He and his wife, Kelly, reside in Connecticut, where he works as Sr. Web Designer/Developer for Cronin and Company. Aaron wrote Chapter 25, *Managing Browser Bugs: Workarounds, Hacks, and Filters*, Chapter 26, *Introduction to JavaScript*, and Chapter 27, *DOM Scripting*.

Todd Marks

Todd Marks is an avid developer, designer, instructor, author, and manager of information display technologies. In 2002, Todd founded MindGrub Technologies, LLC where he created Flash information display systems for clients such as Oracle, Zurich, and ARINC. Todd currently works as a Products Manager for the mediaEdge division of Exceptional Software, where he oversees development of Media Edge's training applications. Todd is a Macromedia Certified Developer, Designer, and Subject Matter Expert and has written and contributed to several books including *Flash MX Video* (Peer Information), *Beginning Dreamweaver MX 2004* (Wrox), *Advanced PHP for Flash MX* (Glasshaus), *Flash MX Most Wanted Components* (Friends of Ed), and other Dreamweaver and Flash-related titles. Todd wrote Chapter 35, *The Flash Platform*.

Technical Reviewers

Lead Technical Editors

Tantek Çelik

Tantek Çelik is Chief Technologist at Technorati (*www.technorati.com*) where he leads the design and development of new standards and technologies. Prior to Technorati, he was a veteran representative to the World Wide Web Consortium (W3C) for Microsoft, where he also helped lead the development of the award-winning Internet Explorer for Macintosh. As cofounder of the *microformats.org* community and the Global Multimedia Protocols Group (*gmpg.org*), as well as Steering Committee member of the Web Standards Project (WaSP, *www.webstandards.org*) and invited expert to the W3C Cascading Style Sheets working group, Tantek is dedicated to advancing open standards and simpler data formats for the Web.

Molly E. Holzschlag

Molly E. Holzschlag is a well-known web standards advocate, instructor, and author. She is Group Lead for the Web Standards Project (WaSP) and an invited expert to the GEO working group at the World Wide Web Consortium (W3C). Among her thirty-plus books is the recent *The Zen of CSS Design* (PeachPit Press, coauthored with Dave Shea. The book artfully showcases the most progressive *csszengarden.com* designs. A popular and colorful individual, you can catch up with Molly's blog at—where else?—*molly.com*.

Technical Reviewers

The following people also reviewed chapters and contributed their expertise to the final product: Bill Sanders (Part II and Chapter 35), Aaron Gustafson (Chapters 7 and 24), Jeremy Keith (Chapters 26 and 27), Jason Carlin (Chapters 16 and 24), Jeffrey Robbins (Chapter 33), and Matthew Klauschie (Chapter 34).

Preface

If you think you can take a web design book written in 2001 and "tweak" it for release in 2006, guess again. I know…I tried.

In my first draft of the XHTML chapters, I took the content from the last edition and just added some pointers to Cascading Style Sheet alternatives for font and a few other elements and attributes. After all (I figured), the (X)HTML Recommendations hadn't changed since 1999, right?

As it turned out, while I was busy doing things like designing corporate identities and having babies (just one baby, actually), a major sea change had taken place in the web design world. My little pointers to CSS alternatives amounted to "band-aids on a gaping wound," as so aptly noted by Molly Holzschlag in her tech review of those initial chapters. I had fallen out of step with contemporary web design, and I had some catching up to do.

I learned that while it was true that the Recommendation was the same, what *had* changed was how the professional web design community was using it. Designers were actually *complying* with the standards. They were no longer using (X)HTML as a design tool, but as a means of defining the meaning and structure of content. Cascading Style Sheets were no longer just something interesting to tinker with, but rather a reliable method for handling all matters of presentation, from fonts and colors to the layout of the entire page. That ideal notion of "keeping style separate from content" that I had been writing about for years had not only become a possibility, it had become a reality.

I spent the next several months immersing myself in the world of standards-driven web design: reading every book I could get my hands on, exploring oceans of online resources, and of course, poring over the details of the W3C (X)HTML and CSS Recommendations themselves.

As a result, *Web Design in a Nutshell* has not been tweaked; it has been transformed. The book now opens with an overview of web standards and the measurable advantages of designing standards-compliant sites. The (X)HTML chapters have all been rewritten from scratch, in a way that promotes the proper semantic use of each element and radically downplays presentational HTML and how elements are rendered by default in browsers. There are now 10 chapters on CSS (the prior edition had only one). Two new chapters on JavaScript and the DOM, written by Aaron Gustafson, treat these topics in a more detailed and useful manner than the previous editions ever offered.

All other sections of the book have been brought up to date as well, reflecting some significant advancements (such as approaches to accessibility, support for the PNG graphic format, and print-specific style sheets, to name a few) as well as minor shifts (such as the guidelines on web graphics and multimedia production) that have taken place since the last edition.

The tale of transformation does not end with the book. This author has been transformed as well. Knowing what I know now, I shudder when I look at that first draft of the book. I shudder more when I look at my sites with their layers of nested tables, spacer-GIFs, and meaningless markup. Am I ashamed? Not especially...I was no different from most other web designers in the late '90s. You have to learn sometime, and for me, writing this book was my wake-up call.

I suspect that for every new web designer who comes along who has never used a table for layout, there are many more like me who need to relearn their craft. That's to be expected in a medium as new and quickly evolving as the Web. I've written this book to be the definitive resource for designers who are onboard with standards-driven web design as well as those who are still making the transition.

Now, if you'll excuse me, I have some sites to redesign.

What's in the Book

This Nutshell book focuses on frontend matters of web design and development: markup, style sheets, image production, multimedia, and so on. Ironically, despite its title, there is little in the way of "design" advice, per se. Rather, it strives to be a thorough reference for all the technical details and requirements that we face in our day-to-day work designing and developing web content.

The book is divided into six parts (plus appendixes), each covering a general subject area.

Part I: The Web Environment

Chapter 1, *Web Standards*, describes the current approach to web design and sets the stage for the entire book. It is essential reading. Chapters on designing for varying browsers and displays provide useful overviews of the unique challenges web developers face. Chapter 5, *Accessibility*, and Chapter 6, *Internationalization*, both serve as introductions to the ways web content may be created to reach all users, regardless of ability, browsing device, or language. Chapter 4, *A Beginner's Guide to the Server*, is a primer on basic server functions, system commands, uploading files, and file types.

Part II: The Structural Layer: XML and (X)HTML

This part of the book is about document markup, commonly referred to as the *structural layer* because it provides the foundation upon which presentation (styles) and behaviors (scripting) are applied. I highly recommend starting with Chapter 7, *Introduction to XML*, as it covers critical concepts that guide the way (X)HTML is handled in contemporary web design. Chapters 8 through 15 focus on HTML and XHTML markup, including detailed descriptions of all the elements and the way they should be used in standards-based web design.

Part III: The Presentation Layer: Cascading Style Sheets

Part III provides a thorough guide to using CSS for controlling the presentation of web content with a focus on visual media. It begins with an overview of the fundamentals (Chapter 16) and an introduction to CSS selectors (Chapter 17). Chapters 18 through 23 provide detailed descriptions of all the visual properties in the CSS 2.1 specification. Finally, examples of how CSS is used in the real world are provided in *CSS Techniques* (Chapter 24) and *Managing Browser Bugs: Workarounds, Hacks, and Filters* (Chapter 25).

Part IV: The Behavioral Layer: JavaScript and the DOM

Part IV is all about adding interactivity to your pages with JavaScript. Chapter 26 is an introduction to JavaScript, covering, syntax, control structures, object-orientation, and the whys and hows of unobtrusive scripting. Chapter 27 introduces the Document Object Model and shows you how to tap into it to manipulate both content and design. As a supplement to Chapter 27, we've included a brief introduction to Ajax techniques that will help you on your way to building rich Internet applications.

Part V: Web Graphics

The chapters in Part V contain essential information on working with RGB color and choosing the appropriate graphic file formats. The chapters dedicated to GIF, JPEG, and PNG graphics offer practical tips for graphic production and optimization based on the compression schemes used by each format. The *Animated GIFs* chapter is a further examination of GIF's animation capabilities.

Part VI: Media

Because the Web is not limited to text and images, Part VI is included to provide a basic introduction to adding audio, video, and Flash movies to web pages. There is also a chapter on printing from web pages using print-specific CSS style sheets as well as an introduction to the PDF format for document distribution.

Appendixes

The Appendixes in this book are sure to get a lot of use. Appendix A is an alphabetical listing of all elements and attributes in the HTML 4.01 Recommendation, as well as a few nonstandard elements that are well supported and in common use. Appendix B is an alphabetical listing of all properties defined in the CSS 2.1 specification. Appendix C lists all the character entities defined in HTML 4.01 and XHTML 1.0 with their numerical references. Appendix D provides a detailed explanation of the color names and RGB color values used both in (X)HTML and CSS. Finally, Appendix E, contributed by Tantek Çelik, describes the future of XHTML and Microformats.

Using Code Examples

This book is here to help you get your job done. In general, you may use the code in this book in your programs and documentation. You do not need to contact O'Reilly for permission unless you're reproducing a significant portion of the code. For example, writing a program that uses several chunks of code from this book does not require permission. Selling or distributing a CD-ROM of examples from O'Reilly books does require permission. Answering a question by citing this book and quoting example code does not require permission. Incorporating a significant amount of example code from this book into your product's documentation does require permission.

We appreciate, but do not require, attribution. An attribution usually includes the title, author, publisher, and ISBN. For example: "*Web Design in a Nutshell*, by Jennifer Niederst Robbins. Copyright 2006 O'Reilly Media, Inc., 0-596-00987-9."

If you feel your use of code examples falls outside fair use or the permission given above, feel free to contact the publisher at *permissions@oreilly.com*.

Conventions Used in This Book

The following typographical conventions are used in this book:

Constant width

> Used to indicate code examples, code references in text (including tags, elements, variables, and so forth), and keyboard commands.

Constant width italic

> Used to indicate replaceable text in code.

Constant width bold

> Used to highlight the code that is being discussed.

Italic

> Used to indicate filenames, directory names, URLs, and glossary terms.

> This icon designates a tip, suggestion, or a general note that is an important aside to its nearby text.

> This icon designates a warning relating to the nearby text.

CSS Property Conventions

The CSS chapters in this book use the same syntax for indicating allowable property values that are used in the W3C CSS 2.1 Recommendation. A few examples are shown here:

```
Value: [<family-name>,]* <family-name>
Value: <uri> [ mix || repeat ]? | auto | none | inherit
Value: [ <border-style> || <border-width> || <border-color> ] | inherit
Value: [<color>|transparent]{1,4}|inherit
```

The notation indicates the value options and requirements, but it is not always intuitive. The various conventions are explained briefly here.

- Words that appear on their own (for example, inherit) are keyword values that must appear literally, without quotes.

- When punctuation such as commas and slashes (/) appear in the option, they must be used literally in the value as indicated.

- Words in brackets give a type of value (such as <color> and <uri>) or a reference to another property (as in <border-style>).

- If a vertical bar separates values (for example, X | Y | Z), then any one of them must occur.

- A double vertical bar (X || Y) means that X, Y, or both must occur, but they may appear in any order.

- Brackets ([...]) are for creating groups of values.

Every word or bracketed group may be followed by one of these modifiers:

- An asterisk (*) indicates the preceding value or group is repeated *zero* or more times.

- A plus (+) sign indicates that the preceding value or group is repeated *one* or more times.

- A question mark (?) indicates that the preceding value or group is optional.

- A pair of numbers in curly braces ({X,Y}) indicates that the preceding value or group is repeated at least X and at most Y times.

Given these syntax rules, the examples above would be interpreted like this:

Value: [<family-name>,]* <family-name>
The value may be a font family name, preceded by zero or more additional font family names, each followed by a comma.

Value: <uri> [mix || repeat]? | auto | none | inherit
The value may be one of the keyword options auto, none, and inherit, or it may be a URI followed (optionally) by the keywords mix, repeat, or both.

Value: [<border-style> || <border-width> || <border-color>] | inherit
The value may be the keyword inherit, or it may be any combination of values for border-style, border-width, and border-color, in any order.

Value: [<color>|transparent]{1,4}|inherit
The value may be the keyword inherit, or it may be one, two, three, or four "color" values. Each "color" value is provided as either the keyword transparent or one of the standard methods for specifying <color> (such as a color name or RGB value).

How to Contact Us

Please address comments and questions concerning this book to the publisher:

O'Reilly Media, Inc.
1005 Gravenstein Highway North
Sebastopol, CA 95472
(800) 998-9938 (in the United States or Canada)
(707) 829-0515 (international/local)
(707) 829-0104 (fax)

There is a web page for this book, which lists errata and additional information. You can access this page at:

http://www.oreilly.com/catalog/wdnut3/

To comment or ask technical questions about this book, send email to:

bookquestions@oreilly.com

For more information about books, conferences, software, Resource Centers, and the O'Reilly Network, see the O'Reilly web site at:

http://www.oreilly.com

Safari® Enabled

 When you see a Safari® Enabled icon on the cover of your favorite technology book, it means the book is available online through the O'Reilly Network Safari Bookshelf.

Safari offers a solution that's better than e-books. It's a virtual library that lets you easily search thousands of top tech books, cut and paste code samples, download chapters, and find quick answers when you need the most accurate, current information. Try it for free at *http://safari.oreilly.com*.

Acknowledgments

As always, this book is a product of the efforts of a small army of people. First, I want to thank my executive editor, Steve Weiss, who kept the big wheels rolling and bought me more time when life got in the way of deadlines. A standing ovation goes to Linda Laflamme, the developmental editor, who kept numerous plates spinning and went above and beyond the call of duty repeatedly without complaint. She was my ally and hero, and I could not have managed this book without her.

Next, I am thrilled to have had two of the most prominent experts and advocates in standards-based web design as technical editors of this edition. I owe heaps of gratitude to Molly Holzschlag, who is the one responsible for turning this ship around. She gave me a firm kick in the pants in the first round of reviews, but it was exactly what the book (and I) needed to get up to speed with contemporary thinking and terminology. I am also enormously grateful to Tantek Çelik for not only the "fine-toothed-comb" treatment he gave the chapters, but also for the positive support and the feeling that I could always rely on him for help. In my most defeated moments, that kept me going.

It's tough writing a book about everything, and I know when I'm out of my league. I consider myself very fortunate to have chapters contributed by some of the top experts in their respective fields. Thanks go to Derek Featherstone for bringing real-world experience and advice to his "Accessibility" chapter and to Todd Marks, a leading author on Flash and Dreamweaver for his solid chapter, "The Flash Platform" (Chapter 35). Last, but by no means least, I want to say a special and heartfelt thanks to Aaron Gustafson who gallantly and competently saved the day more than once. His three consecutive chapters (Chapter 25, *Managing Browser Bugs: Workarounds, Hacks, and Filters,"* Chapter 26, *Introduction to JavaScript,"* and Chapter 27, *DOM Scripting"*) are like an information-packed drum solo in the middle of the book. He also contributed by reviewing chapters and always being available to answer the "CSS question of the day."

Thanks also go to the other really smart people who applied their areas of expertise in reviewing miscellaneous chapters: Bill Sanders, for taking on Flash and all of Part II, Jeremy Keith for his careful review of the JavaScript and DOM chapters, Jason Carlin for reviewing CSS chapters and being my go-to guy for CSS information (as well as what music I should be listening to), and Matthew Klauschie, who knows more than a thing or two about video on the Web.

I want to acknowledge the fine help I received with the figures for this book. Travis Young created the streamlined CSS examples and screenshots for Chapters 18 through 23. A round of applause goes to illustrator Chris Reilley, who took my raw materials and spun them into gold. I've worked with Chris on all my books and am always impressed by his top-notch work.

Producing a book of this size is no small feat, and to do so in record time faced with rounds of later-than-last-minute changes is worthy of applause. Thanks go to my attentive copyeditor, Linley Dolby, and the rest of the production team for bearing with me and making the book look great.

I want to say thanks to Alan, Courtney, Dan, Danielle, Jessica, Jillian, Kate, Megan, Melanie, and the whole gang at Starbucks in Seekonk, MA for pouring the gallons of iced chai that fueled the writing of this edition and doing so in a way that made me feel at home. Thanks also to Jamie, Diane, Joanna, and the other women at Rumford Day Nursery for taking good care of my little boy so his mama could work overtime without worrying. And thank you Seekonk Public Library for getting wireless Internet.

As always, I'd like to thank my Mom, Dad, Liam, and Audrey for the boundless support and inspiration they each provide. Endless thanks and at least a few foot-rubs go to my husband, Jeff Robbins, who put up with a lot this year. I am fortunate to have a husband who will go into "Super-dad" mode to free up my evenings and weekends for writing. Jeff also updated Chapter 33, *Audio on the Web.* Finally, I thank my darling Arlo for the joy he brings me every single day and for reminding me of what is important.

—Jennifer Niederst Robbins
December 2005, Massachusetts

The Web Environment

Web Standards

A great sea change has taken place in web development in the last six or seven years (and since the last edition of this book). Standards compliance is the name of the game in web design these days. After years of browser competition, HTML hacking, and other practices born out of the lack of guiding principles, we are all finally recognizing the benefits of abiding by the rules. That means using clean and logical HTML or XHTML for marking up content, Cascading Style Sheets for all matters of presentation, and a single Document Object Model for scripting.

As of this writing, we are still in a period of transition. New approaches need to be learned; old habits need to be shaken. Eventually, standards-based design will be second nature. The good news is that the developers of the tools we use to view and create web pages are making strides toward full standards support. With everyone on the same page, web production has the potential to be more efficient, less costly, and forward compatible.

This chapter introduces the current web standards and the way they impact web design.

What Are Standards?

The World Wide Web Consortium (W3C) creates and oversees the development of web technologies, including XML, HTML, and their numerous applications. They also keep their eye on higher-level issues such as making content accessible to the greatest number of devices and users, as well as laying a common foundation for future development, thus making web content "forward compatible."

The W3C is not an official standards body, but rather a joint effort by experts in web-related fields to bring order to the development of web technologies. The W3C releases its final word on how various tasks (such as HTML markup) should be handled in documents called "Recommendations." Most of their recommendations become the *de facto* standards for web development. There are other standards bodies that also affect the Web and the Internet at large, including those described next.

ISO (International Organization for Standardization)
> The ISO is a true standards organization that manages more than 10,000 standards, including everything from information systems and character sets to the dimensions of 220-size film and the grain size of coated adhesives. Their seal of approval helps keep commerce and information technologies compatible world wide.

IETF (Internet Engineering Task Force)
> The IETF is an international community of network designers, operators, vendors, and researchers concerned with the evolution of the Internet as a whole. It publishes Request for Comments (RFCs) that define how things are done over the Internet, including FTP, TCP/IP, HTTP, and email.

Ecma International
> Previously known as ECMA (European Computer Manufacturers Association), this is a European association for standardizing information and communication systems. Ecma International manages information technology standards, including ECMAScript, the standardized version of JavaScript.

The Unicode Consortium
> This body manages the Unicode standard for multilingual character sets.

ANSI (American National Standards Institute)
> The ANSI covers a wide range of true standards including ASCII, the American Standard Code for Information Interchange.

The Standards Process

The Internet was built on standards. Because the Internet isn't owned and operated by one person or company, decisions regarding how best to accomplish tasks have traditionally been made by a cooperative effort of invention, discussion, and finally adoption of *the* way to handle a particular task.

Since even before the Web, Internet standards such as protocols, naming systems, and other networking technologies have been managed by the IETF. The process begins when a need for functionality is identified (email attachments, for example) and a person or group proposes a system to make it work. After a discussion phase, the proposal is made public in the form of an RFC. Once the kinks are worked out and agreed upon, the technology becomes the standard. This, of course, is a greatly simplified explanation. If you are interested in learning more about the standards approval process or in finding out what new technologies are currently in development, the IETF site (*www.ietf.org*) provides an excellent overview.

A Bumpy Beginning

The Web was subject to the same development process as any other Internet protocol. The problem was that the explosion of excitement and opportunism of the early Web caused the development of HTML and other technologies to outpace the traditional rate of standards approval. So while the W3C began working on HTML standards in 1994, the browser software companies didn't wait for them.

To gain control of the browser market, the Netscape browser popped up on the scene with its own set of proprietary HTML tags that vastly improved the appearance of web pages. Microsoft eventually responded with its own set of tags and features to compete with Netscape, and thus the Browser Wars were born. Both companies are guilty of give-the-people-what-they-want mentality with little regard for how that would impact the medium in the long term. The problem only got worse as web design grew beyond simple HTML to encompass richer web technologies such as Cascading Style Sheets, JavaScript, and DHTML.

As a result, we have inherited a slew of tags and technologies that work only in one browser or another as well as elements (<font> being the most notorious) that do nothing to describe the structure of the document. This flew in the face of the original intent of HTML: to describe the structure of a document's contents, not its visual presentation. While web standards are better established now, the W3C is still compensating for years' worth of bogus code still in use.

It didn't take long for the development community to say, "Enough is enough!" and demand that browser creators slow down and abide by the Recommendations set forth by the W3C. The champion of this effort is the Web Standards Project (WaSP, *www.webstandards.org*), a collective of web developers established in 1998. They pushed hard on the browser developers, tool developers, and the design community to get on the same page. Their actions seem to be paying off, as over the past several years, the standards effort has certainly gained steam.

Standards Support Today

The good news is that the current version browsers have gotten their acts together in supporting the available HTML and XHTML markup standards. Some browser-specific tags are still rattling around out there, but at least they aren't creating any new ones. The new challenge is consistent support for Cascading Style Sheets. Fortunately, the full Level 1 specification is supported by the latest browsers (and the vast majority of browsers in use). Unfortunately, there is still a bit of chaos around the implementation of Level 2 features such as absolute positioning, and no browser currently supports every available property and value in the CSS 2.1 Recommendation. Nearly every browser out there, even the standards-conformant versions, are known to have quirks and bugs, but all eyes turn to Microsoft Internet Explorer for consistent support, because it makes up the lion's share of web traffic. Browser bugs and the workarounds necessary for dealing with them are treated in detail in Chapter 25.

The Advantages of Standards

We're all still waiting for that ideal day when all browsers faithfully adhere to the W3C Recommendations, but that's no reason to put off creating standards-compliant content yourself. Standards offer wonderful benefits that you can begin taking advantage of right away.

Accessibility

Your web content will certainly be viewed by a variety of browsers and devices. In addition to the graphical browsers we're most familiar with today, it may be displayed by alternative devices such as mobile phones, handheld computers, or assistive devices such as screen readers for the visually impaired. By creating well-structured and logically marked up documents according to the guidelines for accessibility, you provide a better experience for the greatest number of users. See Chapter 2 for a look at issues related to competing browsers. Chapter 5 discusses ways in which the current web standards are being developed with accessibility in mind.

Forward compatibility

Future standards will build on current standards; therefore, content that is strictly compliant today will enjoy longevity into a day when deprecated elements and attributes are no longer supported. Everyone will need to part with their table-based layouts eventually. Why not start building sites the right way immediately?

Simpler and faster development

For years, web developers have needed to jump through hoops to compensate for the differences in browser support, sometimes resorting to creating several different versions of the whole site to cater to browser support quirks. Properly marking up the structure of documents and the strategic use of style sheets enables you to create one version of your content that serves all your visitors. And because the document controlling visual style is separate from the content, the design and editorial development can happen in tandem, potentially shortening production schedules. By cutting time from development schedules, standards compliance can make good business sense.

Faster download and display

Documents that use nonstandard HTML to control presentation (such as tables, font tags, and transparent images) tend to get bloated. Stripping out these elements and using style sheets for controlling presentation typically results in much smaller files that download more quickly and may add up to significant bandwidth savings. On top of that, modern browsers render pages faster in standards mode than in backward-compatible mode. Faster pages mean happier visitors. For additional information on the benefits of style sheets, see Chapter 16.

Current Web Standards

Okay, so standards are great, but what standards are we talking about? This section looks at the current standards for the structural, presentational, and behavioral aspects of web design.

Web design and development is commonly discussed in terms of "layers" (and sometimes, even as a "layer cake," which is more enticing), borrowing a layer model from one commonly used for describing network protocols. The marked up document forms the *structural layer*, which is the foundation on which other layers may be applied. Next comes the *presentation layer*, specified with Cascading Style Sheets, that provides instructions on how the document should look on the screen, sound when it is read aloud, or be formatted when it is printed. On top of these layers, there may also be a *behavioral layer*, the scripting and programming that adds interactivity and dynamic effects to a site. This edition of *Web Design in a Nutshell* is organized according to this new mental model of web design.

The following is a summary of web technology Recommendations (what the W3C calls its final published standards) as of this writing. You can check in with further developments of these technologies at the W3C site (*www.w3.org*).

Structural Layer

After years of browser developers getting jiggy with tag creation, the web community is returning to HTML's original intent as a markup language: to describe the structure of the document, not to provide instructions for how it should look. The structural markup of the document forms the foundation on which the presentational and behavioral layers may be applied.

These are the current standard languages for structural markup:

XHTML 1.0 (Extensible Hypertext Markup Language) and XHTML 1.1
XHTML 1.0 is simply HTML 4.01 rewritten according to the stricter syntax rules of XML. XHTML 1.1 finally does away with deprecated and legacy elements and attributes and has been modularized to make future expansions easier. XHTML 2.0 is currently in development. The last version of HTML was HTML 4.01, which is still universally supported by today's browsers, but is not forward compatible. Part II looks at these languages in detail. Links to the full XHTML 1.0, XHTML 1.1, and HTML 4.01 specifications can be found on this page: *www.w3.org/MarkUp/*.

XML 1.0 (Extensible Markup Language)
XML is a set of rules for creating new markup languages. It allows developers to create custom tag sets for special uses. See Chapter 7 for more information, or go to the source at *www.w3.org/XML/*.

Presentation Layer

Now that all presentation instructions have been removed from the markup standard, this information is the exclusive job of Cascading Style Sheets. Style sheets standards are being developed in phases, as follows.

Cascading Style Sheets (CSS) Level 1
This style sheet standard has been a Recommendation since 1996 and is now fully supported by current browser versions. Level 1 contains rules that control the display of text, margins, and borders.

CSS Level 2.1
This Recommendation is best known for the addition of absolute positioning of web page elements. Level 2 reached Recommendation status in 1998, and the 2.1 revision is a Candidate Recommendation as of this writing. Support for CSS 2.1 is still inconsistent in current browser versions.

CSS Level 3
Level 3 builds on Level 2 but is modularized to make future expansion simpler and to allow devices to support logical subsets. This version is still in development.

You can find links to all three CSS specifications on this page: *www.w3.org/Style/ CSS.* Style sheets are discussed further in Part III in this book.

Behavioral Layer

The scripting and programming of the behavioral layer adds interactivity and dynamic effects to a site.

Object models

The Document Object Model (DOM) allows scripts and applications to access and update the content, structure, and style of a document by formally naming each part of the document, its attributes, and how that object may be manipulated. In the beginning, each major browser had its own DOM, making it difficult to create interactive effects for all browsers.

Document Object Model (DOM) Level 1 (Core)
> This version covers core HTML and XML documents as well as document navigation and manipulation. The DOM Level 1 Specification can be found at *w3c.org/TR/REC-DOM-Level-1/.*

DOM Level 2
> Level 2 includes a style sheet object model, making it possible to manipulate style information. Links to the core and other modules of the DOM Level 2 Specification are available at *www.w3.org/DOM/DOMTR.*

Scripting

Netscape introduced its web scripting language, JavaScript, with its Navigator 2.0 browser. It was originally called "Livescript" but was later co-branded by Sun, and "Java" was added to the moniker. Microsoft countered with its own JScript while supporting some level of JavaScript in its Version 3.0 browser. The need for a cross-browser standard was clear.

JavaScript 1.5/ECMAScript 262
> The W3C is developing a standardized version of JavaScript in coordination with the Ecma International, an international industry association dedicated to the standardization of information and communication systems. According to the Mozilla site, Netscape's JavaScript is a superset of the ECMAScript standard scripting language, with only mild differences from the published standard. In general practice, most developers simply refer to "JavaScript," and the standard implementation is implied.

The full specification can be found at *www.ecma-international.org/publications/ standards/Ecma-262.htm.*

Other XML-Based Technologies

XML is a meta-language used to create other markup languages and applications. This powerful tool has enabled the development of some specialized standards. These are just a few. To see other XML technologies, visit the W3C site. With the modularization of XHTML and other XML specifications, it may be possible to mix and match XML modules within a single document, for example: XHTML, SVG, and MathML.

SVG 1.1 (Scalable Vector Graphics)
This is an XML language for defining two-dimensional vector and mixed vector/raster graphics. SVG is discussed briefly in Chapter 7. For in-depth information, read the specification at *www.w3.org/TR/SVG11/*.

MathML 2.0 (Mathematical Markup Language)
Just as it sounds, this is an XML language for defining the elements of mathematical notation, in both structure and content, for mathematics to be communicated and processed on the Web. More information and the specification can be found at *www.w3.org/Math/*.

SMIL 1.0 (Synchronized Media Integration Language) and SMIL 2.0
SMIL is an XML language for creating multimedia presentations that combine images, text, audio, and video in timed displays. More information and specifications can be found at *www.w3.org/AudioVideo/*.

Standards-Driven Design

Now that standards-compliant browsers are used by the vast majority of web visitors (see Chapter 2 for statistics), it is definitely time for designers and developers to start creating standards-compliant content. The following sections present some quick tips for making the transition to standards-based design.

Separate Presentation from Structure

For web designers and developers, the biggest mind shift towards making standards-compliant sites is keeping presentation separate from structure.

It was difficult to recognize HTML as a structural language when it was full of elements and attributes (like bgcolor, align, and of course, font) that define how elements look on the page. The W3C has deprecated those elements in the HTML 4.01 Recommendation and removed them entirely from XHTML 1.1. What remains is a markup language suited for the original purpose of logically describing the meaning of content elements (semantic markup) and establishing the basic hierarchical outline (or structure) of the document. The way the document is visually (or aurally, in the case of speech browsers) presented should be handled entirely by style sheets.

Following are some guidelines that will get you on the right track for designing with web standards.

Don't choose an element based on how it looks in the browser.
Now that you can make any element look the way you want with a style sheet rule, there is no reason to use an h3 because it looks less clunky than an h1, or a blockquote just because you want an indent. Take the time to consider the meaning or function of each element in your document and mark it up accurately.

Don't leave elements undefined.

Don't merely typeset a page using <font> and <br> tags to create the appearance of headings or lists. Again, consider the meaning of the text and mark it up accordingly. Documents with meaningful semantic markup make sense to the greatest number of viewing devices, including web browsers, cell phones, or screen readers.

Avoid deprecated elements and attributes.

There is a well-supported CSS property to replace every element and attribute that has been deprecated in the HTML 4.01 Specification. Using a style sheet will give you greater control and can potentially make future changes easier.

Avoid using tables for layouts.

Ideally, tables should be used exclusively for tabular data. It is now entirely possible to create rich page layouts using CSS alone with no tables. Chapter 24 includes several examples of multicolumn layouts along with references to CSS design showcases online. In addition to being semantically incorrect, nested tables result in bloated files and take browsers several passes to display. For those accustomed to thinking in terms of tables, it requires relearning page layout from the ground up, but now is the time to start the process.

Use a DOCTYPE Declaration

Every HTML or XHTML document should begin with a DOCTYPE declaration that tells the browser which language your document was written in. An example of a DOCTYPE declaration for a document written in strict XHTML 1.0 looks like this:

```
<! DOCTYPE html PUBLIC "-//W3C//DTD XHTML 1.0 Strict//EN"
"http://www.w3.org/TR/xhtml1/DTD/xhtml1-strict.dtd">
```

Not only is it the correct thing to do according to the W3C, but current browsers have the ability to switch into different rendering modes (e.g., "Standards" "Almost standards," "transitional," and "quirks") based on the DOCTYPE. Omitting the DOCTYPE may adversely affect the way your page renders in the browser. Available DOCTYPE declarations and DOCTYPE switching are discussed in more detail in Chapter 9.

Validate Your Markup

You can't play fast and loose with the strict standards the way you could with old HTML. Code written incorrectly may render strangely or not at all. While HTML was always meant to be validated, it is now more important than ever to validate your markup before you publish your content on the Web.

Some HTML editors, like BBEdit by BareBones Software, have built-in validators. You may also use the W3C's free validation tools for HTML/XHTML (*validator. w3.org*) and CSS (*jigsaw.w3.org/css-validator*).

Be forewarned: the error reports a validator spits out can be overwhelming. One of the problems is that errors are inherited, so if you make a mistake early on (such as forgetting to close a tag) the validator gripes about it in multiple error lines. Try fixing early mistakes and then validating again; chances are, the error list will reduce.

Error messages can also be confusing. The W3C has published a list of common error messages and how to interpret them at *validator.w3.org/docs/errors.html.*

For Further Reading

If this introduction to standards has left you hungry for more detail, you can find plenty of in-depth discussions on the bookshelves and the Web.

Books

Additional books regarding accessibility, HTML, XHTML, CSS (including invaluable books by CSS guru, Eric Meyer) are listed at the ends of the appropriate chapters of this book. For more information on standards, consider these two volumes.

Designing with Web Standards, by Jeffrey Zeldman (New Riders)
This is the place to start if you need guidance and practical advice regarding making the switch to standards. Not only is it extremely thorough and informative, it's actually really fun to read.

Web Standards Solutions: The Markup and Style Handbook (Pioneering Series), by Dan Cederholm (Friends of Ed)
This book offers practical advice on how to create web content with standards, including multiple solutions to common issues.

Web Resources

With so many professionals in the online community learning to design with standards, it's no surprise there are plenty of tips, tutorials, and resources available.

The Web Standards Project (www.webstandards.org)
The Web Standards Project is an organization founded in 1998 to push the industry toward standardization. This site provides numerous compelling articles and helpful resources.

A List Apart (www.alistapart.com)
A List Apart is an online magazine by and for web designers with hundreds of excellent articles on a variety of topics.

"Developing with Web Standards; Recommendations and Best Practices" (www. 456bereastreet.com/lab/developing_with_web_standards/)
This article contains lots of practical information and links to additional online resources. It was essential for the creation of this chapter. Roger Johansson's *456bereastreet.com* site is a recommended resource for issues regarding standards.

The World Wide Web Consortium (www.w3.org)
If you want to know the details about current web standards, go right to the source.

2

Designing for a Variety of Browsers

Most web authors agree that the biggest challenge (and headache) in web design is dealing with a multitude of browsers and their varying support of web standards. Does a page that is designed to be functional on all browsers necessarily need to be boring? Is it possible to please everyone? And if not, where do you draw the line? How many past browser versions do you need to cater to with your designs?

The situation is better than it was a few years ago, but the struggle is not over. For instance, you can now be confident that at least 99% of users have browsers that support nearly all of HTML 4. Unfortunately, there are still inconsistencies in the way Cascading Style Sheets are implemented. And of course, older browser versions that pre-date the current standards take a long time to fade away entirely.

This chapter provides background information, statistics, and current wisdom from professional web designers that may help you deal with browser differences. It focuses on the traditional graphical computer-based browsers that developers generally keep in mind. Web browsing clients for mobile devices are discussed in Chapter 3, and assistive browsing devices for the disabled are addressed in Chapter 5.

Browser History

The story of the browser provides useful context for the way web sites are currently designed and developed. This brief and simplified timeline highlights a few of the significant events in the development of the major browsers that have led to the current web design environment.

If you are interested in the history of browsers and the Web, take a look at the thorough timeline and the old browser emulators at Deja Vu (*www.dejavu.org*).

1991 to 1993: The World Wide Web is born.

Tim Berners-Lee started his hypertext-based information management at the CERN physics research labs. Text-only pages could be viewed using a simple line-mode browser.

1993: NCSA Mosaic is released.

The Mosaic browser was created by Marc Andreessen, a student at the National Center for Supercomputing Applications (NCSA). Although it was not the first browser to allow graphics to be placed on the page, it was certainly the most popular due to its cross-platform availability. The ability to add images to documents was one of the keys to the Web's rapid rise in popularity. Mosaic also supported sound, video, bookmarks, and forms. All web pages at this time were displayed in black text on a gray background.

1994: Netscape 0.9 is released.

Marc Andreessen formed Mosaic Communications Corp. (which later became Netscape Communications) and released the Netscape 0.9 browser. The early browsers were *not* free (except to students and teachers). To offer a superior experience over such freely available browsers as Mosaic and thereby attract customers, Netscape created its own HTML tags without regard for the traditional standards process. For example, Netscape 1.1 included tags for changing the background color of a web page and formatting text with tables.

1996: Microsoft Internet Explorer 3.0 is released.

Microsoft finally got into the Web game with its first competitive browser release, complete with its own set of tags and features. It was also the first browser to support style sheets, which at the time were an obscure authoring technique.

1996 to 1999: The Browser Wars begin.

For years, the web development world watched as Netscape and Microsoft battled it out for browser market dominance. The result was a collection of proprietary HTML tags and incompatible implementations of new technologies, such as JavaScript, Cascading Style Sheets, and Dynamic HTML. On the positive side, the competition between Netscape and Microsoft also led to the rapid advancement of the medium as a whole.

1998: Netscape releases its Communicator code under an open source license.

This bold move enabled the thousands of developers to participate in improving Communicator. In the end, they decided to scrap it all and start from scratch. The Mozilla group, made up in part of Netscape employees, guided the development of the open source browser and soon expanded to a complete application platform.

2000: Internet Explorer 5 for the Mac is released.
This is significant because it is the first browser to fully support the HTML 4.01 and CSS 1 Recommendations, setting the bar high for other browsers in terms of standards compliance. It is also the first browser to fully support the PNG format with alpha transparency.

2000: Netscape is sold to AOL.
This was regarded as Netscape's official loss to Microsoft in the Browser War. Entwined in the operating system of every PC running the Windows operating system, Internet Explorer was a formidable foe. Netscape lost important ground by releasing bloated all-in-one applications and taking several years off to rewrite its browser from scratch for the Netscape 6 release. As of this writing, Netscape is just a blip on the browser usage charts at a mere 1% for all combined versions, compared with approximately 90% for all combined versions of Internet Explorer.

2003: The Mozilla Foundation is formed.
Open source Mozilla code continued development under the newly formed Mozilla Foundation (funded in part by AOL).

2005: Mozilla's Firefox browser is released.
Firefox 1.0 caused much fanfare in the development community due to its strong support of web standards and its improved security over Internet Explorer. Firefox is important because it was the first browser to make a significant dent in Microsoft's share of the browser market.

Rendering Engines

A *rendering engine*, also known as a layout engine, is the code that tells the browser how to display web content and available style information in the browser window. The rendering engine is responsible for the size of an unstyled h1 heading or how a horizontal rule looks on the page. It's also the key to the correct implementation of CSS and other web standards.

The first separate and reusable rendering engine was Gecko, released by the Mozilla developers in 1998. It was notable for its small size and excellent support for standards. Now web developers pay attention to underlying rendering engines as a key to understanding a browser's performance.

The Wikipedia, an online collaborative encyclopedia, has a detailed comparison of rendering engines, where they are used, and what they support at *en. wikipedia.org/wiki/Comparison_of_layout_engines*.

Browser Roll-Call

It is critical that professional web developers be familiar with the most popular browsers in current use and not just the ones on their own desktops. This section provides basic information about the browsers that web developers care about most, whether because of total share of web usage (Internet Explorer 6 for Windows) or because its technology and standards support is important to the development community (Opera). The browsers listed here make up more than 99% of total usage as of this writing.

 There are scores of less common browsers, some with loyal followings, as well as older browser versions that are still in use. Unfortunately, it is not possible to list them all in this chapter. Evolt.org, a site for the web development community, keeps a complete archive of browsers old and new at *browsers.evolt.org*.

Table 2-1 lists the browsers and their release dates, platforms, rendering engines, and level of standards support, while the following sections describe each browser in more detail.

Table 2-1. Various web browsers

Browser	Release date	Platform	Rendering engine	Standards support
Microsoft Internet Explorer 6	2001	Windows, Linux, Unix	Trident IV	CSS 1, some CSS 2, some CSS 3, ECMA-Script, DOM (with proprietary implementations and quirks)
Microsoft Internet Explorer 5 and 5.5 (Windows)	1999 (5), 2001 (5.5)	Windows, Linux, Unix	Trident II (5) and III (5.5)	Most CSS 1, some CSS 2 (with bugs), partial support of ECMAScript/DOM
Microsoft Internet Explorer 5 (Macintosh)	2000	Macintosh	Tasman	CSS 1, some CSS 2, some CSS 3, ECMA-Script, DOM (buggy and not complete)
Netscape Navigator 7	2002	Windows, Macintosh, Linux, Unix	Gecko	CSS 1, most CSS 2, ECMAScript, DOM
Netscape Navigator 4	1997	Windows, Linux, Macintosh, Unix	N/A	Some basic CSS 1, JavaScript, no DOM because it was written after NN4's release
Firefox 1.0	2005 (pre 1.0 release versions available in 2004)	Windows, Linux, Macintosh, Unix	Gecko	CSS 1, most CSS 2, some CSS 3, ECMA-Script, DOM
Opera 8.5	2005	Windows, Linux, Macintosh, Unix	Presto	CSS 1, most CSS 2, ECMAScript, DOM (Opera 7 was the first version with DOM support)
Safari	2002	Macintosh OS X	KHTML	most CSS 1, some CSS 2, some CSS 3, ECMAScript, DOM (with bugs)

Table 2-1. Various web browsers (continued)

Browser	Release date	Platform	Rendering engine	Standards support
America Online	Various	Windows (there is a Mac version, but it isn't as well supported)	Trident	CSS 1, some CSS 2, ECMAScript, DOM (same as Internet Explorer, but expect additional buggy behavior)
Lynx	1993	Unix, Windows, Macintosh	N/A	N/A

Microsoft Internet Explorer 6

Internet Explorer 6 is the browser that comes with Windows XP, although it is also available for older Windows versions. As this book goes to press, Version 6 alone currently accounts for more than half of all web usage. Unfortunately, it is also notorious for inconsistent standards support. Microsoft has plans to release IE 7, which promises better security (the Achilles' heel of previous versions) and better standards support, with special attention to Cascading Style Sheets Level 2.1.

For information on designing for Internet Explorer, visit Microsoft's Internet Explorer Developer Center (part of its MSDN online developer's network) at *msdn.microsoft.com/ie/default.aspx*. Additional information is available on the Microsoft product pages at *www.microsoft.com/windows/ie/*.

Microsoft Internet Explorer 5 and 5.5 (Windows)

Released in early 1999, IE 5 was the first major browser with XML support. Because it is tied to several older Windows versions, it still accounts for 5 to 10% of browser usage as of this writing.

Microsoft Internet Explorer 5 (Macintosh)

Internet Explorer 5 for the Macintosh was released in 2000 and offered never before seen high levels of standards compliance and features that even IE 6 for Windows has yet to match. Microsoft stopped development with Version 5.2.3 but still offers free downloads of the latest versions of IE 5/Mac for OS X (5.2.3) and OS 9 (5.1.7).

Netscape Navigator 7

This latest version of Navigator was released in 2002, with additional 7.x releases in 2003 and 2004. It is essentially the Mozilla browser wrapped in the Netscape brand. It accounts for a startlingly small share of web traffic (less than 1%). Netscape's previous meaningful release was Version 6, which was years in the making, had numerous problems with standards and failed to gain back the market share gobbled up by Internet Explorer during its overlong development. A beta of Version 8 is available as of this writing.

For information about the Netscape browser, go to *browser.netscape.com*. Starting in October 2004, Netscape shut down its online developer resources. Mozilla.org is trying to gain rights to archive and publish those documents.

Netscape Navigator 4

Netscape Navigator and Communicator 4 was once the king of the browser world. Now its user base has dwindled to a fraction of a percent. Even so, web developers may consider a site's performance in Navigator 4 because it is typical of browsers with minimal support for current standards such as Cascading Style Sheets. Also, web developers can assume that users who still use Netscape 4 really have no alternative, for instance, because it is installed by their organization or is built into an application. While designers generally don't worry about matching layouts exactly in Netscape 4, it is critical that no content gets lost and that advanced CSS or scripting techniques don't crash the browser.

Firefox 1.0

Firefox (previously Firebird) is an open source browser based on Mozilla code. Its popularity exploded in the development community for being small, fast, and highly standards compliant. It also offers features such as tabbed browsing, pop-up blockers, integrated Google search, and better security than Internet Explorer, enabling Firefox to be the first browser to take a bite out of IE's market share. Because it is open source, many useful extensions have been created for it (see the sidebar, "Web Developer Extension for Firefox").

Download and find out more about Firefox at the Mozilla web site, *www. mozilla.org*.

Web Developer Extension for Firefox

Web developers are raving about the Web Developer extension for Firefox created by Chris Pederick. The extension adds a toolbar to the browser with tools that enable you to analyze and manipulate any page in the window. For example, you can edit the style sheet for the page you are viewing or apply your own. You can get information about the HTML and graphics on the page. It also allows you to validate the CSS, HTML, and accessibility of a web page.

Download the Web Developer extension at *chrispederick.com/work/firefox/ webdeveloper/*.

For a complete list of Firefox extensions, including others for web developers, go to *https://addons.update.mozilla.org/extensions/?application=firefox/*.

Opera 8.5

Opera is a lean and mean browser created by Opera Software in Oslo, Norway. Opera is respected for its exact compliance with HTML and CSS standards, extremely quick download times, and a small minimum disk requirement. It is free if you don't mind ad banners as part of the interface. To register the browser and get rid of the ads, the price is $29. The general public is not likely to flock to Opera, and it never so much as blips in the browser statistic charts; however, many developers continue to test their sites in Opera to make sure their code is clean. The Opera browser is also an important player in the handheld device market.

For more information about Opera, see *www.opera.com*.

Safari

Safari is the browser that comes with Mac OS X. It uses the KHTML rendering engine originally developed for the Konqueror desktop environment. It is very fast and offers fairly solid support of standards, although it does have its own bugs.

For more information and downloads, go to *www.apple.com/safari/*.

America Online

Beginning with Windows AOL 3.0 (32 bit), the AOL client does not have a browser embedded, but instead uses the Internet Explorer browser users already have installed in their systems. Therefore, browser compatibility is mostly independent of a user's specific AOL version. The scant 1 to 2% of AOL subscribers with Macintoshes use an AOL browser that is built on Gecko.

As of this writing, approximately 97% of AOL users view the Web on Windows machines using Internet Explorer 5.0 or higher. Unfortunately, Internet Explorer's functionality is limited somewhat when used in conjunction with the AOL client. This is due to the way the specific AOL clients interact with the browser and AOL's reliance on proxy servers and image compression techniques.

AOL publishes a site specifically for web developers who want their sites to be accessible and attractive to AOL users. AOL's web developer site can be found at *webmaster.info.aol.com*.

Lynx

Lynx is the best-known text-only browser. It has been around since the beginning of the Web and has been updated to include support for tables, forms, and even JavaScript. Lynx is useful to developers for testing a site's basic functionality in a non-graphical environment. This is important to ensure accessibility for visitors with disabilities who may be using Lynx with a speech or Braille device.

Lynx is not kept current for all platforms, so you may find only a beta or out-of-date version. Another alternative is to view your page in a Lynx emulator online at *www.delorie.com/web/lynxview.html*.

The Extremely Lynx page (*www.subir.com/lynx.html*) is a good starting point for finding developer information for Lynx.

An excellent resource for tracking browser releases and history is Browser News (*www.upsdell.com/browsernews/*).

Gathering Usage Statistics

Web developers pay attention to the breakdown of browser usage, for the Web at large and more relevantly for their specific sites, because it directly affects the way they create their pages. There are several methods for tracking browser usage: free general statistics listings, log analysis tools that you run on your own server, and professional statistics services.

Global Browser Statistics

If you are interested in a general breakdown of overall browser usage, there are a number of web sites that provide listings for free. They also offer usage statistics on other useful criteria such as screen resolution and various web technologies.

The Counter (*www.thecounter.com/stats*) bases its global statistics on millions of visitors using thousands of web sites registered with their service. This is an easy (and free) way to get a good general overview of browser usage.

Another useful resource for browser information, as well as for tutorials on a number of web topics, is the W3 Schools site (*www.w3schools.com/browsers*). Their statistics seem skewed toward the development and technically savvy community, as evidenced by the fact that the Firefox browser makes up nearly 20% of all usage, compared with only 8% at the more general Counter.com as of this writing (September 2005).

Server Log Analysis

The most meaningful statistics are those culled from your own site's usage. There are software tools designed just for this purpose, all of which work basically the same way.

When a browser accesses files from a server, it leaves a record of that transaction on the server, including a little data about itself: specifically, its version and the platform it is running on. This information is known as the *user agent string*, and it is used by analysis software to generate statistics about the browser usage for a site. A typical user agent string might look like this:

```
Mozilla/4.0 (compatible; MSIE 5.5; Windows 98)
```

There are dozens of log analysis tools available at a wide variety of costs. Many hosting companies include some level of server statistics as part of their hosting packages. You may also install special statistics software for better reporting. A web search for "web statistics analysis" will turn up many companies offering statistics analysis.

Another option is to sign up with a service such as The Counter (mentioned earlier) that puts a counter on your web page and provides usage stats in exchange for ad placement on your page.

The Mozilla Legacy

Today, we know Mozilla as the foundation that guides the development of the open source Mozilla software. So it may be confusing to see Mozilla at the beginning of a user agent string for Internet Explorer, as shown in the earlier example.

The Mozilla identifier at the beginning of a typical user agent string is an interesting artifact from the earliest days of the Browser Wars. Netscape first released its browser under the codename Mozilla (a shorthand combination of Mosaic killer and Godzilla). Mozilla, for its time, was a fairly turbo-powered browser, so webmasters began targeting their content to it specifically.

When competing browsers (most significantly, Microsoft Internet Explorer) began featuring similar capabilities, they didn't want to be left out of the targeting action, so they put the word "Mozilla" in their user agent identification as well. Eventually, everyone was doing it, so the only way to truly identify the browser version was to include it in parentheses (such as MSIE 5.5 in the previous example).

The name Mozilla stuck with the Netscape browser through its glory days and continued to its release as open source software. For more information on the Mozilla Foundation, see *www.mozilla.org*.

Targeted Statistics Consulting

If you want fairly accurate browser usage statistics, but your own site isn't up and running yet, you may hire the services of a user trends consultant to analyze usage on similar sites or within a specific business sector. A place to start is the Web Analytics Association (*www.webanalyticsassociation.org*), which offers a listing of members who provide usage trend reports.

Learning from Browser Statistics

However you gather your statistics, they can tell you some important things about your audience and how they may experience the Web. Consider Table 2-2, which provides a set of browser statistics typical of the end of 2005. These statistics may not necessarily be meaningful as you read this book, but if you are completely unfamiliar with the typical browser breakdowns, these will give you a ballpark idea.

Table 2-2. Browser statistics for December 2005 from The Counter.com

Browser	Usage
Microsoft Internet Explorer 6	83%
Microsoft Internet Explorer 5	3%
Mozilla/Firefox	8%
Safari	2%
Unknown	1%

Table 2-2. Browser statistics for December 2005 from The Counter.com (continued)

Browser	Usage
Opera x.x	1%
Netscape 7	1%
Netscape compatible	< 1%
Microsoft Internet Explorer 4.x	< 1%
Netscape 4.x	< 1%
Konqueror	< 1%
Netscape 6 (and older versions)	< 1%

What You Can Learn

Once you have statistics in hand, what conclusions can you draw from them? Even statistics as general as those in Table 2-2 provide a jumping off point for thinking about how they might impact design.

Standards support

The good news is that 99% of browsers in use today support some level of current standards, at least on paper. Unfortunately, the reality is that even browsers with strong standards support have their own quirky implementations and bugs that require developers to jump through hoops, particularly when it comes to CSS, ECMAScript (JavaScript), and the DOM. That's where web design and development can feel like a black art. Techniques for addressing CSS browser bugs are covered in detail in Chapter 25.

Dominance of Windows and Internet Explorer

As of this writing, the vast majority (83%, according to these statistics; others vary) of web traffic is happening on Windows machines running Internet Explorer 6. That means you cannot afford to ignore its unique behaviors and requirements. For example, knowing that more than 80% of your visitors will not be able to zoom text when its size has been specified in pixel units should influence the way you size text with style sheets. Other examples of Internet Explorer's special needs are listed in Chapter 25.

Version 7 is nearing its final release as of this writing, and IE 6 will eventually fall to second in the rank, but it takes several years for old browser versions to fade from use completely.

Persistence of old browser versions

Speaking of old browser versions, the statistics above show that browsers such as Netscape 4, originally released in 1997, are still hanging around. In fact, statistics show that there are still a handful of hits from Netscape 2.

With the vast volume of web traffic, even less than 1% could amount to millions of users. If your revenue depends on them, you must continue to keep them in mind and make sure that your site is, at the very least, functional on even the oldest browsers.

Browser Usage Trends

What the statistics above do not show us are some important browser developments over time. The most drastic trend, of course, is Microsoft's complete domination of the browser arena. In mid-1997, Netscape Navigator enjoyed a comfortable 70 to 80% of overall browser usage (according to statistic sites such as those listed earlier); by 1998, that share was down to 50%. Now, all versions combined make up just 1%.

It seemed Internet Explorer was unstoppable, that was until 2005, when it suffered its first drop in browser usage to Mozilla's free Firefox browser. There was a grass-roots campaign to promote Firefox (*www.spreadfirefox.com*) as an alternative browser to people fed up with IE's security holes. Firefox usage quickly expanded to 5 to 10% of all browser usage (depending on whose stats you use). As of this writing, its rise is slowing. Even so, it has caused Microsoft to recognize the need to improve its security and to continue development of a standalone browser application. Microsoft has plans to integrate web browsing functions so fully into its operating system that browser software as we know it may be obsolete.

Dealing with Browser Differences

How do professional web designers and developers cope with the multitude of browsers and their varying capabilities?

In the past, it required some tough decisions or a lot of extra work. It was common to create multiple versions of a site to ensure similar functionality. Some designers played it safe and avoided any web technology more advanced than basic HTML. On the other end of the spectrum were designers who chose to design cutting edge sites exclusively for the latest version of one specific browser. We can thank the Browser Wars of the late '90s for that chaos.

Web standards—or more important, the fact that the major browser developers have finally started to support them—have simplified the way designers cope with the multitude of browsers in use. Gone are the days of choosing sides or building several versions of the same site. Today, it is possible to create sites that are accessible to 100% of browsers and that look good in the vast majority of them. The trick is following the standards yourself in the way you write, style, and program your content.

Note that I said "possible" in the last paragraph, and not "easy," to create sites for all browsers. As of this writing, the web environment, although inching towards standards compliance, is not there yet. There are still inconsistencies, even in the current browser versions, that require some fancy coding to deliver a consistent cross-browser experience. While we are in this period of transition, there are still some old-school techniques that are common practice or even necessary despite going against W3C recommendations.

Bugs aside, sticking with standards is still the primary tool to ensuring your site is usable for all users on all browsers. Following are some specific strategies for addressing varying browser capabilities.

A Little Help from Authoring Tools

Both Adobe GoLive and Macromedia Dreamweaver provide tools that give you feedback on your design's performance in various browsers. GoLive provides a complete list of browser profiles that change the appearance of the document in the Layout window. Simply select a profile from the View palette and the Layout window simulates how your page will look when viewed with that browser. This can allow you to make certain adjustments in real time, without the need to open multiple browsers for testing.

Dreamweaver has a Check Target Browser feature that checks your code against a list of browser profiles to see if any tags or attributes are unsupported and then generates a report with its findings. To take some of the guesswork out of browser support for scripting, Dreamweaver allows you to set a target browser. Dreamweaver then limits the behaviors you can select to just those supported in that browser. The program also includes built-in functions for performing browser detection.

Dreamweaver users may also be interested in the book *Build Your Own Standards Compliant Website Using Dreamweaver 8*, by Rachel Andrew (Sitepoint).

Document Authoring

It is important to keep in mind that your primary goal on the Web is to communicate. While it may not be possible to make your site look exactly the same on all browsers, you can be sure your content is accessible and usable, at the very least, by following standards recommendations for marking up your content.

Start with good markup
> When an HTML document is written in logical order and its elements are marked up in a meaningful way, it will be usable in even Mosaic 1.0 (try it yourself on the Mosaic emulator at Dejavu.org). Plus, you have to figure that if a visitor is using Netscape 2.0, your page won't look any worse than any other.

Follow accessibility guidelines
> The techniques that make your site accessible to people with disabilities also ensure that your site can be viewed on all browsers, including old versions, text-only browsers, and micro-browsers in handheld devices. See Chapter 5 for more information on accessibility.

Style Sheet Tactics

Now that HTML has resumed the role of providing document structure, Cascading Style Sheets bear the burden of delivering consistent page layouts and formatting. The good news is that the vast majority of browsers support CSS Level 1, so you can do basic text formatting with peace of mind that the majority of your visitors will see it the way you intend.

The bad news is that there are still inconsistencies in the way much of the specification is implemented, even by those browsers who claim full CSS support. So

CSS implementation still requires some extra effort to achieve consistent results. In some cases, it is necessary simply to live with one browser displaying items a few pixels off. Remember, the goal is to communicate. A few pixels shouldn't matter.

The specifics of known bugs, limitations, and workarounds are covered in Chapter 25, so I won't go into detail here. But I can show you a general style sheet strategy for addressing the special needs of all browsers. This technique comes from web standards guru Jeffrey Zeldman. In his book, *Designing with Web Standards* (New Riders), he describes the Best-Case Scenario Design Method.

The crux of the method (in addition to the proper use of XHTML and CSS) is to design for your favorite full-featured, standards-compliant browser. This is a departure from the past practice of checking how pages looked in the lowest common denominator browsers first. Then test your page to make sure it looks and works the same in comparable standards-compliant browsers. If it doesn't look the same, you may need to use some fancy CSS tricks to work out the kinks.

Once you have the design working acceptably in the modern browsers (which are used by the vast majority of users), take a look at it in a noncompliant browser, such as Netscape 4. If it looks okay, you're done. If not, the solution is to separate your style sheet into two separate sheets: one with just the basic CSS features and another with advanced rules features for browsers that understand them. Link the advanced style sheet using @import to hide it from browsers that wouldn't know what to do with it.

Knowing which rules are basic and which are advanced takes research, testing, and practice. With some trial and error, you should be able to design a site that looks the way you want it to in the top-model browsers but still is acceptable in older versions.

Programming

The standards that govern web behaviors are the scripting language ECMAScript (so close to JavaScript 1.5 that it is usually just referred to by the less technical sounding moniker, JavaScript) and the Document Object Model (DOM), which defines the components of a web page that can be manipulated.

There is the same good news/bad news scenario for JavaScript and the DOM. Although 99% of compliant browsers profess to support the standards, they are fraught with bugs and inconsistencies. Some browsers do not support certain JavaScript functions. Microsoft has added its own extensions to the DOM that work only in Internet Explorer. And so on.

For the remaining 1% of browsers that do not support the DOM at all (namely Version 4 browsers), there are no simple workarounds. It is usually necessary to serve an alternative version of the page that uses scripting functions those browsers can understand, or to provide an explanatory page without scripts at all that would work on any browser.

Know Your Audience

Although by following standards-driven development techniques, you ensure that your site is usable for all visitors, you may decide to embrace or steer clear of certain technologies based on knowledge of your audience. Before designing a new site, be sure to spend time up front researching the likely platforms, browsers, technical savviness, and connection speeds of the users you are targeting. If you are redesigning an existing site, spend time with the server logs to analyze past site usage.

There are no browser-support guidelines that can anticipate every design situation; however, the following scenarios should start you thinking:

- If your site is aimed at a consumer audience—for instance, a site that sells educational toys to a primarily parent audience—don't ignore your site's performance and presentation in the AOL browsers or older browser versions over dial-up connections.

- If you are designing for a controlled environment, such as a corporate intranet or, even better, a web-based kiosk, you've got it made! Knowing exactly what browser and platform your viewers are using means you can take full advantage of the bells and whistles (and even proprietary features) appropriate to that browser. If you are designing a standalone kiosk, you may even have the luxury of loading the fonts you want to use. Just be sure your design won't crash the browser, because there won't be anyone there to restart it for you immediately.

- If your site is *about* the technology being used, such as SVG graphics or Flash animations, you have every right to expect users to use the appropriate browser or plug-in to catch up with your content. But it might still be nice to at least provide some screenshots or other alternative content to let the others know what they're missing.

- If you are designing a government site, you are required by law under Section 508 to make your pages accessible to all browsing devices. For more information, see Chapter 5.

Test!

The final word in the dilemma of designing for a variety of browsers is *test*! Always test your site on as many browsers, browser versions, and platform configurations as you can get your hands on.

Professional web design firms run their sites through a vigorous quality assurance phase before going "live." They generally keep a bank of computers of varying platforms and processing powers that run as many versions of browsers (including Lynx) as possible.

Another option is to subscribe to a screen capture service such as Browser Cam. For a monthly fee, you can enter the URL of a page you want to check, and Browser Cam creates screen captures of the page in all the operating systems and browsers you select. This makes it easy to see which browsers are having problems without needing to run copies of all of them yourself. Read more at *browsercam.com*.

If you have extremely limited resources, make the site available on a private test site and take a look at it on your friends' computers. You might view it under corporate conditions (a fast Windows machine with a 6.0 browser and a T1 connection), and then visit a friend at home to see the same site on AOL with a 56K modem. (If nothing else, this is a good excuse to get away from your computer and visit your friends.)

Although your pages will certainly look different in different environments, the idea is to make sure that nothing is outright broken and your content is communicated clearly.

3

Designing for a Variety of Displays

A simple fact of web publishing is that your page is at the mercy of the software and hardware configuration of each individual user. A page that looks great on your machine may look radically different when viewed on another user's setup. This is partly due to the browser's functionality (as discussed in Chapter 2) and the individual user's preferences (font size, colors, etc.), but the display device itself also plays a large part in the user's experience.

This chapter looks at the ways in which design decisions are influenced by a wide range of displays and viewing conditions. The variation in display is a function of the monitor's size (or, more accurately, its resolution), color capabilities, and user's personal preferences. However, it is important to keep in mind that the diversity does not end there. Some users may be watching your web page on TV. Still others may be viewing it in the palm of their hand on a PDA (personal digital assistant) or cell phone. Sight-impaired users may be listening to your page, not viewing it.

How do you create a page that works in a cinema-display computer monitor and a postage-stamp sized cell phone? Once again, web standards are the answer. The W3C guides the development of web technologies in a way that ensures that the Web is accessible to all manner of devices. As designers and developers, our job is to author documents in a way that they make sense in any environment. That means logical, well-structured markup, uncluttered by presentation instructions that may not be appropriate for a particular medium. In fact, Cascading Style Sheets include a function that allows you to create different style sheets targeted to particular media such as print, screen, and handheld.

As most web viewing does take place on computer monitors, this chapter starts with a look at how monitor resolution impacts web page design.

Designing for Unknown Monitor Resolutions

Browser windows can be resized to any dimension, limited only by the maximum size of the monitor. Designing for an unknown amount of browser real estate is a challenge unique to web design and one that is particularly troublesome for designers who are accustomed to the printed page.

Many web designers want to know which monitor resolution to design for. As with most web design issues, there is no "right" way to design for the Web, and your decisions should always be guided by your knowledge of your target audience and the purpose of your site. Still, it is helpful to understand the environment and to know how others are maneuvering within it.

This section looks at the range of monitor resolutions and presents the current wisdom on making appropriate design decisions.

Standard Monitor Sizes and Resolutions

The first step in determining the likely size of your web page is to look at the maximum amount of space provided by the computer monitor. Computer monitors come in a variety of standard sizes, typically measured in inches, ranging from 12" laptop displays all the way up to 30" cinema displays.

A more meaningful measurement, however, is monitor resolution: the total number of pixels available on the screen. The higher the resolution, the more detail can be rendered on the screen. Resolution is related to but not necessarily determined by monitor size. Depending on the video card driving it, a single monitor can display a number of different resolutions. For instance, a 17" monitor can display 800 × 600 pixels, 1024 × 768 pixels, or even higher. The following is a list of some standard monitor resolutions supported by Windows and Macintosh platforms. This is not a complete listing, merely the most commonly occurring configurations.

- 640 × 480
- 800 × 600
- 1024 × 768
- 1152 × 870
- 1280 × 1024
- 1600 × 1200

It is important to keep in mind that the higher the resolution on a given monitor, the more pixels are packed into the available screen space. The result is smaller pixels, which will make your images and page elements appear smaller as well. For this reason, web measurements are made in pixels, not inches. Something that appears to be an inch wide on your system may look smaller or larger on other screens. Chapter 28 further discusses resolution as it applies to graphics.

Live Space in the Browser Window

Knowing the size of the monitor is just the beginning. The operating system and the interface components of the browser itself (known as the browser *chrome*) occupy a fair amount of screen space. The amount of space that is actually available within the browser window, (the browser *canvas*), is dependent on the computer's operating system, the browser being used, and the individual user's preference settings.

Table 3-1 lists the amount of canvas space that is available at standard monitor resolutions. Measurements were taken with the browser maximized to fill the monitor and with all possible chrome elements such as buttons, location bars, and scrollbars visible. In a way, this can be considered a worst case scenario for available space (with the browser maximized).

Bear in mind that these are theoretical extremes, and actual browser window dimensions will vary. Users may have some of the buttons showing, but not all of them. Scrollbars turn on and off automatically, so they are difficult to anticipate. Users with high monitor resolutions (1024 pixels wide and higher) do not necessarily open their browser windows to fill the whole area, but may keep several narrow windows open at the same time.

Table 3-1. Minimum canvas dimensions at various monitor resolutions

Browser	640 × 480	800 × 600	1024 × 768	1280 × 1024
Windows				
Internet Explorer 6	620 × 309	**780 × 429**	1004 × 597	1260 × 853
Firefox 1.0	621 × 291	781 × 421	1005 × 579	1261 × 835
Netscape 7[a]	625 × 258	785 × 378	1009 × 546	1265 × 802
Macintosh[b]				
Safari	625 × 352	785 × 472	1009 × 640	1265 × 896
Firefox 1.0	625 × 328	785 × 448	1009 × 616	1265 × 872
Internet Explorer 5.2	625 × 334	785 × 454	1009 × 622	1265 × 878
Netscape 7[a]	625 × 340	785 × 460	1009 × 628	1265 × 884

[a] Netscape measurements are taken with MySidebar hidden. MySidebar takes up 170 pixels of horizontal space.
[b] Macintosh widths are measured with no launch bar visible on the side of the screen.

The dimensions for Microsoft Internet Explorer on an 800 × 600 monitor are in bold because they represent the available canvas area for a typical lowest common denominator user. Because as much as 80% of web traffic uses Internet Explorer on Windows, and because as many as a quarter of users have 800 × 600 monitors, it is current web design practice to make sure pages fit comfortably within 780 × 429 pixels in order not to alienate this significant percentage of users. Designing to fit specific window sizes is discussed later in this chapter.

Fixed Versus Liquid Web Pages

Closely related to the issue of varying monitor resolutions is the question of whether web pages should be designed to be liquid (resizing and adapting to various window sizes, also called "fluid" design) or fixed at a particular size (giving the designer more control of the page's dimensions). There are very strong opinions on both sides, and there are good reasons for and against each approach, naturally.

You may find that you choose a fixed structure for some sites and allow others to be liquid, or you may have strong convictions that one or the other approach is the only way to go. Either way, it is useful to be familiar with the whole picture and the current opinions of professional web designers (see "The Layout Debate" sidebar). This section attempts to present a balanced overview of the possibilities and the pitfalls.

The Layout Debate

The question of whether fixed or liquid page layouts are most appropriate for web pages has sparked impassioned debate among professionals in the web design community. There is an undeniable trend toward fixed-width layouts (presumably due to the desire to control line lengths), but there are still staunch proponents of liquid designs as best for a medium where the canvas size is unknown. To get caught up with both sides of the debate, start with these articles and blog entries (they all have links to additional points of view):

- "On Fixed vs. Liquid Design," by Doug Bowman (experimenting with fixed-width design at *www.stopdesign.com/log/2003/12/15/fixedorliquid.html*)
- "More on fixed widths," by Richard Rutter (pro–liquid design article at *clagnut.com/blog/269/*)
- "Fixed Fashion," by Jeremy Keith (pro–liquid design post at *www.adactio. com/journal/display.php/20050415012704.xml*)
- "The Benefits of a Fixed Width Design," by Mike Golding (*www.notestips. com/80256B3A007F2692/1/TAIO-5TT34F*)

Liquid Layouts

Web pages are fluid by default. The behavior of the "normal flow" of a web document is to flow into the browser window, filling all available space in the canvas area. When the browser window is resized, the elements reflow to adapt to the new dimensions. Many designers make a conscious decision to construct pages that adapt to the stretching and shrinking of browser windows. This approach comes with advantages and disadvantages.

Advantages and disadvantages of fluid web pages

The advantages of a flexible design include:

- You don't need to worry about choosing a target monitor resolution.
- The whole window is filled, without the potentially awkward empty space left over by many fixed-width designs.
- Designing liquid pages is in keeping with the spirit and the nature of the medium. A "good" web page design by these standards is one that is functional to the greatest number of users.

Keep in mind, though, these potential pitfalls of a flexible design:

- On large monitors, the text line length can get out of hand when the text fills the width of the browser. Long lines of text are particularly uncomfortable to read on a screen. (Note, line length on liquid designs could be controlled by the max-width CSS property, but it is not supported by Internet Explorer 6 or earlier. One day, it will be a tool for addressing the line-length issue.)
- Elements float around on large monitors, making the design less coherent and potentially more difficult to use. Likewise, on very small monitors, elements can get cramped.
- The results of flexible design are unpredictable, and users will have varying experiences of your page.

Creating flexible pages

The key to creating web pages that resize proportionally to fill the browser is using relative measurements, such as percentages) in your style sheets, tables, or frames or not specifying measurements at all and allowing elements to size automatically.

As an example, let's consider a web page that is divided into two sections: a main content column and a links column (Figure 3-1). By using percentage values for the divs, table cells, or frame measurements, the columns and elements will remain proportional to one another. In this example, the main content column takes up 75% of the screen regardless of the size of the browser window. Note that the content of that column reflows to fill the available width.

Using style sheets, you can also set the contents of the page to flex based on the user's text size preference by setting measurements in *ems*, a unit used in printing to refer to the width of one capital letter M. In CSS, an em is equal to the font size; in other words, an em unit in 12-point text is 12 points square. Using em measurements for element dimensions, margins, line-height, and so on ensures that page elements scale proportionally with the user's chosen text preference.

Fixed-Width Design

If you want more control over the layout of a page, you may opt to design a web page with a fixed width that stays the same for all users, regardless of monitor resolution or browser window size. This approach to web design is based on design principles learned in print, such as a constant grid, the relationship of page elements, and comfortable line lengths. It is a popular approach among the stan-

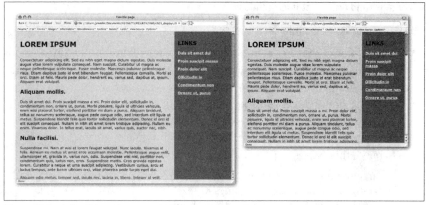

Figure 3-1. A flexible web page with proportional columns

dards-based design crowd as of this writing, but that may only indicate a trend, not that it is the superior approach to web page layout.

Advantages and disadvantages of fixed-width design

These are the advantages of fixed-width design:

- The basic layout of the page remains the same regardless of canvas size. This may be a priority for companies interested in presenting a consistent corporate image for every visitor.
- Fixed-width pages and columns provide better control over line lengths, preventing them from becoming too long when the page is viewed on a large monitor.

Consider also these disadvantages:

- If the available browser window is smaller than the grid for the page, parts of the page will not be visible and may require horizontal scrolling to be viewed. Horizontal scrolling is a hindrance to ease of use, so it should be avoided. (One solution is to choose a page size that serves the most people, as discussed later in this section.)
- Elements may shift unpredictably if the font size in the browser is larger or smaller than the font size used in the design process.
- Trying to exert absolute control over the display of a web page is bucking the medium. The Web is not like print; it has its own peculiarities and strengths.

Creating fixed pages

Fixed web page designs are created by using exact pixel measurements for all the elements on the page. Figure 3-2 shows a two-column web page similar to the one in Figure 3-1; however, this one has been sized to exactly 900 pixels wide, with the two columns set to 700 and 200 pixels, respectively.

Style sheets offer the best set of tools for fixed-measurement layouts. In the past, designers resorted to tricks such as sized transparent graphics to hold

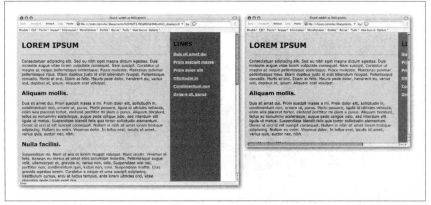

Figure 3-2. A fixed-width web page with exact pixel measurements viewed on large (left) and small (right) monitors

"whitespace" on the page and multiple nested tables to control spacing around elements. Thankfully, these workarounds are no longer necessary.

Style sheets allow you to set specific pixel measurements for the page, columns, margins, indents, and so on. You can also specify the font size in pixels, ensuring the text will wrap similarly for most users.* The CSS Level 2 specification provides tools for the precise positioning of elements on the page, right down to the pixel. For designers looking for control over layout, style sheets are great news.

Some visual HTML authoring tools make it easy to create fixed-width designs. Adobe GoLive (*www.adobe.com/products/golive/main.html*) has an option for designing your page on a grid as though it were a page-layout program. GoLive then automatically generates the corresponding (and often complicated) table. Macromedia Dreamweaver (*www.macromedia.com/software/dreamweaver/*) also includes a layout mode with the option of generating your design using tables or style sheets with absolute positioning.

Left-aligned or centered?

When you set your content to a specific width, you need to consider where it should appear in the browser window. By default, it will be aligned on the left margin, with the extra space in the browser window on the right. Some designers opt to center the page, splitting the extra space over the left and right margins. Centering the page may make it feel as though the page better fills the browser window. Figure 3-3 provides examples of each approach. Neither of these approaches is necessarily better than the other; it's just a design decision you'll need to make.

---

* Using pixel measurements for font size is problematic, because Internet Explorer users (Version 6 and earlier on Windows) cannot resize text set in pixels in the browser window. This could create accessibility problems for sight-impaired users who need to zoom text. Internet Explorer 7 will support this feature, but in the meantime, em units are the best choice for font size. For a more detailed discussion, see Chapter 18.

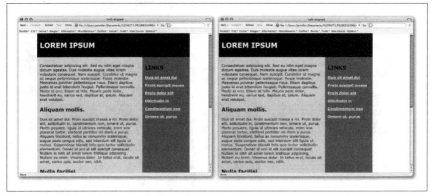

Figure 3-3. Positioning fixed-width content on the page

Be aware that there are a few issues regarding centering content in the browser window in modern browsers. This is discussed in Chapter 21.

Pop-up and resized windows

For the ultimate in control-freak, fixed-width page design, you can specify not only the size of your web page, but also the size of the browser window itself.

One way to get the browser window "just so" is to open a new browser window automatically (known as a *pop-up window*) set to specific pixel dimensions. The drawback to this technique is that pop-up windows have become associated with annoying, force-fed advertising banners. Many users have learned to close a pop-up window before the content even has time to load. The seriously annoyed folks may have taken the time to install a pop-up window blocker on their browser. Others may simply have JavaScript turned off for security or whatever reasons. The lesson here is not to put critical content in a pop-up window, and if you do, label the link accordingly to let people know what to expect.

Another, more drastic, approach is to run a JavaScript that resizes the user's current browser window to accommodate your design. In my opinion, this is just bad manners—like visiting a stranger's house and rearranging their furniture without asking. But I will qualify this statement by saying that no technique is entirely off limits. Sometimes an otherwise bad practice may be the appropriate solution. In this case, automatically resizing the browser window might be a good backup technique to make sure a web-based kiosk window is always sized appropriately.

Combination Pages

Of course, web pages need not be all-fixed or all-flexible. It is certainly possible to create pages that are a combination of the two by setting a specific pixel size for one critical element and allowing the rest of the page to resize to fill the browser window. In Figure 3-4, the right column has been set to stay at 200 pixels so the list of links is always visible, but the main content column is allowed to resize to fill the available browser window space.

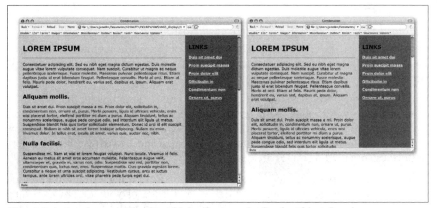

Figure 3-4. A web page with a liquid left column and a fixed-width right column

Choosing a Page Size

Obviously, if you decide to design a web page at a fixed size, you need to make a decision regarding how big to make it. If the page is too wide, you run the risk of users with lower resolution monitors missing some of your content as shown in Figure 3-2. It makes sense to design the page to fit comfortably in the smallest monitors and eliminate the need for horizontal scrolling. This is where web traffic statistics come in handy.

The statistics

Table 3-2 shows the breakdown of users browsing the Web with various monitor resolutions in late 2005, according to TheCounter (*www.thecounter.com*).

Table 3-2. Resolution statistics as of December 2005 (thecounter.com)

Resolution	Usage
640 × 480	< 1%
800 × 600	20%
1024 × 768	56%
1152 × 864	3%
1280 × 1024	14%
1600 × 1200	<1%
Unknown	2%

Of course, this is only an approximation based on traffic to a limited set of web sites. The only worthwhile statistics are those culled from your own server logs. You can install software to check browser resolution yourself, or sign up for a tracking service such as TheCounter (free in exchange for ad placement).

Current practice

Based on these statistics, the only definitive conclusion is that it is finally time not to worry about how your page will appear in 640 × 480 monitors (unless, of course, you know the target audience for your site is likely to have outdated hardware setups).

As of this writing, professional web developers tend to design pages that fit in 800 × 600 monitors. Although the percentage of people with this monitor resolution is steadily shrinking, with just a fifth of all traffic, it is still too large a population to risk alienating. For this reason, you will find that most fixed-width consumer- or business-oriented web sites are designed to be approximately 750 pixels wide.

If you know that the majority of your visitors will have a higher monitor resolution (such as graphic designers), or if the right edge of your design does not contain critical content, then it may be safe to design to fill the live space of a 1024 × 768 monitor. Very few sites today are designed to fill 1280 × 1024.

I suspect as 800 × 600 monitors go the way of 640 × 480, we'll be seeing larger and larger web pages. For now, however, consider 800 × 600 the lowest common denominator monitor resolution.

"Design-to-Size" Developer Tools

There are a few developer tools available that allow you to see how your page will look at varying browser sizes without needing to change the resolution on your monitor.

One of the niftiest tools out there is the Web Developer Extension for Firefox and Mozilla browsers. The extension adds a toolbar to the browser that has a number of useful tools for web developers. One of the tools is Resize, which automatically changes the dimensions of the browser window to your specifications. You can download Web Developer Extension for free at *www.chrispederick.com/work/firefox/webdeveloper/*.

Macromedia Dreamweaver provides a Window Size tool that resizes the document window to a number of standard monitor resolutions. This allows you to see how your page is fitting the available live space as you design it. The window size is listed as a pixel dimension (say, 760 × 420) in the bottom-right corner of the document window. Clicking on the button opens a pop-up menu of standard resolutions.

In Adobe GoLive CS, the dimensions of the page you are working on are displayed in the lower-right corner. There is a pull-down menu that lets you set the layout window to the available space for several standard widths (such as 720 pixels to fit in an 800 × 600 monitor) or add your own. Selecting a resolution resizes the layout window.

Designing "Above the Fold"

Newspaper editors have always designed the front page with the most important elements "above the fold," that is, visible when the paper is folded and sitting in the rack.

Likewise, the first screenful of a web site's homepage is the most important real estate of the whole site, regardless of whether the page is fixed or flexible. It is here that the user makes the decision to continue exploring the site or to hit the Back button and move along. Web designers have adopted the term "above the fold" to apply to the contents that fit in that important first screen.

As discussed throughout this chapter, a "screenful" can be quite different depending on the resolution of the monitor. To play it absolutely safe, consider the space available for the lowest common denominator 800 × 600 monitor—approximately 780 × 400 pixels. That's not much room.

Some elements you should consider placing above the fold include:

- The name of the site.
- Your primary marketing message.
- Some indication of what the site is about. For instance, if it is a shopping site, you might place the credit card logos or shopping cart in the top corner to instantly communicate that "shopping happens here."
- Navigation to other parts of the site. If the entire navigation device (such as a list of links down the left edge of the page) doesn't fit, at least get it started in the first screen; hopefully users will scroll to see the remainder. If it is out of sight completely, it is that much more likely to be missed.
- Any other information that is crucial for visitors to the site, such as a toll-free number or special promotion.
- Banner advertising. Advertisers may require that their ads appear at the top of the page.

Monitor Color Issues

Differences in the number of colors a monitor can display (color depth) and how bright or dark it is (gamma) may also influence your design decisions. Dealing with color issues in web design is discussed in Chapter 28.

Mobile Devices

The increased popularity and usefulness of the Web combined with the growing reliance on handheld communications devices (such as palm-top computers, PDAs, and cellular telephones) has resulted in web browsers squeezing into the coziest of spaces. Advancing technology and lower production costs have made high-resolution color displays and embedded web browsers standard issue on nearly all new phones and PDAs. This comes as a big improvement over the black-and-white, text-only displays of only a few years ago, and it is creating a call for mobile-appropriate web content.

Mobile Display Resolution

Because each manufacturer creates its own displays, there are no clear standard screen resolutions for mobile devices the way there are for computer monitors. But to get you in the ballpark, take a look at some current specifications. On the low end are standard mobile phones with screen dimensions of 128 × 128 pixels. Fuller-featured phones typically have resolutions of 176 × 208, 176 × 220, 208 × 208, or as large as 240 × 320. Handheld devices, such as the ubiquitous Black-Berry, sport screen sizes of 240 × 160 or 240 × 240.

Mobile Browsers

The browsers embedded in mobile phones and PDAs (also known as *microbrowsers*) are designed to accommodate the lower memory capacity, low bandwidth abilities, and limited display area of handheld devices. Some are WAP browsers with limited HTML support (see the sidebar, "WAP and WML"), and some are full-featured browsers that support the current web standards and allow access to all the same web content that is available from a PC browser. (Some of the best-known mobile browsers and their web addresses are listed at the end of this section.)

Support for standards

The significant development in mobile browsing technology is the abandonment of WAP (Wireless Application Protocol) and its authoring language WML (Wireless Markup Language) in favor of the same web authoring standards set forth by the W3C for web content. The Open Mobile Alliance (*www.openmobilealliance. org*), the organization that guides standards for the mobile industry, has been working in cooperation with the W3C to ensure that web technologies take into account the needs of the mobile environment. In fact, the W3C has formed the Device Independence Working Group (*www.w3c.org/2001/di*) to promote access to a "unified Web from any device in any context by anyone."

Modern mobile phones and other handheld devices will support XHTML Mobile Profile (XHTML minus the tags that don't make sense for the mobile environment), ECMAScript Mobile Profile, Wireless CSS, SVG Tiny (a version of Scalable Vector Graphics especially for mobile devices), among other standards. This is big news, because web content developers no longer need to learn a special language to make content accessible to the growing mobile audience. The devices may also continue to support less strictly authored HTML pages as well as legacy WML.

Adapting web content for small screens

What happens when a cell phone accesses a traditional web page? Basically, it does the best it can. One of the biggest challenges for mobile browsers is rendering big web pages on small screens. Browser and device developers have created a few solutions to this problem.

Shrink-to-fit
> The most sophisticated method is to reduce the web page to fit the available width of the device display. They accomplish this by intelligently displaying the contents of the source HTML document sequentially and shrinking graphics to fit. The best known browsers that use this technique are Opera's Small-Screen Rendering technology and Access System's NetFront browser with its SmartFit Rendering.

Allow horizontal scrolling
> Another option is to simply display the web page at its actual size and enable horizontal and vertical scrolling to view it all. Some devices offer an option for users to decide whether they want to scroll the page horizontally (which may be necessary for wide tabular content such as time tables) or make pages flow into the narrow screen width.

Designing for Mobile Devices

It should come as no surprise that the prescription for optimizing your visitors' experience in the mobile environment is creating standards-compliant content. Here are just a couple of tips.

Write clean HTML

The best ways to accommodate the limitations of handheld browsers are to mark up documents semantically and logically and to avoid sinking text in graphics (which you should be avoiding anyway). The goal is to create a page that works and makes sense even with all the graphics and tables stripped away.

One example of how logical semantic markup can serve all audiences is the practice of marking up navigation options as an unordered list in the document source. Cascading Style Sheets can be used to present the list as a horizontal navigation bar (with graphics, too, if you choose) for graphical browsers, but microbrowsers and other alternative browsing devices will see a bulleted list of links. This technique is demonstrated in Chapter 24.

Use media types

What looks good on a PC monitor may not work at all on the small screen of a PDA. Fortunately, you can give the PDA its own set of presentation instructions by creating a style sheet crafted specifically for handheld devices. The HTML media attribute allows you to target a number of media including (but not limited to) screen, print, projection, and handheld. CSS media types are discussed in further detail in Chapter 16.

To create a link to a style sheet that is used only by handheld devices, use the code:

```
<link rel-"stylesheet" href="smaller.css" media="handheld" />
```

Online Resources

For more information on what is happening in the mobile browsing world, see these useful sites.

Mobile standards

These organizations oversee the technology that is continuing to improve the mobile web experience.

* Open Mobile Alliance (*www.openmobilealliance.org*)
* W3C's Device Independence group (*www.w3.org/di*)

Mobile browsers

The following are some of the most popular embedded mobile browsers.

* Opera (Opera Software, *www.opera.com*)
* NetFront (Access Systems, *www.access-sys-eu.com*)
* Nokia (Nokia, *www.forum.nokia.com*)
* Openwave Mobile Browser (Openwave, *www.openwave.com*)
* Pocket Internet Explorer (Microsoft, *www.microsoft.com*)
* Picsel (Picsel Technologies, *www.picsel.com*)

Mobile device manufacturers

The major information appliance manufacturers publish information about their products and technologies for developers. To get you started, a few of the most popular are:

- Forum Nokia (*www.forum.nokia.com*)
- Ericsson Mobility World (*www.ericsson.com/mobilityworld*)
- BlackBerry Developers pages (*www.blackberry.com/developers*)

The Web on TV

Some people access the Web via their television sets using a set-top box that connects to the television and either a cable or modem Internet connection. Although it is not as full-featured or versatile as browsing on PCs, it may offer a convenient and more affordable alternative for some users. Gaming consoles are another option for using the TV as the display for Internet content.

The only significant player in the web TV arena is MSN TV (formerly WebTV, which hit the market in 1996). As of this writing, it remains barely a blip on the radar screen of overall browser usage, but it still has millions of users. Some sites are designed specifically for MSN TV.

MSN TV uses a television rather than a monitor as a display device. The canvas area in the MSN TV browser is a scant 544 × 372 pixels. Principles for designing legible television graphics apply, such as the use of light text on dark backgrounds rather than vice versa and the avoidance of any elements less than two pixels in width. These and other guidelines are provided on MSN TV's special developer site at *developer.msntv.com/*.

Of particular interest is MSN-TV Viewer, which shows you how your web page will look on MSN TV, right from the comfort of your computer. It is available for free for both Windows and Mac (although the Mac version is antiquated and will not be updated). For information on MSN-TV Viewer, go to *developer.msntv.com/ TOOLS/msntvvwr.asp*.

4

A Beginner's Guide
to the Server

Even if you focus primarily on what's commonly referred to as *frontend* web development—HTML documents and web graphics—the server and the way it is configured may impact the way you work. In most cases, there is no way to avoid making firsthand contact with the server, even if it's just to upload files.

For this reason, all web designers should have a basic level of familiarity with servers and what they do. At the very least, this will enable you to communicate more clearly with your server administrator. If you have permission for greater access to the server, it could mean taking care of certain tasks yourself without needing to wait for assistance.

This chapter provides an introduction to server terminology and functions, pathnames, and file (MIME) types. It also discusses uploading files and setting permissions, which designers often need to do.

Servers 101

A *server* is any computer running software that enables it to answer requests for documents and other data. The programs that request and display documents (such as a browser) are called *clients*. The terms *server-side* and *client-side*, in regard to such specific functions refer to which machine is doing the processing. Client-side functions happen on the user's machine; server-side functions occur on the remote machine.

Web servers answer requests from browsers (the client program), retrieve the specified file (or execute a script), and return the document or script results. Web browsers and servers communicate via the Hypertext Transfer Protocol (HTTP).

Popular Server Software

Any computer can be a server as long as it is running server software. Today, there are many server packages available, but the overwhelming leaders are Apache and Microsoft Internet Information Server (IIS).

Apache
> The majority of servers today (approximately 70%) run Apache. Powerful and full-featured, it has always been available for free. It runs primarily on the Unix platform but is also available on other platforms, including Windows NT/2000 and Mac OS X.

> The core installation of Apache has limited functionality, but it can be expanded and customized easily by adding modules. Apache calls on each module to perform a dedicated task, such as user authentication or database queries. You can pick up a copy of the Apache server and its documentation from the Apache home page at *www.apache.org*.

Internet Information Server (IIS)
> This is Microsoft's server package, which is also available without charge. IIS runs on the Windows NT platform. IIS has developed into a powerful and stable server option that is somewhat easier to set up and maintain than its Unix competitor. It has many advanced server features, including ASP (Active Server Pages) for server-side scripting. As of this writing, approximately 20% of sites run on IIS servers. For more information, see the Windows Server System pages at *www.microsoft.com/windowsserversystem/*.

Two good sites for information and statistics on popular servers are ServerWatch (*www.serverwatch.com*) and Netcraft (*www.netcraft.com/survey/*).

The particular brand of server does not impact the majority of things designers do, such as making graphics or developing basic HTML files. It certainly influences more advanced web site building techniques, such as Server Side Includes, adding MIME types (discussed later in this chapter), and database-driven web pages. Be certain to coordinate with your server administrator if you are using your server in ways beyond simple HTML and graphic files storage.

Basic Server Functions

As a web designer, it is important that you have some level of familiarity with the following elements of the web server.

Web root directory

When a browser requests a document, the server locates the document, starting with the server's root directory. This is the directory that has been configured to contain all documents intended to be shared via the Web. The root directory does not necessarily appear in the URL that points to the document, so it is important to know what your root directory is when uploading your files.

For example, if the root directory on *example.com* is */users/httpd/www/* and a browser makes a request for *http://www.example.com/super/cool.html*, the server actually retrieves */users/httpd/www/super/cool.html*. This, of course, is invisible to the user.

Index files

A slash (/) at the end of a URL indicates that the URL is pointing to a directory, not a file. If no specific document is identified, most servers display the contents of a default file (or index file). The index file is generally named *index.html*, but on some servers, it may be named *welcome.html* or *default.html*. Often, there is a hierarchy of index file names that the browser checks for and uses the one that has been given the highest priority. For example, if a directory contains both *index.html* and *index.php*, the server may be set up to display *index.php* automatically. This is another small variation you will need to confirm with your server administrator.

Some servers may be configured to display the contents of the directory if an index file is not found, leaving files vulnerable to snooping. For this reason, it is a good idea always to name some page (usually the main page) in each directory *index.html* (or another specified name). One advantage is that it makes URLs to the index page of each directory more tidy (*www.littlechair.com* rather than *www. littlechair.com/homepage.html*, for example).

 Another variable to confirm with your server administrator is whether your server has been configured to be case sensitive. For case-sensitive servers, the files *index.htm* and *Index.htm* are not equivalent, and can result in missing file errors.

HTTP response header

Once the server locates the file, it sends the contents of that file back to the browser, preceded by some HTTP response headers. The headers provide the browser with information about the arriving file, including its media type (also known as its *content type* or *MIME type*). Usually, the server determines the format from the file's suffix; for example, a file with the suffix *.gif* is taken to be an image file.

The browser reads the header information and determines how to handle the file, either displaying it in the window or launching the appropriate helper application or plug-in. MIME types are discussed further at the end of this chapter.

Server-Side Programming

Web pages and sites have gotten much more interactive since the early days of simple HTML document sharing. Now web sites serve as portals of two-way information sharing, e-commerce, search engines, and dynamically generated content. This functionality relies on programs and scripts that are processed on the server. There are a number of options for server-side programming, of which CGI, ASP, PHP, and Java servlets/JSP are the most common.

CGI (Common Gateway Interface)

Instead of pointing to an HTML file, a URL may request that a CGI program be run. CGI stands for Common Gateway Interface, and it's what allows the web server to communicate with other programs (CGI scripts) that are running on the server. CGI scripts are commonly written in the Perl, C, or C++ language.

CGI scripts are the traditional methods for performing a wide variety of functions such as searching, server-side image map handling, and gaming; however, their most common use is form processing (information entered by the user through entry fields in the document). As other more powerful options for interfacing with databases become available (such as ASP, PHP, and Java servlets), traditional CGI programming is getting less attention.

Most server administrators follow the convention of keeping CGI scripts in a special directory named *cgi-bin* (short for CGI-binaries). Keeping them in one directory makes it easier to manage and secure the server. When a CGI script is requested by the browser, the server runs the script and returns the dynamic content it produces to the browser.

ASP (Active Server Pages)

ASP (Active Server Pages) is a programming environment for Microsoft's Internet Information Server (IIS). It is primarily used to interface with data on the server to create dynamically generated web pages. It can also be configured to process form information.

Often, you'll come across a web document that ends in the *.asp* suffix (as opposed to *.html*). This indicates that it is a text file that contains HTML and scripting (usually written in VBScript) that is configured to interact with ASP on the server.

For more information on ASP, see Microsoft Developer Network's page entitled "ASP from A to Z" at *msdn.microsoft.com/workshop/server/asp/aspatoz.asp*. Another good resource is ASP 101 (*www.asp101.com*).

PHP

PHP is another scripting language that allows you to create dynamically generated web pages (similar to ASP). PHP is a project of the Apache Software Foundation, so it is open source and available for free. PHP works with a variety of web servers, but it is most commonly used with Apache.

PHP code, which is similar to Perl or ASP, can be embedded into the HTML document using special PHP tags. PHP's advantage over CGI scripting is that it is very easy to include short bits of PHP code directly in a web page, to process form data or extract information from a database, for example.

For more information on PHP, go to *www.php.net*, the official PHP web site.

Java servlets and JSP

Although Java is known for its small applications (known as *applets*) for the Web, it is a complete and complex programming language that is more typically used for developing large, enterprise-scale applications. With a Java-enabled web server, a programmer can write Java servlets that produce dynamic web content.

JavaServer Pages (JSP) is a related technology that is similar to ASP. JSP code is embedded directly in web pages; it provides a simple way for web authors to access the functionality of complex servlets that are running on the web server.

For more information on Java servlets and JSP, consult *java.sun.com/products/servlet/* and *java.sun.com/products/jsp/*.

Unix Directory Structures

Because the Web was spawned from the Unix environment, it follows many of the same conventions. Directory structure and pathname syntax are prime examples. It is important for all web designers to have an understanding of how directory structures are indicated on the Unix platform, because pathnames are used in hyperlinks and pointers to images and other resources.

Directories ("places" to store files) are organized into a hierarchical structure that fans out like an upside-down tree. The topmost directory is known as the root and is written as a forward slash (/). The root can contain several directories, each of which can contain subdirectories; each of these can contain more subdirectories, and so on. A subdirectory is said to be the *child* of the directory that holds it (its *parent*). Figure 4-1 shows a system with five directories under the root. The directory *users* contains two subdirectories, *jen* and *richard*. Within *jen* are two more subdirectories, *work* and *pers*, and within *pers* is the file *art.html*.

A *pathname* is the notation used to point to a particular file or directory; it tells you the path of directories you must travel to get to where you want to go. There are two types of pathnames: absolute and relative.

Absolute Pathnames

An *absolute* pathname always starts from the root directory, which is indicated by a slash (/). So, for example, the pathname for the *pers* directory is */users/jen/pers*, as shown in Figure 4-2. The first slash indicates that you are starting at the root and is necessary for indicating that a pathname is absolute.

The advantage to using absolute pathnames in links, image tags, and other places where you provide the URL of a file on the server is mobility. Because the pathname starts at the top of the server hierarchy, you can move the file to another

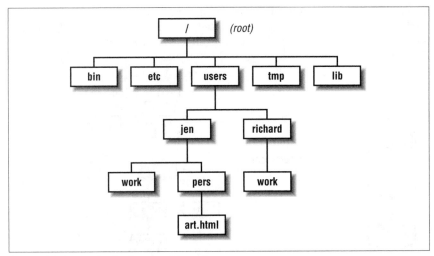

Figure 4-1. Example of a directory hierarchy

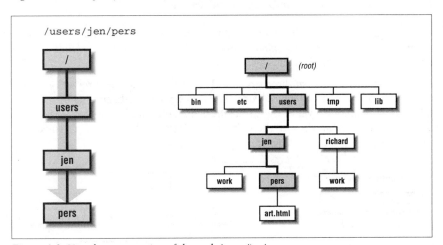

Figure 4-2. Visual representation of the path /users/jen/pers

directory on the server and the links won't break. The downside is that it makes it more difficult to test pages on your local machine, because your machine is likely to have a different root directory than the final destination server.

Relative Pathnames

A *relative* pathname points to a file or directory relative to your current working directory. When building a web site on a single server, relative pathnames are commonly used within URLs to refer to files in other directories on the server.

Unless you specify an absolute pathname (starting with a slash), the server assumes you are using a relative pathname. Starting in your current location (your working directory), you can trace your way up and down the directory hierarchy. This is best explained with an example.

If I am currently working in the directory *jen* and I want to refer to the file *art.html*, the relative pathname is *pers/art.html*, because the file *art.html* is in the directory *pers*, which is in the current directory, *jen*. This is illustrated in Figure 4-3.

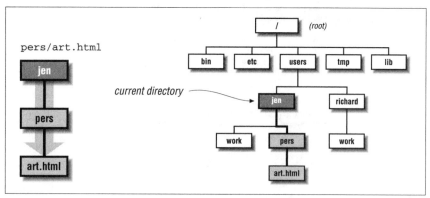

Figure 4-3. The path pers/art.html relative to the jen directory

Going back up the hierarchy is a bit trickier. You go up a level by using the shorthand of two dots (..) for the parent directory. Again, consider an example based on Figure 4-1.

If I am currently in the *jen* directory, and I want to refer to the directory *richard/work*, the pathname is *../richard/work*. The two dots at the beginning of the path take me back up one level to the to the *users* directory, and from there, I find the directory called *richard*, and then the subdirectory called *work*, as shown in Figure 4-4.

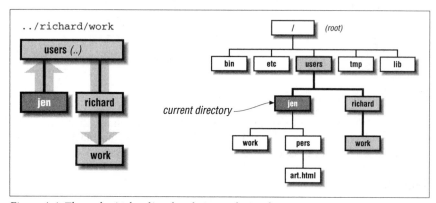

Figure 4-4. The path ../richard/work, relative to the jen directory

If I am currently in my *pers* directory and I want to refer to Richard's *work* directory, I need to go up two levels, so the pathname would be *../../richard/work*, as shown in Figure 4-5.

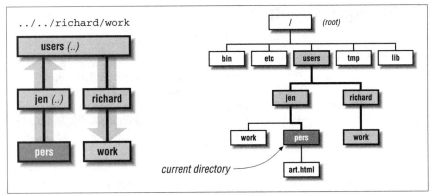

Figure 4-5. The path ../../richard/work, relative to the pers directory

Note that the absolute path */users/richard/work* accomplishes the same thing. The decision whether to use an absolute versus a relative pathname generally comes down to which is easiest from where you are and how likely it is that you will be moving files and directories around. Relative pathnames can break if files or directories are moved.

Using relative pathnames in HTML

When pointing to another web page or resource (such as an image) on your own server, it is common to use a relative URL, one that points to the new resource relative to the current document. Relative URLs follow the syntax for pathnames described above. For example, a hypertext link to *art.html* from another document in the *pers* directory would look like this:

```
<a href="art.html">
```

The URL for the link could also be written starting from the root directory:

```
<a href="/users/jen/pers/art.html">
```

Image tags also use pathnames to point to the graphic file to be displayed. For instance, this image tag in the *art.html* document:

```
<img src="../../daisy.gif">
```

points to a graphic named *daisy.gif* located in the *jen* directory. Two uses of *../* indicate that the graphic file resides in a directory two levels higher than the current document (*art.html*).

If you plan on doing your HTML markup by hand, pathname syntax will come naturally after a little practice. If you are using a WYSIWYG authoring tool (such as Macromedia Dreamweaver, Adobe GoLive, or Microsoft FrontPage), you have the luxury of letting the tool construct the relative URL pathnames for you. Some even have site management tools that automatically adjust the pathnames if documents get moved.

File Naming Conventions

For your files to traverse the network successfully, you must name them in accordance with established file naming conventions:

- Avoid character spaces in filenames. Although this is perfectly acceptable for local files on a Macintosh or Windows machine, character spaces are not recognized by other systems. It is common to use an underscore or hyphen character to visually separate words within filenames, such as *andre_bio.html* or *andre-bio.html*. Hyphens are sometimes preferred because they tend to better enable search engines to index the individual words in a filename.

- Avoid special characters such as ?, %, #, /, and : in filenames. It is best to limit filenames to letters, numbers, underscores (in place of character spaces), hyphens, and periods.

- Use proper suffixes. HTML documents should use the suffix *.html* (*.htm* also works on most servers). GIF graphic files take the suffix *.gif*, and JPEGs should be named *.jpg* or *.jpeg*. If your files do not have the correct suffix, the server might not send the proper HTTP Content-Type header, and thus the browser may not recognize the files as web-based files. Suffixes for a large number of common file types are listed later in this chapter.

- Consistently using all lowercase letters in filenames, while certainly not necessary, may make them easier to remember. In addition, filenames are case-sensitive on some servers, so keeping them all lowercase avoids potential hassles.

- Keep filenames as short as possible. They add to the size of the file (and they can be a nuisance to remember).

Uploading Documents (FTP)

The most common transaction that a web designer will have with a web server is the uploading of HTML documents, graphics, and other media files. Files are transferred between computers over a network via a method called FTP (File Transfer Protocol).

If you are working in a Telnet session on Unix, you can run the FTP program and transfer files with a hefty collection of command-line arguments (not covered in this book).

Fortunately, if you work on a Mac or PC, there are a number of FTP programs with graphical interfaces that spare you the experience of transferring files using the Unix command line. In fact, FTP functions are now built right into full-featured web authoring tools, such as GoLive, Dreamweaver, and FrontPage, among others. On the Mac, dedicated programs that allow drag-and-drop file transfer, such as Fetch and Interarchy (previously Anarchie) are quite popular. On the PC, there are numerous simple FTP programs, such as CuteFTP, WS_FTP, AceFTP, and Transmit. These (and many others) are available for download at *www.shareware.com*; search for "ftp."

The FTP Process

Regardless of the tool you use, the basic principles and processes are the same. Before you begin, you must have an account with permission to upload files to the server. Check with the server administrator to be sure you have a login name and a password.

You don't necessarily need an account to upload and download files if the server is set up as an "anonymous" FTP site. However, due to obvious security implications, be sure that your personal directories are not configured to be accessible to all anonymous users.

1. Launch the FTP program of your choice and open a connection with your server. You'll need to enter the exact name of the server, your account name, and password.

2. Locate the appropriate directory into which you want to copy your files. You may also choose to create a new directory or delete existing files and directories on the remote server using the controls in your FTP program. (Note that some servers allow you to enter the complete pathname to the directory before logging in.)

3. Specify the transfer mode. The most important decision to make during uploading is specifying whether the data should be transferred in binary or ASCII mode.

   ASCII files are composed of alphanumeric characters. Some FTP programs refer to ASCII files as "text" files. Most HTML documents may be transferred as ASCII or text. However, more and more HTML documents are written using Unicode (UTF-8 in particular), and Unicode files may be corrupted if sent as ASCII or text. For such files, see the next section on binary.

   Binary files are made up of compiled data (ones and zeros); some examples are executable programs, graphic images, movies, and so on. Some programs refer to the binary mode as "raw data" or "image." All graphics (*.gif*, *.jpeg*, and so on), multimedia files, and Unicode (e.g., UTF-8) encoded (X)HTML files should be transferred as binary or raw data. Table 4-1 includes a listing of the transfer mode for a number of popular file types.

   In Fetch (available at *www.fetchsoftworks.com*), you may see a *MacBinary* option, which transfers the file with its resource fork (the bit of the file containing desktop icons and other Mac-specific data) intact. It should be used only when transferring from one Mac to another. This resource fork is appropriately stripped out of Mac-generated media files when transferred under the standard raw data mode.

   Some FTP programs also provide an *Auto* option, which enables you to transfer whole directories containing files of both types. The program examines each file and determines whether it should be transferred as text or binary information. This function is not totally reliable on all programs, so use it with caution until you are positive you are getting good results.

Servers

4. Upload your files to the server. Standard FTP uses the terminology *put* (uploading files from your computer to the server) and *get* (downloading files from the server to your computer), so these terms may be used in your FTP program as well. You can also upload multiple files at a time.

5. Disconnect. When you have completed the transfer, be sure to disconnect from the server. You may want to test the files you've uploaded on a browser first to make sure everything transferred successfully.

Setting Permissions

When you upload files to a web server, you need to be sure that the files' permissions are set so that everyone is able to read your files. Permissions control who can read, write (edit), or execute (if it is a program) the file, and they need to be established for the owner of the file, the file's group, and for "everyone." Usually, when you create or upload a file, you are automatically the owner, which may mean that only you can set the permissions. Most web servers honor the operating system's default permissions to determine which files can be read, written, and executed.

Some FTP programs enable you to set the default upload permissions via a dialog box. Figure 4-6 shows Fetch's dialog box for doing this. For most web purposes, you want to grant yourself full permissions but restrict all other users to read-only. You may want to confirm that your server administrator agrees with these settings.

Figure 4-6. Standard permissions settings (using Fetch)

The server needs to be specially configured to recognize these permissions commands, so check with your administrator to see if you can use this easy method. The administrator will give you instructions if any special permissions settings are necessary.

If a CGI or script file does not work properly, permissions are often the culprit. You'll need to enable execution to run these files. Resist the urge to enable all permissions for all files and directories, because it could become possible for users to upload their own script files and run them, allowing them to do such things as delete all of your files, deface your site, or create their own mail server to send out spam.

File (MIME) Types

Servers add a header to each document, which tells the browser the type of file it is sending. The browser determines how to handle the file based on that information—for example, whether to display the contents in the window, or to launch the appropriate plug-in or helper application.

The system for communicating media types closely resembles MIME (Multipurpose Internet Mail Extension), which was originally developed for sending attachments in email. The server needs to be configured to recognize each MIME type to successfully communicate the media type to the browser.

If you want to deliver media beyond the standard HTML files and graphics (such as a Shockwave Flash movie or an audio file), you should contact your server administrator to be sure the server is configured to support that MIME type. Most common formats are built into current versions of server software, but if the format isn't there already, the administrator can easily set it up if you provide the necessary information.

The exact syntax for configuring MIME types varies among server software; however, they all require the same basic information: type, subtype, and extension. Types are the most broad categories for files. They include text, image, audio, video, application, and so on. Within each category are a number of subtypes. For instance, the file type image includes the subtypes gif, jpeg, and the like. The extension refers to the file's suffix, which the server uses to determine the file type and subtype. Not all extensions are standardized.

Table 4-1 lists the MIME type and subtype for common media types. The ASCII/ binary information is provided to aid in making upload decisions.

Of course, new technologies and file types are emerging every day, so keep in mind that it is the web designer's responsibility to make sure that for any new media type, the appropriate information is communicated to the server administrator. For a complete listing of registered MIME types, see the IANA (Internet Assigned Numbers Authority) site at *www.iana.org/assignments/media-types/*.

Table 4-1. MIME types and subtypes

Type/subtype	Extension	Description	ASCII/ binary
application/excel	.xl	Microsoft Excel	B
application/mac-binhex40	.hqx	Mac BinHex archive	B
application/msword	.doc, .dot, .word, .w6w	Microsoft Word document	B

Table 4-1. MIME types and subtypes (continued)

Type/subtype	Extension	Description	ASCII/ binary
application/pdf	`.pdf`	Portable Document Format (Adobe Acrobat file)	B
application/postscript	`.ai`	PostScript viewer	A
application/postscript	`.eps`	Encapsulated PostScript	A
application/postscript	`.ps`	PostScript file	A
application/powerpoint	`.ppt, .pot`	PowerPoint file	B
application/rtf	`.rtf`	Rich Text Format (Microsoft Word)	A
application/vnd.ms-excel	`.xll, .xls`	Microsoft Excel File	B
application/xml	`.xml`	Generic XML	A
application/xml+xhtml	`.htm, .html`	XHTML document	A
application/x-director	`.dcr, .dir, .dxr`	Shockwave files	B
application/x-gzip	`.gz, .gzip`	GNU zip (Unix decompressor)	B
application/x-msdownload	`.exe`	Self-extracting file or executable	B
application/x-perl	`.pl`	Perl source file	A
application/x-sea	`.sea`	Self-extracting archive (StuffIt file)	B
application/x-sit	`.sit`	StuffIt archive	B
application/x-shockwave-flash	`.swf`	Shockwave Flash file	B
application/x-stuffit	`.sit`	StuffIt Archive	B
application/x-tar	`.tar`	Compressed file	B
application/x-zip or application/x-zip-compressed	`.zip`	Compressed file (decompress using WinZip or StuffIt on Mac)	B
audio/aifc	`.aifc`	Compressed AIFF file	B
audio/basic	`.au`	μ-law sound file	B
audio/basic	`.snd`	Digitized sound file	B
audio/midi or audio/x-midi	`.mid`	MIDI audio file	B
audio/x-aiff	`.aif, .aiff`	AIFF file	B
audio/x-mpeg	`.mp3`	MP3 audio file	B
audio/x-ms-wma	`.wma`	Windows Media audio file	B
audio/x-ms-wax	`.wax`	Windows Media audio metafile	B
audio/x-pn-realaudio	`.ra, .ram`	RealAudio file (and metafile)	B
audio/x-pn-realaudio-plugin	`.rpm`	RealAudio (plug-in)	B
audio/x-wav	`.wav, .aiff`	Windows WAV audio file	B
image/gif	`.gif`	Graphic in GIF format	B
image/jpeg	`.jpg, .jpeg, .jpe, .jfif, .pjpeg, .pjp`	Graphic in JPEG format	B

Table 4-1. MIME types and subtypes (continued)

Type/subtype	Extension	Description	ASCII/ binary
image/tiff	*.tif*, *.tiff*	TIFF image (requires external viewer)	B
image/x-MS-bmp	*.bmp*	Microsoft BMP file	B
image/x-photo-cd	*.pcd*	Kodak Photo CD image	B
image/x-pict	*.pic*	PICT image file	B
image/x-png or image/png	*.png*	Graphic in PNG format	B
image/x-portable-bitmap	*.pbm*	Portable bitmap image	B
text/html	*.htm*	HTML document	A
text/plain	*.txt*	ASCII text file	A
text/richtext	*.rtx*	Rich Text Format (Microsoft Word)	A
text/xml	*.xml*	Generic XML document	A
video/avi or video/x-msvideo	*.avi*	AVI video file	B
video/mpeg	*.mpg*, *.mpe*, *.mpeg*, *.m1v*, *.mp2*, *.mp3*, *.mpa*	MPEG movie	B
video/quicktime	*.mov*	QuickTime movie	B
video/quicktime	*.qt*	QuickTime movie	B
video/x-ms-asf	*.asf*	Windows Media (legacy)	B
video/x-ms-asx	*.asx*	Windows Media metafile (legacy)	B
video/x-ms-wmv	*.wmv*	Windows Media video file	B
video/x-ms-wmx	*.wmx*	Windows Media video metafile	B
video/x-sgi-movie	*.movie*	Silicon Graphics movie	B
x-world/x-vrml	*.wrl*, *.wrz*	VRML 3D file (requires VRML viewer)	B

Servers

5

Accessibility

—by Derek Featherstone

At its core, web accessibility is about building web sites, applications, and pages so that there are as few barriers to use as possible for anyone, regardless of ability and the device used to access the information. Web accessibility goes beyond creating a more usable Web for persons with disabilities, too. Many of the techniques and principles designers apply to make web content more accessible to people with disabilities also improve accessibility for those using slower connections who might have the images off as well as increase interoperability with handhelds.

For sites to be accessible, we have to let go the notion that we know how people use our web sites. We have to understand the nature of the medium in which we work. And, we have to be willing to embrace "universal design" and to use web development techniques and code that support accessibility.

Types of Disabilities

There are four broad categories of disabilities that have an impact on how a person interacts with a web site: vision impairment, mobility impairment, auditory impairment, and cognitive impairments.

Vision impairment
> People that are blind or have low vision use a variety of assistive technology to get content from the screen, including screen readers, Braille displays, screen magnifiers, and even some combination of these.

Mobility impairment
> Mobility challenges range from having no use of the hands at all to difficulties with fine motor control. Various hardware solutions include modified mice and keyboards, single-button "switches," foot pedals, head wands, and joysticks, while software solutions range from full voice recognition to face tracking to simple keyboard macros.

Auditory impairment

Auditory impairments may seem to have little to no impact on how people use the Web, as most content is text and images. A person who has never been able to hear, however, may process language completely differently than a hearing person or someone with hearing loss that occurred later. There are requirements for captioning for multimedia and audio files to make this type of media accessible to everyone.

Cognitive impairment

Cognitive impairments, which involve memory, reading comprehension, mathematical processing, visual comprehension, problem solving, and attention, are the least understood of the various accessibility issues. Although there isn't a large body of literature and research available, the common advice is to focus on simplicity and clarity to help address some of these issues. Thinking this way also helps make your web pages, sites, and applications more readily understood by everyone.

Overview of Assistive Technology

Assistive technology is any tool that helps a person with a disability accomplish everyday tasks more easily. A specially designed "rocker" knife that makes it easier to cut food with the use of one hand is considered assistive technology. In computer terms, assistive technology helps people accomplish two fundamental tasks: input and output. These tools are not web specific; web usage is just one component of their overall utility.

 Don't overlook your own computer's capabilities. Windows XP and Mac OS X both include a lot of support for accessibility by default, and Sun Microsystems' Solaris 10 includes full accessibility support with voice capabilities, screen magnification, and onscreen keyboard functions.

Input Devices

Assistive technology for input works to provide the same type of functionality that a keyboard and mouse provide. This means that for the most part, you as a web designer or developer simply need to ensure that what you create is operable by both keyboard and mouse. If you can do that, generally the assistive technology will take care of the rest (although some input considerations are discussed later in the chapter).

Some example technologies are:

Alternative keyboards

Alternative keyboards may provide a more functional key layout, be color-coded for cognitive disabilities, include larger keys, have a keyboard overlay or guide that aids in selection of the proper key, or be designed for one-handed use.

Virtual keyboards

A virtual keyboard is one that is displayed on the screen to help people who may have difficulty typing but are able to use a mouse or some other pointing device effectively. Windows XP comes with a basic onscreen keyboard.

Voice recognition software

Voice recognition software makes use of a computer's audio capabilities to detect a person's voice for two main purposes: transcribing voice to text and listening for operating commands. Voice command recognition is available at the operating system level (Mac OS X) as well as in voice-capable web browsers, such as the most recent versions of the Opera browser.

Voice Recognition Approaches

Voice recognition software has evolved significantly over the last decade. To activate a web link, you might simply say the link text. The voice recognition software then searches through the links it finds in the page, finds the correct one, and simulates a "click" on that link. So, what happens if you have multiple links with the same text? The software might highlight all of the links and overlay a number beside each, allowing you to speak the number of the link you'd like to follow.

To fill in a form, you could speak the name of the field you wish to fill in, and the cursor will automatically be placed in the appropriate text box or form control. As you will see in Chapter 15, form controls must be labeled properly so that the voice recognition software knows exactly which form field should receive the focus.

Some recognition packages enable users to overlay a numbered 3×3 grid on the computer screen by saying "mouse grid." The user then speaks the number of the grid portion of interest. The software overlays another numbered 3×3 grid within that space and the mouse cursor moves on the screen. This process continues until the grid is sufficiently small to put the mouse cursor where the user desires and the user issues the command to click or double-click. For example, to click on a radio button, you might have to say the following: "Mouse grid. Four. Three. Eight. Two. Five. Mouse click."

Head and mouth wands

These wands amount to a stick that is used to type on a regular or modified keyboard. These input devices are regularly used with a common operating system feature known as "sticky keys" that enables the user to press and release a modifier key, such as Ctrl, and then press another key, treating the sequence of keystrokes as if they happened in unison.

Face and eye tracking

This technology generally uses software to follow the eyes or face of a person who has limited mobility and is unable to speak clearly enough to use voice recognition software. As users move their eyes, the mouse cursor follows. Various other actions may be used as a click or double-click. For an example, visit *www.qualilife.com*.

Switches

Adaptive switches are highly specialized mechanisms that may simply serve as a single button mouse or may allow for greater flexibility with a set of foot switches, or a sip and puff mechanism. Again, these may be used in conjunction with specialized software to allow people to have full control of all the functions on their computer, including typing with automatic word-prediction.

Output Devices

The normal sources of output for most everyday computer usage are the monitor and speakers. Captioning or transcripts can be of assistance, or users can turn to:

Screen readers

Most screen readers are programs that interpret and interface with the actions that occur within the operating system and the applications that run on it. They provide extensive functionality through keystroke combinations and offer specific modes for specific functions. For example, Freedom Scientific's JAWS (*www.freedomscientific.com*) has normal reading, tables reading, and forms modes. They generally read some combination of the rendered HTML on the screen and do so based on source order. Other screen readers include: Window Eyes (GW Micro, *www.gwmicro.com*), HAL (Automated Living, *www.automatedliving.com*), and SuperNova (Dolphin Computer Access, *www.dolphincomputeraccess.com*).

Screen magnifiers

Used by people with low vision, screen magnifier software simply provides an enlarged view of the onscreen text and graphics. Examples include Zoom-Text (Ai Squared Software, *www.aisquared.com*), SuperNova, and MAGic (Freedom Scientific).

Aural browsers

Similar in function to screen readers, aural browsers are specialized for web use and provide less functionality than a full screen reader. Some examples are Home Page Reader (IBM, *www-3.ibm.com/able/solution_offerings/hpr.html*), which is a standalone program, and Connect Outloud (Freedom Scientific) and Browsealoud (Texthelp Systems, *www.browsealoud.com*), which are plug-ins for Internet Explorer.

Braille display

These devices convert computer output to Braille, displaying the words via a set of movable pins that represent the current line of display. These devices are often used in conjunction with a screen reader. For example, the speech output from JAWS could be sent to a Braille display.

Who Is Responsible for Accessibility?

Generally speaking, there are four "groups" of people responsible for accessibility. These include:

Web designers

That's right, us: the people who design, program, and build web sites. Using the W3C's Web Content Accessibility Guidelines (WCAG) we can make informed decisions as to how to make sites accessible.

Browser, screen reader, and other user agent manufacturers
> This group is responsible for ensuring the accessibility of their tools for using the Web. The User Agent Accessibility Guidelines (UAAG) help browser manufacturers build their tools so that they can leverage the good content that developers produce.

Software vendors
> Playing a critical role in accessibility, this group creates the tools that developers, designers, and authors use to create web content. This group looks at the Authoring Tool Accessibility Guidelines (ATAG) when they are building their software.

Users
> People with disabilities are not without some responsibility. It is quite reasonable that we expect people using assistive technology to know how to use it properly and efficiently.

So if we as developers, designers, and authors are partly responsible, how do we go about living up to those responsibilities to make our web sites accessible? First, we start with an understanding of what we're trying to achieve, and then we apply that to the way we build our sites. Fortunately, we are guided by the W3C's Web Content Accessibility Guidelines 1.0 (WCAG 1.0).

Web Content Accessibility Guidelines

The Web Content Accessibility Guidelines were created by the Web Accessibility Initiative (WAI) at the W3C. The guidelines were formally made Recommendations in 1999, and a lot has changed since then. Some of the techniques that are advocated in the WCAG 1.0 Techniques resource are outdated and may no longer apply in the same way as when the guidelines were released.

These guidelines have several related checkpoints organized according to three different priority levels from Priority 1 (most critical for web accessibility) to Priority 3 (important but having less impact on overall accessibility). At *www.w3. org/TR/1999/WAI-WEBCONTENT-19990505*, each of the checkpoints are listed following their related guidelines along with their priority level. For a view of the checkpoints organized according to their priority level, go to *www.w3.org/TR/ WCAG10/full-checklist.html*.

Guideline 1: Provide equivalent alternatives to auditory and visual content.
> Following this rule ensures that visually or aurally impaired people have access to the content that they are unable to perceive. "Equivalent alternatives" refers to ensuring that images have appropriate alt text that represents the image, that audio content has captions provided, and that video includes audio description. Remember, when deciding what an equivalent alternative is, you must consider both the content and function of the original.

Guideline 2: Don't rely on color alone.
> When you rely on color alone to present information on a web page, you limit the usefulness of that information. Rather than using color alone to show which fields of a form are required, mark the labels in red and bold, or with an asterisk beside them to ensure that people who can't see the red color

have some other means of getting the same information. Further, provide sufficient contrast between the foreground color and the background color to ensure that text (even as part of a graphic, Flash movie, or other multimedia component) is readable.

Guideline 3: Use markup and style sheets and do so properly.
In other words, validate your code to ensure it has the correct syntax, use appropriate HTML elements for the tasks for which they were designed, and use HTML for your content, CSS for presentation, and ECMAScript for interaction and behavior (JavaScript is the most commonly known implementation of ECMAScript). Not only does this mean using markup the correct way (using <blockquote>...</blockquote> to surround a quote, for example) and enhance accessibility, but it also means not using markup the wrong way (using <blockquote>...</blockquote> to indent text, for example), which can actually reduce accessibility.

Guideline 4: Clarify natural language usage.
Identify the language of the document and mark up such exceptions as foreign words, abbreviations, and acronyms. This makes it easier for speech devices and other assistive technologies to interpret the content. In fact, some screen readers change their language on the fly to speak the content with the correct pronunciation and accents. Of course, a limited number of languages are supported. For further details on language codes, refer to Chapter 6.

Guideline 5: Create tables that transform gracefully.
Five years ago it was common to see tables used for layout purposes, simply because browser support for CSS-based layouts was less than satisfactory. Modern, standards-based web development techniques suggest that we limit the use of tables to the display of tabular data—after all, that is what tables were designed for! Chapter 13 includes tips to help ensure that your tables are as accessible as possible.

Guideline 6: Ensure that pages featuring new technologies transform gracefully.
Think of this guideline as preparing your web page for the worst, ensuring that it is both compatible with future/new technologies as well as backward compatible with technologies.

Following this guideline is like making a contingency plan, preparing for the reality that we don't really know how people will use our sites and web pages. Does the site still work if CSS is disabled, or overridden? Does the site work appropriately when JavaScript is disabled? What about when a particular plug-in is not available? Is there an appropriate alternative in that case?

This guideline is also about making sure that the web pages you implement don't require the use of any specific input device. For example, in addition to allowing a mouse to control or activate certain scripts or controls (such as playing a movie) you must allow a keyboard.

Guideline 7: Ensure user control of time-sensitive changes.
At its most fundamental level, this guideline is about providing all users the control that they need to take in content at their own pace. Consider a web site that includes a news ticker that displays a new headline every two

seconds. What if someone can't finish reading the headline in the allotted time? Allowing the user control over this type of content helps everyone. Another common scenario is the web page that employs a `<meta>` tag and `http-equiv="refresh"` to redirect users to a new page after an allotted time after displaying the message "This page has moved. You will be redirected in five seconds. If you aren't, then click this link." This technique isn't good practice, because it makes the assumption that everyone will be able to read the message that quickly.

In addition to these issues with reading pace and readability in general, this guideline suggests avoiding "flickering" or other blinking and moving content. Not only can these be a distraction to those with reading difficulties, but flickering or flashing in the 4 to 59 flashes per second range may trigger seizures in those with photosensitive epilepsy.

Guideline 8: Ensure direct accessibility of embedded user interfaces.
Essentially this means that if you create your own interface within the browser using Flash or similar technology, the interface should follow all of the basic accessibility principles. The embedded interface should provide device-independent access to any content and controls that it contains, and the content of the embedded interface should be made available to assistive technology such as screen readers.

Guideline 9: Design for device independence.
Generally speaking, web pages written in HTML or XHTML are device independent. You can activate links, move to form fields, and submit forms using either the mouse or keyboard. HTML is device independent by default. It is only when we add non-HTML based elements to the mix—Flash, Java, or even scripting with JavaScript—that the trouble starts. When implementing scripts and other items that go beyond basic HTML, remember that some people rarely use a mouse; they "click" on links with the Enter key on their keyboards or push submit and other buttons with their spacebars. Keep this in mind. Head wands, switches, alternative keyboards, voice recognition, and other input devices generally emulate basic mouse and keyboard typing and clicking. If you can ensure that these two actions are allowed, you don't necessarily have to make other adjustments for assistive technology and alternate input devices.

Many of this chapter's guidelines and associated techniques are coming under question as we more fully understand how people using screen readers and sighted keyboards use the Web. With the growing popularity of standards-based techniques that use CSS for layout, we rarely require the use of the once-common `tabindex` attribute. In most cases, it simply isn't required anymore. There are also several arguments that the use of access keys as recommended by Guideline 9 is not as useful as it first appears.

Guideline 10: Use interim solutions.

One of the most difficult areas of making accessible web pages, this guideline seems to suggest the use of outdated techniques that are designed to compensate for older browsers and screen readers. This is due to literal interpretation of the guidelines without recognizing why the guideline existed in the first place.

All of the guidelines in this section include the phrase "until user agents." This means that when the guidelines were published, the interim solutions suggested were valid and useful, but it was fully recognized that these techniques may no longer be recommended once user agents and assistive technology had "caught up." Ensure that when you read through these solutions, you check to make sure that the techniques are still valid and useful.

Guideline 11: Use W3C technologies and guidelines.

The W3C specifications were designed with accessibility features built into them. So, following these specifications should result in greater accessibility for all.

At its core, this guideline suggests that the lowest common denominator—HTML—is the best and most accessible delivery format. And for the most part, it is true.

However, we know that this is not always possible, nor is it reality. The best advice, then, based on this guideline is to use W3C technologies and make them accessible, and when you use other technologies, use their built-in accessibility features, and provide an alternative version to the non-W3C version that is accessible.

Guideline 12: Provide context and orientation information.

This guideline encompasses using titles for frames to ensure that the purpose of each frame is clearly stated, to use elements, such as optgroup, within a select form control to group related options together, to use fieldset to group related form controls together, to describe the fieldset contents with a legend, and to explicitly associate form controls with their labels.

All of these techniques improve accessibility for everyone by providing information about the components and their relationships to one another.

Guideline 13: Provide clear navigation mechanisms.

Clearly marked navigation menus that are consistent across a site can be enhanced by using a site map, providing metadata by using link relationships and other information about the author, date of publication, and the type of content they contain.

There are implications here for content creation as well: link text should be clear and identify where the link leads, and headings, paragraphs, and lists should provide their distinguishing phrase or content near the beginning.

Guideline 14: Ensure documents are clear and simple.

This guideline is designed to help everyone by making documents more readable and more readily understood. Clarity is often achieved through not words alone, but through the combination of words and well-designed illustrations or images that help get the point across (with appropriate alt text, of course).

Web Content Accessibility Guidelines 2.0 (WCAG 2.0)

At the time of this writing, the W3C's Working Draft of Web Content Accessibility Guidelines 2.0 was entering its final stages of approval.

WCAG 2.0 revolves around four basic principles for web accessibility:

- Content must be perceivable.
- User interface components in the content must be operable.
- Content and controls must be understandable.
- Content must be robust enough to work with current and future technologies.

This is not a radical departure from WCAG 1.0, and the same general principles apply. In many ways, it is a reorganization to make the full gamut of accessibility guidelines more understandable. Further, WCAG 2.0 attempts to provide better guidance to web content authors by eliminating some of the ambiguity in WCAG 1.0. For a comparison of WCAG 1.0 and WCAG 2.0, see *www.w3.org/WAI/GL/2005/06/30-mapping.html*.

Keep in mind, however, that the WCAG 2.0 Working Draft is subject to revision based on review and public comment.

Standards Variations and Section 508

Various other countries have their own versions of web accessibility standards, most of which are derived from WCAG 1.0. Canada, Australia, the U.K., and Europe, for example, have accessibility standards that generally agree with the most important points (Priority 1 and Priority 2) of WCAG 1.0. One of the most well-known standards that is a deviation from this is Section 508 in the U.S., which uses Priority 1 checkpoints, as well as a few other selectively chosen checkpoints.

Many view Section 508 as a more literal and strict interpretation of the Priority 1 and 2 checkpoints. Fundamentally, though, Section 508 principles are generally consistent with Priority 1 of WCAG 1.0, though the wording may be slightly different.

The following list is excerpted from subsection 1194.22 of Section 508 standards for Web-based intranet and Internet information and applications (*www.section508.gov/index.cfm?FuseAction=Content&ID=12#Web*). You'll notice that the items (a) through (k) consistently map to the Priority 1 checkpoints of WCAG 1.0, whereas the subsequent items do not.

- (a) A text equivalent for every nontext element shall be provided (e.g., via alt, `longdesc`, or in element content).
- (b) Equivalent alternatives for any multimedia presentation shall be synchronized with the presentation.
- (c) Web pages shall be designed so that all information conveyed with color is also available without color, for example, from context or markup.

- (d) Documents shall be organized so they are readable without requiring an associated style sheet.

- (e) Redundant text links shall be provided for each active region of a server-side image map.

- (f) Client-side image maps shall be provided instead of server-side image maps except where the regions cannot be defined with an available geometric shape.

- (g) Row and column headers shall be identified for data tables.

- (h) Markup shall be used to associate data cells and header cells for data tables that have two or more logical levels of row or column headers.

- (i) Frames shall be titled with text that facilitates frame identification and navigation.

- (j) Pages shall be designed to avoid causing the screen to flicker with a frequency greater than 2 Hz and lower than 55 Hz.

- (k) A text-only page, with equivalent information or functionality, shall be provided to make a web site comply with the provisions of this part, when compliance cannot be accomplished in any other way. The content of the text-only page shall be updated whenever the primary page changes.

- (l) When pages utilize scripting languages to display content, or to create interface elements, the information provided by the script shall be identified with functional text that can be read by assistive technology.

- (m) When a web page requires that an applet, plug-in, or other application be present on the client system to interpret page content, the page must provide a link to a plug-in or applet that complies with [subsection]1194.21(a) through (l).

- (n) When electronic forms are designed to be completed online, the form shall allow people using assistive technology to access the information, field elements, and functionality required for completion and submission of the form, including all directions and cues.

- (o) A method shall be provided that permits users to skip repetitive navigation links.

- (p) When a timed response is required, the user shall be alerted and given sufficient time to indicate more time is required.

Web Accessibility Techniques

Official guidelines and checkpoints are vital, but they don't give us much in the way of best practice advice or implementation techniques. To help you, the W3C provides reference documents with overviews of HTML, CSS, and core techniques at *www.w3.org/WAI/intro/wcag.php*.

Here are some good starting points that will help you make your web sites more accessible.

Start with meaning.

In other words, use HTML elements for the purposes for which they were designed: to provide a semantic description of a document's content. As discussed in the guidelines earlier in this chapter, make use of headings (h1 through h6), lists, quotes, and blockquotes to provide structure to your pages. Use table markup appropriately as shown in Chapter 13. Screen readers and other software infer meaning and provide functionality based on this markup.

Provide alternatives.

Ensure that you provide some type of alternative—alt text, longdesc, transcripts for audio files, and captions for video—for users with various disabilities. Formerly cost prohibitive, captioning and transcripting can now be outsourced at a very reasonable cost and provide significant benefit to users that require alternative media types.

Use Zoom layouts.

Typically used by low-vision users, a Zoom layout is an alternative view of the same content. Users of screen magnification software have a limited view of what is on the screen, making multiple columns difficult to follow. A single-column format can be very useful. For more information on Zoom layouts, Joe Clark's web site (*www.joeclark.org/access/webaccess/zoom/to*) is an excellent starting point.

Remember that order counts.

Ensuring a logical order within a page and the components within the page makes your life simpler and can be very beneficial to users of screen readers and Zoom layouts. A screen reader or aural browser tends to read things in the order of the source (although there are exceptions). Ensure that a logical order applies not only to the entire page, but also to components of the page, such as groups of links or form fields.

Make your forms explicit.

Although various pieces of assistive technology can make guesses as to which form fields go with which labels, you're better off making the relationship explicit than relying on a guess. Best practice for forms also includes using fieldset and legend to group related form controls. If nothing else, use the label element for every form control. For more information, see Chapter 15. Where it is undesirable to have the label visible on the screen, either hide the label from the visible screen using CSS positioning, or use the title attribute instead to provide a prompt text for the form control.

Test JavaScript extensively.

When using JavaScript in your pages, you should test with JavaScript support both on and off to ensure greatest interoperability. Do not let this fool you into thinking that if the page works under both of these conditions that you are finished, however. Remember that screen reader users are likely using Internet Explorer with scripting on. The interaction between what happens with the scripts and the screen reader might surprise you; testing with real people using screen readers is a must if you are doing any serious scripting in your pages or applications.

Facilitate users moving around the page.

This includes all users, but it is particularly useful for visually impaired and mobility impaired people who rely on keyboard navigation. Providing "in-page" links to various parts of the page has become a best practice. This includes a "skip to main content" link or "skip to navigation" link, depending on whether you present content or navigation first in the source order of your page. A skip-to-main content link can be visible on the page to everyone:

```
<a href="#content">Skip to main content</a>
```

visible only to screen readers through CSS positioning:

```
<a style="position: absolute; left: -999em; " href="#content">Skip to
main content</a>
```

or visible only to screen readers through using an image-based alt text:

```
<a href="#content"><img src="1x1.gif" alt="Skip to main content" /></a>
```

Each of these techniques has its advantages and disadvantages. The most accessible and useful is when the link is available to all users and not just focused on screen readers.

Allow text to scale.

Despite the fact that pixels are a relative unit, specifying text in your CSS using pixel units means that users of Internet Explorer for Windows (Versions 6 and earlier) will not be able to scale their text without what amounts to an intervention. Specifying text sizes in em or % units allows text to scale in IE for Windows as well as other modern browsers and is considered to be current best practice.

Make use of the focus state for links.

When a keyboard user navigates a page's links via a browser's built-in mechanism, we can provide visual feedback to show the user which link is currently selected or has the focus. This makes the web page easier to use. This is typically seen in menu bars that add in a CSS hover effect for mouse users:

```
a:link {
    color: #000;
    background-color: #fff;
}
a:hover {
    color: #fff;
    background-color: #000;
}
```

To provide the same feedback for keyboard users, add the code:

```
a:focus {
    color: #fff;
    background-color: #000;
}
```

Although the :focus technique works for links in modern standards-compliant browsers, Internet Explorer for Windows doesn't recognize the :focus pseudoclass selector. Instead, you must use the :active pseudoclass to provide the same visual feedback:

```
a:active {
    color: #fff;
    background-color: #000;
}
```

Handle colors intelligently.

Declare your colors *in pairs* and to do so *only* in CSS. If you are specifying a background color in the CSS and a foreground color in the HTML, there is room for conflict if style sheets are off, not supported, or overridden by the end user. In addition, when you declare your background and foreground colors in CSS, be sure that there is a reasonable contrast between them. (See the color contrast analyzers available at JuicyStudio for more: *http://juicystudio.com/services/colourcontrast.php*.)

Use CSS background images carefully.

Creative techniques for using background images in CSS help provide for accessibility as they allow us to use text for buttons, tabs, and other places formerly the province of graphics. This provides for scaling of text and doesn't require alt text. There is one catch: if the image contains content, do not use it as a background image, as there is no means to specify alternative text for background images as there is for images placed inline with the img element. The exceptions are various image replacement techniques, whose usefulness is often debated.

When using a CSS background image, be sure to specify a background-color as well, to ensure that there is enough contrast between the foreground text and the background while images are off, or do not load.

Testing for Accessibility

One of the best ways to ensure successful implementation of these guidelines is through testing. How else will you know when you've hit the mark in terms of providing accessible content? There are four primary methods of testing for accessibility: by developers, by expert review, with real users, and with automated tools.

Testing by Developers

You can find accessibility testing tools online and on the desktop for everything from smaller scale testing to enterprise level tools that allow you to track progress over time, automate reporting, and allow for manual review in conjunction with automated tests.

These items should be in every web developer's toolkit. In addition to their use for informal accessibility testing, they are often useful for general web development as well.

*Web Developer Toolbar for Firefox/Mozilla (addons.mozilla.org/extensions/
moreinfo.php?id=60)*

An extension for Firefox and Mozilla, the Web Developer Toolbar provides a
host of tools that are useful for low-level accessibility testing. It allows you to
easily disable CSS and JavaScript, as well as replace images with their alt
text. Quick access to these tools helps assess your work against the guidelines presented in this chapter.

*Accessibility Toolbar for Internet Explorer (www.nils.org.au/ais/web/resources/
toolbar/)*

Similar to the Web Developer Toolbar, the Accessibility Toolbar is designed
to work in Internet Explorer for Windows. It provides quick access to many
of the same types of tools found in the Web Developer Toolbar, as well as
one-click launching of several online services that allow you to roughly
analyze readability of passages of text, color contrast analysis, various other
vision-related disabilities, and online automated testing tools.

Opera browser (www.opera.com)

The Opera browser is actually quite a good testing tool on its own. It includes
quick access to various browser "modes" that are useful for demonstrating
and testing a text-based view of the web site. It also includes both voice
recognition of commands and speech capabilities in its browser, which are
useful for quick demonstration and testing.

WAT-C online tools and services (www.wat-c.org/tools/)

In September of 2005, a group of web developers and accessibility specialists
formed the Web Accessibility Tool Consortium (WAT-C) to provide a series
of tools under a general public license agreement that can be used for both
testing accessibility and educational purposes. These tools include the Accessibility Toolbar for IE and many useful online services developed by Gez
Lemon of Juicy Studio (*www.juicystudio.com*).

Expert Review

Expert review testing involves one or more accessibility specialists reviewing a
web site, page, or set of pages to perform a heuristic analysis and evaluation of
conformance against a set of criteria, such as W3C or Section 508 standards. The
analysis is based on experience and common "rules of thumb" in terms of accessibility issues.

Once the review is completed, the reviewers usually prepare a report that outlines
specific accessibility issues, methods for improving accessibility, and areas that
need to be tested further by users with various disabilities (often referred to as
"pan-disability" testing). They may or may not assign a "severity" to each issue,
but will likely make prioritized recommendations on those items that should be
fixed first and those that should be fixed but may be less critical.

Testing with Users

Although it is fine for an expert to review a site, feedback is that much more meaningful and powerful when it comes from people who use assistive technology every day.

User testing falls into two categories: general review and testing of specific tasks. General review tends to be focused on providing a general impression of the accessibility of a site but without particular goals in mind. Although this can be useful for finding "obvious" accessibility issues such as missing alt text, spelling mistakes, and confusing content or reading order, it may not be as useful as testing for such specific tasks as:

- Logging into the application
- Finding the email address for support/help
- Performing a typical transaction, such as determining your current bank balance or purchasing a specific item and having it shipped to your address
- Creating a new account

User testing that provides an overall impression of the accessibility of a site can be useful, but it pales in comparison to actually watching users attempt to complete tasks that are critical to their use of the application or site.

Several things often happen during these facilitated tests: an observer makes notes about difficult areas, ranks task completion (completed, completed with difficulty, completed with assistance, not completed, for example), and code is reviewed to identify areas for improvement.

User testing should not be seen as a final stage of development; it should be done early in the development process, conducted with multiple users with various disabilities, and repeated after improvements are made.

In some cases, however, we don't have that luxury. So, how much accessibility testing should you do? As much as you can! Some is better than none. If all you can manage is expert review, or testing with a handful of users, then do that, and do it well.

Automated Testing Tools

If used with appropriate caution and judgment, automated tools can be very useful in determining accessibility problems in a site, in tracking progress over time, and for identifying possible issues that bear further investigation. The W3C maintain an extensive list of tools that are available for use in testing at *www.w3. org/WAI/ER/existingtools.html*. Keep in mind, however, that ability and disability are relative terms, so testing with black-and-white absolutes is sometimes problematic and always controversial.

It is important to remember with all of the automated testing tools that in some cases, you may see issues that do not apply to your particular site or that are difficult to test. For example, after scanning a page with JavaScript, many automated testing tools will state that you have used JavaScript in the page and therefore must include an alternate by using a `<noscript>...</noscript>` block in your page.

The problem is that the automated test does not know what the script is doing, and what the result will be if the page is used with JavaScript both on and off.

As another simple example to illustrate the point: an automated testing tool can test for the presence of alternative text for an image. It can even test to see if there are other images with the same alternative text, and it can test to see if that image is part of a link. However, it cannot run any test that will determine whether or not the alternative text is appropriate for the image in question.

Therein lies the problem with automated testing. Human judgment is still required and must be factored into testing time as automated testing on its own is simply not the answer.

For best testing, a combination of automated testing methods, browser-based tools, expert review, and user task completion should be what you aim for.

6

Internationalization

If the Web is to reach a truly worldwide audience, it needs to be able to support the display of all the languages of the world, with all their unique alphabets and symbols, directionality, and specialized punctuation. The W3C's efforts for internationalization (often referred to as "i18n"—an i, then 18 letters, then an n) ensure that the formats and protocols defined by the W3C are usable worldwide in all languages and writing systems.

You often hear the terms *internationalization* (or *globalization*) and *localization* used together. The W3C defines localization as the process of adapting a technology or content to meet the language, cultural, and other requirements of a particular culture, region, or language. Internationalization refers to the design and development of web content and technologies that enables easy localization for target audiences. Localization entails more than simple language translation. It also takes into account details including, but not limited to:

- Date and time formats
- Currency
- Keyboard usage
- Cultural interpretations of symbols, icons, and colors
- Content that may be subject to misinterpretation or viewed as insensitive
- Varying legal requirements

Creating multilingual web sites and localized versions of site content is well beyond the scope of this Nutshell book. This chapter addresses two primary issues related to internationalization. First is the handling of alternative character sets that take into account all the writing systems of the world, including character encoding and character references. Second is the features built into HTML 4.01 and CSS 2.1 for specifying languages and their unique presentation requirements.

Character Sets and Encoding

The first challenge in internationalization is dealing with the staggering number of unique character shapes (called *glyphs*) that occur in the writing systems of the world. This includes not only alphabets, but also all ideographs (characters that indicate a whole word or concept) for such languages as Chinese, Japanese, and Korean. There are also invisible characters that indicate particular functionality within a word or a line of text, such as characters that indicate that adjacent characters should be joined.

To understand character encoding as it relates to HTML, XHTML, and XML, you must be familiar with some basic terms and concepts.

Character set
> A *character set* is any collection or *repertoire* of characters that are used together for a particular function. Many character sets have been standardized, such as the familiar ASCII character set that includes 128 characters mostly from the Roman alphabet used in modern English.

Coded character set
> When a specific number is assigned to each character in a set, it becomes a *coded character set*. Each position (or numbered unit) in a coded character set is called a *code point* (or *code position*). In Unicode, (discussed in more detail later) the code point of the greater-than symbol (>) is 3E in hexadecimal or 62 in decimal. Unicode code points are typically denoted as U+hhhh, where hhhh is a sequence of at least four and sometimes six hexadecimal digits.

Character encoding
> Character encoding refers to the way characters and their code points are converted to bytes for use by computers. The character encoding transforms the character stream in a document to a byte stream that is interpreted by user agents and reassembled again as a character stream for the user.
>
> The number of characters available in a character set is limited by the bit depth of its encoding. For example, 8 bits are capable of describing 256 (2^8) unique characters, 16 bits can describe 65,536 (2^{16}) different characters, and so on.

Many character sets and their encodings have been standardized for worldwide interoperability. The most relevant character set to the Web is the comprehensive Unicode (ISO/IEC 106460-1), which includes more than 50,000 characters from all active modern languages. Unicode is discussed in appropriate detail in the next section.

Web documents may also be encoded with more specialized encodings appropriate to their authoring languages. Some common encodings are listed in Table 6-1. Note that all of these encodings are 8-bit (256 character) subsets of Unicode.

Table 6-1. Common 8-bit character encodings

Encoding	Description
ISO 8859-1 (a.k.a. Latin-1)	Latin characters used in most Western languages (includes ASCII)
ISO 8859-5	Cyrillic
ISO 8859-6	Arabic
ISO 8859-7	Greek
ISO 8859-8	Hebrew
ISO-2022-JP	Japanese
SHIFT_JIS	Japanese
EUC-JP	Japanese

HTML 2.0 and 3.0 were based on the 8-bit Latin-1 (ISO 8859-1) character set. Even as HTML 2.0 was being penned, the W3C was aware that 256 characters were not adequate to exchange information on a global scale, and it had its sights set on a super–character set called Unicode. Unfortunately, Unicode wasn't ready for inclusion in an HTML Recommendation until Version 4.0 (1996). Without further ado, it's time to talk Unicode.

Unicode (ISO/IEC 10646-1)

SGML-based markup languages are required to define a *document character set* that serves as the basis for interpreting characters. The document character set for HTML (4 and 4.01), XHTML, and XML is the *Universal Character Set (UCS)*, which is a superset of all widely used standard character sets in the world.

The USC is defined by both the Unicode and ISO/IEC 10646 standards. The code points in Unicode and ISO/IEC 10646 are identical and the standards are developed in parallel. The difference is that Unicode adds some rules about how characters should be used. It is also used as a reference for such issues as the bidirectional text algorithm for handling reading direction within text. The Unicode Standard is defined by the Unicode Consortium (*www.unicode.org*).

 In common practice, and throughout this book, the Universal Character Set is referred to simply as "Unicode."

Because Unicode is the document character set for all (X)HTML documents, numeric character references in web documents will always be interpreted according to Unicode code points, regardless of the document's declared encoding.

Unicode code points

Unicode was originally intended to be a 16-bit encoded character set, but it was soon recognized that 65,536 code positions would not be enough, so it was extended to include more than a million available code points (not all of them are assigned, of course) on supplementary planes.

The first 16 bits, or 65,536 positions, in Unicode are referred to as the *Basic Multi-lingual Plane (BMP)*. The BMP includes most of the more common characters in use, such as character sets for Latin, Greek, Cyrillic, Devangari, hirgana, katakana, Cherokee, and others, as well as mathematical and other miscellaneous characters. Most ideographs are there, too, but due to their large numbers, many have been moved to a *Supplementary Ideographic Plane*.

Unicode was created with backward compatibility in mind. The first 256 code points in the BMP are identical to the Latin-1 character set, with the first 128 matching the established ASCII standard.

Unicode encodings

Many character sets have only one encoding method, such as the ISO 8859 series. Unicode, however, may be encoded a number of ways. So although the code points never change, they may be represented by 1, 2, or 4 bytes. The encoding forms for Unicode are:

UTF-8
> This is an expanding format that uses 1 byte for characters in the ASCII set, 2 bytes for additional character ranges, and 3 bytes for the rest of the BMP. Supplementary planes use 4 bytes. UTF-8 is the recommended Unicode encoding for web documents and other Internet technologies.

UTF-16
> Uses 2 bytes for BMP characters and 4 bytes for supplementary characters. UTF-16 is another option for web documents.

UTF-32
> Uses 4 bytes for all characters.

So while the code point for the percent sign is U+0025, it would be represented by the byte value 25 in UTF-8, 00 25 in UTF-16, and 00 00 00 25 by UTF-32. There are other things at work in the encoding as well, but this gives you a feel for the difference in encoding forms.

Choosing an encoding

The W3C recommends the UTF-8 encoding for all (X)HTML and XML documents because it can accommodate the greatest number of characters and is well supported by servers. It allows wide-ranging languages to be mixed within a single document.

Not all web documents need to be encoded using UTF-8 however. If you are authoring a document in a language that uses a lot of non-ASCII characters, you may want to choose an encoding that minimizes the need to numerically represent ("escape") these special characters.

Bear in mind, however, that regardless of the encoding, all characters in the document will be interpreted relative to Unicode code points.

For more information on how character sets and character encodings should be handled for web documents, see the W3C's Character Model for the World Wide Web 1.0 Recommendation at *www.w3.org/TR/charmod/*.

Specifying Character Encoding

The W3C encourages authors to specify the character encoding for all web documents, even those that use the default UTF-8 Unicode encoding, but it is particularly critical if an alternate encoding is used. There are several ways to declare the character encoding for documents: in the HTTP header delivered by the server, in the XML declaration (for XHTML and XML documents only), or in a meta element in the head of the document. This section looks at each method and provides guidelines for their use.

HTTP headers

When a server sends a document to a user agent (such as a browser), it also sends information about the document in a portion of the document called the *HTTP header*. A typical HTTP header looks like this:

```
HTTP/1.x 200 OK
Date: Mon, 14 Nov 2005 19:45:33 GMT
Server: Apache/2.0.46 (Red Hat)
Accept-Ranges: bytes
Connection: close
Transfer-Encoding: chunked
Content-Type: text/html; charset=UTF-8
```

Notice that one of the bits of information that the server sends along is the Content-Type of the document using a MIME type label. For example, HTML documents are always delivered as type text/html. (The MIME types for XHTML documents aren't as straightforward, as discussed in the sidebar, "Serving XHTML.") The Content-Type entry may also contain the character encoding of the document using the charset parameter, as shown in the example.

The method for setting up a server with your preferred character encoding varies with different server software, so it is best to consult the server administrator for assistance. For Apache servers, the default character encoding may be set for all documents with the *.html* extension by adding this line to the *.htaccess* file.

```
AddType 'text/html; charset=UTF-8' html
```

The advantages to setting character encodings in HTTP headers are that the information is easily accessible to user agents and the header information has the highest priority in case of conflict. On the downside, it is not always easy for authors to access the server settings, and it is possible for the default server settings to be changed without the author's knowledge.

It is also possible for the character encoding information to get separated from the document, which is why it is recommended that the character encoding be provided within the document as well, as described by the next two methods.

Serving XHTML

XHTML 1.0 documents may be served as either XML or HTML documents. Although XML is the proper method, many authors choose to deliver XHTML 1.0 files with the text/html MIME type used for HTML documents for reasons of backward compatibility, lack of browser support for XML files, and other problems with XHTML interpretation. When XHTML documents are served in this manner, they may not be parsed as XML documents.

XHTML 1.0 files may also be served as XML, and XHTML 1.1 files must always be served as XML. XHTML documents served as XML may use the MIME types application/xhtml+xml, application/xml, or text/xml. The W3C recommends that you use application/xhtml+xml only.

Whether you serve an XHTML document as an HTML or XML file type changes the way you specify the character encoding, as covered in the upcoming "Choosing the declaration method" section.

XML declaration

XHTML (and other XML) documents often begin with an XML declaration before the DOCTYPE declaration. The XML declaration is not required. The declaration may include the encoding of the document, as shown in this example.

```
<?xml version="1.0" encoding="UTF-8"?>
<!DOCTYPE html PUBLIC "-//W3C//DTD XHTML 1.0 Strict//EN"
    "http://www.w3.org/TR/xhtml1/DTD/xhtml1-strict.dtd">
```

The XML declaration may be provided even for XHTML documents served as text/html.

Because the default encoding for all XML documents is UTF-8 or UTF-16, encoding information in the XML declaration is not required for these encodings, and thus can be omitted as a space-saving optimization.

In addition, although it is technically correct to include the XML declaration in such documents, Appendix C of the XHTML 1.0 specification, "HTML Compatibility Guidelines," recommends avoiding it, and many authors choose to omit it because of browser-support issues. For example, when Internet Explorer 6 for Windows detects a line of text before the DOCTYPE declaration, it converts to Quirks Mode (see Chapter 9 for details), which can have a damaging effect on how the documents styles are rendered. (This is reportedly fixed in IE 7.) It is required only if your document uses an encoding other than UTF-8 or UTF-16 and if the encoding has not been set on the server.

The meta element

For HTML documents as well as XHTML documents served as text/html, the encoding should always be specified using a meta element in the head of the document. The http-equiv attribute passes information along to the user agent as though it appeared in the HTTP header. Again, the encoding is provided with the charset value as shown here:

```
<head>
    <meta http-equiv="content-type" content="text/html; charset=utf-8" />
    <title>Document Title</title>
</head>
```

Although the meta element declaring the content type is not a required element in the HTML and XHTML DTDs, it is strongly recommended for the purpose of clearly identifying the character encoding and keeping that information with the document. This is particularly helpful for common text editors (such as BBEdit), which use the meta element to identify the character encoding of the document when opening the document for editing. With this method, all character encodings must be explicitly specified, including UTF-8 and UTF-16.

Choosing the declaration method

The declaration method you use depends on the type of document you are authoring and its encoding method.

HTML documents
> The encoding should be specified on the server and again in the document with a meta element. This makes sure the encoding is easily accessible and stays with the document should it be saved for later use.

XHTML 1.0 documents served as HTML
> The encoding should be specified on the server and again in the document with a meta element. If the encoding is something other than UTF-8 or UTF-16, and the document is likely to be parsed as XML (not just HTML), then also include the encoding in an XML header. Be aware that the inclusion of the XML declaration may cause rendering problems for some browsers.

XHTML (1.0 and 1.1) documents served as XML
> The encoding should be specified on the server and by using the encoding attribute in the XML declaration. Although not strictly required for UTF-8 and UTF-16 encodings, it doesn't hurt to include it anyway.

 This strategy for declaring character encodings is outlined in a tutorial on the W3C's Internationalization site (*www.w3.org/ International/tutorials/tutorial-char-enc/*). For another approach, see the article "WaSP Asks the W3C: Specifying Character Encoding" on the Web Standards Project site (*webstandards.org/learn/ askw3c/dec2002.html*).

Character References

HTML and XHTML documents use the standard ASCII character set (these are the characters you see printed on the keys of your keyboard). To represent characters that fall outside the ASCII range, you must refer to the character by using a character reference. This is known as *escaping* the character.

In HTML and XML documents, some ASCII characters that you intend to be rendered in the browser as part of the text content must be escaped in order not to be interpreted as code by the user agent. For example, the less-than symbol (<) must be escaped in order not to be mistaken as the beginning of an element start tag. Other characters that must be escaped are the greater-than symbol (>), ampersand (&), single quote ('), and double quotation marks ("). In XML documents, all ampersands must be escaped or they won't validate.

There are two types of character references: Numeric Character References (NCR) and character entities.

Numeric Character References

A *Numeric Character Reference* (NCR) refers to the character by its Unicode code point (introduced earlier in this chapter). NCRs are always preceded by &# and end with a ; (semicolon). The numeric value may be provided in decimal or hexadecimal. Hexadecimal values are indicated by an x before the value.

For example, the copyright symbol (©), which occupies the 169th position in Unicode (U+00A9), may be represented by its hexadecimal NCR © or its decimal equivalent, ©. Decimal values are more common in practice. Note that the zeros at the beginning of the code point may be omitted in the numeric character reference.

> Handy charts of every character in the Basic Multilingual Plane are maintained as a labor of love by Jens Brueckmann at his site J-A-B. net. The Unicode code point and decimal/hexadecimal NCR is provided for every character. It is available at *www.j-a-b.net/web/char/char-unicode-bmp*.

Character Entities

Character entities use abbreviations or words instead of numbers to represent characters that may be easier to remember than numbers. In this sense, entities are merely a convenience. Character entities must be predefined in the DTD of a markup language to be available for use. For example, the copyright symbol may be referred to as ©, because that entity has been declared in the DTD. The character entities defined in HTML 4.01 and XHTML are listed in Appendix C (a list of the most common is also provided in Chapter 10). XML defines five character entities for use with all XML languages:

<
> Less than (<)

>
> Greater than (>)

&
> Ampersand (&)

'
> Apostrophe (')

"
> Quotation mark (")

Escapes in CSS

It may be necessary to escape a character in a style sheet if the value of a property contains a non-ASCII character. In CSS, the escape mechanism is a backslash followed by the hexadecimal Unicode code point value. The escape is terminated with a space instead of a semicolon. For example, a font name starting with a capital letter C with a cedilla (Ç) needs to be escaped in the style rule, as shown here.

```
p { font-family: \C7 elikfont; }
```

When the special character appears in a style attribute value, it is possible to use its NCR, entity, or CSS escape. The CSS escape is recommended to make it easier to move it to a style sheet later.

 For guidelines on declaring character encodings and using escapes, see the W3C's Authoring Techniques for XHTML & HTML Internationalization available at *www.w3.org/TR/i18n-html-tech-char/*.

Language Features

Coordinating character sets is only the first part of the challenge. Even languages that share a character set may have different rules for hyphenation, spacing, quotation marks, punctuation, and so on. In addition to character shapes (glyphs), issues such as directionality (whether the text reads left to right or right to left) and cursive joining behavior have to be taken into account. This section introduces the features included in HTML 4.01 and XHTML 1.0 and higher that address the needs of a multilingual Web.

Language Specification

Authors are strongly urged to specify the language for all HTML and XHTML documents. To specify a language for XHTML documents, use the xml:lang attribute in the html root element. HTML documents use the lang attribute for the same purpose. To ensure backward compatibility, the convention is simply to use both attributes, as shown in this example, which specifies the language of the document as French.

```
<html xml:lang="fr" lang="fr" xmlns="http://www.w3.org/1999/xhtml" >
```

 Users can set language preferences in their browsers. This language preference information is passed to the server when the user makes a request for a document. The server may use it to return a document in the preferred language if there is a document available that matches the language description.

The language attributes may be used in a particular element to override the language declaration for the document. In this example, a long quotation is provided in Norwegian.

```
<blockquote xml:lang="no" lang="no">...</blockquote>
```

Language Values

The value of the lang and xml:lang attributes is a language tag as defined in "Tags for the Identification of Languages" (RFC 3066). Language tags consist of a primary subtag that identifies the language according to a two- or three-letter language code (according to the ISO 639 standard), for example, fr for French or no for Norwegian. When a language has both a two- and three-letter code, the two-letter code should be used.

The complete list of ISO 639 language codes is available at the Library of Congress web site at *www.loc.gov/standards/iso639-2/langcodes.html*. The more common two-letter codes are provided in Table 6-2 at the end of this section.

A language tag may also contain an optional subtag that further qualifies the language by country, dialect, or script, as shown in these examples.

en-GB
> English as spoken in Great Britain

en-scouse
> English with a scouse (Liverpool) dialect

bs-Cyrl
> Bosnian with Cyrillic script (rather than Latin script, bs-Latn)

Codes for country names are provided by the standard ISO 3166 and are available at *www.iso.org/iso/en/prods-services/iso3166ma/02iso-3166-code-lists/list-en1.html*. Dialect and script language tags are registered with the IANA (Internet Assigned Numbers Authority) and are available at *www.iana.org/assignments/language-tags*.

Table 6-2. Two-letter codes of language names

Language	Code	Language	Code	Language	Code
Afar	aa	Esperanto	eo	Georgian	ka
Abkhazian	ab	Spanish	es	Kongo	kg
Avestan	ae	Estonian	et	Kikuyu	ki
Afrikaans	af	Basque	eu	Kuanyama	kj
Akan	ak	Persian	fa	Kazakh	kk
Amharic	am	Fulah	ff	Greenlandic	kl
Aragonese	an	Finnish	fi	Cambodian	km
Arabic	ar	Fiji	fj	Kannada	kn
Assamese	as	Faroese	fo	Korean	ko
Avaric	av	French	fr	Kanuri	kr
Aymara	ay	Frisian	fy	Kashmiri	ks
Azerbaijani	az	Irish	ga	Kurdish	ku
Bashkir	ba	Scots Gaelic	gd	Komi	kv
Belarusian	be	Galician	gl	Cornish	kw
Bulgarian	bg	Guarani	gn	Kirghiz	ky
Bihari	bh	Gujarati	gu	Latin	la
Bislama	bi	Manx	gv	Luxembourgish	lb
Bambnara	bm	Hausa	ha	Ganda	lg
Bengali; Bangla	bn	Hebrew (formerly iw)	he	Limburgan	li
Tibetan	bo	Hindi	hi	Lingala	lm
Breton	br	Hiri Motu	ho	Lingala	ln
Bosnian	bs	Croatian	hr	Laothian	lo
Catalan	ca	Haitian	ht	Lithuanian	lt
Chechen	ce	Hungarian	hu	Luba Katanga	lu
Chamorro	ch	Armenian	hy	Latvian	lv
Corsican	co	Hetero	hz	Malagasy	mg
Cree	cr	Interlingua	ia	Marshallese	mh
Czech	cs	Indonesian (formerly in)	id	Maori	mi
Old Slavic	cu	Interlingue	ie	Macedonian	mk
Chuvash	cv	Igbo	ig	Malayalam	ml
Welsh	cy	Sichuan Yi	ii	Mongolian	mn
Danish	da	Inupiak	ik	Moldavian	mo
German	de	Icelandic	is	Marathi	mr
Divehi	dv	Italian	it	Malay	ms
Dzongkha	dz	Inuktitut	iu	Maltese	mt
Ewe	ee	Japanese	ja	Burmese	my
Greek	el	Javanese	jv	Nauru	na
English	en	Javanese	jw	Nepali	ne

Table 6-2. Two-letter codes of language names (continued)

Language	Code	Language	Code	Language	Code
Ndonga	ng	Sardinian	sc	Tagalog	tl
Dutch	nl	Sindhi	sd	Setswana	tn
Nynorsk	nn	Northern Sami	se	Tonga	to
Norwegian	no	Sangho	sg	Turkish	tr
Ndebele	nr	Serbo-Croatian	sh	Tsonga	ts
Navaho	nv	Sinhalese	si	Tatar	tt
Chichewa	ny	Slovak	sk	Twi	tw
Occitan	oc	Slovenian	sl	Tahitian	ty
Ojibwa	oj	Samoan	sm	Uighur	ug
(Afan) Oromo	om	Shona	sn	Ukrainian	uk
Oriya	or	Somali	so	Urdu	ur
Ossetian	os	Albanian	sq	Uzbek	uz
Punjabi	pa	Serbian	sr	Venda	ve
Pali	pi	Swati	ss	Vietnamese	vi
Polish	pl	Sesotho	st	Volapuk	vo
Pashto, Pushto	ps	Sundanese	su	Walloon	wa
Portuguese	pt	Swedish	sv	Wolof	wo
Quechua	qu	Swahili	sw	Xhosa	xh
Rhaeto-Romance	rm	Tamil	ta	Yiddish (formerly ji)	yi
Kirundi	rn	Telugu	te	Yoruba	yo
Romanian	ro	Tajik	tg	Zhuang	za
Russian	ru	Thai	th	Chinese	zh
Kinyarwanda	rw	Tigrinya	ti	Zuni	zu
Sanskrit	sa	Turkmen	tk		

Directionality

HTML 4.01 and XHTML take into account that many languages read from right to left and provide attributes for handling the directionality of text. Directionality is part of a character's encoding within Unicode.

The dir attribute is used for specifying the direction in which the text should be interpreted. It can be used in conjunction with the lang attribute and may be added within the tags of most elements. The accepted value for direction is either ltr for "left to right" or rtl for "right to left." For example, the following code indicates that the paragraph is intended to be displayed in Arabic, reading from right to left:

```
<p lang="ar" xml:lang="ar" dir="rtl">...</p>
```

The bdo element, introduced in HTML 4.01, also deals specifically with documents that contain combinations of left- and right-reading text (bidirectional text, or bidi, for short). The bdo element is used for "bidirectional override," in other words, it specifies a span of text that should override the intrinsic direction (as inherited from Unicode) of the text it contains. The bdo element uses the dir attribute as follows:

```
<bdo dir="ltr">English phrase in an otherwise Hebrew text</bdo>...
```

Cursive Joining Behavior

In some writing systems, the shape of a character varies depending on its position in the word. For instance, in Arabic, a character used at the beginning of a word looks completely different when it is used as the last character of a word. Generally, this joining behavior is handled within the software, but there are Unicode characters that give precise control over joining behavior. They have zero width and are placed between characters purely to specify whether the neighboring characters should join.

HTML 4.01 provides mnemonic character entities for both these characters, as shown in Table 6-3.

Table 6-3. Unicode characters for joining behavior

Entity	Numeric	Name	Description
&zwnj;	&#8204;	zero-width non-joiner	Prevents joining of characters that would otherwise be joined.
&zwj;	&#8205;	zero-width joiner	Joins characters that would otherwise not be joined.

Style Sheets Language Features

The first version of Cascading Style Sheets (CSS) did not include any mechanisms for dealing with anything but standard western, left-to-right languages.

CSS Level 2 introduced a few controls that specifically address multilingualism.

Directionality
> The direction and unicode-bidi properties in CSS 2 allow authors to specify text direction, similar to the dir and bdo elements in HTML.

Quotation marks
> The quotes property is used to specify quotation marks appropriate to the current language of the text. Generated quotation marks are discussed in Chapter 23.

CSS Level 3 addresses advanced foreign language attributes such as detailed specification of international numbering schemes, vertical text, and language-based text justification. International numbering schemes are published in the CSS 3 Lists Module (*www.w3.org/TR/css3-lists/*). Text effects that accommodate internationalization efforts are published in the CSS 3 Text Effects Module (*www.w3.org/TR/css3-text/*).

CSS 3 also includes a module for dealing with Ruby text. *Ruby* text is a run of text that appears alongside another run of text (the base). It serves as an annotation or pronunciation guide, as in the case of phonetic Japanese characters that run above the pictorial kanji symbols to aid readers who do not understand the symbols. More information can be found at *www.w3.org/TR/css3-ruby/*.

For Further Reading

If you are interested in learning more, the W3C Internationalization Activity Home Page (*www.w3.org/International/*) makes a great jumping-off point for further exploration.

Another good resource is Babel, an Alis Technologies/Internet Society joint project to internationalize the Internet. It is available at *alis.isoc.org/index.en.html*.

II

The Structural Layer: XML and (X)HTML

7

Introduction to XML

If you are thinking about skipping this chapter, please reconsider. While you may never need to be an XML expert, the basic concepts covered here will illuminate why things are done the way they are in the world of web document authoring. Furthermore, if you "get" XML, you'll understand the reasoning that influences all contemporary web design and related W3C Recommendations, from XHTML to CSS 2 and beyond.

XML (Extensible Markup Language) is a W3C standard for text document markup. It is not a language in itself (like HTML), but rather a set of rules for creating other markup languages. In other words, it is a meta-markup language. Languages written according to XML syntax are called *XML applications* (a confusing use of the word "application" to be sure, but such is the legacy jargon that SGML has left us). If this sounds a bit abstract, think of it this way: XML provides the tools for making up custom sets and subsets of tags.

Although XML began as an effort to improve information structure and handling on the Web, it has quickly taken the entire computing world by storm. In fact, today there is more XML used outside the Web than on it. XML is used for document sharing and data storage in fields as diverse as finance, retail, physics, travel, insurance, and academia, just to name a few. There are also XML files working behind the scenes in an increasing number of software applications, such as Microsoft Office, Macromedia Flash, and Apple iTunes. This is just a testament to the flexibility and robust nature of XML.

XML is having some of its intended impact on the Web as well. It is the cornerstone of the W3C's vision for the future of information exchange over networks.

XML is a complex topic, well beyond the scope of this web design book. This chapter provides an introduction to XML, focusing on the aspects of XML that are useful to web designers and developers, such as how it works, the basic syntax, terminology, and web-based XML applications.

The best way to get a feel for XML is to look at a quick example.

XML Basics

Here is a very simple XML document that is marked up with tags I made up to describe the liner notes for my famous end-of-the-year music compilations. (I could call it JenML).

```
<?xml version="1.0"?>
<compilation >
<title>Oh Baby! Jen's Favorites</title>
<year>2005</year>
<image source="ohbabycover.jpg"/>
<tracklist>
  <track number="1">
    <artist>The Wrens</artist>
    <song>
      <song_title>Hopeless</song_title> from
      <album_title>The Meadowlands</album_title>,
      <label>Absolutely Kosher Records</label>,
      <release_date>2003</release_date>
    </song>
    <comments>I love The Wrens, both musically and personally.</comments>
  </track>
  <!--more tracks added here -->
</tracklist>
</compilation>
```

Certain things about this example should look familiar to anyone who has seen an HTML document. First, it is a plain-text document. As such, it can be created or edited in any text editor. It also uses tags in brackets to indicate the start and end of content *elements* in the document. Consider this element from the example:

```
<artist>The Wrens</artist>
```

The element includes the *content* (in this case, the character data "The Wrens") and its *markup* (the start tag <artist> and end tag </artist>). In XML, tags are case-sensitive, so <ARTIST>, <Artist>, and <artist> would be parsed as three different elements. Elements may contain character data, other elements, or both. Some elements are *empty*, which means they have no content. <meta/> is an example of an empty element in XHTML. Elements may be clarified or enhanced with *attributes* that provide extra information about that element. In the example, the image element uses the source attribute to provide the location of the image file.

Meaningful Markup

The most significant thing to note here is that the tags describe the information they contain in a meaningful way. In XML, element names are intended to be simple, descriptive, and easily readable by human beings as well as machines. Notice also that the tags do not provide any indication of how the document should look when it is displayed. Their purpose is to provide a *semantic* description (the meaning) of their contents. XML documents rely on style sheets to handle all matters of presentation.

Together, the elements in a document create its *structure*. Notice in the example that some elements contain other elements, which may contain yet more elements. This hierarchy is referred to as the *document tree*. It starts with a *root element* (compilation in the example) and branches out in layers of *parent/child* relationships. Every XML document *must* have exactly one root element, and the root element has no ancestors. Document structure is covered in more detail in Chapter 16.

 The concepts of *semantic markup* and *document structure* are directly relevant to web design. HTML and XHTML are markup languages for describing text documents whose "data" consists of paragraphs, headings, lists, and so on. In proper HTML markup, elements should accurately describe their contents, and should not be chosen to achieve a particular visual effect in a browser. Additionally, an awareness of a document's structure will be a major advantage when planning and writing style sheets.

Text as Data, Data as Text

It is easy to see even from our simple example how XML markup treats content in a text document like data. So while this document can be displayed in a page format, it can just as easily be stored in a database (which is a common use of XML-formatted information).

On the flip side, XML allows data to be stored in a plain-text format. This is the key to XML's rampant success in the computing world. Data that had previously been stored in proprietary, device-specific formats can now be marked up in a text file and shared between incompatible systems. Longevity is improved as well. XML documents are self-defining, intuitive, and not tied to a format or system that may grow obsolete.

How It Works

XML has four basic components:

- A document marked up in an XML language
- An optional Document Type Definition or XML Schema that defines the elements and the rules for their use in that language
- Style sheets for presentation instructions
- Parsers that interpret the XML document

Take a closer look at each.

XML Documents

XML documents may be used for a wide variety of content. A document might be text based (such as a magazine article), or it might contain only numerical data to be transferred from one database or application to another. An XML document might also contain an abstract structure, such as a particular vector graphic shape (as in SVG) or a mathematical equation (as in MathML).

A Brief XML History

Both XML and HTML have roots in *SGML* (Standard Generalized Markup Language). SGML is a comprehensive set of syntax rules for marking up documents and data that has existed as an ISO standard since 1986. It is the big kahuna of meta-languages. For information on SGML, including its history, see *www.oasis-open.org/cover/general.html*.

When Tim Berners-Lee needed a markup language that told browsers how to display content, he used SGML to create HTML. In other words, HTML is an SGML application, albeit a very simplified one.

As the Web matured, there was a clear need for more versatile markup languages. SGML provided a good model, but it was too vast and complex; it had many features that were redundant, overly complicated, or simply weren't useful. XML is a simplified and reduced form of SGML.

Much of the credit for XML's creation can be attributed to Jon Bosak of Sun Microsystems, Inc., who started the W3C working group responsible for scaling down SGML to its portable, Web-friendly form. Other big players include James Clark, the technical lead of the working group, and Tim Bray, Michael Sperberg-McQueen, and Jean Paoli, the co-editors of the XML specification.

XML 1.0 became a W3C Recommendation on February 10, 1998 and it was revised three times, with the third edition released in 2004. At that time, the W3C released XML 1.1, which addressed issues with Unicode, among other things. Developers are still encouraged to use XML 1.0 if they do not need the newer features. Various aspects and modules of XML are still in development. For more information and updates on XML progress, see the W3C's site at *www.w3.org/XML*.

It is important to note that an XML document is not limited to one physical file. It may be made up of content from multiple files that are integrated via special markup, or it may exist only as records in a database that are assembled on the fly. The end result is always marked-up text content.

Document Type Definition (DTD)

Some XML languages also use a *Document Type Definition (DTD)* that defines each element allowed in the document along with its attributes and rules for use. An XML-compliant application may check the document against its DTD to "decode" the markup and make sure that it follows its own rules. A document that conforms to its DTD is said to be *valid*. DTDs are discussed in detail later in this chapter.

An updated method for defining XML elements and document structure is *XML Schemas*. A particular instance of an XML Schema is called an *XML Schema Definition (XSD)*. The difference is that XSDs are XML-based, while DTDs (an older form of schema) are created according to the rules of SGML. XSDs are more powerful in describing XML languages, but the price is that they also tend to be more complicated and difficult to read and write. XML Schemas are outside the scope of this introductory chapter, but you can find information on the W3C site at *www.w3c.org/XML/Schema*.

Style Sheets and XML

A markup language describes only the structure of a document; it is not concerned with how it looks. Like HTML, XML documents can use Cascading Style Sheets for presentation. In fact, the CSS Level 2 Recommendation has been broadened for use with all XML applications, not just web documents. CSS is covered in Part III of this book.

Another style sheet language called the *Extensible Stylesheet Language (XSL)* exists for XML documents. XSL creates a large overhead in processing, whereas CSS is fast and simple, making it generally preferable.

XSL is useful when the contents of the XML document need to be "transformed" before final display. Transforming generally refers to the process of converting one XML language to another, such as turning a particular XML language into XHTML on the fly, but it can also be used for transformations as simple as replacing words with other words. An *Extensible Stylesheet Language for Transformations (XSLT*, a subset of XSL) style sheet works as a translator in the transformation process. XSL is not covered in this chapter; for more information, see the XSL information on the W3C site at *www.w3.org/Style/XSL/*.

Parsers

Software that interprets the information in XML documents is called an *XML parser* or *processor*. Parsers are generally built into other XML-compliant applications (such as web browsers or database servers), although standalone, command-line XML parsers do exist. It's the parser's job to pass elements and their contents to the application piece by piece for display or execution.

One of the things the parser does is make sure that the XML document is *well-formed*, that is, that it follows all of the rules of XML markup syntax correctly. If a document is not well-formed, parsers are instructed not to process it (although some are more forgiving than others). Well-formedness is discussed in the following section. Some parsers are also *validating parsers*, meaning they check the document for validity against a DTD.

XML Document Syntax

Now let's look at some of the particulars of XML syntax using this simple XML document:

```
<?xml version="1.0" encoding="US-ASCII" standalone="no"?>
<!DOCTYPE accounts SYSTEM "simple.dtd">
<accounts>
<customer>
   <name>
      <firstname>Bobby</firstname>
      <lastname>Five</lastname>
```

```
    </name>
    <accountNumber>4456</accountNumber>
    <balance>111.32</balance>
  </customer>
  <!-- more customers will be added soon -->
  <?php  print date ('Fj,Y') ?>
</accounts>
```

 Because XHTML is an XML application, all of the following syntax conventions apply to web documents written in XHTML.

XML Declaration

The first line of the example is the *XML declaration*.

```
<?xml version="1.0" encoding="US-ASCII" standalone="no"?>
```

The XML declaration contains special information for the XML parser. First, the version attribute tells the parser that it is an XML document that conforms to Version 1.0 of the XML standard (which, incidentally, is the only available option).

In addition, the encoding attribute specifies which character encoding the document uses. By default, XML use the UTF-8 encoding of the Unicode character set (the most complete character set including glyphs from most of the world's languages). Alternate encodings may also be specified, such as ISO-8859-1 (Latin-1), which is a set containing characters from most Western European languages. Character encodings are discussed in more detail in Chapter 6.

Finally, the optional standalone="no" attribute informs the program that an outside DTD is needed to correctly interpret the document. If the value of standalone is yes, it means there is no DTD or the DTD is included in the document.

XML documents should begin with an XML declaration, but it is not required.

In XHTML documents, the presence of an XML declaration will cause Internet Explorer 6 for Windows to render in Quirks mode, even when a proper DOCTYPE declaration is provided (see Chapter 9 for information on Quirks versus Standards mode and DOCTYPE switching). For this reason, it is commonly omitted. This problem has been fixed in IE 7. Some other browsers may render the XML declaration or have other problems. Avoid using the XML declaration in your XHTML documents if possible.

Document Type Declaration

The example also includes a document type (DOCTYPE) declaration.

```
<!DOCTYPE accounts SYSTEM "simple.dtd">
```

The purpose of the DOCTYPE declaration is to refer to the DTD against which the document should be compared for validity. The declaration identifies the root element of the document (accounts, in the example). It also provides a pointer to the DTD itself. DOCTYPE declarations are discussed in the "DTD Syntax" section later in this chapter and again in Chapter 9 as they apply to XHTML.

Together, the XML declaration and DOCTYPE are often referred to as the *document prolog*. For XML languages that don't use DTDs, the entire prolog is optional. For languages with DTDs, the DOCTYPE declaration is required for the document to validate.

Comments

You can leave notes within an XML document in the form of a comment. Comments begin with <!-- and end with -->. If you've used comments in HTML, this syntax should be familiar. The example document contains the comment:

```
<!-- more customers will be added soon -->
```

Comments are not elements and, therefore, do not affect the structure of the document. They may be placed anywhere in a document except before an XML declaration or within a tag or another comment.

Processing Instructions

A processing instruction is a method for passing information to applications that may read the document. It may also include the program or script itself. Unlike comments, which are intended for humans, processing instructions are for computer programs or scripts. Processing instructions are indicated by <? at the beginning and ?> at the end of the instruction.

The example document includes a processing instruction for a simple PHP command that displays the current date.

```
<?php print date('Fj, Y'); ?>
```

Entity References

Isolated markup characters (such as <, &, and >) are not permitted in the flow of text in an XML document and must be escaped using either a Numeric Character Reference or a predefined character entity. This is to avoid having the XML parser interpret any < symbol as the beginning of a new tag. In addition to using entity references in the content of the document, you must use them in attribute values.

XML defines five character entities for use in all XML languages, listed in Table 7-1. Other entities may be defined in a DTD.

Table 7-1. Predefined character entities in XML

Entity	Char	Notes
&	&	Must not be used inside processing instructions
<	<	Use inside attribute values quoted with "
>	>	Use after]] in normal text and inside processing instructions
"	"	Use inside attribute values quoted with '
'	'	Use inside attribute values quoted with "

If you have a document that uses a lot of special characters, such as an example of source code, you can tell the XML parser that the text is simple character data (CDATA) and should not be parsed. To protect content from parsing, enclose it in a CDATA section, indicated by <![CDATA[...]]>. This XHTML example uses a CDATA section to display sample markup on a web page without requiring every < and > character to be escaped:

```
<p>This is sample SMIL markup:</p>
<![CDATA[
<audio src="audio_file.mp3" begin="0s" />
    <seq>
            <img src="image_1.jpg" begin="0s" />
            <img src="image_2.jpg" begin="5s" />
    </seq>
]]>
```

The five reserved characters (listed in Table 7-1) are also put to frequent use when writing scripts (such as JavaScript), making it necessary to designate those blocks of content as CDATA so they will be ignored by XML parsers.

Well-Formed XML

Browsers often recover from sloppily written or illegal HTML. This is not the case with XML documents. Because XML languages vary, the rules for coding the document need to be followed to the letter to ensure proper interpretation by the XML client. In fact, the XML specification strictly prohibits XML parsers from trying to read or render documents with syntax errors. When a document follows the XML markup syntax rules, it is said to be *well-formed*. Documents that have incorrect syntax are referred to as *malformed*.

The primary rules for a well-formed XML document are:

- There may be no whitespace (character spaces or line returns) before the XML declaration, if there is one.
- An element must have both an opening and closing tag, unless it is an empty element.
- If an element is empty, it must contain a closing slash before the end of the tag (for example, <br/>).
- All opening and closing tags must nest correctly and not overlap.
- There may not be whitespace between the opening < and the element name in a tag.
- All element attribute values must be in straight quotation marks (either single or double quotes).
- An element may not have two attributes with the same name.
- Comments and processing instructions may not appear inside tags.
- No unescaped < or & signs may occur in the character data of an element or attribute.
- The document must have a single root element, a unique element that encloses the entire document. The root element may be used only once in the document.

This is by no means a complete list. There are over a hundred criteria that must be met for a document to be well-formed, but many of them follow common sense; for example, there must be at least one character between the brackets <>. But because the syntax rules must be read by machines (without common sense), the rules need to be explicit.

You can check whether the syntax of your XML document is correct using a well-formedness checker (also called a *non-validating parser*). There is a list of them at the Web Developer's Virtual Library at *wdvl.com/Software/XML/parsers.html*.

Document Type Definition (DTD)

A Document Type Definition (DTD) is a file associated with SGML and XML documents that defines how markup tags should be interpreted by the application reading the document. The DTD uses SGML syntax to explain precisely which elements and attributes may appear in a document and the context in which they may be used. DTDs were briefly introduced earlier in this chapter. In this section, we'll take a closer look.

A DTD is a text document that contains a set of rules, formally known as *element declarations*, *attlist* (attribute) *declarations*, and *entity declarations*. DTDs are most often stored in a separate file (with the *.dtd* suffix) and shared by multiple documents; however, DTD information can be included inside the XML document as well. Both methods are demonstrated later in this section.

Document Type Declarations

XML documents specify which DTD they use via a *document type declaration* (also called a *DOCTYPE declaration*).

When the DTD is an external document, the DOCTYPE declaration identifies the root element for the document, lists the method used to identify the DTD (SYSTEM or PUBLIC), and then finally provides the location or name of the DTD itself. When using an external DTD, it is recommended that you include the standalone attribute set to "no" in the XML declaration.

A SYSTEM identifier points to the DTD file by location (its URI), as shown in this example:

```
<?xml version="1.0" standalone="no"?>
<!DOCTYPE compilation SYSTEM "http://www.littlechair.com/notreal/comp.dtd">
```

DTDs that are shared by a large community or are hosted at multiple sites may have a PUBLIC ID that specifies the XML application. When public IDs are used, it is common practice to supply an additional SYSTEM URI because it is better supported. Web developers who write documents in XHTML will be familiar with the following DOCTYPE declaration that indicates the root element (html) and the public identifier for XHTML Strict. This declaration also specifies its URL as a backup method.

```
<?xml version="1.0" standalone="no?">
<!DOCTYPE html PUBLIC "-//W3C//DTD XHTML 1.0 Strict//EN"
    "http://www.w3.org/TR/xhtml1/DTD/xhtml1-strict.dtd">
```

As an alternative, the DTD may be included in the XML document itself, rather than as an external *.dtd* document. This is done by placing the DTD within square brackets in the document type declaration as shown here:

```
<?xml version="1.0"?>
<!DOCTYPE phonebook [
    <!ELEMENT listing (name, number)>
    <!ELEMENT name    (#PCDATA)>
    <!ELEMENT number  (#PCDATA>
]>
```

An XML document may combine external and internal DTD subsets.

Valid XML

When an XML document conforms to all the rules established in the DTD, it is said to be *valid*, meaning that all the elements are used correctly.

 A well-formed document is not necessarily valid, but if a document proves to be valid, it follows that it is also well-formed.

When your document uses a DTD, you can check it for mistakes using a *validating parser*. The parser checks the document against the DTD for contextual errors, such as missing elements or improper order of elements. Some common parsers are Xerces from the Apache XML Project (available at *xml.apache.org*) and Microsoft MSXML (*msdn.microsoft.com/xml/default.asp*). A full list of validating parsers is provided by Web Developer's Virtual Library at *wdvl.com/Software/XML/parsers.html*.

As an alternative to downloading your own parser, you can use a free online parsing service. Just enter the locations of your documents at these sites:

- The Brown University Scholarly Technology Group's XML Validation Form at *www.stg.brown.edu/service/xmlvalid/*
- W3Schools XML Validator (based on MSXML) at *www.w3schools.com/dom/dom_validate.asp*

XML Names

When naming elements and attributes (and other less common XML constructs), you must follow the rules for XML names:

- Names may contain letters, numbers, or non-English character glyphs (such as Ø).
- Names may contain these three punctuation characters: _ (underscore), - (hyphen), or . (period). No other punctuation characters are permitted.
- Names may not start with a number or punctuation (exception: _ (underscore) is allowed at the start).
- Names must not start with "xml."
- Names may not contain whitespace of any kind (space, carriage return, line feed, or non-breaking space).

DTD Syntax

The following example is made up of lines taken from the XHTML Strict DTD (the full DTD is over 1,500 lines long). It contains samples of element, attlist (attribute), and entity declarations.

```
<!ELEMENT title (#PCDATA)>
<!ELEMENT meta EMPTY>
<!ELEMENT ul (li)+>

<!ENTITY % i18n
 "lang          %LanguageCode; #IMPLIED
  xml:lang      %LanguageCode; #IMPLIED
  dir           (ltr|rtl)      #IMPLIED"
 >

<!ATTLIST title
  %i18n;
  id            ID             #IMPLIED
  >

<!ATTLIST meta
  %i18n;
  id            ID             #IMPLIED
  http-equiv    CDATA          #IMPLIED
  name          CDATA          #IMPLIED
  content       CDATA          #REQUIRED
  scheme        CDATA          #IMPLIED
  >
```

Element declarations

Element declarations are the core of the DTD. Every element must have an element declaration in order for the document to validate. Consider the parts of this declaration for the title element.

```
<!ELEMENT title (#PCDATA)>
```

!ELEMENT identifies the line as an element declaration (no surprise there). The next part provides the element name (in this case, title) that will be used in the markup tag. Finally, the material within the parentheses identifies the content model for the element, or in other words, what type of content it may contain. In this example, the content model for the title element must be #PCDATA, which stands for *parsed character data*. This means the content is character data that may or may not include escaped character entities (such as < and & for < and &, respectively), but it may *not* include other elements.

Other content models include:

Single child elements
> You may also put other element names in the parentheses. In the following (non-XHTML) element declaration, the content of the birth element must be exactly one year element.

```
<!ELEMENT birth (year)>
```

Sequences
> More often, elements will contain multiple elements. When element names are separated by commas in the parentheses, it means they must appear in exactly the provided order. No listed element may be omitted or the document will be invalid.

```
<!ELEMENT birth (month, year)>
```

The number of child elements

DTD syntax allows you to indicate varying numbers of element instances using the following suffixes:

?   Permits zero or one of the element

*   Permits zero or more of the element

+   Permits one or more of the element

In the XHTML example, the following declaration indicates that the unordered list element (ul) may contain one or more list item elements (li), as indicated by the + suffix. A ul with no li elements would be invalid.

```
<!ELEMENT ul (li)+>
```

A list of options

A list of elements separated by vertical bars indicates available options, only one of which may be used. In this (non-XHTML) example, the season element may contain exactly one of the child elements named winter, spring, summer, or fall.

```
<!ELEMENT season (winter|spring|summer|fall)>
```

Combinations of options and/or sequences

Options and sequences may be grouped in parentheses to be combined with other options or suffixes. In this (non-XHTML) example, the martini element starts with either a gin or vodka element, followed by zero or more of either olive or onion, followed by an optional vermouth element.

```
<!ELEMENT martini ((gin|vodka),(olive|onion)*,vermouth?)>
```

Mixed content

It is common for elements to contain a mix of character data and child elements. This is declared by combining #PCDATA and the permitted child elements in an option group. The * suffix permits zero or more of the chosen element, in no specified order. In this (non-XHTML) example, the description element may include text and/or any number of date children. There is no method for specifying the particular order or number of child elements for an element with mixed content.

```
<!ELEMENT description (#PCDATA|date)*>
```

Empty elements

Empty elements don't have any content. They are indicated by the keyword EMPTY. In the XHTML example, the meta element is empty.

```
<!ELEMENT meta EMPTY>
```

Attlist (attribute) declarations

ATTLIST (attribute) declarations are used to declare the attributes permitted for a particular element. The following attribute declaration from the previous XHTML example says that the meta element may use the attributes id, http-equiv, name, content, and scheme. %i18n is an entity that represents still more available attributes (more on entities next).

```
<!ATTLIST meta
  %i18n;
  id          ID       #IMPLIED
  http-equiv  CDATA    #IMPLIED
  name        CDATA    #IMPLIED
  content     CDATA    #REQUIRED
  scheme      CDATA    #IMPLIED
>
```

After each attribute name is its attribute type, which provides an indication of the type of information its value may contain. The most common attribute types are CDATA (character data) and an enumerated list of possible values (for example (left|right|center)). Other attribute types include ID, IDREF, IDREFS, NMTOKEN, NMTOKENS, ENTITY, ENTITIES, NOTATION, and xml: (a predefined XML value).

Finally, a default value is provided for each attribute. The default value itself may be listed, or there may be an indication of whether the attribute is required within the element (#REQUIRED), optional (#IMPLIED), or fixed (#FIXED *value*).

Entity declarations

In XML, an entity is a string of characters that stands for something else. An entity can be used to represent a single character or a selection of marked up content, such as a footer containing copyright information. Entity declarations provide the name of the entity (which must be a legal XML name; see the earlier sidebar "XML Names") and its replacement text. The five character entities proved by XML were listed in Table 7-1.

General entities insert replacement text into the body of an XML document. The syntax for declaring general entities is:

```
<!ENTITY address "1005 Gravenstein Highway, North Sebastopol, CA 95472">
```

As a result, wherever the author places an &address; entity in the XML source, it will be replaced by the full address upon display. The content may include markup tags. (Be sure that when double quotes are used to delimit the entity value, single quotes are used in the enclosed content, or vice versa.) The content of an entity may also reside in a separate, external file that is referenced in the entity declaration by its URL.

The XHTML sample at the beginning of this section includes another kind of entity called a *parameter entity*, shown here:

```
<!ENTITY % i18n
  "lang       %LanguageCode; #IMPLIED
   xml:lang   %LanguageCode; #IMPLIED
   dir        (ltr|rtl)      #IMPLIED"
>
```

Parameter entities are used only within the DTD itself to declare groups of elements or entities that are repeated throughout the DTD. They are indicated by the % symbol (rather than &). The entity declaration above creates a parameter entity called %i18n (shorthand for "internationalization") that includes three language-related attributes. Because these three attributes apply to nearly every XHTML element, instead of repeating them in every ATTLIST declaration, a parameter entity is used instead to reduce repetition. You can see it in use in the attribute declaration for the meta element.

When to Use a DTD

If you create a markup language in XML, it is not mandatory that it have a DTD. In fact, DTDs come with a few disadvantages. A DTD is useful when you have specific markup requirements to apply across a large number of documents. A DTD can ensure that certain data fields are present or delivered in a particular format. You may also want to spend the time preparing a DTD if you need to coordinate content from various sources and authors. Having a DTD makes it easier to find mistakes in your code.

The disadvantages to DTDs are that they require time and effort to develop and are inconvenient to maintain (particularly while the XML language is in flux). DTDs slow down processing times and may be too restrictive on the user's end. Another problem with DTDs is that they are not compatible with the namespace convention (discussed next). Elements and attributes from another namespace won't validate under a DTD unless the DTD explicitly includes them. If you are creating just a few XML documents, you may choose not to create a DTD. If you are using namespaces and it is necessary to have documentation of your XML vocabulary, you must use an XML Schema.

Because XHTML is a markup language that is used on a global scale, it was necessary to define the language and its various versions in DTDs. An XHTML document must include a DOCTYPE declaration to specify which DTD it follows in order to validate.

XML Namespaces

An XML document may use tags that come from different XML applications or vocabularies. For example, you might have an XHTML document that also contains some math expressions written using MathML. But in this case, the parser needs to differentiate between an a element coming from XHTML (an anchor) and an a element that might come from MathML (an absolute value).

The W3C anticipated such conflicts and responded by creating the namespace convention (see the Recommendation at *www.w3.org/TR/REC-xml-names*). A *namespace* provides a name for a particular XML *vocabulary*, the group of element and attribute names used in an XML application. This allows several XML vocabularies to be used in a single XML document.

When you reference elements and attributes in your document, the browser looks them up in the namespace to find out how they should be used. Namespaces have names that look just like URLs (they are not links to actual documents, however) to ensure uniqueness and provide information about the organization that maintains the namespace.

Namespaces are declared in an XML document using the xmlns attribute. You can establish the namespace for a whole document or an individual element. Typically, the value of the xmlns attribute is a reference to the URL-like namespace.

This example establishes the default namespace for the document to be transitional XHTML:

```
<html xmlns="http://www.w3.org/1999/xhtml">
```

If you need to include math markup, you can apply the xmlns attribute within the specific tag, so the browser knows to look up the element in the MathML DTD (not XHTML):

```
<a xmlns="http://www.w3.org/1998/Math/MathML">46/100</a>
```

If you plan to refer to a namespace repeatedly within a document, you can declare the namespace and give it a label just once at the beginning of the document. Then refer to it in each tag by placing the label before the tag name, separated by a colon (:). For example:

```
<html xmlns="http://www.w3.org/1999/xhtml"
      xmlns:math="http://www.w3.org/1998/Math/MathML">
```

The full namespace can now be shortened to math later in the document, resulting in tidier code and smaller file sizes:

```
<math:a>46/100</math:a>
```

XML on the Web

As mentioned earlier, XML turned out to have uses that reach far beyond web documents, but it is still the W3C's primary tool for optimizing information exchange over the Web. XML is put to use on the Web in several ways.

The most common is XHTML, a reformulation of HTML according to the stricter syntax rules of XML. XHTML is formally introduced in the next section and is discussed in detail in the Chapters 8 through 15.

XHTML 1.1 can be combined in documents with other XML vocabularies such as MathML and SVG (Scalable Vector Graphics; discussed next). Namespaces help the parser keep track of which elements belong to which application (note that this requires a browser that supports namespaces).

XML documents may also be displayed directly in web browsers that support XML. The "Browser Support" section provides more information on how browsers deal with XML.

Finally, one of the most widespread uses of an XML-based format for web content is in the form of RSS feeds that allow summaries of web content (or the content itself) to be shared on other sites or read with a special reader. RSS is discussed in detail in the following section.

The W3C keeps a directory of Recommended DTDs to use in web documents at *www.w3.org/QA/2002/04/valid-dtd-list.html*.

Browser Support

All of the current browser versions produced by Microsoft, Mozilla, and Opera support XML in some form. Table 7-2 lists each of the browsers and the XML features they support.

Table 7-2. Browser support for XML

Browser	XML 1.0	XML+CSS	XSL	Namespaces
Internet Explorer 6 for Windows	Yes	Yes	Yes	Yes
Internet Explorer 5 for Macintosh	Yes	Yes	Yes	No
Internet Explorer 5 and 5.5 for Windows	Yes	No	No	No
Firefox 1.0	Yes	Yes	Yes	Yes
Mozilla 1.8	Yes	Yes	Yes	Yes
Netscape 8	Yes	Yes	Yes	Yes
Netscape 6 and 7	Yes	Yes	No	Yes
Opera 7 and 8	Yes	Yes	No	Yes
Safari 2.0	Yes	Yes	Yes	Yes

Viewing XML in Web Browsers

When an XML-compliant browser encounters an XML document that doesn't have a style sheet, it typically displays the contents of the file, including the markup. All of the browsers in Table 7-2 also use some sort of color-coding to improve readability, either to make markup stand out from the content or to indicate parent/child relationships (Netscape 6 color-codes only when you select View Page Source). All of them except Opera also display plus (+) and minus (-) signs next to parent elements that allow the user to expand or collapse the element's contents. Figure 7-1 shows an unstyled XML document in Firefox 1.0.

If the XML document has a CSS style sheet, browsers that support XML+CSS use the style sheet to display the document's contents according to the presentation instructions. When a style sheet is in use, the markup is hidden. Figure 7-2 shows the same XML document, this time referencing a CSS style sheet. XML documents with XSLT style sheets may be converted to XHTML before being displayed in the browser.

Web-Related XML Applications

XML is already being put to powerful uses on the Web. Some languages, like XHTML and RSS, are expanding the possibilities of web-based content and changing the way we use the Web itself. Others have found small niche uses (such as SMIL and MathML) or have yet to live up to their promised potential (such as SVG). This section introduces these XML languages and others that are relevant to the Web.

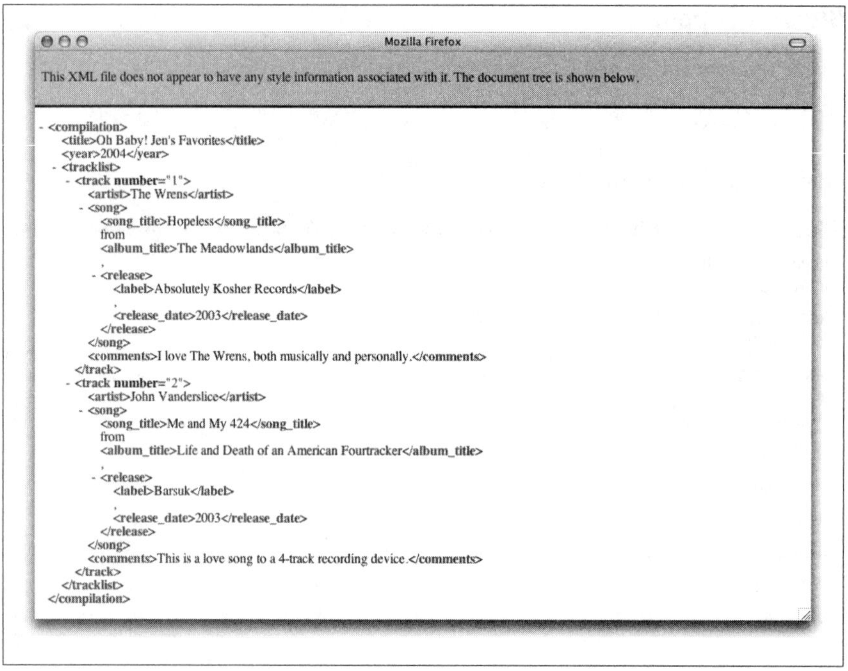

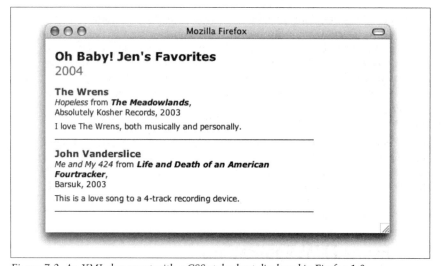

Figure 7-1. An unstyled XML document displayed in Firefox 1.0

Figure 7-2. An XML document with a CSS style sheet displayed in Firefox 1.0

XHTML (Extensible Hypertext Markup Language)

In the context of XML, *XHTML* is a language for describing the content of hypertext documents intended to be viewed or read in some sort of browsing client. It uses a DTD that declares such elements as paragraphs, headings, lists, and hyper-links. It uses the namespace http://www.w3.org/1999/xhtml.

In the context of web design, XHTML is the updated version of HTML and is the current W3C recommendation for authoring web pages. It has all the same elements and attributes as the HTML 4.01 Recommendation, but where HTML was written according to the broader rules of SGML, XHTML has been rewritten according to XML syntax. That means that XHTML documents need to be well-formed, requiring more stringent markup practices. XHTML is by far the dominant use of XML on the Web.

XHTML is discussed in great detail in Chapters 8 through 15.

RSS (Really Simple Syndication or RDF Site Summary)

RSS is an XML language and file format for syndicating web content. The elements in the RSS vocabulary provide metadata about content (such as its head-line, author, description, and originating site) that allows content to be shared as data, known as an *RSS feed*. While originally intended for headlines and short summaries, some RSS feeds now contain the full content of each posting, including marked-up XHTML content. The content of the feed is up to the discre-tion of the author.

RSS feeds can be used to display information from other sites on a web page, such as headlines from Slashdot on a technology-related site. RSS feeds can also be read using special programs called *feed readers* (or *news readers*). Readers may be web-based or standalone desktop applications. Web sites that combine feeds from many sources in one place are sometimes called *aggregators*.

Some popular RSS feed readers include SharpReader (Windows), NetNewsWire (Mac), and the web-based Bloglines. A web search for "RSS readers" will turn up many more. Some browsers, such as Firefox 1.0 and Safari RSS, come with built-in RSS readers.

How it works

To understand how RSS works, consider this possible scenario. Say you have a favorite news site that is updated frequently throughout the day and you want to make sure you don't miss their Oscar nomination announcement. You could use your web browser to visit the site every 20 minutes and scan through it for new posts, but that would waste a lot of time. But, if that site is RSS-enabled (and most news sites are), every time they post an article to the site, a listing of that article simultaneously appears in RSS feed readers that have subscribed to the site and are themselves checking the site once an hour or so. Using a news reader, you could keep an eye on new articles as they are posted and take a break only when you see Oscar in the title.

Originally developed to create web "channels" during the days of web push tech-nologies, news sites were the first to put RSS to widespread use. But it wasn't until the *weblog* (or *blog*) phenomenon that the RSS acronym became as familiar as HTML.

Because blog creation software such as Blogger and Movable Type made it easy to publish content as an RSS feed, most bloggers make their site content available both on a web page and via an RSS feed (watch for the ubiquitous orange RSS or XML icon). That means that you can use a news reader to see when your friends post without having to check every blog, every day. Furthermore, you can often read the content right there in the reader, without skipping from site to site.

Many web users have integrated spending time with their RSS feed readers into their daily routines. Bloggers are finding that an increasing number of visitors are reading their sites via RSS feeds rather than in the context of a designed page. In this way, RSS has made a significant impact on how information is produced and consumed.

Trouble over an RSS standard

The story of the development of RSS has all the makings of a daytime drama. Along the way, RSS developers divided into two camps, both claiming right to the initials "RSS" for their specifications. The result is that we, indeed, now have two recent standards, RSS 1.0 and RSS 2.0, that sound sequential, but are actually conflicting. In addition, there are several older incompatible flavors of RSS (0.91, 0.92, 0.93, and others) that are still in use.

The history of the RSS "fork" is well documented, and it makes for some interesting reading. Check out Mark Pilgrim's blow-by-blow account taken from actual message board and mailing list posts at *diveintomark.org/archives/2002/09/06/history_of_the_rss_fork*. You can also find a more general RSS history by Joseph Reagle at *goatee.net/2003/rss-history.html*.

RSS 1.0 is the product of the RSS-DEV Working Group, a committee of individuals, some of whom had worked on various incarnations of RSS since its inception. Their vision for RSS (*RDF Site Summary*) is that it should take full advantage of RDF (a metadata syntax discussed below) and XML namespaces in order to harness the full power of XML. They added these features into the developing RSS 0.91 spec in development and called the result RSS 1.0.

On the other side of the debate is David Winer (of Userland Software) who maintains that the reason RSS became so popular in the first place is because it was so simple to author and use. It achieved this simplicity specifically because it *didn't* include RDF or namespaces, and David and others wanted it to stay that way. David made minor changes to RSS 0.91 and called the result RSS 2.0 (for *Really Simple Syndication*). RSS 2.0 is not RDF based, but does address namespaces.

Developers on both sides of the RSS controversy agree that the technology is far too useful to suffer from conflicting and confusing standards. As of this writing, everyone has agreed to work toward a unified method, or at least distinctive names, for web syndication.

Enter Atom

In June 2003, Sam Ruby set up a wiki to discuss and design "a well-formed log entry." Many of those frustrated with both the political drama and technical limitations of RSS joined the effort, and in June 2004 formally set up the Atompub Working Group at the IETF (Internet Engineering Task Force, a volunteer organization that develops Internet standards) to develop and formalize a new feed format and publishing protocol called *Atom* (formerly Echo). The Atompub Working Group's goal is to create a single standard for syndicated content feeds based on experience gained with RSS.

As of this writing, Atom 1.0 has been published and accepted as a proposed standard. Atom is being backed and implemented by some important syndication tool developers and indexers (e.g., Google and Technorati).

For further reading

For more information on RSS and Atom, visit these online resources:

web.resource.org/rss/1.0/
  RSS 1.0 specification

blogs.law.harvard.edu/tech/rss
  RSS 2.0 specification

www.intertwingly.net/slides/2003/rssQuickSummary.html
  A comparison of RSS specifications

ietf.org/html.charters/atompub-charter.html
  IETF's Atom Publishing Format and Protocol Charter

www.intertwingly.net/wiki/pie/FrontPage
  The Atom Project

RDF (Resource Description Framework)

RDF is an XML application used to define the structure of metadata for documents; for example, data that is useful for indexing, navigating, and searching a site. A standard method for describing the contents of a web site, page, or resource could be useful to automated agents that search the Web for specific information.

Metadata could be used in the following ways:

- For descriptions of resources to provide better search engine capabilities
- In cataloging, for describing the content and content relationships available at a particular web site, page, or digital library
- In describing collections of pages that represent a single logical "document"
- For digital signatures that allow electronic commerce, collaboration, and other "trust"-based applications

A simple RDF document that provides author information about a book looks like this (this example is taken from and describes the O'Reilly book *XML in a Nutshell*):

```
<rdf: RDF xmlns:rdf="http://www.w3.org/1999/02/22-rdf-syntax-ns#">
<rdf:Description about="urn:isbn:0596000588">
  <author>Elliotte Rusty Harold</author>
```

```
    <author>W. Scott Means</author>
  </rdf:Description>
</rdf:RDF>
```

The first line of code declares the namespace for RDF as `http://www.w3.org/1999/02/22-rdf-syntax-ns#`.

For more information about RDF, see the W3C's pages at *www.w3.org/RDF/*.

SVG (Scalable Vector Graphics)

The W3C is developing the Scalable Vector Graphics (SVG) standard for describing two-dimensional graphics in XML. SVG allows for three types of graphic objects: vector graphic shapes (paths consisting of straight lines and curves), images, and text. The following sample SVG code (taken from the W3C Recommendation) creates an SVG document fragment that contains a red circle with a blue outline (stroke):

```
<?xml version="1.0" standalone="no"?>
<!DOCTYPE svg PUBLIC "-//W3C//DTD SVG 20001102//EN"
"http://www.w3.org/TR/2000/CR-SVG-20001102/DTD/svg-20001102.dtd">
<svg width="12cm" height="4cm">
   <desc>Example circle01 - circle expressed in physical units</desc>
   <circle cx="6cm" cy="2cm" r="1cm"
           style="fill:red; stroke:blue; stroke-width:0.1cm" />
</svg>
```

The SVG standard provides ways to describe paths, fills, a variety of shapes, special filters, text, and basic animation. When using SVG within another XML document type, identify its namespace as `http://www.w3.org/2000/svg`.

To view SVG graphics, you must have an SVG viewer installed. The most popular is Adobe's SVG Viewer (available as a free download at *www.adobe.com*), which allows SVG documents to display in a browser window. Adobe also includes tools for creating SVG files in Illustrator and GoLive. (As of this writing, it is unclear whether Adobe will continue to support GoLive now that it has acquired Macromedia.)

For more information on SVG and lists of all available viewers, editors, and converters, see the W3C pages at *www.w3.org/Graphics/SVG*. Or, if you want your information in book form, try *SVG Essentials* by J. David Eisenberg (O'Reilly) or *Fundamentals of SVG Programming: Concepts to Source Code* by Oswald Campesato (Charles River Media).

SMIL (Synchronized Multimedia Integration Language)

SMIL (pronounced "smile") is an XML language for combining audio, video, text, animation, and graphics in a precise, synchronized fashion. A SMIL file instructs the client to retrieve media elements that reside on the server as standalone files. Those separate elements are then assembled and played by the SMIL player.

The SMIL 1.0 Recommendation, released in June of 1998, was one of the first XML-based DTDs proposed by the W3C. The SMIL 2.0 Recommendation, released in January 2005, greatly expands upon the functionality established in the initial specification. It is broken into modules to be used with XHTML 1.1.

How SMIL works

The best way to get a quick understanding of SMIL is to look at a simple example. The following SMIL code creates a 15-second narrated slideshow, in which an audio track plays as a series of three images displayed in sequence.

```
<par dur="15s">
<audio src="audio_file.mp3" begin="0s" />
    <seq>
        <img src="image_1.jpg" begin="0s" />
        <img src="image_2.jpg" begin="5s" />
        <img src="image_3.jpg" begin="10s" />
    </seq>
</par>
```

Looking at the code, it is easy to pick out the audio and image elements. Each points to a separate media file on the server.

All elements contained within the <par> element are played in parallel (at the same time); therefore, the audio will continue playing as the images are displayed. The image elements are contained in the <seq> element, which means they will be played one after another (in sequence). The begin attribute gives timing instructions for when each element should be displayed. In the example, the images will display in slideshow fashion every five seconds.

For more information on SMIL, take a look at *SMIL 2.0: Interactive Multimedia for Web and Mobile Devices* by Dick C.A. Bulterman and Lloyd Rutledge (Springer). Or you can check out these online resources.

W3C SMIL resources
Go right to the source for a good starting place for research or to keep up to date on the latest developments. See *www.w3.org/AudioVideo/*. For a thorough explanation of all SMIL elements and their supported attributes and values, make your way through the SMIL 2.0 Recommendation at *www.w3. org/TR/smil20/cover.html*.

JustSMIL Home (now part of Streaming Media World)
This is a great site containing tutorials, product reviews, news, tips, and other useful SMIL information. See *smw.internet.com/smil/smilhome.html*.

MathML (Mathematical Markup Language)

MathML is an XML application for describing mathematical notation and capturing both its structure and content. The goal of MathML is to enable mathematics to be served, received, and processed on the World Wide Web. The MathML 2.0 Recommendation was released by the W3C Recommendation in October 2003.

Because there is no way to reproduce mathematical equations directly using HTML, authors had resorted to inserting graphical images of equations into the flow of text. This effectively removes the information from the structure of the document. MathML allows the information to remain in the document in a meaningful way. With adequate style sheets, mathematical notation can be formatted for high-quality visual presentation. Several vendors offer applets and plug-ins that allow the display of MathML information in browser windows.

For examples of MathML, see the Recommendation at *www.w3.org/TR/2003/REC-MathML2-20031021*. The main MathML page (*www.w3.org/Math*) is a good starting place for information.

Other XML Applications

There are far too many XML applications to list in a book. However, you may find that the more languages you are aware of, the better your grasp of XML's possibilities. The following are just a handful of the XML applications you may hear about.

DocBook
> DocBook is a DTD for technical publications and software documentation. DocBook is officially maintained by the DocBook Technical Committee of OASIS, and you can find the official home page located at *www.oasis-open.org/committees/docbook/*.

Chemical Markup Language (CML)
> CML is used for managing and presenting molecular and technical information over a network. For more information, see *www.xml-cml.org*.

Open Financial Exchange (OFX)
> OFX is a joint project of Microsoft, Intuit, and Checkfree. It is an XML application for describing financial transactions that take place over the Internet. For more information, see *www.ofx.net/ofx/default.asp*.

Where to Learn More

If you are interested in learning more about XML, you will want to check out *Learning XML* by Erik T. Ray and *XML in a Nutshell* by Elliotte Rusty Harold and W. Scott Means, both published by O'Reilly.

The growth and development of XML is well documented online in resources such as the following:

World Wide Web Consortium (www.w3.org)
> The World Wide Web Consortium's official web site is the best place to go for the latest news on new XML standards and proposals.

XML.com (www.xml.com)
> XML.com, part of the O'Reilly Network, is a clearinghouse of great articles and information on XML.

The XML Cover Pages (www.oasis-open.org/cover/xml.html)
> The Cover Pages hosted by Oasis provide a comprehensive reference on all XML-related topics.

8

HTML and XHTML Overview

HTML (Hypertext Markup Language) is the markup language used to turn text documents into web pages. HTML allows authors to identify elements that give the document structure, such as headings, paragraphs, lists, and so on. Other elements act as mechanisms for adding hypertext links, interactive forms, and media such as audio and video to web pages.

HTML has undergone quite a journey since its creation by Tim Berners-Lee in 1991 as a simple way to indicate the meaning and structure of hypertext documents. It didn't take long for competing browser developers to add on to the initial minimal set of HTML elements or for the first crop of web designers to co-opt HTML as a visual design tool.

XHTML is a reformulation of HTML in XML. In other words, it uses the same vocabulary (the same elements and attributes) as HTML, but the syntactical rules are pulled from XML, which is stricter than HTML. XHTML is discussed in detail later in this chapter.

Before we delve into HTML and XHTML syntax, let's take a moment to look at the important role (X)HTML plays as well as the recent groundswell of respect it has earned in the new standards-driven web design environment.

The W3C

Seeing the need to bring order to the development of HTML, Berners-Lee founded the World Wide Web Consortium (W3C) in 1994. The W3C continues to oversee HTML and related web technologies and has been releasing updated and standardized versions of HTML in publications known as "Recommendations" since 1995. The current standards are HTML 4.01 (1999) and XHTML 1.0 (2000).

The Role of HTML

The marked up HTML document is said to be the *structural layer* of a web page. It is the foundation upon which the *presentation layer* (instructions for how the elements should be delivered or displayed) and the *behavioral layer* (scripting and interactivity) are applied.

Did you happen to read the preceding XML chapter? It may seem off the topic of HTML, but there are some critical XML-based concepts there that guide the way HTML is perceived and handled in contemporary web design. One guiding concept is that the fundamental purpose of HTML as a markup language is to provide a *semantic* description (the meaning) of the content and establish a document *structure*. It is not concerned with *presentation*, such as how the document will look in a browser. Presentation is the job of Cascading Style Sheets, which is covered in Part III.

That presentational instructions should be kept separate from the semantic and structural markup is nothing new. It has been the intent of HTML from its beginning as an application of SGML (Standardized General Markup Language) as noted in the upcoming sidebar. What *is* new is that the web community is recognizing that there are measurable advantages (in terms of time and money) to using HTML for what it was designed to do, and nothing more.

Keeping Presentation Separate from Document Structure

Before HTML, there was SGML (Standard Generalized Markup Language), which established a complex language for describing documents in terms of their structure, independent of appearance. SGML is a vast set of rules for developing markup languages such as HTML, but it is so all-encompassing that HTML uses only a small subset of its capabilities.

Because HTML is one instance of an SGML markup system, this principle of keeping presentation information separate from the structure of the document remains inherent to the HTML purpose. Over the early years of the Web's development, this ideal was compromised by the creation of HTML tags that contain explicit style instructions, such as the font element and bgcolor attribute.

The W3C has been taking measures to get HTML back on track. First, the creation of Cascading Style Sheets gives authors a robust solution for specifying style information and keeping it out of the document's content. In addition, with each new HTML Recommendation, the elements and attributes related to presentation have been deprecated and finally eliminated.

With this system in place, the W3C is more diligent than ever to clean up the HTML standard to make it work the way it was intended. Slowly the browser and authoring tool developers are getting on board. Now it is up to web developers and designers to start creating clean content.

Starting with "Good" Markup

In the interest of building a solid foundation, writing presentation-free, logical, and well-structured (X)HTML documents has become a cornerstone of modern standards-compliant web design. Web authors are encouraged to work toward four separate, yet related, goals when marking up content for distribution on the Web.

Write standards-compliant documents

That means using HTML or XHTML markup according to the rules set forth in the Recommendations and making sure that your documents validate against a declared DTD. Following the standards will ensure your documents are forward compatible as web technologies and browser capabilities evolve.

Use semantic markup

It is also important to mark up elements in your document semantically, that is, in a way that is descriptive and meaningful. There is a renewed emphasis on choosing elements to appropriately describe the content and not purely for their presentational effects in the browser. Techniques that once were common, such as marking up content as a list just to get the text to indent, are now deemed completely unacceptable.

Semantic markup is not the same as standards compliance. It is possible to create a document out of font, br, and i elements that validates entirely, but that does zilch for making the content meaningful. A semantically marked up document ensures accessibility in the widest range of browsing environments, from desktop computers to cell phones to screen readers. It also allows nonhuman readers, such as search engine indexing functions, to correctly parse your content and make decisions about how to handle it.

Structure documents logically

Make sure that your content reads in a logical order in the source to improve its readability across all browsing environments. Information that should be read first should be at the beginning of the document. You can always use style sheets to position elements where you want them for visual display.

Keep presentation separate from structure

Use style sheets to control presentation. Keeping all presentation information in a separate style sheet document makes it easier to redesign or repurpose content. In terms of markup, this means avoiding presentational (X)HTML elements and attributes that are still hanging around in the Recommendations (such as b for bold text), and using an appropriate semantic alternative (e.g., strong) with a style sheet rule.

Markup Basics

An HTML or XHTML document is an ASCII (plain text), or more often, Unicode (e.g., UTF-8) document that has been marked up with tags that indicate elements and other necessary declarations (such as the markup language it is written in). An *element* is a structural component (such as a paragraph) or a desired behavior (such as a line break). This section introduces the key components and behaviors of HTML documents, including elements, attributes, how elements may be nested, and information in a document that is ignored by browsers.

Elements

Elements are denoted in the text source by the insertion of special bracketed HTML tags. Most elements follow this syntax.

```
<element-name>content</element-name>
```

The element name appears in the start tag (also called the opening tag) and again in the end (or closing) tag, preceded by a slash (/). The end tag works something like an "off" switch for the element. Nothing within the brackets is displayed by the browser or other user agent. It is important to note that the element includes both the content *and* its markup (the start and end tags).

In XHTML, all element and attribute names must be lowercase. HTML is not case sensitive.

Consider this example of HTML markup that identifies the content at the beginning of this section as a second-level heading element and a paragraph element:

```
<h2>Elements</h2>

<p>Elements are denoted in the text source by the insertion of special
bracketed HTML tags. Most elements follow this syntax.</p>
```

In HTML 4.01 and earlier, the end tag for some elements is optional, and the browser determines when the tag ends by context. This practice is most common with the p (paragraph) element. Most browsers automatically end a paragraph when they encounter a new start tag. In XHTML, end tags are always required.

Some elements do not have content because they are used to provide a simple directive. These elements are said to be *empty*. The image element (img) is an example of such an element; it tells the browser to call a graphic file from an external location into the current page. Other empty elements include the line break (br), horizontal rule (hr), and elements that provide information about a document and don't affect its displayed content, such as the meta and base elements. Table 8-1 lists all the empty elements in HTML.

In HTML 4.01 and earlier, empty elements simply didn't have a closing tag. In XML, termination is required for all elements. The convention is to use a trailing slash within the tag to signify the element's termination, as in <img/>, <br/>, and <hr/>. For reasons of backward compatibility, it is recommended to add a space before the slash, as shown in Table 8-1. The space is necessary if you are sending your XHTML with the HTTP Content-Type of text/html.

Table 8-1. Empty elements

`<area />`	`<frame />`	`<link />`
`<base />`	`<hr />`	`<meta />`
`<basefont />`	`<img />`	`<param />`
` `	`<input />`	
`<col />`	`<isindex />`	

 An excellent resource for HTML element information is Index DOT Html (*www.blooberry.com/indexdot/html/*), which was created and is maintained by Brian Wilson. It provides an alphabetical listing of every HTML element and its attributes, with explanations, standards details, and browser support information.

Attributes

An *attribute* clarifies or modifies an element's actions. Attributes are indicated by attribute name and value pairs added to the start tag of the element (end tags never contain attributes). Attribute names and their accepted values are declared in the DTD; in other words, you cannot make up your own. You can add multiple attributes within a single opening tag. Attributes, if any, go after the tag name, each separated by one or more spaces. Their order of appearance is not important.

The syntax for an element with attributes is as follows:

```
<element attribute="value">content</element>
```

The following are examples of elements that contain attributes:

```
<head profile="http://gmpg.org/xfn/11">...</head>
<img src="graphics/pixie.gif" alt="pixie" />
<table summary="This is a conference schedule.">...</table>
```

Most browsers cannot handle attribute values more than 1,024 characters in length. Values may be case-sensitive, particularly filenames or URLs.

XHTML requires that all attribute values be enclosed in quotation marks. Single or double quotation marks may be used, as long as they are used consistently throughout the document.

In HTML 4.01 and earlier, some values are permitted to go unquoted; for instance, if the value is a single word containing only letters (a–z or A–Z), digits (0–9), hyphens (-), periods (.), underscores (_), and colons (:). It is the best practice to quote all values, regardless of the Recommendation you are following.

 Be careful not to leave out the closing quotation mark, or all the content from the opening quotation mark until the browser encounters a subsequent quotation mark will be interpreted as part of the value and won't display in the browser. This is a simple mistake that can cause hours of debugging frustration.

Nested Elements

HTML elements may contain other elements. This is called *nesting*, and to do it properly, the entire element (including its markup) must be within the start and end tags of the containing element (the *parent*). Proper nesting is one of the criteria of a well-formed document (a requirement for XHTML).

In this example, list items (li) are nested within an unordered list element (ul).

```
<ul>
  <li>Example 1</li>
  <li>Example 2</li>
</ul>
```

A common mistake made when nesting elements is to close the parent element before the element it contains (its *child*) has been closed. This results in an incorrect overlapping of elements that would make an XHTML document *malformed* and may cause rendering problems for HTML documents. In this example, the elements are incorrectly nested because the strong element should have been closed before the a (anchor).

```
INCORRECT:  <a href="#">Click <strong>here.</a></strong>
```

Information Browsers Ignore

Some information in an HTML document, including certain markup, is ignored or has little to no impact on presentation when the document is viewed in a browser or other user agent. These include:

Line breaks
> Line returns in the HTML document are treated as spaces, which then typically collapse with other spaces (see next point). Text and elements wrap continuously until they encounter a p or br element within the flow of the document text. Line breaks are displayed, however, when text is marked up as a preformatted (pre) element or styled with the white-space: pre property in a style sheet.

Tabs and multiple spaces
> When a user agent encounters more than one consecutive blank character space in an HTML document, it displays it as a single space. So, if the document contains:

```
far,            far             away
```
> the browser displays:

> far, far away

> Extra spaces can be added within the flow of text by using the non-breaking space character entity ( ). Multiple spaces are displayed, however, when text is marked up as preformatted text (pre) or with the white-space: pre property in a style sheet. Tabs in the source document are problematic for some browsers and are best avoided.

Empty p elements

Empty paragraph elements (`<p>...</p>` or `<p>` alone) with no intervening text are interpreted as redundant by all browsers and displayed as though they were only a single paragraph break. Most browsers display multiple br elements as multiple line breaks.

Unrecognized element

A browser simply ignores any element it doesn't understand or that was incorrectly specified. Depending on the element and the browser, this can have varied results. Browsers typically display the contents of the element and its markup as though it were normal text, although some older browsers may display nothing at all.

Text in comments

Browsers do not display text between the special `<!--` and `-->` elements used to denote a *comment*. Here is a sample comment:

```
<!-- This is a comment -->
<!-- This is a
multiple line comment
that ends here. -->
```

There must be a space after the initial `<!--` and preceding the final `-->`, but you can put nearly anything inside the comment otherwise. You cannot nest comments. Comments are useful for leaving notes within a long HTML file, for example:

```
<!-- navigation table starts here -->
```

HTML markup that is contained within comments will not display, therefore comments may be useful for temporarily hiding content without permanently removing it from the document.

Introduction to XHTML

With the finalization of the XML Recommendation in hand (see Chapter 7), the W3C had a streamlined and web-friendly standard for defining markup languages. It should come as no surprise that one of the top priorities was reformulating HTML (an SGML application) into an XML application. XHTML is the result.

XHTML 1.0 contains the same list of elements and attributes as HTML 4.01. It even has the same three associated DTDs: Strict, Transitional, and Frames. The difference is that, as for all XML applications, correct syntax is suddenly critical. So while browsers are forgiving of a certain amount of looseness in HTML, XHTML documents are required to be well-formed. The syntax requirement differences between HTML and XHTML are listed in the upcoming "Well-Formed XHTML" section. The W3C recognizes the benefit of having a stricter professional standard and a more relaxed standard that is accessible to anyone who wants to publish on the Web, so both HTML and XHTML standards are currently maintained and supported by current browsers.

The XHTML Family

XHTML is not just one, but a family of document types. Between January 2000 and June 2001, the W3C turned out four XHTML Recommendations: XHTML 1.0, XHTML Basic, the Modularization of XHTML, and XHTML 1.1. They are currently reviewing XHTML 2.0 and XHTML-Print, both based on modular XHTML. This section takes a brief look at each one. You can find detailed and up-to-date information on the W3C site at *w3c.org/MarkUp*. (For example, on May 27, 2005, the seventh working draft of XHTML 2.0 was published.)

XHTML 1.0

The XHTML 1.0 Recommendation (released in January 2000) is just a reformulation of the HTML 4.01 specification according to the rules of XML. Like HTML 4.01, XHTML 1.0 comes in three varieties—Strict, Transitional, and Frames—each defined by a separate Document Type Definition (DTD). These are discussed in the next section.

The Modularization of XHTML

In a world where HTML content is being used on devices as varied as cell phones, desktop computers, refrigerator panels, dashboard consoles, and more, a "one-size-fits-all" content markup language will no longer work. Modularization is the solution to this problem. Instead of one comprehensive set of elements, this Recommendation defines a way to break XHTML into task-specific modules. A *module* is a set of elements that handle one aspect or type of object in a document.

Modularization is the way of the future for markup standards. This approach has a number of benefits:

- Special devices and applications can mix and match modules based on their requirements and restraints.
- It prevents spin-off, device-specific languages. Authors can create their own XML modules, leaving the XHTML standard unscathed.
- It allows "hybrid" documents in which several DTDs are used in combination. For instance, in theory, it allows web documents to have SVG (Scalable Vector Graphics) modules or MathML modules mixed in with the XHTML content, though the details of making this work have yet to be figured out as of the time of this writing.

The Modularization of XHTML Recommendation was initially released in April 2001. A Second Edition of the Recommendation was introduced as a Working Draft in February 2004.

XHTML Basic

The XHTML Basic Recommendation (released in December 2000) is a stripped-down version of modularized XHTML. It is a subset of XHTML elements that are appropriate to such mobile web clients as cell phones, handheld devices, and other information appliances. The definition of a standard, yet extensible, set of XHTML modules for developers of mobile applications and clients allows this document type to be shared across those development communities. It gives them a common starting point. See *www.w3.org/TR/xhtml-basic/* for more information.

XHTML 1.1

The XHTML 1.1 Recommendation, released in 2001, is a reformulation of XHTML 1.0 (Strict) using the XHTML modules. It is also the first markup language to be fully liberated from legacy functionality of HTML by completely eliminating the elements and attributes that control presentation. Authors are required to put all style and layout information in Cascading Style Sheets.

Some examples of modules in XHTML 1.1 include structure, text, hypertext, lists, object, image, forms, tables, objects, and image maps.

As of this writing, few browsers support an XHTML 1.1 document when it is properly identified as an XML application media type. For this reason, although XHTML 1.1 is the most recent Recommendation, most professional developers use XHTML 1.0 because it can be labeled as HTML text. XHTML media types are discussed further in Chapter 9.

XHTML-Print

This document specifies a simple XHTML-based data stream suitable for printing in environments where it is not feasible or desirable to install a printer-specific driver and where some variability in the formatting of the output is acceptable. It is designed to print basic content without regards to layout or presentation. This Recommendation is in development.

XHTML 2.0

XHTML 2.0 is a markup language intended for rich, portable web-based applications. It is not intended to be backward compatible with its earlier versions. As of this writing, XHTML 2.0 is in development as a Working Draft.

Three Flavors of HTML 4.01 and XHTML 1.0

Although the W3C has ideas on how HTML *should* work, they are also aware that it is going to be a while before old browsers are phased out and web authors begin to mark up documents properly. For that reason, both the HTML 4.01 and XHTML 1.0 Recommendations encompass three slightly different specification documents: one "Strict," one "Transitional," and one just for framed documents. These documents, called *Document Type Definitions* (or *DTDs*), define every element, attribute, and entity along with the rules for their use. The XHTML DTDs are written following the rules and conventions of XML (Extensible Markup Language), while the HTML DTDs follow SGML syntax. See Chapter 7 for more on XML. The browser uses the DTD to "decode" the markup and check it for validity.

Strict DTD

This version excludes all deprecated elements and attributes (such as font and align) to reinforce the separation of document structure from presentation. Ideally, documents should be tagged strictly for meaning and structure, leaving all presentation to be handled by style sheets.

Transitional DTD

The Transitional DTD includes all deprecated elements and attributes in order to be backwards compatible with the legacy behavior of most browsers. Deprecated elements and attributes are permitted but discouraged from use. This DTD provides a way to ease web authors out of their current habits and toward abiding by standards. Many web authors today choose to use the Transitional DTD while the industry waits for current browsers to offer perfect and consistent CSS support and for older browsers to fade away.

Frameset DTD

The Frameset DTD includes the same elements as the Transitional DTD, with the addition of elements for creating framed web pages (frameset, frame, and noframe). The Frameset DTD is kept separate because the structure of a framed document (where frameset replaces body) is fundamentally different from regular HTML documents. Frames are discussed in Chapter 14.

It is important to specify which version you are using in your document using a DOCTYPE declaration, as modern browsers can use this information to turn on "strict" standards-compliant formatting (Standards Mode), as opposed to the "quirky" behavior of older, nonstandard HTML (Quirks Mode). Of course, if you do specify the DTD, you must stick to it exactly so that your document will be valid (in other words, don't break any rules defined by the DTD). DOCTYPE declarations and switching are discussed further in Chapter 9.

Which Standard Is Right for You?

With so many co-existing Recommendations, it may be difficult to choose which one is best for your purposes. The following is a quick summary that will put all of these options into perspective.

XHTML 1.0 Transitional

Use this standard if your authoring style makes use of any of the deprecated elements (such as font) or attributes (such as bgcolor or align) and you have the discipline (or authoring tools) it takes to make sure the document is well-formed. This is the most popular choice for professional web developers because it is forward compatible, yet still allows some of the legacy techniques required to control presentation in current browsers.

XHTML 1.0 Strict

Use XHTML Strict if you are committed to using style sheets for all presentation and layout because all of those deprecated tags have been removed from this Recommendation. Documents must be well-formed as well, of course.

HTML 4.01
> Use Transitional, Strict, or Frames if you aren't concerned with site longevity, if you are not using updated authoring tools, or if you can't bring yourself to close an li element.

XHTML 1.0 Frames or HTML 4.01 Frames
> Use if you are creating a framed site. All deprecated attributes are still in there.

XHTML 1.1
> This is available for use, but it is difficult to make it work effectively due to lack of browser support for the XML identifiers that a compliant XHTML 1.1 document requires. For this reason, it is not commonly used by developers as of this writing.

Well-Formed XHTML

Web browsers are forgiving of sloppy HTML, but XHTML (being an XML application) requires that you play by the rigid rules of XML markup syntax. What makes XHTML documents different from HTML documents is that you need to be absolutely sure that your document follows the syntax rules of XML correctly (in other words, that it is *well-formed*). The sections below summarize the requirements of well-formed XHTML as well as some tips for backward compatibility with older browsers.

All-Lowercase Element and Attribute Names

In XML, all elements and attribute names are case-sensitive, which means that `<img>`, `<Img>`, and `<IMG>` are parsed as different elements. In the reformulation of HTML into XHTML, all elements were interpreted to be lowercase. When writing XHTML documents (and their associated style sheets), be sure that all tags and attribute names are written in lowercase. Attribute values are not required to be case-sensitive.

 If you want to convert the upper- and mixed-case tags in an existing HTML file to well-formed, all-lowercase tags, try the HTML Tidy utility (*tidy.sourceforge.net/*) or Barebones Software BBEdit (Macintosh only, *www.bbedit.com*), which can automate the process.

Quoted Attribute Values

XHTML requires that all attribute values be contained in quotation marks. Double or single quotation marks are acceptable, as long as they are used consistently throughout the document. So where previously it was okay to omit the quotes around single words and numeric values, now you need to be careful that every attribute value is quoted.

Element Termination

In HTML, it is okay to omit the end tag for certain block elements (such as p and li). The beginning of a new block element is enough to trigger the browser to parse the previous one as closed. Not so in XHTML. To be well-formed, every container element must have its end tag, or it registers as an error and renders the document noncompliant.

Empty Elements

This need for termination extends to empty elements as well. So instead of just inserting a line break as <br>, XHTML requires the element to be terminated. You can simply add a slash before the closing bracket, indicating the element's ending. So in XHTML, a line break is entered as <br/>.

The notion of closing empty elements can cause some browsers (namely Netscape 4) to complain, and even new browsers to have problems when content is sent as text/html, so to keep your XHTML digestible to those browsers, be sure to add a space before the closing slash (<br />). This allows the closed empty tag to slide right through. See Table 8-1 for a complete list of empty elements.

Explicit Attribute Values

XML (and therefore XHTML) does not support *attribute minimization*, the SGML practice in which certain attributes can be reduced to just the attribute value. So while HTML has many minimized attributes such as checked and nowrap, in XHTML, the values need to be explicitly declared as checked="checked" and nowrap="nowrap". Table 8-2 lists the attributes that were minimized in HTML but require values in XHTML.

Table 8-2. Explicit attribute values

checked="checked"	disabled="disabled"	noresize="noresize"
compact="compact"	ismap="ismap"	nowrap="nowrap"
declare="declare"	multiple="multiple"	readonly="readonly"
defer="defer"	noshade="noshade"	selected="selected"

Nesting Requirements

It has always been a rule in HTML that elements should be properly nested within one another. The closing tag of a contained element should always appear before the closing tag of the element that contains it. In XHTML, this rule is strictly enforced. So be sure that your elements are nested correctly, like this:

```
<p>I can <em>fly!</em></p>
```

and not overlapping like this:

```
<p>I can <em>fly!</p></em>
```

In addition, XHTML enforces other nesting restrictions that have always been a part of the HTML specification. The XHTML DTD includes a special "Content Models for Exclusions" note that reinforces the following:

- An a element cannot contain another a element.
- The pre element cannot contain img, object, applet, big, small, sub, sup, font, or basefont.
- The form element may not contain other form elements.
- A button element cannot contain a, form, input, select, textarea, label, button, iframe, or isindex.
- The label element cannot contain other label elements.

Character Entities

XHTML (as a function of XML) is extremely fussy about special characters such as <, >, and &. All special characters should be represented in the XHTML document by their character entities instead. Common character entities are listed in Table 10-3, and the complete list appears in Appendix C.

Character entity references should be used in place of characters such as < and & in regular text content, as shown in these examples:

```
<p> the value of A &lt; B </p>
<p> Laverne &amp; Shirley </p>
```

In places where it was common to use special characters, such as in the title of a document or in an attribute value, it is now necessary to use the character entity instead. For instance, the following worked just fine in HTML, despite being invalid:

```
<img src="puppets.jpg" alt="Crocco & Lynch">
```

But in XHTML, the value must be written like this:

```
<img src="puppets.jpg" alt="Crocco &amp; Lynch" />
```

This applies to ampersands that occur in URLs as well.

```
<a href="mailto: jen@example.com ? subject=subject&amp;cc=person ">
    Email Jen<a/>
```

Protecting Scripts

It is common practice to enclose scripts and style sheets in comments (between <!-- and -->). Unfortunately, XML software thinks of comments as unimportant information and may simply remove the comments from a document before processing it. To avoid this problem, use an XML CDATA section instead. Content enclosed in <![CDATA[...]]> is considered simple text characters and is not parsed (for more information, see Chapter 7). For example:

```
<script language="JavaScript">
<![CDATA[
...JavaScript here...
]]>
</script>
```

The problem with this method is backward compatibility. HTML browsers ignore the contents of the XML CDATA section, while XML browsers ignore the contents of comment-enclosed scripts and style sheets. So you can't please everyone. One workaround is to put your scripts and styles in separate files and reference them in the document with appropriate external links. The common practice is to avoid CDATA and comments altogether and keep scripts and style externalized. Although not required, it is heavily recommended as part of XHTML and document management.

id and name Attributes

In HTML, the name attribute may be used for the elements a, applet, form, frame, iframe, img, and map. The name attribute and the id attribute may be used in HTML to identify document fragments.

In XML, only id may be used for fragments and there may only be a single id attribute per element. XHTML documents must use id instead of name for identifying document fragments in the aforementioned elements. In fact, the name attribute for these elements has been deprecated in the XHTML 1.0 specification.

Once again, we run into an issue with browser compatibility. Some legacy browsers (namely Netscape 4) do not recognize the id attribute as an identifier for a document fragment (current standards-conformant browsers handle it just fine). If your fragment identifiers must work in Netscape 4, use both name and id. Unfortunately, this is likely to cause validation errors if you are complying to XHTML 1.0 Strict or XHTML 1.1, and therefore you should use only the id attribute when possible for fragment identifiers. The only remaining valid use of the name attribute is for form submission semantics on form control elements like input.

Web Authoring Tools

HTML documents are simple text files, which means you can use any minimal text editor to write them. Fortunately, there are a number of tools that make the process of generating HTML documents more quick and efficient. They fall into two main categories: HTML editors and WYSIWYG (What-You-See-Is-What-You-Get) web authoring tools.

HTML/XHTML Editors

HTML editors are text editing tools designed especially for writing HTML. They require that you know how to compose HTML by hand; however, they save time by providing shortcuts for such repetitive tasks as setting up documents, compiling tables, or simply applying styles to text.

There are scores of simple HTML editors available, and many of them are free. Just enter "HTML Editor" in the search field of Shareware.com (*www.shareware.com*) and wade through the results. For purposes of brevity, I'm going to cut to the chase.

Windows users should check out Macromedia HomeSite. For more information and to download a demo copy, see *www.macromedia.com/software/homesite/*.

If you're working on a Macintosh, check out BBEdit, a commercial HTML editor from Bare Bones Software, Inc. For more information and to download a demo version, see *www.bbedit.com*.

WYSIWYG Authoring Tools

WYSIWYG HTML editors have graphical interfaces that make writing HTML more like using a word processor or page layout program. So for instance, if you want to add an image, just drag it from the desktop onto the page; the authoring tool creates all the HTML coding needed to accomplish the effect on the screen. In addition to simple style and format shortcuts, many of these tools automate more complex tasks, such as creating Cascading Style Sheets, adding JavaScript, and adding PHP functionality.

WYSIWYG tools offer several benefits:

- They offer considerable time savings over writing code by hand.
- They are good for beginners. They can even be useful for learning HTML, because you can lay out the page the way you want and then view the resulting code.
- They are good for quick prototyping. You can try out design ideas on the fly.
- They provide a good head start for creating style sheets, JavaScript behaviors, and other features.

On the downside, they are expensive and have steep learning curves. Some experienced web authors feel that the markup these tools spit out is not as efficient as markup carefully crafted by hand.

If you are a professional web designer and developer, a web authoring tool won't excuse you from learning HTML altogether. In many cases, you will need to do some manual fine-tuning to the resulting HTML code.

Some of the most popular tools as of this writing are:

Macromedia Dreamweaver
> Dreamweaver has emerged as the industry-standard HTML authoring tool due to its advanced features and better standards compliance. For more information, see *www.macromedia.com/software/dreamweaver*.

Adobe GoLive
> Another powerful and professional-level authoring tool, GoLive is well integrated into the suite of Adobe design tools. For more information, see *www.adobe.com/products/golive/main.html*.

 In April, 2005, Adobe announced that it would be acquiring Macromedia. As of this writing, there is no word on the future of the Dreamweaver and GoLive products and brands. It is unclear whether they will both be maintained, if only one will survive, or if they will be rolled together into some turbo-charged hybrid. Consult the Adobe web site for updates. In this edition, all Adobe and Macromedia product names are listed as they currently exist in the market.

Microsoft FrontPage (Windows only)

FrontPage, part of the Microsoft Office software package, is easy for beginners to learn and is popular with the business community. It offers wizards, themes, and tools that make web page creation easy. FrontPage still produces code that many professional web authors consider to be unsatisfactory due to inefficient and proprietary code. Some FrontPage functions are closely integrated with Microsoft's Internet Information Server (IIS), so check with your hosting service for possible conflicts. For more information, see *www. microsoft.com/frontpage/*.

Good Authoring Practices

This section offers some guidelines for writing "good" HTML documents—markup that will be supported by a wide variety of browsers, handled easily by browsers expecting correct syntax, and extensible to emerging technologies built on the current HTML specification.

Choose elements that accurately and meaningfully describe the content. Making sure that your document is semantically sound improves accessibility under the wide range of web browsing environments. If something is a list, mark it up as a list. If you don't want bullets, it's not a problem. You can use a style sheet to change the presentation of the list to be anything you want, be it bullet-less or a graphical horizontal navigation bar (see Chapter 24 for this technique).

Avoid choosing elements based on the way that they render in the browser. For example, don't use a `blockquote` just to achieve indented text and don't use a series of `br`s or `<p> </p>` for extra whitespace. Again, you can use a style sheet for such presentational effects.

Avoid using deprecated elements and attributes. This is actually a round-about way of saying "use style sheets instead of presentational HTML," because most elements and attributes have been deprecated in favor of style sheet controls.

Write compliant, valid documents.. Even if you are using HTML 4.01, it is a good idea to follow the XHTML Recommendations for a compliant, valid document. Although once it was fine to omit closing tags and quotation marks, browsers in the future may not be so forgiving.

Validate your HTML. To be absolutely sure about how you're doing conformance-wise, you should run your HTML code through an HTML validator, such as the one at the W3C site (*validator.w3.org*). For a list of other validator services, see The Web Design Group page at *www.htmlhelp.com/links/ validators.htm*.

Avoid extra returns and character spaces. These extra keystrokes add to the size of your document because blank spaces are transmitted just like all other characters. Not only that, line breaks and extra spaces can create unwanted whitespace in certain contexts. For instance, extra spaces within and between table cells (`td` elements) can add unwanted spaces in a table. Adding a line break between consecutive `img` elements will introduce whitespace between the images. It is best to keep your file as compact as possible.

Use comments to delineate sections of markup so that you can find them quickly. HTML documents can get long and complicated. Adding comments to label portions of the document can make things easier to find at a glance and may allow you to keep the document compact without a lot of extra space.

Follow proper filenaming conventions. Consider these guidelines:

- Use the proper HTML document suffix *.html* or *.htm*. Suffixes for a number of common file types can be found in Table 4-1.

- Avoid spaces and special characters such as ?, %, #, and so on in filenames. It is best to limit filenames to letters, numbers, underscores (in place of spaces), hyphens, and periods.

- Filenames may be case-sensitive on your server. Consistently using all lowercase letters in filenames, although certainly not necessary, may help avoid confusion and make them easier to remember.

- Keep filenames as short as possible. Extra characters add to the file size of the document.

9

Document Structure

Before marking up your actual content, it is necessary to establish the proper global structure of the (X)HTML document itself. An (X)HTML document is composed of three parts: a *declaration* of the HTML or XHTML version used, a *header* containing information about the document, and the *body* containing the document's content.* This chapter takes a look at each of these components and, in doing so, introduces these elements used for establishing the global structure of the document:

html	Root element of an (X)HTML document
head	Header
body	The body of the document
title	Document title
meta	Meta data (information about the document)

If you use a professional web authoring tool to create web pages, chances are you're accustomed to the minimal document structural markup inserted for you when you select "New File." This chapter will give you the tools necessary to peek under the hood and decide if the automatically generated declarations accurately represent the mode in which you intend to author.

Minimal Document Structure

This markup sample shows the structure of a minimal XHTML document as specified in the XHTML 1.0 Recommendation. It provides important context to upcoming discussions of global document structure.

---

* Not all documents have a body. Framed documents are composed of a declaration, header, and a frameset that establishes the number and structure of its frames. Framed documents are discussed in Chapter 14.

```
<?xml version="1.0" encoding="UTF-8"?>
<!DOCTYPE html PUBLIC "-//W3C//DTD XHTML 1.0 Strict//EN"
    "http://www.w3.org/TR/xhtml1/DTD/xhtml1-strict.dtd">

<html xmlns="http://www.w3.org/1999/xhtml" xml:lang="en" lang="en">

  <head>
    <title>Document Title</title>
  </head>

  <body>
    <p>Content of document...</p>
  </body>

</html>
```

 This example begins with an *XML declaration* that identifies the version of XML and the character encoding of the document. XML declarations are encouraged for XHTML documents; however, they are not required when the character encoding is the UTF-8 default as in the above example. Because XML declarations are problematic for current browsers as of this writing, even those that are standards-compliant, they are generally omitted.

Now, take a closer look at the four major components of XHTML (and HTML) documents.

Document type declaration
```
<!DOCTYPE html PUBLIC "-//W3C//DTD XHTML 1.0 Strict//EN"
    "http://www.w3.org/TR/xhtml1/DTD/xhtml1-strict.dtd">
```

The document type (DOCTYPE) declaration tells the browser which DTD to use to parse the document. This example specifies XHTML Strict. If this example were an HTML document, it would use one of the HTML DTDs. The upcoming "Document Type Declaration" section provides more information on the DTD options and uses for this information.

Root element
```
<html xmlns="http://www.w3.org/1999/xhtml" xml:lang="en" lang="en">...
    </html>
```

html is the root element for all HTML and XHTML documents. The html element and its declarative attributes shown here are discussed in the upcoming section, "The Root Element."

Document header
```
<head>
    <title>Document Title</title>
</head>
```

The head element, or header, contains information about the document that is not considered part of the document content. The header must include a descriptive title in order to validate. Document headers are covered in more detail later in this chapter.

Document body
```
<body>
    Content of Document...
</body>
```

The body element contains all of the content of the document—the part that displays in the browser window or is spoken in a speech browser. The body of an (X)HTML document might consist of just a few paragraphs of text, a single image, or a complex combination of text, images, tables, and multimedia objects. What you put on the page is up to you.

Document Type Declaration

To be valid, an (X)HTML document must begin with a document type declaration that identifies which version of HTML or XHTML is used in the document. This is done using a DOCTYPE declaration that names the *document type definition* (DTD) for the document. A DTD is a text document that lists all the elements, attributes, and rules of use for a particular markup language. See Chapter 7 for more information on DTDs.

The inclusion of a document type declaration has always been a requirement of valid HTML documents. With no DOCTYPE declaration, there is no set of rules to validate against. In the years of fast and loose HTML authoring, the DOCTYPE declaration was commonly omitted. However, now that standards compliance is a priority in the web development community, and because there are so many DTDs to choose from, authors are strongly urged to include the DTD declaration and validate their documents. The DOCTYPE declaration (or its omission) also triggers different browser behaviors, as discussed in the upcoming "DOCTYPE Switching" section.

DTD Options

HTML 4.01 and XHTML 1.0 offer three DTD versions:

- Strict
- Transitional
- Frameset

XHTML 1.1 has only one DTD. The DTD documents live on the W3C server at a stable URL.

The `<!DOCTYPE>` (document type) declaration contains two methods for pointing to DTD information: one is a publicly recognized document identifier; the other is a specific URL in case the browsing device does not recognize the public identifier. Descriptions and specific markup for each HTML and XHTML version are listed here.

HTML 4.01 Strict
   The Strict DTD omits all deprecated elements and attributes. If you are authoring according to the strict DTD, use this document type definition:

```
<!DOCTYPE HTML PUBLIC "-//W3C//DTD HTML 4.01//EN"
   "http://www.w3.org/TR/HTML4.01/strict.dtd">
```

HTML 4.01 Transitional
> The Transitional DTD includes everything from the Strict DTD, plus all deprecated elements and attributes. If your document includes some deprecated elements or attributes, point to the Transitional DTD using this DOCTYPE declaration:

```
<!DOCTYPE HTML PUBLIC "-//W3C//DTD HTML 4.01 Transitional//EN"
 "http://www.w3.org/TR/HTML4.01/loose.dtd">
```

HTML 4.01 Frameset
> If your document contains frames—that is, it uses frameset instead of body for its content—then identify the Frameset DTD. The Frameset DTD is the same as the Transitional version (it includes deprecated yet supported elements and attributes), with the addition of frame-specific elements. The content-containing HTML documents that are displayed within the frames do not need to use the Frameset DTD.

```
<!DOCTYPE HTML PUBLIC "-//W3C//DTD HTML 4.01 Frameset//EN"
 "http://www.w3.org/TR/HTML4.01/frameset.dtd">
```

XHTML 1.0 Strict
> The same as HTML 4.01 Strict, but reformulated according to the syntax rules of XML.

```
<!DOCTYPE html PUBLIC "-//W3C//DTD XHTML 1.0 Strict//EN"
 "http://www.w3.org/TR/xhtml1/DTD/xhtml1-strict.dtd">
```

XHTML 1.0 Transitional
> The same as HTML 4.01 Transitional, but reformulated according to the syntax rules of XML.

```
<!DOCTYPE html PUBLIC "-//W3C//DTD XHTML 1.0 Transitional//EN"
 "http://www.w3.org/TR/xhtml1/DTD/xhtml1-transitional.dtd">
```

XHTML 1.0 Frameset
> The same as HTML 4.01 Frameset, but reformulated according to the syntax rules of XML.

```
<!DOCTYPE html PUBLIC "-//W3C//DTD XHTML 1.0 Frameset//EN"
 "http://www.w3.org/TR/xhtml1/DTD/xhtml1-frameset.dtd">
```

XHTML 1.1
> There is only one DTD for XHTML 1.1. It omits every deprecated element and attribute. It differs from XHTML 1.0 Strict in these ways:
>
> * The lang attribute has been replaced with the xml:lang attribute.
> * The name attribute for the a and map elements has been replaced with id.
> * A *ruby* collection of elements has been added. The W3C defines ruby as "short runs of text alongside the base text, typically used in East Asian documents to indicate pronunciation or to provide a short annotation."
>
> ```
> <!DOCTYPE html PUBLIC "-//W3C//DTD XHTML 1.1//EN"
>  "http://www.w3.org/TR/xhtml11/DTD/xhtml11.dtd">
> ```

The W3C makes these document type declarations and more available for your copy-and-paste convenience at *www.w3.org/QA/2002/04/valid-dtd-list.html*.

DOCTYPE Switching

Years of lax authoring practices and techniques for dealing with inconsistent browser behaviors resulted in millions of web pages built in a way that *worked*, but were far from valid against the current standards. Browser developers were faced with a difficult dilemma: get rigorous about standards conformance and break nearly every web site in existence, or maintain the status quo.

When building Internet Explorer 5 for the Macintosh, development lead Tantek Çelik invented and coded a stop-gap solution that served two communities of authors: those writing standards-compliant documents and those who were authoring web documents based on familiar browser rendering behaviors.

The method now known as *DOCTYPE switching* uses the inclusion and content of a DOCTYPE declaration to toggle the rendering mode in certain browsers. If a modern DOCTYPE declaration is detected, it indicates that the author is standards-aware, and the browser switches into a standards-compliant rendering mode (*Standards mode*). If no (or if an older) declaration is detected, the browser reverts to *Quirks mode*. Quirks mode mimics the rendering behavior of old browsers, allowing for nonstandard code, hacks, and workarounds that are common in legacy web authoring practices. There is a third mode that some browsers implement known as *Almost Standards mode* that is different from true Standards mode in that it implements vertical sizing of table cells traditionally and not according to the CSS 2 specification.

Browser support

You can use the DOCTYPE declaration to switch rendering modes in the following browsers:

- Internet Explorer 6 and 7 (Windows)
- Internet Explorer 5 (Mac)
- Netscape 6 and higher
- Opera 7 and higher
- Mozilla (and Mozilla-based browsers like Firefox)
- Safari
- Konqueror 3.2 and higher

Making the switch

Although all of the browsers listed above do some sort of switching, the requirements for switching them into Standards or Almost Standards mode varies somewhat by browser and is influenced by the DTD version and the presence of the complete URL for that DTD. For XHTML documents, the presence of the XML declaration will cause Internet Explorer 6 for Windows and Konqueror to switch into Quirks mode even if the proper DOCTYPE declaration has been provided.

Figuring out which DOCTYPE triggers which mode in every browser can get pretty confusing. For a thorough comparison of browsers' responses to every possible (X)HTML DTD and URL combination, see the chart created and maintained by Henri Sivonen at *http://hsivonen.iki.fi/doctype/*.

To summarize here, these are your best bets for triggering Standards or Almost Standards mode in the most browsers that do DOCTYPE switching:

- XHTML 1.0 Strict or Transitional or XHTML 1.1, with a complete URL (including `http://`) and *without* the XML declaration. If the URL is omitted or incomplete, some browsers revert to Quirks mode. Including the XML declaration causes Internet Explorer 6 to revert to Quirks mode, however, this has been corrected in IE 7.

- HTML 4.0 or 4.01 Strict DTD, with or without the URL. (Omitting the URL triggers Quirks mode in IE 5/Mac with the 4.01 Strict DTD only.)

- HTML 4.0 or 4.01 Transitional DTD, with the URL `http://www.w3.org/TR/html4/loose.dtd` (for all browsers but Konquerer 3.2). Including `http://www.w3.org/TR/1999/REC-html401-19991224/loose.dtd` triggers Quirks mode in Netscape 6 and Konqueror.

The Root Element

XML and SGML documents have one and exactly one root element. It is the element that encloses all following elements. XHTML and HTML define `html` as the root element.

html

`<html>...</html>`

Attributes

> *Internationalization attributes:* `lang`, `xml:lang`, `dir`
> `id="text"` *(XHTML only)*
> `xmlns="http://www.w3.org/1999/xhtml"` *(Required; XHTML only)*
> `version="-//W3C//DTD HTML 4.01//EN"` *(Deprecated in HTML 4.01)*

All elements in the document are contained within the root element (they are said to be *descendants* of the root element). As the root element, `html` may have no ancestors (in other words, it may not be contained within any other element).

This example shows the root element from a minimal XHTML document:

`<html xmlns="http://www.w3.org/1999/xhtml" xml:lang="en" lang="en" >`

Because this example is an XHTML document, the `html` element is also used to identify the XML namespace and language for the document, as discussed next. HTML documents do not use namespaces.

Namespace

An XML *namespace* is a collection of element and attribute names as defined by the DTD of a particular markup language. In XML documents, you must explicitly identify the namespace so the client (in this case, the browser) knows that you intend the q element in your document to be a "quote" and not a "question" from some other (theoretical) XML language for exams.

The namespace is specified using the xmlns attribute in the html root element. The value is the location of an online documentation of that namespace. The namespace identifier for XHTML 1.0 and 1.1 is xmlns="http://www.w3.org/1999/xhtml".

Language

Because this Web of ours is "World Wide," the HTML specifications take into account that documents are published in a variety of languages. For that reason, it is important to identify the language in which the document is written (as in lang="en") and the language of the XML version (as in xml:lang="en"). These attributes are placed in the html root element along with the namespace identifier. The XHTML 1.0 Recommendation suggests you include both attributes in the interest of backward compatibility. See Chapter 6 for a complete list of two-letter language codes.

The Document Header

The header provides a place to include important information about the document to users, browsers, and search engines. It is also a common place to stow scripts and embedded style sheets. This section looks at the head element and the elements it contains.

head

<head>...</head>

Attributes

> *Internationalization attributes:* lang, xml:lang, dir
> id="text" (XHTML only)
> profile="URLS"

Every head element must include a title element that provides a description of the document. The head element may also include any of the following elements in any order: script, style, meta, link, object, isindex, and base. The head element merely acts as a container of these elements and does not have any content of its own.

It is recommended that HTML documents (and XHTML documents without an XML declaration) also include a meta element that specifies the content type and character encoding for the document, although this element is not required. The meta element is discussed in the upcoming "Providing Meta Data" section.

Titles

The most important (and only required) element within the header is the document title, which provides a description of the page's contents.

title

<title>...</title>
This element is required.

Attributes

Internationalization: lang, xml:lang, dir

Starting in HTML 4.01, the title element is required, which means that every HTML document must have a meaningful title in its header in order to be valid. The title is typically displayed in the top bar of the browser, outside the regular content window.

Titles should contain only ASCII characters (letters, numbers, and basic punctuation). Special characters (such as &) should be referred to by their character entities within the title, for example:

<title>The Adventures of Peto & Fleck</title>

The title is what is displayed in a user's bookmarks or favorites list. Descriptive titles are also a key tool for improving accessibility, as they are the first thing a person hears when using a screen reader. Search engines rely heavily on document titles as well. For these reasons, it's important to provide thoughtful and descriptive titles for all your documents and avoid vague titles, such as "Welcome" or "My Page." You may also want to keep the length of your titles in check so they are able to display in the browser's title area.

Other Header Elements

Other useful HTML elements also placed within head of the document include:

base
> This element establishes the document's base location, which serves as a reference for all pathnames and links in the document. For more information, see Chapter 11.

isindex
> *Deprecated.* This element was once used to add a simple search function to a page. It has been deprecated by HTML 4.01 in favor of form inputs.

link
> This element defines the relationship between the current document and another document. Although it can signify such relationships as index, next, and previous, it is most often used to link a document to an external style sheet (see Chapter 16).

script
> JavaScript and VBScript code may be added to the document within its header using this element. For examples of using the script element, see Chapter 27.

style

> One method for attaching a style sheet to an HTML document is to embed it in the head of the document with the style element. For more information, see Chapter 16.

meta

> The meta element is used to provide information about a document, such as keywords or descriptions to aid search engines. It is discussed in detail in the next section.

Providing Meta Data

The meta element has a wide variety of applications but is primarily used to include information about a document, such as the character encoding, creation date, author, or copyright information.

meta

```
<meta />
```

Attributes

> *Internationalization:* lang, xml:lang, dir
> id="*text*" *(XHTML only)*
> content="*text*" *(Required)*
> http-equiv="*text*"
> name="*text*"
> scheme="*text*"

The data included in a meta element is useful for servers, web browsers, and search engines but is invisible to the reader. It must always be placed within the head of the document.

A document may have any number of meta elements. There are two types of meta elements, using either the name or http-equiv attribute. In each case, the content attribute is necessary to provide a value (or values) for the named information or function. These examples show the syntax of both meta types:

```
<meta http-equiv="name" content="content" />
<meta name="name" content="content" />
```

http-equiv

Information provided by an http-equiv attribute is processed as though it had come from an HTTP response header. HTTP headers contain information the server passes to the browser just before it sends the HTML document, such as media type information and other values that affect the action of the browser. Therefore, the http-equiv attribute provides information that will, depending on the description, affect the way the browser handles your document.

An *HTTP header* is not the same as the header indicated by the head element within the HTML document. HTTP headers exist outside the HTML text document and are tacked on by the server. When a document is requested via an HTTP request (that is, via the Web), the HTTP header goes along for the ride to give the browser a heads-up on what kind of document to expect. Its contents are not displayed.

There is a large number of predefined http-equiv types available. This chapter introduces just a few of the most useful. For a complete listing, see the Dictionary of HTML META Tags at *vancouver-webpages.com/META*.

name

The name attribute is used to insert hidden information about the document that does not correspond to HTTP headers. For example:

```
<meta name="author" content="Jennifer Niederst Robbins" />
<meta name="copyright" content="2006, O'Reilly Media" />
```

You can make up your own names or use one of the names put forth by search engine and browser companies for standardized use. A few of the accepted and more useful meta names are discussed later in this section.

Identifying media type and character encoding

It is recommended (although not required) that the media type and character encoding be specified within (X)HTML documents as a way to keep that information with the document. (For more information on declaring character encodings, see Chapter 6.)

This is done using the meta element, as shown in this example:

```
<meta http-equiv="content-type" content="text/html; charset=UTF-8" />
```

The parts are broken down as follows:

Media type identification
> The media type, very similar to MIME types used for sending email attachments, is another bit of information sent in the HTTP header. For HTML documents, the media type is always text/html. That one is easy. XHTML documents, on the other hand, are not as straightforward.
>
> XHTML 1.0 documents may be served as either XML or HTML documents. Although XML is the proper method, due to lack of browser support for XML files, many authors choose to deliver XHTML 1.0 files with the text/html MIME type used for HTML documents. When XHTML documents are served in this manner, they may not be parsed as XML documents.
>
> XHTML 1.0 files may also be served as XML using the MIME types application/xhtml+xml, application/xml, or text/xml. The W3C recommends that you use application/xhtml+xml only.
>
> XHTML 1.1 documents are *not* permitted to use the text/html media type. This poses a problem because some browsers do not know what to do with

the non-text/html media types. This is another reason why XHTML 1.1 is still difficult to implement properly and why developers generally opt for the XHTML 1.0 standard.

For more information on the W3C's recommended media types, see *www. w3.org/TR/xhtml-media-types/*.

Character encoding

It is recommended, although not required, that the character encoding be specified for all documents. The character encoding describes the set of actual glyphs, or character shapes, that your document uses. Sets of characters are standardized: you can refer to them by identifying standard numbers. For example, in documents written in English, the most common character encoding is ISO-8859-1, which consists of all the characters in Western European languages. For more information on character encoding, see Chapter 6.

Character encoding should be set on the server as part of the HTTP header. It may also be set in the XML declaration for XHTML documents that use a character encoding other than the XML standard UTF-8 or UTF-16. For instances when it is necessary to override or guarantee the server setting (and if the XML declaration is not used), the character encoding may be provided with a meta element, as shown in the example.

For more information on the preferred methods of specifying character encoding, see Chapter 6 and the Web Standards Project article at *www.webstandards.org/learn/askw3c/dec2002.html*.

Using the meta element for client-pull

Client-pull refers to the ability of the browser (the client) to automatically request (pull) a new document from the server. The effect for the user is that the page displays, and after a period of time, automatically refreshes with new information or is replaced by an entirely new page. This technique can be used to automatically redirect readers to a new URL (for instance, if an old URL has been retired).

Be aware, however, that the W3C strongly discourages the use of this method for automatic forwarding in favor of server-side redirects for reasons of accessibility.

Client-pull uses the refresh attribute value, first introduced by Netscape. It tells the browser to wait a specified number of seconds (indicated by an integer in the content attribute) and then to load a new page. If no page is specified, the browser just reloads the current page. The following example instructs the browser to reload the page after 15 seconds (assume there's something fancy happening on the server side that puts updated information in the HTML document):

```
<meta http-equiv="refresh" content="15" />
```

To reload a different file, provide the URL for the document within the content attribute:

```
<meta http-equiv="refresh" content="1; url=http://doc2.html" />
```

Note that there is only a single set of quotation marks around the value for content. Although URLs usually require their own quotation marks, these are omitted within the context of the content attribute.

Other uses of http-equiv

Here are some other uses of the http-equiv attribute:

expires

> Indicates the date and time after which the document should be considered expired. Web robots may use this information to delete expired documents from a search engine index. The date and time format (as shown below) follows the date/time standard for HTTP headers because the http-equiv attribute is intended to mimic an HTTP header field.
>
> ```
> <meta http-equiv="expires" content="Wed 12 Jun 2001 10:52:00 EST" />
> ```

content-language

> This may be used to identify the language in which the document is written. The browser can send a corresponding Accept-Language header, which causes the server to choose the document with the appropriate language.
>
> This example tells the browser that the document's natural language is French:
>
> ```
> <meta http-equiv="content-language" content="fr" />
> ```
>
> The W3C now recommends using the lang and xml:lang attributes in the html element for language specification, but this method may be used for backward compatibility. For more information on internationalization and a listing of two-letter language codes, see Chapter 6.

meta names for search engines

Search engines introduced several meta names that aid their search engines in finding pages. Note that not all search engines use meta-data, but adding them to your document won't hurt. There is a blurry distinction between name and http-equiv in this case, so most of these meta names also work as http-equiv definitions.

description

> This provides a brief, plain-language description of the contents of your web page, which is particularly useful if your document contains little text, is a frameset, or has extensive scripts at the top of the HTML document. Search engines that recognize the description may display it in the search results page. Some search engines use only the first 20 words of descriptions, so get to the point quickly.
>
> ```
> <meta name="description" content="Jennifer Robbins' resume
>     and web design samples" />
> ```

keywords

> You can supplement the title and description of the document with a list of comma-separated keywords that would be useful in indexing your document. Note: Search engines have largely abandoned meta keywords in

practice due to both spam and deterioration. There is a larger trend away from invisible metadata in general for these reasons, and toward more visible data in the contents themselves of web pages.

```
<meta name="keywords" content="designer, web design, branding,
    logo design" />
```

author
Identifies the author of the web page.

```
<meta name="author" content="Jennifer Robbins" />
```

copyright
Identifies the copyright information for the document.

```
<meta name="copyright" content="2005, O'Reilly Media" />
```

robots
This value was created as an alternative to the *robots.txt* file, and both are used to prevent your page from being indexed by search engine "spiders." This value is not as well supported as the *robots.txt* file, but some people like to include it anyway. The content attribute can take the following values: index (the default), noindex (prevents indexing), nofollow (prevents the search engine from following links on the page), and none (the same as setting "noindex, nofollow"). The advantage of using this attribute instead of the *robots.txt* file is that it can be applied on a page-by-page basis (whereas *robot. txt* applies to an entire site if it's located in the root directory).

```
<meta name="robots" content="noindex, nofollow" />
```

The Document Body

The body of the document comes after the document header. Although the body element markup is optional in previous versions of HTML, in XHTML it is required. The content of the body element is what gets displayed in the browser window (or read by a speech browser).

body

```
<body>...</body>
```

Attributes

Core attributes: id, class, style, title
Internationalization: lang, xml:lang, dir
Intrinsic Events: onload, onunload, onclick, ondblclick, onmousedown, onmouseup, onmouseover, onmousemove, onmouseout, onkeypress, onkeydown, onkeyup

Deprecated Attributes

alink="#*rrggbb*" or "*color name*"
background="*URL*"
bgcolor="#*rrggbb*" or "*color name*"
link="#*rrggbb*" or "*color name*"

```
text="#rrggbb" or "color name"
vlink="#rrggbb" or "color name"
```

The body element may include any combination of block-level elements, inline elements, and forms. In other words, it contains all the elements in the normal document flow. For visual browsers, the body acts as a canvas where the content appears. Audio user agents may speak the content of the body.

The HTML 3.0 Recommendation added a number of presentational attributes for the body element that had been introduced by browser developers and were in common use. At the time, they were the only mechanism for setting the color for all the links and text in the document or for adding a background color or image to the page. A single body opening tag may contain a number of specific attributes, as shown here:

```
<body text="color" link="color" vlink="color" alink="color">
```

Today, of course, style sheets are the correct way to handle matters of presentation, so all of the presentational attributes for the body element are officially deprecated and are discouraged from use.

Because they are still in the Transitional DTD and universally supported in browsers, brief explanations of the deprecated body attributes are provided in Table 9-1. The CSS alternatives are provided.

Table 9-1. Deprecated body attributes

Body attribute	Description	Equivalent CSS style
text="color"	Sets the color for all the regular text in the document	body {color: color}
link="color"	Sets the color for hyperlinks	a:link {color: color}
vlink="color"	Sets the color for links that have already been clicked	a:visited {color: color}
alink="color"	Sets the color for a link while it is in the process of being clicked	a:active {color: color}
bgcolor="color"	Sets the color of the background for the entire page	body {background-color: color}
background="url"	Specifies an image to be used as a tiling background for the page	body {background-image: url(filename.gif)}

10

Text Elements

This chapter gets to the real meat and potatoes of document markup: elements used to structure text content. It's no surprise that nearly half of all the elements in the (X)HTML Recommendation are introduced in this chapter. The elements and discussions are organized as follows:

Block elements		Generic elements	
h#	Heading	div	Block division
p	Paragraph	span	Span of inline content
pre	Preformatted text	**Lists**	
address	Contact information	ul	Unordered list
blockquote	Lengthy quotation	ol	Ordered list
Inline elements		li	List item
abbr	Abbreviation	dl	Definition list
acronym	Acronym	dt	Term
cite	Citation or reference	dd	Definition
code	Code fragment	menu	Menu list
dfn	Defining term	dir	Directory
em	Emphasized text	**Presentational elements**	
q	Short inline quotation	b	Bold
strong	Strongly emphasized	big	Big text
samp	Sample output	i	Italic
kbd	Text entered by a user	s	Strike-through
var	Variable or program argument	strike	Strike-through
sub	Subscript	tt	Teletype
sup	Superscript	u	Underlined

Line breaks		Presentational elements (*continued*)	
br	Inserts line break	font	Font face, color, and size
Edit notation		basefont	Sets default font face
ins	Inserted text	nobr	No break
del	Deleted text	wbr	Word break
		hr	Horizontal rule

Choosing Text Elements

This chapter, jam-packed as it is with text elements, is a good opportunity for a reminder about the importance of well-structured and meaningful (semantic) markup.

In the early years of web design, it was common to choose elements based on their default formatting in the browser. Don't like the size of the h1? Hey, use an h4 instead. Don't like bullets on your list? Make something list-like using br elements. Need indents? Blockquote it! Those days are over and gone.

Now we have Cascading Style Sheets (CSS) to visually format any element any way we like, at last liberating us from the browsers' default rendering styles. That means you must choose elements that accurately describe your content. If you don't like how it looks, change it with a style sheet. If you don't see an HTML element that fits, use a generic div or span element to add appropriate structure and meaning.

Additional tips on good markup are listed in Chapter 8.

A Word on Deprecated Elements

Many elements and attributes in this book are marked as "deprecated," which means they are being phased out of HTML and are discouraged from use. Most of the deprecated elements and attributes are presentational and have analogous style sheet properties that should be used instead. Others are simply obsolete or poorly supported.

The W3C needed a way to get the HTML specification back on track while acknowledging legacy browser capabilities and the authoring methods that catered to them. Rather than yanking them all at once, causing virtually every site in the world to be invalid, they put the deprecated elements and attributes in a "transitional" DTD that is available while browsers get up to speed with standards and web authors (and authoring tools) change their markup practices.

Now that style sheet alternatives to presentational HTML are widely supported, it is time to start phasing deprecated elements out of your documents as well.

The Building Blocks of Content

Text elements fall into two broad categories: inline and block. *Inline elements* occur in the flow of text and do not cause line breaks by default (they are covered later in this chapter). *Block-level elements*, on the other hand, have a default presentation that starts a new line and tends to stack up like blocks in the normal flow of the document. Block elements make up the main components of document structure.

Compared to inline elements, there are relatively few block elements. This section looks at heading levels, paragraphs, blockquotes, preformatted text, and addresses. Lists and list items are also block elements, and they are discussed later in this chapter, as is the generic div element used for defining custom block elements. The other block-level elements are tables and forms, which are treated in their own respective chapters.

Headings

Headings are used to introduce ideas or sections of text. (X)HTML defines six levels of headings, from h1 to h6, in order from most to least important.

h1 through h6

`<hn>...</hn>`

Attributes

> *Core* (id, class, style, title), *Internationalization, Events*

Deprecated attributes

> `align="center|left|right"`

This example defines the element as a first-level heading.

```
<h1>Camp Sunny-Side Up</h1>
```

HTML syntax requires that headings appear in order (for example, an h2 should not precede an h1) for proper document structure. Doing so not only improves accessibility, but aids in search engine optimization (information in higher heading levels is given more weight). Using heading levels consistently throughout a site—using h1 for all article titles, for example—is also recommended.

Browsers generally render headings in bold text in decreasing size, but style rules may be applied to easily change their presentation.

Paragraphs

Paragraphs are the most rudimentary elements of a text document. They are indicated by the p element.

p

```
<p>...</p>
```

Attributes

Core (id, class, style, title), *Internationalization, Events*

Deprecated attributes

```
align="center|left|right"
```

Paragraphs may contain text and inline elements, but they may not contain other block elements, including other paragraphs. The following is an example of a paragraph marked up as a p element.

```
<p>Paragraphs are the most rudimentary elements of a text
document. They are indicated by the p element.</p>
```

Because paragraphs are block elements, they always start a new line. Most browsers also add margins above and below block elements. Text is formatted flush-left, ragged right for left-to-right reading languages (and flush-right for right-to-left reading languages). Style sheets may be used to override any default browser rendering.

HTML 4.01 allows the end </p> tag to be omitted, leaving user agents to parse the beginning of a new block element as the end of the previous paragraph. In XHTML, however, all elements must be terminated, and omitting end tags will cause the document to be invalid. For reasons of forward compatibility, it is recommended that you close paragraphs and all elements regardless of the markup language you are using.

Quotations (blockquote)

Use the blockquote element for lengthy quotations, particularly those that span several paragraphs and require line breaks.

blockquote

```
<blockquote>...</blockquote>
```

Attributes

Core (id, class, style, title), *Internationalization, Events*
cite="*URL*"

It is recommended that content within a blockquote be contained in other block-level elements, such as paragraphs, headings, lists, and so on, as shown in this markup example.

```
<blockquote cite="http://www.jenandtheneverendingstory.com">
<p>This is the beginning of a lengthy quotation (text continues...) </p>
<p>And it's still going on and on (text continues...) </p>
</blockquote>
```

The cite attribute is intended to be used to provide information about the source from which the quotation was borrowed, but it has very limited browser UI support (only Netscape 6+ as of this writing) and is not currently in common use.

The HTML specification recommends that blockquotes be displayed as indented text, which, in fact, they usually are. The blockquote element should not be used merely to achieve indents.

Preformatted Text

Preformatted text is used when it is necessary to preserve the whitespace in the source (character spaces and line breaks) when the document is displayed. This may be useful for code or poetry where spacing and alignment is important for meaning. Preformatted text is indicated with the pre element.

pre

```
<pre>...</pre>
```

Attributes

Core (id, class, style, title), Internationalization, Events

Deprecated Attributes

width="number"

Preformatted text is unique in that it displays exactly as it is typed in the HTML source code—including all line returns and multiple character spaces. Long lines of text stay intact and are not reflowed. The pre element in this example displays as shown in Figure 10-1. The second part of the figure shows the same content marked up as a p element for comparison.

```
<pre>
This is               an               example of

       text with a          lot of
                            curious
                            whitespace.
</pre>

<p>
This is               an               example of

       text with a          lot of
                            curious
                            whitespace.
</p>
```

Preformatted text is meant to be displayed in a fixed-width font to preserve the alignment of columns of characters. Authors are discouraged from changing the font face and whitespace settings with style sheets. Preformatted elements may include any inline element with the exception of img, object, big, small, sub, sup, and font, all of which would disrupt the column alignment of the fixed-width font.

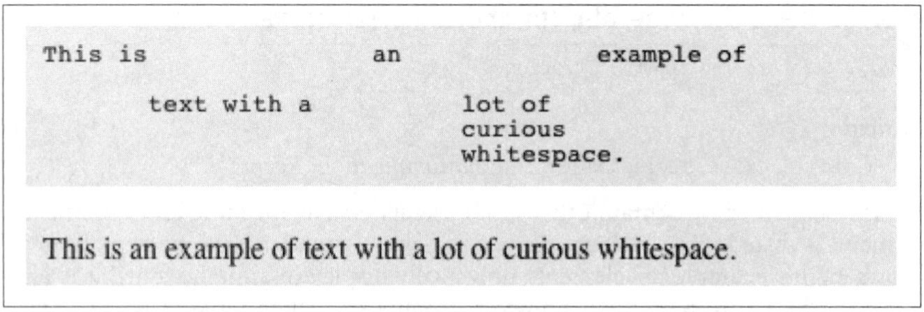

```
This is              an            example of

     text with a          lot of
                          curious
                          whitespace.
```

This is an example of text with a lot of curious whitespace.

Figure 10-1. Preformatted text compared to a paragraph

Addresses

The address element is used to provide contact information for the author or maintainer of the document. It is not appropriate for all address listings. It is generally placed at the beginning or end of the document, or associated with a large section of content (such as a form).

address

`<address>...</address>`

Attributes

> *Core* (id, class, style, title), *Internationalization, Events*

An address might be used as shown in this markup example.

```
<address>
Contributed by <a href="../authors/robbins/">Jennifer Robbins</a>,
<a href="http://www.oreilly.com/">O'Reilly Media</a>
</address>
```

Inline Elements

Most text elements are *inline* elements (spans of characters within the flow of text). Inline elements by default do not add line breaks or extra space.

This section introduces the semantic text elements that describe the enclosed text's meaning, context, or usage. These elements leave the specific rendering of the element to style sheets, either the author's or the browser's default rendering. There are other inline elements in the XHTML specification that are concerned with presentation (for example, the b element for bold text). They are briefly discussed at the end this chapter.

Phrase Elements

HTML 4.01 and XHTML 1.0 and 1.1 define a collection of *phrase* elements (also called *logical* elements) for adding structure and meaning to inline text. Because phrase elements share syntax and attributes, they are aggregated into one element listing here.

abbr, acronym, cite, code, dfn, em, kbd, samp, strong, var

`<abbr>...</abbr>, <acronym>...</acronym>, etc.`

Attributes

Core (id, class, style, title), *Internationalization, Events*

Phrase elements may contain other inline elements. The meaning and use of each element is listed here. When elements have a standardized presentation in browsers (for example, em elements universally display in an italic font), it is also noted. Authors are reminded, however, to choose elements based on meaning, not a desired rendering effect.

em
> Indicates emphasized text. em elements are nearly always rendered in italics.

strong
> Denotes strongly emphasized text. Strong elements are nearly always rendered in bold text.

abbr
> Indicates an abbreviated form.

acronym
> Indicates an acronym.

cite
> Denotes a citation: a reference to another document, especially books, magazines, articles, and so on. cites are commonly rendered in italics.

dfn
> Indicates the defining instance or first occurrence of the enclosed term. It can be used to call attention to the introduction of special terms and phrases. Defining terms are often rendered in italics.

code
> Denotes a program code sample. By default, code is rendered in the browser's specified fixed-width font (usually Courier).

kbd
> Stands for "keyboard" and indicates text entered by the user. It may be useful for technical documents. Keyboard text is typically rendered in a fixed-width font.

samp
> Indicates sample output from programs, scripts, etc. It may be useful for technical documents. Sample text is usually rendered in a fixed-width font by default.

var
> Indicates the instance of a variable or program argument. This is another element that will be most useful for technical documents. Variables usually render in italics.

Indicating emphasis

The em and strong elements are used for indicating emphasis and even stronger emphasis, as demonstrated in this example.

```
<p>We <em>really</em> need to leave <strong>right now</strong>!</p>
```

Although emphasized text renders reliably in italics, it is not always an appropriate substitute for the i element. For example, if you want to italicize the title of a book, the cite element is the better choice. If there is no good match, create your own meaningful element using a generic span element and apply italics with the font-style style property. To use another example, it is a convention to display words from another language in italics, but that doesn't necessarily mean that those words are emphasized.

A good rule of thumb is to consider how your document would sound if it were read aloud (as it might be). Do you want the italic words to be read louder or at a different pitch from the rest of the sentence? If the answer is no, then it is probably best to find an alternative to em. The same logic applies to the strong element.

Acronyms and abbreviations

The abbr element indicates that text is an abbreviation: a shortened form of a word ending in a period, such as Mass., Inc., or etc. Acronyms (indicated with the acronym element) are abbreviations formed from the initial letters or groups of letters of words in a phrase, such as WWW and USA. An acronym may be pronounced as a word (NATO) or letter by letter (FBI).

The title attribute may be added to either element to provide the full name or longer form. The value of the title attribute may be displayed as a "tool tip" by visual browsers, or read aloud by a speech device.

```
<acronym title="National Aeronautics and Space Administration">NASA
  </acronym>
<abbr title="Tablespoons">Tbs.</abbr>
```

Marking up shorthand terms such as abbreviations and acronyms provides useful information on how they should be interpreted by user agents such as spellcheckers, aural devices, and search-engine indexers. It also improves the accessibility of the content.

The CSS 2.1 specification provides the informative speak aural property that allows authors to specify whether an acronym should be read as a word or spoken letter by letter, as shown here:

```
acronym#FBI {speak: spell-out;}
```

The speak property is documented in Appendix B.

Short Quotations

HTML 4 introduced the q element for indicating short inline quotations, such as "To be, or not to be." Longer quotations should use the blockquote element listed earlier.

q

```
<q>...</q>
```

Attributes

Core (id, class, style, title), *Internationalization, Events*
cite="*url*"

The HTML Recommendation suggests that user agents should automatically insert quotation marks before and after q elements, therefore, authors are advised to omit them in the source. As of this writing, Internet Explorer 5 for Macintosh, Netscape 6, and Opera do insert generic double quotation marks, but Internet Explorer 6 for Windows does not.

```
As mother always said, <q>a guest is no one to criticize.</q>
```

Ideally, when used with the lang (language) attribute, the browser may insert language-specific quotation marks. Contextual quotation marks will be better handled with CSS-based generated text, as described in Chapter 23, once browser support improves.

The cite attribute is intended to provide a link to additional information about the source of the quote, but it is not well supported as of this writing. Netscape 6.1 makes the cite link available in a contextual menu accessed by right-clicking the quotation.

Deleted and Inserted Text

The ins and del elements are used to mark up changes to the text and indicate parts of a document that have been inserted or deleted (respectively). They may be useful for legal documents and any instance where edits need to be tracked.

As HTML elements, ins and del are unusual in that they may be used to indicate both block-level and inline elements. They may contain one or more words in a paragraph or one or more elements like paragraphs, lists, and tables. When ins and del are used as inline elements (as in within a p), they may not contain block-level elements because that violates the allowable content of the paragraph.

del, ins

```
<del>...</del>, <ins>...</ins>
```

Attributes

Core (id, class, style, title), *Internationalization, Events*
cite="*URL*"
datetime="*YYYY-MM-DDThh:mm:ssTZD*"

The following markup indicates that one name has been deleted and another one inserted in its place.

```
Chief Executive Officer: <del title="retired">Peter Pan</del> <ins>Pippi
Longstockings</ins>
```

Browsers that support the ins and del elements may give it special visual treatment (for example, displaying deleted text in strike-through text), but authors are encouraged to use style sheets to provide presentational instructions.

The title attribute may be used with del or ins to provide a short explanation for the change that may be displayed as a "tool tip" on visual browsers. The cite attribute provides a way to add links to longer explanations, but it is poorly supported as of this writing.

The datetime attribute may be used to indicate the date and time the change was made (although it, too, is poorly supported). Dates and times follow the format listed above where YYYY is the four-digit year, MM is the two-digit month, DD is the day, hh is the hour (00 through 23), mm is the minute (00 through 59), and ss is the seconds (00 through 59). The TZD stands for Time Zone Designator and its value can be Z (to indicate UTC, Coordinated Universal Time), an indication of the number of hours and minutes ahead of UTC (such as +03:00), or an indication of the number of hours and minutes behind UTC (such as –02:20). This is the standard format for date and time values in HTML. For more information, see *www.w3.org/TR/1998/NOTE-datetime-19980827*.

Generic Elements (div and span)

The generic div and span elements provide a way for authors to create custom elements. The div element is used to indicate block-level elements, while span indicates inline elements. Both generic elements rely on id and class attributes to give them a name, meaning, or context.

The Versatile div

The div element is used to identify and label any block-level division of text, whether it is a few list items or an entire page.

div

```
<div>...</div>
```

Attributes

    Core (id, class, style, title), *Internationalization, Events*

Deprecated attributes

    align="center|left|right"

By marking a section of text as a div and giving it a name using id or class attributes, you are essentially creating a custom HTML element. In this example, a heading and a list are enclosed in a div identified as "sidebar."

```
<div id="sidebar">
    <h1>List of links</h1>
    <ul>
        <li>Resource 1</li>
```

```
        <li>Resource 2</li>
        <li>Resource 3</li>
     </ul>
  </div>
```

Because a div is a block-level element, its contents will start on a new line (even text not contained within other block-level elements). Otherwise, div elements have no inherent presentation qualities of their own.

The div really shines when used in conjunction with Cascading Style Sheets. Once you've marked up and named a div, you can apply styles to all of its contents or treat it as a box that can be positioned on the page, for instance, to form a new text column. A div may also be called on by script, applet, or other processing by user agents.

The Useful span

Like the div element, span allows authors to create custom elements. The difference is that span is used for inline elements and does not introduce a line break.

span

```
<span>...</span>
```

Attributes

Core (id, class, style, title), *Internationalization, Events*

This is a simple example of a span used to identify a telephone number.

```
Jenny: <span class="telephone">867.5309</span>
```

Markup like this has a number of uses. Most commonly, it is a "hook" that can be used to apply style sheet rules. In this example, all elements labeled as telephone may receive the same presentational instructions, such as to be displayed in bold, blue text.

The span also gives meaning to an otherwise random string of digits to user agents who know what to do with telephone information. This is discussed a bit more in the next section.

Element Identifiers (class and id)

The previous examples show how the id and class attributes are used to turn generic div and span elements into elements with specific meanings and uses. It should be pointed out that class and id attributes may be used with nearly all (X)HTML elements, not just div and span. This section discusses the id and class element identifiers and their distinct uses.

id identifier

The id attribute is used to give an element a specific and unique name in the document. In the earlier div example, id was used to label a section of the page as "sidebar." That means there may be no other element with id="sidebar" in that document (although, it is okay if it appears in other documents on the same site). ID values must be unique.

The HTML 4.01 Recommendation specifies the following uses for id attribute:

- As a style sheet selector
- As a target anchor for links (with the same functionality as <a name="">)
- As a means to access an element from a script
- As the name of a declared object element
- For general purpose processing by user agents, essentially treating the element as data

class identifier

The class attribute is used for grouping similar elements. Multiple elements may be assigned the same class name, and doing so enables them to be treated similarly.

In the span example above, the telephone number was identified as telephone with the class attribute. This implies that there may be many more telephone numbers in the document. A single style sheet rule could then be used to make them all bold and blue. Changing them all to green requires editing just one line of code. This offers an obvious advantage over changing color one by one with the deprecated font element. In addition to being inefficient to maintain, font doesn't add any semantic cues for user agents.

According to the HTML 4.01 specification, the class attribute may be used:

- As a style sheet selector
- For general purpose processing by user agents

In HTML 4.01, id and class attributes may be used with all elements except base, basefont, head, html, meta, param, script, style, and title. In XHTML, id support has been added to those elements.

Tips on using class

There is a heady exhilaration that comes with the ability to create your own custom elements using id and class. The class attribute in particular is prone to misuse. These tips should provide some basic guidance for keeping your markup clean.

Keep class *names meaningful.*
The value of the class attribute should provide a semantic description of a div or span's content. Choosing names based on the intended presentation of the element—for example, class="indented" or class="bluetext"—does little toward giving the element meaning and reintroduces presentational information to the document. It is also short-sighted. Consider what happens when, in an inevitable future design change, all elements classified as bluetext are rendered in green.

Don't go class-*crazy.*

It's easy to go overboard in assigning class names to elements. In many cases, other types of selectors, such as contextual or attribute selectors, may be used instead. For example, instead of labeling every h1 element in a sidebar as class="sideread", a contextual selector could be used, like this:

```
div#sidebar h1 {font: Verdana 1.2em bold #444;}
```

Lists

Humans are natural list-makers, so it makes sense that mechanisms for creating lists of information have been part of HTML since its birth. This section looks at the types of lists defined in (X)HTML:

- Unordered information
- Ordered information
- Terms and definitions

Unordered Lists

Unordered lists are used for collections of related items that appear in no particular order. Most lists fall into this category. Just about any list of examples, components, thoughts, or options should be marked up as an unordered list. Most notably, unordered lists are the element of choice for navigational options. Unordered lists for navigation are discussed later in this section.

In (X)HTML, unordered lists are denoted with the ul element. The content of a ul is limited to one or more list items (li). List items may contain either block-level or inline elements, or both. Unordered lists and their list items are block elements, so each will display starting on a new line.

ul

```
<ul>...</ul>
```

Attributes

> *Core* (id, class, style, title), *Internationalization, Events*

Deprecated attributes

> compact
> type="disc|circle|square"

li

```
<li>...</li>
```

Attributes

> *Core* (id, class, style, title), *Internationalization, Events*

Deprecated attributes

```
type="format"
value="number"
```

Unordered list syntax

This example shows the markup for a basic unordered list.

```
<ul>
    <li>Unordered information</li>
    <li>Ordered information</li>
    <li>Terms and definitions</li>
</ul>
```

In HTML 4.01, the end tags for list items are optional, but in XHTML, all end tags are required. It is good practice to close all elements regardless of the version of HTML you are using.

Unordered list presentation

By default, user agents insert a bullet before each list item in an unordered list. Leaving an unordered list unstyled (that is, applying no style sheet properties to it) is a reliable shortcut to having your information appear as an indented bulleted list.

But that sells the usefulness of the unordered list element short. By applying style properties, an unordered list may be presented however you like. You can change the shape of the bullets with the list-style-type property (this property replaces the deprecated type attribute that is discouraged from use). The list-style-image property allows you to use your own image as a bullet. Style properties for lists are discussed in Chapter 23.

And that's just the beginning. You can set lists to display horizontally, too. You can even use unordered list markup as the structure underlying a rich graphical navigation toolbar with rollover effects, all accomplished with Cascading Style Sheets. These techniques are outlined in Chapter 24.

Ordered Lists

Ordered lists are used for lists in which the sequence of the items is important, such as step-by-step instructions or endnotes. Ordered lists are indicated by the ol element and must include one or more list items (li). Like all lists, ordered lists and their list items are block-level elements.

ol

`<ol>...</ol>`

Attributes

Core (id, class, style, title), *Internationalization, Events*

Deprecated attributes

```
compact
start="number"
type="1|A|a|I|i"
```

Ordered lists have the same basic structures as unordered lists, as shown in this simple example.

```
<ol>
    <li>Get out of bed</li>
    <li>Take a shower</li>
    <li>Walk the dog</li>
</ol>
```

By default, user agents automatically number the list items in ordered lists. There is no need to add the number in the source.

Style sheets may be used to change the numbering system (list-style-type) as described in Chapter 23. The list-style-type property replaces the deprecated type attribute that specifies the numbering system for lists, as shown in Table 10-1.

Table 10-1. Values of the deprecated type attribute

Type value	Generated style	Sample sequence
1	Arabic numerals (default)	1, 2, 3, 4
A	Uppercase letters	A, B, C, D
a	Lowercase letters	a, b, c, d
I	Uppercase Roman numerals	I, II, III, IV
i	Lowercase Roman numerals	i, ii, iii, iv

Use the deprecated start attribute to start the counting of the list items at a particular number. This markup example creates an ordered list using lowercase letters that starts counting at 10.

```
<ol type="a" start="10">
<li>See quirksmode.org/css/tests/</li>
<li>According to the W3C Working Group</li>
<li>See the XHTML 1.1 Working Document</li>
</ol>
```

The resulting list would look like this, because "j" is the tenth letter in the alphabet:

j. See quirksmode.org/css/tests/
k. According to the W3C Working Group
l. See the XHTML 1.1 Working Document

There is a CSS alternative to the start attribute using the counter-reset property, but it is poorly supported by browsers at this time.

Definition Lists

Use a *definition list* for lists that consist of term and definition pairs.

Definition lists are marked up as dl elements. The content of a dl is some number of terms (indicated by the dt element) and definitions (indicated by the dd element). The dt (term) element may contain only inline content, but a dd may include block-level or inline elements. All three elements used in definition lists are block-level elements and will start on a new line by default.

dl

```
<dl>...</dl>
```

Attributes

> *Core* (id, class, style, title), *Internationalization, Events*
> compact

dd

```
<dd>...</dd>
```

Attributes

> *Core* (id, class, style, title), *Internationalization, Events*

dt

```
<dt>...</dt>
```

Attributes

> *Core* (id, class, style, title), *Internationalization, Events*

The markup structure for definition lists is a little different from the lists discussed so far. The entire list, made up of dt and dd elements, is contained within the dl element, as shown here.

```
<dl>
    <dt>em</dt>
    <dd>Indicates emphasized text. em elements are nearly always rendered in
italics.</dd>

    <dt>strong</dt>
    <dd>Denotes strongly emphasized text. Strong elements are nearly always
rendered in bold text.</dd>

    <dt>abbr</dt>
    <dd>Indicates an abbreviated form.</dd>

    <dt>acronym</dt>
    <dd>Indicates an acronym.</dd>
</dl>
```

Terms and definitions are not required to appear in alternating order. In other words, it is fine to introduce two terms and apply one definition, or supply two or more definition elements for a single term. The HTML 4.01 Recommendation provides an informal example of definition list dialogues, where the speaker corresponds to the term and the spoken words correspond to the definition. Many semantic (X)HTML experts consider this particular example to be an abuse of the semantics of definitional lists and thus it should be avoided.

The presentation of definition lists should be controlled with style sheet properties. By default, user agents generally display the definitions on an indent.

Nesting Lists

List elements may be nested within other lists. For example, you can add an unordered list within a definition list, or a numbered list as an item within an unordered list. This example shows just one variation. The resulting list is shown in Figure 10-2.

```
<ol>
<li>Mix Marinade
    <ul>
    <li>2 slices ginger <em>(smashed)</em></li>
    <li>1 T. rice wine or sake</li>
    <li>1 t. salt</li>
    <li>2 T. peanut oil</li>
    </ul>
</li>
<li>Saute the seasonings</li>
<li>Add fish sauce</li>
</ol>
```

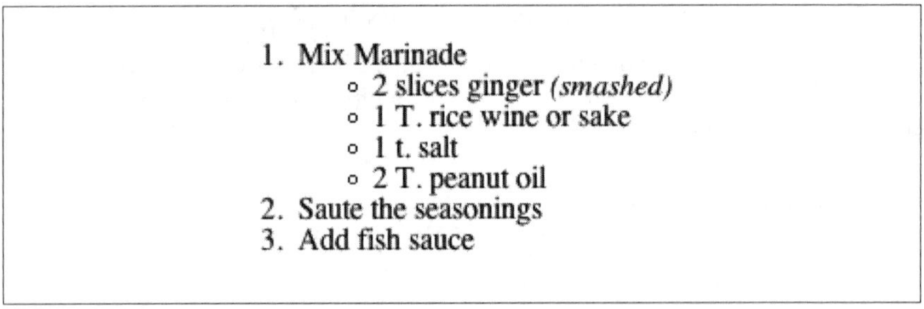

1. Mix Marinade
   - 2 slices ginger *(smashed)*
   - 1 T. rice wine or sake
   - 1 t. salt
   - 2 T. peanut oil
2. Saute the seasonings
3. Add fish sauce

Figure 10-2. Nested lists

Note that in order for the list markup to be valid, ul and ol elements may contain only li elements. That means the nested list must be contained within a list item (li) and may not be a child of the ul or ol element. Authors should also be careful to close all elements so they are nested properly and do not overlap.

When unstyled unordered lists (ul) are nested within each other, browsers automatically display a different bullet for each consecutive level, usually disc, then circle, then square. Nested ordered lists all receive the default Arabic numbering system (1, 2, 3, etc.). Use style sheets to specify the marker system for each nested list level, as appropriate.

Deprecated List Elements

The HTML and XHTML Transitional Recommendations include two deprecated list elements, dir and menu. The dir (directory) element was designed for use in multicolumn displays. The menu element was designed to be used as a single-column list of menu options. The W3C strongly discourages the use of these elements and instructs authors to use unordered lists (ul) instead.

Presentational Elements

There are a handful of (X)HTML elements that are explicitly presentation oriented. Sometimes called "physical" styles, they provide instructions for the size, weight, or style of the font used to display the element.

If you've been paying attention, you already know that Cascading Style Sheets are now the preferred way to specify presentation instructions. Table 10-2 lists the presentational inline elements, along with the preferred alternative for achieving the same visual effect.

Table 10-2. Presentational inline elements and style sheet alternatives

Element	Description	Alternative
b	Bold	Use the strong element instead if appropriate, or use the font-weight property: font-weight: bold
big	Big	Use a relative font-size keyword to make text display slightly larger than the surrounding text: font-size: bigger
i	Italic	Use the em element instead if appropriate, or use the font-style property: font-style: italic
s (*deprecated*)	Strike-through	Use the text-decoration property to make text display with a line through it: text-decoration: line-through
small	Small	Use a relative font-size keyword to make text display slightly smaller than the surrounding text: font-size: smaller
strike (*deprecated*)	Strike-through	Use the text-decoration property to make text display with a line through it: text-decoration: line-through

Element	Description	Alternative
tt	Teletype	Use the font-family property to select a specific or generic fixed-width font: `font-family: "Andale Mono", monospace;`
u (*deprecated*)	Underline	Use the text-decoration property to make text display with a line under it: `text-decoration: underline`

Font Elements

The font element—an inline element used to specify the size, color, and font face for the enclosed text using the size, color, and face attributes, respectively—is the poster child for what went wrong with HTML. It was first introduced by Netscape Navigator as a means to give authors control over font formatting not available with HTML at the time (and for good reason). Netscape was rewarded with a temporary slew of loyal users, but the HTML standard and web development community paid a steep price in the long run.

Another deprecated font-related element, basefont, is used to set the font face, color, and size for an entire document when it is in the head of the document or for subsequent text when it is placed in the body.

The font element is emphatically deprecated, and you will be ridiculed by your peers for using it. I'm not kidding. Don't use it. For the sake of historical reference and thoroughness in documenting the HTML and XHTML Transitional DTDs, it is included in this chapter with some basic explanation.

font

`<font>...</font>`

This element is deprecated.

Attributes

Core (id, class, style, title), *Internationalization*

Deprecated attributes

`color="#RRGGBB"` or `"color name"`
`face="typeface"` (or list of typefaces)
`size="value"`

basefont

`<basefont>`

This element is deprecated.

Attributes

`id="text"`

Deprecated attributes

```
color="#RRGGBB" or "color name"
face="typeface" (or list of typefaces)
size="value"
```

The font element adds no semantic value to a document and mixes presentation instructions in with the document structure. Furthermore, it makes updating a site more labor intensive, because each and every font element needs to be hunted down and changed, unlike style sheets that enable elements throughout a site to be reformatted with one simple edit.

The font element has three attributes, all of which have been deprecated as well:

color

Specifies the color of the text using a hexadecimal RGB value or color name.

face

Specifies a font or list of fonts (separated by commas) to be used to display the element.

size

Specifies the size for the font. The default text size is represented by the value "3." Values may be provided as numbers (1 through 7) or as values relative to 3 (for example, the value −1 is the same as the value 2, the value +3 is the same as 6).

A single font element may contain all of these attributes as shown:

```
<font face="sans-serif" size="+1" color="white"><em>...</em></font>
```

All of the functionality of the font element has been replaced by style sheet properties. The font element in the example could be handled with these style properties:

```
em {font-family: sans-serif;
    font-size: 120%;
    color: white; }
```

For more information on using style sheets to control the presentation of fonts, see Chapter 18, and kiss your font tags goodbye forever.

Subscript and Superscript

The subscript (sub) and superscript (sup) elements cause the selected text to display in a smaller size and positioned slightly below (sub) or above (sup) the baseline. These elements may be helpful for indicating chemical formulas or mathematical equations.

sub, sup

```
<sub>...</sub>, <sup>...</sup>
```

Attributes

Core (id, class, style, title), *Internationalization, Events*

Figure 10-3 shows how these examples of subscript and superscript render in a browser.

```
<p>H<sub>2</sub>0</p>
```

```
<p>E=MC<sup>2</sup></p>
```

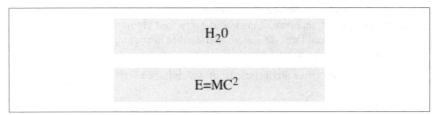

Figure 10-3. Subscript and superscript

Line Breaks

Line breaks may be added in the flow of text using the br element. The text following the br element begins on a new line with no extra space added above. It is one of the few presentational elements preserved in the XHTML 1.0 Strict and XHTML 1.1 DTDs.

---

br

```
<br />
```

Attributes

Core (id, class, style, title)

Deprecated Attributes

```
clear="none | left | right | all "
```

The br element is straightforward to use, as shown in this example.

```
<p>This is a paragraph but I want <br />this text to start on a new line in
the browser.</p>
```

The clear attribute is used with the br element to specify where the next line should appear in relation to floated elements. For example, if an image has been floated to the right, then adding the markup <br clear="right" /> in the flow of text causes the new line to begin *below* the image on the right margin. The value left starts the next line below any floated objects on the left margin. The value all starts the next line below floats on both margins. The default, none, causes the next line to start where it would normally.

Word Wrapping

Another text quality that is inherently presentational is word wrapping: the way lines break automatically in the browser window. In CSS, you can prevent lines from wrapping by setting the white-space property to nowrap. The HTML and

---

XHTML Recommendations define no element for preventing lines from wrapping. However, there are two nonstandard elements, nobr and wbr, that were introduced by Netscape and are sometimes used to control whether and where lines wrap.

The nobr element, which stands for "no break," prevents its contents from wrapping. The wbr (word break) element allows authors to specify the preferred point at which a line should break. These have never been adopted into an HTML Recommendation, but they are still in use and supported by Internet Explorer (all versions) and Mozilla. They are not supported in Safari and Opera.

Text and graphics that appear within the nobr element always display on one line, and are not wrapped in the browser window. If the string of characters or elements within the nobr element is very long, it continues off the browser window, and users must scroll horizontally to the right to see it. Adding a br within a nobr element text causes the line to break.

The esoteric word-break element (wbr) is used to indicate a recommended word-break point within content if the browser needs to do so. This may be useful if you have long strings of text (such as code or URLs) that may need to fit in tight spaces like table cells. If the table cell is wide enough, the text stays on one line, but if it is scaled smaller on someone's browser, the browser will wrap the line at the wbr. All of these nonstandard presentational elements should be avoided as well.

There are standard character entities for "soft hyphen" that should perform the same function, but they are inconsistently supported (the following section provides more information on character entities). The  entity causes a conditional line break in Mozilla, Safari, and Opera, but not Internet Explorer. The ­ entity works for Opera and Internet Explorer on Windows but is buggy on Safari and is not supported by Mozilla.

 Thanks go to Peter-Paul Koch for his wbr testing and summary on Quirksmode.org.

Horizontal Rules

In some instances, it is useful to add a visual divider between sections of a document. (X)HTML includes the hr element for adding a horizontal rule (line) to a web page.

hr

```
<hr />
```

Attributes

Core (id, class, style, title), *Internationalization, Events*

Deprecated attributes

```
align="center|left|right"
noshade="noshade"
size="number"
width="number" or "number%"
```

The hr element is a block-level element, so it always appears on its own line, usually with a bit of space above and below as well. By default, browsers render a horizontal rule as a beveled dimensional line, as shown in Figure 10-4.

```
<p>These are some deep thoughts.</p>
<hr />
<p>And this is another paragraph of deep thoughts.</p>
```

These are some deep thoughts.

And this is another paragraph of deep thoughts.

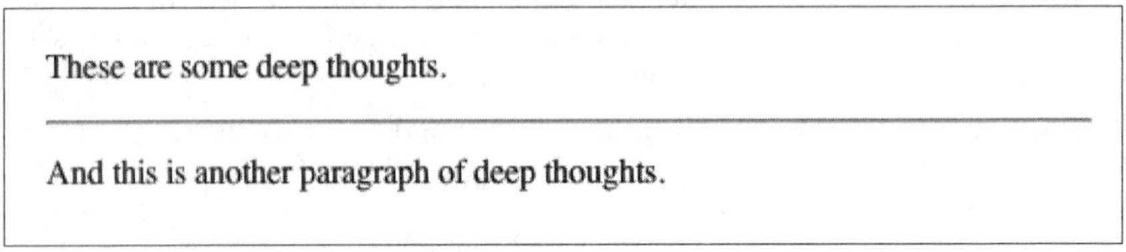

Figure 10-4. A horizontal rule (default rendering)

The hr element includes a number of deprecated attributes for controlling the presentation of the rule.

size
> Specifies the length of the rule in pixels or percentages.

width
> Specifies the thickness of the rule in pixels.

align
> Specifies the horizontal alignment of horizontal rules that are not the full width of the containing element.

noshade
> Turns off the dimensional shading on the rule and renders it in black.

It is possible to control the presentation of an hr with style sheets, as shown in this example, that make the rule a one-pixel solid blue line. Note that the color and background colors are specified for cross-browser compatibility.

```
hr {height: 1px;
    width: 100%;
    color: blue;
    background-color: blue; }
```

The preferred method is to keep the presentational hr element out of the document entirely and specify horizontal dividers using borders on the top or bottom edges of specific block elements, such as before h1s.

```
h1 {border-top: 1px solid blue;
    padding-top: 3em; }
```

Character Entity References

Characters not found in the normal alphanumeric character set, such as < and &, must be specified in HTML and XHTML documents using character references. This is known as *escaping* the character. Using the standard desktop publishing keyboard commands (such as Option-G for the © symbol) within an HTML document will not produce the desired character when the document is rendered in a browser. In fact, the browser generally displays the numeric entity for the character.

In (X)HTML documents, escaped characters are indicated by character references that begin with & and end with ;. The character may be referred to by its Numeric Character Reference (NCR) or a predefined character entity name.

A Numeric Character Reference refers to a character by its Unicode code point in either decimal or hexadecimal form (for more information on Unicode and code points, see Chapter 6). Decimal character references use the syntax &#*nnnn*;. Hexadecimal values are indicated by an "x": &#x*hhhh*;. For example, the less-than (<) character could be identified as < (decimal) or < (hexadecimal).

Character entities are abbreviated names for characters, such as < for the less-than symbol. Character entities are predefined in the DTDs of markup languages such as HTML and XHMTL as a convenience to authors, because they may be easier to remember than Numeric Character References.

XHTML includes the XML entity declaration for the apostrophe ('). In HTML, the apostrophe character entity was curiously omitted, so its numeric reference (&039;) must be used instead.

Table 10-3 presents the (X)HTML character entities and numeric character references for commonly used special characters. The complete list of character entities defined in HTML 4.01 and XHTML 1.0/1.1 appears in Appendix C.

Table 10-3. Common special characters and their character entities

Character	Description	Entity	Decimal	Hex
	Character space (nonbreaking space)			&#x00A0;
&	Ampersand	&amp;	&#038;	&#x26;
<	Less-than sign (useful for displaying markup on a web page)	&lt;	&#060;	&#x3C;
>	Greater-than sign (useful for displaying markup on a web page)	&gt;	&#062;	&#x3E;
'	Apostrophe	' (*XHTML only*)	&#039;	&#x27;
"	Left curly quotes	&ldquo;	&#8220;	&#x201C;
"	Right curly quotes	&rdquo;	&#8221;	&#x201D;
™	Trademark	&trade;	&#8482;	&#x2122;
£	Pound symbol	&pound;	&#163;	&#xA3;

Table 10-3. Common special characters and their character entities (continued)

Character	Description	Entity	Decimal	Hex
¥	Yen symbol	&yen;	&#165;	&#xA5;
©	Copyright symbol	&copy;	&#169;	&#xA9;
®	Registered trademark	&reg;	&#174;	&#xAE;

XML Character Entities

XML 1.0 defines five character entities that must be supported by all XML processors. The XHTML DTDs explicitly declare these entities as well, in keeping with recommended practice for XML languages.

Less than (<) < <

Greater than (>) > >

Ampersand (&) & &

Apostrophe (') ' '

Quotation mark (") " "

The only significant change is that XHTML includes an entity for the apostrophe character ('), which was curiously omitted from HTML. For backward compatibility, it is recommended that authors use the numeric reference for apostrophe (') instead.

11

Creating Links

The HTML 4.01 specification puts it simply and clearly: "A link is a connection from one web resource to another." This ability to create hyperlinks from one document to another is what makes HTML unique among document markup languages and is the key to its widespread popularity. You can create a link to any web resource, including (but not limited to) another HTML document, an image, a program, or a particular element within an HTML document.

This chapter focuses on these HTML elements related to linking and building relationships between documents.

a	Anchor (link)
base	Provides a base pathname
link	Establishes relationship between documents

Simple Hypertext Links

The anchor (a) element is used to identify a string of text or an image that serves as a hypertext link to another document.

a

`<a>...</a>`

Attributes

Core (id, class, style, title)
Internationalization
Events (plus onfocus, onblur)
accesskey="*character*"
charset="*charset*"
coords="*x,y coordinates*"

```
href="URL"
id="text"
hreflang="language code"
name="text"
rel="relationships"
rev="relationships"
shape="rect|circle|poly|default"
tabindex="number"
target="text"
type="media type"
```

The href attribute provides the pathname (URL) of the document to which you want to link. URLs can be absolute or relative, as discussed in the next sections.

A text link is marked up like this:

```
I am <a href="link.html">linking</a> to you!
```

To make an image a link, enclose the image element in an anchor as follows:

```
<a href="link.html"><img src="pixies.gif"></a>
```

By default, most graphical browsers display linked text underlined and in blue, but this presentation can be altered with style sheets. Linked images appear with a blue border by default unless you change this setting with the border style property or the deprecated border attribute in the img element.

Absolute URLs

An *absolute URL* is made up of the following components: a protocol identifier, a hostname (the name of the server machine), and the path to the specific filename. When you are linking to documents on other servers, you need to use an absolute URL. The following is an example of a link with an absolute URL:

```
<a href="http://www.littlechair.com/web/index.html">...</a>
```

Here, the protocol is identified as *http* (HyperText Transfer Protocol, the standard protocol of the Web), the host is *www.littlechair.com*, and the pathname is *web/index.html*.

Relative URLs

A *relative URL* provides a pointer to another document relative to the location of the current document. The syntax is based on pathname structures in the Unix operating system, which are discussed in Chapter 4. When pointing to another document within your own site (on the same server), it is common to use relative URLs.

For example, if I am currently in *resume.html* (identified here by its full pathname):

```
www.littlechair.com/web/work/resume.html
```

and I want to put a link on that page to a document named *bio.html* that is in the same directory:

```
www.littlechair.com/web/work/bio.html
```

I could use a relative URL as the href attribute value as follows:

```
<a href="bio.html">...</a>
```

Using the same example, to link to the file *index.html* in a higher-level directory (*web*), I could use the relative pathname to that file as shown:

```
<a href="../index.html">
```

This relative URL is the equivalent to the absolute URL *http://www.littlechair.com/web/index.html*.

Establishing a base

By default, a relative URL is based on the current document. You can change that by placing the base element in the document header (head) to state explicitly the base URL for all relative pathnames in the document.

base

```
<base />
```

Attributes

```
id="text"  (XHTML only)
href="url"  (Required)
target="name"
```

The base element may appear only in the head of the document, and it should appear before any other element with an external reference. The browser uses the specified base URL (not the current document's URL) to resolve relative URLs. The base element is also useful in specifying a target frame for relative links in a framed document (see Chapter 14).

Linking Within a Document

By default, when you link to a page, the browser displays the top of that page. You may also link to a particular point in a web page (called a *fragment*).

Linking to document fragments is most often used as a navigational aid by creating a hyperlinked table of contents at the top of a very long scrolling web page. Users can see the major topics at a glance and quickly get to the portions that interest them. When linking down into a long page, it is generally a good idea to add links back to the top of the page or to the table of contents. You can also link to fragments in other documents (as long as they have been named).

Linking to specific destinations in a document is a two-step process in which you give an identifying name to an element and then make a link to that marker.

Naming a Fragment

HTML provides two ways to identify a document fragment: by inserting an anchor (a) element with the name attribute (instead of href) or by adding the id attribute to any HTML element. Both methods act as a marker that can be referenced from a link later.

XHTML documents must use the id attribute for all fragment identifiers in order to be well-structured XML. Unfortunately, the id attribute is not universally supported by all browsers for this purpose (support is lacking in Version 4 browsers). To ensure maximum backward and forward compatibility, the XHTML Recommendation suggests redundant markup using both id and name in the a element.

In this example, a named anchor is used to let users link directly to a "Stock Quotes" section of a web document called *dailynews.html*. First, the heading is marked up as a named anchor with the name "stocks." Named anchors receive no special style treatment by default (in other words, they are not underlined like anchors with the href attribute).

```
<h1><a name="stocks" id="stocks">Daily Stock Quotes</a></h1>
```

The same fragment might also be identified right in the h1 element as shown here (if Version 4 browsers don't need to be supported).

```
<h1 id="stocks">Daily Stock Quotes<h1>
```

The value of the name and id attributes must be unique within the document (in other words, two elements can't be given the same name).

Linking to a Fragment

The second step is to create a link to the fragment using a standard anchor element with its href attribute. Fragment identifiers are placed at the end of the pathname and are indicated by the hash (#) symbol (formally known as an *octothorpe*).

To link to the stocks fragment from within *dailynews.html*, the markup would look like this:

```
<a href="#stocks">Check out the Stock Quotes</a>
```

Linking to a Fragment in Another Document

You can create a link to a named fragment of any document on the Web by using the complete pathname immediately followed by the fragment identifier. Of course, the fragment identifiers would have to be in place already. To link to the stocks section from another document in the same directory, use a relative pathname as follows:

```
<a href="dailynews.html#stocks">Go to today's Stock Quotes</a>
```

Use an absolute URL to link to a fragment on another site, as in:

```
<a href="http://www.website.com/document.html#fragment">...</a>
```

Targeting Windows

The problem with a hypertext medium is that when users click on an interesting link that takes them off your page, they might never come back. One solution to this problem is to make the target document appear in a second browser window that opens automatically. In that way, your page is still readily available in the background.

This technique is not without controversy, however. Windows that open automatically, also known as *pop-up* windows, are now strongly associated with intrusive web advertising. The population's distaste for them is so strong that there are a slew of pop-up blocker programs on the market and even built right into browsers. Consider whether a pop-up window is the best solution given the fact that some users may not see that content. Pop-up windows are also problematic from the standpoint of usability and accessibility. If you do use a pop-up window, it is advised that you let users know what to expect by adding a comment such as "link opens in new window."

 The following technique simply opens a new browser window but does not control its size. To do that, you must use JavaScript.

To launch a new browser window for the linked document, use the `target` attribute in the a element. Setting the `target` attribute to the standardized `"_blank"` value causes the browser to open a fresh browser window. For example:

```
<a href="http://www.oreilly.com/" target="_blank">...</a>
```

Note that _blank opens a new browser window every time. So if you set every link on your page to target a _blank window, every link will launch a new window, potentially leaving your user with a mess of open windows.

A better method, especially if you have more than one link, is to give the targeted window a specific name, which can then be reused by subsequent links. The following link will open a new window called "display":

```
<a href="http://www.oreilly.com/" target="display">...</a>
```

All links that target a window called "display" will now load into that same browser window.

The target attribute is most often used in conjunction with framed documents. The syntax and strategy for using the target attribute with framed documents is discussed in Chapter 14.

Alternative Protocols

Linking to other web pages using the HTTP protocol is by far the most common type of link, but there are several other types of transactions that can be made using other standard Internet protocols.

Mail Link (mailto:)

The `mailto` protocol can be used in an a element to automatically send an email message to the recipient, using the browser's email application or an external email application. Note that the browser must be configured to support this protocol, so it will not work for all users. The `mailto` protocol has the following components:

```
mailto:username@domain
```

A typical mail link might look like this:

```
<a href="mailto:jen@oreilly.com">Send Jennifer email</a>
```

You can also experiment with adding information within the `mailto` URL that automatically fills in standard email fields such as Subject or cc:.

```
mailto:username@domain?subject=subject
mailto:username@domain?cc=person1
mailto:username@domain?bcc=person2
mailto:username@domain?body=body
```

Additional variables are appended to the string with an ampersand (&) symbol as shown:

```
mailto:username@domain?subject=subject&cc=person1&body=body
```

In XHTML, the ampersand (&) symbol must be escaped—that is, expressed as a character entity (&) in the string—for the document to be valid. The same link in XHTML would be marked up like this:

```
mailto:username@domain?subject=subject&amp;cc=person1&body=body
```

Spaces within subject lines need to be written as %20 (the space character in hexadecimal notation). The following sample mail link employs these additions:

```
<a href="mailto:jen@oreilly.com?subject=Like%20your%20book">Email for
    Jen</a>
```

 When you put a link to an email address on a web page, the address is prone to getting "spidered" (automatically indexed) and added to spam mailing lists. To avoid getting spammed, do not put your intact email address in the source document, either as a mailto link or in the content itself. An alternative is to spell out the email address (such as "jen at oreilly dot com") so it is understandable to humans but not recognizable to spambots.

FTP Link (ftp://)

You can link directly to a file on an FTP server. When the user clicks on the link, the file downloads automatically using the browser's built-in FTP functions and is saved on the user's machine. If the document is on an anonymous FTP server (no account name and password are required), the FTP link is simple:

```
<a href="ftp://server/pathname">...</a>
```

To link to an FTP server that requires the user to log in, the format is:

```
<a href="ftp://user:password@server/pathname">...</a>
```

For security purposes, it is highly recommended that you never include both the username and password to a server within an HTML document. If you use the syntax user@server/path, the users will be prompted to enter their passwords in a dialog box.

By default, the requested file is transferred in binary format. To specify that the document should be transferred as an ASCII file, add ;type=a to the end of the URL:

```
<a href="ftp://user:password@server/pathname;type=a">...</a>
```

The variable type=d identifies the pathname as a directory and simply displays its contents in the browser window. The variable type=i specifies image or binary mode, which is the default but may also be given explicitly.

Here are some examples of FTP links:

```
<a href="ftp://pete@ftp.someserver.com/program.exe">...</a>
<a href="ftp://ftp.superwarehouse.com/games;type=d">...</a>
```

Other Links

Table 11-1 lists URL types that are not as well known or useful as mailto or ftp://, but are available. As with other links, place these URLs after the href attribute within the anchor element.

Table 11-1. Alternative link protocols

Type	Syntax	Use
File	file://server/path	Specifies a file without indicating the protocol. This is useful for accessing files on a contained site such as a CD-ROM or kiosk application, but it is less appropriate over networks (such as the Internet).
News	news:newsgroup news:message_id	Accesses either a single message or an entire newsgroup within the Usenet news system. Some browsers do not support news URLs, so you should avoid using them.
NNTP	nntp://server:port/ newsgroup/article	Provides a complete mechanism for accessing Usenet news articles. The article is served only to machines that are allowed to retrieve articles from this server, so this URL has limited practical use.
Telnet	telnet:// user:password@server:port/	Opens a Telnet session with a desired server. The user and password@ elements are optional and follow the same rules as described for ftp://.
Gopher	gopher://server:port/path	Accesses a document on a gopher server. The gopher document retrieval system was eclipsed by the World Wide Web, but some gopher servers are still operating.

Linking Documents with link

The link element defines a relationship between the current document and another external document. It is not the same as a hypertext link because it is not accessible by clicking or otherwise selecting a hyperlink. It is always placed in the header (head) of the document. There can be multiple link elements in a document.

link

```
<link />
```

Attributes

Core (id, class, style, title), *Internationalization, Events*
charset="*charset*"
href="*URL*"
hreflang="*language code*"
media="all|screen|print|handheld|projection|tty|tv|projection|braille|
aural"
rel="*relationships*"
rev="*relationships*"
target="*name*"
type="*resource*"

The most important attributes are href, which points to the linked file, and rel, which describes the relationship(s) from the source document to the target document. The rev attribute describes the reverse relationship(s) (from the target back to the source).

A variety of attributes make the link element very versatile, but it is not currently used to its full potential. By far, the most popular application of the link element is for referring to an external style sheet. In this example, the type attribute identifies the MIME content type of the linked document as a Cascading Style Sheet, which is required in XHTML:

```
<head>
<link href="wholesite.css" rel="stylesheet" type="text/css" />
</head>
```

Note the use of the "/" at the end of the link element to explicitly mark it as an empty element for XHTML, while leaving a space before the "/" for compatibility with Version 4 browsers.

Another use as recommended in the HTML 4.01 specification is to refer to an alternate version of the document in another language. The following example creates a link to a French version of the document:

```
<head>
<link rel="alternate" href="translations/french.html"
      type="text/html" hreflang="fr" />
</head>
```

By using the next and prev values for the rel attribute, you can establish the document's position in a sequence of documents, as shown in the next example. This information could be used by browsers and other tools to build navigation menus, tables of contents, or other link collections.

```
<head>
<title>Chapter 11: Creating Links</title>
```

```
<link rel="prev" href="chapter10.html" />
<link rel="next" href="chapter12.html" />
</head>
```

Table 11-2 lists the accepted values for the rel and rev attributes and their uses. These attributes and values can be used in the a element as well as link to define relationships for a specific link. Again, these features are not widely used, nor are they well supported by browser user interfaces.

Table 11-2. Link types using the rel attribute

Value	Relationship
alternate	Substitute version of the current document, perhaps in another language or optimized for another display medium. This value is used frequently in style sheet switching.
stylesheet	External Cascading Style Sheet; used with type="text/css".
start	The first document in a collection or series.
next	The next document in a series.
prev	The previous document in a series.
contents (or toc)	A document providing a table of contents.
index	A document providing an index for the current document.
glossary	A document containing a glossary of terms.
copyright	A document containing copyright information for the current document.
chapter	A document serving as a chapter in a collection of documents.
section	A document serving as a section in a collection of documents.
subsection	A document serving as a subsection in a collection of documents.
appendix	A document serving as an appendix.
help	A help document.
bookmark	A document that serves as a bookmark; the title attribute can be used to name the bookmark.

12

Images and Objects

In addition to text content, web pages may include a wide range of multimedia objects, including images, image maps, Java applets, video, Flash movies, even other HTML documents. This chapter focuses on the (X)HTML elements defined for adding images and media objects, including:

img	Adds an image
map	The map used for an image map
area	A geometric region in an image map
object	A generic media object
param	Specifies values for an object necessary at runtime
embed	Embeds media requiring plug-ins *(nonstandard)*
noembed	Content displayed if embedded media is not supported *(nonstandard)*
applet	Adds an applet *(deprecated)*
iframe	A floating frame that displays an external HTML document

Inline Images

Inline images are images that occur in the normal flow of the document's content. As inline elements, they affect the visual display of other elements in the flow, unlike background images, which render behind elements. Images are added to the document with the img element. Images are considered to be replaced elements because the actual content resides in external files rather than in the source document.

The HTML 4.01 Recommendation allows images to be added using the generic object element, as demonstrated later in this chapter. Because the object method is not universally supported, the img element is still the primary element used to place images in web documents.

img

```
<img />
```

Attributes

Core (id, class, style, title), *Internationalization, Events*
alt="*text*" *(Required)*
ismap
height="*number*"
longdesc="*URL*"
lowsrc="*URL*"
name="*text*"
src="*URL*" *(Required)*
usemap="*URL*"
width="*number*"

Deprecated attributes

align="absbottom|absmiddle|baseline|bottom|center|left|middle|
right|top"
border="*number*"
hspace="*number*"
vspace="*number*"

Images and
Objects

Image Formats and Usage

Web images must be in one of the three web-compatible formats: GIF, JPEG, or
PNG. Furthermore, the files should be named with the proper suffixes—*.gif*, *.jpeg*
or *.jpg*, and *.png*, respectively—so that your web server sends the proper Content-
Type—image/gif, image/jpeg, and image/png, respectively—which the browser
uses to recognize the image format. These graphic file formats, as well as other
requirements for putting images online, are discussed in detail in Part V.

Inline images are used in a variety of ways:

As a simple image
An image can be used on a web page much as it is used in print—as a static
image that adds information, such as a company logo or an illustration.

As a link
An image can also be used to link to another document as an alternative to
text links.

As an image map
An image map is a single image with multiple "hotspots" that link to other
documents. There is nothing special about the image itself; it is an ordinary
inline image. Special HTML markup and map files link pointer coordinates
with their respective URLs. The upcoming "Image Maps" section of this
chapter includes a full explanation of how image maps work and how to
create them.

Images (transparent GIFs, in particular) have also been used as spacing devices, but now that we have better control of space and alignment with Cascading Style Sheets, this use of spacer images is outdated and must be avoided in contemporary web design.

With the emergence of standards-driven web design in recent years, there has been a shift away from using inline images for purely decorative purposes. Images that are not part of the content and only contribute to the presentation of the page are commonly placed as background images using CSS instead. Images may be applied to the background of any element (not just body) using the background-image or shortcut background style properties and they *don't* need to tile. Chapter 24 includes examples of several CSS image replacement techniques.

There are several benefits to specifying decorative images only in an external style sheet and keeping them out of the document structure. Not only does it make the document cleaner and more accessible, it also makes it easier to make changes to the look and feel of a site than when presentational elements are interspersed in the content. See Chapter 20 for more details on CSS background images. For inspiration on how visually rich a web page can be with no img elements at all, see the CSS Zen Garden site at *www.csszengarden.com*.

Without further ado, it is time to look at an example of img element markup.

img Element Syntax

There are over a dozen attributes that can be applied to the img element to affect its display, but the only required attributes are src, which provides the URL of the image file, and alt for providing text for browsers that cannot (or have been asked not to) display images. The syntax for a minimal image element looks like this:

```
<img src="url of image" alt="alternative text" />
```

The URL provided by the src attribute may be absolute (including the protocol and domain name) or relative to the current document (using a relative path-name). The conventions for relative pathnames are described in detail in Chapter 4.

Figure 12-1 shows an inline image resulting from this markup.

```
<p>Star light <img src="star.gif" alt="star" /> Star bright.</p>
```

Figure 12-1. An image placed within a line of text

Default presentation

As the example makes clear, because img is an inline element, it does not introduce any line breaks or extra space. By default, the bottom of an image aligns with the baseline of surrounding text. The alignment and position of the image may be changed with style sheet rules as discussed in Chapters 18 and 21. There are also a number of deprecated attributes for controlling the presentation of images that are briefly introduced later in this chapter.

Alternative text

There is no guarantee that an image will be displayed. It may be corrupted or not found, or users may be using a text-only or speech browser that doesn't support images. When an image is not displayed, graphical browsers display a generic broken image icon in its place. Non-graphical browsers generally just write out "[image]." Either of these instances can be a dead end for users and make certain content inaccessible.

The alt attribute allows you to specify a string of alternative text to be displayed in place of the image when the image is unavailable. It is also what non-graphical browsers write in place of images. Figure 12-2 shows one possible rendering for this markup if the image file should fail to load.

```
<p>First star <img src="star2.gif" alt="star illustration" /> I see tonight.
</p>
```

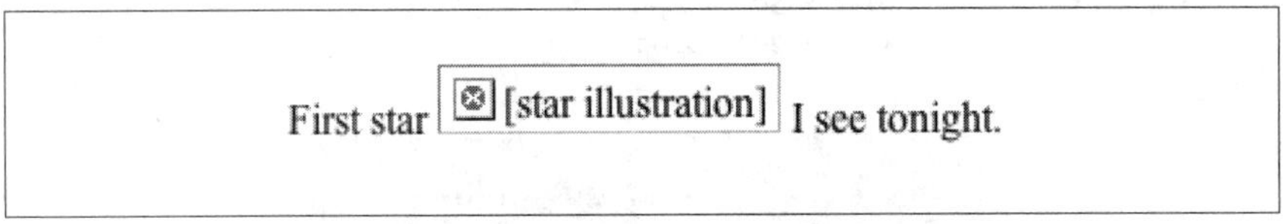

First star ⊗ [star illustration] I see tonight.

Figure 12-2. Alternative text may be displayed when an image is unavailable

Firefox displays the alternative text as though it were in the text flow. The Safari browser does not display alternative text for missing graphics. Some browsers display alternative text as a pop-up "tool tip" when the mouse rests on the image area, but such behavior is nonstandard and is not something to depend on.

The HTML 4.01 specification declared alt to be a required attribute within the img element (although an image will still display without it). Taking the extra time to provide alternative text for your images is the simplest way to make your page accessible to the greatest number of readers.

The W3C recommends that alternative text be provided only when the image contains content relevant to the document, not when the image is purely decorative. For example, the alternative text "red line" is not useful and only slows down document processing and may be frustrating for users using spoken browsing devices. An alt attribute with an empty string (alt="") is recommended instead.

Specifying Width and Height

Although src and alt are the only required attributes in the img element, width and height are often used because they speed up page display. The width and height attributes simply indicate the dimension of the image in pixels, such as:

```
<img src="star.gif" width="50" height="50" />
```

With this information, the browser can lay out the page before the images download.

 CSS width and height properties are preferred to the presentational attributes, and will also ensure that the page can be assembled before the images arrive.

Without width and height values, the page may be redrawn several times, first without images in place, and again each time new images arrive. It is worthwhile to take the time to include accurate width and height information in every img element.

If the width and height values specified are different than the actual dimensions of the image, the browser resizes the image to match the specified dimensions. If you specify a percentage value for width and height, some later browsers resize the image to the desired proportions.

Although this effect may be convenient and prevent an extra trip to the image editor, in some browsers, it just results in a pixelated, poor quality image, as shown in Figure 12-3.

```
<img src="star.gif" width="50" height="50" />
<img src="star.gif" width="200" height="50" />
```

Figure 12-3. Resizing an image with width and height attributes

 Reducing the dimensions of an image with markup is a bad practice and is strongly discouraged. In addition to resulting in poor image quality, it forces an unnecessarily large file download on the user when a much smaller file would do. Changing the image dimensions for the final presentation does not reduce the file size.

Deprecated img Attributes

There are a number of attributes in the Transitional DTDs that have been deprecated because they control presentational aspects of the image. As with most deprecated attributes, they have been replaced with more versatile style sheet properties. This section provides an introduction to these attributes and suggests style sheet alternatives.

If you are authoring using the XHTML Strict or XHTML 1.1 DTDs, using any of these attributes will cause your document to be invalid. Use the style sheet methods listed instead.

Vertical alignment

By default, the bottom of an image aligns with the baseline of the surrounding text (see Figure 12-1), but there are ways to change the vertical alignment. The preferred method is to use style sheets. Using HTML markup alone, the HTML 4.01 Recommendation includes the deprecated align attribute with the values top, middle, and bottom for vertical alignment. The HTML 3.2 Recommendation also included the values texttop, absmiddle, baseline, and absbottom, but they were dropped from future specifications and are only partially supported by modern browsers. Figure 12-4 shows the effects of these alignment values.

Figure 12-4. Vertical alignment values

The preferred CSS method for specifying vertical alignment is via the vertical-align property, which may be used to change the alignment of an image relative to the baseline or the height of the line it occupies. The accepted values are top, text-top, bottom, text-bottom, middle, sub, super, and baseline (the default), as well as specific length or percentage values. See Chapter 18 for explanations of vertical alignment with CSS.

Horizontal alignment

The align attribute is also used to align an image on the left or right margin of the page by using the values left or right, respectively. What makes left and right alignment special is that, in addition to placing the image on a margin, it allows the text to wrap around it. This is called *floating* the image. Figure 12-5 shows how images are displayed when set to align to the left and right.

```
<p><img src="leaf.gif" alt="" align="left" />An Oak and a Reed were arguing
about their strength...</p>
<p><img src="leaf.gif" alt="" align="right" />An Oak and a Reed were arguing
about their strength...</p>
```

The CSS float property is the preferred method for positioning images (or any element) against the right or left edges of the containing block and allowing the following content to wrap around it. Chapter 21 discusses floating elements.

Adding space around aligned images

When text flows around an image, browsers allow it to bump up against the image's edge. Usually, it is preferable to have a little space between the image and the surrounding text. In HTML, you provide this space by using the vspace and hspace attributes within the img element.

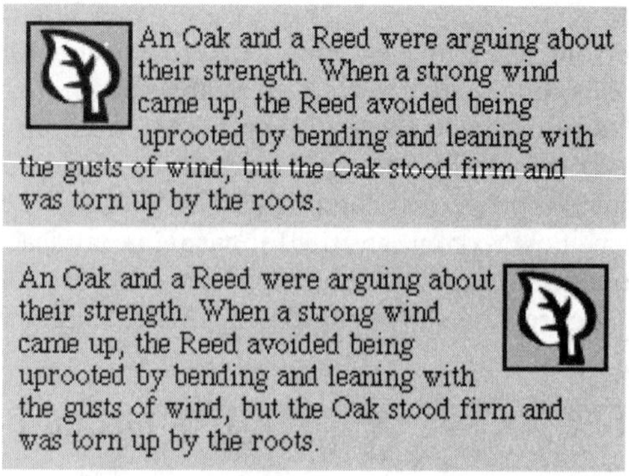

An Oak and a Reed were arguing about their strength. When a strong wind came up, the Reed avoided being uprooted by bending and leaning with the gusts of wind, but the Oak stood firm and was torn up by the roots.

An Oak and a Reed were arguing about their strength. When a strong wind came up, the Reed avoided being uprooted by bending and leaning with the gusts of wind, but the Oak stood firm and was torn up by the roots.

Figure 12-5. Text wraps around floated images

Right Alignment Without Text Wrap

Using the align="right" attribute to place an image against the right margin automatically results in text wrapping around the image. If you want to move an image to the right without the wrap, put the image in a paragraph (p), and then align the paragraph to the right, as shown:

```
<p align="right"><img src="leaf.gif" /></p>
<p>An Oak and a Reed were arguing...</p>
```

In CSS, to align an element with no text wrap, apply the text-align property to a block-level element that contains the image.

The vspace (vertical space) attribute holds a specified number of pixels of space above and below an aligned image. Space to the left and the right is added with hspace (horizontal space). Note that space is always added symmetrically (both top and bottom, or on both sides), and it is not possible with these attributes to specify an amount of space along a particular side of the image (you can, however, do this with style sheets). Figure 12-6 shows an image aligned with the hspace attribute set to 12.

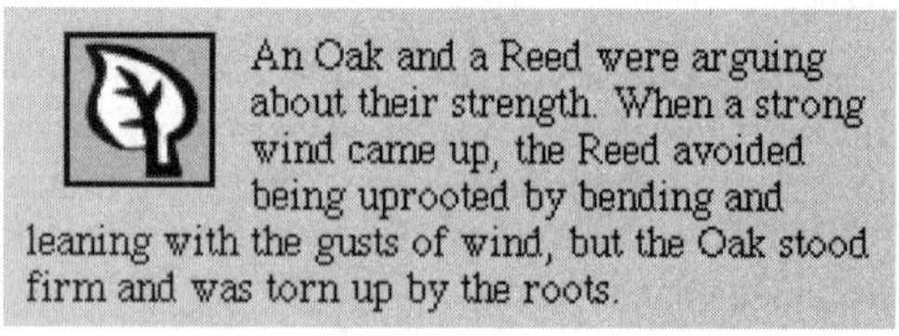

An Oak and a Reed were arguing about their strength. When a strong wind came up, the Reed avoided being uprooted by bending and leaning with the gusts of wind, but the Oak stood firm and was torn up by the roots.

Figure 12-6. Image alignment with horizontal spacing

The preferred CSS method for adding space around the sides of the image is to simply apply an amount of margin around it. The various `margin` properties allow you to apply different amounts of space to each side of the floated image. CSS margins are discussed in Chapter 19.

Stopping text wrap

Text automatically wraps to fill the space along the side of an aligned image (or other inline object). To stop the text from wrapping and start the next line against the margin (instead of against the image), insert a line break (`br`) with the `clear` attribute.

The `clear` attribute gives the browser directions on where to place the new line. It has three possible values: `left`, `right`, and `all`. If an image is aligned right, insert `<br clear="right" />` to begin the text below the image against the right margin. For left-aligned images, use `<br clear="left" />`. The `<br clear="all" />` element starts the text below the image on both margins, so it may be the only value you'll ever need. Figure 12-7 shows the result of this markup.

```
<p><img src="leaf.gif" alt="leaf illustration" align="left" hspace="12" />An
Oak and a Reed were arguing about strength. <br clear="all" />When a strong
wind came up,...
```

An Oak and a Reed were arguing about their strength.

When a strong wind came up, the Reed avoided being uprooted by bending and leaning with the gusts of wind, but the Oak stood firm and was torn up by the roots.

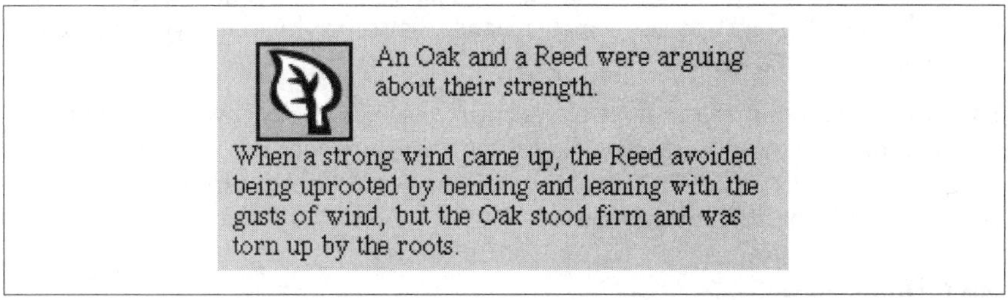

Figure 12-7. The clear attribute starts the next line below an aligned image

The preferred CSS method for preventing the following element from starting next to the floated image is to apply the `clear` property to the following element and specify the side (`left`, `right`, or `both`) that you want to start below any floated objects. Clearing is discussed in Chapter 21.

Borders

By default, when an image is linked, most browsers display a two-pixel-wide border around the image in the same color as the text links on the page (bright blue by default). In most cases, this blue border is visually unappealing, particularly around an image with transparent edges, but it is quite simple to turn it off using the `border` attribute.

The `border` attribute specifies the width of the border in number of pixels. Specifying a value of zero turns the borders off:

```
<a href="document.html"><img src="picture.gif" border="0" /></a>
```

Of course, if you are fond of the borders, you could just as easily make them really wide by setting a higher number value.

In the preferred CSS method, you set the border width for all the images in a document with one simple style rule using the border property:

```
img {border: 0;}
```

For more information on controlling the borders around images, see Chapter 19.

Image Loading Techniques

A couple of simple practices, which may not be obvious from simply looking at HTML markup, can help you optimize your pages and improve response time.

Reuse images whenever possible

When a browser downloads an image file, it stores it in the disk cache (a space for temporarily storing files on the hard disk). That way, if it needs to redisplay the page, it can just pull up a local copy of the HTML and image files without making a new trip out to the remote server.

When you use the same image repetitively in a page or a site, the browser only needs to download the image once. Every subsequent instance of the image is grabbed from the local cache, which means less traffic for the server and faster display for the end user.

The browser recognizes an image by its entire pathname, not just the filename, so if you want to take advantage of file caching, be sure that each instance of your image is pointing to the same image file on the server (not multiple copies of the same image file in different directories).

Link to large images

Remember that when designing for the Web, you must always consider the time it takes to download files. Images are particularly bandwidth-hungry, so you should use them with care. One successful strategy for providing access to very large images (with correspondingly large file sizes) is to provide a postage-stamp–size preview image that links to the full-size image. Be sure to provide information necessary to help users decide whether they want to spend the time clicking the link, such as a description of what they're going to get and the file size of the image (so they can make an estimate of how long they'll need to wait).

Image Maps

Ordinarily, placing an image within an anchor element makes the entire image a link to a single document when the user clicks anywhere on the image. As an alternative, you can create an *image map* that contains multiple links, or "hotspots," within a single image. The effect is created with HTML markup (some image maps also use scripts on the server) and an ordinary image that serves as a backdrop for the pixel coordinates.

Favicons

Another type of image you often see in association with web sites is the *favicon*, a small icon that appears with the name or URL of a site in the Favorites list (in Internet Explorer 6), or the location bar and tabs in a tabbed browsing interface (Mozilla and Safari). Favicons are not related to (X)HTML image markup as discussed in this chapter, but this is as logical a point as any to discuss how to create a favicon for your site.

Creating the Icon

A favicon must be saved in the Windows *.ico* format. The *.ico* format is capable of storing several images and is typically used to hold several size variations of the same image. The favicons that appear in the browser location bar or favorites list are 16×16 pixels. Some designers also include a 32×32 pixel version that may be used for as desktop shortcut icon.

Once you have designed an icon, it is recommended to save it as a PNG (to take advantage of transparency) and then convert it to *.ico* format. File converters for both Windows and Mac are listed at the end of the sidebar. When you save the file, it must be named exactly *favicon.ico* to be recognized by all favicon-supporting browsers.

Installing the Favicon

The simplest way to install a favicon is simply to upload the *favicon.ico* file to the root directory of the site. It is also possible to install favicons to other directories for instances when you wish to use different icons for different areas of the site. While some browsers will find the favicon with no markup at all, to play it safe, include link elements in the head of the document that point to the icon you intend to use. A relative URL may also be provided, such as */favicon. ico*.

```
<link rel="shortcut icon" href="http://domain.tld/path/favicon.ico"
type="image/x-icon" />
<link rel="icon" href=" http://domain.tld/path/favicon.ico" type="image/x-
icon" />
```

Providing links for "icon" and "shortcut icon" covers all bases of browser compatibility. A relative URL may also be provided, such as */favicon.ico*.

Favicon Resources

For an in-depth tutorial on creating favicons, I recommend *www.december14. net/ways/rest/favicon.shtml*.

To convert a graphic to ICO format on a Macintosh, try the IconBuilder plug-in for Photoshop, available from IconFactory (*www.iconfactory.com/iconbuilder. asp*).

—Continued—

Windows users have more options, including RealWorld Icon Editor (*www.rw-designer.com/3D_icon_editor.php*) and IconCool Studio (*www.iconcool.com/iconcoolstudio.htm*). There is also a free command-line converter, called *png2ico*, by Matthias Benkmann, which is available at *www.winterdrache.de/freeware/png2ico/index.html*.

There are two types of image maps: client-side and server-side. For *client-side image maps*, the coordinate and URL information necessary to create each link is contained right in the document. The process of putting the pieces together happens in the browser on the user's machine (thus, client-side). For *server-side image maps*, as the name suggests, the map information resides on the server and is processed by the server or a separate CGI script.

Client-side image maps are far more prevalent than server-side, which are rarely used due to critical accessibility issues. In fact, due to new techniques and philosophies in web design, even client-side image maps are waning in popularity. Image maps generally require text to be sunk into an image, which is sternly frowned upon. In terms of site optimization, they force all regions of the image to be saved in the same file format, which may lead to unnecessarily large file sizes.

That said, take a look at what it takes to make a client-side image map.

Creating Image Maps

The key to making image maps work is a text-based map that associates pixel coordinates with URLs. This map is handled differently for client-side and server-side (as outlined in the following sections), but the outcome is the same. When the user clicks somewhere within the image, the browser passes the coordinates of the mouse pointer to the map, which, in turn, generates the appropriate link.

Available tools

Although it is possible to put together image map information manually, it is much easier to use a tool to do it.

If you use any of the Macromedia or Adobe web design software packages, you're in luck, because there are image map tools built into both their HTML editors and web image programs. The image map tools in Dreamweaver and GoLive are particularly handy because you can create the image map right in the current document window.

 As of this writing, the future of these specific products is unclear based on the initial announcement of Adobe's acquisition of Macromedia. It is fairly certain that some sort of image map tool will be available when the dust settles.

There are also standalone image map creation utilities available as shareware. One popular option is MapEdit, by Tom Boutell, available at *www.boutell.com/mapedit/*. It costs $10 and is available for Windows, Mac OS X, and Unix. A search for "image map tool" on your search engine of choice will turn up many more options.

Creating the map

Regardless of the tool you're using, and regardless of the type of image map you're creating, the process for creating the map information is basically the same. Read the documentation for your image map tool to learn about features not listed here.

1. Open the image in an image map program.

2. Define areas within the image that should be clickable by using the appropriate shape tools: rectangle, circle, or polygon (for tracing irregular shapes).

3. While the outline of the area is still highlighted, enter a URL for that area in the text entry field provided, as shown in Figure 12-8.

4. Continue adding shapes and their respective URLs for each clickable area in the image.

5. For server-side image maps, you also need to define a default URL, which is the page that displays if users click outside a defined area. Many tools have a prominent field for entering the default URL, but on others, you may need to look for it under a pull-down menu.

6. Select the type of image map (client- or server-side) you want to create. Note that server-side image maps are strongly discouraged.

7. Save or export the map information. Server-side image maps are saved in a map definition file (*.map*) that resides on the server. For client-side image maps, you may need to copy and paste the resulting map code into your HTML file.

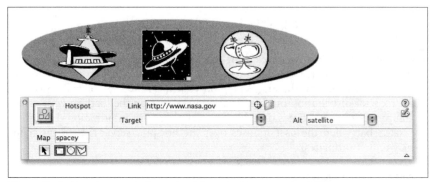

Figure 12-8. Creating map information (shown in Dreamweaver MX)

If you do not have an image map tool, it is possible to write out the map information by hand following the examples in this chapter. Simply note the pixel coordinates of the shapes as indicated in an image editing program (in Photoshop, they are provided in the Info palette) and type them into the appropriate place in the map file.

Client-Side Image Maps

Client-side image maps have three components:

- An ordinary image file (*.gif*, *.jpeg*, or *.png*)
- A map delimited by the map element containing the coordinate and URL information for each clickable area (described by area elements contained within the map element)
- The usemap attribute within the image element (img) that indicates which map to reference

map

`<map>...</map>`

Attributes

Core (id, class, style, title), *Internationalization, Events*
id="*text*"
name="*text*"

area

`<area />`

Attributes

Core (id, class, style, title), *Internationalization, Events, Focus*
alt="text" *(Required)*
coords="values"
href="url"
nohref
shape="rect|circle|poly|default"
target="*text*"

There are many advantages to using client-side image maps. They are self-contained within the HTML document and do not rely on a server to function. This means you can test the image map on your local machine or make working site demos for distribution on disk. It also cuts down on the load on your server and improves response times. In addition, complete URL information displays in the status bar when the user mouses over the hotspot (server-side image maps display only coordinates).

Sample client-side image map

This is the markup for the client-side image map pictured in Figure 12-9. While most authors use a web authoring tool to generate map markup such as this, it is helpful to have an understanding of what is happening in the map, area, and img elements. Each component of the image map will be discussed in turn.

```
<map name="spacey">
<area shape="rect" coords="203,23,285,106"
href=http://www.nasa.gov alt=""/>
```

```
<area shape="circle" coords="372,64,40" href="mypage.html" alt=""/>
<area shape="poly"
coords="99,47,105,41,94,39,98,34,110,35,115,28,120,35,133,38,133,
42,124,42,134,58,146,56,157,58,162,63,158,67,141,68,145,72,155,
73,158,75,159,80,148,83,141,83,113,103,87,83,72,83,64,80,64,76,
68,73,77,72,79,63,70,59,67,53,68,47,78,45,89,45,99,47"
href="yourpage.html" alt=""/>
</map>

<img src="orbit.gif" width="500" height="125" border="0" usemap="#spacey" />
```

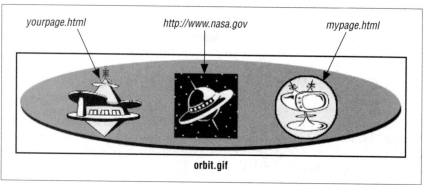

Figure 12-9. An image map

`<map name="spacey">`

This marks the beginning of the map. You must give the map a name. Within the map element there are area elements for each hotspot within the image.

`<area shape="rect" coords="203,23,285,106" href=http://www.nasa.gov alt=""/>`

Each area element contains the shape identifier (shape), pixel coordinates (coords), and the URL for the link (href). In this case, the shape is the rectangle (rect) that corresponds to the black square in the center of the image. The value of the coords attribute identifies the top-left and bottom-right pixel positions of the rectangle (coords="x1,y1,x2,y2"). Some browsers also support the nonstandard rectangle as an equivalent to rect, but this is not widely supported.

In each area element, the alt attribute provides the alternative text for that region of the image. The alt attribute is a required attribute for the area element.

`<area shape="circle" coords="372,64,40" href="mypage.html" alt=""/>`

This area corresponds to the circular area on the right of the image in Figure 12-9. Its shape is circle. For circles, the first two coordinates identify the position of the center of the circle and the third value is its radius in pixels (coords="x,y,r"). Some browsers also support the nonstandard circ as an equivalent to circle.

```
<area shape="poly"
coords="99,47,105,41,94,…additional coordinates omitted to save space… "
    href="yourpage.html" alt=""/>
```
This is the area element for the irregular (polygon) shape on the left of the image in Figure 12-9. For polygons, the coordinates are pairs of x,y coordinates for each point or vertex along the path that surrounds the area (`coords="x1,y1,x2,y2,x3,y3..."`). At least three pairs are required to define a triangle; complex polygons generate a long list of coordinates. Some browsers also support the nonstandard polygon as an equivalent to poly.

```
<img src="orbit.gif" width="500" height="125" border="0" usemap=
    "#spacey" />
```
The usemap attribute is required within the image element to indicate that this image is an image map that uses the map named "spacey."

Server-Side Image Maps

In the first years of the Web, all image maps were server-side image maps (client-side image maps were introduced later). Because they rely on the server, they are less portable and the information is not self-contained, which introduces serious accessibility problems if the server is not available. As of this writing, the use of server-side image maps is strongly discouraged.

For historical interest, a description of how they work is provided here. Server-side image maps have four elements:

- An ordinary image file (*.gif*, *.jpeg*, or *.png*).
- HTML markup in the document: the ismap attribute within the img element and an anchor (a) element that links the image to the *.map* file on the server.
- A map definition file (*.map*) containing the pixel coordinate and URL information for each clickable area; the *.map* file resides on the server, usually in a directory called *cgi-bin*. The map file format is server-dependent and may be formatted as either "NCSA" or "CERN."
- A CGI script that runs on the server (or a built-in function of the server software) that interprets the *.map* file and sends the correct URL to the HTTP server.

Within the HTML file, the image map is set up as shown in this example:

```
<a href="/cgi-bin/imagemap/spacey.map"><img src="x.gif" ismap /></a>
```

Embedded Media

Images aren't the only things that can be displayed as part of a web page. You can also include content such as QuickTime movies, interactive Flash files, all manner of Java applets, and more. The browser renders embedded media files using the provided self-contained code (as in the case of an applet), using its built-in display devices (as for GIF or JPEG images), or by taking advantage of a plug-in or helper application (as for Windows Media or Flash).

The elements that embed media in (X)HTML are:

object
> The W3C recommended element for all media

applet
> For Java applets; deprecated in HTML 4.01 and XHTML 1.0

There is a third nonstandard (and therefore, nonvalidating) element for embedding media that is still used by browsers that use Netscape's plug-in architecture:

embed
> For plug-in dependent media; not part of any HTML Recommendation

Now, take a closer look at each of these elements and their uses.

The object Element

According to the HTML 4.01 Recommendation, the object element is an all-purpose object-placer. It can be used to place a variety of object types on a web page, including applets, movies, interactive objects (Flash), and even plain old images. As of this writing, browser support does not quite fulfill the W3C's vision for this element (for example, it still may not be used reliably as a replacement for the img element), however, the object element is still used for a wide range of embedded media.

object

```
<object>...</object>
```

Attributes

> *Core* (id, class, style, title), *Internationalization, Events*
> archive="*URLs*"
> classid="*URL*"
> codebase="*URL*"
> codetype="*codetype*"
> data="*URL*"
> declare="declare"
> height="*number*"
> name="*text*"
> standby="*message*"
> tabindex="*number*"
> type="*type*"
> usemap="*URL*"
> width="*number*"

Deprecated attributes

> align="baseline|bottom|left|middle|right|top"
> border="*number*"
> hspace="*number*"
> vspace="*number*"

param

```
<param />
```

Attributes

id="*text*"
name="*text*" *(Required)*
value="*text*"
valuetype="data|ref|object"
type="*content type*"

The object element began as a proprietary element in Internet Explorer to support ActiveX and later Java applets. Netscape Navigator initially supported only embed and applet (discussed later in this chapter) for embedding media, but added limited object support in its Version 4 release, and improved (yet still improperly implemented) support in Version 6. The W3C intends the object element, now part of the HTML 4.01 and XHTML Recommendations, to be a replacement for the more specific img and applet elements as well as the nonstandard embed and bgsound (used for background sounds).

The attributes required for the object element vary with the type of content it is placing. The object element may also contain a number of param elements that pass important information to the object when it displays or plays. Not all objects require additional parameters.

The object and param elements work together to allow authors to specify three types of information:

The implementation of the object.   That is, the executable code that runs in order to render the object. This may be a tool or player required to display an external file (such as the QuickTime plug-in for showing a *.mov* file), or it may be the object itself, such as a self-contained clock applet. The implementation is specified with the classid attribute.

The data to be rendered.   The data attribute specifies the URL of the data; in most cases, an external file, such as a movie or a PDF file. According to the HTML 4.01 spec, the data attribute may also be used to provide the raw data right there in the object element.

Additional settings required by the object at runtime.   Some embedded media objects require additional settings that get called into play when the object plays or is rendered. For example, when placing a Windows Media movie, authors have the option of adding a variety of controls, turning the "AutoStart" feature on or off, and many more features specific to the Windows Media Player. The runtime settings are provided with param elements within the object. Examples of the param element are provided later in this section.

Authors may not need to provide all three types of information for an object. For example, for a self-contained applet, you may only need to specify the implementation. If you know that the browser has built-in capacities to render an object (such as a GIF image), then only the data for the image and a description of the data type are required. And as noted above, not all objects require additional parameters.

Specifying data and type

To get a basic idea of how the object element works, take a look at this minimal markup example that uses the object element to place an inline image.

```
<object data="daffodil.gif" type="image/gif">
A color photograph of a daffodil.
</object>
```

Here, the data attribute provides the URL for the source for the embedded object (in this case an image file) and type tells the browser that the content type is a GIF image. When a type attribute is provided, the browser uses that information to determine how (and if) to render the object. The browser's preferences contain a list that specifies how to handle each content type, be it via native support, a plug-in player, or an external helper application. If the type is not recognized, the browser may not be able to render the object. In this example, the browser can render a GIF image without the need of a special player.

 While the syntax exists for adding images with the object element, the img element is still the most common way to go due to lack of browser support of object for image placement.

Specifying an implementation

The object element is also commonly used with the classid attribute for specifying the implementation, such as an ActiveX control, Java applet, or Python applet. This example shows an object element used to place a Java applet on a page. (Note that some applets require placement with the applet element for proper functionality.)

```
<object classid="java:calendar.class" codetype="application/java"
standby="Calendar loading..." width="200" height="150" title="basic
calendar">...</object>
```

The Java applet is called with the classid attribute. The optional codetype attribute specifies the content type of the data that will be downloaded by the classid. A browser may use the value of the codetype attribute to avoid downloading information for a content type it does not support. The optional standby attribute provides a message to be displayed while the applet is loading.

Some plug-in media and applets require width and height values in order to play correctly, so be sure to read any documentation provided for your media type. It is good practice to provide width and height measurements for every object element.

Adding parameters

These days, it is more common to see the object element used to place an ActiveX control (Internet Explorer's version of plug-ins) than an applet. ActiveX controls are identified by the naming scheme clsid, followed by a long string of characters specific to the ActiveX control required to render the media object. ActiveX controls typically require additional settings used to control the display or playback of the object. These settings are provided by param elements as shown in this example for embedding a Windows Media movie.

```
<object classid="clsid:6BF52A52-394A-11d3-B153-00C04F79FAA6" height="280"
width="320" codebase="http://activex.microsoft.com/activex/controls/mplayer/
en/nsmp2inf.cab#version=6,4,7,111">
  <param name="URL" value="movies/europe.wmv" />
  <param name="autoStart" value="false" />
  <param name="UIMode" value="full" />
</object>
```

Here, the classid attribute points to the ActiveX control for the Windows Media Player 9. The codebase attribute is intended to be used to provide a base path used to resolve relative URIs specified by the classid, data, and archive attributes. In practice, however, it has come to be (mis)used as a pointer to a location for downloading the current ActiveX control or plug-in if it is not installed on the user's computer, as is the case in this example.

Within the object element, there are three param elements that pass important information to the ActiveX control. The parameters and values are provided by the name and value attributes, respectively. In this example, the URL parameter provides the location of the movie itself, autoStart is set to false, so the user needs to click to start playback, and the UIMode setting instructs the player to display the full control panel for playing the movie.

Parameter names and their values are specific to the media object, so these name/value pairs do not work with any other media type (not even older versions of Windows Media Player).

Providing alternate content

If the browser determines that it cannot render the specified object, it then proceeds to render the content of the object element. In the example from earlier in this section, should the browser not have the capacity to render the GIF, it will display the alternative content ("A color photograph of a daffodil") instead.

```
<object data="daffodil.gif" type="image/gif" width="150" height="125">
A color photograph of a daffodil.
</object>
```

The alternative content may also be another object element. Authors may provide several layers of alternate content by nesting objects with different implementations. The user agent will keep looking inside each object element until it finds an object that it can render.

In this example, borrowed from the HTML 4.01 Recommendation, a Python applet is embedded on the page with the object element. If the browser can't render the applet, an MPEG video is provided as a backup. If the video cannot be rendered, there is a static GIF image, and finally, a text description is provided if all else fails.

```
<object title="The Earth as seen from space" classid="http://www.observer.
mars/TheEarth.py">
    <object data="TheEarth.mpeg" type="application/mpeg">
        <object data="TheEarth.gif" type="image/gif">
```

```
                The Earth as seen from space.
            </object>
        </object>
    </object>
```

Cross-browser compatibility

In an ideal world, authors could embed objects by simply specifying the data and data type for the media file and perhaps a few additional parameters, as shown in this example that should be sufficient for placing a QuickTime movie:

```
<object type="video/quicktime" data="/movies/arlo.mov" width="320"
height="256">
    <param name="autostart" value="false" />
    <param name="controller" value="true" />
</object>
```

Unfortunately, while most standards-compliant browsers correctly interpret the object element, the markup required to make embedded media play correctly with all their features on all browsers is determined by the individual media players, not the browsers. For example, as of this writing, the QuickTime plug-in player does not accept settings from param elements, so it still requires the nonstandard embed element for all but the default playback settings. The embed element is discussed further in the next section.

To ensure that the embedded media renders or plays for the widest range of browsers and platforms, developers use this strategy that takes advantage of nesting within object elements for providing alternate content:

- Typically, the top-level object element contains the classid for an ActiveX control that will do the trick for the 80% or so of users with Internet Explorer on Windows.

- Within that object, provide an alternate object specifying the data and data type that allows other browsers to choose their own method for rendering the object based on the data type.

There is a bug in Internet Explorer for Windows that causes both object elements to be rendered, even though according to the HTML 4.01 Recommendation, only the first supported object element should appear. Therefore, it is necessary to take measures to make sure only one object appears, such as those in these examples:

- A tutorial on standards-compliant QuickTime embedding uses style sheets to hide the redundant object element (*realdev1. realise.com/rossa/rendertest/quicktime.html*).

- This exploration on the "right" way to embed Flash movies uses Internet Explorer's conditional comments to display just one object based on browser version (see *weblogs. macromedia.com/accessibility/archives/2005/08/in_search_of_a. cfm*). The resulting code is provided in the example below.

- At this point, the page should be tested for full functionality on all the browsers that must be supported. If the object renders or plays fine, you're done. If not, there is one more option...

- The ultimate fallback is the embed element that works with all browsers that use the Netscape plug-in architecture. An embed element with attributes for controlling runtime parameters may be used within or in place of the inner data/type object. While this ensures that the media will play in most browsers, the trade-off is that it is a nonstandard element that will cause your document to be invalid. Authors must determine whether their greatest priority is a valid (X)HTML document or complete media support for users without IE for Windows.

The following examples show two approaches to providing alternate content for an embedded Flash movie that ensures the widest browser support. The first uses the default code generated by the Flash authoring tool for embedding the Flash object on the page. It uses the object element with an ActiveX classid for Internet Explorer and the nonstandard embed element for browsers that use plug-ins.

```
<object classid="clsid:D27CDB6E-AE6D-11cf-96B8-444553540000"
codebase="http://download.macromedia.com/pub/shockwave/cabs/flash/swflash.
cab#version=6,0,40,0"
        width="300" height="120">
    <param name="movie" value="/flash.swf" />
    <param name="quality" value="high" />
    <param name="bgcolor" value="#FFFFFF" />

        <embed src="/flash.swf" type="application/x-shockwave-flash"
            quality="high" bgcolor="#FFFFFF" width="300" height="120"
            pluginspage="http://www.macromedia.com/go/getflashplayer">
        <noembed>You need the Flash player</noembed>
        </embed>
</object>
```

This version uses standards-compliant nested objects with Microsoft's proprietary conditional comments to make sure only the correct object renders in Internet Explorer. The inner object may be used by Gecko-based browsers.

```
<object classid="clsid:D27CDB6E-AE6D-11cf-96B8-444553540000"
codebase="http://download.macromedia.com/pub/shockwave/cabs/flash/swflash.
cab#version=6,0,40,0"
        width="300" height="120">
    <param name="movie" value="/flash.swf" />
    <param name="quality" value="high" />
    <param name="bgcolor" value="#FFFFFF" />

    <!--[if !IE]> <-->
    <object data=" /flash.swf" type="application/x-shockwave-flash"
width="300" height="120" >
        <param name="quality" value="high" />
        <param name="bgcolor" value="#FFFFFF" />
        <param name="pluginurl" value="http://www.macromedia.com/go/
getflashplayer" />
```

```
        You need the Flash player.
    </object>

    <!--> <![endif]-->

    </object>
```

 There are other methods for ensuring cross-browser compatibility that use JavaScript and browser-sniffing techniques, but they are beyond the scope of this chapter.

The embed Element

The nonstandard embed element was addressed briefly in the previous section. Here it is covered in more detail. The embed element was originally created by Netscape for use with plug-in technologies. It is currently supported by most browsers; however, because it is not included in any HTML Recommendation, it will cause (X)HTML documents to be invalid. Whenever possible, authors are advised to use object for multimedia objects and use embed as a last resort fallback. All available attributes for the embed element are described in Appendix A.

embed

<embed>...</embed> or (<embed />)

Attributes

```
align="left|right|top|bottom"
height="number"
hidden="yes|no"
name="text"
palette="foreground|background"
pluginspage="URL"
src="URL" (Required)
width="number"
```

Netscape Navigator only

```
border="number"
frameborder="yes|no"
hspace="number"
pluginurl="URL"
type="media (MIME) type"
vspace="number"
```

There is conflicting documentation inline as to whether the embed element requires an end tag. Some sources say an end tag is required, as shown here:

```
<embed src="url" type="content-type" height="n-pixels" width="n-pixels">
</embed>
```

Microsoft documentation shows embed as an empty element and modern browsers seem to support the empty embed syntax, shown here:

```
<embed src="url" type="contenttype" height="n-pixels" width="n-pixels" />
```

The src attribute is required to tell the browser the location of the media file to be played. The type attribute specifies the content type of the embedded media. The browser uses the content-type information (or the suffix of the media file) to find the appropriate plug-in to render or play the file. Many media types require that width and height values (the dimensions of the plug-in element in pixels) be specified in order for the plug-in to function.

The optional pluginspage attribute provides the URL of a page where the user can download information for the required plug-in should it not be found on the client machine. Netscape 4.0 introduced the pluginurl attribute, which specifies a link to a function that installs the plug-in automatically. To hide the media file or object from view, use the hidden attribute with a value of yes.

The embed element uses special attributes and their values for additional runtime settings (the same settings provided with param elements in the object element). These attributes are specific to the media type and the plug-in. For example, the autoplay and playeveryframe attributes are used by the QuickTime player only. (The attributes listed for the embed element work for all embedded media.)

noembed

The noembed element is used within the embed element and provides alternative content that displays if the browser cannot display the specified media file.

noembed

```
<noembed>...</noembed>
```

Attributes

> None

In the following example, the browser would display a GIF image and brief message in place of the media object.

```
<embed src="movies/vacation.mov" width="240" height="196" autoplay="false"
pluginspage="http://www.apple.com/quicktime/download/">
    <noembed><img src="vacation.gif"> You do not seem to have the plugin.
    </noembed>
</embed>
```

Using embed

Although the embed element is still in common use as of this writing, and is actually recommended by multimedia format developers such as Macromedia and Apple, eventually full plug-in functionality will be possible using the standard object element alone. If you do use embed elements, consider making a note of where they appear so you can clean up your documents and make them valid when that day arrives.

Java Applets

Java is an object-oriented programming language developed by Sun Microsystems. It is *not* related to JavaScript, which is a scripting language developed by Netscape to run within an HTML document in a browser. Because Java is a full programming language (like C or C++), it can be used to create whole applications.

Java's primary contribution to web content, however, has been in the form of *Java applets*, which are self-contained, mini-executable programs. These programs, named with the *.class* suffix, can be placed right on the web page, like an image. Java applets can be used for all sorts of interactive and multimedia gadgets, such as clocks, calculators, spreadsheets, scrolling marquees, games, text effects, and digital "guitars," just to name a few.

There was a great buzz among web developers when Java applets first hit the scene, but since then, enthusiasm has waned in the face of performance issues (applets take a long time to initialize and tend to crash browsers) and the dominance of Flash for multimedia and interactivity.

Where to Get Applets

If you need a customized applet for your site, your best bet is to hire a programmer to create one to your specifications. However, there are a number of applets available for free or for a licensing fee that you can download from libraries on the Web.

A good place to start is the applets section of Sun's Java site at *java.sun.com/applets/*. This page provides a list of links to applet-related resources.

If you are looking for cool applets you can use right away, try the JavaBoutique at *javaboutique.internet.com*. Here you will find hundreds of applets available for download as well as clear instructions for their use. It's a great way to add interactivity to your site without learning any programming.

Adding an Applet to a Page

There are currently two methods for adding an applet to a web page: the object element, recommended by HTML 4.01, and the better supported, though deprecated, applet element.

applet

```
<applet>...</applet>
```

This element is deprecated.

Attributes

> *Core* (id, class, style, title)
> alt="*text*"
> archive="*URLs*"
> code="*class*" *(Required)*

```
codebase="URL"
height="number"
name="text"
object="text"
width="number"
```

Deprecated attributes
```
align="left|right|top|middle|bottom"
hspace="number"
vspace="number"
```

The W3C has deprecated the applet element and all its attributes in favor of the object element. Despite this, the applet element may still be the better choice, because browser support for object-embedded applets is so inconsistent that it is difficult to find an approach that works in all browsers. In addition, some applets require that applet be used, so read the documentation for the applet first. This section looks at both methods.

Adding applets with applet

The applet element is a container for any number of parameter (param) elements. The following is an example of how an applet element for a game might look:

```
<applet codebase=class code="Wacky.class" width="300" height="400">
  <param name="Delay" value="250" />
  <param name="Time" value="120" />
  <param name="PlaySounds" value="YES" />
</applet>
```

The applet element contains a number of standard attributes:

code

> Tells the browser which applet will be used. Applets end with the suffix *.class* or *.jar*. This attribute is required.

codebase

> This tells the browser in which directory to find the applets. If the applets are in the same directory as the page, the codebase attribute is not necessary.

width, height

> These specify the pixel dimensions of the "window" the applet will occupy. These attributes are required for the Java applet to function properly.

The applet element may also use many of the same attributes used for images, such as alt for providing alternative text if the applet cannot be displayed, and presentational attributes such as align (for positioning the applet in the flow of text), and hspace/vspace (used in conjunction with align).

Special parameters for the applet are provided by any number of parameter elements (sometimes there are none). The param element always contains the name of the parameter (name) and its value (value). Parameters provide special settings and controls that are specific to the particular applet, so you need to follow the parameter coding instructions provided by the programmer of the applet.

Adding applets with object

You can add a simple, self-contained applet to an HTML document using the object element like this:

```
<object classid="applet.class" codebase="http://somedomain.com/classes/">
An applet with some useful function should display in this space.
</object>
```

The classid attribute points to the applet itself (its implementation). It has the same function as the code attribute in the applet element when used for Java applets. classid may not contain any pathname information, so the location of the class file is provided by the codebase attribute.

When using object for Java applets, the object element may contain a number of parameter (param) elements, as with the applet element. (Note that Netscape 4.0 does not support param elements within object, so it may not play applets correctly if placed this way.)

Inline (Floating) Frames

Microsoft Internet Explorer 3.0 introduced a feature called *inline frames* (also called floating frames) that are identified with the iframe element. They enable an HTML document to be embedded within another HTML document, viewed in a scrollable frame. An iframe is placed in the document flow as an inline element, much like an image.

iframe

```
<iframe> ... </iframe>
```

Attributes

```
Core (id, class, style, title)
frameborder="1|0"
height="number"
longdesc="URL"
marginheight="number"
marginwidth="number"
name="text"
scrolling="yes|no|auto"
src="URL"
width="number"
```

Deprecated attributes

```
align="top|middle|bottom|left|right"
```

Nonstandard attributes

```
hspace="number"
vspace="number"
```

The iframe element is part of the HTML 4.01 and XHTML 1.0 Transitional DTD. As such, it is also included in the Frameset DTD, but it is not a frameset-related element. It is supported by standards-compliant browsers. It is however deprecated, and the preferred strict alternative is to use the object element instead, its type attribute explicitly set to text/html, and its data attribute set to the URL of the external document. Inline frames do not work in Netscape 4, but that accounts for a less than .5% of users as of this writing.

The iframe element places an external HTML document on a web page in a scrolling window. The src attribute provides the URL of the external document. The width and height attributes provide the dimensions of the floating frame. Figure 12-10 shows the resulting inline frame specified in this markup example.

```
<body bgcolor="black" text="white">

<h1>Inline (Floating) Frames</h1>

<p><iframe src="list.html" width="200" height="100" align="left">
Your browser does not support inline frames. Read the list <a href="list.
html">here</a>.</iframe></p>

<p>Consectetuer adipiscing elit. Sed eu nibh eget magna dictum egestas...
</p>
</body>
```

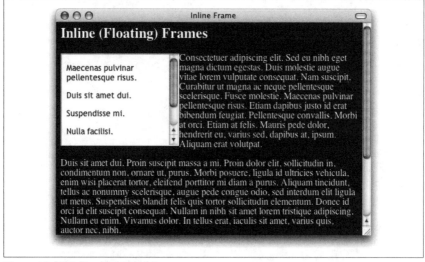

Figure 12-10. Inline (floating) frame

13

Tables

HTML table elements, first introduced in Netscape 1.1, were developed to give authors a way to present rows and columns of tabular data. In fact, that has always been and remains their intended use. But it didn't take long for designers, fed up with the one-column, full-width web pages, to co-opt tables as a tool for controlling page layout. For the last 10 years, complex table-based layouts have been the norm. Nobody cared much that it was a misuse of the table elements—there weren't any other options. Today, we do have an option. Cascading Style Sheets offer the ability to create multicolumn pages and sophisticated layouts that were previously achievable only with tables. With improved browser support, pure style sheet layouts are finally a viable solution.

So tables-for-layout are out, but that doesn't mean that the whole set of table elements has been tossed in the dustbin. In fact, tables are still the appropriate markup choice for real tabular data, such as schedules, statistics, and so on.

This chapter takes on the topic of HTML tables, starting with their basic structure and markup and moving on to methods that make data tables accessible when rendered non-visually. Tips for using layout tables responsibly are included as well. Along the way, the following table-related elements will be addressed.

table	Establishes a table
tr	Table row
td	Table cell
th	Table header cell
caption	Provides a table caption
thead	Identifies a table header
tbody	Identifies the body of the table
tfoot	Identifies a table footer
col	Declares a column
colgroup	Declares a group of columns

Table Uses

HTML tables fall into two broad categories: data tables and layout tables. This section takes a look at both types.

Data Tables

Data tables, the arrangement of information in rows and columns, are the intended use of HTML table elements. In visual browsers, the arrangement of data in rows and columns gives users an instant understanding of the relationships between data cells and their respective header labels. These relationships may be lost for users without the benefit of visual presentation unless care is taken to author the data table with accessibility in mind. These techniques are discussed in the upcoming "Accessible Tables" section.

Tables may be used to present calendars, schedules, statistics, or other types of information as shown in Figure 13-1. Note that "data" doesn't necessarily mean numbers. A table cell may contain any sort of information, including numbers, text elements, even images or multimedia objects.

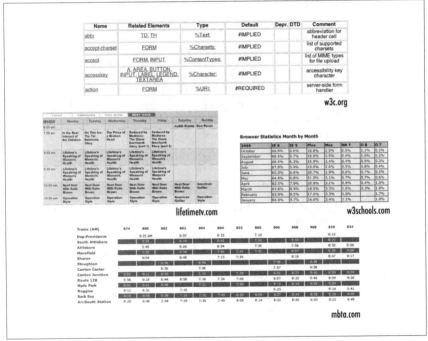

Figure 13-1. Examples of data tables

Layout Tables

Layout tables, unlike data tables, are used purely as a presentational device for controlling the layout of a page. The HTML 4.01 Recommendation specifically discourages this use of tables, but it wasn't until CSS became a viable alternative that they have been condemned by the professional web community at large as well.

You can't turn around on the Web without bumping into a site—even big-name sites—that still uses tables for layout. Some sites use tables as a minimal framework; others have complex tables nested several layers deep to hold things together. Figure 13-2 shows just a few examples of layout tables of varying levels of complexity. The borders have been enhanced to reveal the table structure. (As not to point any fingers, these "old-school" examples are all my own work; I assure you, I've changed my ways.)

Figure 13-2. Examples of layout tables

While we are still in a period of transition from table-based design to totally CSS-based design (with flawless browser support, of course), some authors still choose to use tables to establish the basic column structure of the page. While not ideal, it can be done responsibly by using style sheets to keep the table markup minimal and with a mind toward accessibility. These strategies are discussed in the "Responsible Layout Tables" section at the end of this chapter.

Basic Table Structure

Put simply, web tables are made up of cells (which is where the content goes), arranged into rows. The HTML table model is said to be "row primary" because rows are identified explicitly in the document structure, while columns are just implied. The following examples illustrate the basic structure of an HTML table.

Rows and Cells

The minimum elements for defining a table are table, for establishing the table itself, tr for declaring a table row, and td for creating table cells within the row. Explanations and examples of how these elements fit together follow these element and attribute listings.

table

```
<table>...</table>
```

Attributes

    Core (id, class, style, title), *Internationalization, Events*
    border="*number*"
    cellpadding="*number of pixels or %*"
    cellspacing="*number of pixels or %*"
    frame="void|above|below|hsides|lhs|rhs|vsides|box|border"
    rules="all|cols|groups|none|rows"
    summary="*text*"
    width="*number, percentage*"

Deprecated attributes

    align="left|right|center"
    bgcolor="*#rrggbb*" or "*color name*"

Nonstandard attributes

    height="*number, percentage*"

tr

```
<tr>...</tr>
```

Attributes

    Core (id, class, style, title), *Internationalization, Events*
    align="left|center|right|justify|char"
    char="*character*"
    charoff="*length*"
    valign="top|middle|bottom|baseline"

Deprecated attributes

    bgcolor="*#rrggbb*" or "*color name*"

td

```
<td>...</td>
```

Attributes

Core (id, class, style, title), *Internationalization, Events*
abbr="*text*"
align="left|right|center|justify|char"
axis="*text*"
char="*character*"
charoff="*length*"
colspan="*number*"
headers="*id references*"
rowspan="*number*"
scope="row|col|rowgroup|colgroup"
valign="top|middle|bottom|baseline"

Deprecated attributes

bgcolor="*#rrggbb*" or "*color name*"
height="*pixels, percentage*"
nowrap="nowrap"
width="*pixels, percentage*"

To see how the basic table elements are applied, consider a simple table with two rows and two columns (four content or "data" cells). The diagram on the left in Figure 13-3 shows the table with its cells and rows labeled in the way they are recognized in HTML. The diagram on the right shows the HTML elements that correspond with each component.

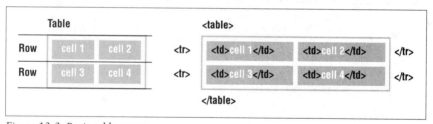

Figure 13-3. Basic table structure

Written out in an HTML source document, the markup for the table in Figure 13-3 would look more like this:

```
<table>
<tr>
    <td>cell 1</td><td>cell 2</td>
</tr>
<tr>
    <td>cell 3</td><td>cell 4</td>
</tr>
</table>
```

The entire table is indicated by the table element, which has no content of its own, but acts as a containing element for one or more of table row elements (tr). The table in the example contains two rows. Each tr element, in turn, contains two *data cells*, which are indicated by the td elements. The cells are the elements that contain real content; the table and tr elements are purely for table structure. A table cell may contain any data that can be displayed in a document, including formatted text, images, multimedia elements, and even other tables.

As mentioned earlier, the table system in HTML is row-primary. Rows are labeled explicitly, but the number of columns is just implied by the number of cells in the longest row. In other words, if all the rows have three cells (three td elements), then the table has three columns. If one row contains four td elements and all the others contain two, the browser displays the table with four columns, adding blank cells to the shorter rows. HTML 4.01 introduced an advanced standard system for describing table structure that includes explicit column elements. This system is discussed in the "Columns and Column Groups" section of this chapter.

Spanning Rows and Columns

Data cells in a table can occupy more than one space in the grid created by the rows and columns. You expand a td element horizontally or vertically using the colspan and rowspan attributes, respectively.

Column span

In Figure 13-4, <td colspan="2"> tells the browser to make "cell 1" occupy the same horizontal space as two cells—to make it "span" over two columns. The resulting spanned cell is indicated in Figure 13-4. Note that the row containing the spanned cell now only has one td element instead of two.

```
<table>
<tr>
<td colspan="2">Cell 1</td>
</tr>
<tr>
<td>Cell 3</td><td>Cell 4</td>
</tr>
</table>
```

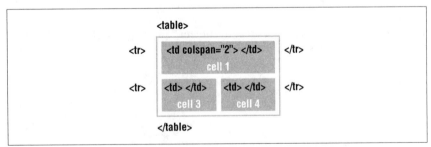

Figure 13-4. The colspan attribute expands cells horizontally to the right

Setting the colspan to a number greater than the actual number of columns (such as colspan="4" for the example) may cause some browsers to add empty columns to the table, possibly throwing your elements out of alignment.

Row span

Similar to colspan, the rowspan attribute stretches a cell to occupy the space of cells in rows below. Include the rowspan attribute in the row where you want the cell to begin and set its value equal to the number of rows you want it to span downward.

In Figure 13-5, note that the bottom row now contains only one cell. The other has been incorporated into the vertical spanned cell. Browsers ignore overextended rowspan values. There can never be more rows than explicitly stated tr elements.

```
<table>
<tr>
<td rowspan="2">Cell 1</td><td>Cell 2</td>
</tr>
<tr>
<td>Cell 4</td>
</tr>
</table>
```

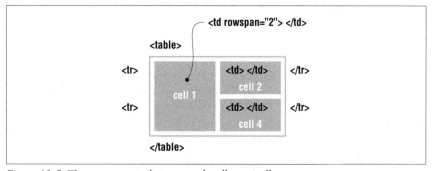

Figure 13-5. The rowspan attribute expands cells vertically

 You may combine colspan and rowspan attributes to create a cell that spans both rows and columns.

Descriptive Elements

The basic table model also includes two elements that provide descriptions of the table's contents. Table header cells (th) are used to describe the cells in the row or column that they precede. The caption element gives a title to the whole table.

Table headers

Table header cells (indicated by the th element) are used to provide important information or context about the cells in the row or column that they precede. The th element accepts the same list of attributes as td.

th

<th>...</th>

Attributes

> *Core* (id, class, style, title), *Internationalization, Events*
> abbr="*text*"
> align="left|right|center|justify|char"
> axis="*text*"
> char="*character*"
> charoff="*length*"
> colspan="*number*"
> headers="*id references*"
> rowspan="*number*"
> scope="row|col|rowgroup|colgroup"
> valign="top|middle|bottom|baseline"

Deprecated attributes

> bgcolor="*#rrggbb*" or "*color name*"
> height="*pixels, percentage*"
> nowrap="nowrap"
> width="*pixels, percentage*"

In terms of markup and table structure, headers are placed in the tr element, the same as a td, as shown in this example.

```
<table>
<tr><th>Planet</th><th>Distance from Earth</th></tr>
<tr><td>Venus</td><td>pretty darn far</td></tr>
<tr><td>Neptune</td><td>ridiculously far</td></tr>
</table>
```

User agents usually render the contents of table headers slightly differently than regular table cells (most often in bold, centered text); however, their appearance may easily be changed with style sheets.

The difference between th and td elements is not merely presentational, however. Table headers perform an important function in binding descriptive labels to table cells for non-visual browsers. They are discussed in more detail in the "Accessible Tables" section later in this chapter. Table header elements should not be used in layout tables.

Captions

The caption element provides a title or brief description of the table.

caption

`<caption>...</caption>`

Attributes

Core (id, class, style, title), *Internationalization, Events*

Deprecated attributes

`align="top|bottom|left|right"`

The caption element must immediately follow the opening table tag and precede all other table elements, as shown in this example and Figure 13-6.

```
<table>
<caption>Planetary Distances</caption>
<tr><th>Planet</th><th>Distance from Earth</th></tr>
<tr><td>Venus</td><td>pretty darn far</td></tr>
<tr><td>Neptune</td><td>ridiculously far</td></tr>
</table>
```

Planetary Distances	
Planet	**Distance from Earth**
Venus	pretty darn far
Neptune	ridiculously far

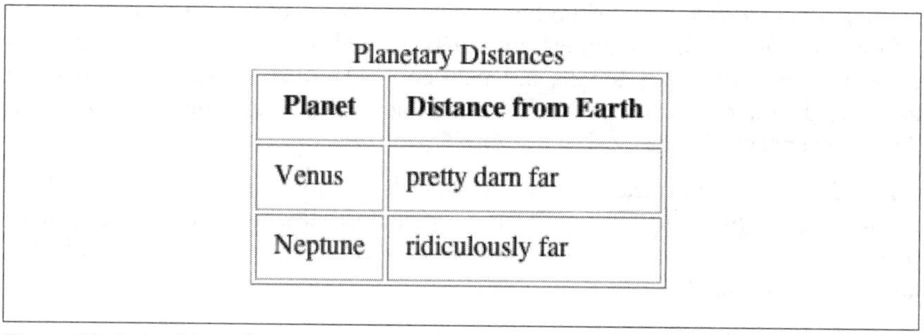

Figure 13-6. A table with a caption

By default, the caption appears at the top of the table. Its width is determined by the width of the table. You can use the `caption-side` style property to move the caption below the table. There is also a deprecated `align` attribute that does the same thing. The `left` and `right` values are not well supported, so authors generally have the option of putting the caption above or below the table.

Captions are a useful tool for table accessibility and will be addressed again briefly in the "Accessible Tables" section later in this chapter.

Row Groups

HTML and XHTML define three "row group" elements that enable authors to organize rows into a table header (thead), footer (tfoot), and a table body (tbody). Because these elements share syntax and attributes, they have been aggregated into one element listing, presented here.

thead, tbody, tfoot

`<thead>...</thead>`, `<tbody>...</tbody>`, `<tfoot>...</tfoot>`

Attributes

Core (`id`, `class`, `style`, `title`), *Internationalization, Events*
`align="left|center|right|justify|char"`
`char="`*character*`"`
`charoff="`*length*`"`
`valign="top|middle|bottom|baseline"`

Internet Explorer 3.0 first introduced this system for grouping rows so they can be treated as units by user agents or style sheets. The W3C included the row group elements in the HTML 4.0 Recommendation as a way to allow more meaningful labeling, improve accessibility, and provide more flexibility for applying style sheet properties. Row groups are advantageous for data tables but should be avoided for layout tables.

The rows in a table may be grouped into a table head (thead), a table footer (tfoot), and one or more table bodies (tbody). The head and footer should contain information about the document and may someday be used to display fixed elements while the body scrolls independently. Another possibility is that the table head and foot would print on every page of a long table that has been divided over several pages.

The W3C requires that the tfoot element (if there is one) appear before tbody in the markup so the table can render the foot before downloading all the (potentially numerous) rows of data. An example of a simple table marked up with row groups is shown here.

```
<table>

<thead>
<tr><th>Employee</th><th>Salary</th><th>Start date</th></tr>
</thead>

<tfoot>
<tr><td colspan="3">Compiled by Buster D. Boss</td></tr>
</tfoot>

<tbody>
<tr><td>Wilma</td><td>5,000</td><td>April 6</td></tr>
<tr>... more data cells...</tr>
<tr>... more data cells...</tr>
</tbody>

</table>
```

Columns and Column Groups

As mentioned earlier in this chapter, the columns in a table are just implied by the number of cells in the longest row. In some instances, however, it is desirable to identify conceptual columns of data cells or groups of columns. The col (column) and colgroup (column group) elements allow authors to conceptually join a group of cells that appear in a column (or columns).

Column and column groups offer a number of conveniences. Their original intent was to speed up the display of tables in visual user agents. By specifying the width of each column, the user agent does not need to parse the contents of the entire table in order to calculate column and table. Columns and column groups are also useful for applying attributes (such as width or align) to all the cells they include. They may also be used as "hooks" for a limited number of style properties (see note). When used with the scope attribute (discussed in the upcoming accessibility section), they may also provide helpful context for screen readers and other non-visual browsing devices.

 The CSS 2.1 Recommendation states that only the following four style properties may be applied to the col and colgroup elements: border, background, width, and visibility. For an in-depth explanation of why this is the case, read Ian Hickson's blog entry, "The mystery of why only four properties apply to table columns" at *ln. hixie.ch/?start=1070385285&count=1*. See also Chapter 22 of this book for more information on style properties for tables.

col

```
<col />
```

Attributes

Core (id, class, style, title), *Internationalization, Events*
align="left|center|right|justify|char"
char="*character*"
charoff="*length*"
span="*number*"
valign="top|middle|bottom|baseline"
width="*pixels, percentage, n**"

colgroup

```
<colgroup>...</colgroup>
```

Attributes

Core (id, class, style, title), *Internationalization, Events*
align="left|center|right|justify|char"
char="*character*"
charoff="*length*"
span="*number*"
valign="top|middle|bottom|baseline"
width="*pixels, percentage, n**"

The col element is used to label or to apply attribute specifications to an individual column (or across several columns via the span attribute) without actually grouping the columns together structurally or conceptually. An empty element, col is used only to apply attributes or styles to the columns to which it refers.

The colgroup element defines a conceptual group of columns. The number of columns included in the group is indicated with the span attribute or by the total of col elements (with their span values) within the column group. Attributes, such as width or align, applied to the colgroup element apply to every column within that group.

The colgroup and/or col elements must appear before any row or row group elements. They are placed either immediately after the table start tag or immediately after the caption element, if there is one. In this example, column group information has been added to the previous sample table markup.

```
<table>

<colgroup id="employinfo">
   <col span="2" width="100" />
   <col span="1" width="50" class="date" />
</colgroup>

<thead>
<tr><th>Employee</th><th>Salary</th><th>Start date</th></tr>
</thead>

<tfoot>
<tr><td colspan="3">Compiled by Buster D. Boss</td></tr>
</tfoot>

<tbody>
<tr><td>Wilma</td><td>5,000</td><td>April 6</td></tr>
<tr>... more data cells...</tr>
<tr>... more data cells...</tr>
</tbody>

</table>
```

The colgroup element identifies the three columns as part of the same structural group. (There may be many column groups in a table, but for simplicity's sake, this example has just one.) Within the colgroup, the first col element identifies two columns (span="2"), each with a width of 100 pixels. The remaining col has a width of 50 pixels. If all the columns in the table were to be the same width, the width could have been specified in the colgroup element. The third column is identified with a class attribute that could later be targeted with a style property (such as background).

Table Presentation

As for all matters of presentation, style sheets are the preferred method for changing the appearance of tables and offer more fine-tuned control than HTML attributes. See Chapter 22 for more information on CSS specifically for tables.

That said, there are a number of non-deprecated attributes that may be used to control cell spacing, dimensions, borders, and alignment (although, even most of those have style sheet alternatives). This section takes a look at those presentation-related attributes and also points out the preferred CSS methods.

Table Cell Spacing

There are two types of space that can be added in and around table cells: cell padding and cell spacing. The `cellpadding` and `cellspacing` attributes are used with the `table` element and apply to the whole table; you can't specify padding or spacing for individual cells using HTML alone.

Cell spacing

Cell spacing refers to the amount of space that is held between the cells in a table. It is specified with the `cellspacing` attribute in the `table` element. Values are specified in number of pixels. Increasing the cell spacing results in wider shaded borders between cells. In the second image in Figure 13-7, the darker gray areas indicate the 10 pixels of cell spacing added between cells. The default value for `cellspacing` is 2; therefore, if no `cellspacing` is specified, browsers will automatically place two pixels of space between cells.

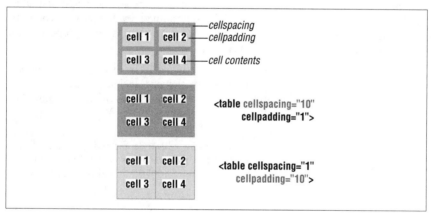

Figure 13-7. Cell spacing versus cell padding

Cell padding

Cell padding refers to the amount of space between the cell's border and the contents of the cell (as indicated by the third image in Figure 13-7). It is specified using the `cellpadding` attribute in the `table` element. Values are specified in number of pixels; the default value is 1. Relative values (percentages of available space) may also be used.

CSS alternatives

Cell padding may be handled by applying the `padding` property to the `td` element. By using `class`, `id`, or more specific selectors, it is possible to apply different amounts of padding to different cells within a table (the `cellpadding` attribute applies the same amount of padding to all cells).

There is no CSS property that is exactly equivalent to the `cellspacing` attribute, although you can adjust the amount of space between cells by setting the border-collapse property for the table to separate and then use the `border-spacing` property to specify the amount of space between cell borders. The difference is that with the `cellspacing` attribute, the border is rendered thicker between cells, while the `border-spacing` property adds empty space between them.

Unfortunately, the `border-spacing` property is not supported by Internet Explorer 6 and earlier (support in IE 7 is not documented as of this writing), so authors are left with no practical CSS `cellspacing` substitute for the time being.

Many authors also explicitly set both the cellspacing and cellpadding to 0 (zero) to override default browser settings and clear the way for style sheet properties.

Table and Cell Dimensions

By default, a table will render just wide enough to contain all of its contents. You can explicitly specify the width of a table using the `width` attribute in the `table` element. The HTML specifications provide no way to specify the height of a table, preferring the height to be automatically determined by the table's contents. However, there is a nonstandard `height` attribute that is well-supported for providing minimum height for the overall table.

You can control the width and height of individual cells by using the (you guessed it) `width` and `height` attributes in the `td` or `th` element. Height values are considered to be minimum heights and cells may expand downward to accommodate their contents.

The width and height attributes have been deprecated for td and th elements, but they are not deprecated for use in the table element. Style sheet properties are still the preferred method for specifying table dimensions.

CSS alternative

Use the `width` and `height` properties to set the size of any table-related element. Heights set on table and table cells are considered minimum heights, and the actual height may expand to fit the content.

Borders

The `table` element accepts the following attributes for controlling borders and rules between cells and around the table. All of the attributes introduced here apply to the `table` element only. None of these attributes are deprecated, but authors are urged to use CSS for drawing borders around table elements instead.

border
Controls the width of the frame around the table. The default value is 1.

frame
Specifies the sides of the table on which the frame should render. By default, the frame is rendered as a shaded, 3D style rule. The frame attribute uses these keyword values: void (no frame), above (top side only), below (bottom side only), hsides (horizontal sides), lhs (lefthand side), rhs (righthand side), vsides (vertical sides), box (all four sides), and border (all four sides).

rules
Specifies which rules render between the cells of the table. One use for this attribute might be to display rules only between certain sets of columns or rows, as defined by colgroup or the row group elements (thead, tbody, and tfoot). The accepted values for the rules attribute are all, cols, groups, none, and rows.

CSS alternative

The collection of border properties in CSS allows you to specify the style (such as solid, dotted, dashed, and so on), color, and width of borders around any table-related element. With style sheets, it is possible to apply different borders to different sides of tables, their rows, or cells. See Chapter 19 for details on the border properties and Chapter 22 for how borders are handled in tables specifically.

Cell Content Alignment

The align and valign attributes are used to specify the horizontal and vertical alignment (respectively) of content within cells. Alignment may be specified for the following elements: td, th, tr, thead, tbody, tfoot, col, and colgroup.

Adding the align attribute to the table element aligns the entire table in the width of its containing element and does not affect the alignment within the cells.

Horizontal alignment

The align attribute accepts the usual values left, right, center, and justify. Text is left-justified by default in left-to-right reading languages.

The align attribute also includes the char value that specifies that the table contents should be aligned on a specific character, such as a decimal point for a column of currency amounts. The character used for alignment is provided by the char attribute. The charoff attribute specifies the offset distance to the first alignment character. Although it's a nifty idea, the char and charoff attributes are not supported by current browsers.

Alignment settings for individual cells (td or th) always override settings at the higher levels. Alignment set on elements within a cell (a p element, for example) override the cell's alignment. If the table includes a col or colgroup, the align settings on the columns override any alignment applied to a row or row group element.

Vertical alignment

The valign attribute is used to vertically position the contents of the cell at the top, bottom, or middle of the cell. The baseline value of valign ensures that the first lines of each cell in a row share the same baseline.

CSS alternatives

Authors may use the text-align property to specify the horizontal alignment for the contents of any table element (including the table element itself). The text-align property may also be applied to any element contained within a table cell, thus overriding the cell- or row-level alignment settings.

For vertical centering, applying the vertical-align style property to the td or th element has the same effect as the valign attribute. The available values for vertical-align when applied to table cells are baseline, top, middle, and bottom.

Backgrounds

The (X)HTML Recommendations have deprecated the bgcolor attribute used to apply background colors to cells, rows, and tables. Use the background style sheet property to apply colors and background images instead. The background property is explained in Chapter 20, and background behavior in tables is covered in Chapter 22.

Accessible Tables

Presenting data in rows and columns is a highly effective device in visual media for adding meaning to data. Consider the simple table example in Figure 13-8.

Planet	Diameter measured in earths	Orbital period in years	Moons
Mercury	.38	.24	0
Venus	.95	.62	0
Jupiter	317.8	11.9	63

Figure 13-8. A simple table example

Sighted users can easily trace up a column or across a row to a header cell that explains the data's meaning and context. Blind or severely sight-impaired users do not have this luxury. When using a screen reader or Braille device, the contents of each cell may be read one after another (a process called *linearization*). The table in Figure 13-8 might be presented like so: "Planet Diameter measured in earths Orbital period in years Moons Mercury .38 .24 0 Venus .95 .62 0 Jupiter 317.8 11. 9 63." It's easy to lose track of the meaning of each statistic for a table as simple as this. For complex data tables, such as those pictured in Figure 13-1, it's nearly impossible.

The (X)HTML specification provides several mechanisms for adding meaning to cell data even when the table is presented non-visually. This section outlines the basics of authoring accessible data tables. For more in-depth tutorials, see these online resources:

- "Techniques for Accessible HTML Tables" (from Papers on Section 508), by Steve Ferg (*www.ferg.org/section508/accessible_tables.html*)
- "Bring on the Tables," by Roger Johansson (*www.456BereaStreet.com/ archive/200410/bring_on_the_tables/*)
- "Creating Accessible Tables," at WebAIM (*www.webaim.org/techniques/ tables/2*)

Table Metadata

The first step in making a table accessible is to provide descriptions of the table using the caption element and summary attribute.

The caption element introduced earlier in this chapter provides a short descriptive title for the table. Visual browsers display the contents of the caption element above or below the table, as specified by an attribute or style property.

The summary attribute in the table element may provide a more lengthy description of the table. It is analogous to the alt attribute for images. Unlike the caption element, the value of the summary attribute is not rendered by visual browsers.

The summary may give visually impaired users a better understanding of the table's contents and organization that sighted users could understand at a glance. This alleviates the need to read through several rows of data to decide whether a table will be useful. Although the summary is available for longer descriptions, authors are advised to keep summary descriptions clear and succinct and use them only when necessary.

The table in Figure 13-8 might be given the following caption and summary (note that summaries are more useful for tables that are more complex than this one).

```
<table summary="A comparison of major features for each planet in the solar
system, relative to characteristics of the Earth.">
<caption>Solar System Summary</caption>
<tr> (table continues...)
```

Table Headers

The most important element in creating accessible data tables is the table header (th). Table headers provide a description or context for the data cells in a column or row. Non-visual user agents rely on the th element for descriptions of each table cell. While it is possible to use styles to make the first row of table cells (td) *look* like headers (for example, by making them bold and arranging them in shaded boxes), a td element alone will not perform the same function as a th, and important information will be lost.

Here is the same table from the previous figure rewritten with table headers (Figure 13-9). Notice that by default, browsers render headers in bold, centered text, but you can easily change the way they look with CSS properties. By all means, do not avoid using th elements properly just because you don't like the browser's default rendering.

```
<table summary="A comparison of major features for each planet in the solar
system, relative to characteristics of the Earth.">
<caption>Solar System Summary</caption>
  <tr>
    <th>Planet</th>
    <th abbr="diameter">Diameter measured in earths</th>
    <th abbr="orbit">Orbital period in years</th>
    <th>Moons</th>
  </tr>
  <tr>
    <td>Mercury</td><td>.38</td><td>.24</td><td>0</td>
  </tr>
  <tr>
    <td>Venus</td><td>.95</td><td>.62</td><td>0</td>
  </tr>
  <tr>
    <td>Jupiter</td><td>317.8</td><td>11.9</td><td>63</td>
  </tr>
</table>
```

	Solar System Summary		
Planet	**Diameter measured in earths**	**Orbital period in years**	**Moons**
Mercury	.38	.24	0
Venus	.95	.62	0
Jupiter	317.8	11.9	63

Figure 13-9. A table with a caption and table header elements

With headers in place, a screen reader may be configured to read each row of data like this: "Planet: Mercury, Diameter measured in earths: .38, Orbital period in years: .24, Moons: 0," and so on. It is clear how headers alone go a long way toward attaching meaning to the data in each cell.

It is also easy to see how this might be cumbersome, particularly if the header titles are long. The abbr attribute allows authors to provide an alternate version of the header title that may be used instead, as shown in example.

```
<th abbr="diameter">Diameter measured in earths</th>
```

Instead of repeating "Diameter measured in earths" before each measurement, a screen-reader could say simply "diameter" instead.

Associating Headers with Data

As table structure gets more complex, additional markup is required to keep the associations between table headers and their respective data clear. The remaining attributes for the th element, scope and headers, are used to conceptually attach headers to groups of data cells.

Scope

In the simple table shown in Figure 13-9, it is easy to tell that the headers apply to their respective columns of data. In more complex tables, the relationships between headers and data may not be so straightforward. The scope attribute in the th element is used to explicitly declare associations between table headers and the rows, columns, row groups, or column groups in which they appear (using the values row, column, rowgroup, and colgroup, respectively)

The table example in Figure 13-10 has been altered slightly to include table headers for each row.

Solar System Summary			
	Diameter measured in earths	**Orbital period in years**	**Moons**
Mercury	.38	.24	0
Venus	.95	.62	0
Jupiter	317.8	11.9	63

Figure 13-10. Table with row and column headers

In this case, it is desirable to make it clear that the headers in the left column apply to each data cell in the rows in which they appear. It is helpful to indicate the relationship of the cells with their respective column header as well. This revised markup shows how the scope attribute is used to indicate these relationships.

```
<table summary="A comparison of major features for each planet in the solar
system, relative to characteristics of the Earth.">
<caption>Solar System Summary</caption>
  <tr>
    <td> </td>
    <th scope="column" abbr="diameter">Diameter measured in earths</th>
    <th scope="column" abbr="orbit">Orbital period in years</th>
    <th scope="column">Moons</th>
  </tr>
  <tr>
    <th scope="row">Mercury</th>
    <td>.38</td>
    <td>.24</td>
    <td>0</td>
  </tr>
```

```
  <tr>
    <th scope="row">Venus</th>
    <td>.95</td>
    <td>.62</td>
    <td>0</td>
  </tr>
  <tr>
    <th scope="row">Jupiter</th>
    <td>317.8</td>
    <td>11.9</td>
    <td>63</td>
  </tr>
</table>
```

This line from the table markup example extends the description "Mercury" to all the cells in that row. The relationship may be visualized as shown in Figure 13-11.

```
<th scope="row">Mercury</th>
```

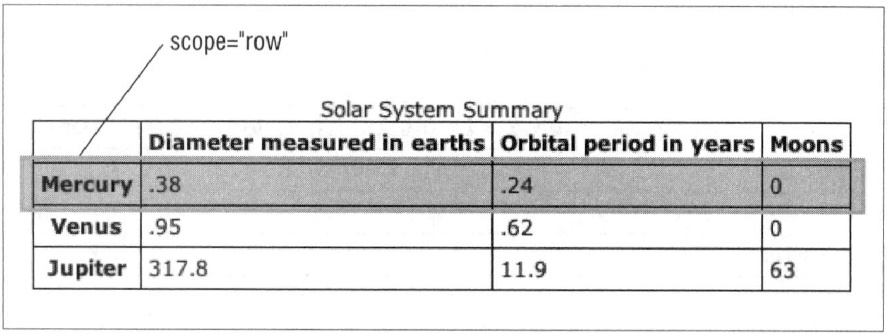

Figure 13-11. A header is associated with a row with the scope attribute

The scope attribute may also be used in a data cell element (td) to apply its content as a label to the remaining cells in its row, column, row group, or column group. This is useful for cells that contain data themselves but also carry meaning about other data cells, such as the planet names in the sample table. If the "Planets" table header were reinserted, the planet names could go back to being regular td elements yet still be associated with each row.

ID and headers

In Figure 13-11, it was possible to indicate the scope of the header by drawing a box across the row. The same would be true when applying scope to columns or groups: the scope extends in a rectangle that encompasses the specified table cells.

For very complex tables with spanned and/or nested table headers, the relationships between headers and the data they describe may not fit into neat rectangles. The headers attribute is used to associate data cells with specific table headers by referencing them by name (provided in an id value).

The solar system table has been altered once again to include a (fairly contrived) nested header as shown in Figure 13-12.

Solar System Summary			
	Measurements relative to Earth		**Moons**
	Diameter measured in earths	**Orbital period in years**	
Mercury	.38	.24	0
Venus	.95	.62	0
Jupiter	317.8	11.9	63

Figure 13-12. Table with a nested header

The first step in using this method to associate headers and cells is to give each table header (th) element a name using the id attribute. Then, each td uses the headers attribute to specify the table headers that apply to it. The value may include several header names, separated by spaces, as shown in this example.

```
<table  cellpadding="4" summary="A comparison of major features for each
planet in the solar system, relative to the Earth's characteristics.">
<caption>Solar System Summary</caption>
  <tr>
    <td rowspan="2"></td>
    <th colspan="2" id="measure" abbr="measurements">Measurements relative
        to Earth</th>
    <th rowspan="2" id="moons">Moons</th>
  </tr>
  <tr>
    <th id="diameter" abbr="diameter">Diameter measured in earths</th>
    <th id="orbit" abbr="orbit">Orbital period in years</th>
  </tr>
  <tr>
    <th id="mercury">Mercury</th>
    <td headers="mercury measure diameter">.38</td>
    <td headers="mercury measure orbit">.24</td>
    <td headers="mercury moons">0</td>
  </tr>
  <tr>
    <th id="venus">Venus</th>
    <td headers="venus measure diameter">.95</td>
    <td headers="venus measure orbit">.62</td>
    <td headers="venus moons">0</td>
  </tr>
  <tr>
    <th id="jupiter">Jupiter</th>
    <td headers="jupiter measure diameter">317.8</td>
    <td headers="jupiter measure orbit">11.9</td>
    <td headers="jupiter moons">63</td>
  </tr>
</table>
```

The headers method is complicated—even for a simple table such as the one in this example—and should be used only when scope won't adequately do the trick.

Responsible Layout Tables

You've surely heard (throughout this book and elsewhere) that table-based layout has been replaced by CSS for positioning elements on the page. However, during this time of transition, as browser developers work out the kinks in CSS support, some authors still choose to use tables to establish the basic grid of the page. It is possible to rely on a table for layout, but be in line with the current trends of standards compliance and accessibility in contemporary web design.

Layout tables are not inherently evil (or even inaccessible), as long as they are handled the right way. This section recommends ways to use layout tables that do the least harm.

Stick to Basic Table Elements

When using a table strictly for layout, use only the minimal table elements:

table
> Use to establish the table

tr
> Use for table rows

td
> Use for table cells

Captions, table headers, row groups, and all features for improving table accessibility as listed in the previous section should be avoided. They will only serve to confuse or slow down readers with assistive devices.

Keep It Simple and Lightweight

The problem with most layout tables in terms of accessibility is complexity. It is not uncommon for tables aiming to achieve pixel-precise layouts to use techniques such as:

- Tables nested within tables, some many levels deep
- Empty rows inserted for the sole purpose of establishing column widths
- Table cells that contain only one-pixel GIFs used for spacing
- Numerous spanned rows and columns
- Repetitive presentational table attributes

These typically result in overly complicated table structures and bloated markup. Non-sighted users may become disoriented trying to navigate from cell to cell in an attempt to make sense of the content. The complexity and size of the source document isn't doing any favors for visual browsers either.

An example of a typically convoluted table-based layout is shown in Figure 13-13 (another one of my own old-school designs). The borders have been enhanced to reveal the complexity of the table structure.

By contrast, responsible layout tables are simple and lightweight. The table in Figure 13-14 contains similar content to the example in Figure 13-13, but a single

Figure 13-13. An overly complex nested table layout

stripped-down layout table is used to establish the basic grid structure of the page. The borders have been turned on to reveal the table structure. There are no nested tables, and every table cell is filled with real content. All matters of visual formatting are handled with style sheets (as discussed in the next section).

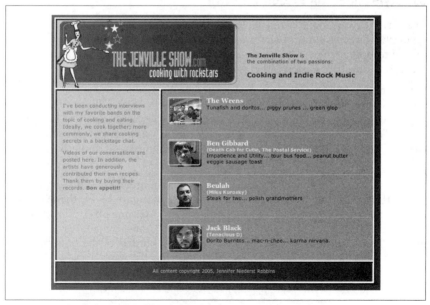

Figure 13-14. A lightweight table used for layout

The markup for the table in Figure 13-14 is shown here. It has been simplified to reveal the structure of the table markup.

```
<table>
  <tr>
    <td colspan="2" id="masthead">
    <div id="welcome">The Jenville Show is ...</div>
    </td>
  </tr>

  <tr>
    <td id="intro">
      <p>I've been conducting interviews...</p>
    </td>

    <td id="bandlist">
      <ul>
        <li id="wrens">...</li>
        <li id="gibbard">...</li>
        <li id="beulah">...</li>
        <li id="jackblack">...</li>
      </ul>
    </td>
  </tr>

  <tr>
    <td colspan="2"><p class="copyrt">All content...</p></td>
  </tr>
</table>
```

Use Style Sheets for Presentation

The secret to keeping a layout table simple and streamlined is to use it only to establish a basic layout grid and to use Cascading Style Sheets for everything else related to presentation. The good news is with style sheets, the need for most of the layout table hacks listed earlier is eliminated.

For example, one of the main reasons for nesting tables was to get different amounts of cell padding in different parts of the table. With CSS, padding can be applied on a cell-by-cell basis. Similarly, where once it was necessary to put text in a single-celled table to display it in a colored box, style sheets now allow any element to be presented in that fashion by setting dimensions and a background color.

In the complicated layout in Figure 13-13, the list of artists is held together in a two-part nested table. In the lightweight example in Figure 13-14, the bands are now marked up semantically as an unordered list. The one-pixel rules that had been created with table cells filled with one-pixel transparent GIFs and background colors are now created simply by applying borders to the bottom of list item (li) elements.

Using the background images, image replacement, and rounded-corner techniques listed in Chapter 24, this single-table layout could be made to approximate the look and feel of the original even further.

These are just a few examples of how style sheets could be used in tandem with a minimal layout table. The table takes care of the structure, and style sheets handle the presentation of all the content in a way that alleviates the need for additional tables and table cells. Once you've weaned yourself this far, it's not a big leap to CSS positioning and table-free design.

Check for Linearization

When creating a layout table, it is important to be aware of how well your table will linearize when presented in a non-visual browser. *Linearization* refers to the order of the content when all the table formatting is removed. Screen readers read content in the order in which it appears in the source document, as though there were no markup there at all.

Tables are said to linearize well when their contents appear in a logical order in the source document. In general, it is preferable to get readers to the main content as quickly as possible. Unfortunately, the way many layout tables are constructed leads to the side column content (long lists of links and other sidebar-like information) appearing before the main content. The table in Figure 13-15 shows a typical (albeit simple) three-column layout table with a masthead.

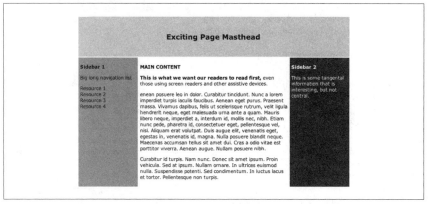

Figure 13-15. A typical layout table

While it is perfectly clear what to read first when rendered visually, a look at the source reveals that users with screen readers will need to listen to the big long navigation list in "Sidebar 1" before they hear the main feature. This is a simplified example of a table that does not linearize well. Complex layout tables that are typical in everyday practice have far more egregious linearization problems.

```
<table width="700" border="0" cellpadding="4">
  <tr>
    <td colspan="3">
      <h2>Exciting Page Masthead </h2>
    </td>
```

```
    </tr>
    <tr>
      <td><p><strong>Sidebar 1</strong></p>
         <p>Big long navigation list</p>
            ...
      </td>

      <td><p><strong>MAIN CONTENT</strong></p>
         <p><strong>This is what we want our readers to read first,</strong> even
    those using screen readers and other assistive devices.</p>...
      </td>

      <td><p><strong>Sidebar 2</strong></p>
         <p>This is some tangental information ... </p>
      </td>
    </tr>
  </table>
```

Layout tables can be designed to linearize in a logical order, but it takes some careful planning, and at times, a little finagling. One technique that works for the three-column layout shown in the example is to put the main content cell in a new row just after the masthead and use the rowspan attribute to present it side by side with the sidebar cells, as shown in this example. The resulting table is shown in Figure 13-16.

```
  <table>
    <tr>
      <td colspan="3"><div align="center">
         <h2>Exciting Page Masthead </h2>
      </div></td>
    </tr>

    <tr>
      <td></td>
      <td rowspan="2"><p><strong>MAIN CONTENT</strong></p>
         <p><strong>This is what we want our readers to read first....</strong></p>
      </td>
      <td></td>
    </tr>

    <tr>
      <td><p><strong>Sidebar 1</strong></p>
      <p>Big long navigation list</p>...
      </td>
      <td><p><strong>Sidebar 2</strong></p>
      <p class="style1">This is some tangental information...</p></td>
    </tr>

  </table>
```

The empty table cells in the second row have been left unstyled in this example to reveal the table's structure, but obviously, they could be minimized by tinkering with styles. The important thing to notice is that the main content is now the first thing users read after the masthead when the table is linearized.

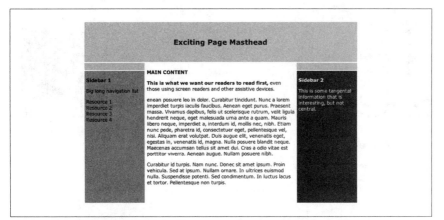

Figure 13-16. A table with preferred linearization

Creating tables that linearize logically can be a tricky business and may require rethinking the design. As an alternative, using CSS with absolute positioning allows you to start with markup that is in the preferred order and then place each element wherever you want on the page. This may be another motivation for cutting the tether to table-based design.

14

Frames

Frames are a method for dividing the browser window into smaller subwindows, each displaying a different HTML document. This chapter covers the structure and creation of framed documents, controls for affecting their display and function, and some advanced tips and tricks. The following frame-related elements will be addressed.

frame	Defines a single frame
frameset	Establishes the structure for frames or other framesets
noframes	Content displayed if frames are not supported

Introduction to Frames

Frames allow authors to display several HTML documents in the browser window at one time, each in its own scrollable subwindow. Introduced by Netscape Navigator 2.0, frame support was soon added by other popular browsers. The HTML 4.01 and XHTML 1.0 Recommendations include a Frameset DTD for framed documents. XHTML 1.1 omits all frame elements.

Framed documents are typically used as a navigation device in which all of the navigation options stay put in one frame while the linked content documents are displayed in another frame. Because frames may include scrollbars and scroll independently of one another, frames are a method for making sure one page component stays put on the page while the rest of the page is free to scroll.

It is important to note that frame-like functionality (in which one element stays fixed and the rest of the page scrolls) can also be accomplished with CSS using the position: fixed property. Unfortunately, Internet Explorer 6 for Windows and earlier do not support fixed positioning, but there are workarounds as noted in Chapter 25.

Due to reliable browser support, frames are still an option for navigation and other uses. However, they do present certain problems and peculiarities that have led to their currently controversial status. Like most things, frames are neither all good nor all bad. It is your responsibility to be familiar with both sides of the coin so you can help present the best solution for your or your clients' needs.

Advantages

Consider these advantages to using frames:

- They enable parts of the page to remain stationary while other parts scroll. This is useful for elements you may not want to scroll out of view, such as navigational options or banner advertising.

- Frames unify resources that reside on separate servers. For instance, you may use frames to combine your own material (and navigation graphics) with threaded discussion material generated by software on a vendor's server.

- With the noframes element, you can add alternative content for browsers that do not support frames. This accessibility feature is built into the frames system.

Disadvantages

Also keep in mind these disadvantages:

- Frames may make site production more complicated because you need to produce and organize multiple files to fill one page.

- Navigating through a framed site may be prohibitively challenging for some users (especially users with disabilities who are using alternative browsing devices).

- Documents nested in a frameset may be more difficult to bookmark.

- A large number of frames on a page may significantly increase the load on the server because so much of the load on a server is initial document requests. Four requests for 1K files (the frameset and the contents of three frames) is more work for your server than a single request for a 4K document.

- Multiple documents for each web page makes the site more difficult to manage and update.

- Framed documents can be a nuisance for search engines. Content-level documents may be missed in searches. If a contained document is found by a search engine, it will probably be displayed out of context of its frameset, potentially losing important navigational options.

- It is more difficult to track actual page (or ad) impressions when the pages are part of a framed document.

With the pros and cons in mind, take a look at how framed documents are constructed.

Basic Frameset Structure

A web page that is divided into frames is held together by a top-level frameset document.

Frameset documents are fundamentally different from other HTML documents in that they use the frameset element instead of a body element. The frameset element may not contain any content, but instead defines and names some number of frames (or other framesets), arranged in rows and/or columns. Each frame is indicated with a frame element within the frameset. A frameset document contains a regular header portion (as indicated with the head element).

frameset

`<frameset>...</frameset>`

Attributes

    Core (id, class, style, title), *onload, onunload*
    cols="*list of lengths*" *(number, percentage,* or **)*
    rows="*list of lengths* " *(number, percentage,* or **)*

Nonstandard attributes

    border="*number*"
    bordercolor="*#rrggbb*" or "*color name*"
    frameborder="1|0"; "yes|no" *(NN 3)*

This is an example of a minimal frameset document in XHTML. The resulting frameset, shown in Figure 14-1, has two frames occupying two columns of equal width.

```
<!DOCTYPE html PUBLIC "-//W3C//DTD XHTML 1.0 Frameset//EN"
    "http://www.w3.org/TR/xhtml1/DTD/xhtml1-frameset.dtd">

<html xmlns="http://www.w3.org/1999/xhtml" xml:lang="en" lang="en">
<head>
<title>Simple Framed Document</title>
</head>

<frameset cols="*,*">
   <frame src="left.html" />
   <frame src="right.html" />
</frameset>

<noframes>
<body>
<p>Your browser does not support frames.</p>
<p><a href="left.html">Go to the left</a></p>
<p><a href="right.html">Go to the right</a></p>
</body>
</noframes>

</html>
```

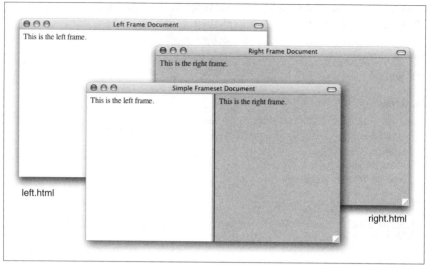

right.html

Figure 14-1. Basic frameset document

The frameset document is displaying two external HTML documents, each in its own frame. The job of the frameset document is simply to build a framework that holds them together. It also includes the noframes element for providing alternative content for browsers that don't support frames.

Take a look for a moment at the frameset source document. It begins with the DOCTYPE declaration that tells the browser to use the XHTML 1.0 Frameset DTD when rendering this file. Next is the html root element and an ordinary header containing the document's title.

> A DOCTYPE declaration that points to a Frameset DTD will throw browsers that support DOCTYPE switching into Quirks mode. That means that most browsers will support nonstandard and deprecated elements and attributes. For more information on DOCTYPE switching, see Chapter 9.

This is the point at which a frameset document diverges from regular HTML documents. Instead of a body, it uses the frameset element that specifies that the document should display in two columns (cols) of equal width. The frameset is merely a container for two frame elements. The primary job of the frame element is to provide the URL of the document that should display in that frame. The example above has two frames. One pulls in a document called *left.html* and the other displays *right.html*.

It is important to note that *left.html* and *right.html* are ordinary (X)HTML documents, each consisting of a head and body element. In other words, documents that are displayed *within* a frame are not frameset documents and do not need to use the Frameset DTD. They may be authored according to the Strict or Transitional DTDs. It is possible to display another frameset document in a frame;

however, there are more efficient methods for nesting frames as discussed in the "Nesting Frames" section later in this chapter.

frame

```
<frame />
```

Attributes

> *Core* (id, class, style, title)
> frameborder="1|0" (*IE 3+ and W3C Rec.*); "yes|no" (*NN 3+*)
> longdesc="*URL*"
> marginwidth="*number*"
> marginheight="*number*"
> name="*text*"
> noresize="noresize"
> scrolling="yes|no|auto"
> src="*URL*"

Nonstandard attributes

> bordercolor="*#rrggbb*" or "*color name*" *(Nonstandard)*

Alternate Content

The sample frameset document contains one other element in addition to frameset. The noframes element contains content that will be displayed in browsers and devices that don't support frames; therefore, it is an important tool for ensuring the accessibility of framed documents.

noframes

```
<noframes> ... </noframes>
```

Attributes

> *Core* (id, class, style, title), *Internationalization, Events*

The noframes element must be placed within the frameset element in order to be valid.

```
<noframes>
<body>
<p>Your browser does not support frames.</p>
<p><a href="left.html">Go to the left</a></p>
<p><a href="right.html">Go to the right</a></p>
</body>
</noframes>
```

The content of the noframes element might be just a few lines or an entire page of information.

Ideally, the content of the noframes element is a complete alternative to the framed interface. It should include the entire content of the page within a body element. If the complete content is too large (in terms of byte size), opt for the list of descriptions and links instead.

At minimum, `noframes` content should provide a brief description of each frame with a link to access the individual (X)HTML documents. Without links, the frameset document is a dead end to users and search engines.

Establishing Rows and Columns

Rows (horizontal frames) and columns (vertical frames) are established with the `frameset` element, using the `rows` and `cols` attributes, respectively. These attributes divide the frameset in a grid-like manner. Frames are filled from left to right for columns and from top to bottom for rows.

The number of rows or columns in the frameset is determined by the number of size values provided. For example, to create a frameset with three columns, you write `cols="25%,50%,25%"` (or three other size values). In this case, the user agent creates a column for each of the provided measurements. Rows work in the same manner. Figure 14-2 shows a simple framed document divided into two equalsized rows (on the left) and columns (right).

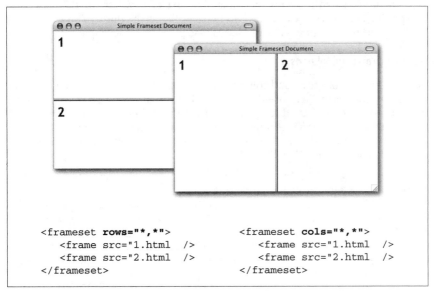

```
<frameset rows="*,*">                  <frameset cols="*,*">
   <frame src="1.html" />                 <frame src="1.html" />
   <frame src="2.html" />                 <frame src="2.html" />
</frameset>                             </frameset>
```

Figure 14-2. Simple horizontal and vertical frameset layouts

Specifying sizes

Frame size can be listed in one of three ways:

Absolute pixel values
> The browser interprets an integer as an absolute pixel value. The frameset element `<frameset cols="150,650">` creates two columns, one exactly 150 pixels wide and the other exactly 650 pixels wide. If the browser window is larger than the total specified pixels, it enlarges each frame proportionally to fill the window.

Percentages

Percentages are based on the total width of the frameset. The total should add up to 100%. The frameset element `<frameset rows="25%,50%,25%">` creates three rows; the top and bottom frames each always occupy 25% of the height of the frameset, and the middle row makes up 50%, regardless of how the browser window is resized.

Relative values

Relative values, indicated by the asterisk (*) character, are used to divide up the remaining space in the frameset into equal portions (as shown in Figure 14-2). For instance, the frameset `<frameset cols="100,*">` creates two columns—the first is 100 pixels wide, and the second fills whatever portion is left of the window.

You can also specify relative values in multiples of equal portions and combine them with other measurement values. For example, the frameset defined by `<frameset cols="25%,2*,*">` divides the window into three columns. The first column always occupies 25% of the window width. The remaining two divide up the remaining space; however, in this case, the middle column will always be two times as big as the third. (You may notice that this results in the same division as the percentages example.)

Combining rows and columns

You can specify both rows and columns within a single frameset, creating a grid of frames, as shown in Figure 14-3. When both `cols` and `rows` are specified for a frameset, frames are created left to right in each row, in order. Rows are created top to bottom. The order of appearance of `frame` elements within the `frameset` determines where their contents display. The order in which documents are displayed is demonstrated in Figure 14-3.

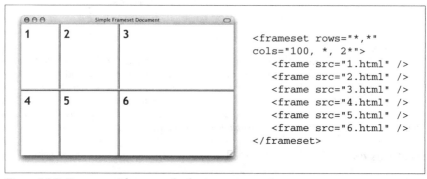

Figure 14-3. Frameset with rows and columns

Nesting Frames

It is possible to nest a frameset within another frameset, which means you can take one row and divide it into several columns (or, conversely, divide a column into several rows), as shown in Figure 14-4. Nesting gives you more page layout flexibility and complexity than simply dividing a frameset into a grid of rows and columns.

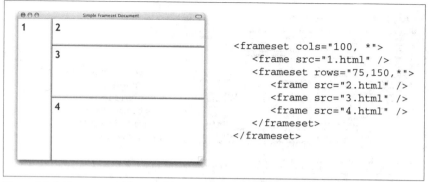

```
<frameset cols="100, *">
    <frame src="1.html" />
    <frameset rows="75,150,*">
        <frame src="2.html" />
        <frame src="3.html" />
        <frame src="4.html" />
    </frameset>
</frameset>
```

Figure 14-4. Document with nested framesets

In Figure 14-4, the top-level frameset specifies two columns. The first column is a frame 100 pixels wide. The second column (which occupies the remainder of the window) is filled with another frameset, this one with three rows.

There is no technical limit on the number of levels that frames can be nested, only practical ones. If you nest frames, be careful to close each successive frameset or the document will not display correctly.

Frame Function and Appearance

By default, frames are separated by borders with 3D beveled edges, and each frame has a scrollbar if its contents do not fit in their entirety. You may want to change these settings using the attributes for controlling frame functionality and presentation.

Scrolling

The scrolling attribute within the frame element controls whether scrollbars appear within the frame, regardless of the frame's contents.

The default setting is auto, which behaves like any browser window—no scrollbars display unless the contents are too big to fit entirely within the frame. The yes value should make scrollbars appear, even for mostly empty frames, however, most current browsers seem to treat it the same as auto. To make sure scrollbars never appear, even when the content is larger than the available space, set scrolling="no".

In Figure 14-5 both frames display the same text document, but scrolling is set to auto in the top and no in the bottom frame.

Disabling Resize

By default, any user can resize your frames—overriding your size settings—simply by clicking and dragging on the border between frames. You can prevent users from doing that by adding the noresize attribute to the frame element.

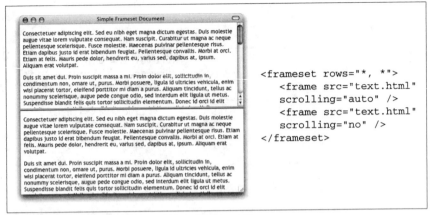

```
<frameset rows="*, *">
    <frame src="text.html"
    scrolling="auto" />
    <frame src="text.html"
    scrolling="no" />
</frameset>
```

Figure 14-5. Setting scrollbars with the scrolling attribute

Be careful that you're not disabling functionality the user needs, though; if the frame contains text, chances are good that some users may need to resize.

Frame Margins

As you probably already know, browsers hold a margin space on all sides of the browser window, preventing a document's contents from displaying flush against the edge of the window. The width of the margin varies from browser to browser.

Frames have margin attributes that allow you to control (or remove) the margins on any frame-enabled browser. To adjust the top and bottom margins of a frame, specify a number of pixels for the marginheight attribute. Use the marginwidth attribute to specify the amount of space for the left and right margins. They can be combined as shown in the example in Figure 14-6.

The example shows the same HTML document (containing only a graphic) loaded into two frames within a frameset. The left frame has specific margins set. The right frame has its margins set to zero, allowing the contents of the frame to be positioned right up against the edges of the frame.

Frame Borders

By default, framed documents display with a 3D border between each frame. These borders visually divide the sections and also serve as a handle for resizing. The HTML 4.01 specification allows for borders to be controlled only at the frame level (in the frame element).

Most browsers also support the nonstandard method of setting borders and border thicknesses for the whole page in the frameset element. Bear in mind that this nonstandard use of border attributes will cause a document to be invalid because it does not conform to any DTD.

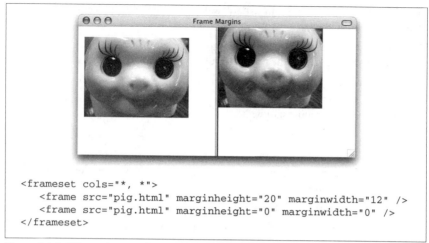

```
<frameset cols="*, *">
    <frame src="pig.html" marginheight="20" marginwidth="12" />
    <frame src="pig.html" marginheight="0" marginwidth="0" />
</frameset>
```

Figure 14-6. Effects of setting frame margins

Browsers vary in their support of border attributes. It is best to do plenty of testing (including in older browsers) to be sure you can live with the different results.

Turning borders on and off

The frameborder attribute is used to turn the 3D borders between frames on (with a value of 1) and off (0), like a toggle switch. The W3C Recommendations specify that the frameborder attribute should be used for each individual frame element, but most browsers support frameborder in the frameset element as well (see previous note). Applying a frame border to a single frame draws the border on all sides of that frame. It will look as though the neighboring frames have their borders turned on as well, even if they are turned off.

Border thickness

You can use the nonstandard border attribute in the frameset element to specify the thickness of the frame borders in pixels. The default thickness varies by browser. Although border is not part of the Frameset DTD, it is fairly well supported by current browsers.

 Turning the frameborder off removes only the 3D border, but it leaves a gap between the frames. To remove this gap and give the page a smooth, seamless appearance, use the border attribute with a setting of 0 pixels: <frameset frameborder="0" border="0">

Targeting Frames

One of the challenges of managing a framed document is coordinating where linked documents display. By default, a linked document loads into the same window as the link; however, it is often desirable to have a link in one frame load a page into a different frame in the frameset. For instance, this is the desired effect for a list of navigation links in a narrow frame that loads content into a larger main frame on the page.

To load a new linked page into a particular frame, you first need to assign a name to the targeted frame using the name attribute in the frame element, as follows:

```
<frame src="original.html" name="main" />
```

 Names must start with a letter (upper- or lowercase).

Now you can specify that frame by name within any anchor (a) element with the target attribute, as shown in this example:

```
<a href="new.html" target="main">...</a>
```

In this example, the document *new.html* will load into the frame named "main."

If a link contains a target name that does not exist in the frameset, a new browser window is opened to display the document, and that window is given the target's name. Subsequent links targeted to the same name will load in that window.

The base Element

If you know that you want all the links in a given document to load in the same frame (such as from a table of contents into a main display frame), you can set the target once using the base element instead of setting the target within every link in the document (saving a lot of typing and extra characters in the HTML document).

Placing the base element in the head of the document, with the target frame specified by name, causes all the links in the document to load into that frame. The following is a sample targeted base element:

```
<head>
<base target="main" />
</head>
```

Targets set in individual links override the target set in the base element at the document level.

Reserved Target Names

There are four standard target names for special redirection actions. Note that all of them begin with the underscore (_) character. Do not give your frames names beginning with an underscore, as they will be ignored by the browser (names must start with a letter). The four reserved target names are:

_blank
    A link with target="_blank" opens a new, unnamed browser window to display the linked document. Each time a link that targets _blank is opened, it launches a new window, potentially leaving the user with a mess of open windows. Note that this value can be used with any link, not just those in a frames context.

Opening pages in new windows is problematic for accessibility. When opening a document in a new window, be sure to include a note that says "link opens in a new window" or something similar. This gives all users, but particularly those with non-visual browsers who won't see a new window open, a heads-up that the context of the page is going to change.

_self

This is the default target for all a elements; it loads the linked document into the same frame or window as the source document. Because it is the default, it is not necessary to use it with individual a elements, but it may be useful for the base element.

_parent

A linked document with target="_parent" loads into the parent frame (one step up in the frame hierarchy). If the link is already at the top-level frame or window, it is equivalent to _self. Figure 14-7 demonstrates the effects of a link targeting the parent frame.

The _parent target name works only when the nested framesets are in separate documents. It does not work for multiple nested framesets within a single frameset document as shown in Figure 14-4.

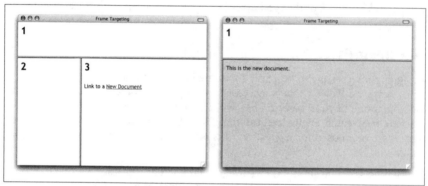

Figure 14-7. In nested framesets, the _parent target links to the parent frameset

_top

This causes the document to load at the top-level window containing the link, replacing any frames currently displayed. A linked document with target="_top" "busts out" of its frameset and is displayed directly in the browser window, as shown in Figure 14-8.

 Links to other web sites should use the target attribute set to _top or another named window to prevent the site from loading within the current frameset.

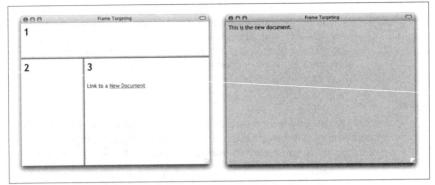

Figure 14-8. Linking with the _top target replaces the entire frameset

Frame Design Tips and Tricks

Perhaps the most common bit of design advice regarding frames is "don't use them." Although frames once had their heyday, they are no longer used in professional, standards-driven web design.

If you do choose to use frames for a project, there are a few pointers and tricks you should be aware of that go beyond a simple familiarity with the elements and attributes.

All-Purpose Pages

Designing a web page to be part of a framed document doesn't guarantee that it will always be viewed that way. Keep in mind that some users might end up looking at one of your pages on its own, out of the context of its frameset (this is possible if a search engine returns the URL of the content, for example). Since frames are often used for navigation, this orphaned content page could be a dead end for a user.

For that reason, you should try to design your content pages so that they stand up on their own. Adding a small amount of redundant information to the bottom of each page can make a big difference in usability. First, indicate the name of the site with a link to its home page on each content document. This helps to orient a newcomer who may have just dropped in from a search engine.

It is important to pay particular attention to the navigational options available on content pages viewed without their frameset. At the very least, provide a small link on every page to a more appropriate (and framed) starting point, such as the top level of your site. Be sure to set the target="_top" attribute so the link won't load the home page frameset within the current frameset.

External Links

By default, any link within a frame loads the new document into that same frame. To prevent external links from loading into the current frame, be sure to add target="_top" to all your external links; the new site will open in the full browser window. As an alternative, set the target to "_blank" to open the link in a new browser window.

 As noted earlier, always provide a note or some indication that a link is going to open in a new window so as not to confuse your users.

It is never appropriate to load whole external sites into the context of another framed document, unless you are doing so with the expressed permission of the owners and operators of the external site.

Improving Frame Accessibility

Framed content, while accessible to screen readers, may be disorienting. The content may be read from each frame in a linear fashion (users may skip to each frame with a keyboard shortcut) or it may be presented as a list of links to the individual HTML documents.

There are a few measures you can take to improve the accessibility of your site.

Give frames titles

One of the best ways to make framed content easier to use for visitors with alternative browsing devices is to give each frame a short but descriptive title using the title attribute in the frame element, as shown here:

```
<frame src="navigation.html" title="navigation options" name="links" />
<frame src="welcome.html" title="main content" name="main" />
```

Users can use the titles to decide whether to access that frame. In the absence of titles, the name attribute may be used, but authors typically give frames names that are minimal and not adequately descriptive.

Provide complete noframes content

Framesets should always include a noframes element to provide content if the user cannot or chooses not to view the framed content. It is a good idea to make the complete content from the framed page available in the noframes element and to enclose it in the body element. At the very least, the noframes content should be as descriptive as possible rather than just "you need frames to see this site."

Adding links to the individual HTML documents, particularly those containing links to the other parts of your site, helps users get to your content without relying on the frameset.

Helping Search Engines

Search engines all work differently but pretty much uniformly do not understand frames or any content within a frameset or frame element. This means search engines will not find any links that require burrowing through a site for indexing purposes, and all the content of your framed site will be missed.

The same measures for improving accessibility for users with non-visual browsing devices (i.e., providing frame titles and complete noframes content) will also make it easier for search engines to index your content.

In addition, you may include a meta element with information about your site in the frameset document. Although not all search engines use meta information, meta elements can be useful tools for those that do. If your top-level frameset document contains limited noframes content, you can use the meta element to add a site description and keywords to the page for the search engine to index. Values for the meta element related to search engines are provided in Chapter 9.

For more information about search engines and how they work, see the Search Engine Watch site at *www.searchenginewatch.com* (from which the previous information was gathered).

 For information on how MSN TV handles frames, see *developer. msntv.com/Develop/Frames.asp.*

15

Forms

Forms provide an interface allowing users to interact in some way with your site. In most cases, they are used to gather data, either for later use or to provide a customized response on the fly. Forms have a wide range of uses, from functions as simple as search boxes, mailing list signups, guestbooks, and surveys to as complex as online commerce systems.

Forms collect input via controls, such as buttons, text fields, or scrolling menus. Controls are placed on the page using special elements in the markup. These elements are merely an interface for collecting user information and do not actually process the data. The real work is done by forms-processing applications on the server, such as CGI scripts, ASP, ASP.NET, ColdFusion, PHP, or Java servlets.

The programming necessary for form processing is beyond the scope of this book. This chapter focuses on the frontend aspects of forms: the elements and attributes for building the form interface as well as the elements used to improve accessibility.

form	Establishes the form
input	Creates a variety of controls
button	Generic input button
textarea	Multiline text entry control
select	Multiple-choice menu or scrolling list
option	An option within a select control
optgroup	Defines a group of options
label	Attaches information to controls
fieldset	Groups related controls and labels
legend	Assigns a caption to a fieldset

The Basic Form Element

The form element is used to designate an area of a web page as a form.

form

```
<form> ... </form>
```

Attributes

Core (id, class, style, title), *Internationalization, Events,* onsubmit,
onreset, onblur
accept="*content-type-list*"
accept-charset="*charset list*"
action="*URL*" *(Required)*
enctype="*content type*"
method="get|post"
name="*text*" *(Deprecated in XHTML in favor of* id *attribute)*
target="*name*"

The form may contain any web content (text, images, tables, and so on), but its
function is to be a container for a number of controls (checkboxes, menus, text-
entry fields, buttons, and the like) used for entering information. It also has the
attributes necessary for interacting with the form-processing program. You can
have several forms within a single document, but they cannot be nested, and you
must be careful they do not overlap.

When the user completes the form and presses the "submit" button, the browser
takes the information, arranges it into name/value pairs, encodes the information
for transfer, and then sends it off to the server.

Figure 15-1 shows the form resulting from this simple form markup example.

```
<h2>Sign the Guestbook:</h2>
<form action="/cgi-bin/guestbook.pl" method="get">
<p>
First Name: <input type="text" name="first" /><br />
Nickname: <input type="text" name="nickname" /><br />
<input type="submit" /> <input type="reset" />
</p>
</form>
```

The action Attribute

The action attribute in the form element provides the URL of the program to be
used for processing the form. In the example in Figure 15-1, the form information
is going to a Perl script called *guestbook.pl*, which resides in the *cgi-bin* directory
of the current server (by convention, CGI programs are usually kept in a directory
called *cgi-bin*).

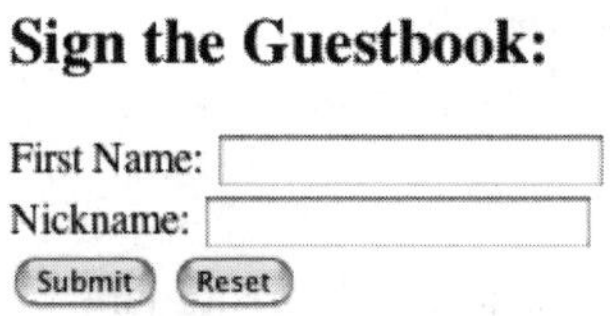

Sign the Guestbook:

First Name: [   ]
Nickname: [   ]
(Submit) (Reset)

```
<h2>Sign the Guestbook:</h2>
<form action="/cgi-bin/guestbook.pl" method="get">
<p>
First Name: <input type="text" name="first" /><br />
Nickname:   <input type="text" name="nickname" /><br />
<input type="submit" /> <input type="reset" />
</p>
</form>
```

Figure 15-1. A simple form

The method Attribute

The method attribute specifies one of two methods, either get or post, for submitting the form information to the server. Form information is typically transferred in a series of variables with their respective content, separated by the ampersand (&), as shown here:

```
variable1=content1&variable2=content2&variable3=content3
```

The name attributes of form control elements provide the variable names. The content the user enters makes up the content assigned to the variable.

Using the form in Figure 15-1 as an example, if a user entered "Josephine" next to "First Name" and "Josie" next to "Nickname," the form passes the variables on in this format:

```
name=Josephine&nickname=Josie
```

With the get method, the browser transfers the data from the form as part of the URL itself (appended to the end and separated by a question mark) in a single transmission. The information gathered from the nickname example would be transferred via the get method as follows:

```
get http://www.domainname.com/cgi-bin/guestbook.pl?name=
Josephine&nickname=Josie
```

The post method transmits the form input information separated from the URL, in essentially a two-part message. The first part of the message is simply the special header sent by the browser with each request. This header contains the URL from the form element, combined with a statement that this is a post request, plus some other headers we won't discuss here. This is followed by the actual form data. When the server sees the word "post" at the beginning of the message, it stays tuned for the data. The information gathered with the name and nick-name form would read as follows using the post method:

```
post http://www.domainname.com/cgi-bin/guestbook.pl HTTP1.0
... [more headers here]
name=Josephine&nickname=Josie
```

Whether you should use post or get may depend on the requirements of your server. In general, if you have a short form with a few short fields, use the get method. Conversely, long, complex forms are best sent via post. If security is an issue (such as when using the input type="password" element), use post, because it offers an opportunity for encryption rather than sending the form data straight away tacked onto the URL. One advantage of get is that the request can be book-marked, because everything in the request is in the URL. This isn't true with post.

 It is possible to send a *query string* via a URL in the document source, as shown here:

```
<a href="http://www.domainname.com/cgi-bin/guestbook.
pl?name=Josephine&amp;nickname=Josie">...</a>
```

Note that in XHTML documents, it is necessary to escape the ampersand character (that is, provide its character entity, &) in the URL. It will be correctly parsed as an ampersand by the processing agent.

Encoding

Another behind-the-scenes step that happens in the transaction is that the data gets encoded using standard URL encoding. This is a method for translating spaces and other characters not permitted in URLs (such as slashes) into their hexadecimal equivalents. For example, the space character translates to %20, and the slash character is transferred as %2F.

The default encoding format, the Internet Media Type (application/x-www-form-urlencoded), will suffice for most forms. If your form includes a file input type (for uploading documents to the server), you should use the enctype attribute to set the encoding to its alternate setting, multipart/form-data.

Form Controls

A variety of form control elements (also sometimes called "widgets") are used for gathering information from a form. This section looks at each control and its specific attributes. Every form control (except submit and reset) requires that you give it a name (using the name attribute) so the form-processing application can sort the information. For easier processing of form data on the server, the value of name should not have any character spaces (use underscores or periods instead).

The name attribute works like a variable name. The value provided for name becomes the variable's name. The content entered by the user into the form control is then assigned to the variable. Of all the attributes, the name attribute is key in passing data from the HTML form to any other place in the page, another page, or out through middleware to a database.

Input Controls

The input element is used to create a variety of form input controls, including:

- Single-line text entry fields
- Password entry fields
- Hidden controls
- Checkboxes
- Radio buttons
- Submit and reset buttons
- File upload mechanisms
- Custom and image buttons

The type attribute in the input element specifies the control type. The value of the type attribute also determines which other attributes may be used with the element. The input element and all of its accepted attributes appears here. Control-specific attribute listings appear along with the discussion of each control type.

input

```
<input />
```

Attributes

Core (id, class, style, title), *Internationalization, Events,* onfocus, onblur, onselect, onchange
alt="*text*"
accept="*MIME type*"
accesskey="*character*"
checked="checked"
disabled="disabled"
maxlength="*number*"
name="*text*" *(Required by all input types except submit and reset)*
readonly="readonly"
size="*number*"
src="*URL*"
tabindex="*number*"
type="text|password|checkbox|radio|submit|reset|file|hidden|
      image|button"
value="*text*"

Text entry field

The simplest type of form element is the text entry field (type="text"). Text is the default setting for the input element.

input type="text"

Attributes

> Core (id, class, style, title), *Internationalization, Events,*
> *Focus* (accesskey, tabindex, onfocus, onblur)
> disabled="disabled"
> maxlength=number
> name="text" *(Required)*
> readonly="readonly"
> size="number"
> value="text"

This field allows the user to enter a single word or a line of text. By default, the browser displays a text-entry box that is 20 characters wide, but you can set it to be any length using the size attribute.

By default, the user can type an unlimited number of characters into the field (the display scrolls to the right if the text exceeds the width of the supplied box), but you can set a maximum number of characters using the maxlength attribute.

Use the value attribute to specify the initial value, that is, the text to appear when the form is loaded. The user can change this default text. If you have a form that consists of only one text input element, pressing the Enter key submits the form without requiring a specific Submit button in the form. The following markup creates a text field with a size of 15 characters, a maximum length of 50 characters, and the text "enter your name" displayed in the field (Figure 15-2).

```
<p>What is your name?</p>
<input type="text" name="name" size="15" maxlength="50" value="enter your
name" />
```

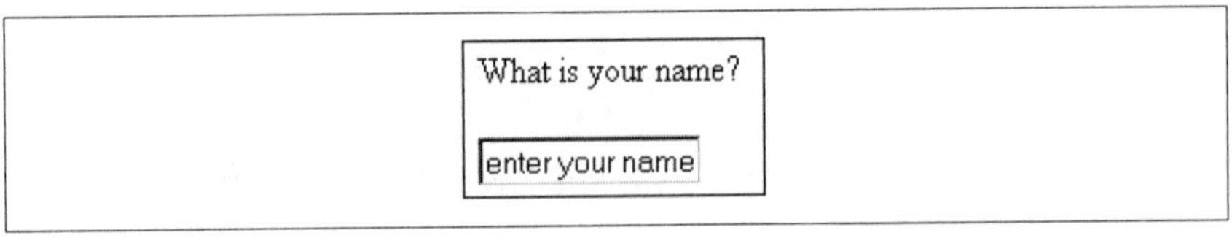

Figure 15-2. Text entry input control

Password text entry

A password field (type="password") works just like text entry, except the characters are obscured from view using asterisk (*) or bullet (•) characters (or another character determined by the user agent).

input type="password"

Attributes

> Core (id, class, style, title), *Internationalization, Events,*
> *Focus* (accesskey, tabindex, onfocus, onblur)
> disabled="disabled"

```
maxlength="number"
name="text" (Required)
readonly="readonly"
size="number"
value="text" (Required)
```

The attributes and syntax for password entry fields are the same as for the text input type. The only difference is that values (such as the one provided as an initial value in this markup) are replaced with neutral characters, as shown in Figure 15-3.

```
<p>What is your password?</p>
<input type="password" name="password" size="8" maxlength="8"
value="abcdefg" />
```

Figure 15-3. Password input control

 Although the characters entered into the password field are not visible to casual onlookers, the form does *not* encrypt the information entered and should not be considered to be a real security measure.

Hidden entry (type="hidden")

The hidden input (type="hidden") adds a control that isn't displayed in the browser, but is supplied to the form processor when the form is submitted.

input type="hidden"

Attributes

```
accesskey="character"
tabindex="number"
name="text" (Required)
value="text" (Required)
```

Hidden controls are useful for sending information to be processed along with the user-entered data, such as labels used by the script to sort forms. Users cannot see or alter hidden controls. Some scripts require specific hidden fields be added to the form in order to function properly. Here is a hidden element (Figure 15-4):

```
<p>This is a hidden element</p>
<input type="hidden" name="extra_info" value="important" />
```

> This is a hidden element

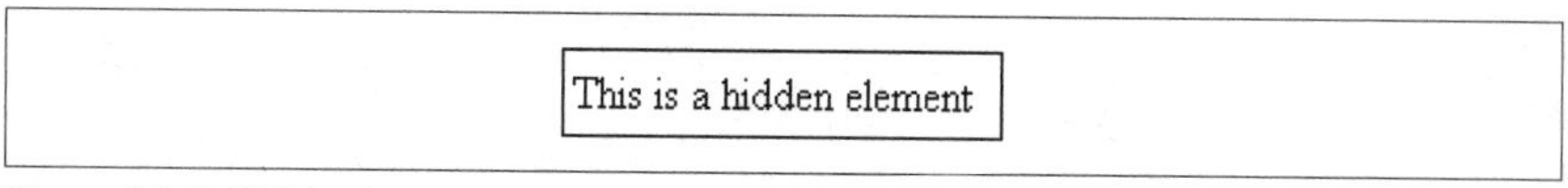

Figure 15-4. Hidden input

Checkbox (type="checkbox")

Checkboxes (type="checkbox") are like on/off switches that can be toggled by the user. Several checkboxes in a group may be selected at one time, which makes them useful for multiple-choice questions where more than one answer is acceptable. When a form is submitted, only the "on" checkboxes submit values to the server.

input type="checkbox"

Attributes

Core (id, class, style, title), *Internationalization, Events, Focus* (accesskey, tabindex, onfocus, onblur)
align="left|right|top|texttop|middle|absmiddle|baseline|bottom|
    absbottom"
checked="checked"
disabled="disabled"
name="*text*" *(Required)*
readonly="readonly"
value="*text*" *(Required)*

Checkboxes can be used individually to transmit specific name/value coordinates to the server when checked. By default, a checkbox is not checked; to make it checked when the page loads, simply add the checked attribute to the corresponding input element. In XHTML, you must provide a value for every attribute, so the correct syntax is checked="checked".

When the box is checked, the corresponding value is transmitted with the form to the processing program on the server. The values for unchecked boxes are not sent.

If you assign a group of checkboxes the same name, they behave like a multiple-choice list in which the user can select more than one option for a given property, as shown in the following markup and in Figure 15-5.

```
<p>Which of the following operating systems have you used?</p>
<input type="checkbox" name="os" value="WinXP" /> Windows XP
<input type="checkbox" name="os" value="Linux" checked="checked" /> Linux
<input type="checkbox" name="os" value="OSX" checked="checked" /> Macintosh
OSX
<input type="checkbox" name="os" value="DOS" /> DOS
```

Which of the following operating systems have you used?

⌐ Windows XP ☑ Linux ☑ Macintosh OSX ⌐ DOS

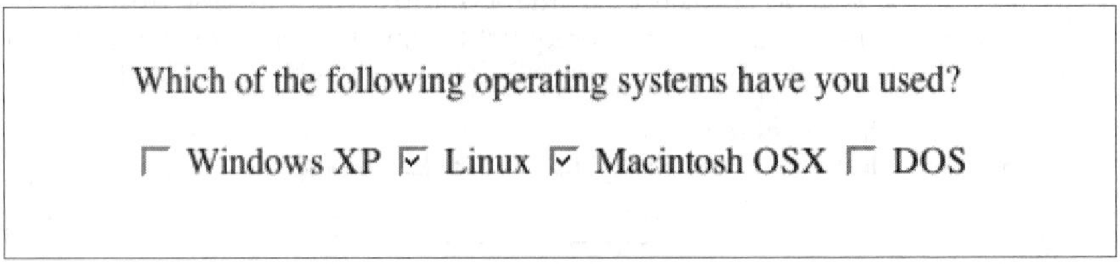

Figure 15-5. Multiple checkboxes in a group may be selected

Radio button

Radio buttons (type="radio") are another kind of button that users can toggle on and off. Unlike checkboxes, when a group of radio buttons share the same control name, only one button within the group can be "on" at one time, and all the others are "off." They are used when the options are mutually exclusive.

input type="radio"

Attributes

Core (id, class, style, title), *Internationalization, Events,*
Focus (accesskey, tabindex, onfocus, onblur)
checked="checked"
disabled="disabled"
name="*text*" *(Required)*
readonly="readonly"
value="*text*" *(Required)*

In this example (Figure 15-6), only one operating system may be selected. The checked attribute makes the button "on" by default when the page loads. Only data from the "on" radio button is sent when the form is submitted.

```
<p>Which of the following operating systems have you used?</p>
<input type="radio" name="os" value="WinXP" /> Windows XP
<input type="radio" name="os" value="Linux" /> Linux
<input type="radio" name="os" value="OSX" checked="checked" /> Macintosh OSX
<input type="radio" name="os" value="DOS" /> DOS
```

Which of the following operating systems have you used?

    ⊙ Windows XP   ⊙ Linux   ⦿ Macintosh OSX   ⊙ DOS

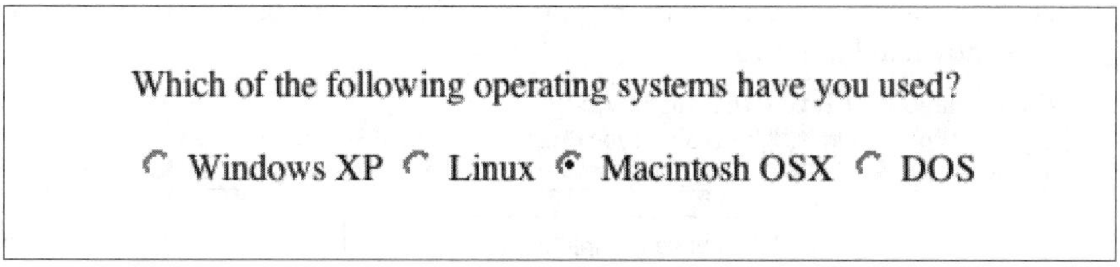

Figure 15-6. Only one radio button in a group may be selected

Submit and reset buttons

Submit buttons, used for sending the form data to the processing agent, are added with the submit input element type. Reset buttons return all form controls to their initial values and are added with the reset input element type.

input type="submit"

Creates a submit button control; pressing the button immediately sends the information in the form to the server for processing.

Attributes

> *Core* (id, class, style, title), *Internationalization, Events,*
> *Focus* (accesskey, tabindex, onfocus, onblur)
> disabled="disabled"
> name="*text*"
> value="*text*"

input type="reset"

Creates a reset button that clears the contents of the elements in a form (or sets them to their default values).

Attributes

> *Core* (id, class, style, title), *Internationalization, Events,*
> *Focus* (accesskey, tabindex, onfocus, onblur)
> disabled="disabled"
> value="*text*"

Every form (unless it consists of exactly one text field) needs a submit button control to initiate the transmission of information to the server. A form may have more than one submit button. By default, the submit button (type="submit") says "Submit" or "Submit Query," but you can change it by adding your own text after the value attribute.

The reset button (type="reset") reverts all form controls back to the state they were in when the form loaded (either blank or with values provided by the author with the value attribute). The default value (and hence the label for the button) is "Reset," but like the submit button, you can change its text by specifying its value, as shown in Figure 15-7.

```
<p>You have completed the form.</p>
<input type="submit" /><input type="reset" value="Start Over" />
```

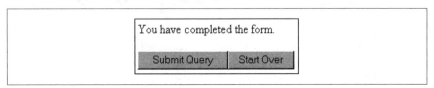

Figure 15-7. Submit and reset buttons

Some developers opt to leave the reset button out entirely, because there is no error-checking mechanism. If a user presses it accidentally, all the data already entered is lost. This isn't an uncommon occurrence.

Custom button

Authors may create a custom "push" button for use with client-side scripting (JavaScript) controls by setting the input type to button.

input type="button"

Attributes

Core (id, class, style, title), *Internationalization, Events,*
Focus (accesskey, tabindex, onfocus, onblur)
align="left|right|top|texttop|middle|absmiddle|baseline|bottom|
    absbottom"
disabled="disabled"
name="*text*"
value="*text*"

This button (type="button") has no predefined function, but rather is a generic tool that can be customized with a scripting language such as JavaScript (the scripting language should be declared with a meta element). Use the value attribute to write your own text on the button, as shown in the following markup and in Figure 15-8. The data from a type="button" input element is never sent when a form is submitted; this type is useful only with script programs on the browser.

```
<p>This does something really exciting.</p>
<input type="button" value="Push Me!" />
```

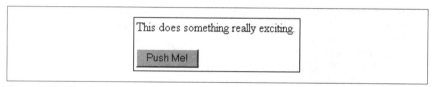

Figure 15-8. Custom button

Image button

If you want to use your own image for a submit button, use the image input type.

input type="image"

Attributes

Core (id, class, style, title), *Internationalization, Events,*
Focus (accesskey, tabindex, onfocus, onblur)
align="top|middle|bottom"
alt="*text*"
disabled="disabled"
name="*text*" *(Required)*
src="*URL*"

You can replace the submit button with a graphic of your choice by using the image input (type="image"), as shown in the markup example and in Figure 15-9. Clicking on the image submits the form to the server and includes the coordinates of the mouse click with the form data. You must provide the URL of the graphic with the src attribute. It is recommended that you use alternative text (with the alt attribute) for image buttons.

```
<input type="image" src="graphics/sendme.gif" alt="Send me" />
```

Figure 15-9. Using an image for a button

File selection

The file input type allows users to submit external files with their form submission. The form control includes a text field and a "Browse" button that accesses the contents of the local computer.

input type="file"

Attributes

Core (id, class, style, title), *Internationalization, Events, Focus* (accesskey, tabindex, onfocus, onblur)
accept="*MIME type*"
disabled="disabled"
maxlength="*number*"
name="*text*" *(Required)*
readonly="readonly"
size="*number*"
value="*text*"

The file-selection form field (type="file") lets users select a file stored on their computer and send it to the server when they submit the form. It is displayed as a text entry field with an accompanying "Browse" button for selecting the file, as shown in the following markup and in Figure 15-10. As for other text fields, you can set the size and maxwidth values as well as the field's default text. When using the file input type, you should specify enctype="multipart/form-data" in the form element.

```
<form enctype="multipart/form-data">
<p>Send this file with my form information:</p>
<input type="file" size="28" />
</form>
```

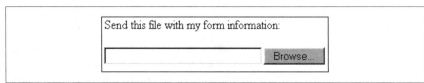

Figure 15-10. The file-selection form field

Multiline Text Areas

The textarea element creates a multiline, scrollable text entry box that allows users to input extended text entries.

textarea

```
<textarea>...</textarea>
    Core (id, class, style, title), Internationalization,
    Events, plus onselect, onchange
    Focus (accesskey, tabindex, onfocus, onblur)
    cols="number" (Required)
    disabled="disabled"
    name="text" (Required)
    readonly="readonly"
    rows="number" (Required)
```

A textarea form control and its markup are presented here (Figure 15-11).

```
<p>What did you dream last night?</p>
<textarea name="dream" rows="4" cols="45">Tell us your dream in 100 words or
less</textarea>
```

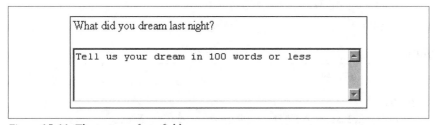

Figure 15-11. The textarea form field

Specify the number of lines of text the area should display using the rows attribute. The cols attribute specifies the width (measured in characters). These attributes are required. Scrollbars are provided if the user types more text than fits in the allotted space.

The text that appears within the textarea element is the initial content of the text entry window when the form is displayed. When the form is transmitted, the browser sends the text along with the name specified by the required name attribute.

Creating Menus with the select Element

The select element creates a menu of options that is more compact than group-ings of checkboxes or radio buttons. A menu displays as either a pull-down menu or as a scrolling list of choices, depending on how the size is specified. The select element works as a container for any number of option elements. It may also contain one or more optgroups, which are used to define a logical group of option elements.

select

```
<select> ... </select>
```

Attributes

> *Core* (id, class, style, title), *Internationalization, Events*, onfocus, onblur,
> onchange
> disabled="disabled"
> multiple="multiple"
> name="text" *(Required)*
> size="*number*"
> tabindex="*number*"

option

```
<option> ... </option>
```

Attributes

> *Core* (id, class, style, title), *Internationalization, Events*
> disabled="disabled"
> label="*text*"
> selected="selected"
> value="*text*"

optgroup

```
<optgroup>...</optgroup>
```

Attributes

> *Core* (id, class, style, title), *Internationalization, Events*
> disabled="*disabled*"
> label="*text*" *(Required)*

Pull-down menus

The select element displays as a pull-down menu of options when no size specification is listed (the default) or when size="1". In a pull-down menu, only one item may be selected at a time. (Note that adding the multiple attribute turns the menu into a scrolling list, as described in the next section.) Clicking on the arrows or bar pops up the full menu, as shown in Figure 15-12.

```
<p>What is your favorite ice cream flavor?</p>
<select name="ice_cream">
<option>Rocky Road</option>
<option>Mint Chocolate Chip</option>
<option>Pistachio</option>
<option selected="selected">Vanilla</option>
<option>Chocolate</option>
<option value="swirl">Fudge Ripple</option>
<option label="Praline Pecan">Super-duper Praline Pecan Smashup</option>
<option>Bubblegum</option>
</select>
```

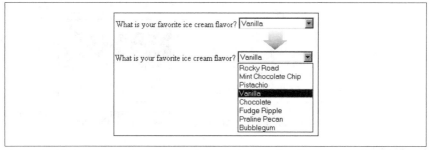

Figure 15-12. Items in a select menu can be set to display after the menu is collapsed

By default, the first option element in the list displays when the form loads. Use the selected attribute in an option element to make it the default value for the menu (the option will be highlighted when the form loads).

The text within each option element is the value that is sent to the server. If you want to send a value for that choice that is not displayed in the list, provide it with the value attribute in the option element. In the sixth option element in the example, users will see "Fudge Ripple," but the value "swirl" will be sent to the form processing agent.

The label attribute, when provided, is displayed instead of the option element content. In the seventh option in the example, users will see "Praline Pecan," but the form will send the data "Super-duper Praline Pecan Smashup," because it is the default value provided in the option element.

Scrolling menus

To make the menu display as a scrolling list, simply specify the number of lines you'd like to be visible in the list using the size attribute, or add the multiple attribute to the select element, as shown in the following markup and in Figure 15-13. The multiple attribute makes it possible for users to select more than one option from the list.

```
<p>What are your favorite ice cream flavors?</p>
<select name="ice_cream" size="6" multiple="multiple">
<option>Rocky Road</option>
<option>Mint Chocolate Chip</option>
<option>Pistachio</option>
<option selected="selected">Vanilla</option>
<option selected="selected">Chocolate</option>
<option value="swirl">Fudge Ripple</option>
<option>Super-duper Praline Pecan Smashup</option>
<option>Bubblegum</option>
</select>
```

This example also uses the selected attribute to preselect options and the value attribute for providing a value for the option that is different from the displayed text.

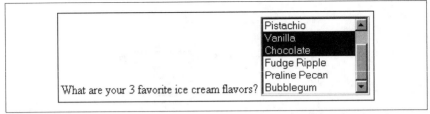

Figure 15-13. Use the size attribute to display a select menu as a scrolling list

Option groups

Conceptual groups of options may be organized into option groups, indicated with the optgroup element. This could be used by browsers to display hierarchical cascading menus. The value of the required label attribute is displayed as a heading for the following options.

The content of the optgroup element is one or more option elements. An optgroup element may not contain other optgroup elements. This example shows how the optgroup element could be used to structure a list of ice cream flavors similar to those in the previous examples. The label attribute provides a name for the group of options.

```
<p>What are your favorite ice cream flavors?</p>
<select name="ice_cream" size="6" multiple="multiple">
<optgroup label="traditional">
    <option>Vanilla</option>
    <option>Chocolate</option>
    <option>Mint Chocolate Chip</option>
    <option>Pistachio</option>
    <option>Fudge Ripple</option>
</optgroup>
<optgroup label="specialty">
    <option>Inside-out Rocky Road</option>
    <option>Super-duper Praline Pecan Smashup</option>
    <option>Bubblegum</option>
</optgroup>
</select>
```

When a user selects an option from the list (such as "Pistachio" from the example), the content of that option is passed on with the variable name specified in the select element:

```
ice_cream=Pistachio
```

Buttons

The button element defines a custom "button" that functions similarly to buttons created with the input tag. The button element may contain images (but not image maps) and any other content with the exception of a, form, and form control elements. Buttons may be rendered as shaded "3D" buttons with up/down motion when clicked (like submit and reset buttons), unlike the image input type, which is just a flat image.

button

```
<button> ... </button>
```

Attributes

Core (id, class, style, title), *Internationalization, Events,*
Focus (accesskey, tabindex, onfocus, onblur)
disabled="disabled"
name="*text*"
value="*text*"
type="submit|reset|button"

This example shows button elements used in place of "submit" and "reset" buttons. Note that the button elements include both images and text content.

```
<button type="submit" name="submit"><img src="thumbs-up.gif" alt="thumbs-up
icon" /> Finished. Ready for step two.</button>
```

```
<button type="reset" name="reset"><img src="thumbs-down.gif" alt="thumbs-
down icon" /> Try again.</button>
```

Notice that the text that appears in the button (for example, "Try again") does not necessarily have to match the variable name (reset). Usability experts recommend using clear and descriptive labels for buttons such as "Please press when completed." The variable name for that button that is passed along for processing can be more utilitarian.

Accessibility Features

Forms

The HTML 4.01 Recommendation added a few form elements and attributes that aid in accessibility. Some provide improved ways to group and label form structure and content. Others provide keyboard alternatives for selecting and activating (such as bringing *focus* to) form fields.

 The added benefit of elements that describe the structure and relationships within form content is that they provide good "hooks" for applying style sheet rules, as addressed briefly at the end of this chapter.

Labels

The label element is used to associate some descriptive text with a form field. This provides important context for users accessing the form with a speech-based browser. Each label element is associated with exactly one form control.

label

```
<label> ... </label>
```

Attributes

> *Core* (id, class, style, title), *Internationalization,*
> *Events, plus* onfocus, onblur
> accesskey="*character*"
> for="*text*"

There are two ways to apply a label to a form control. One is to nest the control and its associated description within the label element. Following is an example of labels being applied to a simple form with this method.

```
<form action="/cgi-bin/guestbook.pl" method="GET">
<label>Login account: <input type="text" name="login" /></label>
<label>Password: <input type="password" name="password" /></label>
<input type="submit" />
</form>
```

The other method is to associate the label with an id value specified in the input form. The for attribute says which control the current label is for. This method is useful for form fields that are not juxtaposed with their descriptions, such as when they span across different table cells. The following is an example of the label element referencing an id.

```
<form action="/cgi-bin/guestbook.pl" method="GET">
<label for="log">Login account:</label>
<input type="text" name="login" id="log" />

<label for="pswd">Password:</label>
<input type="password" name="password" id="pswd" />
<input type="submit" />
</form>
```

---

id and name in Form Elements

When applied to form control elements (such as input, select, etc.), the id and name attributes have different and distinct functions. The value of the name attribute is passed to the forms processor when the form is submitted. The id attribute is used to give the element a unique identifier that may be accessed by a style sheet rule, script, or the label element as shown in the previous example. An id attribute may not be used in place of name, because its value will not be submitted with the form.

This is not the case for the form element itself. For the form element, id and name have a similar role in assigning a unique name to the form. Which one you use depends on the markup language you are using. In HTML, the name attribute may be used to give the form a name to make it accessible to scripts. In XHTML, only id may be used, and the name attribute has been removed from the DTD.

---

fieldset and legend

The `fieldset` element is used to create a logical group of form controls. The `fieldset` may contain a `legend` element, a description of the enclosed fields that may be useful for non-visual browsers.

fieldset

```
<fieldset> ... </fieldset>
```

Attributes

Core (id, class, style, title), *Internationalization, Events*

legend

```
<legend> ... </legend>
```

Attributes

Core (id, class, style, title), *Internationalization, Events*
accesskey="*character*"
align="top|bottom|left|right" *(Deprecated)*

The following form is structured into groups using `fieldset` elements and includes descriptive legends.

```
<form>
<fieldset>
  <legend>Customer Information</legend>
  <label>Full name <input type="text" name="name" /></label>
  <label>Email Address <input type="text" name="email" /></label>
  <label>State <input type="text" name="state" /></label>
</fieldset>

<fieldset>
  <legend>Mailing List Sign-up</legend>
  <label>Add me to your mailing list <input type="radio" name"list"
value="yes"  checked="checked" /></label>
  <label>No thanks <input name"list" value="no" /></label>
</fieldset>
</form>
```

accesskey and tabindex

As part of the W3C's efforts to improve the accessibility of web content and interactivity to users without visual browsers or traditional point-and-click browser capabilities, the HTML 4.01 Recommendation introduced several attributes designed to make selecting form fields easier from the keyboard. To use a form control, it must be selected and active. In the web development world, this state is called *focus*. The following attributes bring focus to a form element without the traditional method of pointing and clicking on it with the mouse. Every user can enjoy these shortcuts for moving around in a form.

The accesskey attribute specifies a character to be used as a keyboard shortcut to an element. The actual functionality of the access key may require a keystroke combination such as Alt-*key* (Windows) or Command-*key* (Macintosh).

The accesskey attribute can be used with the button, input, label, legend, and textarea form control elements. Netscape 4 and other pre-standards browsers do not support access keys. When an access key brings focus to a label element, the focus is passed onto the respective form control.

Authors should provide some indication of the access key, such as providing an access key legend in the site or pointing out the access key in context by putting it in parentheses or making it bold or underlined, as shown in the following example.

```
<b>A</b>ddress<input type="text" name="address" accesskey="1" />
```

Accessibility specialists suggest using numbers instead of letters so as not to conflict with other software keystroke combinations. Others suggest that access keys should not be used because they are not transparent to the user and rely on the author providing access key legends or cues.

Another method for bringing focus to form fields is by hitting the Tab button to move from one field to the next. By default, browsers that support tabbing will tab through in order of appearance in the document. Use tabindex if you want to rearrange the order of focus without rearranging the source markup. It may be used with the button, input, select, and textarea elements. Elements with a tabindex of zero (0) are accessed after elements with positive specified values. Elements with negative tabindex values are left out of the tabbing order. Disabled elements are also left out. Adding tabindex is very straightforward.

```
Address <input type="text" name="address" tabindex="1" />
Zip code <input type="text" name="zip" tabindex="3" />
Phone number <input type="text" name="phone" tabindex="2" />
```

Although tabindex is intended to be an accessibility feature, many accessibility experts don't necessarily recommend it. In most cases, the order of appearance of form controls in the document source should be logical and sufficient. Changing that order may defy the user's expectations, potentially leading to confusion. Take care using tabindex and only use it with good reason.

As of this writing, tab indexing is poorly supported in Safari 1.0 and Firefox 1.0 on the Macintosh OS X. Because of bugs and incomplete implementation, tabindex may be assumed to apply to text-input fields only in these browsers.

title Attribute

Another attribute for improving the accessibility of form fields (as well as links, images, and other resources) is title. Use it to provide a description of the field or special instructions. Speech browsers may speak the title when the form field is brought into focus. Visual browsers may render titles as "tool tips" that appear when the pointer pauses over the control.

disabled and readonly

The disabled and readonly attributes inhibit the user's ability to select or change the form field. When a form element is disabled, it cannot be selected. Visual browsers may render the element as grayed-out. The disabled state can only be changed with a script. This is a useful attribute for restricting access to some form fields based on data entry earlier in the form.

The readonly attribute prevents the user from changing the value of the form field (although, it can still be selected). This enables developers to set values for controls contingent on other data entry using a script.

Affecting Form Appearance

The way a form control appears in the browser depends on that browser's rendering engine. In HTML alone, there are no attributes for affecting the presentation of a form control other than specifying character lengths for text fields. We are left with the knowledge that controls will be rendered slightly differently on different browsers and platforms.

Using Cascading Style Sheets to change the presentation and positioning of the form controls, you can take measures to improve the appearance of your forms. Layout tables have also traditionally been used to align form elements, but tables for layout are no longer the preferred option now that CSS is better supported.

Styling Form Controls with CSS

As for any HTML element, you can use Cascading Style Sheets to alter the font, colors, and size of form controls. The form element and the form control elements accept the id, class, and style attributes, so you can alter the font, size, color, and so on as you would for any other web page element. The label, fieldset, and legend elements intended for accessibility also make useful "hooks" for styling form content.

Some browsers, particularly old versions, do not support resizing fields or positioning forms with style sheets, so do so with caution and test thoroughly. Cascading Style Sheets are explained in Part III.

This simple example uses an inline style to create a black submit button with white text in the Impact font face (Figure 15-14):

```
<input type="submit" value="SUBMIT" style="font-family: Impact, sans-serif;
color: white; font-size: 14px; background: black" />.
```

Figure 15-14. A submit button altered with style sheets

In this example, a style sheet is used to highlight the required fields (last name and phone number) using class attributes in a minimal form (Figure 15-15):

```
<!-- Style information in head of document -->
<style type="text/css">
input.required { background-color: darkred; color: white }
</style>

<!-- In the form... -->

<p>First Name: <br />
<input type="text" name="first" size="30"></p>
<p>Last Name: <br />
<input type="text" name="last" size="30" class="required" value="Last name
required" /></p>
<p>Phone Number: <br />
<input type="text" name="number" size="12" class="required" value="required
field" /></p>
```

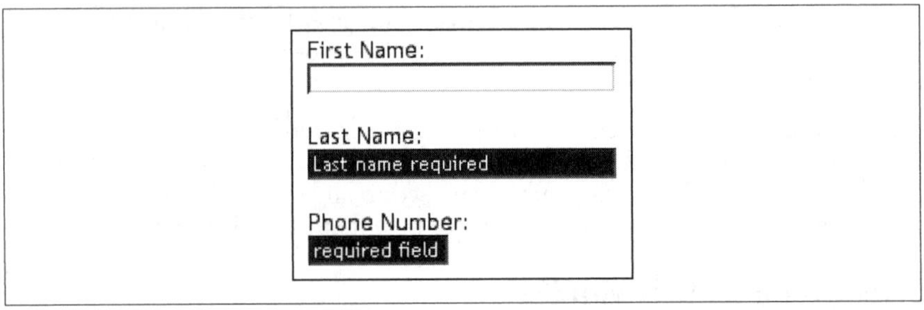

Figure 15-15. Style sheets alter the appearance of certain fields

Aligning Form Elements

A page with lots of form elements can get ugly in a hurry. The best favor you can do for a form is to align the elements in some orderly fashion.

Layout tables

The traditional method (and most reliable if you choose to support Version 4 browsers) is to align form content with tables, as shown in Figure 15-16. When laying out a form with a table, it usually works best to put the table element in the form element (rather than the other way around). Keep in mind that unstyled form controls will render at varying sizes depending on the user's browser and preferences, so allow for a certain amount of flexibility. If you do use tables for layout, make sure that they use minimal markup and linearize well. (See Chapter 13 for tips on layout tables.)

CSS-only alignment

You can align form elements in a similar fashion using CSS alone, without applying layout tables, as shown in the simple example in Figure 15-17.

This is the minimal and semantic markup for the form. Each component of the form uses a label and input element, except for the submit button, which has an input element only.

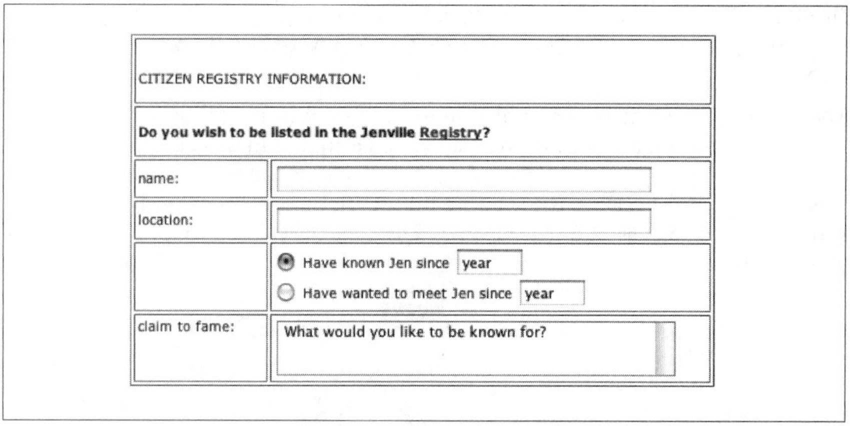

Figure 15-16. Using a table to align a form

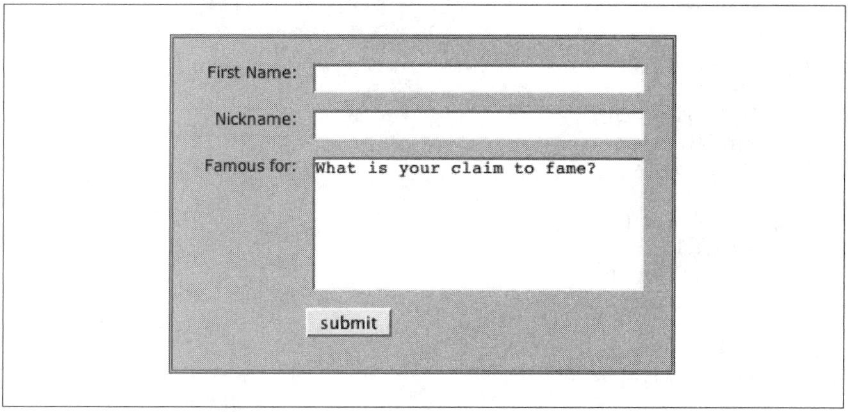

Figure 15-17. Using CSS to align a form

```
<form action="/cgi-bin/guestbook.pl" method="get">
    <fieldset id="signup">
        <label for="first">First Name:</label>
        <input type="text" name="firstname" id="first" /><br />

        <label for="nick">Nickname: </label>
        <input type="text" name="nickname" id="nick" /><br />

        <label for="desc">Famous for:</label>
        <textarea rows="10" cols="25" id="desc">What is your claim to
            fame?</textarea><br />

        <input type="submit" value="submit" id="subbutton" />
    </fieldset>
</form>
```

The goal for this form was to have the label and inputs appear side by side, with
the labels on a right alignment. This is handled by floating both the label and

input elements so they are adjacent, and then changing the text-align on the label to right. A margin on the label element keeps the label text from bumping into the inputs.

When using the float property, it is important to clear the following elements to make them start on a new line after the floated element. In this example, the clear property is applied to both the label and br elements for cross-browser compatibility. Note that because the submit button does not have a label, its float property is set to none and it is cleared. The style sheet used to align the form is provided here.

```
fieldset {
    font-family: Verdana, Arial, Helvetica, sans-serif;
    font-size: 12px;
    background-color: #CCCCCC;
    padding: 12px;
    border: medium double #666;
    width: 30em; }

label {
    width: 6em;
    float: left;
    text-align: right;
    margin: .5em 1em;
    clear: both; }

input, textarea {
    float: left;
    margin: .5em 0;
    width: 250px; }

#subbutton {
    float: none;
    width: auto;
    margin-bottom: 1em;
    margin-left: 7em;
    clear: both; }

br {clear: both; }
```

The Presentation Layer: Cascading Style Sheets

16

Cascading Style Sheets Fundamentals

Cascading Style Sheets (CSS) is a W3C standard for defining the presentation of web documents. *Presentation* refers to the way a document is displayed or delivered to the user, whether it's on a computer monitor, a cell phone display, or read aloud by a screen reader. This book focuses primarily on the visual aspects of presentation, such as typography, colors, alignment, layout, and so on. CSS is the mechanism for providing these types of style instructions to elements in a document that has been marked up with XHTML, HTML, or any XML language. Most important, CSS keeps these presentation instructions separate from the content and its structural and semantic markup.

Before CSS, web designers were at the mercy of the browser's rendering engine and internal style sheets for the way HTML elements looked in the browser window. Presentational elements and attributes added to HTML, such as the font tag and the bgcolor attribute, granted some additional control over visual display, but the integrity of markup suffered. Cascading Style Sheets (or just "style sheets" in these chapters) hand visual display decisions back to designers and authors. This comes as good news both for designers who want more control over presentation and for those who are eager to see HTML get back to the exclusive business of defining document structure and meaning. Style sheets make both of these goals possible.

CSS in a Nutshell

The chapters in this section provide a solid overview and reference of CSS and its properties. This book focuses on CSS used with documents written in (X)HTML, although CSS can also be used with any XML language.

This chapter lays an important foundation for understanding how CSS works, including rule syntax and how style sheets are applied to documents. It also covers some critical key concepts at the core of CSS, such as inheritance, handling conflicting styles (the cascade), how elements display, and the box model.

Browser issues are briefly addressed as well. The chapter finishes with a section on specifying values in CSS.

Chapter 17 explains all the various ways elements can be targeted for style application, and Chapters 18 through 23 cover the CSS visual display properties as they are specified in the CSS 2.1 Recommendation. These chapters document how CSS is designed to work. Browser support varies, of course, so this book provides notes if a property or its values are particularly problematic in a browser.

Finally, Chapters 24 and 25 put everything together in real-world applications. Chapter 24 is a cookbook of some of the most popular CSS techniques, such as CSS rollovers and multicolumn layouts. All of the browser-related problems and solutions are aggregated in Chapter 25, making it a handy reference if you encounter problems down the road.

In the interest of keeping everything "in a nutshell," the chapters in this section stick to visual media properties. The CSS properties related to interface, paged media, and aural (speech) media are included in Appendix B.

The Benefits of CSS

The benefits of using web standards for web page production were covered in detail in Chapter 1, however, it won't hurt to start off with a refresher of the advantages style sheets offer.

Greater typography and page layout controls
> With style sheets, you can specify traditional typography features that you could never do with HTML alone (even with its presentational extensions).

Less work
> Not only can you format all similar elements in a document with a single style rule, external style sheets make it possible to edit the appearance of an entire site at once with a single style sheet edit.

Potentially smaller documents
> Redundant font tags and nested tables make for bloated documents. Stripping presentational HTML out of the document saves on file size.

Potentially more accessible documents
> Well-structured and semantically rich documents are accessible to a wider variety of devices and the people who use them. Techniques based on presentational (X)HTML, such as using the font element to format headings and breaking up content into complex nested tables, damage the integrity of the source document.

Presentational HTML is on its way out
> The W3C has deprecated all presentational elements and attributes in the HTML and XHTML specifications. One day, browsers will not be required to support them.

It's well supported

As of this writing, nearly every browser in current use supports nearly all of the CSS 1 specification. Most also support the majority of the Level 2 and 2.1 Recommendations.

As for the disadvantages...there aren't any, really. Some people complain that style sheets can be misused, but you can't fault CSS for that. There are some lingering hassles from inconsistent browser support that require workarounds and extra planning (see Chapter 25), but that is by no means an argument against using style sheets for presentation right away.

How CSS Works

What follows is a simplified explanation of how style sheets work. At its heart, the process actually is this simple.

1. Start with an XHTML (or HTML) document. Ideally, this document will have been given a logical structure and semantic meaning using the appropriate XHTML elements. The XHTML markup is commonly referred to as the *structural layer* of the web page. It forms the foundation upon which the *presentation layer* is applied.

2. Write style rules for how each element should ideally look. Each rule targets the element by name, and then lists properties—such as font, color, and so on—to be applied to the element. The specifics of writing style rules are covered in the upcoming "Rule Syntax" section.

3. Attach the styles to the document. The style rules may be gathered up into a separate document and applied to a whole site, or they may appear in the header and apply only to that document. Style instructions may appear within an XHTML element itself as well. Each of these methods for attaching style rules to the content document is discussed in the "Adding Styles to a Document" section in this chapter.

Needless to say, there's a bit more to each step than is described here. The next section begins to get into the nitty gritty of style sheets by looking at the parts of a style rule.

Rule Syntax

Style sheets consist of one or more rules for describing how a page element should be displayed. The following example contains two rules. The first rule makes all the h1s in a document gray; the second specifies that paragraphs should be set in 12-pixel high Verdana or some sans-serif font:

```
h1 {color: #eee;}
p {font-size: 12px;
    font-family: Verdana, sans-serif; }
```

Figure 16-1 shows the components of a style sheet rule.

The two main sections of a style sheet rule are the *selector* (which identifies the element to be styled) and the *declaration* (the style or display instructions to be

CSS History and Standards Development

HTML was never intended to be a presentational language, so the idea of using separate style sheets with HTML documents (in the manner style sheets were used in desktop publishing) has been around since 1990 when the Web was just a twinkle in Tim Berners-Lee's eye. As early as 1993, before the release of the Mosaic browser, there were already several HTML style sheet proposals in circulation.

Cascading Style Sheets as we know them got their start in 1994 when Håkon Lie published his first draft of *Cascading HTML Style Sheets*. He was quickly joined by Bert Bos, who had been working with a similar style sheet system for his Argo browser. What set their style sheet proposal apart was the notion that the system must strike a balance between author and reader style preferences and that it must have a mechanism for dealing with multiple style sheets and conflicting styles (thus, the "cascade," discussed in an upcoming section in this chapter).

After presentations at WWW conferences and much lively discussion in the *www-style* mailing list, development of Cascading Style Sheets continued. In 1995 when the World Wide Web Consortium (W3C) became operational, an official working group dedicated to CSS was formed. By this time, "HTML" had been dropped from its title, because it was recognized early on that other languages would need a presentation language as well.

The first formal CSS Recommendation was CSS Level 1, released in 1996, which contains all the basics for attaching font, color, and spacing instructions to elements on a page. The first browser to implement aspects of CSS 1 was Internet Explorer 3, followed soon after with a half-hearted effort to stay competitive by Netscape 4.

CSS Level 2 was released in 1998. It is most notable for the addition of properties for positioning elements on the page (originally released as CSS-P, then later rolled into CSS Level 2), but it also introduced media types, table layout properties, aural style sheets, and more sophisticated methods for selecting elements, among other features.

As of this writing, there are two other Recommendations in the works. CSS Level 2, Revision 1 is a working draft (downgraded from Candidate Recommendation) that makes minor adjustments to CSS2 based on experience working with it from 1998 to 2004. It fixes errors, deletes properties that were not adopted by the CSS community, and moves some unsupported features to the upcoming CSS 3 specification.

—Continued—

The module-based CSS Level 3 Recommendation adds support for vertical flowing text, improved table handling, international languages, and better integration with other XML technologies such as SVG (Scalable Vector Graphics), MathML, and SMIL (Synchronized Multimedia Interchange Language). The W3C is also working on special CSS sets targeted to specific media such as CSS Mobile, CSS Print, and CSS TV. It is clear that CSS is an integrated part of the W3C's vision for the future of web content.

To keep up to date with the W3C's CSS-related activities, visit *www.w3.org/ Style/CSS/*.

Figure 16-1. Parts of a style sheet rule

applied to that element). In the previous sample code, the h1 and p elements are the selectors. The complete list of selectors in the CSS 2.1 specification is covered in Chapter 17.

The declaration is made up of a *property* and its *value*. The curly braces allow for multiple declarations, which make up a *declaration block*. A property is a stylistic parameter that can be defined, such as color, font-family, or line-height. Properties are separated from their values by the colon (:) character followed by a space. Style properties are the real meat of CSS; therefore, they are treated in detail in Chapters 18 through 23.

A declaration may contain several property/value pairs. Multiple properties must be separated by semicolons (;), as shown in this example.

```
p {font-size: 11px; font-weight: bold; color: #C06; }
```

Note that because CSS ignores whitespace and line returns, this same rule could be written like this to make the properties easier to find on the page.

```
p {
    font-size: 11px;
    font-weight: bold;
    color: #C06;
}
```

Technically, the last property in a declaration block does not require a semicolon, but developers usually include it anyway to make it easy to append the rule later. In addition, the inclusion of the trailing semicolon avoids a rare bug in older browsers.

Properties take several types of values, including predefined keywords, percentage values, specific length measurements, color values, integers, and URLs. When using a style property, it is critical to know which values it accepts. Accepted values for each property are provided with the property listings in each CSS chapter as well as in Appendix B. The syntax for length measurement and color values is discussed in the upcoming "Specifying Values" section of this chapter.

Adding Styles to a Document

Style rules can be applied to documents in three ways: as inline style directions, as style elements embedded at the top of the document itself, and as external files that can be either linked to or imported into the document.

 When attaching styles to a document, it is important to keep in mind that other style sheets may apply to your document as well. User agents, such as browsers, have built-in style sheets for rendering content. In addition, individual users may create their own style sheets and apply them to a single site or to all the sites they visit in order to make the text comfortable to read or to meet special needs. Which style sheet takes precedence is covered in the upcoming "Document Structure and Inheritance" section.

Inline Styles

You can add style information to an individual element by using the style attribute within the HTML tag for that element. The value of the style attribute is one or more standard style declarations, as shown here:

```
<h1 style="color: red">This Heading will be Red</h1>

<p style="font-size: 12px; font-family: 'Trebuchet MS', sans-serif">
This is the content of the paragraph to be set with the
described styles.</p>
```

Note that if the style attribute uses double quotation marks as shown, quoted values within the list (such as the font name "Trebuchet MS" in the example) must use single quotation marks. The reverse is also valid: if the document uses single quotes for attributes, then contained quoted values require double quotes.

Although a perfectly valid use of style information, inline styles are equivalent to the font extension to HTML in that they pollute the document with presentation information. With inline styles, presentation information is still tied to individual content elements, so any changes must be made in each individual tag in every file. Inline styles are best used only occasionally to override higher-level rules. In fact, the style attribute has been deprecated in XHTML 1.1 and does not appear in other XML languages.

Embedded Style Sheets

A more compact method for adding style sheets is to embed a style block in the top of the HTML document using the style element summarized here.

style

```
<style> ... </style>
```

Attributes

Internationalization (lang, dir, xml:lang)
media="all|aural|braille|handheld|print|projection|screen|tty|tv"
title="*text*"
type="*content type*" (*Required*)

The following example shows these sample rules embedded in an XHTML document:

```
<!DOCTYPE html PUBLIC "-//W3C//DTD XHTML 1.0 Strict//EN"
    "http://www.w3.org/TR/xhtml1/DTD/xhtml1-strict.dtd">
<html xmlns="http://www.w3.org/1999/xhtml" xml:lang="en" lang="en">
<head>
<style type="text/css">
   h1 {color: #666;}
   p  {font-size: 90%;
       font-family: Verdana, sans-serif; }
</style>
<title>Style Sheets</title>
</head>
...
</html>
```

The style element must be placed within the head tags in the document. Currently, Cascading Style Sheets is the only widely supported style sheet language, but the W3C has prepared for the possibility of additional languages to be added in the future by providing the type attribute within the style element. The only viable style type as of this writing is text/css. The type attribute is required in both HTML and XHTML; if it is omitted, some browsers may ignore the entire style sheet.

In addition, the media attribute in the style element (not shown in the example) may be used to target the medium (screen, print, handheld, etc.) to which the style sheet should be applied. If it is not present, the default is "all" media. The media attribute is discussed in the "CSS for Other Media" section.

 Browsers that do not support style sheets (such as Version 2 browsers) will not recognize the style element and may display the style rules on the page. If for some reason you need to support non-CSS browsers, you can prevent the contents from displaying by placing them within comments, as shown in this example:

```
<style type="text/css">
<!--
   h1 {color: #36C;}
-->
</style>
```

Although once standard markup, the inclusion of comments in the style element is no longer conventional as older browsers disappear from use.

External Style Sheets

The most powerful way to use CSS is to collect all the style rules in a separate text document and create links to that document from all the pages in a site. In this way, you can make stylistic changes consistently across a whole site by editing the style information in a single document. This is a powerful tool for large-scale sites (and small ones, too, for that matter).

Style sheet content

The style sheet document is a plain-text document that contains at least one style sheet rule. It may *not* contain HTML tags (after all, it isn't an HTML document) and so including HTML tags may cause parts of the style sheet to be ignored. HTML comments are also not permitted, however, comments may be inserted in the style sheet by using the CSS comment syntax shown here:

```
/* This is the end of the chapter */
```

There are two ways to refer to external style sheets (which should be named with the *.css* suffix) from within a document: the link element and the @import directive.

Using link

The best-supported method for referring to external style sheets is to create a link to the CSS document using the link element in the head of the document, as shown in this example:

```
<head>
<link rel="stylesheet" href="/pathname/stylesheet.css" type="text/css" />
</head>
```

The rel attribute defines the linked document's relation to the current document—a "style sheet." The href attribute provides the URL of the style sheet document. Authors may link to more than one style sheet in a document and both will apply.

Importing

An alternative to linking is to import an external style sheet into a document using the @import function in the style element:

```
<style type="text/css">
<!--
  @import url(http://pathname/stylesheet.css);
  p {font-face: Verdana;}
-->
</style>
```

In this example, an absolute URL is provided, but a relative URL may also be used. @import commands must come *before* anything else (except @charset).

Importing allows multiple style sheets to be applied to the same document. When additional @import functions are added within the style element, the style information from the last file read (the one at the bottom of the list) takes precedence over the previous ones.

The @import directive may also be used in the style sheet itself to reference information in other external *.css* files. See the sidebar "Modular Style Sheets" for more information.

@import is not supported by Netscape 4, Internet Explorer 3, and Opera 3. This limitation is often used as part of a technique for hiding unsupported style information from these browsers. Fortunately, they make up a small fraction of browsers in use as of this writing.

CSS for Other Media

CSS 2 introduced the ability to target style sheets to specific presentation media. This is done using the media attribute in the link element or @media or @import

Modular Style Sheets

The @import command may also be used within a style sheet document (the .css file) to pull style information in from other style sheets. With this method, one external style sheet attached to the HTML document accesses style rules from multiple .css files. This functionality is used strategically as a way to modularize styles and reuse them efficiently.

For example, frequently used styles related to navigation could be stored in a navigation style sheet. Basic typography settings could be stored in another, form styles in another, and so on. These style modules are added to the main style sheet with the @import command as shown here:

```
/* basic typography */
@import url("type.css");

/* form inputs */
@import url("forms.css");

/* navigation */
@import url("list-nav.css");
```

rules in a style sheet. The complete list of accepted values for the media attribute follows, but currently, only screen, print, and all are widely supported. Support for handheld is getting a lot of attention by the W3C's Mobile Web Initiative. Multiple values may be provided in a comma-separated list.

all
> Used for all media.

aural
> Used for screen readers and other audio versions of the document. This value is deprecated in favor of speech in future versions of CSS.

braille
> Used when rendering the document with a Braille device.

embossed
> Used with Braille printing devices.

handheld
> Used for web-enabled cell phones or PDAs.

print
> Used for printing the document or for displaying a "print preview."

projection
> Used for projection media such as a slideshow presentation.

screen
> Used for display on a computer monitor. This is the media that applies to all browsers running on computers.

speech
> This value is reserved for spoken output in the CSS 2.1 Recommendation. Its properties, however, will be defined in a later CSS Level release.

tty
> Used for teletype printers or similar devices.

tv
> Used for presentation on a television.

Key Concepts

To become comfortable with the way CSS behaves, it is important to have an understanding of its guiding concepts. This section provides a basic introduction to these fundamental ideas:

- Document structure and inheritance
- Conflicting style rules: the "cascade"
- Element types
- The box model

Document Structure and Inheritance

XML, XHTML, and HTML documents have an implicit structure or hierarchy. For instance, the html root element usually contains a head and a body, and the body, in turn, contains some number of block-level elements, such as paragraphs (p). A paragraph may include inline elements such as anchors (a) or emphasized text (em). This hierarchy can be visualized as a tree, branching out from the root. Figure 16-2 shows the document tree structure of a very simple XHTML document.

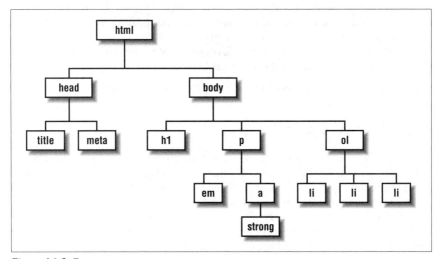

Figure 16-2. Document tree structure

The parent-child relationship

The document tree becomes a family tree when it comes to referring to the relationship between elements. An element that is directly contained by another element is said to be the *child* of that element. In Figure 16-2, the p element is the child of body, and body is said to be its *parent*. Elements that have the same parent are called *siblings*. In the example, the li element is the child of ol, its parent, and the other li elements are its siblings. This parent-child relationship is fundamental to how CSS works.

Notice in the example that the p element contains an a element, which in turn contains the inline element strong. Technically, the strong element is contained by the p element as well. All the elements a given element contains are said to be its *descendants*. To be considered a child, an element needs to be directly under its parent element in the hierarchy (therefore, a child is just a special kind of descendant). As you might expect, the terminology extends in the other direction as well, as all elements higher than a particular element in the hierarchy are known as its *ancestors*. The root element is called the root element because it has no ancestors.

This may all seem academic, but as you'll see, an awareness of the structure tree of your document comes into play in practical ways when working with CSS.

Inheritance

Related to structural relationships is the concept of *inheritance*, in which most styles are passed down from an element to its descendants. In other words, a child may *inherit* property values from its parent. For example, if a style rule applies a text color to a ul list, then every list item (li) within that list will be that color as well, because they inherit the property from their parent element. In CSS, most properties are inherited, but some (such as margins and backgrounds) are not. Inheritance is noted in the property descriptions throughout this book.

Styles applied to specific elements override settings higher in the hierarchy. With planning, inheritance can be used to make style specification more efficient. For example, if you'd like all the text on the page to be blue except for list items, you can set the color property at the body level to apply to the whole document and then use another rule to make lis a different color.

This notion of some rules overriding others brings us to an important concept: the cascade.

Conflicting Style Rules: The Cascade

It is possible (even common) for elements in a document to get presentation instructions from several sources. Conflicts are certain to arise. The working group that developed CSS anticipated this situation and devised a hierarchical system that assigns different weights to various sources' style information. The *cascade* (of *Cascading* Style Sheets) refers to what happens when several sources of style information vie for control of the elements on a page; style information is passed down until it is overridden by a style command with more weight.

The cascade order provides a set of rules for resolving conflicts between competing style sheets. When a user agent (such as a browser) encounters an element, it looks at all of the style declarations that might possibly apply to it, and then sorts them all out according to style sheet origin, selector specificity, and rule order to determine which one applies.

Style sheet origin

At the top level, user agents look at the origin of the style declarations. Browsers give different weight to style sheets from the following sources, listed from the least weight to greatest:

User agent style sheets
> This is the style information that is built into the browsing device for rendering HTML elements and sets their default appearance.

Reader style sheets
> The reader (or user) may also create a style sheet. Reader style sheets override the default browser styles.

Author style sheets
> When the author of a document attaches a style sheet to it, those declarations take precedence over the reader and user agent style sheets (with an "important" exception, listed next).

Reader !important *style declarations*
> In CSS 2, reader style declarations marked as !important (see the sidebar "Assigning Importance") trump all style declarations, even those from author style sheets.

 In CSS 1, any style marked as "important" by the author took precedence over all reader styles. This was reversed in CSS 2.

After considering the source of the style sheet, there is another hierarchy of weights applied to style sheets created by the document's author. As discussed in this chapter, authors may attach style information to documents as inline styles, an embedded style element, or one or more external style sheets. These points of origin within the author style sheets are given varying weights as well (remember, all author styles override reader and user agent styles unless the reader marks a style !important). The following list indicates the weight of various author style declarations, from least to most weight. In other words, style rules farther down in the list override those higher in the list.

Linked external style sheets (using the link *element)*
> If there are multiple linked style sheets, the style rules in style sheets listed lower in the document take precedence over those listed above it. For example, if an HTML document links to two style sheets, like this:

```
<head>
<link rel="stylesheet" href="style1.css" type="text/css" />
<link rel="stylesheet" href="style2.css" type="text/css" />
</head>
```

Assigning Importance

If you want a rule not to be overridden by a subsequent conflicting rule, include the !important indicator just after the property value and before the semicolon for that rule. For example, to always set all paragraph text to blue, use the following rule in a style sheet for the document:

```
p {color: blue !important;}
```

Even if the browser encounters an inline style later in the document (which should override a document-wide style sheet), like this one:

```
<p style="color: red">
```

that paragraph will still be blue, because the rule with the !important indicator cannot be overridden by other styles in the author's style sheet.

The only way an !important rule may be overridden is by a conflicting rule in a reader (user) style sheet that has also been marked !important. This is to ensure that special reader requirements, such as large type for the visually impaired, are never overridden.

Based on the previous style examples, if the reader's style sheet includes this rule:

```
p {color: black;}
```

the text would still be blue, because all author styles (even those not marked important) take precedence over the reader's styles. However, if the conflicting reader's style is marked !important, like this:

```
p {color: black !important;}
```

the paragraphs will be black and cannot be overridden by any author-provided style.

If a style rule provided in *style2.css* conflicts with a style rule in *style1.css*, the rule located in *style2.css* will take precedence because that style sheet is listed lower in the source document.

Imported external style sheets (using @import*)*
Imported style information overrides linked styles. If there are multiple @import directives, the rules provided in the style sheets lower in the list override the ones above.

Embedded style sheets (with the style *element)*
Styles applied to a specific document override those set externally.

Inline styles (using the style *attribute in an element tag)*
Inline styles override all other style declarations that may reference that element, with one exception.

Style declarations marked as !important

Any style marked as !important overrides all other conflicting style rules. The only thing that can override an important rule in an author style sheet is an important rule created by the user (as noted earlier).

Selector specificity

So far, we've looked at the priorities given to various sources of style information and methods for attaching style to markup. Once the set of applicable style rules has been chosen, there may still be conflicts. For this reason, the cascade continues at the rule level.

In the following example, there are two rules that reference the strong element.

```
strong {color: red;}
h1 strong {color: blue;}
```

The user agent assigns different levels of weight to the various selector types. The more specific the selector, the more weight it is given to override conflicting declarations. In the previous example, all the strong text in the document will render in red. However, if the strong text appears within a first-level heading, it will be blue instead, because an element in a particular context is more specific and carries more weight than the element alone.

The following is a list of selector types in order by weight from least to most. The selector types and terminology are explained in Chapter 17.

- Individual element and pseudoelement selectors (e.g., p, or :first-letter)
- Contextual selectors (e.g., h1 strong)
- Class selectors (e.g., p.special)
- ID selectors (e.g., p#intro)

Keep in mind that any rule marked !important will override conflicting rules regardless of specificity or order.

Rule order

Finally, once styles have been sorted by author, attachment method, and specificity, there may still be conflicts within a single style sheet source. When a style sheet contains several conflicting rules of identical weight, whichever one comes last has the most weight and overrides the others in the list. For instance, in the following example, all of the first-level headings in the document would be red, because the last rule wins.

```
h1 {color: green;}
h1 {color: blue;}
h1 {color: red;}
```

This "last-one-listed wins" scenario was mentioned earlier in relation to multiple link elements and @import commands. It also applies within a single declaration block. In the following example, the first declaration makes the border on all sides of a div gray using the shorthand border-color property. The second declaration conflicts with the first by specifying that the top border should be black. Because

Calculating Specificity

There is more to the story of how specificity is determined. The W3C developed a numbering system that expresses a selector's weight value in four parts (a, b, c, d), in which each part is a tally of the selector's particular components:

- a equals 1 if the rule is a style attribute value rather than a selector. For rules using selectors, a=0. In this way, inline styles will always win out over embedded or external style sheets.
- b equals the number of ID attributes given in the selector.
- c equals the number of class attributes, attribute selections, or pseudoclasses in the selector.
- d equals the number of every element and pseudoelement in the selector.

Here are a few simple examples to show specificity calculation at work. These rules are listed in order from least to most weight:

- p {color: #FFFFFF;}: One element selector (0,0,0,1)
- ol li em {color: red;}: Three element selectors (0,0,0,3)
- .hot {color: red;}: One class selector (0,0,1,0)
- #tip em {color: blue;}: One ID selector, one element selector (0,1,0,1)

Weight is calculated from left to right, so the last example (#tip em) with a 1 in the *b* slot would have more weight than the second example (p em) with a 3 in the *d* slot. That means if there were an em element that matched both these rules, it would be blue, because the selector with the 0,1,0,1 weight value wins.

For more information on calculating selector specificity, see the CSS Recommendation at *www.w3.org/TR/CSS21/cascade.html#specificity*. Eric Meyer provides a lengthier, illustrated explanation in his book *Cascading Style Sheets: The Definitive Guide* (O'Reilly).

the declaration listed second overrides the first, the resulting div will have a black top border and gray borders on the three remaining sides.

```
div#side {border-color: gray;
          border-color-top: black; }
```

Block and Inline Elements

If you are familiar with (X)HTML, you already know something about block-level and inline elements. CSS uses the terms "block" and "inline" as well, but it is important to understand that it is not the same as what makes elements either block or inline in (X)HTML.

In (X)HTML, the distinction between block-level and inline elements is based on containment rules, or in other words, what elements can be nested within what other elements. In general, block-level elements may contain both block and inline elements, while inline elements may contain only data and other inline elements. Paragraphs (p), headings (such as h1), lists (ol, ul, dl), and divs are the most common block-level elements. However even some of those block-level elements must obey special rules in (X)HTML; e.g., paragraphs, headings, and address (<address>) may only contain inline elements and content. Emphasized text (em) and anchors (a) are examples of common inline elements. It is invalid markup to nest a paragraph within an anchor element, for example.

In CSS, however, the notion of block-level and inline is purely presentational. block and inline are two possible *display roles* that are used to tell user agents how to present the element in the layout. Display roles are assigned using the display property. The following descriptions summarize the presentational differences between block-level and inline elements in CSS.

A *CSS block-level* element (display: block) always generates breaks before and after itself. It fills the available width of the parent element that contains it, whether it's the full width of the body of the document or a smaller defined space like a sized div. You can't place anything next to a block element in the normal flow of the document.

CSS Inline-level elements (display: inline) do not generate any line breaks. They appear in the flow of the line and will break only when they run out of room, at which point they wrap onto a new line.

Unlike the XHTML notions of block and inline, a CSS block-level element may be nested inside an inline-level element and vice versa. Using CSS, any (X)HTML (or XML for that matter) element may be made block-level or inline-level.

There are other values for the display property. The most commonly used and well supported is none, which causes the element not to display at all and essentially removes it from the document flow. Other values include list-item (like a block item, only it displays a number or bullet), run-in (makes an otherwise block element, like a heading, run into the following element, like a paragraph), and a collection of table-related display roles. Table display values are discussed in Chapter 22.

It is worthy of note that elements defined as block-level elements in (X)HTML typically also have a default presentation of display: block when rendered in browsers. Likewise, the default display role of HTML inline elements is display: inline. It is possible to override the default display roles of (X)HTML elements using the CSS display property. In fact, making list items (li) display inline instead of block-level (their default) is a common web design practice (see Chapter 24).

However, bear in mind that changing the presentation of an HTML element with CSS does not change the definition of that element as block-level or inline in HTML. Putting a block-level element within an inline element will always be invalid (X)HTML, regardless of the display role.

While (X)HTML elements have default display roles, elements in other XML languages typically do not. The display property is the tool authors may use to explicitly declare display roles for individual elements.

Authors are advised not to reassign display roles for table-related (X)HTML elements.

Having an awareness of an element's display role is useful for understanding the CSS box model, discussed in the next section.

Introduction to the Box Model

The *box model* forms the cornerstone of the CSS visual formatting system. It is a critical concept for understanding how style sheets work. This section provides only a basic introduction to the box model. The specifics of applying styles and laying out pages using the box model are provided in Chapters 19 and 21.

According to the box model, every element, whether block or inline, generates a rectangular box around itself called an *element box* (although block and inline boxes are handled somewhat differently). Properties such as borders, margins, and backgrounds (among others) can be applied to an element's box. Boxes can also be used to position elements and lay out the page. Figure 16-3 shows the resulting boxes for this small sample of markup.

```
<body>
<h1>Headline</h1>
<p>This is a paragraph of text. <em>Lorem ipsum</em> dolor sit amet,
consecteteur adipiscing elit. Praesent tellus ante, laoreet in, ultrices at,
vehicula ut, leo. <strong>Vivamus velit.</strong> Nullam massa odio,
condimentum ut, porttitor in, suscipit eu, risus.</p>
<ul>
    <li>This is a list of list items</li>
    <li>And another item</li>
    <li>And another item</li>
</ul>
</body>
```

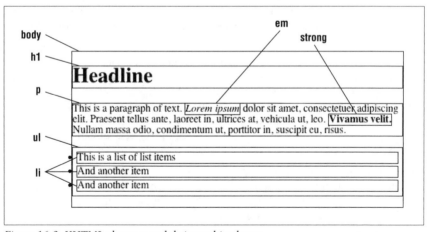

Figure 16-3. XHTML elements and their resulting boxes

Element boxes are made up of four main components. At the core of the box is the element's content. The content is surrounded by some amount of padding, then the border, which is surrounded by the margin, as shown in Figure 16-4.

There are a few fundamental characteristics of the box model worth pointing out:

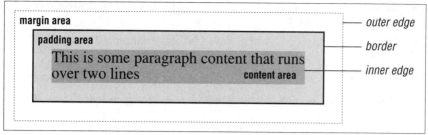

Figure 16-4. Structure of an element box

- Padding, borders, and margins are optional. If you set their values to zero, they are effectively removed from the box.

- The padding area is the space between the edge of the content area and the border (if there is one). Any background color or image applied to the element will extend into the padding area.

- Borders are generated by style properties that specify their style (such as solid or dashed), width, and color. When a border has gaps, the background color or image shows through those gaps. In other words, backgrounds extend behind the border to its outer edge.

- Margins are always transparent, which means that the background color or pattern of the parent element will show through. The boundary of the margin (the element's outer edge) is not visible, but is a calculated amount.

- The width of an element applies to the width of the content area only. This means that when you specify that an element should be 200 pixels wide, the actual contents will display 200 pixels wide, and the cumulative widths of the padding, border, and margins will be added to that amount. (Internet Explorer 5 for Windows is notorious for implementing the width of the box incorrectly. See Chapter 25 for details.)

- The top, right, bottom, and left sides of an element box may be styled independently of one another. For example, you can add a border to only the bottom of an element, or to only the left and right sides.

This should get you started visualizing your document according to the CSS model, but it's only the beginning. To put these ideas into practical use, see the box properties and positioning discussions in Chapters 19, 21, and 24.

Specifying Values

It is important to use the proper syntax for specifying length and color values in style sheet rules.

Length Units

CSS allows measurements to be specified in a variety of units. Some of the units (such as em and pica) are taken from the traditional print publishing world. When specifying lengths, keep the following in mind:

- Do not add space between the number and the two-letter unit abbreviation. It must be 24px, not 24 px.
- The only value that does not require a unit abbreviation is 0 (zero).
- Measurements may contain decimal fractions, such as 14.5cm.
- Some properties, such as margins, accept negative values: margin: -500px

Table 16-1 lists units of measurements that you can specify in style sheet values.

Table 16-1. Units of measurements for style sheet values

Code	Unit	Description
px	Pixel	Pixel units are relative to the monitor resolution.
pt	Point	A traditional publishing unit of measurement for type. In CSS, a point is equal to 1/72 of an inch.
pc	Pica	A traditional publishing unit of measurement equal to 12 points (or 1/6 of an inch).
em	Em	A relative unit of measurement that traditionally equals the width of the capital letter "M" in the current font. In CSS, it is equal to the point size of the font (e.g., an em space in 24pt type is 24 points wide) and is used for both vertical and horizontal measurements.
ex	Ex	A relative unit of measurement that is the height of the lowercase letter "x" for that font (approximately half the length of an em).
in	Inches	Standard unit of measurement in the U.S.
mm	Millimeters	Metric measurement.
cm	Centimeters	Metric measurement.

Specifying Color

As in HTML, there are two methods for specifying color in style sheets: by name and by numerical value.

By name

You can specify color values by name as follows:

    h1 {color: olive;}

The CSS 2.1 specification accepts only 17 color names for use in style sheets (CSS 1 and CSS 2 had only 16 names; orange was added in Version 2.1.) The color names are:

aqua	green	orange	white
black	lime	purple	yellow
blue	maroon	red	
fuchsia	navy	silver	
gray	olive	teal	

Other names from the complete list of color names may be supported by some browsers. For the complete list, see Appendix D.

By RGB value

Within style sheets, RGB colors can be specified by any of the following methods:

```
{color: #0000FF;}
{color: #00F;}
{color: rgb(0,0,255);}
{color: rgb(0%, 0%, 100%);}
```

The first method uses three two-digit hexadecimal RGB values (for a complete explanation, see Appendix D). The second method uses a three-digit syntax, which is essentially converted to the six-digit form by replicating each digit (therefore, #00F is the same as #0000FF).

The last two methods use a functional notation specifying RGB values as a comma-separated list of regular values (from 0 to 255) or percentage values (from 0 to 100%). Note that percentage values can use decimals, e.g., rgb(0%, 50.5%, 33.3%).

Percentage Values

Percentage values are indicated by a number followed by the percentage sign (%). Percentage values are calculated relative to other values in the document. When specifying percentage values for measurements, it is important to pay attention to how they will be calculated for the given property. Sometimes percentages are relative to the current element. In other instances, they are calculated based on the properties of the parent element. The CSS Recommendation specifies how percentage values are calculated for each value, and there are notes provided in the descriptions in this book as necessary.

Keyword Values

Most properties also have values that are described in *keywords*. You'll find keywords for each property in the property listing in the CSS Recommendation and throughout this book. Note that a keyword like normal may have different functions depending on the context of the property to which it is applied.

All properties in CSS 2.1 have the keyword inherit that forces the value of the property to be the same as that of the parent element. Most properties inherit by nature, but the inherit keyword is a tool for overriding assigned styles when necessary.

Browser Support

For years, web designers and developers grappled with inconsistencies in the ways browsers supported HTML, but eventually, reliable support for nearly the entire HTML 4.01 Recommendation arrived. Now, the browser developers are working on getting up to speed with CSS, so support of some features (particularly in the newer CSS 2.1 Recommendation) are buggy and inconsistent across browsers.

Chapter 25 specifically addresses the most notorious browser bugs and how to deal with them, but you'll also find browser alert notes when appropriate for each property in Chapters 18 through 23.

No browser support chart is provided with this book, because it would no doubt be obsolete before this book is retired. However, there are several excellent online resources that publish CSS browser support information.

West Civ Browser Support Page (www.westciv.com/style_master/academy/browser_support/index.html)
West Civ provides free support charts online for properties tested on IE, Netscape, and Opera. A complete, more detailed report is available for a nominal fee.

Index DOT Css, by Brian Wilson (www.blooberry.com/indexdot/css/index.html)
This is a remarkably thorough site (albeit somewhat out of date) that documents browser support for every CSS selector, property, and value for Internet Explorer, Netscape/Mozilla, and Opera browsers. It also provides notes on particular bugs and behaviors.

Internet Explorer Blog (blogs.msdn.com/ie/)
Here you can keep up with what the developers are up to at Microsoft.

For Further Reading

CSS is a rich topic. Not surprisingly, there are mountains of information about it in print and on the Web. These are just a few resources that I found invaluable in writing the CSS chapters of this book.

Books

There are many good books on CSS on the shelves these days. These are the ones that helped me out the most and that I recommend wholeheartedly.

- *Cascading Style Sheets: The Definitive Guide, Second Edition*, by Eric Meyer (O'Reilly)
- *Web Standards Solutions: The Markup and Style Handbook*, by Dan Cederholm (Friends of Ed)
- *The Zen of CSS Design: Visual Enlightenment for the Web*, by Dave Shea and Molly E. Holzschlag (New Riders)
- *Eric Meyer on CSS: Mastering the Language of Web Design*, by Eric A. Meyer (New Riders)

Online Resources

These sites are good starting points for online exploration of style sheets.

W3C (www.w3c.org/Style/CSS)
The World Wide Web Consortium is where the standards, including CSS, are developed and overseen. Go right to the source for the nitty-gritty details and latest developments.

A List Apart (www.alistapart.com)
> This online magazine features some of the best thinking and writing on cutting-edge, standards-based web design. It was founded in 1998 by Jeffrey Zeldman and Brian Platz.

css-discuss (www.css-discuss.org)
> This is a mailing list devoted to talking about CSS and how to use it.

Inspirational CSS showcase sites

If you are looking for excellent examples for what can be done with CSS and standards-based design, check out these sites:

CSS Zen Garden (www.csszengarden.com)
> This is a showcase site for what can be done with CSS, a single HTML file, and the creative ideas and techniques of hundreds of designers. Its creator and keeper is standards expert Dave Shea. See the companion book listed above.

CSS Beauty (www.cssbeauty.com)
> A showcase of excellent sites designed with CSS.

The Weekly Standards (www.weeklystandards.com)
> This web site highlights recently launched corporate web sites that take advantage of standards-based development techniques.

Informative personal sites

Some of the best CSS resources on the Web are the blogs and sites of individuals with a passion for standards-based design. Most feature articles, tutorials, and lists of links to other great online resources. These are only a few of the many inspirational blogs, but from these, it's easy to access the CSS community network.

Stopdesign (www.stopdesign.com)
> Douglas Bowman, CSS and graphic design guru, publishes articles and trend-setting tutorials.

Quirksmode (www.quirksmode.org)
> His own description says it best: "QuirksMode.org is the personal and professional site of Peter-Paul Koch, freelance web developer in Amsterdam, the Netherlands. It contains more than 150 pages with CSS and JavaScript tips and tricks, and is one of the best sources on the WWW for studying and defeating browser incompatibilities."

Mezzoblue (www.mezzoblue.com)
> This is the personal site of Dave Shea, the creator of the CSS Zen Garden.

Meyerweb.com (www.meyerweb.com)
> This is the personal site of the king of CSS, Eric Meyer.

Tantek Çelik (tantek.com/log)
Tantek was the developer of Internet Explorer 5 for the Mac, an author of the W3C CSS Recommendations, and the creator of the famous "Box Model Hack." He's got his finger on the pulse, to say the least.

Molly.com (www.molly.com)
This is the blog of prolific author and web-standards activist, Molly E. Holschlag.

Simplebits (www.simplebits.com)
This is the personal site of standards guru and author, Dan Cederholm.

17

Selectors

The *selector* is the part of the style rule that identifies the element (or elements) to which the presentation instructions are applied. For instance, if you want all of the h1s in a document to be green, write a single style rule with h1 as the selector. But that's just the beginning. CSS provides a variety of selector types to improve flexibility and efficiency in style sheet authoring. This chapter introduces the selectors included in the CSS 2.1 specification, including:

- Type (element) selectors
- Contextual selectors (descendant, child, and adjacent sibling)
- Class and ID selectors
- Attribute selectors
- Pseudoclasses
- Pseudoelements

Not all of these forward-thinking selectors are supported by today's browsers, so if a particular selector is not quite ready for prime time, it will be noted.

The W3C Selectors specification introduces additional selectors above and beyond those in CSS 2.1, which modern browsers are still in the process of implementing. This book does not describe them. For more information on those new selectors in particular, see the W3C Selectors specification (*www.w3.org/TR/css3-selectors*).

Type (Element) Selector

The most straightforward selector is the *type selector* that targets an element by name, as shown in these examples:

```
h1 {color: blue;}
h2 {color: blue;}
p {color: blue;}
```

Type selectors can be grouped into comma-separated lists so a single property will apply to all of them. The following code has the same effect as the previous code:

```
h1, h2, p {color: blue;}
```

CSS 2 introduced a universal element selector (*) that matches any element (like a wildcard). The style rule * {color: gray} makes every element in a document gray. The universal selector may be a useful tool when used in relation to other elements, as discussed in the next section.

 The universal selector causes problems with form controls in some browsers. If your page contains form inputs, the safest bet is to avoid the universal selector.

Contextual Selectors

Type selectors, such as those in the previous example, apply to all instances of that element found in a document. By contrast, *contextual selectors* allow you to apply style properties to select elements, based on their context or relation to another element. There are several types of contextual selectors: descendant, child, and adjacent sibling. This is where being familiar with the document tree structure of your document comes in handy.

Contextual selectors use a specific character to signify the type of relationship between the elements in the selectors. This character is known as the *combinator*.

Descendant Selector

Descendant selectors target elements that are contained within (therefore descendants of) another element. They are indicated in a list separated by a character space (the combinator for descendant selectors), starting with the higher-level element. For example, the following rule specifies that em elements should be olive, but only when they are descendants of a list item (li). All other em elements are unaffected by this rule.

```
li em {color: olive;}
```

Like simple type selectors, contextual selectors can be grouped together in comma-separated lists. The following code makes emphasized (em) text red only when it appears in the context of a first-, second-, or third-level heading:

```
h1 em, h2 em, h3 em {color: red;}
```

Descendant selectors may also be nested several layers deep, as shown in this example that targets only emphasized text (em) within anchors (a) within ordered lists (ol).

```
ol a em {font-weight: bold;}
```

Child Selector

A *child selector* is similar to the descendant selector, but it targets only direct children of a given element. In other words, the element must be contained directly within the higher-level element with no other element levels in between. Child selectors are separated by the greater-than symbol (>). The rule in the following example makes the background of emphasized text gray, but only when it is the child of a paragraph:

```
p > em {background-color: gray;}
```

Therefore, in the following markup example, only the first instance of em receives a gray background, because the second one is the child of an intervening strong element:

```
<p>I've got <em>laser</em> eyes, and <strong>I know what you're <em>
thinking.</em></strong></p>
```

Adjacent Sibling Selector

The *adjacent sibling selector* is used to target an element that comes immediately after another element with the same parent element. The combinator for adjacent sibling selectors is a plus (+) sign. For example, if you wanted to give special presentation treatment to the first paragraph following a first-level heading, the resulting rule would look like this:

```
H1 + p {padding-left: 40;}
```

 Browser alert: Child selectors and adjacent sibling selectors are not supported by Netscape 4 or Internet Explorer Version 6 and earlier. Support in Internet Explorer 7, in beta as of this writing, is not yet documented.

Class and ID Selectors

So far, all of the selectors we've seen have been tied to specific elements. *Class selectors* and *ID selectors* give you the opportunity to target elements that you've named yourself, independent of the document element.

Elements are named using the class and id attributes. They can be applied to all XHTML elements except base, head, html, meta, script, style, and title. In addition, class may not be used in basefont and param. Class and ID selectors work in slightly different ways.

class Selector

Use the class attribute to identify a number of elements as being part of a conceptual group. Elements in a class can then be modified with a single style rule. For instance, you can identify all the items in a document that you classify as "special":

```
<h1 class="special">Attention!</h1>
<p class="special">You look marvelous today.</p>
```

To specify the styles for elements of a particular class, add the class name to the type selector, separated by a period (.).

```
h1.special {color: red;}
p.special {color: red;}
```

To apply a property to all the elements of the same class, omit the tag name in the selector (be sure to leave the period—it is the character that indicates a class):

```
.special {color: red;}
```

Note that class names cannot contain spaces; use hyphens or underscores instead if necessary (although underscores are discouraged due to lack of support in some browsers).

When choosing a name for a class, be sure that it is meaningful. For example, naming a class redtext merely reintroduces presentational information to the document and does nothing to describe the type of information in the element. It may also be confusing if in a future redesign, the color of those elements changes to blue.

Authors should resist going overboard with class creation (a syndrome commonly referred to as "class-itis"). In many cases, other types of selectors with higher specificity, such as contextual or attribute selectors, may be used instead.

id Selector

The id attribute is used similarly to class, but it is used for targeting a single element rather than a group. id must be used to name an element uniquely (in other words, two elements can't have the same id name in the same document). It is not a problem for an id value to be used in multiple documents across a site; it only needs to be unique within each document. If you have several elements that need a similar treatment, use class instead.

The following example gives a paragraph a specific ID (note that the value of an id attribute must always begin with a letter):

```
<p id="j042801">New item added today</p>
```

ID selectors are indicated by the octothorpe (#) symbol within the style sheet as follows:

```
p#j061998 {color: red;}
```

The element name may be omitted:

```
#j061998 {color: red;}
```

In modern web design, id attributes are frequently used to identify main sections (usually divs) within a page. Some common id values for this purpose are content, header, sidebar, navigation, and footer. Establishing sections of the page makes it easier to create contextual selectors so that elements can be styled based on where they appear on the page without the need to create extra classes.

Like class attributes, id names should be chosen based on the semantic role of the element, not its presentation. For example, for a sidebar on the left side of the page that contains news, it is preferable to name the div id="sidebar-news" rather than id="sidebar-left".

 The id attribute is also used in scripting to identify and access unique page objects.

Attribute Selectors

CSS 2 introduced a system for targeting specific attribute names or values. This may be useful for XML languages other than XHTML that may not contain class and id attributes. There are plenty of uses for attribute selectors within XHTML as well, but unfortunately, attribute selectors are not widely supported at this time.

 Browser alert: Attribute selectors are not supported by Internet Explorer Versions 6 and earlier. As of this writing, support is rumored in IE 7, but it has not been documented. Gecko-based browsers (Mozilla and Netscape 6+), Safari, and Opera 7 do support them, but represent a smaller portion of browser usage.

There are four variations on attribute selectors:

Simple attribute selection
> The broadest attribute selector targets elements with a particular attribute regardless of its value. The syntax is as follows:
>
>   element[attribute]
>
> Example: img[title] {border: 3px red;}
>
> Specifies that all images in the document that include a title attribute get a red border.

Exact attribute value
> This selects elements based on an attribute with an exact attribute value.
>
>   element[attribute="exactvalue"]
>
> Example: img[title="first grade"] {border: 3px red;}
>
> Only images with the title value first grade are selected. The value must be an exact character string match.

Partial attribute value
> For attributes that accept space-separated lists of values, this attribute selector allows you to look for just one of those values (rather than the whole string). The tilde (~) in the selector differentiates this selector from those that match an exact value.
>
>   element[attribute~="value"]
>
> Example: img[title~="grade"] {border: 3px red;}
>
> This selector looks for images that contain the word grade in the list of title values. Images with the attributes title="first grade" or title="second grade" would be selected by the example selector.

Hyphen-separated attribute value
> This selector is intended to target hyphen-separated values. The selector matches the value you specify, or that value followed by a hyphen. This type

CSS: Selectors

of attribute selector is indicated by a vertical bar (|). This will make more sense in the example.

```
element[attribute|="value"]
```

Example: *[hreflang|="es"] {color: red;}

This selector looks for all elements in which the hreflang attribute is es or begins with es-. Elements with the language of their target href identified as es, es-ar, or es-es would be selected (in other words, it finds all variations on the Spanish language). Selecting language subcodes is a common use for this type of attribute selector (e.g., to put language flags next to hyperlinks that link to sites and pages of a different language), but by no means its only application.

Pseudoselectors

Style rules are normally attached to elements in the document tree structure, such as those we've discussed in the chapter so far. But some elements are not necessarily found in the document markup, such as which links have been visited or the first line of a paragraph. To apply style to these instances in a document, CSS provides several pseudoselectors. Instead of targeting a particular element in the document, pseudoselectors are interpreted by the browser based on context and function. Pseudoselectors are indicated by the colon (:) character. Pseudoselectors are divided into pseudoclasses and pseudoelements.

Pseudoclasses

As the name implies, *pseudoclasses* work as though there is a class applied to a group of elements, most often the anchor (a) element. These "phantom" classes (to use Eric Meyer's term) do not appear in the markup, but rather are based on the state of those elements or the document itself.

Anchor pseudoclasses

There are several pseudoclasses that can be used to apply styles to various states of a link:

```
a:link {color: red;}
a:visited {color: blue;}
a:hover {color: fuchsia;}
a:active {color: maroon;}
```

Similar to their body attribute counterparts in the body element, :link applies to hypertext links that have not been visited, :visited applies to links to pages that have been visited, and :active applies during the act of clicking. The difference is that you can do much more than just change color with CSS. Following are popular rules for turning off the underline under linked text.

```
a:link {color: red; text-decoration: none;}
a:visited {color: blue; text-decoration: none;}
```

The :hover selector is used to create rollover effects in which the link changes in appearance when the mouse pointer moves over it. The examples above turned off underlines for links. The following rule uses :hover to make the underline appear as a rollover.

```
a:link {color: red; text-decoration: none;}
a:hover {color: red; text-decoration: underline;}
```

 According to CSS 2, :active and :hover may be used with elements other than anchors, but this use is not supported in Internet Explorer (through Version 6) or Netscape 4.

Love, HA!

Anchor pseudoclasses need to appear in a particular order in a style sheet in order to function properly. The initials LVHA (or according to a popular mnemonic, *love, HA!*) remind developers that the correct order is :link, :visited, :hover, :active. This has to do with order and specificity. Putting :link or :visited last would override the :hover and :active states, preventing those styles from appearing.

Other CSS 2.1 pseudoclasses

In addition to the anchor pseudo-classes, the CSS 2 specification introduced additional pseudoclass selectors. Be warned, however, that they are not well supported at this time.

:focus

This targets elements that have focus, such as a form element that is highlighted and accepting user input. Although CSS 2 permits :focus to be applied to any element, it is currently only supported for use with the form elements. Netscape 6 supports :focus with a, input, textarea, and select.

Example: input:focus {background-color: yellow;}

:first-child

This targets an element that is the first occurring child of a parent element. It allows you to select the first paragraph of a div or the first li in a ul, for example.

Example: li:first-child {font-weight: bold;}

:lang( )

This targets an element that targets elements for which a language has been specified. It functions the same as the lang|= attribute selector, but may be more robust.

Example: p:lang(de) {color: green;}

Browser alert: Internet Explorer for Windows does not support
:focus or :first-child in Versions 6 and earlier. Support in IE 7 (in
beta as of this writing) is undocumented. Internet Explorer 5 for
Macintosh, Netscape 6+ and Opera 7+ do support them. Internet
Explorer 5 for Macintosh is the only browser that supports the
:lang pseudoclass as of this writing.

Pseudoelements

Pseudoelement selectors work as though they are inserting fictional elements into
the document structure for styling. Pseudoelements are generally parts of an
existing element based on context, such as its first line or first letter. Four pseudoelements are included in CSS 2.1:

:first-line
> As it sounds, this selector applies a style rule to the first line of the specified
> element. The properties for the :first-line pseudoelement are limited to
> color, font, background, word-spacing, letter-spacing, text-decoration,
> vertical-align, text-transform, line-height, and text-shadow.

> The following code adds extra letter spacing in the first line of text for every
> paragraph:

> ```
> p:first-line {letter-spacing: 6pt;}
> ```

:first-letter
> Attaches a style to the first letter of an element. The properties for :first-
> letter are limited to font, color, background, margin, padding, border, text-
> decoration, vertical-align, text-transform, line-height, and float. CSS 2.1
> added the letter-spacing and word-spacing properties to this pseudoclass.

> The following sample makes the first letter of any paragraph classified as
> "opener" big and red:

> ```
> p.opener:first-letter {font-size: 300%; color: red;}
> ```

:before *and* :after
> CSS 2 introduced these pseudoelements that insert generated content before
> and/or after a specified element and declare a style for that content.

> This example inserts exaggerated quotation marks before and after a block-
> quote (&8220; and &8221; are the character entities for left and right curly
> quotation marks):

> ```
> blockquote:before {content: "&#8220;"; font-size: 24px; color: purple;}
> blockquote:after {content: "&#8221;"; font-size: 24px; color: purple;}
> ```

Browser alert: Internet Explorer does not support generated content (:before or :after) in Versions 6 and earlier. Support in IE 7,
in beta as of this writing, is doubtful but is not specifically documented. Netscape 6+, Firefox/Mozilla, and Opera 7+ do support
generated content.

All current CSS-compliant browsers support the :first-letter and
:first-line pseudoelement selectors reasonably well.

Selector Summary

Table 17-1 provides a quick summary of the selectors covered in this chapter. Put a sticky-note on this page.

Table 17-1. Summary of selectors

Selector	Type of selector	Description
*	Universal selector	Matches any element. `* {font-family:serif;}`
A	Type selector	Matches the name of an element. `div {font-style: italic;}`
A B	Descendant selector	Matches element B only if it is a descendant of element A. `blockquote em {color: red;}`
A>B	Child selector	Matches any element B that is a child of any element A. `div.main>p {line-height:1.5;}`
A+B	Adjacent sibling selector	Matches any element B that immediately follows any element A. `p+ul {margin-top:0;}`
.classname A.classname	Class selector	Matches the value of the `class` attribute in all elements or a specified element. `p.credits {font-size: .8em;}`
#idname A#idname	ID selector	Matches the value of the `id` attribute in an element. `#intro {font-weight: bold;}`
A[att]	Simple attribute selector	Matches any element A that has the given attribute defined, whatever its value. `table[border] {background-color: white;}`
A[att="val"]	Exact attribute value selector	Matches any element B that has the specified attribute set to the specified value. `table[border="3"] {background-color: yellow;}`
A[att~="val"]	Partial attribute value selector	Matches any element B that has the specified value as one of the values in a list given to the specified attribute. `table[class~="example"] {background-color: orange;}`
A[hreflang|="es"]	Hyphenated prefix attribute selector	Matches any element A that has an attribute `hreflang` with a hyphen-separated list of values beginning (from the left) with "es". `a[hreflang|="es"] {background-image: url(flag-es.png);}`
a:link	Pseudoselector	Specifies a style for links that have not yet been visited. `a:link {color: purple;}`
a:visited	Pseudoselector	Specifies a style for links that have already been visited. `a:visited {color: gray;}`
:active	Pseudoselector	Applies a style to elements (typically links) while in their active state. `a:active {color: red;}`

CSS: Selectors

Table 17-1. Summary of selectors (continued)

Selector	Type of selector	Description
:after	Pseudoselector	Inserts generated text at the end of the specified element and applies a style to it. `p.intro:after {content: "fini"; color: gray;}`
:before	Pseudoselector	Inserts generated text at the beginning of the specified element and applies a style to it. `p.intro:before {content: "start here "; color: gray;}`
:firstchild	Pseudoselector	Specifies a style for an element that is the first child of its parent element in the flow of the document source. `p:firstchild {text-style: italic;}`
:first-letter	Pseudoselector	Specifies a style for the first letter of the specified element. `p:first-letter {font-size: 60px;}`
:first-line	Pseudoselector	Specifies a style for the first line of the specified element. `p:first-line {color: fuchsia;}`
:focus	Pseudoselector	Specifies a style for elements (typically form controls) that have focus (selected and ready for user input). `input[type="text"]:focus {background-color: yellow;}`
:hover	Pseudoselector	Specifies a style for elements (typically links) that appears while the pointer is over them. `a:hover {text-decoration: underline;}`
:lang(ab)	Pseudoselector	Specifies a style for an element for which its language matches the given language code (or language code prefix). `a:lang(de) {color: green;}`

18

Font and Text Properties

Cascading Style Sheets offer a degree of control over text formatting that approaches desktop publishing. This certainly comes as a relief after years of misusing HTML markup for presentation purposes. Controls for specifying fonts and text formatting are undeniably the most popular use of style sheets and they are the properties that browsers support the most reliably.

This chapter discusses the challenges of typography on the Web and introduces the following text-related CSS 2 properties:

font-family	text-decoration	letter-spacing
font-size	text-transform	word-spacing
font-weight	line-height	white-space
font-style	text-indent	direction
font-variant	text-align	unicode-bidi
font	vertical-align	

 Text color is discussed in the "Foreground Color" section of Chapter 20.

Typography on the Web

For those accustomed to print, the Web offers some unique challenges, usually requiring the relinquishing of control. Typography is a prime example. In print, designers may choose a typeface and point size for headlines and body copy, and as long as the proper font is provided when the printed piece is output, everything looks just the way the designer intended. On the Web, it's not so easy.

Font Issues

Specifying fonts for use on web pages is made difficult by the fact that browsers are limited to displaying fonts that are already installed on the user's local hard drive. So, even though you've specified text to be displayed in the Frutiger font, if users do not have Frutiger installed on their machines, they will see the text in whatever their default browser font happens to be. Fortunately, CSS allows you to specify a list of alternative fonts if your first choice is not found (as discussed in the section "Font Family").

This problem is compounded by the fact that fonts are named inconsistently across platforms and based on the foundry they come from. So even though you want text to show up in plain Times, the font name for that typeface may be Times New Roman or TimesNR or Times Roman. Browsers don't know the difference. This makes it difficult to find a font face even if it (or something like it) is in fact there.

Type Size Issues

The other web typography challenge is type size. Size is problematic due to varying screen resolutions and different default font sizes built into browsers and operating systems. What looks perfectly fine on your monitor may be too small to read for someone else. On top of that, to keep content accessible, text should be sized in a way that allows the end user to resize it (usually larger) to meet special needs. The specific problems of setting text size along with recommendations will be covered in the upcoming "Font Size" section, but for now, suffice it to say that it is not as straightforward as print. It requires knowledge of the medium and occasionally some tough decisions.

Alternatives to Browser Text

Although CSS offers far more control over text formatting than any presentational HTML hack, keep in mind that it is still working in an environment that is somewhat hostile to—or, at the very best, naïve about—typography. From the Web's earliest days, there have been efforts to circumvent the limitations and achieve beautiful typography on web pages. After more than 10 years of trying, there is still no ideal solution, but there are a few options to be aware of.

Text in graphics

It didn't take long for designers (this author included) to start replacing ugly browser text with text set in an inline graphic. For a while, it was not uncommon to run across sites with all every last word of their "content" sunk into a graphic. While this may achieve the short-term goal of preserving the intended font design, it comes at a steep cost. Not only does it increase the file size of the page, but the content is essentially removed from the document. Alternative text (using the `alt` attribute) helps, but does not solve the problem.

Image-replacement techniques

In modern, CSS-based web design, there is a new way to replace text with an image that preserves the text in the source document. There are several variations, but all image-replacement techniques are based on applying the image as a background in the text element and then finding a way to hide the text using CSS. The various image-replacement techniques are covered in detail in Chapter 24.

sIFR text

One of the most interesting web typography solutions to come along is *sIFR*, which stands for Scalable Inman Flash Replacement. It draws inspiration from the image-replacement techniques that were growing popular in CSS-based designs, but uses small Flash movies instead of bitmapped GIF, JPEG, or PNG images. The advantage is that text in Flash movies is vector-based, so it is smooth, anti-aliased, and able to resize with the page. Using a combination of CSS, JavaScript, and Flash technology, sIFR allows authors to "insert rich typography into web pages without sacrificing accessibility, search engine friendliness, or markup semantics."

sIFR (in Version 2.0 as of this writing) was created by Mike Davidson, who built upon the original concept developed by Shaun Inman (the "I" of sIFR). Here's how the process works (taken from the official sIFR site at *www.mikeindustries. com/sifr*).

1. A normal (X)HTML page is loaded into the browser.

2. A JavaScript function is run that first checks that Flash is installed and then looks for whatever tags, IDs, or classes you designate.

3. If Flash isn't installed (or obviously if JavaScript is turned off), the (X)HTML page displays as normal and nothing further occurs. If Flash is installed, Java-Script traverses through the source of your page, measuring each element you've designated as something you'd like "sIFRed."

4. Once measured, the script creates Flash movies of the same dimensions and overlays them on top of the original elements, pumping the original browser text in as a Flash variable.

5. ActionScript inside of each Flash file then draws that text in your chosen typeface at a 6 point size and scales it up until it fits snugly inside the Flash movie.

In optimal browser conditions, this all happens in a split-second, so all of the checking, replacing, and scaling is not visible to the user. Some browsers may struggle with sIFR.

sIFR is not perfect, but it is a promising technique that could lead to more powerful typography solutions. To find out more about sIFR, visit *www. mikeindustries.com/sifr*. There is also an interesting historical document with the history of web typography and the first release of sIFR at *www.mikeindustries. com/blog/archive/2004/08/sifr*.

Embedded fonts

In the mid-1990s, there were concerted efforts made by Microsoft and Bitstream (partnered with Netscape) to develop embedded font technologies. With embedded fonts, a separate file containing the necessary character set for the document is provided with the HTML document via the link element.

Not surprisingly, at the height of the Browser Wars, there was no spirit of cooperation in the embedded font field, so the result was two competing and incompatible embedded font technologies. Microsoft's Embedded Open Type worked only on Internet Explorer on Windows. Bitstream (a font design company) created TrueDoc Dynamic fonts that were initially supported by Netscape 4, but then dropped in Gecko-based Netscape 6. Bitstream has since thrown in the towel on TrueDoc technology for the Web due to lack of browser support. For now, embedded fonts are largely an ignored technology.

For information on Embedded Open Type, see *www.microsoft.com/typography/web/embedding/default.aspx*. For information on Bitstream's TrueDoc technology, see *www.truedoc.com*.

Font Family

The CSS specification provides the font-family property for specifying the font face for text elements.

font-family

Values: [[<family-name> | <generic-family>] [,<family-name> | <generic-family>]*] | inherit

Initial value: Depends on user agent (the default font in the browsing device)

Applies to: All elements

Inherited: Yes

Use the font-family property to specify any font (or list of fonts, separated by commas), as shown in these examples:

```
h1 {font-family: Arial; }
tt {font-family: Courier, monospace; }
p {font-family: "Trebuchet MS", Verdana, sans-serif; }
```

The value of the property is one or more font names, separated by commas. This allows authors to provide a list of fonts, starting with a first choice, followed by a list of alternates. The user agent (typically a browser) looks for the first font on the user's machine and, if it is not found, it continues looking for the next font in the list until a match is made.

Note that in the third example, the "Trebuchet MS" is enclosed in quotation marks. Font names that contain character spaces must be enclosed in quotation marks (single or double). If the font name appears in an inline style, be sure to use single quotes if the style attribute uses double (or vice versa).

Generic Font Families

You should include a generic font family as the last option in your list so that if the specified fonts are not found, a font that matches their general style will be substituted. Generic family names must never be enclosed in quotation marks.

The five possible generic font family values are:

serif *(e.g., Times New Roman)*
> Serif typefaces have decorative serifs, or slab-like appendages, on the ends of certain letter strokes (Figure 18-1, left).

sans-serif *(e.g., Helvetica or Arial)*
> San-serif typefaces have straight letter strokes that do not end in serifs (Figure 18-1, right).

monospace *(e.g., Courier or New Courier)*
> In monospaced typefaces, all characters take up the same amount of horizontal space on a line (Figure 18-2). For example, a capital W will be no wider than a lowercase i. Compare this to normal typefaces that allot different widths to different characters.

cursive *(e.g., Zapf-Chancery or Comic Sans)*
> Cursive fonts emulate a script or handwritten appearance.

fantasy *(e.g., Western, Impact, or some display-oriented font)*
> Fantasy fonts are purely decorative and would be appropriate for headlines and other display type. Fantasy is not commonly used for web sites, because it is difficult to anticipate which font will be used and whether it will be legible online.

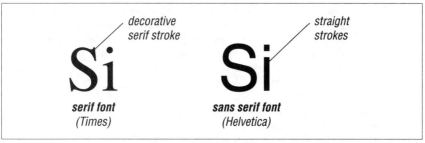

Figure 18-1. Serif and sans-serif font characters

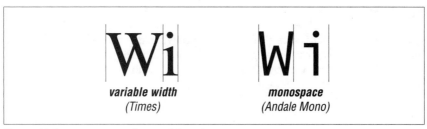

Figure 18-2. Monospace and normal font characters

Commonly Available Fonts

Because a font will display only if it is available on a user's hard drive, it makes sense to design with the most commonly available fonts, particularly for sites with wide-reaching audiences. So, which fonts can you rely on?

In general web design practice, designers tend to specify fonts from Microsoft's Core Web Fonts collection. This is a set of TrueType fonts (for both Windows and Mac) that have been specially designed to be easy to read on screens at small sizes. Microsoft released the fonts in 1996 and initially made them available for download. Today, they are installed automatically with Internet Explorer and other Microsoft software, so you can count on the majority of users having them available. Table 18-1 lists the fonts in the Core Web Fonts collection.

Table 18-1. Core Web Fonts from Microsoft

Serif	Georgia
	Times New Roman
Sans Serif	Arial Arial Black
	Trebuchet MS
	Verdana
Monospace	Courier New
	Andale Mono
Miscellaneous	Comic Sans MS
	Impact
	Webdings

 Microsoft publishes an interesting online resource that lists which fonts are installed with its various popular applications and each version of the Windows operating system. There are also lists of the fonts that come installed with Macintosh OS X, Unix systems, and Adobe Type Manager. You'll find the font lists at *www.microsoft. com/typography/fonts/default.aspx*.

If you know your audience might have more specialized fonts installed, by all means, make a statement and go off the beaten path. You can always provide a more commonly available font as a backup in the list of font names.

Font Size

CSS provides the font-size property for specifying the size of text. There are many value options for specifying font size, each with its own pros and cons. This section discusses the various keyword and unit options and their impact on usability.

font-size

Values: xx-small | x-small | small | medium | large | x-large |
xx-large | smaller | larger | <length> | <percentage> | inherit

Initial value: medium

Applies to: All elements

Inherited: Yes

These examples demonstrate the font-size property used with several different value types.

```
p.copyright {font-size: x-small;}
strong {font-size: larger;}
h2 {font-size: 1.2em;}
p#intro {font-size: 120%;}
```

Absolute Versus Relative Sizes

Before diving into the details of specifying type size, it is worth pausing to clarify the difference between absolute and relative sizes. *Absolute sizes* have predefined meanings or an understood real-world equivalent. In CSS, absolute values may be expressed as keywords, such as small or x-large (discussed next) or by using absolute length values, such as cm (centimeter), in (inch), or pt (point, 1/72 of an inch).

Relative sizes, on the other hand, are based on the size of something else, like the parent element or the em measurement of the text (see the sidebar "A Word About Ems"). Relative values, such as em and percentages, are generally preferred for web text for reasons that are covered in the upcoming sections.

Absolute Size Keywords

Absolute sizes are descriptive terms that reference a table of sizes kept by the browser. There are seven absolute size keywords in CSS: xx-small, x-small, small, medium, large, x-large, and xx-large. The keywords do not correspond to a particular measurement, but rather are scaled consistently in relation to one another. The default size is medium in current standards-conformant browsers.

Figure 18-3 shows how the following examples of text sized with absolute keywords look in Firefox 1.0.

```
<span style="font-size: xx-small">xx-small</span>
<span style="font-size: x-small">x-small</span>
<span style="font-size: small">small</span>
<span style="font-size: medium">medium</span>
<span style="font-size: large">large</span>
<span style="font-size: x-large">x-large</span>
<span style="font-size: xx-large">xx-large </span>
```

A Word About Ems

In traditional typography, the em has been a measurement of width approximately equal to the width of the capital letter M for the given typeface. Using that measurement, you arrive at the width of an em-space or an em-dash.

As typography has adapted to digital media, the em has become a measure of width and height, or often height alone. For purposes of CSS, the em is calculated as the distance between the baselines when the font is set without any additional *interlinear space*, also called *leading* (extra space added between lines of text for legibility).

This distance forms the basis of an implied *em-square* measurement based on the design of the typeface (also called the *em-box*). It is possible that ascenders and descenders of a particular typeface may exceed the boundaries of the em-square, or that no characters of another face fill it completely. The font's em-box measurement can be used as a relative unit of measurement.

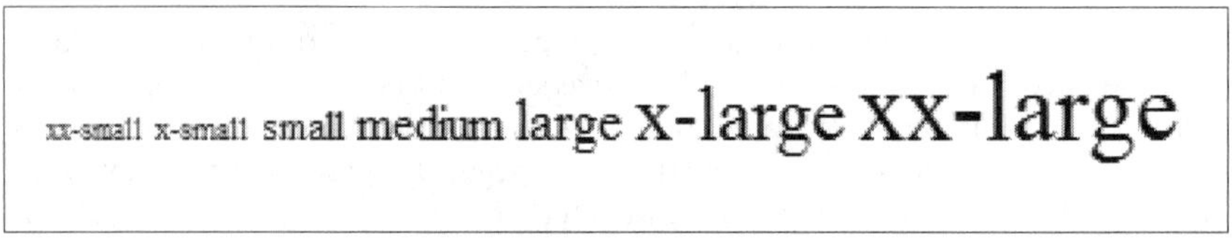

xx-small x-small small medium large x-large xx-large

Figure 18-3. Text sized with absolute keywords

This figure and other figures in this book use inline styles as a means to save space on the page. In the real world, inline styles should be avoided in favor of external or embedded style sheets.

The CSS 2.1 specification leaves the scaling factor (how much each consecutive keyword is enlarged or reduced) up to the user agent. Chances are, it will be somewhere around 1.2 (the most recent recommended scaling factor) or as large as 1.5 (the CSS 1 recommended scaling factor), varying between different browsers.

At a scaling factor of 1.2, if medium (default) text is 16 pixels, then large text would be 19 pixels (after some rounding). The upshot of it all is absolute size keywords vary in size from browser to browser, so they are not the best option if you are looking for consistency.

Internet Explorer 5 and 5.5 for Windows use small as the default, which can seriously throw off an attempt to use absolute size keywords throughout a document.

Relative Size Keywords

There are two relative keywords: larger and smaller. They are used to shift the size of the text relative to the parent object according to the seven-step absolute-size scale (using the same scaling factor). For example, if the text of a paragraph is set to large, applying the keyword smaller to a child em element would cause the emphasized text to display at medium size. Figure 18-4's examples use relative size keywords.

```
There are two relative keywords: <span style="font-size: larger">larger</
span> and <span style="font-size: smaller">smaller</span>. They are used...
```

There are two relative keywords: larger and smaller. They are used to shift the size of the text relative to the parent object according to...

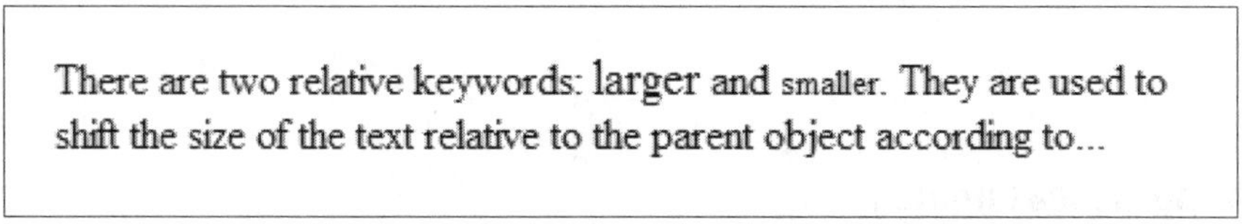

Figure 18-4. Relative size keywords

Percentage Measurements

One fairly reliable way to specify text size is in percent values. Percent values are calculated relative to the inherited size of the parent text. That "inherited" part is important, because it means that if you nest similar elements with percentage values, the affect is cumulative. It doesn't take many levels of nesting before the text is unreadable.

In Figure 18-5, the ul element is set to a relative size of 80%. If the body of the document is 16 pixels, that means the ul text will be 13 pixels (after rounding). The nested ul within that list takes the same size setting (80%), but this time it is applied to its inherited size (13 pixels), resulting in 10 pixel text, and so on for each nested level.

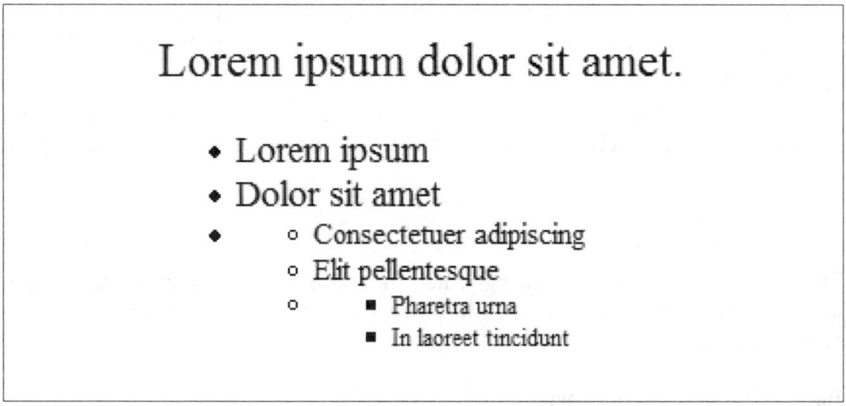

Lorem ipsum dolor sit amet.

- Lorem ipsum
- Dolor sit amet
  - Consectetuer adipiscing
  - Elit pellentesque
    - Pharetra urna
    - In laoreet tincidunt

Figure 18-5. Nested elements with percentage size values

Style sheet
```
body {font-size: 24px;}
ul {font-size: 80%;}
```

Markup
```
Lorem ipsum dolor sit amet.
<ul>
  <li>Lorem ipsum</li>
  <li>Dolor sit amet</li>
  <li><ul>
      <li>Consectetuer adipiscing</li>
      <li>Elit pellentesque</li>
        <ul>
          <li>Pharetra urna </li>
          <li>In laoreet tincidunt</li>
        </ul>
      </ul>
  </li>
</ul>
```

Length Measurements

The final way that type size may be specified is in a specific number of units. Some units are absolute and some are relative.

The absolute length units are:

- pt (points, 1/72 of an inch in CSS 2.1)
- pc (picas, 1 pica is equal to 12 points)
- mm (millimeters)
- cm (centimeters)
- in (inches)

The relative length units are:

- em (distance from baseline to baseline with no extra line space),
- ex (approximately the height of the letter "x" in the font)
- px (pixels; in CSS, pixels are relative because their actual size can vary by display resolution when the resolution is very different from the typical 75–100 dpi, e.g., on 300 dpi printers)

Specifying a unit length with the font-size property is simple. Just be sure that the value is immediately followed by the unit abbreviation, with no extra space between, like this:

```
p {font-size: 12px; }
h1 {font-size: 1.6em; }
```

The tricky part comes in knowing which units are the most appropriate for the job. Some units are problematic in terms of accessibility while others are victims of browser inconsistencies.

The problem with absolute values

Because real-world measurements, such as inches and picas, aren't relevant on computer screens (see Chapter 26 for an explanation of why inches are useless), none of the absolute values make sense for web page text. If you are creating a style sheet for print, however, absolute length units may be just the ticket.

Recommendation: Avoid pt, pc, mm, cm, and in measurements for web pages.

The problem with pixels

You may be thinking that because elements on web pages are measured in numbers of pixels, and because pixels are considered a relative measurement, that they are the answer to all font size problems. It would be nice if they were. For some designers, control over text at the pixel level is intoxicating.

Unfortunately, there are a few reasons why pixels have come to be shunned for text size. We know that all pixels are not created equal, so that means that what is tidy yet readable on your monitor may require a magnifying glass on someone else's screen.

On most current browsers, starting with Internet Explorer 5 for Macintosh in March 2000, that is not a problem, because users have a "text zoom" function that allows them to increase the size of text regardless of the style sheet settings. Ironically, Internet Explorer for Windows (Version 6 and earlier) does not allow text zoom on text specified in pixels (it will resize text set in ems and percentages). IE 7 (in beta as of this writing) promises a zoom function on pixels, but for the time being, there is a significant percentage of users who cannot override pixel size settings. This is a big no-no in terms of accessibility.

Recommendation: If accessibility is important to you (and it should be), avoid using px measurements for text until IE 5 for Windows and IE 6 for Windows are just a memory.

The problem with ems

Ems turn out to be the best length unit for the Web, but they too have a couple of potential snags. The first is that em measurements are relative to the browser's base size. For most browsers, the default base size is 16 pixels, which is quite large. Designers tend to want to reduce the text size slightly across a whole page or a whole site.

But that 16 pixel base size is not a sure thing. Some users may have reset their base text smaller already in the browser preferences, in which case, making text smaller again in the author style sheet may make it unreadable. Fortunately, all current version browsers allow text zoom on text specified in ems, so users can make the text large enough to read easily (that is, if they know about the zoom function).

The other issue with ems is that, due to rounding errors, there is a lot of inconsistency among browsers and platforms when text size is set in fractions of an em. One or two pixels can make a big difference when text is displayed at low resolutions. Not only that, some browsers have problems with text set at less than one em. Percentages are a more reliable way to provide relative measurements, but then you may run into problems with cumulative resizing.

Recommendation: One popular solution is to use a combination of percentages and ems to avoid the problems associated with both. This method was first introduced by Owen Briggs as a conclusion to his deep exploration of browser font-size differences. The method works by making the text slightly smaller with a percentage at the body level. Then use ems on the individual elements that you'd like to be larger than the surrounding text. Here is an example using his suggested values:

```
body {font-size: 76% }   /* results in 12 pixel text when the base size is 16
pixels */
p {font-size: 1em; }
h1 {font-size: 1.5em; }
```

The advantage is that the percentage value gives you more fine-tuned control, and the em sizing doesn't compound the way percentages do. The disadvantage is that if the base size is less than 16 pixels, everything may appear too small. However, because the sizes are specified in ems, resizing text in the browser is an option for users.

 See all 264 of Owen Briggs' screenshots, as well as solutions for dealing with inconsistent font sizing, at *thenoodleincident.com/ tutorials/box_lesson/font/index.html.*

Other Font Settings

Compared to the hassles of font-face and font-size, the other font-related properties are a walk in the park (albeit, a short walk). This section introduces style properties for adjusting font weight, style, and "small caps" display.

Font Weight

The font-weight property specifies the weight, or boldness, of the type.

font-weight

Values:	normal | bold | bolder | lighter | 100 | 200 | 300 | 400 | 500 | 600 | 700 | 800 | 900 | inherit
Initial value:	normal
Applies to:	All elements
Inherited:	Yes

Font weight can be specified either as a descriptive term (normal, bold, bolder, lighter) or as one of the nine numeric values listed above. The default font weight is normal, which corresponds to 400 on the numeric scale. Typical bold text corresponds to 700 on the numeric scale. There may not be a font face within a family that corresponds to each of the nine levels of boldness (some may come in only normal and bold weights). Figure 18-6 shows the effect of each of the values on the

---

popular Verdana web font face in the Firefox browser (note that bold kicks in at 600, not 700).

It is evident that the numeric font-weight values are not useful when multiple weights are not available for the font. There's no harm in using them, but don't expect them to change the weights of an existing font. It merely looks for font weights that are already available.

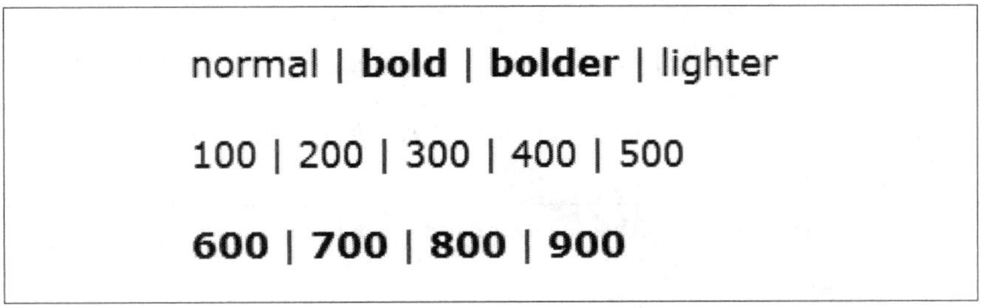

normal | **bold** | **bolder** | lighter

100 | 200 | 300 | 400 | 500

600 | **700** | **800** | **900**

Figure 18-6. The effect of font-weight values

Unfortunately, the current browsers are inconsistent in support of the font-weight property, mainly due to the lack of available fonts that fit the criteria. The values that are intended to make text lighter than normal weight are particularly unsuccessful. Of the possible values, only bold and bolder will render reliably as bold text. Most developers stick to those values and ignore the rest.

Font Style

font-style controls the *posture* of the font, that is, whether the font is italic, oblique, or normal.

font-style

Values:	normal | italic | oblique | inherit
Initial value:	normal
Applies to:	All elements
Inherited:	Yes

Italic and oblique are both slanted versions of the font. The difference is that the italic version is usually a separate typeface design with more curved letter forms, while oblique text takes the normal font design and displays it on a slant using mathematical calculations, as shown in Figure 18-7 (top). At small text sizes on low resolution monitors, italic and oblique text may look exactly the same (Figure 18-7, bottom).

```
<p style="font-style: oblique">This is a sample of oblique Times as rendered
in a browser.</p>
<p style="font-style: italic">This is a sample of italic Times as rendered
in a browser. </p>
```

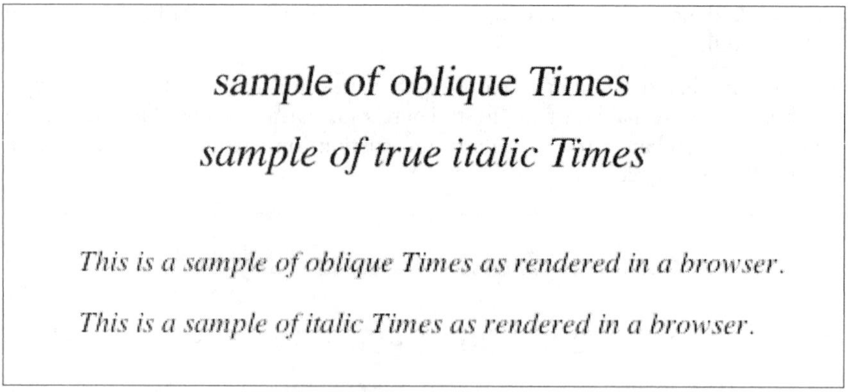

> *sample of oblique Times*
>
> *sample of true italic Times*
>
> *This is a sample of oblique Times as rendered in a browser.*
>
> *This is a sample of italic Times as rendered in a browser.*

Figure 18-7. Comparison of oblique and italic type set with the font-style property

Font Variant

The sole purpose of the font-variant property is to specify that text should appear as small caps. Small caps fonts use smaller uppercase letters in place of lowercase letters. More values may be supported for this property in future style sheet versions.

font-variant

Values:	normal	small-caps	inherit
Initial value:	normal
Applies to:	All elements
Inherited:	Yes

If a true small caps font face is not available, the browser may simulate small caps by displaying all caps at a reduced size. Figure 18-8 shows such a simulation using this style rule.

```
<span style="font-variant: small-caps">lorem ipsum dolor sit amet,</span>
consectetuer adipiscing elit. Pellentesque pharetra, urna in laoreet
tincidunt, nunc quam eleifend libero, a tincidunt purus augue eu felis.
Phasellus quis ante. Sed mi.
```

> LOREM IPSUM DOLOR SIT AMET, consectetuer adipiscing elit. Pellentesque pharetra, urna in laoreet tincidunt, nunc quam eleifend libero, a tincidunt purus augue eu felis. Phasellus quis ante. Sed mi.

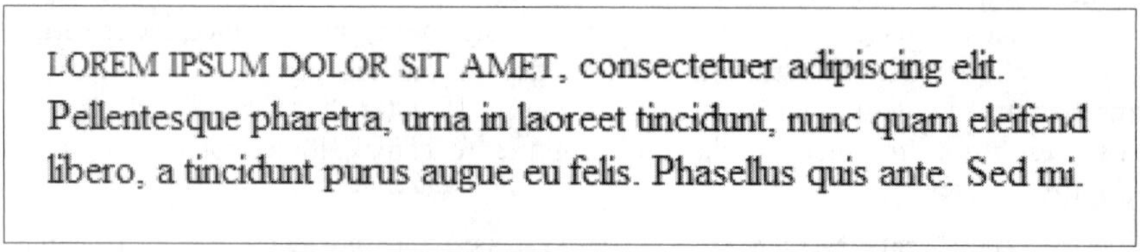

Figure 18-8. Using font-variant for small caps

Unlike a true small caps typeface design, the proportions of the capital and small cap letters do not blend well because the line weight of the small caps has been reduced. One use of small caps typefaces in the print world is to reduce the size of acronyms so they do not stand out like sore thumbs in the flow of text. Unfortunately, the font-variant property only transforms lowercase letters, so it cannot be used for this purpose.

 There are two additional font-related properties in CSS 2 that were dropped in CSS 2.1 due to lack of support. The font-stretch property was for making a font's characters wider or more narrow using these keyword values: normal, wider, narrower, ultra-condensed, extra-condensed, condensed, semi-condensed, semi-expanded, expanded, extra-expanded, ultra-expanded, and inherit. The other dropped property is font-size-adjust, which was intended to compensate for the varying x-heights of fonts at the same size settings.

Putting It All Together with the font Property

Specifying multiple font properties for each text element could get repetitive and lengthy, so the authors of CSS provided the shorthand font property that compiles all the font-related properties into one rule. Technically, font is more than just a shorthand property, because it is the only property that allows authors to specify fonts from the operating system of the user agent.

font

Values:	[[<'font-style'> || <'font-variant'> || <'font-weight'>]? <'font-size'> [/<'line-height'>]? <'font-family'>] | caption | icon | menu | message-box | small-caption | status-bar | inherit
Initial value:	Uses individual property default values
Applies to:	All elements
Inherited:	Yes

When using the font property as shorthand for a number of font properties, the order in which the property values appear is important. All of these font rules show correct usage of the font property.

```
h1 { font: 1.75em sans-serif; } /* minimum value list for font */
h1 { font: 1.75em/2 sans-serif; }
h1 { font: bold 1.75em sans-serif; }
h1 { font: oblique bold small-caps 1.75em Verdana, Arial, sans-serif; }
```

The rule may include values for all of the properties or a subset, but it *must* include font-size and font-family, in that order, as the last two properties in the list. Omitting one or putting them in the wrong order causes the entire rule to be invalid. These examples are invalid:

```
h1 { font: sans-serif; } /* font-size omitted */
h1 { font: 1.75em/2 sans-serif oblique; } /* size and family come first */
```

Once you've met the font-size and font-family requirement, the rule may also include optional font-style, font-variant, or font-weight properties at the beginning of the rule. They may appear in any order, as long as they precede font-size. Another optional value is the line-height property (for adding space between lines) that appears just after font-size, separated by a slash (/), as shown here:

```
p { font: italic 12px/18px Georgia, Times, Serif }
```

It is important to know that when you use the shorthand font property, any property that is omitted will be reset to the initial setting (default) for that property. Be aware that an incomplete shorthand rule could accidentally override settings made earlier in the style sheet by resetting the values to the default.

Using System Fonts

The font property provides a number of keywords that allow authors to apply font styles from the operating system into their web documents. This may be a useful tool for making a web application blend in with the surrounding desktop environment. The values are:

caption
> The font used for captioned controls (e.g., buttons, drop-down menus, etc.)

icon
> The font used to label icons

menu
> The font used in menus (e.g., drop-down menus and menu lists)

message-box
> The font used in dialog boxes

small-caption
> The font used for labeling small controls

status-bar
> The font used in window status bars

Choosing one of these keywords applies all aspects of that font (family, size, weight) at once, although they may be overridden with specific font properties. If a particular font is not found, the user agent should approximate the font or substitute a default font. System font values are well-supported by current standards-compliant browsers.

Text Transformation (Capitalization)

The font-variant property uses capital letter shapes for lowercase letters, but doesn't really affect the capitalization of the text, only the character shapes of the font. There is another CSS property, text-transform, for altering the capitalization of text without needing to retype it in the source document. It works by toggling between the upper- and lowercase characters as specified.

text-transform

Values: none | capitalize | lowercase | uppercase | inherit

Initial value: none

Applies to: All elements

Inherited: Yes

Use the text-transform property to change the capitalization of an element without retyping it in the source. This can make changing capitalization of a particular element (like headers) for an entire site as easy as changing one style sheet rule.

The default value is none, which leaves the text as it appears in the source (and resets any inherited value). The capitalize value displays the first letter in each word of the element in uppercase. The lowercase value makes all letters in the element lowercase, and likewise, the uppercase value makes all characters uppercase. The effects of these text-transform property examples are shown in Figure 18-9.

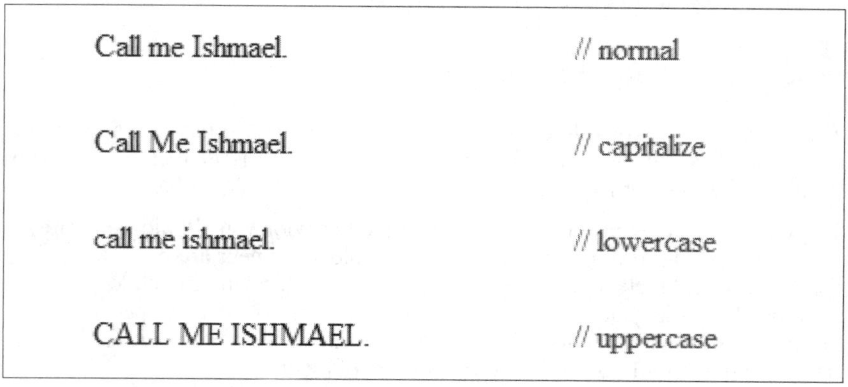

Call me Ishmael.	// normal
Call Me Ishmael.	// capitalize
call me ishmael.	// lowercase
CALL ME ISHMAEL.	// uppercase

Figure 18-9. The text-transform property

Text Decoration

Use the text-decoration element to specify underlines, overlines (a line over the text), strike-throughs, and the blinking effect.

text-decoration

Values: none | underline | overline | line-through | blink

Initial value: none

Applies to: All elements

Inherited: No, but a text decoration is "drawn through" any child elements (see explanation in this section).

The values for `text-decoration` are fairly intuitive: `underline` causes an element to be underlined, `overline` draws a line over the element, and `line-through` draws a line through the middle of the element and replaces the deprecated `strike` and `s` elements in HTML. `text-decoration` variations are shown in Figure 18-10.

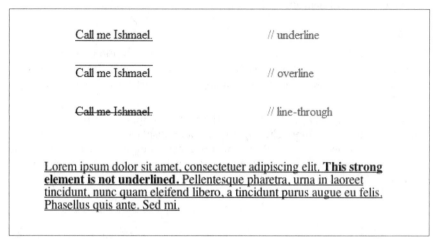

Figure 18-10. The text-decoration property

There is also an optional `blink` value that causes the text to flash on and off like the dreaded Netscape `blink` element (the `blink` value is deliberately still not supported by Internet Explorer).

The `text-decoration` property has one strange behavior you should be aware of. Although `text-decoration` values applied to a block element are not inherited by the block's child elements, the line gets drawn through the child elements anyway. The line (such as an `underline`, `overline`, or `line-through`) will go through the inline elements even if they explicitly have `text-decoration` set to none, as shown in this example and the bottom of Figure 18-10.

```
<p style="text-decoration: underline">Lorem ipsum dolor sit amet,
consectetuer adipiscing elit. <strong style="text-decoration: none">This
strong element is not underlined.</strong> Pellentesque pharetra, urna in
laoreet tincidunt, nunc quam eleifend libero, a tincidunt purus augue eu
felis. Phasellus quis ante. Sed mi. </p>
```

There is currently no way to turn decoration off for child elements. The solution is to apply the style to spans in the desired parts of the text instead of the block element itself.

The most popular use of the `text-decoration` property is to turn off the underlines that automatically appear under links by setting `text-decoration` to none, as shown here:

```
a:link, a:visited { text-decoration: none; }
```

This should be done with some care, however, as the underline is a strong visual cue that text is clickable. Removing the underline may cause the link to be missed. If you turn the underline off, be sure that other cues such as color or weight contrast compensate.

Similarly, because underlines have become so associated with hypertext, adding an underline to text that is not a link may be misleading and even frustrating. In the days of typewriters, underlines were used in place of italic text. Consider whether italics may be an acceptable alternative to underlines.

Line Height

In CSS, the line-height property defines the minimum distance between the baselines of adjacent lines of text. A *baseline* is the imaginary line upon which the bottoms of characters sit. Line height is analogous to *leading* or *interlinear space* (the amount of space between lines) in traditional typesetting. Adjusting the line height can change the *color* of a block of text. In this case "color" refers not to hue (like blue or green), but rather the overall density or darkness of the text.

This section looks at both the line-height property and the method by which CSS calculates the actual height of lines. CSS line height handling has an impact on vertical alignment within text, discussed later.

line-height

Values:	normal | <number> | <length> | <percentage> | inherit
Initial value:	normal
Applies to:	All elements
Inherited:	Yes

These examples demonstrate three alternative methods for specifying the same amount of line spacing. If the font size is 10 pixels, the resulting line height for each of the examples listed would be 20 pixels. Figure 18-11 shows the results (bottom) compared to a paragraph with the default line height (top).

```
p.open {line-height: 2; }      /* uses a scaling factor */
p.open {line-height: 2em; }    /* unit of length */
p.open {line-height: 200%; }   /* percentage */
```

The default value is normal, which most browsers display at 120% of the font size. When a number is specified alone (as in the first example), it acts as a scaling factor that is multiplied by the current font size to calculate the line-height value. Line heights can also be specified using any of the length units. Relative values (em, ex, and %) are calculated by the font size of the element. Negative values are allowable and will cause the lines of text to overlap.

It is important to note that child elements inherit the *computed* line height value from their parent element, not the specified value. For example, the line height for

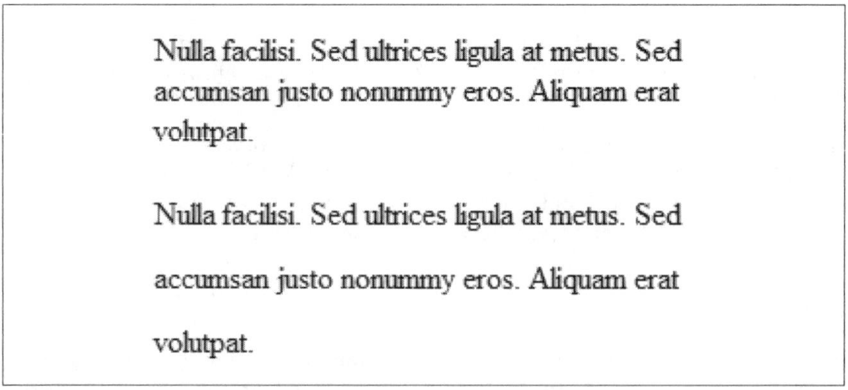

Nulla facilisi. Sed ultrices ligula at metus. Sed accumsan justo nonummy eros. Aliquam erat volutpat.
Nulla facilisi. Sed ultrices ligula at metus. Sed accumsan justo nonummy eros. Aliquam erat volutpat.

Figure 18-11. The line-height property

a `div` with a font size of 12 and a line height of 1 em calculates to 12 pixels. A paragraph element that is the child of that `div` will inherit the 12-pixel line height, not the relative 1 em value. If that paragraph happens to have a font size larger than 12 pixels, the lines of text will overlap.

The same is not true for scaling factors. When you specify a numerical scaling factor, that value is applied to the selected element and all of its child elements.

Calculating Line Height

Although specifying line heights numerically is fairly straightforward, it is worthwhile to take a look under the hood to see how CSS is actually handling the calculation.

The difference between the line height and the font size values is the leading. Half of the leading is applied above the text's content area and the other half is placed below. The net result is the same as the baseline-to-baseline measurement for line height. Figure 18-12 shows how leading is distributed for text with a font size of 14 pixels and a line height of 22 pixels.

4 px half-leading above and below
22 px line box height
14 px content height
A typical line of text

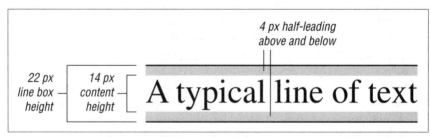

Figure 18-12. Line height and leading

When there is an odd number of pixels, the user agent decides where the larger value is placed (although, most place the extra pixel below the content area).

The text's content area plus its leading form an implied *inline box*, which is the total amount of vertical space the text occupies in a line. Being able to visualize the inline box will come in handy later when we discuss vertical alignment.

Text Alignment Properties

One of the ways text can be formatted to improve visual hierarchy and readability is through alignment. CSS provides several properties for adjusting the horizontal and vertical alignment of text.

Indents

Use the text-indent property to specify an amount of indentation for the first line of text in an element.

text-indent

Values:	`<length>` | `<percentage>` | `inherit`
Initial value:	0
Applies to:	Block-level elements and table cells
Inherited:	Yes

The value of text-indent may be any unit of length or a percentage value (calculated as a percentage of the parent element width), as shown in these examples and Figure 18-13:

```
p#1 { text-indent: 3em; }
p#2 { text-indent: 50%; }
p#3 { text-indent: -20px; }
```

The third rule in this list shows an allowable negative text-indent value. Negative values can be used to create hanging-indent effects. This feature should be used with care, as it may cause text to disappear off the left edge of the browser (add left padding to compensate) or may not be supported properly in older browser versions.

One last thing to know about indents is that a child element inherits the computed indent value from its parent, not the specified value. So if a div is set to 800 pixels wide with a 10% margin, the computed indent will be 80 pixels. A paragraph within the div will inherit the 80-pixel indent, not the 10% text-indent value.

 Designers may be accustomed to specifying indents and margins in tandem, but to be consistent with the CSS model, margins will be discussed in relation to the box model in Chapter 19.

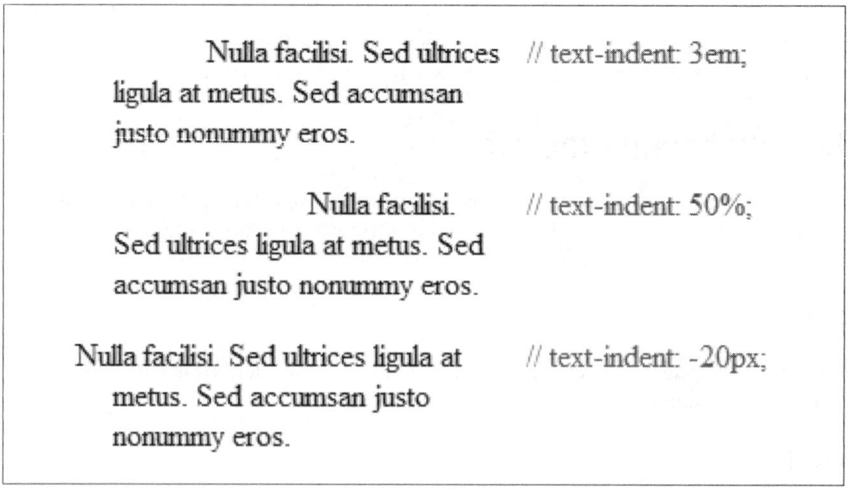

> Nulla facilisi. Sed ultrices   // text-indent: 3em;
> ligula at metus. Sed accumsan
> justo nonummy eros.
>
>   Nulla facilisi.   // text-indent: 50%;
> Sed ultrices ligula at metus. Sed
> accumsan justo nonummy eros.
>
> Nulla facilisi. Sed ultrices ligula at   // text-indent: -20px;
> metus. Sed accumsan justo
> nonummy eros.

Figure 18-13. The text-indent property

Horizontal Alignment

Use the text-align property to adjust the horizontal alignment of text within block elements.

text-align

Values:	left | right | center | justify | inherit
Initial Values:	left *for languages that read left to right* right *for languages that read right to left*
Applies to:	Block-level elements and table cells
Inherited:	Yes

The resulting text behavior of the various text-align property keyword values should be fairly intuitive as illustrated in Figure 18-14.

```
p { text-align: left; }
p { text-align: right; }
p { text-align: center; }
p { text-align: justify; }
```

It is worth pointing out that the text-align property controls the horizontal alignment of the inline elements within the element, not the alignment of the element itself. In other words, it is not equivalent to the deprecated center element. Notice that the paragraph elements in Figure 18-14 remain aligned on the left margin.

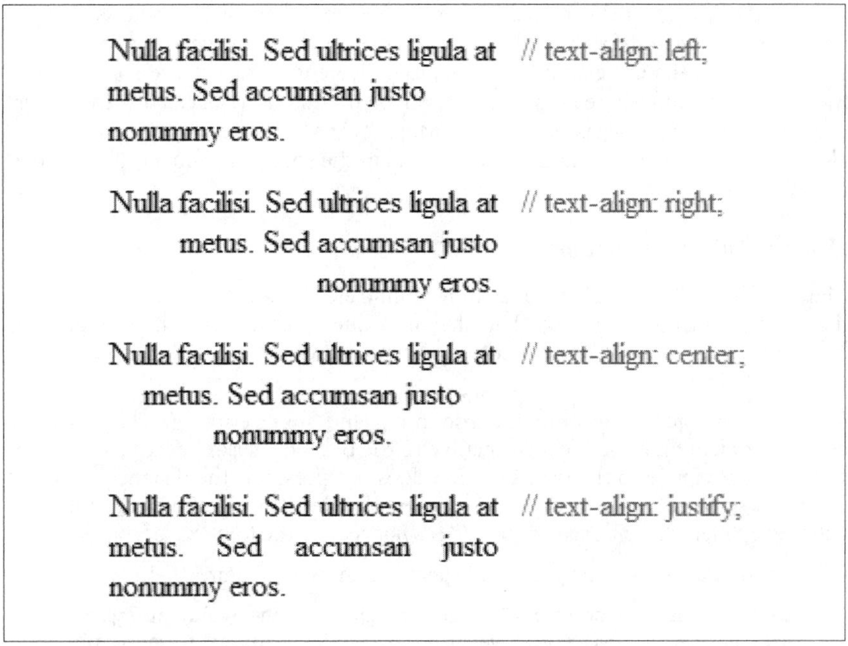

Nulla facilisi. Sed ultrices ligula at   // text-align: left;
metus. Sed accumsan justo
nonummy eros.

Nulla facilisi. Sed ultrices ligula at   // text-align: right;
            metus. Sed accumsan justo
                        nonummy eros.

Nulla facilisi. Sed ultrices ligula at   // text-align: center;
    metus. Sed accumsan justo
            nonummy eros.

Nulla facilisi. Sed ultrices ligula at   // text-align: justify;
metus.   Sed   accumsan   justo
nonummy eros.

Figure 18-14. The text-align property

The proper way to horizontally align elements is through manipulation of their left and right margins, as discussed in Chapter 19.

Vertical Alignment

Use the `vertical-align` property to specify the vertical alignment of an inline element. Vertical alignment values are relative to the baseline, text height (font size), or the total height of the text line. In the course of looking at vertical alignment values, this section introduces other important CSS concepts such as replaced elements and the inline box model.

vertical-align

Values:	baseline | sub | super | top | text-top | middle | text-bottom | bottom | <percentage> |<length> | inherit
Initial value:	baseline
Applies to:	Inline elements and table cell elements
Inherited:	No

The `vertical-align` property applies to inline text elements as well as nontext elements that may appear in the flow of text, such as images or form inputs. Images and inputs are examples of *replaced* elements, because the source document contains only a reference to the element that is replaced by the actual content when the page is assembled. Most XHTML elements are *non-replaced* elements, which means their content appears in the source document, like the text of a paragraph (p).

Aligning relative to the baseline

Many of the `vertical-align` values move inline elements with respect to the baseline of the surrounding text. The default value is `baseline`, which aligns the baseline of text—or the bottom edge of a replaced element—with the baseline of the parent element.

The sub and super values allow subscripting and superscripting. The sub value causes the element to be lowered relative to the baseline. super causes the element to be raised relative to the baseline. CSS does not prescribe the distance it should be raised or lowered, so it depends on the browser. It is significant to note that aligning an element with sub or super does *not* reduce the font size of the element.

These examples of baseline, sub, and super are shown in Figure 18-15.

```
<p>Aliquam erat <span style="vertical-align: baseline">volutpat</span></p>
<p>Aliquam erat <span style="vertical-align: sub">volutpat</span></p>
<p>Aliquam erat <span style="vertical-align: sup">volutpat</span></p>
```

Aliquam erat volutpat   // baseline

Aliquam erat volutpat   // sub

Aliquam erat volutpat   // super

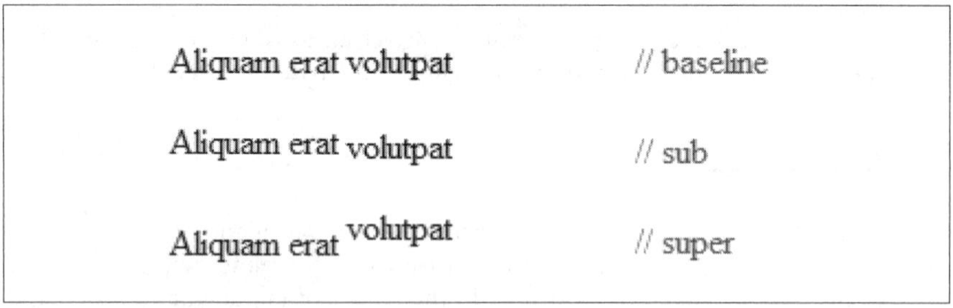

Figure 18-15. vertical-align relative to baseline

Aligning relative to text height

The `text-top` and `text-bottom` values align an element relative to the top and bottom edges of the surrounding text, respectively. Although it depends on the font design, the "top" of text corresponds roughly to the top of the ascenders and the "bottom" of text corresponds roughly to the bottom of the descenders. More accurately, it is the top and bottom of the text box for that font and is derived from the font size of the parent element. Replaced elements in the line are ignored in the calculation of the top and bottom of the text box.

The inline box model for the calculation of line height is discussed in detail in Chapter 19.

Figure 18-16 shows elements aligned with text-top and text-bottom. It is easy to see that the aligned elements are positioned relative to the text and not to the overall height of the line.

```
<p>A tall <img style="vertical-align: middle" src="img/placeholder_tall.gif"
alt="" /> image and a short <img style="vertical-align: text-top" src="img/
placeholder_short.gif" alt="" /> image.</p>
```

```
<p>A tall <img style="vertical-align: middle" src="img/placeholder_tall.gif"
alt="" /> image and a short <img style="vertical-align: text-bottom"
src="img/placeholder_short.gif" alt="" /> image</p>
```

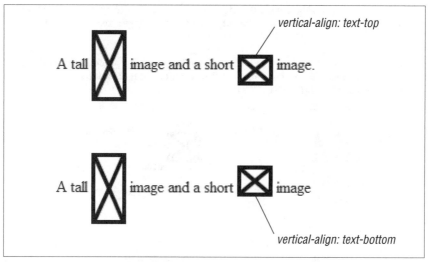

Figure 18-16. Text-top and text-bottom

The final text-based alignment is middle, which aligns the vertical midpoint of the element (typically an image) with an imaginary line drawn through the middle of the x-height of the parent. A font's x-height is the height of its lowercase letters, but browsers usually calculate it as .5 em. According to the specification, then, the line against which an element will be vertically centered is only .25 em above the baseline, as indicated by the gray line in Figure 18-17.

```
<p>A tall <img style="vertical-align: middle" src="img/placeholder_tall.gif"
alt="" /> image and a short <img style="vertical-align: middle" src="img/
placeholder_short.gif" alt="" /> image.</p>
```

Figure 18-17. Text aligned with the middle value

CSS: Font/Text
Properties

Aligning relative to line height

The top and bottom values align elements relative to the top and bottom of the line box for that line. The line box is an implied box that is generated for each line of text in a block element. It is drawn high enough to enclose the tallest inline element, including its leading. Replaced elements, like images, are included in the calculation of the line box height, so they influence the position of elements aligned with top and bottom.

Figure 18-18 shows elements aligned with top and bottom in relation to the line box.

```
<p>A tall <img style="vertical-align: middle" src="img/placeholder_tall.gif"
alt="" /> image and a short <img style="vertical-align: top" src="img/
placeholder_short.gif" alt="" /> image.</p>
```

```
<p>A tall <img style="vertical-align: middle" src="img/placeholder_tall.gif"
alt="" /> image and a short <img style="vertical-align: bottom" src="img/
placeholder_short.gif" alt="" /> image</p>
```

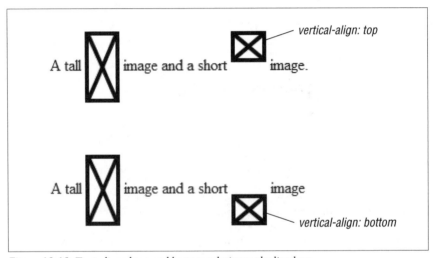

Figure 18-18. Text aligned top and bottom relative to the line box

Aligning with percentage values

When you use a percentage value with vertical-align, the baseline of the element is moved by your specified amount relative to the baseline. The distance is calculated as a percentage of the element's line-height value. Both positive and negative percentage values are accepted.

Text Spacing

CSS provides several tools for adjusting the space between words or characters in text. Adding space within a line is another way to affect the character or color of a block of text. For example, adding a little extra space between letters is a common technique for calling more attention to a headline or the first line of text on a page. This section introduces the letter-spacing, word-spacing, and white-space properties.

Letter Spacing

Use the letter-spacing property to specify an amount of space to be added between characters.

letter-spacing

Values:	normal | <length> | inherit
Initial value:	normal
Applies to:	All elements
Inherited:	Yes

Figure 18-19 shows an example of a style sheet rule that adds 8 pixels of extra space between the characters in the first line of text.

```
p {letter-spacing: 8px; }

<p>Nunc a nisl.</p>
```

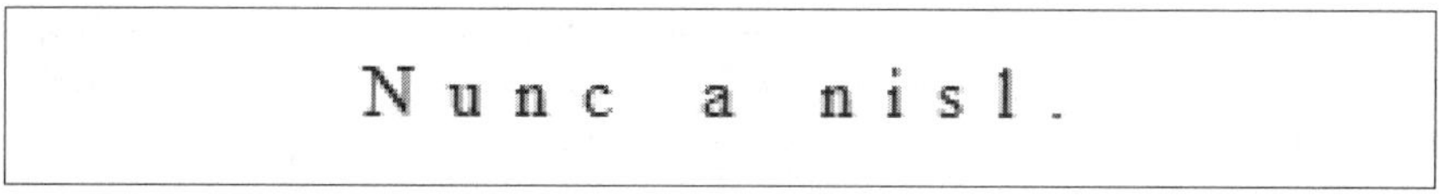

N u n c   a   n i s l .

Figure 18-19. Letter spacing

The default value normal is equivalent to a numeric setting of zero (0). In other words, whatever value you specify is added to the standard character-spacing text. Negative values are permitted and will cause the characters to overlap.

Note that when specifying relative lengths (such as em, which is based on font size), the *calculated* size will be passed down to child elements, even if they have a smaller font size than the parent.

Word Spacing

Use the word-spacing property to specify an additional amount of space to be placed between the words of the text element.

word-spacing

Values:	normal | <length> | inherit
Initial value:	normal

Applies to: All elements

Inherited: Yes

Similar to `letter-spacing`, the value of `word-spacing` gets added to the standard space between words. A setting of zero (0) is equivalent to `normal` and will leave the word spacing unaltered. These examples of word spacing are shown in Figure 18-20.

```
p {word-spacing: 1em;}

<p>Nunc a nisl.</p>
```

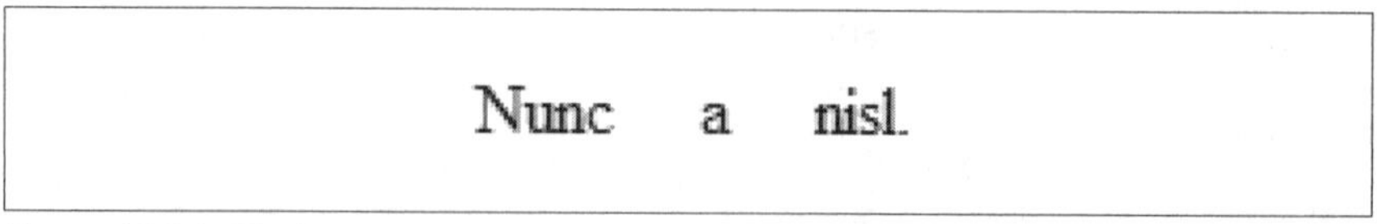

$$\text{Nunc} \quad \text{a} \quad \text{nisl.}$$

Figure 18-20. Word spacing

Note that when specifying relative lengths (such as em, which is based on font size), the calculated size will be passed down to child elements, even if they have a smaller font size than the parent.

Whitespace

By default, strings of character spaces in the source for an element are collapsed down to one space and line breaks are ignored. In XHTML, the `pre` element preserves that whitespace and displays the source just as it is typed. The `white-space` property in CSS does the same thing, and more.

white-space

Values: `normal | pre | nowrap | pre-wrap | pre-line | inherit`

Initial value: `normal`

Applies to: All elements (as of CSS 2.1)

Inherited: Yes

The `normal` value treats text normally, with consecutive spaces collapsing to one. The `pre` value displays multiple characters, like the `pre` element in (X)HTML, except that it has no effect on the font of the element (browsers tend to display `pre` elements in the monospace font).

Figure 18-21 shows a simple use of the `white-space` property as specified in this example style and markup.

```
p.haiku {white-space: pre; }

<p class="haiku">
    Love's pure silver flame
```

```
          gives each innermost spirit
      invisible warmth.
  </p>
```

Love's pure silver flame

gives each innermost spirit

invisible warmth.

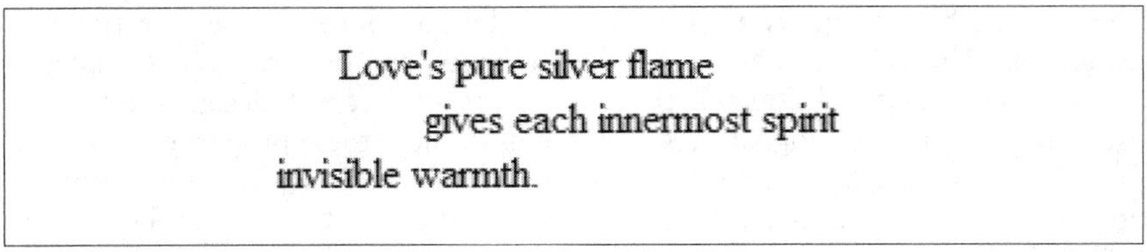

Figure 18-21. The white-space property

nowrap prevents the text element from wrapping unless designated by a <br />. Without a <br />, the text may extend beyond the browser window, requiring horizontal scrolling.

CSS 2.1 introduced two new values for white-space. The pre-wrap value preserves multiple character spaces but allows long lines of text to wrap. Line breaks in the source are also honored. The pre-line value makes multiple character spaces collapse to one, but it preserves new lines in the source. As of this writing, no browser supports the pre-line and pre-wrap values for white-space.

Text Direction

To accommodate languages that read right to left, such as Hebrew and Arabic, the CSS Recommendation provides two properties that affect the direction of the flow of text.

direction

Values:	ltr | rtl | inherit
Initial value:	ltr
Applies to:	All elements
Inherited:	Yes

The direction property affects the direction of text in a block-level element. It also changes the order of column layout, the behavior of text overflow, and margin alignment for justified text. The default is ltr (left to right) unless the browser has an internal style sheet for displaying text from right to left.

unicode-bidi

Values:	normal | embed | bidi-override | inherit
Initial value:	normal

Applies to: All elements

Inherited: No

The unicode-bidi property is provided to take advantage of the directionality features in Unicode. Unicode and directionality are discussed in Chapter 6. Setting directionality falls outside the realm of the average web designer, but it is a useful feature for multilingual sites. For details on how these properties work, see the CSS 2.1 specification online at *www.w3.org/TR/CSS21/*. For more information on the internationalization efforts at the W3C, see *www.w3c.org/ International*.

19

Basic Box Properties

The box model was briefly introduced in Chapter 16 as one of the fundamental concepts of CSS visual formatting. According to the box model, every element in a document generates a box to which such properties as width, height, margins, padding, and borders may be applied.

These element box properties (as well as those for positioning as discussed in Chapter 21), are at the heart of CSS-driven layout and design. Effects that once required tables, such as putting text in a colored box, can now be handled entirely with style sheets. This is just one way that style sheets have liberated developers from the inappropriate use of (X)HTML elements for visual effects. And that's just scratching the surface. Many visual effects created with CSS box properties simply weren't possible before using (X)HTML alone.

The box model is also at the core of some of the most notorious headaches for web developers, namely, the fact that all versions of Internet Explorer for Windows (except IE 6 and 7 running in Standards mode, as described in Chapter 9) interpret the width of the box differently than all other CSS-compliant browsers. This has made it necessary for web developers to jump through all sorts of hoops to replicate layouts consistently on all browsers. For more on the IE/Windows box model problem, see Chapter 25.

This chapter covers the box model in more depth and introduces the basic box properties for specifying size and adding margins, borders, and padding, as listed next.

height	border-top-style	border-top
width	border-right-style	border-right
max-height	border-bottom-style	border-bottom
max-width	border-left-style	border-left
min-height	border-style	border
min-width	border-top-width	padding-top
margin-right	border-right-width	padding-right
margin-left	border-bottom-width	padding-bottom
margin-top	border-left-width	padding-left
margin-bottom	border-width	padding
margin	border-top-color	
	border-right-color	
	border-bottom-color	
	border-left-color	
	border-color	

The box model will be addressed again in Chapter 21 as it relates to positioning and the layout of the page.

The Box Model, Revisited

According to CSS, every element in a document, both block-level and inline-level, generates a rectangular box called an *element box*. Figure 19-1 shows all the areas and boundaries defined by the CSS box model.

At the core of the element box is the content itself, called the *content area*. Its sides are referred to as the *inner edges* of the element box. The width and height of an element are calculated as the distance between these inner edges.

The *padding* is the area held between the content area and an optional border. The *border* is one or more lines that surrounds the element and its padding.

Background colors and images applied to an element are visible in the padding and extend behind the border (if there are gaps in the border style, the background color will show through).

Finally, on the outside of the element border, there is an optional amount of *margin*. The margin area is always transparent, which means that the background of the parent element shows through.

The outside edges of the margin area make up the *outer edges* of the element box. The total width that an element box occupies on the page is measured from outer edge to outer edge and includes the width of the content area plus the total amount of padding, border, and margins.

Keep in mind that when you specify the width value for an element, that sets the width of the content area only, so there's some extra math to do before you know the total width of the element. This calculation may be critical for positioning elements precisely on a page.

Here is where the IE/Windows box model problem comes into play. With the exception of IE 6 and 7 in Standards mode, Internet Explorer for Windows

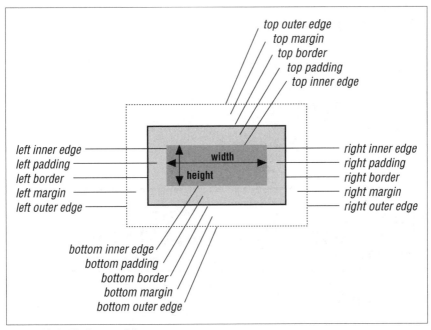

Figure 19-1. The box model

applies the width property to the entire width of the element box, from outer edge to outer edge. When margins, borders, or padding are also applied, this results in potentially large discrepancies between how the element should be sized and how it will appear in IE/Windows.

Inline Boxes

The element box is not the only implied box in the CSS visual formatting model. Every character and element in a line of text also generates a box on the fly. These *inline boxes* are used by the user agent (the browser) behind the scenes to calculate the height of each line in the flow of text and the space around elements. Line boxes and inline boxes are not elements, they are merely a device of the visual layout model. Therefore, you cannot use a selector to target line or inline boxes and apply styles to them (you can apply styles to inline elements, of course).

Having a familiarity with the various inline boxes at work behind the scenes is useful for predicting and controlling line height as well as for specifying the vertical alignment of inline elements. They also come into play when specifying box properties, particularly to inline elements. Figure 19-2 highlights the various inline boxes for a line of text.

The four invisible boxes that the user agent keeps track of when formatting each line of text include:

Em box
> In CSS, the this is a square unit that is equal to the font-size of the element. Its relation to the actual characters in the font is dependent on the typeface design, but in general, it encloses the ascenders and descenders of the font.

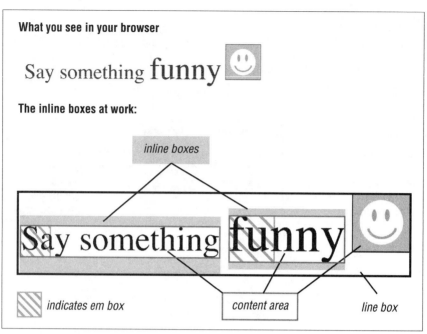

Figure 19-2. Inline boxes

Content area

Every element in a line has a content area box that corresponds to the content area in the box model (Figure 19-1). For text elements (also called *non-replaced elements* because their content appears in the source), the height of the content area is determined by the element's font-size. For anonymous text (text not specifically contained within an inline element), the font-size is inherited from the parent element. For images (and other replaced elements), the content area is the width and height of the image in pixels.

Inline box

The height of the inline box is calculated as the total of the element's content area plus the *leading* added above and below it (see Figure 18-12 in Chapter 18). Leading is the difference between the element's font-size and line-height values. It may be a negative value, which means that lines may overlap. For images (and replaced elements), the inline box is the height of the image in pixels, plus the height of any added borders and margins on the img element.

Line box

The line box is drawn around the top of the highest inline box and the bottom of the lowest inline box. It represents the total required vertical space for the line and all its elements. The vertical-align values top and bottom are relative to the top and bottom edges of the line box.

In the sections that follow, we'll see how the line box (the total height of a line) is affected (or not affected) by the addition of margins, borders, and padding on inline elements.

Width and Height

Use the width and height properties to specify the dimensions of a block-level element or an inline replaced element (like an image). The width and height properties do *not* apply to inline text (non-replaced) elements and will be ignored by standards-conformant browsers. In other words, you cannot specify the width and height of an anchor (a) or a strong element unless you change its display role to a block-level display value like block, list-item, or inline-block.

height

Values:	<length> | <percentage> | auto | inherit
Initial value:	auto
Applies to:	Block-level elements and replaced elements (such as images)
Inherited:	No

width

Values:	<length> | <percentage> | auto | inherit
Initial value:	auto
Applies to:	Block-level elements and replaced elements (such as images)
Inherited:	No

Using the height and width properties is straightforward, as shown in these examples and Figure 19-3.

```
div#tall {width:100px; height:200px; }
div#wide {width:200px; height:100px; }

<div id="tall" style="position:absolute;">
  Lorem ipsum ...
</div>

<div id="wide" style="position:absolute; left: 205px;">
  Lorem ...
</div>
```

There are only a few special behaviors to be aware of:

- width and height properties apply to the content area of the element only. Padding, borders, and margins are added onto the width and height values to arrive at the total element box dimensions. (See the sidebar "The IE/Windows Box Model Problem" for details regarding the notoriously incorrect implementation of box model measurements in Internet Explorer for Windows.)

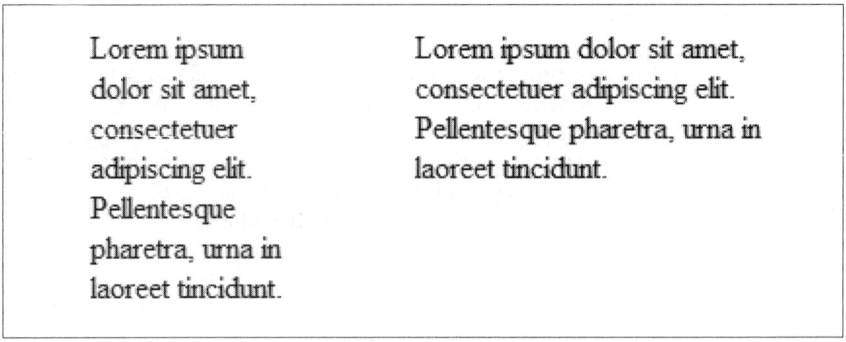

Lorem ipsum dolor sit amet, consectetuer adipiscing elit. Pellentesque pharetra, urna in laoreet tincidunt.

Lorem ipsum dolor sit amet, consectetuer adipiscing elit. Pellentesque pharetra, urna in laoreet tincidunt.

Figure 19-3. The height and width properties

- An element's height is calculated automatically and is just large enough to contain the element's contents; therefore, it is less common to specify height. The height of the content may change based on font-size, user settings, or other factors. If you do specify a height for a text element, be sure to also consider what happens should the content not fit (the overflow property is discussed in Chapter 21).

- For images, it is recommended that both width and height values be provided.

- CSS 2 introduced percentage values for width and height. Percentage values are calculated as a percentage of the width of the parent element. This means that if the size of the parent element changes, the width and height of its child elements will change proportionately.

The IE/Windows Box Model Problem

One of the most notorious browser inconsistencies is that Internet Explorer for Windows (all versions except IE 6 and 7 running in Standards mode) has its own implementation of the box model. In these versions of IE/Windows, the width property is applied to the entire element box, from outer margin edge to outer margin edge, not just the content area, as it should be. This causes valid CSS layouts that apply padding, borders, and margins to elements of a specific width to be rendered inconsistently. By using a proper DOCTYPE declaration, you can switch IE 6 and 7 into Standards mode, and widths and heights will apply to the content area, as expected (see Chapter 9 for details on DOCTYPE switching).

Until all versions of IE 5.x/Windows fade away completely, there is the "box model hack," a well-known workaround developed by Tantek Çelik that serves up a separate set of width values just for IE. This and other browser workarounds are discussed in Chapter 25.

Maximum and Minimum Heights

CSS 2 introduced properties for setting minimum and maximum heights and widths for block elements. They may be useful if you want to put limits on the size of an element when positioning it on a page.

max-width, max-height

Values:	<length> | <percentage> | none | inherit
Initial value:	none
Applies to:	All elements except non-replaced elements (i.e., inline text elements) and table elements
Inherited:	No

min-width, min-height

Values:	<length> | <percentage> | none | inherit
Initial value:	none
Applies to:	All elements except non-replaced elements (i.e., inline text elements) and table elements
Inherited:	No

There are a few behaviors of the minimum and maximum size properties to keep in mind:

- These properties are for use with block-level and replaced elements (like images) only.
- Once again, the measurements apply only to the content area of the element. If you add padding to an element, it will be applied on the outside of the content area and make the overall element box larger, even if a maximum height and width have been specified.

Internet Explorer through Version 6 does not support the min-width, min-height, max-width, and max-height properties. The CSS community has devised some workarounds for the min-height problem. These resources are a good starting point for investigation:

- Dustin Diaz's "Min-height Fast Hack" at *www.dustindiaz.com/ min-height-fast-hack/*
- Dave Shea's Mezzoblue.com: *www.mezzoblue.com/dailies/ 2005/01/05/index.php*
- Grey Wyvern's solution at *www.greywyvern.com/code/min- height-hack.html*

Margins

Margins are an amount of space that may be added around the outside of the element's border. There are properties for specifying a margin amount for one side at a time or by using the shorthand margin property.

margin-top, margin-right, margin-bottom, margin-left

Values: `<length> | <percentage> | auto | inherit`

Initial value: 0

Applies to: All elements (except elements with table display types other than table and inline-table)

Inherited: No

margin

Values: `[<length> | <percentage> | auto]{1,4} | inherit`

Initial value: See individual properties

Applies to: All elements (except elements with table display types other than table and inline-table)

Inherited: No

With the margin-top, margin-right, margin-bottom, and margin-left properties, you can specify a margin for one side of an element. Margin size may be specified in any of the accepted units of length. Negative values are permitted. Figure 19-4 shows examples of adding margins to individual sides of an element. Note that the dotted lines are a device to point out the outer edge of the margin and would not display in the browser.

```
h1 { margin-top: 3px; }
h1 { margin-right: 20px; }
h1 { margin-bottom: 3px; }
h1 { margin-left: 20px; }
```

Percentage values are also permitted, but be aware that percentages are calculated based on the *width* of the parent element. If the parent element gets narrower (perhaps as the result of the browser window resizing) the margins on all sides of the child elements will be recalculated.

Margins may also be set using the keyword auto, which allows the user agent to fill in the amount of margin necessary to fit or fill the containing block.

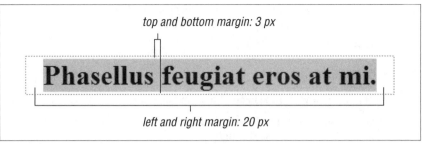

Figure 19-4. Individual margin settings

The proper way to horizontally center an element in CSS is to set the left and right margins to auto. This technique (as well as the workaround required for Internet Explorer in anything but Standards mode) is addressed in Chapter 24.

The Shorthand margin Property

As an alternative to setting margins one side at a time, there is the shorthand margin property. The accepted values are the same as those previously listed. What changes slightly is the syntax as the margin property provides a lot of flexibility for specifying values.

In the values listed for margin above, the {1,4} notation means that you can provide one, two, three, or four values for a single margin property. Here's how it works.

When you provide four values, the values are applied around the edges of the element in clockwise order, like this (some people use the mnemonic device "TRouBLe" for the order Top, Right, Bottom, Left):

```
{ margin: top right bottom left }
```

The four margin properties listed in Figure 19-4 could be condensed using the margin property as so:

```
{ margin: 3px 20px 3px 20px; }
```

When one or more of the four values is missing, certain provided values are replicated for the missing values.

If three values are provided, it is assumed the value for the left margin is missing, so the value for right is used for left ({margin: top right/left bottom}). This rule, therefore, is equivalent to the previous example:

```
{ margin: 3px 20px 3px; }
```

If two values are provided, the right value is replicated for the missing left value, and the top value is replicated for the missing bottom value ({margin: top/bottom right/left}). Again, the same effect achieved by the previous two examples could be accomplished with this rule:

```
{ margin: 3px 20px; }
```

Finally, if only one value is provided, it is replicated for all four values. This declaration applies 20 pixels of space on all sides of an element:

```
{ margin: 20px; }
```

Margin Behavior

It is helpful to be aware of these general margin behaviors.

- Margins are always transparent, allowing the background color or image of the parent element to show through.
- Elements may have negative margins, which may cause elements to break out of containing blocks of their parent elements or overlap other elements on the page.
- The vertical (top and bottom) margins of adjacent block elements in the normal document flow will *collapse*. That means that the space held between adjacent block elements will be the larger of the two margin values, rather than the sum of their margin values. The collapsing margins in the following examples are demonstrated in Figure 19-5.

```
h2#top {margin: 10px 20px 10px 20px;}

h2#bottom {margin: 20px 20px 20px 20px; }
```

```
<h2 id="top" >Lorem ipsum dolor sit amet,</h2>
<h2 id="bottom" >consectetuer adipiscing elit.</h2>
```

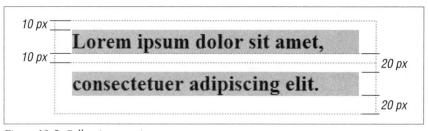

Figure 19-5. Collapsing margins

- The vertical margins do not collapse for floated elements, absolutely positioned elements, and inline block elements.
- In CSS 2.1, horizontal (left and right) margins never collapse.
- Top and bottom margins applied to non-replaced inline elements (text elements such as em or strong) have no effect on the height of the line. In other words, top and bottom margins are not calculated as part of the element's inline box or the height of the line box for that line.
- Left and right margins applied to non-replaced inline (text) elements *do* cause the specified amount of space to be held before and after (to the left of the first character and right of the last character) the inline element, even if it is broken over two lines.

- Top and bottom margins applied to replaced inline elements (i.e., images and form inputs) *do* affect the height of the line. In other words, the margin is included in the inline box for replaced elements, and the line box is drawn larger to accommodate it.
- When an image has a margin, the bottom outer edge of the margin is placed on the baseline of the line (unless placement is altered with the vertical-align property on the img). The image in Figure 19-6 has 20 pixels of margin on all sides. The result is that the image is raised off the baseline by 20 pixels and the line height opens up to accommodate the image and its margin.

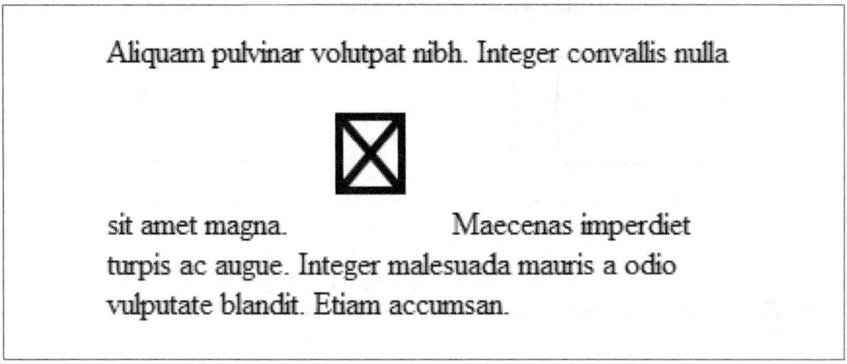

Aliquam pulvinar volutpat nibh. Integer convallis nulla

sit amet magna.   Maecenas imperdiet
turpis ac augue. Integer malesuada mauris a odio
vulputate blandit. Etiam accumsan.

Figure 19-6. Margin settings on inline images

Borders

A border is simply a line drawn around the content area of an element and its (optional) padding. The three aspects of a border that can be specified are its style, width (thickness), and color. As for margin, each of these qualities may be specified for an individual side at a time or for several sides at once using short-hand properties.

There are only a few things to know about border style behavior:

- Borders are drawn on top of an element's background, so the background color or image will show through the gaps in the intermittent border styles.
- Borders applied to non-replaced inline elements (text elements) have no effect on the line height for that line. In other words, they are not included in the inline box for the element.
- Borders applied to replaced elements, however, do affect line height, just as margins do.

Border Style

The border style is the most important of the border qualities because, according to the CSS specification, if there is no border style specified, the border does not exist. In other words, you must always declare the style or other border settings will be ignored.

Figure 19-7 shows the nine border styles you have to choose from.

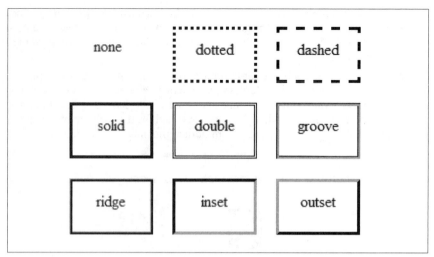

Figure 19-7. The nine available border styles

 There is a bug in Internet Explorer 6 for Windows that causes borders specified as dotted to render as dashed.

Border styles can be applied one side at a time or by using the border-style shortcut property.

border-top-style, border-right-style, border-bottom-style, border-left-style

Values: none | dotted | dashed | solid | double | groove | ridge | inset | outset

Initial values: none

Applies to: All elements

Inherited: No

border-style

Values: [none | dotted | dashed | solid | double | groove | ridge | inset | outset]{1,4} | inherit

Initial value: Not defined

Applies to: All elements

Inherited: No

As you might expect, the `border-top-style`, `border-right-style`, `border-bottom-style`, and `border-left-style` properties allow you to specify a border style to one side of the element. If you do not specify a width for the border, the `medium` width value (the default) will be used. If there is no color specified, it uses the foreground color of the element (i.e., the text color). This example shows single-side border attributes in action (Figure 19-8).

```
div {border-top-style: solid;
     border-right-style: dashed;
     border-bottom-style: dotted;
     border-left-style: double; }
```

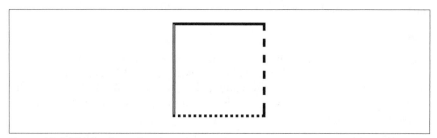

Figure 19-8. The border-style property

The `border-style` shortcut property works the same as the `margin` shortcut described earlier. Border style values for each side are provided in clockwise order: top, right, bottom, left. If fewer values are provided, some values are replicated. The right value will be used for a missing left value, the top value will be replicated for a missing bottom value; and if only one border style is provided, it will be applied to all four sides of the element.

The same effect shown in Figure 19-8 can be replicated using this `border-style` declaration:

```
div {border-style: solid dashed dotted double; }
```

Border Width (Thickness)

The thickness of the rule is controlled with one of the border width properties. As we've seen for `margin` and `border-style`, you can control the width of each individual side or use the `border-width` shorthand property to specify several sides at once. The shorthand values are provided in clockwise (top, right, bottom, left) order and replicate as described for the `margin` shorthand property earlier in this chapter.

border-top-width, border-right-width, border-bottom-width, border-left-width

Values: thin | medium | thick | <length> | inherit

Initial values: medium

Applies to:	All elements
Inherited:	No

border-width

Values:	[thin | medium | thick | <length>]{1,4} | inherit
Initial value:	Not defined
Applies to:	All elements
Inherited:	No

The properties may use the keyword values thin, medium, and thick, in order of increasing width. The actual pixel value for each keyword is left up to the user agent, but must be consistent throughout the document. Border width can be specified in units of length as well (pixels are common). Negative length values are not permitted for borders.

Figure 19-9 shows an example of keyword and pixel-measurement border widths.

```
div {border-style: solid;
    border-top-width: thin;
    border-right-width: medium;
    border-bottom-width: thick;
    border-left-width: 12px; }
```

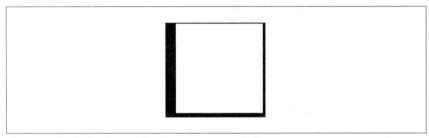

Figure 19-9. The border-width property

Border Color

Use one of the side-specific color properties or the border-color shorthand to specify a color for the border. Values for border-color are provided in clockwise (top, right, bottom, left) order and replicate as described for the margin shorthand property earlier in this chapter.

border-top-color, border-right-color, border-bottom-color, border-left-color

Values:	<color> | transparent | inherit
Initial values:	The value of the color property for the element

Applies to:	All elements
Inherited:	No

border-color

Values:	[<color> | transparent]{1,4} | inherit
Initial value:	Not defined
Applies to:	All elements
Inherited:	No

Colors values may be specified in any of the methods outlined in Chapter 16 and Appendix D. If no border color is declared, the default is the foreground color for the element (i.e., the text color for text elements).

The border-color shorthand property is demonstrated in this example and in Figure 19-10.

```
div {border: 6px solid;
    border-color: #333 #666 #999 #CCC; }
```

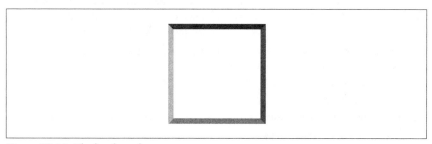

Figure 19-10. The border-color property

CSS 2 added the transparent value that allows the background of the parent element to show through the border, yet holds the width of the border as specified. This may be useful when creating rollover effects with CSS (this technique is explained in Chapter 24), because the space where the border will appear is maintained when the mouse is not over the element.

 Unfortunately, the transparent value is not supported in Internet Explorer for Windows through Version 6. Support in IE 7 (in beta as of this writing) is possible, but not documented.

Combining Style, Width, and Color

There is no shortage of shortcuts for specifying border appearance. Once again, we have rules that apply combinations of style, width, and color to one side at a time and the border property that applies the values to all sides of the element.

border-top, border-right, border-bottom, border-left

Values: [<border-style> || <border-width> || <border-color>] | inherit

Initial value: Not defined

Applies to: All elements

Inherited: No

border

Values: [<border-style> || <border-width> || <border-color>] | inherit

Initial value: Refer to individual properties

Applies to: All elements

Inherited: No

The side-specific and the shorthand border properties may include a `border-style` value, a `border-width` value, and a `border-color` value. They do not need to be in any particular order. You do not need to declare all three border qualities, but keep in mind that if the `border-style` is not declared, there will be no border.

The border shorthand is somewhat different from the other shorthand properties discussed so far in that it can be used to apply border properties to all four sides of the element only. It does not provide a way to target certain borders and there is no system of value replication.

The rules listed here are all valid examples of the border shortcut properties.

```
h1 {border-left: .5em solid blue; }
h1 {border-left: solid blue .5em; }
h1 {border-left: solid .5em; }

p.example {border: 2px dotted #666633; }
p.example {border: dotted 2px; }
```

Padding

The *padding* area is an optional amount of space held between the content area of an element and its border. If you are putting a border on an element, it is usually a good idea to add a bit of padding as well to keep the border from bumping against the content.

Now that you've seen margins and borders at work, the padding properties should look familiar. There are side-specific properties for setting an amount of

Overriding Shorthand Properties

One of the principles of the cascade is that rules that appear later in a style sheet override previous rules. You can use this principle to override shorthand settings for one side of an element box.

In this example, all four sides of a box are given a solid red border, but then the right edge is immediately overridden by a rule that sets the border to none (thus removing it).

```
p.tip { border: solid red 3px;
        border-right: none; }
```

In addition to borders, this trick can be used with any of the shorthand and side-specific properties in this chapter.

padding on each side by name, and a shorthand padding property that applies padding to combinations of four sides.

padding-top, padding-right, padding-bottom, padding-left

Values:	<length> | <percentage> | inherit
Initial value:	0
Applies to:	All elements
Inherited:	No

padding

Values:	[<length> | <percentage>]{1,4} | inherit
Initial value:	0
Applies to:	All elements
Inherited:	No

The padding properties specify the width of the padding area. Values may be provided in units of length or as percentages. Negative values are not permitted for padding.

It is important to note that, as for margins, percentage values are always calculated based on the width of the parent element (even for top and bottom padding). So if the width of the parent element should change, so will the percentage padding values on all sides of the child element.

Figure 19-11 shows examples of element padding.

```
h2#A {padding: 4px; background: #CCC;}
h2#B {padding: 20px; background: #CCC;}

<h2 id="A">Sed ultrices ligula at metus.</h2>
<h2 id="B">Sed ultrices ligula at metus.</h2>
```

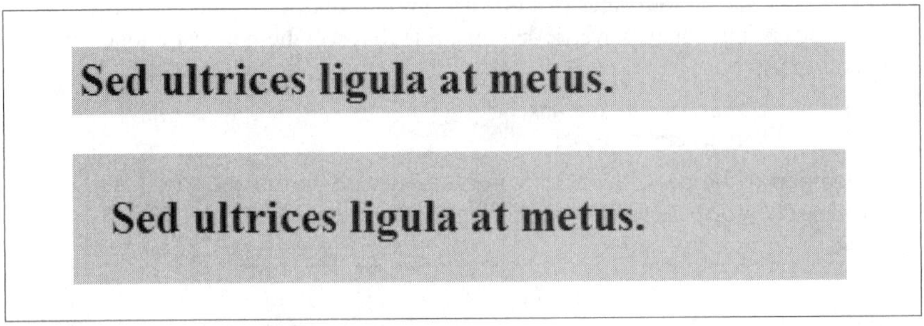

Figure 19-11. Adding padding around elements

Background colors and images applied to an element will display in its padding area (this sets it apart from margins, which are always transparent). So if you want an element to appear in a colored box, with or without an explicit border, padding is the way to put a little space between the edge of the box and the content.

Padding does not collapse as margins do. The total padding between elements will be the sum of the padding for the adjacent sides of the elements.

Color and Backgrounds

Once upon a time in 1993, when Mosaic was the only widely distributed browser in town, all web pages had black text on a gray background with blue hyperlinks and purple visited hyperlinks (unless the user changed it in the browser preferences to something more jazzy—say, lime green on purple). Then in 1994, along came Netscape, and HTML extensions for coloring text and backgrounds were born. Even those limited controls came as a welcome relief to web designers and users clamoring for color.

CSS offers control over color and backgrounds that is worlds away from the effects possible with HTML extensions alone. This chapter introduces the properties for adding color and backgrounds to elements listed here.

```
color                          background-position
background-color               background-attachment
background-image               background
background-repeat
```

Foreground Color

Say goodbye to <font color=> forever. You can pitch the text, link, vlink, and alink attributes for the body element while you're at it.

The color property is used to describe the text (a.k.a. "foreground") color of an element. The foreground color is also used for an element's border unless it is specifically overridden with a border color rule.

color

Values: <color> | inherit

Initial value: Depends on user agent

Applies to: All elements

Inherited: Yes

Color Values

The value of the color property is any of the valid color types and system colors. Here's a refresher.

RGB colors can be specified in any of the following formats:

```
{color: #0000FF;}
{color: #00F;}
{color: rgb(0,0,255);}
{color: rgb(0%, 0%, 100%);}
```

The first example uses three two-digit hexadecimal RGB values (for a complete explanation, see Appendix D). The second example uses a shorthand three-digit syntax, which is converted to the six-digit form by replicating each digit (therefore, 00F is the same as 0000FF).

The last two formats use a functional notation specifying RGB values as a comma-separated list of regular values (from 0 to 255) or percentage values (from 0 to 100%). Note that percentage values can use decimals, e.g., rgb(0%, 50.5%, 33.3%).

CSS 1 and 2 also recognize 16 valid color names: aqua, black, blue, fuchsia, gray, green, lime, maroon, navy, olive, purple, red, silver, teal, white, and yellow. The CSS 2.1 Recommendation adds orange, for a total of 17.

The color property is easy to use, as shown in these examples (Figure 20-1). Unfortunately, in this book we are limited to the full spectrum of gray.

 Note that this example and others in this chapter use inline styles purely as a space-saving device, not as a recommended markup practice. It is preferable to put style information in an external or embedded style sheet in the head of the document.

```
<p style="color: #000">Aenean congue bibendum ligula.</p>
<p style="color: #666">Aenean congue bibendum ligula.</p>
<p style="color: #CCC">Aenean congue bibendum ligula.</p>
```

Despite being fairly straightforward, there are still a few aspects of the foreground color property and the way browsers interpret it to keep in mind.

- The color property is inherited. It makes sense that when you set a color to the text of a paragraph, any emphasized or strong text within it would be that color, too.

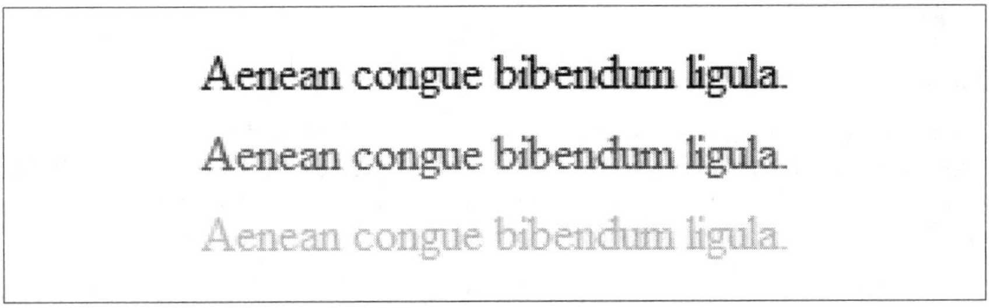

Aenean congue bibendum ligula.

Aenean congue bibendum ligula.

Aenean congue bibendum ligula.

Figure 20-1. Changing the foreground color

- It is valid to add a foreground color to images. The content of the image won't be affected by it, of course, but the color will be used for the image border if one is specified.

- If there is both a foreground color and a border color property applied to an element, the border-color property always overrides color for the border color.

- If you want to change the color of all the text in a document, apply the color property to the body element. Color may be assigned globally to the html element or by using the universal selector (*) as well, but this is less common due to irregularities in inheritance and problems with form elements in some browsers. Be aware, however, that on some older browsers, table elements do not properly inherit properties from the body, so text within tables would go back to the default text color. To be on the safe side, you can make a color declaration for body and the relevant table elements, like this:

  ```
  body, table, td, th { color: fuchsia; } /* ok, maybe not fuchsia */
  ```

- You can apply the color property to form input elements like buttons and pull-down menus. Although it's valid use of CSS, it is not supported consistently across browsers. Make sure that your design is legible even if your chosen form input colors do not display the way you intended.

Background Color

It's been common practice to add a background color to a page using the bgcolor attribute in the body element in HTML. With CSS, not only can you provide a background color for a whole page, but for any element in the document, both block-level and inline. Boxes of color anywhere you want them…and no tables required!

Background color is declared with the (no surprise here) background-color attribute.

background-color

Values:	<color> | transparent | inherit
Initial Value:	transparent

Applies to: All elements

Inherited: No

Background properties are applied to the "canvas" behind an element. With regard to the box model, background colors fill the content area, the padding area, and extend behind the border to its outer edge. This means that if the border has gaps, the background color will show through.

Background properties are not inherited, but because the default value is transparent, the parent's background color shows through its child elements. Figure 20-2 shows an example of the background-color property. Note how a little padding added to the element gives the content a little breathing room inside the resulting rectangular colored box.

```
p {padding: 5px;}
p.a {background-color: #333333;}
p.b {background-color: #666666;}
p.c {background-color: #CCCCCC;}

<p class="a">Fusce rhoncus facilisis sapien.</p>
<p class="b">Fusce rhoncus facilisis sapien.</p>
<p class="c">Fusce rhoncus facilisis sapien.</p>
```

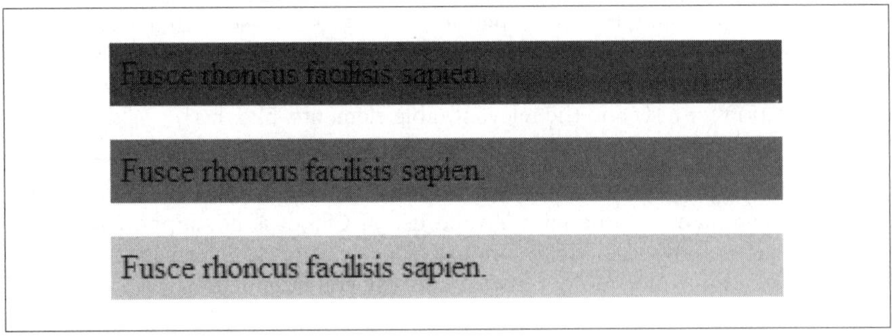

Figure 20-2. The background-color property

Background Images

Once again, CSS beats HTML hands down in the background department (but then, HTML was never intended to be fussing around with things like background images). With CSS, you're not stuck with a repeating tile pattern, and you can position a background image wherever you like. You can also apply a background image to any element in the document.

This section covers the CSS properties for adding and manipulating background images, with the basic background-image property as a starting point and moving on to more advanced background image behaviors such as controlling repeating patterns, positioning the image within the element, and preventing the image from scrolling off the page.

Background Image Tips

When working with background images, keep these guidelines and tips in mind:

- Use an image that won't interfere with the legibility of the text over it.
- As usual for the Web, it is important to keep the file size as small as possible for background images, which may lag behind the display of the rest of the page.
- Provide a background-color that matches the primary color of the image in the background. If the background image fails to display, at least the overall design of the page will be similar. This is particularly important if the text color would be illegible against the default white (or light gray) browser background.

---

background-image

Values: <uri> | none | inherit

Initial value: none

Applies to: All elements

Inherited: No

background-image is the basic property for adding an image to the background (the "canvas") of an element. When applied to the body element, it functions just like the background attribute, causing the image to tile horizontally and vertically until it fills the browser window. Unlike the background attribute, the background-image property can be applied to any element in the document, both block and inline.

Figure 20-3 shows background images applied to a whole page and to an individual paragraph using these style rules.

```
body {background-image: url(stripes.gif);}
p.highlight {background-image: url(dots.gif);}
```

The background-image property is not inherited (in fact, none of the background properties are). Instead, the pattern merely shows through the descendant elements because their background colors are transparent by default. If tiling images were inherited, the result would be a mess in which a new tiling pattern would begin in the top-left corner of each new element on the page.

If a background-color property is also specified, the image is overlaid on top of the color. Always provide a similar background color for an element when you add a background image. That way, if the image fails to load, the text and foreground elements maintain a readable contrast against the background.

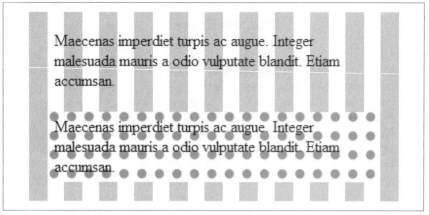

Figure 20-3. The background-image property applied to an entire page and a single paragraph

Background Tiling (Repeat)

Use the background-repeat property to prevent the background image from tiling (repeating) or to make it tile in one direction only.

background-repeat

Values:	repeat | repeat-x | repeat-y | no-repeat | inherit
Initial value:	repeat
Applies to:	All elements
Inherited:	No

By default, background images tile both horizontally and vertically. You can turn this behavior off and make the image appear just once by using the no-repeat keyword value as shown in Figure 20-4.

```
div.ringo {background-image: url(starr.gif); background-repeat: no-repeat}
```

Phasellus feugiat eros at mi. Integer leo tellus, hendrerit non, euismod non, condimentum in, sem. Fusce suscipit, ligula eget tempus dignissim, velit odio faucibus diam, vel nonummy ligula velit ac dolor. Curabitur quis tellus. Proin consequat, nunc ac condimentum lobortis, dui felis tincidunt ligula, nec ullamcorper quam nunc eget orci. Ut nec metus ut nulla lacinia tincidunt. Integer suscipit. Nullam iaculis lacus ac urna. Phasellus malesuada nisi vitae pede.

Figure 20-4. Turning off tiling with no-repeat

repeat-x allows the image to repeat only horizontally. Similarly, repeat-y allows the image to repeat only on the vertical axis. Examples of both are shown in Figure 20-5.

```
div.horiz {background-image: url(starr.gif); background-repeat: repeat-x;}
div.vert {background-image: url(starr.gif); background-repeat: repeat-y;}
```

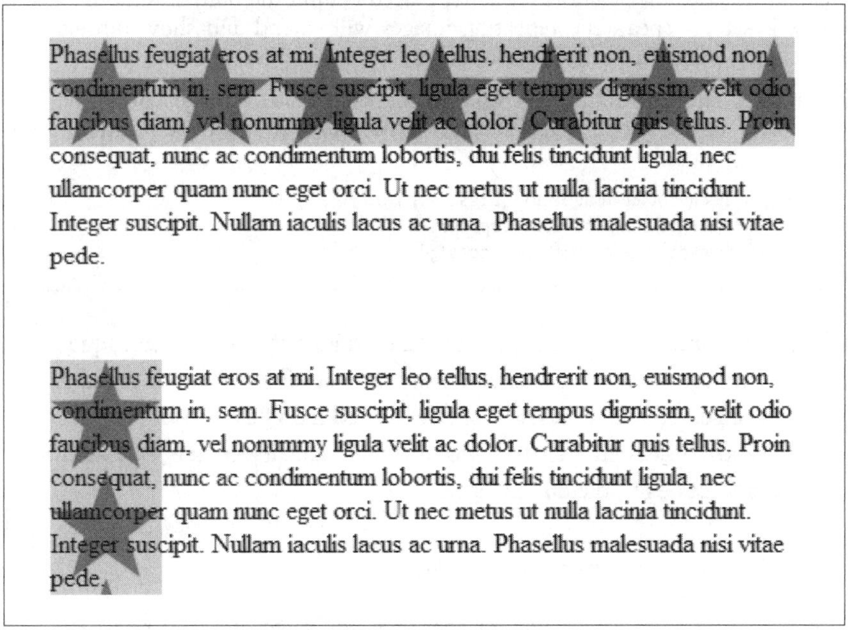

Phasellus feugiat eros at mi. Integer leo tellus, hendrerit non, euismod non, condimentum in, sem. Fusce suscipit, ligula eget tempus dignissim, velit odio faucibus diam, vel nonummy ligula velit ac dolor. Curabitur quis tellus. Proin consequat, nunc ac condimentum lobortis, dui felis tincidunt ligula, nec ullamcorper quam nunc eget orci. Ut nec metus ut nulla lacinia tincidunt. Integer suscipit. Nullam iaculis lacus ac urna. Phasellus malesuada nisi vitae pede.

Phasellus feugiat eros at mi. Integer leo tellus, hendrerit non, euismod non, condimentum in, sem. Fusce suscipit, ligula eget tempus dignissim, velit odio faucibus diam, vel nonummy ligula velit ac dolor. Curabitur quis tellus. Proin consequat, nunc ac condimentum lobortis, dui felis tincidunt ligula, nec ullamcorper quam nunc eget orci. Ut nec metus ut nulla lacinia tincidunt. Integer suscipit. Nullam iaculis lacus ac urna. Phasellus malesuada nisi vitae pede.

Figure 20-5. Horizontal and vertical tiling

Notice that in the examples in Figure 20-4 and Figure 20-5, the tiling begins in the top-left corner of the viewing area (in most cases, the browser window). But the background image doesn't necessarily need to start there, as discussed next.

Background Position

The background-position property specifies the position of the *origin image* in the background of the element. You can think of the origin image as the first image that is placed in the background. It's also the starting point from which repeated (tiling) images extend.

background-position

Values:	[[<percentage> | <length> | left | center | right] [<percentage> |<length> | top | center | bottom]? } | [[left | center | right] || [top | center | bottom]]] | inherit
Initial value:	0% 0% /* same as left top */

Applies to: All elements

Inherited: No

The background-position property specifies the initial position of the origin image. Measurements are relative to the top-left corner of the padding area for the element (the default position). It is not placed behind the border, although if the image is set to repeat, the repeating images will extend and show through the border area when the border style has gaps.

Figure 20-6 shows a simple example of the background-position property, The background-repeat property has been set to no-repeat to make the position of the origin image clear.

```
body { background-image: url(bigstar.gif);
       background-position: top center;
       background-repeat: no-repeat; }
```

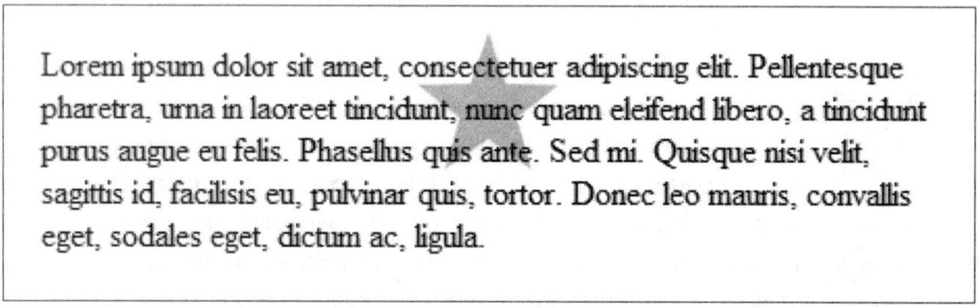

Lorem ipsum dolor sit amet, consectetuer adipiscing elit. Pellentesque pharetra, urna in laoreet tincidunt, nunc quam eleifend libero, a tincidunt purus augue eu felis. Phasellus quis ante. Sed mi. Quisque nisi velit, sagittis id, facilisis eu, pulvinar quis, tortor. Donec leo mauris, convallis eget, sodales eget, dictum ac, ligula.

Figure 20-6. The background-position property

There are a number of methods for specifying the value of background-position. The options after "Values" above may look like gobbledy-gook, but it boils down to three general systems: keywords, lengths, and percentages.

Keyword positioning

The *keyword values* for positioning are left, right, top, bottom, and center. Each value (except center) places the specified edge of the image all the way to the respective edge of the element. For example, the left value pushes the left edge of the image all the way to the left edge of the background area. The center value places the center of the image in the center of the element. And so on.

Keywords are usually used in pairs, as in these examples:

```
{background-position: left top;}
{background-position: right center;}
{background-position: center bottom;}
```

Each of these positions is demonstrated in Figure 20-7.

The order of the keywords is not important according to the CSS 2 Recommendation, but Netscape 6 and related browsers require that the horizontal measurement be provided first, so it's good practice to provide them in horizontal/vertical order just to be safe.

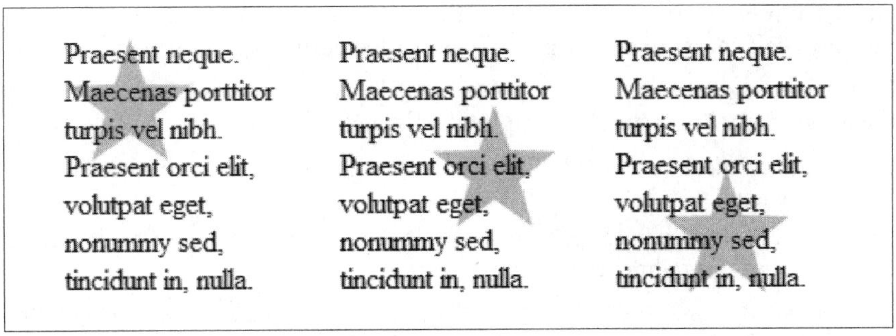

Figure 20-7. Positioning with keywords

If you only provide one keyword, the missing keyword is assumed to be center. Therefore the second and third previous examples could also be written like this:

```
{background-position: right;}
{background-position: bottom;}
```

Length measurements

It is also possible to specify the position of the origin image in units of length. When length units are provided, they are interpreted as the distance from the top-left corner of the padding area to the top-left corner of the image. Length values must be provided with the horizontal measurement first.

In this example, the top-left corner of the image will start 150 pixels from the left edge and 15 pixels from the top of the intro paragraph, as shown in Figure 20-8.

```
p.intro { background-image: url(something.gif);
          background-position: 150px 15px;
          background-repeat: no-repeat;}
```

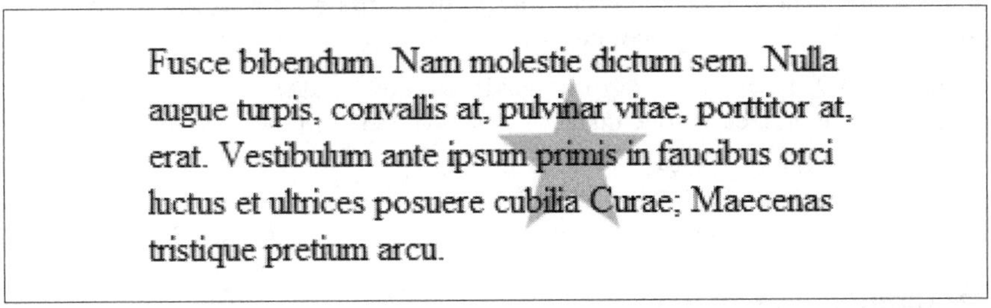

Figure 20-8. Positioning with length measurements

It is valid CSS to specify negative length measurements, thus pulling the image out of the visible background area of the element. Not all browsers currently support negative background image values, so be sure to test on your targeted browsers.

Percentage values

Percentage values follow the same basic positioning model as keywords, but they provide a more fine-tuned control over the image placement. Percentage values are given in horizontal/vertical pairs, with a default value of 0% 0%, which places the upper-left corner of the image in the upper-left corner of the element.

Each percentage value specified applies to both the background canvas area and the image itself. A few simple examples should make this clear.

- The percentage values 50% 50% place the center of the image in the center of the element.

- The percentage values 100% 100% place the bottom-right corner of the image in the bottom-right corner of the element.

- The percentage values 10% 25% match a point that is 10% from the left and 25% from the top edge of the image with the same point in the element.

As for keywords, when only one percentage value is provided, the other is assumed to be 50%.

It is fine to mix length and percentage values, which makes it easy to specify that an image should be centered horizontally in the element but appear exactly 25 pixels from its top edge. CSS 2.1 also allows length and keywords to be combined, but not all browsers support that combination as of this writing.

Positioning repeating images

In the previous examples, the background-repeat property was set to no-repeat for the sake of clarity. The principles of positioning do not change when the image is allowed to tile. When both properties are provided, the positioned origin image functions as the starting point for the repeating pattern.

It is significant to note that the tile pattern extends in both directions from the origin image. Therefore, if an image is positioned in the center of the element and the repeat is set to horizontal, the tiles will repeat on both the left and right of the centered image. Similarly, a vertical pattern extends both up and down from the origin image. There is currently no way to make the repeat go in one direction only in CSS 2.1, but that functionality may be added to a later specification.

In Figure 20-9, both the background-position and background-repeat properties are used to guarantee that one image is always centered in the browser window.

```
body { background-image: url(something.gif);
       background-position: center;
       background-repeat: repeat-x; }
```

Background Attachment

The default behavior for a background image in CSS is to scroll along with the document when the document scrolls, as though it is stuck to the element. This is the also the way background images applied with the body element function.

CSS provides the background-attachment property that frees the background image from the content and allows it to stay in a fixed position when the content of the document scrolls. In effect, it disconnects the image from the content flow and attaches it to the viewing area (typically a browser window).

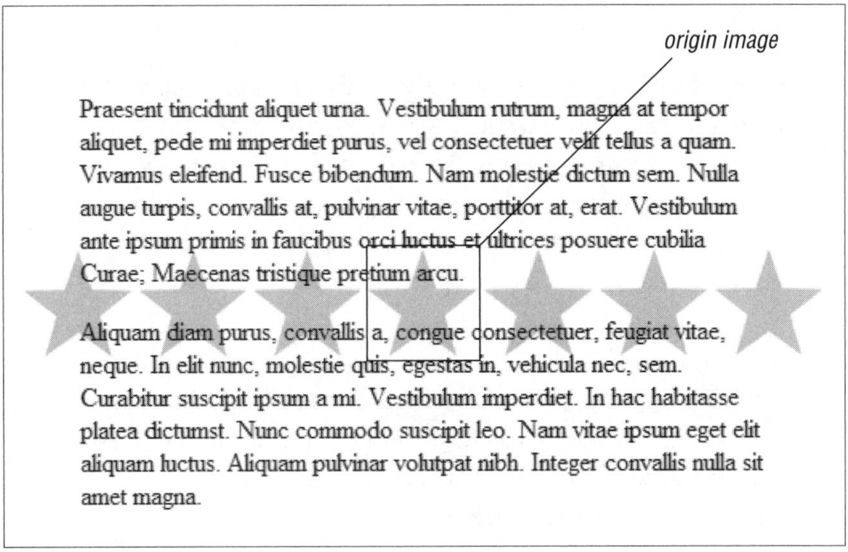

origin image

Praesent tincidunt aliquet urna. Vestibulum rutrum, magna at tempor aliquet, pede mi imperdiet purus, vel consectetuer velit tellus a quam. Vivamus eleifend. Fusce bibendum. Nam molestie dictum sem. Nulla augue turpis, convallis at, pulvinar vitae, porttitor at, erat. Vestibulum ante ipsum primis in faucibus orci luctus et ultrices posuere cubilia Curae; Maecenas tristique pretium arcu.

Aliquam diam purus, convallis a, congue consectetuer, feugiat vitae, neque. In elit nunc, molestie quis, egestas in, vehicula nec, sem. Curabitur suscipit ipsum a mi. Vestibulum imperdiet. In hac habitasse platea dictumst. Nunc commodo suscipit leo. Nam vitae ipsum eget elit aliquam luctus. Aliquam pulvinar volutpat nibh. Integer convallis nulla sit amet magna.

Figure 20-9. Combining position and tiling

background-attachment

Values:	scroll | fixed | inherit
Initial value:	scroll
Applies to:	All elements
Inherited:	No

The default value is scroll, so the origin image will scroll if you do not specify the background-attachment property. The other alternative is fixed, which fixes the image in one place relative to the viewing area.

In this example, the background image is fixed, as demonstrated in Figure 20-10.

```
body { background-image: url(img/star.gif);
       background-position: top;
       background-repeat: no-repeat;
       background-attachment: fixed; }
```

The other primary difference between a fixed origin image and a scrolling one is that for fixed images, the values of background-position are relative to the top-left corner of the viewing area, not the element itself.

This creates an interesting effect when a fixed background pattern is applied to an element other than body. The image stays in the same place and the element's containing box reveals a rectangular slice of the background at a time. Unfortunately, Internet Explorer for Windows Versions 6 and earlier do not support fixed background images on elements other than body. Non-body support is promised in Version 7, in beta as of this writing.

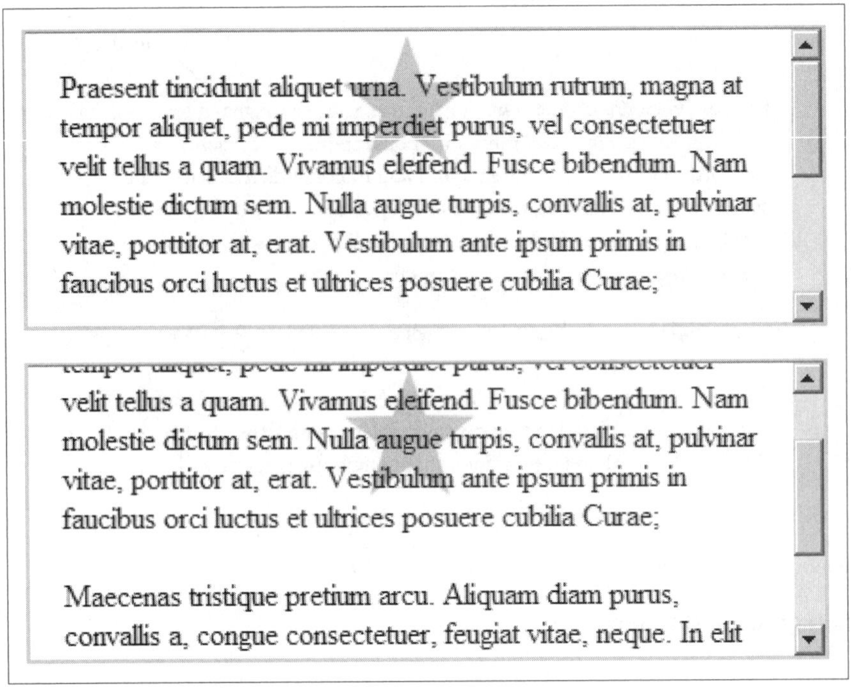

Praesent tincidunt aliquet urna. Vestibulum rutrum, magna at tempor aliquet, pede mi imperdiet purus, vel consectetuer velit tellus a quam. Vivamus eleifend. Fusce bibendum. Nam molestie dictum sem. Nulla augue turpis, convallis at, pulvinar vitae, porttitor at, erat. Vestibulum ante ipsum primis in faucibus orci luctus et ultrices posuere cubilia Curae;

tempor aliquet, pede mi imperdiet purus, vel consectetuer velit tellus a quam. Vivamus eleifend. Fusce bibendum. Nam molestie dictum sem. Nulla augue turpis, convallis at, pulvinar vitae, porttitor at, erat. Vestibulum ante ipsum primis in faucibus orci luctus et ultrices posuere cubilia Curae;

Maecenas tristique pretium arcu. Aliquam diam purus, convallis a, congue consectetuer, feugiat vitae, neque. In elit

Figure 20-10. Preventing scrolling with the background-attachment property

Eric Meyer demonstrates some interesting effects using fixed images as backgrounds for several elements on a page on his page *www.meyerweb.com/eric/css/edge/complexspiral/glassy.html*. To see the full effect, make sure you are using a standards-compliant browser other than Internet Explorer.

Combining Background Properties

CSS provides a handy background shorthand property that allows all the background properties to be combined in one style rule, similar to the font shorthand property (see Chapter 18).

background

Values:	[<'background-color'>||<'background-image'>|| <'background-repeat'>||<'background-attachment'>|| <'background-position'>]|inherit
Applies to:	All elements
Inherited:	No

The background shorthand property takes a value from any of the background-related properties. There are no required values, and the values may appear in any order. The only restriction is that if two values are provided for background-position they must appear together and with the horizontal value first, followed immediately by vertical.

The following are valid examples of the background shorthand property:

```
body {background: url(superstar.gif) fixed top center no-repeat; }
div.intro {background: repeat-x url(topborder.gif) red; }
p {background: #336600; }
```

Watch for Accidental Overrides

Bear in mind that because background is a shorthand property, values that are omitted will be reset to the default for those properties. That combined with the fact that later rules in a style sheet override previous rules makes it easy to accidentally override previously declared background properties with the defaults. In this example, the background image *dots.gif* will not be applied to h3 elements, because by omitting a value for background-image, it essentially set that value to none.

```
h1, h2, h3 { background: red url(dots.gif) repeat-x;}
h3 {background: blue; }
```

To override particular properties, be sure to use the specific background property you intend to change (background-color would be appropriate for the h3 in the example). When using the background (or any shorthand) property, pay attention to related rules earlier in the style sheet, or be sure that every property is specified.

21

Floating and Positioning

CSS isn't limited to just "prettying up" elements in the flow of the document. You can also use it to achieve basic page layout such as multiple columns, text wrap, and even positioning with pixel precision. This chapter introduces *floating* and *positioning*, the CSS methods for arranging elements on the page.

It should be noted that this chapter covers the CSS 2.1 specification for layout-related properties as they are intended to work. There are some notorious browser bugs that make implementing the tools illustrated here challenging. Browser issues will be noted here, but the details about specific browser problems and how to compensate for them are discussed further in Chapter 25.

This chapter covers these CSS 2.1 properties for controlling the positioning of elements.

```
float       bottom      overflow
clear       top         clip
position    left        visibility
bottom      right       z-index
```

Normal Flow

Before jumping into methods for positioning elements, it is useful to have an understanding of what is meant by the "normal flow" of a document according to the CSS layout model. In the normal flow, text elements are laid out from top to bottom, and from left to right in left-to-right reading languages (or from right to left in right-to-left reading languages). This is the default behavior of the web browser.

In the normal flow, block-level elements stack on top of one another and inline elements fill the available space. When the browsing window is resized, the block elements expand or contract to the new width, and the inline content reflows to fit. Objects in the normal flow influence the position of the surrounding content (sibling elements).

In CSS positioning, blocks are defined as being either in the normal flow or removed from the normal flow. Floating and positioning elements changes their relationship to the normal flow, as discussed in the following sections.

Floating

If you've ever aligned an image to the right or left margin and allowed text to wrap around it, then you understand the concept behind floats in CSS. In fact, that is precisely the functionality that the float property was created to provide. The primary difference is that you can float any element with CSS (paragraphs, lists, divs, and so on), not just images.* It is important to note that floating is not a positioning scheme; it is a unique feature with some interesting behaviors to be aware of, as discussed later in this section.

CSS: Floating/Positioning

Floats are useful for far more than just occasionally pushing an image off to one side. In fact, they are one of the primary tools used in modern CSS-based web design. Floats are used to create multicolumn layouts, navigation toolbars from unordered lists, table-like alignment without tables, and more. See Chapter 24 for examples.

To make an element float to the left or right and allow the following text to wrap around it, apply the float property to the element.

float

Values:	left | right | none | inherit
Initial value:	none
Applies to:	All elements
Inherited:	No

In this simple example, the float property is used to float an image to the right (Figure 21-1).

```
img {float: right; margin: 20px;}

<p><img src="img/placeholder.gif">Aliquam pulvinar volutpat...</p>
```

As you can see in Figure 21-1, the float property applied to the img element effectively replaces the deprecated align attribute. In this image example, the margin does the work of the deprecated hspace and vspace attributes. The advantage of margin is that you can apply different amounts of margin space on each side of the

---

* Some browsers allow table elements to be floated with the align attribute as well.

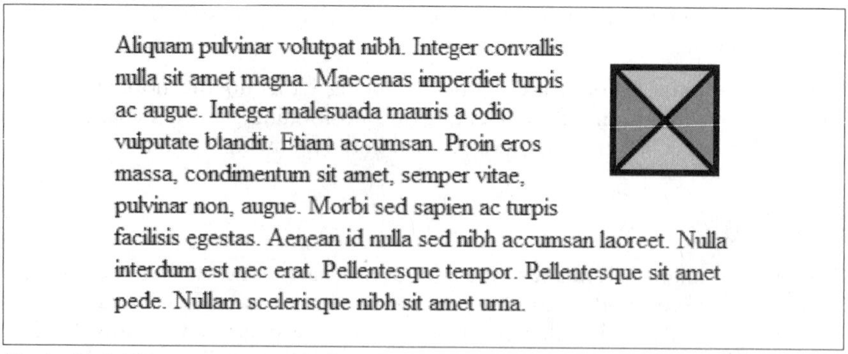

Aliquam pulvinar volutpat nibh. Integer convallis nulla sit amet magna. Maecenas imperdiet turpis ac augue. Integer malesuada mauris a odio vulputate blandit. Etiam accumsan. Proin eros massa, condimentum sit amet, semper vitae, pulvinar non, augue. Morbi sed sapien ac turpis facilisis egestas. Aenean id nulla sed nibh accumsan laoreet. Nulla interdum est nec erat. Pellentesque tempor. Pellentesque sit amet pede. Nullam scelerisque nibh sit amet urna.

Figure 21-1. Floating an image to the right

image (hspace and vspace apply the same amount of space on opposite sides). Padding may also be used to add space around the contents of a floated element.

Although the behavior in this example should be familiar to those who have worked with HTML, it is quite interesting when considered in terms of the CSS visual layout model. Floated elements are removed from the normal flow of the document, yet they still have an effect on other elements in the layout— surrounding content is reflowed to stay out of their way. To use one popular analogy, they are like islands in a stream—they are out of the normal flow, but the stream has to flow around them. Floated elements are unique in this regard, because elements removed from the flow normally cease to have influence on other elements (this will be discussed in the upcoming positioning sections).

Floating Basics

The float property is not limited to images; it can be applied to any element. In this slightly more ambitious example shown in Figure 21-2, the float property is applied to a selection of text (known in CSS as an "inline non-replaced element"). Note that the dotted lines are a device for pointing out the parts of the element boxes in this figure and would not actually appear in the browser.

```
span.note {
    float: right;
    width: 200px;
    margin: 20px;
    background-color: #999;
    font-weight: bold; }

p {border: solid 2px #666; padding: 30px;}

<p><span class="note">I'm going to go over here for a little while. Don't
mind me. </span> Lorem ipsum dolor sit amet, consectetuer  . . .
```

The results reveal some basic behaviors of element floating:

- All floated elements (even inline elements, as shown in the example) take on block behaviors. It is equivalent to setting display: block (although it is not necessary to do so).

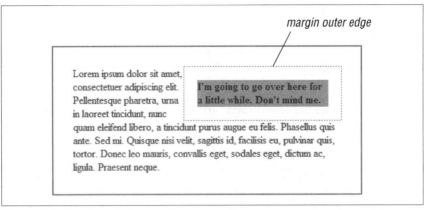

margin outer edge

Lorem ipsum dolor sit amet, consectetuer adipiscing elit. Pellentesque pharetra, urna in laoreet tincidunt, nunc quam eleifend libero, a tincidunt purus augue eu felis. Phasellus quis ante. Sed mi. Quisque nisi velit, sagittis id, facilisis eu, pulvinar quis, tortor. Donec leo mauris, convallis eget, sodales eget, dictum ac, ligula. Praesent neque.

I'm going to go over here for a little while. Don't mind me.

Figure 21-2. Floating an inline text element

- When floating a non-replaced (i.e., text) element, it is necessary to specify the width for the element. Not doing so can result in the content area box collapsing to its narrowest possible width.
- The floated element stays within the content area of its *containing block* (the nearest block-level ancestor element). It does not cross into the padding.
- Margins are maintained on all sides of the floated element. In other words, the entire element box (from outer edge to outer edge) is floated, and the surrounding content flows around it.
- Unlike normal elements, margins around floated elements never collapse (even vertically).

The elements following the floated element exhibit unusual behavior as well. In the following example and Figure 21-3, the floated graphic is taller than its parent paragraph element and hangs down over the following paragraph. The second paragraph (named "boxed") has been given a background and border to show the boundaries of its element box compared to its contents.

```
img { float: left; }
p.boxed { background-color: #999; border: solid 2px #333; }
```

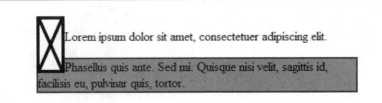

Lorem ipsum dolor sit amet, consectetuer adipiscing elit.

Phasellus quis ante. Sed mi. Quisque nisi velit, sagittis id, facilisis eu, pulvinar quis, tortor.

Figure 21-3. Wrapped element behavior

The border and background position show that the position of the second paragraph's element box is unchanged by the presence of the floated image element. Only its content moves over to make way for the floated image. Notice also that the floated image overwrites (appears "in front of") the background and border for the following paragraph. This is the prescribed behavior for floated elements. Other overwriting behaviors are discussed in the "Negative Margins and Overlap" section ahead.

Floating Behavior

The CSS 2.1 specification provides eight precise rules restricting the positioning of floated objects, which are summarized here. If you need the details, go right to the source, at *www.w3.org/TR/CSS21/visuren.html#float-position*. Eric Meyer provides a useful translation and illustration of the rules in his book *Cascading Style Sheets: The Definitive Guide* (O'Reilly).

In addition to requiring that floated elements stay within the inner edge (or content area) of their containing blocks, there are a number of rules designed to prevent the overlapping of floated objects.

 Browsers (even current standards-conformant browsers) may be inconsistent in the way they handle floated objects due to a certain amount of leeway in the specification and because they follow historical and expected practice. Be sure to test.

Floated elements in close proximity in the source document are not permitted to overwrite one another. Instead, the rules prescribe:

- If elements are floated in the same direction, each subsequent floated object should move in that direction until it reaches the inner edge of the containing block or until it bumps into another floated element. This rule results in multiple floated elements accumulating against the targeted edge.

- If there is not enough room for floated elements to appear side by side, then the second floated object should move down until there is enough room for it to display without overlapping the first object.

The effects of these rules are demonstrated in Figure 21-4.

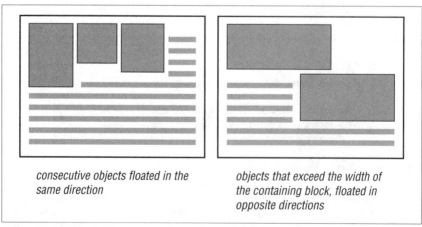

consecutive objects floated in the same direction

objects that exceed the width of the containing block, floated in opposite directions

Figure 21-4. Floated objects accumulate or bump down instead of overlapping

Other rules restrict how high the top edge of a floated element may be positioned.

- The top of a floated element must stay within the top inner edge of its parent element.

- The top of a floated element that is not contained in a block element may not be higher than a preceding block-level element. The float is essentially "blocked" from floating above it.

- The top of a floated element may not start higher than a floated element that precedes it in the document source.

- If a floated element starts in the middle of the text flow of an element, it does not float to the top of that element, but rather starts at the top of the line box for the surrounding text (Figure 21-5).

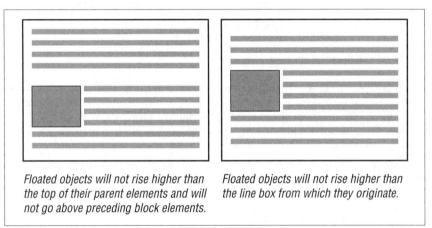

Floated objects will not rise higher than the top of their parent elements and will not go above preceding block elements.

Floated objects will not rise higher than the line box from which they originate.

Figure 21-5. Top edge restrictions on floated elements

Floating elements are also not permitted to stick out of the edge of their containing elements, unless they are too wide to fit (like a wide image). This prevents sequential floated elements from accumulating against an edge and growing wider than the containing block. When the stack grows too wide, the element that doesn't fit gets bumped down so that it clears the floated elements above.

The final two rules state, given all of the established restrictions, floated objects should be put as far left or right (as specified) and as far upward as possible until they reach a defined constraint. A higher position is preferable to one that is farther left or right. I like to picture floated objects on a page jockeying for position, pushing upward and outward until they bump into the edge of the containing block, another floated element, or an imposed ceiling from a previous block element or the like.

Negative Margins and Overlap

The two big rules for the placement of floated objects are that they should never go beyond the content area of their containing block and they should not overlap other elements. These guidelines seemingly get tossed out the window when you apply negative margins to a floated element, as shown in this example and in Figure 21-6.

```
img { float: left; margin: -10px; }
```

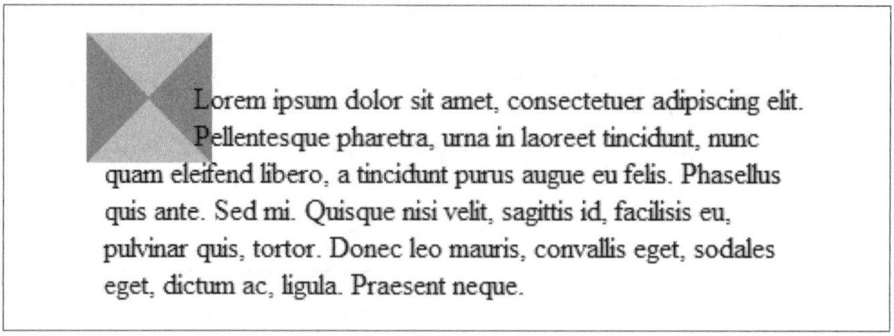

Figure 21-6. A floated element with negative margins

The negative margin setting pulls the content area of the floated element out of its positioned element box, allowing the content to fall outside the confines of the containing block. There are no rules preventing elements with negative top margins from overwriting preceding content that has already been displayed, so negative vertical margins are best avoided.

Negative margins may also cause the flowed content to overlap the floated object. In these instances, the CSS 2.1 specification prescribes different rules for inline boxes and block boxes.

- When an inline box overlaps with a float, the entire element box (including the content, background, and border) overwrites or appears "in front of" the floated element. Be prepared that if you have a floated element with negative margins and you apply backgrounds or borders to inline elements in the wrapped text, those inline boxes may obscure the floated element.

- When block boxes overlap a float, the content of that box appears "in front of" the floated element, but the background and border of the element are overwritten by (appear "behind") the float. This is consistent with the example in Figure 21-3, but allows the text to go in front of the float in the instance of negative margins.

Clearing

Wrapping can be a nice, space-saving layout effect, but it is not always appropriate. There are certainly cases in which you want the area on the side of the floated element to be held clear and the following element to start at its normal position in the containing block. For those instances, use the clear property to prevent an element from appearing next to a floated element.

clear

Values: left | right | both | none | inherit

Initial value:	none
Applies to:	Block-level elements
Inherited:	No

The clear property may be applied only to block elements. It is best explained with a simple example. The left value starts the element below any elements that have been floated to the left edge of the containing block. The rule in this example ensures that all first-level headings in the document start below left-floated elements, as shown in Figure 21-7.

```
img {float: left; margin-right: 10px; }
h1 {clear: left; top-margin: 2em;}
```

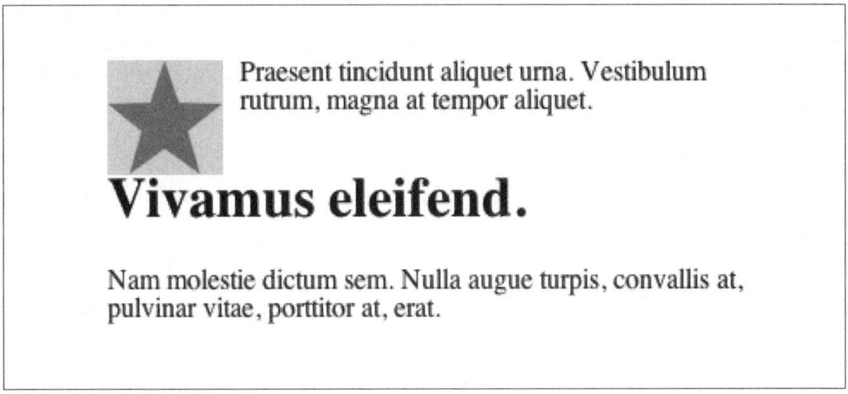

Praesent tincidunt aliquet urna. Vestibulum rutrum, magna at tempor aliquet.

Vivamus eleifend.

Nam molestie dictum sem. Nulla augue turpis, convallis at, pulvinar vitae, porttitor at, erat.

Figure 21-7. Clearing a left-floated element

As you might guess, the right value works in a similar manner and prevents an element from appearing next to an element that has been floated to the right. The value both moves the element down until it is clear of floated elements on both sides. User agents are instructed by CSS 2.1 to add an amount of *clearance* space above the margins of block elements until the top edge of the content fits below the float.

Notice in Figure 21-7, that although there is a top margin applied to the h1 element, the text is touching the bottom of the floated image. That is a result of collapsing vertical margins on the h1 block element. If you want to be sure that there is space below a floated element, add a bottom margin to the float itself, because margins on floated elements never collapse. This remains true when a floated element is set to clear other floated elements on the same side of the page. In that case, adjacent margins of the floated elements add up and don't collapse.

Positioning Basics

It is obvious by how readily web designers co-opted HTML tables that there was a need for page-like layout on web pages. Cascading Style Sheets provides several methods for positioning elements on the page relative to where they would normally appear in the document flow.

If you thought tables were tricky to manage, get ready for CSS positioning! While the positioning properties are fairly simple at face value, inconsistent and buggy browser implementation can make it challenging to achieve the results you're after on all browsers. If fact, positioning can be complicated even when the CSS Recommendation is followed to the letter. It's a recipe for frustration unless you get to know how positioning *should* behave and then know which browsers are likely to give you trouble (some notorious browser bugs are listed in Chapter 25). This section introduces the positioning-related properties as they are defined in CSS 2.1 as well as some key concepts.

Types of Positioning

To get the ball rolling, we'll look at the various options for positioning elements and how they differ. There are four types of positioning, specified by the position property.

position

Values:	static | relative | absolute | fixed | inherit
Initial value:	static
Applies to:	All elements
Inherited:	No

The position property identifies that an element is to be positioned and selects one of four positioning methods (each will be discussed in detail in upcoming sections in this chapter):

static
> This is the normal positioning scheme in which element boxes are rendered in order as they appear in the document flow.

relative
> Relative positioning moves the element box, but its original space in the document flow is preserved.

absolute
> Absolutely positioned objects are completely removed from the document flow and are positioned relative to their containing block (discussed in the next section). Because they are removed from the document flow, they no longer influence the layout of surrounding elements, and the space they once occupied is closed up. Absolutely positioned elements always take on block behaviors.

```
fixed
```

Fixed positioning is like absolute positioning (the element is removed from the document flow), but instead of a containing element, it is positioned relative to the viewport (in most cases, the browser window).

Containing Blocks

The CSS 2.1 Recommendation states that "The position and size of an element's box(es) are sometimes calculated relative to a certain rectangle, called the *containing block* of the element." It is critical to have an awareness of the containing block for the element you want to position.

Unfortunately, it's not entirely straightforward and depends on the context of the element. CSS 2.1 lays out a number of rules for determining the containing block.

- The containing block created by the root element (html) is called the *initial containing block*. The rectangle of the initial containing block fills the dimensions of the viewport. The initial containing block is used if there is no other containing block present. Note that some browsers base the initial containing block on the body element; the net result is the same in that it fills the browser window.

- For elements (other than the root) that are set to static or relative, the containing block is the *content edge* of the nearest block-level, table cell, or inline-block ancestor.

- For absolutely placed elements, the containing block is the nearest ancestor element that has a position other than static. In other words, the ancestor element must be set to relative, absolute, or fixed to act as a containing block for its children. Once an ancestor element is established as the containing block, its boundaries differ based on whether it is a block-level or inline element.

- For block-level elements, the containing block extends to the element's *padding edge* (just inside the border).

- For inline-elements, the containing block is set to the *content edge*. Its boundaries are calculated based on the direction of the text. For left-to-right languages, it begins in the top-left corner of the first line generated by the element and ends in the bottom-right corner of the last line generated by the element. For right-to-left languages, it goes from top-left corner of the first line to bottom-left corner of the last line.

- If there are no ancestor elements, then the initial containing block is used.

Specifying Position

Once the positioning value has been established, the actual positioning is done with the four offset properties.

top, right, bottom, left

Values: \<length> | \<percentage> | auto | inherit

Initial value:	auto

Applies to:	Positioned elements (where position value is relative, absolute, or fixed)

Inherited:	No

The values provided for each of the offset properties defines the distance that the element should be offset from that edge. For instance, the value of top defines the distance from the outer edge of the positioned element to the top edge of its containing block. Positive values move the element down (toward the center of the block); negative values move the element up (and out of the containing block). Similarly, the value provided for the left property specifies a distance from the left edge of the containing block to the left outer edge of the positioned element. Again, positive values push the element in toward the center of the containing block while negative values move the box outward.

 CSS 2 positioned elements from their content edges, not their margin edges, but this was changed in 2.1.

This rather verbose explanation should be made clearer with a few examples of absolutely positioned elements. In this example, the positioned element is placed in the bottom-left corner of the containing block using percentage values (Figure 21-8).

```
div {position: absolute; height: 120px; width: 300px; border: 1px solid
#000;}
img {position: absolute; top: 100%; left: 0%;}
```

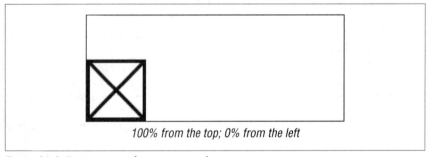

Figure 21-8. Positioning with percentage values

In this example, pixel lengths are provided to place the positioned element at a particular spot in the containing element (Figure 21-9).

```
div.a {position: absolute; height: 120px; width: 300px; border: 1px solid
#000; background-color:#CCC}

div.b {position: absolute; top: 20px; right: 30px; bottom: 40px; left: 50px;
border: 1px solid #000; background-color:#666}

<div class="a">
```

```
            <div class="b"></div>
        </div>
```

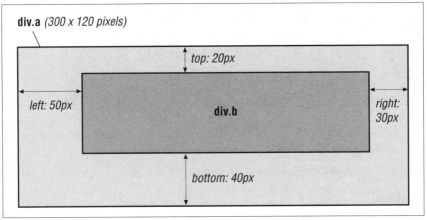

Figure 21-9. Positioning with pixel values

Notice that it is possible to set the dimensions of an element indirectly by defining the positions of its four sides relative to the containing block. The space that is leftover becomes the width and height of the element. If the positioned element also has specified width and height properties that conflict with that space, a set of CSS rules kicks in for settling the difference (these are addressed in the upcoming "Calculating Position" section).

> Setting the width and height of elements is covered in Chapter 19.

This final example demonstrates that when negative values are provided for offset properties, the element can break out of the confines of the containing box (Figure 21-10).

```
div.a {position: absolute; height: 120px; width: 300px; border: 1px solid
#000; background-color:#CCC}

div.b {position: absolute; top: -20px; right: -30px; bottom: 40px; left:
50px; border: 1px solid #000; background-color:#666}

<div class="a">
    <div class="b"></div>
</div>
```

Handling Overflow

When an element is set to a size that is too small to contain all of its contents, it is possible to specify what to do with the content that doesn't fit using the overflow property.

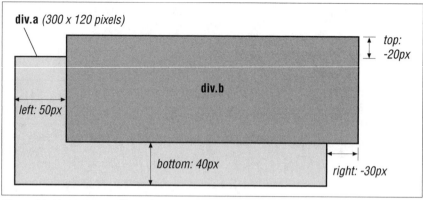

Figure 21-10. Negative offset values

overflow

Values: visible | hidden | scroll | auto | inherit

Initial value: visible

Applies to: Block-level and replaced elements

Inherited: No

There are four values for the overflow property:

visible
> The default value is visible, which allows the content to display outside its element box.

hidden
> When overflow is set to hidden, the content that does not fit in the element box gets clipped and does not appear beyond its edges.

scroll
> When scroll is specified, scrollbars (or an alternate scrolling mechanism) are added to the element box to allow scrolling through the content while keeping the content visible in the box area only. Be aware that the scroll value causes scrollbars to be rendered even if the content fits comfortably in the content box.

auto
> The auto value allows the user agent to decide how to handle overflow. In most cases, scrollbars are added only when the content doesn't fit and they are needed.

Figure 21-11 shows examples of each of the overflow values as applied to an element that is 150 pixels square. The gray background color makes the edges of the content area clear.

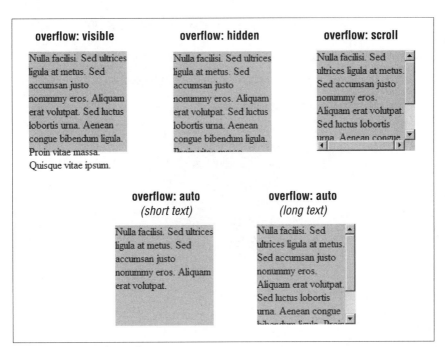

Figure 21-11. Overflow values

Clipping Areas

When the overflow of an absolutely positioned element box is set to hidden, scroll, or auto, the CSS specification allows you to restrict which part of the content is visible by creating a *clipping area* for the element. A clipping area is a rectangular area—like the mat in a picture frame—that lets the content show through. Other shapes may be included in future CSS versions. Specify the size and position of the clipping area with the clip property.

clip

Values:	rect(*top, right, bottom, left*) | auto | inherit
Initial value:	auto
Applies to:	Absolutely positioned elements
Inherited:	No

The default auto property sets the edge of the clipping path at the content edge for the given side. Values for clip must be provided in length values (percentage values are not permitted).

It is important to note that the top, right, bottom, and left values for the clip property are measured from the top-left *corner* of the element, not the sides as is the case for the offset properties. For languages that read right to left, distances are measured from the top-left corner.

This is a simple example of a clipping area applied to an element (Figure 21-12).

```
div.a {position: absolute; height: 150px; width: 150px; background-
color:#CCC;
    clip: rect(10px, 130px, 130px, 10px);}
```

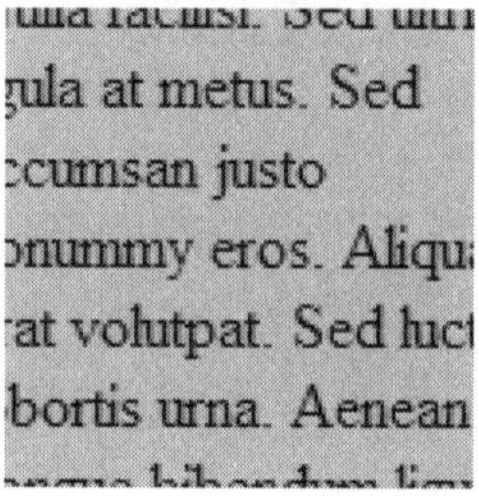

Figure 21-12. A clipping area

Visibility

The visibility property is used to make an entire element invisible.

visibility

Values:	visible | hidden | collapse | inherit
Initial value:	visible
Applies to:	All elements
Inherited:	Yes

Obviously, if the value of visibility is visible (the default), the element will be visible. When it is set to hidden, the element is invisible, but it maintains its spot in the document flow; you just can't see it. This makes it distinctly different from display: none, which removes the element from of the document flow completely and closes up the space it once occupied.

In this example, an inline text element is hidden (Figure 21-13). It is easy to see that the space for its element box is preserved. Notice also that all aspects of the element (including its content, background, and border) are invisible as well.

```
span.a {background-color:#CCCCCC; border: 1px solid #000;  visibility:
visible;}
span.b {background-color:#CCCCCC; border: 1px solid #000;  visibility:
hidden;}
```

```
<p>Aliquam pulvinar volutpat nibh. Integer convallis nulla sit amet magna.
<span class="a"> Maecenas imperdiet turpis ac augue. Integer malesuada
mauris a odio vulputate blandit. Etiam accumsan. </span> Proin eros massa,
condimentum sit amet, semper vitae, pulvinar non, augue. </p>

<p>Aliquam pulvinar volutpat nibh. Integer convallis nulla sit amet magna.
<span class="b"> Maecenas imperdiet turpis ac augue. Integer malesuada
mauris a odio vulputate blandit. Etiam accumsan. </span> Proin eros massa,
condimentum sit amet, semper vitae, pulvinar non, augue. </p>
```

Aliquam pulvinar volutpat nibh. Integer convallis nulla sit amet magna. Maecenas imperdiet turpis ac augue. Integer malesuada mauris a odio vulputate blandit. Etiam accumsan. Proin eros massa, condimentum sit amet, semper vitae, pulvinar non, augue.

Aliquam pulvinar volutpat nibh. Integer convallis nulla sit amet magna.
Proin eros
massa, condimentum sit amet, semper vitae, pulvinar non, augue.

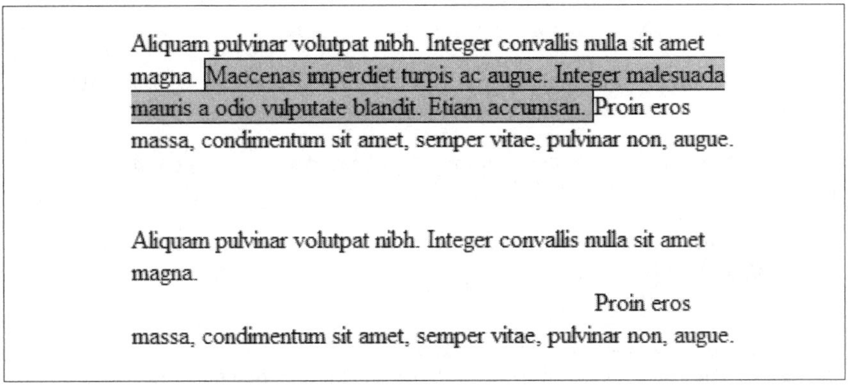

Figure 21-13. Setting visibility to hidden

The collapse property value is recommended for use with CSS table row and column elements. Applying the collapse value to a non-table element may make it hidden, but it is best avoided. Internet Explorer 6 for Windows and earlier does not support collapse (support has not been confirmed in Version 7, which is in beta as of this writing).

Stacking Order

One of the side effects of positioning is that elements can overlap each other. By default, elements stack in the order in which they appear in the document, with later elements rendering on top of preceding elements in the source. You can change the stacking order for an element by setting the z-index property. You can picture the direction of the z-axis as a line that runs from your nose through this page and out the other side.

z-index

Values:	<integer> | auto | inherit
Initial value:	auto
Applies to:	Positioned elements

Inherited: No

The value of the z-index is any integer (whole number), positive or negative. The higher the number, the higher the element will appear in the stack. Lower numbers and negative values move the element lower in the stack.

Consider this source and style sheet that changes the stacking order for three positioned paragraphs (Figure 21-14). Although Paragraph 1 appears first in the source and would normally be overlapped by the subsequent positioned elements, it has been set to render on top by assigning it a higher z-index value.

```
p {position: absolute; padding: 5px; color: #000;}

#p1 {top: 70px; left: 140px; width: 300px; z-index:19; background-color:
#666;}

#p2 {top: 30px; left: 30px; width: 300px; z-index: 1; background-color:
#999;}

span.b {position: absolute; top: 96px; z-index: 72; font-weight: bold;
background: #999;}


<p id="p1">PARAGRAPH 1: Z-INDEX=19<br />Integer convallis nulla sit amet
magna. Maecenas imperdiet turpis ac augue. Integer malesuada mauris a odio
vulputate blandit.</p>

<p id="p2">PARAGRAPH 2: Z-INDEX=1<br /><span class="b">Z-INDEX=72 Integer
convallis nulla</span> sit amet magna. Maecenas imperdiet turpis ac augue.
Integer malesuada mauris a odio vulputate blandit.</p>
```

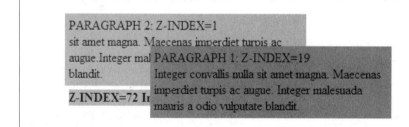

Figure 21-14. Adjusting stacking order with z-index

There are a few other points of interest in this example. First, notice that the z-index values don't need to be consecutive. If you want to guarantee that an element is always on top, you can give it an extremely high z-index value that isn't likely to be topped.

It is also important to note that each positioned element creates its own z-index context. Although the strong text contained in Paragraph 2 has a very high z-index of 72, it still appears behind Paragraph 1 with its z-index of 19. That's because the z-index settings within each element are relative only to the other descendants of that element. In effect, the strong element in Paragraph 2 shares the z-index value of its parent in relation to its parent's siblings.

Absolute Positioning

There have been examples of absolute positioning throughout this chapter, but this section examines this popular method of positioning in more detail.

An absolutely positioned element has these basic characteristics:

- It is declared using {position: absolute;}.
- It is positioned relative to the edges of its containing block using one or more of the offset properties (top, right, bottom, left). Properties that are not specified are set to auto (the default). The offset values apply to the outer edge of the element box (including the margin value, if there is one).
- It is completely removed from the document flow. The space it would have occupied in the normal flow is closed up and it no longer has an affect on other elements (for instance, text won't wrap around it).

These points are demonstrated in this simple example of an absolutely positioned list element (Figure 21-15).

```
div {position: absolute; background-color: #999; width: 440px;}
ul {position: absolute; left: 60px; top: 30px; background-color: #CCC;
margin: 0px;}

<div>
    <p>Phasellus feugiat eros at mi. Integer leo tellus, hendrerit non,
euismod non, condimentum in, sem. </p>
    <ul>
        <li>Lorem ipsum dolor</li>
        <li>Sit amet, consectetuer</li>
        <li>Adipiscing elit</li>
        <li>Vel nonummy ligula</li>
        <li>Tempus dignissim</li>
    </ul>
    <p>Fusce suscipit, ligula eget tempus ...</p>
</div>
```

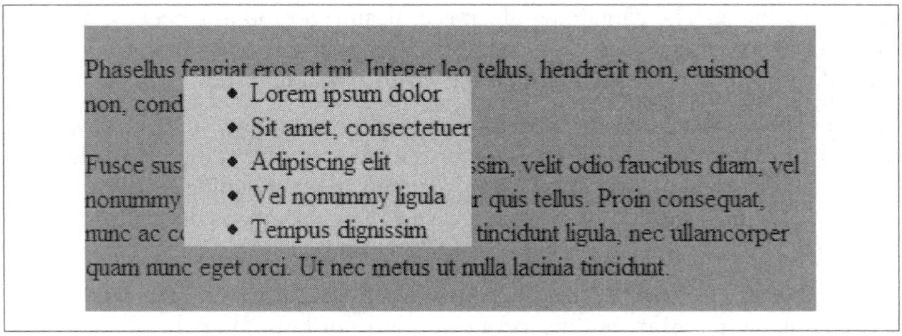

Figure 21-15. Absolute positioning

In all of the previous examples, elements have been positioned using length measurements for the offset property values. The auto value has some interesting behavior that bears attention. When any of the offset properties other than bottom are set to auto, the edge of the element box is positioned in its "static" position, that is, where it would have been in the normal document flow. In Figure 21-16, the dollar sign slug will always stay next to its line of origin, because its top offset property is set to auto.

```
p {position: relative; margin-right: 10px; left: 10px;"}
```

```
<p>Lorem ipsum dolor sit amet, consectetuer adipiscing elit. Pellentesque
<span style="position: absolute; top: auto; left: -1em; background-color:
#CCC;">$</span>pharetra, urna in laoreet tincidunt,...</p>
```

Lorem ipsum dolor sit amet, consectetuer adipiscing elit.

$ Pellentesque pharetra, urna in laoreet tincidunt, Proin consequat, nunc ac condimentum lobortis, dui felis tincidunt ligula, nec ullamcorper quam nunc eget orci. Ut nec metus ut nulla lacinia tincidunt

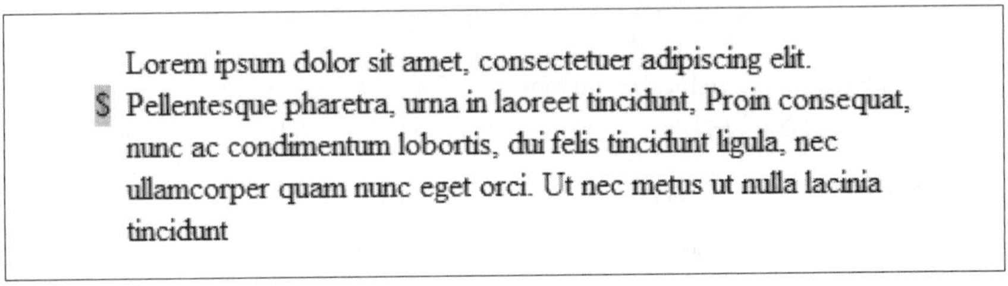

Figure 21-16. Setting offset properties to auto

Notice that the top of the positioned element is in the vertical position that it would have had if the element were still in the line. Only its horizontal position has been changed, as specified. Notice also that the space that the element occupied on the line has been closed up because it has been absolutely positioned. If the left offset property had been set to auto as well, the left edge of the element would be placed in the spot at which the content originated, but it would overlap with the following text (because its space is closed up).

This can be a useful method for adding margin notes that stay with their respective text. Just be sure that there are few or no constraints on the other positioning and sizing properties that might override the auto placement.

Absolute Positioning and Containing Blocks

The first step to absolutely positioning an element is to identify or create its containing block. The containing block is critical to positioning because all absolute measurements are based on its sides. Containing blocks were discussed in more detail earlier in this chapter, but it's worth a brief refresher.

For an ancestor element to be a containing block, it must have a position value of absolute, relative, or fixed (in other words, it must not be static, either declared or by default). If no ancestor element qualifies as a containing block, then the initial containing block is used (html, body, or the viewport, as determined by the user agent).

In the example in Figure 21-15, the containing block for the list is a div that has its position set to relative (but its position has not been altered). It is common practice to declare the position of an ancestor element as relative explicitly and leave it in place, or to insert a new positioned element (like a div) to set up the containing block for absolutely positioned elements.

 To force the browser to use the body element as the initial containing block, add this style rule:

```
body {position: relative;}
```

Another important thing to note is that by setting the position of the unordered list element (ul) to absolute, it thereby becomes the containing block for its descendant elements. If an li element were to be absolutely positioned, its offset properties become relative to the sides of the ul, as shown here and in Figure 21-17.

```
div {position: absolute; background-color: #999; width: 440px;}
ul {position: absolute; left: 60px; top: 30px; background-color: #CCC;
margin: 0px;}
li#callout {position: absolute; left: 60px; top: 30px; background-color:
#CCC; margin: 0px;}

<div>
   <p>Phasellus feugiat eros at mi. Integer leo tellus, hendrerit non,
euismod non, condimentum in, sem. </p>
   <ul>
       <li>First list item</li>
       <li id="callout">Second list item</li>
       <li>Third list item</li>
       <li>Fourth list item</li>
       <li>Fifth list item</li>
   </ul>
   <p>Fusce suscipit, ligula eget ...<p>
</div>
```

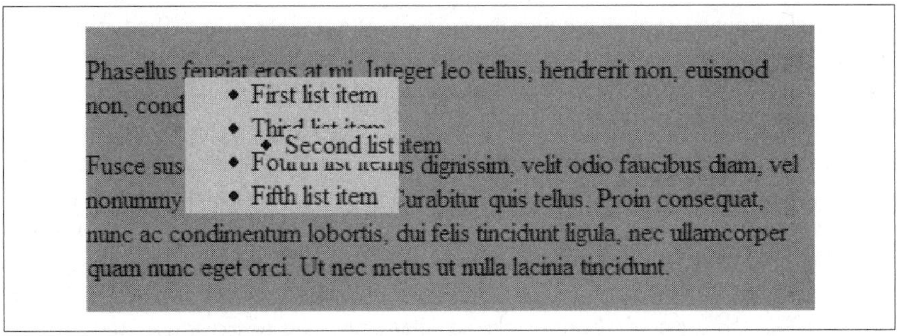

Figure 21-17. The absolutely positioned list becomes the containing block for the positioned list item

Calculating Position

While specifying a position using the offset properties is a fairly straightforward affair, things can get complicated when offset measurements are combined with the margins and content width of the element and the width constraints of the containing block. In fact, the CSS 2.1 specification provides a dizzyingly detailed list of rules and constraints for dealing with conflicting and unspecified values.

In the interest of brevity, this section provides a general and practical summary of those rules that should serve you well in most instances.

The CSS 2.1 specification provides a formula for all the values that make up the width of a containing block. It is presented in Figure 21-18 in graphical form because it is helpful to visualize the values that span across a containing block. Bear in mind that the calculated sum of all the interior values must be equal to the width of the containing block. This same structure applies in the vertical direction as well.

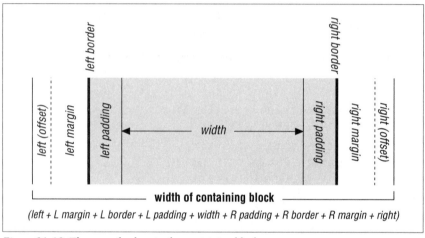

Figure 21-18. The sum of values in the containing block

In very generalized terms, when values are conflicting or unspecified, the space tends to be adjusted on the right side for left-to-right (ltr) languages (or the left side for right-to-left languages). Height issues are resolved by adjusting the space at the bottom of the positioned element.

- In instances where all values have been specified (i.e., none of them are auto), and the values do not add up to the width of the containing block, user agents are instructed to just ignore the right (for ltr languages) and bottom offset values and make up the discrepancies on those sides.

- If the width of the positioned element is specified, it is not altered. However, if the width for a text (non-replaced) element is set to auto, the content area will "shrink to fit" and be just wide enough to accommodate the contents. For replaced elements such as images, the inherent pixel dimensions of the object are used when width is auto.

- The width of an element's content area gets resized only when it is set to auto and all the other properties have specific measurement values. As the only parameter set to auto, the element width is the last resort and gets resized.

- User agents look for an auto value (on the margin or offset) on the right side first (for ltr languages) to make necessary space adjustments. For vertical adjustments, adjustments are made to properties set to auto on the bottom.

- When the top and left properties are set to auto, the element is placed in its "static" position (as mentioned above). This is overridden only as a last resort when all of the other parameters have specific values and left (for horizontal placement) and top (for vertical placement) are the only available auto values. Only then is space adjusted on those sides.

Given these constraints and behaviors, the most simple and predictable approach to absolute positioning is to provide a specific width for the positioned element and specific top and left offsets. That way, the margins on the positioned object will be preserved and the space on the right and bottom can flex as necessary to fit in the containing block. Granted, this won't work for all situations, but it's a starting point. It usually involves a bit of math to get it right.

 These positioning rules are based on the correct behavior as defined in the CSS 2.1 spec and describe the basic behavior of standards-compliant browsers. Be aware, however, that because of a problem with the box model implementation in Internet Explorer for Windows (all versions except IE 6 and 7 running in Standards mode), these browsers have a different method of calculating position based on applying the padding, borders, and margin within the specified width.

Fixed Positioning

Fixed positioning is essentially the same as absolute positioning, only the containing block is the viewing area (or viewport; typically the browser window). The distinguishing feature of fixed elements is that they do not scroll with the document, but are persistent on the page. On printed pages, fixed elements may appear in the same place on all pages.

In addition to not scrolling, fixed elements share these basic characteristics:

- They are declared using {position: fixed;}.
- They are positioned relative to the edges of the viewport (browser window) using one or more of the offset properties (top, right, bottom, left). Properties that are not specified are set to auto (the default). The offset values apply to the outer edge of the element box (including the margin value, if there is one).
- Like absolutely positioned elements, they are completely removed from the document flow, and the space they would have occupied is closed up.

Fixed elements can be used to create frame-like interfaces or to place persistent elements on the page. In this example, a fixed element is used as a short sidebar that stays put as the document scrolls (Figure 21-19).

```
ul {position: fixed; top: 0px; left: 0; width: 100px; background-color:
#999; margin: 0; padding: 10;}
p, h1 {margin-left: 150px;}
```

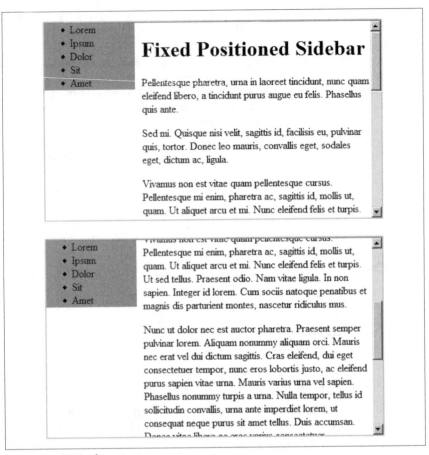

Figure 21-19. Fixed positioning

Internet Explorer 6 and earlier for Windows does not support fixed positioning. Objects with fixed positioning are treated as though they are static, and therefore behave as though they have not been positioned at all. There are workarounds available; to find them, search for "CSS fixed position in IE" or something similar in your favorite search engine. Support in IE 7 for Windows (in beta as of this writing) has not been confirmed.

Relative Positioning

Relative positioning works differently than absolute and fixed positioning. The critical difference is that although the element is moved around, the space where it would have appeared in the normal flow is preserved and continues to influence the elements that surround it.

Relatively positioned elements have these characteristics:

- They are declared using {position: relative;}.

- They are positioned relative to their initial position in the normal flow using one or more of the offset properties (top, right, bottom, left). Properties that are not specified are set to auto (the default).

- Their original space in the document flow is preserved.

- Because they are positioned elements, they can potentially overlap other elements.

This example of a relatively positioned emphasized (em) element demonstrates the basic syntax and behavior of relative positioning (Figure 21-20). Notice that when the element is moved, its space is left behind and the surrounding elements behave as though it is still there.

```
em {position: relative; top: -36px; right: -36px; background: #ccc; }
```

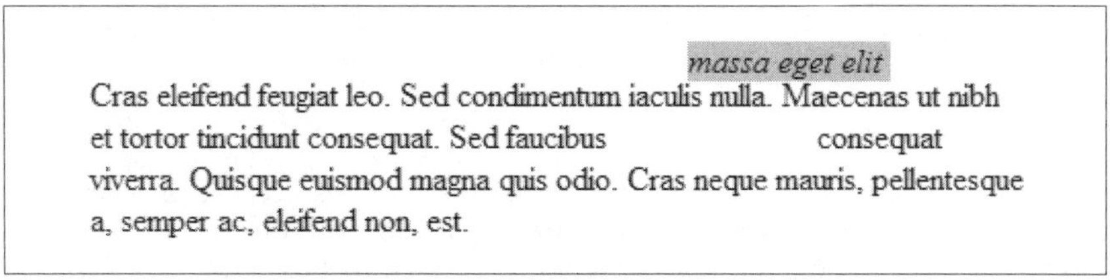

massa eget elit

Cras eleifend feugiat leo. Sed condimentum iaculis nulla. Maecenas ut nibh et tortor tincidunt consequat. Sed faucibus   consequat viverra. Quisque euismod magna quis odio. Cras neque mauris, pellentesque a, semper ac, eleifend non, est.

Figure 21-20. Relative positioning

In relative positioning, the top, right, bottom, and left properties move the element relative to its original position. Specifying a positive value for top moves the element down by that amount. Specifying a value for left moves the element to the right, and so on, such that a positive value for one side is equivalent to a negative value on the opposite side (the computed values are right=-left and bottom=-top).

The CSS 2.1 specification advises that when conflicting values are provided, the provided value for right is ignored in left-to-right languages (left is ignored for right-to-left languages) and is understood to be -left. When top and bottom values conflict, the provided bottom value is ignored and reset to -top. As such, this overconstrained style rule:

```
em {top: 10; bottom: 50; left: 50: right -4;}
```

would be rendered as though it had specified like this:

```
em {top: 10: bottom: -10; left: 50; right: -50;}
```

Relative positioning is often used to establish a containing block by specifying the position of the element as relative, but not altering its position. The result is that its child elements can then be absolutely positioned relative to the rectangle created by the element.

22

CSS for Tables

Tables have gotten a bad reputation in web design circles because of their notorious misuse as page layout devices. Although CSS now offers alternatives to tables for presentation purposes, it's not necessary to kick tables to the curb entirely. In fact, they serve an important purpose: the presentation of tabular data. Using CSS table properties with the full set of HTML table elements allows tables to go back to their original calling, but with more sophisticated tools for handling them.

This chapter explains these CSS 2 properties for controlling table presentation:

caption-side	border-spacing
table-layout	empty-cells
border-collapse	display (table-related values)

The Essence of Tables

If you are familiar with table structure in HTML, then the way CSS handles tables should not be a big surprise. For reasons of backward compatibility, the CSS specification used the row-based table layout model as the starting point for additional layout models and properties for controlling presentation. CSS is broader in its scope, however, because it is designed to work with document languages other than just HTML and XHTML. The system for providing table layout capabilities for non-HTML languages is discussed in the "Table Display Values" section at the end of this chapter.

The CSS 2.1 Recommendation is very detailed in its description of the defined behaviors for the table layout model. For a deeper look into the CSS table model, read the specification online at *www.w3.org/TR/CSS21/tables.html*. Once again, Eric Meyer's *Cascading Style Sheets: The Definitive Guide* (O'Reilly) is the book to turn to for making sense of the spec.

This section provides a summary of some of the key concepts of the CSS table model.

Rows and Columns

At the most basic level, tables are divided into rows and columns. CSS 2.1 describes the model as *row primary*, because rows are identified explicitly in the document structure. Cells are always descendants of rows, not columns. Columns are merely derived based on the number of cells in the rows.

The intersection of all the rows and columns in a table forms a grid and defines a basic *grid cell* unit. The actual *cells* (the boxes that contain the content) in the table may be composed of more than one grid cell, as is the case when cells are set to span rows or columns. Figure 22-1 shows the structure of the CSS table model.

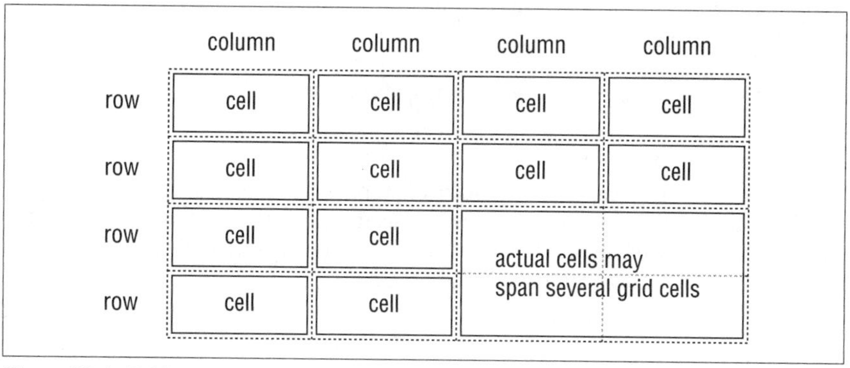

Figure 22-1. Table structure

In addition to cell boxes, the CSS visual box model for tables generates (implied) boxes around rows, row groups, columns, column groups, and the table itself. These boxes correspond to the row, rowgroup, col, colgroup, and table elements in HTML. The table caption (identified with the caption element) is treated as its own box as well (as discussed later in this chapter).

One last table box to be aware of is the *inline table*. Inline tables are block elements that can appear inline (tables are normally block-level elements). Inline tables are created by setting the display property to inline-table. They are not discussed in detail in this chapter, but are sometimes referenced in terms of property application. Only the Opera browser supports this display role as of this writing.

Internal Table Elements

CSS 2.1 makes a distinction between table elements and internal table elements. A *table element* is any part of a table (including table and caption). *Internal elements* are just those elements that generate a cell (such as td or th), a row (tr), a row group (rowgroup), a column (col), or a column group (colgroup).

Internal table elements may have content, padding, and borders. Internal elements may *not* have margins and any margin settings provided will be ignored.

Table Captions

HTML 4.0 introduced the caption element for providing a descriptive title to a table. CSS 2.1 assigns it special behaviors and its own property, caption-side, for positioning the caption above or below the table.

 Internet Explorer for Windows (Versions 6 and earlier) do not support the caption-side property. Support in IE 7, in beta as of this writing, is currently undocumented.

caption-side

Values: top | bottom | inherit

Initial value: top

Applies to: Table-caption elements (caption in HTML)

Inherited: Yes

By default, the table caption is placed on top of the table block (top), but the caption-side property allows it to be placed below the table (bottom). Table captions are block elements, but they have some peculiarities. Figure 22-2 shows the relationship of the caption to the table body.

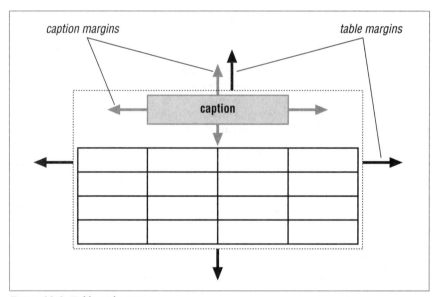

Figure 22-2. Table and caption

As block elements, they can be given their own properties, such as margins. However, they are also treated as children of the table element, and therefore will inherit properties applied to the table. So although it occupies a separate block with its own margins, if the color of the table is set to blue, the caption will be blue as well.

The margins between the caption and table block collapse to equal the greater specified value.

There is an implied or (anonymous) box that encloses the table box and the caption box. It is this anonymous box that is used when the table element is positioned with properties such as float, position, margin-*, top, right, bottom, or left.

Stacking Order

In the visual formatting model for tables, the various table elements are understood to occupy separate superimposed layers. These are used to determine which backgrounds are visible. Elements are transparent by default, allowing the backgrounds of the layers "below" to show through. A background applied to a particular element will be visible if all the elements "above" it are transparent.

The stacking order for table element layers is, from "top" to "bottom": cell, row, row group, column, column group, table, as shown in the diagram in Figure 22-3.

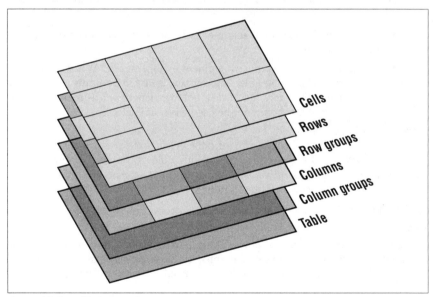

Figure 22-3. Table layer order

Or in other words, applying a background color in a cell will paint over any backgrounds provided in rows, row groups, and so on. This system is similar to the way in which color attributes in HTML table cells (td) override row settings (tr), which in turn override settings at the table level (table). One significant aspect of the CSS model is that table rows and row groups are given precedence over columns and column groups.

Styling Tables

For the most part, you don't need any special properties to control the presentation of tables and their content. Most of the properties listed in the previous chapters apply to table elements as well, although some may have different values when applied to table objects. This list is an overview of the styles to use for formatting typical aspects of a table and its content.

Text content
> Style the text content within tables, rows, and cells as you would any other text element in a document. You can apply the following properties to any table element.
>
> - font and all font-related properties
> - All text-formatting properties
> - color (changes the text color)

Alignment of content in cells
> You can use style properties to adjust the horizontal and vertical placement of cell content. Note that applying text-align: center to the table element does not center the table on the page, but rather centers all the content within each table cell.
>
> - text-align for horizontal alignment within a cell. The values left, right, and center apply.
> - vertical-align for vertical alignment within a cell. When used with tables, the values baseline, top, bottom, and middle apply. The values sub, super, text-top, and text-bottom; length measurements; and percentage values should not be used with table elements.

Background color and images
> You can change the background of table cells, rows, row groups, columns, column groups, or the entire table with color or a background image. Whether the background is visible or overridden is related to the table layer order discussed in the previous section.
>
> - background and all background-related properties

Borders
> You can apply borders to tables and cells at any time. Borders may *not* be applied to rows, row groups, columns, and column groups when the table uses the separated border model (discussed in the upcoming "Borders" section).
>
> - border and all border-related properties (see the special table border properties later in this chapter)

Margins
> Apply a margin around the outside of the table element with any of the margin properties. Margins may not be applied to such internal elements as cells, rows, and columns.
>
> - margin and all margin-related properties (see Chapter 19)

Padding

To add extra space around the content in table cells, add padding to the cell (td). The table element, although it may have a margin, does not accept padding. This may take some getting used to if you are accustomed to controlling cellpadding at the table level in HTML. The good news is that, with CSS, you can specify padding amounts cell by cell, not just globally for all the cells in the table.

- padding and padding-related properties may be applied to table cells.

Cell spacing

In (X)HTML, space between cells is specified with the cellspacing attribute. It is most commonly used to remove extra spacing between cells (cellspacing="0"). There is no directly analogous CSS property for handling space between cells.

The closest thing to cellspacing is to set the border-collapse property to separate and use the border-spacing property to add space between cells. The difference is that with cellspacing, browsers render 3D borders between the cells, while with the CSS border-spacing property, the space is held blank. Unfortunately, border-spacing is not supported in Internet Explorer (Versions 6 and earlier), so it is not a viable alternative at this time. Support in IE 7, in beta as of this writing, is undocumented.

Table size and positioning

It is possible to position a table as you would any other block element. Position measurements apply to the anonymous box that contains both the table and caption boxes (see Figure 22-2). Applying float to a table cell may remove it from the table and is not advised.

- All positioning properties
- width (except rows and row groups)
- height (may not be used on table columns and column groups)

Column properties

Table cells are always descendants of table rows, however, CSS 2.1 describes four permissible column properties that influence cells (each with qualifications).

- border (using the collapsing border model, discussed in the next section)
- background (colors applied to row groups, rows, and cells override column backgrounds)
- width (values provided are minimum values only)
- visibility (when the value is set to collapse, the whole column will not display and any spanned cells it contains will be clipped)

 For an in-depth explanation of why columns support only four properties, read Ian Hickson's blog entry, "The mystery of why only four properties apply to table columns" at *ln.hixie.ch/ ?start=1070385285&count=1*.

Borders

There are two models for handling borders in CSS 2.1. In one, the borders around cells are separated from each other. In the other, borders are said to "collapse" and are continuous from one cell to the next. The `border-collapse` property allows authors to choose which model the table should follow.

border-collapse

Values:	collapse | separate | inherit
Initial value:	collapse
Applies to:	table and inline-table elements
Inherited:	Yes

The Separated Borders Model

In the separated borders model, the border is drawn on all four sides of each cell (or as specified by the border properties), and an amount of space can be added between cells with the `border-spacing` property.

 The `border-spacing` property is not supported by Internet Explorer Versions 6 and earlier. Support in IE 7, in beta as of this writing, is not documented.

border-spacing

Values:	<length> <length>? | inherit
Initial value:	0
Applies to:	table and inline-table elements
Inherited:	Yes

The values for `border-spacing` are two length measurements. The horizontal spacing value comes first and is applied between the cells in each row of the table. The vertical value always comes second and is applied between cells in each column. If you provide just one value, it will be applied both horizontally and vertically. The table in Figure 22-4 uses the separated border model.

```
table {border-collapse: separate;
       border-spacing: 10px 3px;
       border: none;}

td { border: 1px solid black; }
```

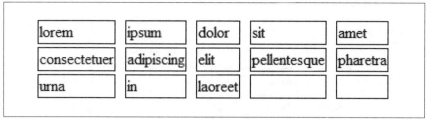

lorem	ipsum	dolor	sit	amet
consectetuer	adipiscing	elit	pellentesque	pharetra
urna	in	laoreet		

Figure 22-4. A table with border-spacing

The default value for border-spacing is 0, which causes adjacent borders to touch, essentially "doubling up" the borders on the inside grid of the table.

When using the separated border model, rows, row groups, columns, and column groups cannot have borders.

If you have a few years of web design experience, you may remember how Netscape 4 required every cell in a table to have content in it or the cell would collapse and the background wouldn't display. In the CSS separated borders model, you get to decide whether you want empty cells to display their backgrounds and borders or whether they should be hidden using the empty-cells property.

> Internet Explorer for Windows (Versions 6 and earlier) do not support the empty-cells property. IE 5 for the Mac shows and hides cells as expected, but it makes the empty cells too large. Support in IE 7, in beta as of this writing, is currently undocumented.

empty-cells

Values: show | hide | inherit

Initial value: show

Applies to: Table cell elements

Inherited: Yes

The default value for empty-cells is show, which shows the background and borders for cells that do not contain any content. The hide value hides the cell's background and borders and is equivalent to visibility: hidden.

For a cell to be "empty," it may not contain any text or replaced elements, non-breaking spaces ( ) or whitespace. It may contain carriage returns (CR), line feeds (LF), and space characters.

Figure 22-5 shows the previous table border example, this time with empty elements set to hide.

```
table {border-collapse: separate;
       border-spacing: 10px 3px;
       empty-cells: hide;
```

```
        border: none;}

  td { border: 1px solid black; }
```

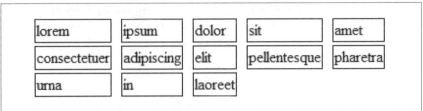

Figure 22-5. Empty cells hidden with the empty-cells property

 The empty-cells property is not supported by Internet Explorer through Version 6. Version 7 promises improved support of CSS 2. 1, but as of this writing, support for empty-cells is not specifically documented.

The Collapsing Border Model

In the collapsing border model, the borders of adjacent borders "collapse" so that only one of the borders is visible and extra space between borders is removed. Figure 22-6 shows the table from the previous examples, only this time, the border-collapse property has been set to collapse.

```
  table {border-collapse: collapse;
         border: none;}

  td { border: 1px solid black; }
```

Figure 22-6. A table with collapsed borders

Borders between cells are centered on the grid lines between cells. Therefore, if two adjacent cells have a border that is eight pixels wide, four pixels will fall in one cell and four pixels will fall in the other. If a border has an odd number of pixels, it is left to the user agent to decide where the extra pixel goes. Wide borders on the outside edge of the table may extend into the table's margin.

Explicitly declaring border-collapse: collapse for tables removes any extra space and little gaps in the border that may be automatically inserted by the browser.

Border pecking order

If there can only be one border between each pair of cells, what happens when neighboring cells have conflicting border styles? The authors of CSS anticipated this problem and devised a system for resolving border conflicts.

- Borders with `border-style` set to `hidden` take precedence over all other border styles, so the border will not display.

- Borders with a style of `none` have the lowest priority. That means that if there is any border specified at all, it will win out and display on the edge of a cell with borders set to `none`.

- Wider borders win over narrower ones, regardless of the border style.

- If the neighboring borders are the same width, then it comes down to a battle of styles. The CSS 2.1 specification establishes this pecking order for border styles (in order from most to least precedence): `double`, `solid`, `dashed`, `dotted`, `ridge`, `outset`, `groove`, and (the lowest) `inset`. That means if one cell has a five-pixel dashed border and its neighbor has a five-pixel groove border, the dashed border will "win" and display between the cells.

- If the border styles differ only in color, then it comes down to the table layer order (Figure 22-3) to determine which border is visible. Styles set on cells win out over rows, and row settings win over row groups, columns, column groups, and finally table.

Table Layout (Width and Height)

User agents (typically browsers) may use one of two algorithm-driven approaches to calculate the width of a table: fixed-width layout and automatic-width layout. Web page authors may specify which layout approach to use for a specific table using the `table-layout` property.

table-layout

Values:	auto | fixed | inherit
Initial value:	auto
Applies to:	table and inline-table elements
Inherited:	No

Fixed-Width Layout

The `fixed` value for `table-layout` tells the browser or other user agent to calculate the size of the table using the "fixed" algorithm. This method requires the least work of the user agent because the table width is determined by the `width` values of the table, columns, and cells within the table.

First, the user agent takes the widths of column elements that are set to a specific width (not auto). Then it looks at the cells in the first row of the table. Cells with specific width values (not auto) set the width for their columns. Any remaining columns that have the width set to auto are sized so their widths are roughly equal to fill the remaining space in the table.

The final width of the table is the sum of the column widths or the table element's width value, whichever is greater.

The important aspect of this model is that only width values provided for cells in the *first row* of the table apply. Therefore, if the top cell in a table is set to 200 pixels and another cell farther down in the same column is set to 350 pixels, the column will be 200 pixels wide. The setting in the lower row is simply ignored in the fixed layout model.

The advantage of the fixed-width layout is that it's much faster than the automatic method. Because it depends on declared width values for the table and columns, and because it only takes into consideration the first row of cells, there is no need to parse and calculate sizes for the entire table content to arrive at a size calculation.

For web developers, declaring the table-layout as fixed may speed up display rates. Just be sure that all column widths are declared explicitly or that cell widths are provided in the first row.

Automatic Layout

The automatic layout model is essentially the same model used for HTML tables for years in which tables expand to fit the width of the content. In CSS, the auto value for table-layout ensures this method will be used to size the table regardless of the browser default.

Because automatic layout is content dependent, the browser must calculate the width of the content in every cell. The real process is fairly complicated, but what it boils down to is this:

- First, the browser calculates the minimum and maximum width of every cell in the table.
- A comparison of the cells in a column sets the minimum and maximum width for that column. The result is that columns are forced to be as wide as their widest cell.
- Once the column widths are determined, the browser turns to the table width setting. If the table width is auto, then the width of the table will be the sum of the column widths, borders, and cell spacing. In other words, it will only be as wide as it needs to be to accommodate the content.
- If it is something other than auto, then the sum of the columns plus borders and spacing are compared to the computed width of the table (the width of the table based on other page criteria such as browser window width). If the table's computed width is larger, then the columns are expanded equally to fill the space.

Even with this brief summary of the automatic width calculation method, it is easy to see why this method is more labor-intensive for the browser. Despite the extra processing time, it may still be desirable to have tables and cells resize automatically to fit the content.

Table Display Values

CSS was designed to work with all XML document languages, not just XHTML. It's likely that other languages may have the need for tabular layouts, but will not have elements like `table`, `td`, or `tr` in their vocabularies.

To this end, the CSS 2.1 specification allows authors to assign table element roles to any element using the `display` property. The `display` property was discussed in Chapter 16 in relation to block and inline elements. This section covers the values listed in bold.

display

Values:	inline | block | list-item | run-in | inline-block | **table** | **inline-table** | **table-row-group** | **table-header-group** | **table-footer-group** | **table-row** | **table-column-group** | **table-column** | **table-cell** | **table-caption** | none | inherit
Initial value:	inline
Applies to:	table and inline-table elements
Inherited:	No

Using the table-related display values, the elements from any markup language can be "mapped" to table elements. A simple example should make this clear. Consider this markup written in a hypothetical XML language.

```
<platter>
  <cheese>
    <name>Brie</name>
    <origin>France</origin>
  </cheese>
  <cheese>
    <name>Manchego</name>
    <origin>Spain</origin>
  </cheese>
</platter>
```

By attaching these style rules:

```
platter { display: table; }
cheese { display: table-row; }
name, origin { display: table-cell; }
```

The example would display in the user agent as though it were marked up like this:

```
<table>
 <tr>
   <td>Brie</td>
   <td>France</td>
 </tr>
 <tr>
   <td>Manchego</td>
   <td>Spain</td>
 </td>
</table>
```

The complete list of table display values is provided here. Their HTML equivalents are listed in parentheses.

table
    Makes an element a block-level table element (table).

inline-table
    Makes the element an inline table. Inline tables are rectangular blocks that behave as inline objects (there is no HTML equivalent).

table-row
    Specifies that the element is a row of cells (tr).

table-row-group
    Specifies that the element is a group of one or more rows (rowgroup).

table-header-group
    Like a row group, only it is always displayed before other rows and after captions. For print, it may be repeated at the top of each page (thead).

table-footer-group
    Like a row group, but it is always displayed after the other rows and before any bottom captions. It may be repeated at the bottom of each page (tfoot).

table-column
    Specifies that the element is a column (col).

table-column-group
    Specifies that the element is a group of columns (colgroup).

table-cell
    Makes the element a table cell (td, th).

table-caption
    Specifies a caption for the table (caption).

Anonymous table elements

Because other languages may not have all the elements necessary to make up the table layout model used by CSS, missing elements are assumed for the layout to work. According to the CSS 2.1 specification, a table element will automatically generate necessary anonymous table objects (a table, row, or cell) around itself.

Anonymous table objects are a function of the user agent's rendering engine—no code is changed. To use the earlier example and its table display values, if the row-equivalent element is missing, the browser generates an anonymous table-row object between the cells and the table level.

```
<platter>
[begin anonymous table-row object]
  <name>Brie</name>
  <origin>France</origin>
[end anonymous table-row object]
</platter>
```

For a more detailed explanation of how anonymous table elements function, see the CSS 2.1 specification online at *www.w3.org/TR/CSS21/tables.html*.

23

Lists and Generated Content

One of the advantages to using an ordered list element on a web page is that the browser numbers list each item automatically. This makes it easier to add, delete, or move list items around without manually editing the numbers, because they aren't in the source document in the first place—they're generated by the user agent. CSS 2.1 provides a number of properties for controlling the style, content, and position of numbers and bullets (called *markers*) used for unordered and ordered lists.

The creators of the CSS 2.1 specification realized there might be other instances in which it would be useful to have user agents generate content that isn't actually present in the document tree. The generated content features of CSS 2.1 provide a mechanism for inserting any specified text or counters (automatic numbering) before or after any element in an (X)HTML or XML document.

This chapter covers the CSS 2.1 properties related to controlling markers for list items as well as the properties associated with generated content.

list-style-type	list-style
list-style-image	display: list-item
list-style-position	content
quotes	counter-reset
counter-increment	

CSS for Lists

Bulleted and numbered lists have been around since the very beginning of HTML.[*] Extensions to the ul and ol elements gave designers the ability to choose a bullet shape or numbering format, but beyond that, authors have had little control over

---

[*] One of the earliest documentations of the HTML language (dated 1992) defines the ul tag and describes ordered lists. To learn about HTML's humble beginnings, visit *www.w3.org/History/19921103-hypertext/hypertext/WWW/MarkUp/Tags.html*.

list presentation. CSS 2.1 offers some improvements, most notably the ability to replace bullets with your own images.

 In modern standards- and accessibility-driven web design, lists are being used in interesting ways to create navigation that previously would have been created with graphics and JavaScript (see Chapter 24).

Choosing a Marker

Ordered and unordered lists are unique elements in that they automatically add a *marker* (a bullet or a number) to the page that isn't part of the document source. Use the list-style-type property to select the type of marker that appears with each list item. This property replaces the deprecated type attribute in XHTML.

list-style-type

Values:	disc | circle | square | decimal | decimal-leading-zero | lower-roman | upper-roman | lower-greek | lower-latin | upper-latin | lower-alpha | upper-alpha | none | inherit
Initial value:	disc
Applies to:	Elements whose display value is list-item (in XHTML, the ul, ol, and li elements)
Inherited:	Yes

Three values for list-style-type (disc, circle, and square) generate a bullet shape, just as browsers have been doing for unordered lists for years. The actual design and rendering of each bullet shape is left to the user agent. In other words, there is no way to alter the color, size, or other presentation attributes of a generated bullet. Figure 23-1 shows each of the bullet markers.

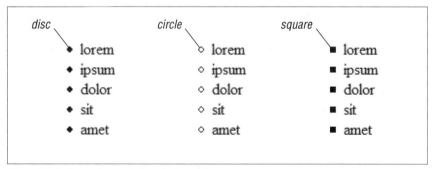

Figure 23-1. list-style-type: disc, circle, and square

The remaining value keywords specify various numbering and lettering styles. Table 23-1 lists the keyword and numbering types provided in CSS 2.1.

Table 23-1. Lettering and numbering system keywords in CSS 2.1

Keyword	System
decimal	1, 2, 3, 4, 5 …
decimal-leading-zero	01, 02, 03, 04, 05 …
lower-alpha	a, b, c, d, e …
upper-alpha	A, B, C, D, E …
lower-latin	a, b, c, d, e … (same as lower-alpha)
upper-latin	A, B, C, D, E … (same as upper-alpha)
lower-roman	i, ii, iii, iv, v …
upper-roman	I, II, III, IV, V …
lower-greek	Lowercase classical Greek symbols

A handful of numbering keywords that were included in CSS 2 were removed from 2.1 due to the difficulty in implementing them and the resulting poor browser support. They include: hebrew, cjk-ideographic, and the Japanese numbering systems katakana, katakana-iroha, hiragana, and hiragana-iroha. Additionally, the values armenian and georgian were in a CSS 2.1 Candidate Recommendation but at risk of being dropped due to lack of implementation. The various international list numbering styles are defined in far more detail in the CSS 3 Lists Module.

The user agent controls the presentation of the generated numbers and letters, although they usually match the font properties of the associated list items. There is no way to change the font, size, color, or other presentation features of number or letter markers. When numbers run several digits long, the user agent determines whether the markers should be left or right justified.

The CSS specification also does not specify what should be done when a lettering system runs out of letters. For long lists, true numbering systems are recommended.

If you want to turn the marker off for a list item, choose the value none. Setting the list-style-type to none for an item or items does not prevent that item from being counted by the counting mechanism; it merely causes the number not to display.

Be aware that even though list-style-type is an inherited property, it may be necessary to explicitly declare styles for each level of nested list element in order to override browsers' built-in style sheets for nested list marker types.

Marker Position

By default, the marker hangs outside the content area for the list item, usually displaying as a hanging indent. The list-style-position property allows you to pull the bullet inside the content area so it runs into the list content.

list-style-position

Values: inside | outside | inherit

Initial value: outside

Applies to: Elements whose display value is list-item (in XHTML, the ul, ol, and li elements)

Inherited: Yes

Figure 23-2 shows the difference between the outside and inside marker positions as indicated by the following styles. Note that the dotted lines are a device to indicate the edges of the content area only and would not actually display.

```
li.one {list-style-position: outside;}
li.two {list-style-position: inside; }
```

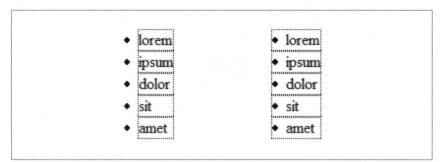

Figure 23-2. list-style-position

Unfortunately, that's about all you can do with list-style-position. It does not provide a way for authors to adjust the distance or position of the marker relative to the list item. CSS 2.1 leaves the distance to the user agent. Interestingly, CSS 2 included the marker-offset property for this very purpose, but it was dropped in CSS 2.1 because it was determined not to be the best solution for the problem. Look for improved control over marker placement in CSS Level 3.

 Internet Explorer for Windows always includes the bullet in the content area box. This can cause some inconsistent results when positioning list blocks or adding borders, padding, and margins to list items.

Make Your Own Bullets

The one juicy feature that CSS does provide for list presentation is the ability to provide an image to be used as a bullet. In the past, to use images, the list needed to be faked with line breaks or a table. Now the markup can remain semantically and structurally intact while a style sheet swaps the browser's bullet for one of your own.

To specify an image to be used as a marker, use the list-style-image property.

list-style-image

Values:	<uri> | none | inherit
Initial value:	none
Applies to:	Elements whose display value is list-item (in XHTML, the ul, ol, and li elements)
Inherited:	Yes

This example shows the syntax for providing the URL of an image for use as a marker. The list-style-type is set to disc as a backup in case the image doesn't display or the property can't be interpreted by the user agent. The resulting list is shown in Figure 23-3.

```
ul { list-style-image: url(happy.gif);
     list-style-type: disc;
     list-style-position: outside; }
```

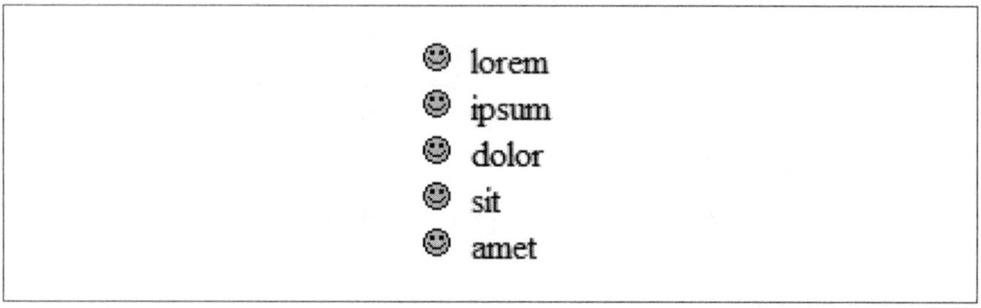

> ◉ lorem
> ◉ ipsum
> ◉ dolor
> ◉ sit
> ◉ amet

Figure 23-3. Using an image as a marker

 Remember that the URL is always interpreted as relative to the style sheet, whether it's embedded in the document or in an external *.css* file elsewhere on the server. Make sure that relative URLs are correct or use absolute URLs (including *http://* and the domain) to be safe.

list-style Shorthand Property

The three list properties (type, position, and image) can be combined in the shorthand list-style property.

list-style

Values:	[<list-style-type> || <list-style-image> || <list-style-position>] | inherit
Initial value:	See individual properties

Applies to:	Elements whose display value is list-item (in HTML and XHTML, the ul, ol, and li elements)

Inherited: Yes

The values for each property may be provided in any order and any may be omitted. Keep in mind that omitted properties are reset to their default values in shorthand properties. Be careful not to override list-style declarations earlier in the style sheet. Each of these examples of list-style duplicates the effects of the separate rules provided in the example shown in Figure 23-4.

```
ul {list-style: url(skull.gif) disc outside;}
ul {list-style: disc outside url(skull.gif);}
ul {list-style: url(skull.gif) disc;}
```

List-item Display

You may have noticed that all of the properties in this chapter apply to "elements whose display value is list-item." In XHTML, there are explicit elements for lists and list items (ol, ul, and li), but in other XML languages, that may not be the case. The CSS specification allows any element to perform like a list item, complete with marker, by setting its display property to list-item. This applies to other elements within XHTML as well, as shown here and in Figure 23-4.

```
p.bulleted {
    display: list-item;
    list-style-type: disc;
    list-style-position: inside; }

<p>Aliquam pulvinar volutpat nibh. ...</p>
<p>Etiam accumsan. Proin eros ...</p>
<p>Aenean id nulla sed nibh accumsan ...</p>
```

- Aliquam pulvinar volutpat nibh. Integer convallis nulla sit amet magna. Maecenas imperdiet turpis ac augue. Integer malesuada mauris a odio vulputate blandit.

- Etiam accumsan. Proin eros massa, condimentum sit amet, semper vitae, pulvinar non, augue. Morbi sed sapien ac turpis facilisis egestas.

- Aenean id nulla sed nibh accumsan laoreet. Nulla interdum est nec erat. Pellentesque tempor. Pellentesque sit amet pede. Nullam scelerisque nibh sit amet urna.

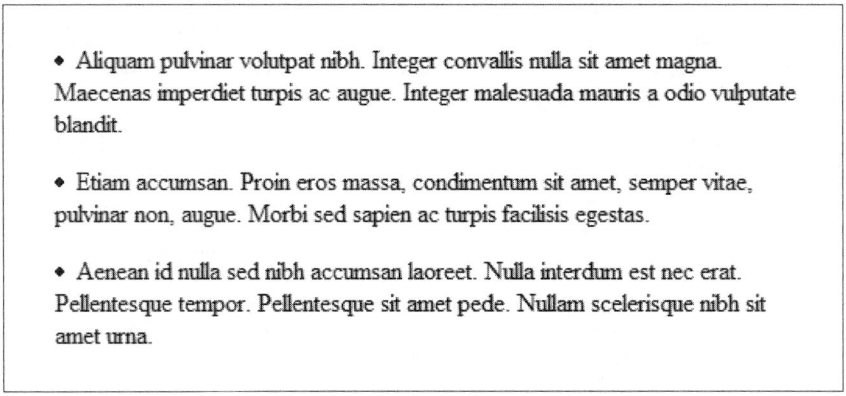

Figure 23-4. Using another element as a list-item

Generated Content

Generated content refers to content that is not in the document tree, yet is inserted in the page when it is displayed in a browser window, printed on paper, projected on a screen, read aurally, or otherwise delivered. Generated content may be specified text, images, or other media (or even the values of attributes) added before or after an element. It could be used to insert the name of the person making an edit after deleted text (del element). Used together with media-specific style sheets, generated content could be used to write out the URL after links only when the document is printed, or to say "end of table" at the end of a long table only when the document is read aurally.

There are also several properties that control *counters*, the mechanisms that keep track of the numbering for ordered list. Used together with generated text, it is possible to insert the word "Section" before each automatically numbered section heading. Allowing the user agent to automatically insert labels and numbers makes it easier to reorganize and relabel long documents because the numbers don't need to be edited manually in the source.

 Unfortunately, no version of Internet Explorer as of this writing supports generated content, because IE doesn't support the :before and :after pseudoselectors. If you do specify generated content, IE will just ignore it, so it does no harm. You can begin using it immediately to provide a richer experience for users with browsers that do support it (Mozilla, Firefox, Netscape 6+, Opera). Safari offers partial support as noted in the chapter.

Inserting Generated Content

Generated content is specified in the style sheet with the :before and :after pseudoelements (pseudoelements are discussed in Chapter 17). The :before selector inserts content (most commonly, but not limited to, text characters, an image, or quotation marks) immediately before the targeted element. The :after pseudoelement inserts the generated content just after the targeted element.

Both pseudoelements are used in conjunction with the content property, which is used to specify where the generated content is to be inserted.

content

Values:	normal	[<string>	<uri>	<counter>	attr(<identifier>)	open-quote	close-quote	no-open-quote	no-close-quote]+	inherit
Initial value:	normal
Applies to:	:before and :after pseudoelements
Inherited:	No

The values for content fall into three broad categories: counters, quotation marks, and "whatever." Counters and quotation marks are discussed in upcoming sections. This section takes on "whatever," which more formally refers to character strings, URIs, and attribute values.

The simplest example of generated text is to insert a string of text before or after an element. In this example, initials are inserted after each del element (indicating deleted text) to show who made the change. The resulting page is shown in Figure 23-5.

```
del:before { content: "[JNR] "; }
del { text-decoration: line-through; border: solid 1px; padding: 2px; }

<p>Praesent tincidunt aliquet urna. vel consectetuer velit tellus a quam.
<del>Vestibulum rutrum,</del> magna at tempor aliquet, pede mi imperdiet
purus,
Vivamus eleifend. Fusce bibendum. Nam molestie dictum sem.</p>
```

Praesent tincidunt aliquet urna. vel consectetuer velit tellus a quam. [JNR] Vestibulum rutrum, magna at tempor aliquet, pede mi imperdiet purus, Vivamus eleifend. Fusce bibendum. Nam molestie dictum sem.

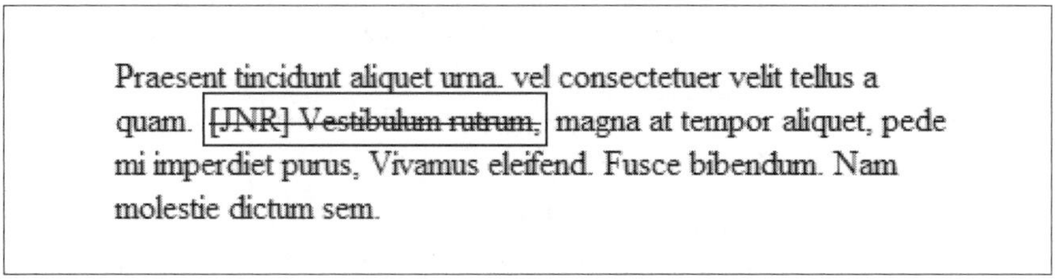

Figure 23-5. Inserting text before an element

You can tell from the border applied to the del element that the generated content is included in the content area for the element. It also inherits whatever styles are applied to the targeted element, such as line-through in the example.

There are a few syntax requirements when inserting text strings:

- By default, the inserted text will butt right against the beginning or end of the targeted element. If you want space between them, add a character space to the value of content. For example, it was necessary to explicitly add a character space after the closing bracket within the value of the content property, as shown here:

  ```
  content: "[JNR] ";
  ```

  If that space were omitted, the closing bracket would be placed right next to the "V" in the element.

- The value of content is not parsed, which means that if you add HTML markup or character entities, it will appear on the final page just as it's typed in.

- To insert a line break in generated text, it is necessary to use the string \A (the CSS way of inserting a new line when the br element isn't an option). If you have a long selection of content that must break over multiple lines in the source, escape out the line feeds with the \ character at the end of each line. The text will wrap as normal when it displays. Unfortunately, escaped content is not well supported by current browsers.

It is also possible to use the value of an element's attribute as the generated text by specifying attr(*attribute-name*) in the value of the content property. One very practical use is to display the URL for links when the document is printed so the reader can follow up on linked resources later.

The styles in this example appear in a style sheet that gets used only when the document prints (print style sheets are discussed in detail in Chapter 36). The markup is also provided.

```
a {text-decoration: none;
a[href]:after {content: " (" attr(href) ")";}


<p>Read my <a href="http://www.oreilly.com">book</a>.</p>
<p>Visit my <a href="http://www.jenville.com">site</a>.</p>
<p>Visit my <a href="http://www.littlechair.com">other site</a>.</p>
```

The a[href] attribute selector applies the rule only to anchors that have the href attribute and not to named anchors used to identify document fragments.

The value of the content property directs the user agent to generate this content after the a element:

1. Insert a character space and an open parentheses character.

2. Insert the value of the href attribute.

3. Insert a closing parentheses character.

When the document is printed, the URL will be written out, as shown in Figure 23-6.

Read my book (http://www.oreilly.com).

Visit my site (http://www.jenville.com).

Visit my other site (http://www.littlechair.com).

Figure 23-6. Inserting the attribute value of href

Quotation Marks

The content property also provides a way to insert quotation marks automatically before and after an element using the open-quote, close-quote, no-open-quote, and no-close-quote values. They are designed to work in tandem with the quotes property, which is used to specify which style of quotation marks to use before and after elements. It will be helpful to cover the quotes property first, then demonstrate the content values mentioned earlier.

quotes

Values: [<string><string>]+ | none | inherit

Initial value: Depends on user agent

Applies to: All elements

Inherited: Yes

The quotes property allows authors to specify which characters to use as quotation marks before and after elements. This may be useful for delivering documents with different styles of quotation marks based on audience (and style sheet) without having to go back and edit the document.

The value of quotes is one or more pairs of character strings. The first value is applied at the beginning of the quote, and the last value is applied at the close of the quote. This example specifies standard English double quotes at the open and close of a quote element.

```
q {quotes: '"' '"'; }
```

Additional pairs specify quotation styles for each consecutive nesting level, as shown in this style rule. Notice that the quotation marks that enclose the provided values must not match the specified quotation character (in other words, when specifying a single quote, use double quotes, and vice versa).

```
q {quotes: '"' '"' "'" "'"; }
```

The double and single quotes specified in this example render as the straight up-and-down ASCII characters. For curly quotes and other more sophisticated quotation characters, the characters must be escaped. In style sheets, characters are escaped with a backslash (\) preceding the hexadecimal Unicode code point (number). The (X)HTML method of escaping characters (&#nnn;) is not valid in style sheets. Character escaping is discussed further in Chapter 6.

This example specifies curly double quotes before and after quotations.

```
q {quotes: '\201C' '\201D'; }
```

Table 23-2 lists the Unicode equivalents for common quotation characters.

Table 23-2. Unicode equivalents for quotation mark glyphs

Character	Unicode (hex)	Description
"	0022	Quotation mark (the ASCII double quotation mark)
'	0027	Apostrophe (the ASCII single quotation mark)
‹	2039	Single left-pointing angle
›	203A	Single right-pointing angle
«	00AB	Left-pointing double angle
»	00BB	Right-pointing double angle
'	2018	Left single curly quotation mark
'	2019	Right single curly quotation mark

Table 23-2. Unicode equivalents for quotation mark glyphs (continued)

Character	Unicode (hex)	Description
"	201C	Left double curly quotation mark
"	201D	Right double curly quotation mark
„	201E	Double low quotation mark

Once the quotation mark characters have been specified, the content property with the open-quote and close-quote keyword values applies the quotation marks at the beginning and end of the quote.

```
q {quotes: '\201C' '\201D'; }
q:before { content: open-quote; }
q:after  { content: close-quote; }
```

The standard treatment for long quotations that span several paragraphs is to omit the closing quotation mark at the ends of paragraphs (except the final paragraph of the quotation). The no-close-quote value allows you to specify that the quotation mark should be omitted from the end of the element, but it closes the quotation such that the proper nesting levels are preserved. When using the no-close-quote value, you must specifically add a quote to the last paragraph in the quote. Similarly, the no-open-quote value maintains the nesting level as though there were a quotation mark there, but it suppresses the display of the quotation character.

Automatic Numbering and Counters

If you have ever used an ordered list in a web page, then you have some basic experience with counters. The CSS 2.1 specification provides properties that allow counters to be added to any element, not just lists. With these tools, you could automatically number the headings in a document and never need to edit the source when new headings are inserted.

Unfortunately, as of this writing, CSS counters are only supported by Opera Versions 5 and higher (a very small slice of web traffic). For that reason, this section provides only a brief introduction to the properties and how they are used. For more information, see the CSS 2.1 specification online (*www.w3.org/TR/ CSS21/generate.html*). Once again, *Cascading Style Sheets: The Definitive Guide* by Eric Meyer (O'Reilly) provides an excellent tutorial on using counters.

Automatic numbering is controlled by the counter-reset and the counter-increment properties used in conjunction with the content property for generated content. counter-reset establishes a starting point for the numbering.

counter-reset

Values: [<identifier> <integer>?]+ | none | inherit

Initial value: Depends on user agent

Applies to:	All elements

Inherited:	No

The value of the `counter-reset` property is an identifier (a label set by the author such as "chapter" or "section") and an optional number that serves as the starting number. The default is zero (0), so simply declaring an identifier for counter-reset sets it to 0. Any integer may be specified as the starting number, including negative values. In this simple example, a "chapter" counter is established and starts at 3.

```
h1 {counter-reset: chapter 3; }
```

Now that a starting point has been established, the `counter-increment` property is used to indicate that an element triggers the counter to go up.

counter-increment

Values:	[<identifier> <integer>?]+	none	inherit

Initial value:	Depends on user agent

Applies to:	All elements

Inherited:	No

The value of `counter-increment` provides the name of the identifier (such as "chapter" or "section") and an optional number that serves as the increment amount. The default is 1, so each instance of the element adds 1 to the counter unless it is specified otherwise. It is possible to specify negative values to make the counter count backward. In this example, the "chapter" counter from the previous example is given the default counter increment of 1.

```
h1 {counter-increment: chapter; }
```

This is the same as specifying

```
h1 {counter-increment: chapter 1; }
```

These counter functions are useful only when used with the `counter()` and `counters()` values of the content property.

The provided values for `counter()` are the identifier name and an optional style (one of the `list-style-type` values such as `upper-alpha`). The counter style is decimal (1, 2, 3, etc.) by default. In this example, the content property is used to insert the automatic counter and the colon character (:) followed by a space before each h2 element in a document.

```
h2:before {counter(section) ": "
          counter-increment: section; } /* defaults to 1 */
```

The `counters()` function is used to specify counters that are several levels deep (e.g., 1.0, 1.1., 1.2., 1.3., 2.0, 2.1., 2.1.1, 2.1.2, 2.1.3., and so on) without needing to specify counter rules for each nesting level individually. The hitch is that they must all be given the same identifier name. It is a good idea to provide a separator character such as a period or a comma to visually separate the string of counters.

Consider for a moment what happens when you put an ordered list inside an ordered list in HTML. By default, the nested ordered list starts counting at "1" by default. That is because lists are self-nesting. When the user agent detects a new nesting level (or "scope," to use the lingo), the counters( ) function knows to trigger the appropriate counter in the string.

This example creates a nested-counter style that counts sections and two levels of subsections (as listed above).

```
ol {counter-reset: ordered;}
ol li:before {counter-increment: ordered;
              content: counters(ordered, ".");}
```

The counting mechanisms provided by CSS 2.1 are much more powerful than the tiny glimpse provided in this section. One day, when browsers catch up in support, they'll be a useful tool for content handling.

24

CSS Techniques

The previous chapters introduced the CSS tools available in web designers' tool-belts: the properties and values provided in the CSS specification. This chapter puts them together in a few of the most popular design and layout techniques used in CSS-driven web design, including:

- Centering a fixed-width page
- Multicolumn layouts
- Boxes with rounded corners
- Replacing text with background images
- CSS rollovers
- List-based navigation

As in so many web-related tasks, there are seemingly endless variations on accomplishing the same goal. Each example in this chapter represents just one solution (you may know of better approaches). The intent is to demonstrate basic style sheet strategy and to provide "starter kits" for achieving basic visual and layout effects with CSS. There is usually much more to be said about each technique, so references to additional resources are provided when available. The "CSS Techniques Resources" section at the end of the chapter lists recommended reading for those interested in learning more about what can be done with CSS-driven design.

Centering a Page

As a strategy for controlling the width of a page while allowing for varying monitor resolutions, it is common for web designers to create fixed-width pages that are then centered in the width of the browser window. In the past, this was achieved by slapping a center tag (or `<div align="center">...</div>`) around a table. In this section, we'll look at three CSS methods for centering a fixed-width page: the official CSS way, a way that works in Internet Explorer, and an effective "hack." All three examples have the effect shown in Figure 24-1.

Figure 24-1. Centering a fixed-width page element

In CSS, the proper way to center a fixed-width element is to specify a width for the element that contains all the page's contents (a div is the usual choice), and then set the left and right margins to auto. According to the CSS visual formatting model, this will have the net effect of centering the element in the initial containing block.

```
div#page {
    width: 500px;
    margin-left: auto;
    margin-right: auto; }
```

This method works for all current standards-compliant browsers, including Internet Explorer 6 for Windows when it is in "Standards" mode (see Chapter 2 about triggering standards-compliance mode in browsers using the DOCTYPE declaration). It will not work with in IE 6/Windows in "Quirks" mode or any earlier version.

An alternative, yet inelegant, solution is to center the whole page using the text-align property on the body element. This technique ultimately amounts to a hack, because it takes a text property and uses it to center any number of items.

The problem with this method is that because horizontal alignment is inherited, all the text on the page will be centered in its element boxes. It is necessary to override the inherited centering by also specifying left alignment for every descendant of the body element. In this example, the universal selector (*) targets all elements that appear within the body of the document and sets text-align to left. Notice also that the margin-left and margin-right values have been replaced in the example with the margin shorthand property. Although not necessary, this reduces the amount of code and keeps the style sheet lean and mean.

```
body { text-align: center; }

body * {text-align: left; }

div#page {
    width: 500px;
    margin: 0 auto; }
```

The third centering method uses negative margins to effectively center a containing block on the page for all browsers that support basic absolute positioning (including Netscape 4). First, the "page" (the name of the div in the examples) is absolutely positioned so its left edge is 50% across the initial containing block (i.e., the width of the browser window). Then, a negative left margin is applied that pulls the page back to the left by half its width, thus aligning the midpoint of the block with the midpoint of the window. And voilà, it's centered. (This method is taken from *The Zen of CSS Design* by Dave Shea and Molly E. Holzschlag [Peachpit Press]. It was originally used by Jon Hicks in his Zen Garden submission.)

```
div#page {
    position: absolute;
    left: 50%
    width: 500px;
    margin-left: -250px; }     /* half the width measurement */
```

Two-Column Layouts

Multicolumn layouts that once required HTML tables are now achievable using CSS alone. Column layouts can be done using floats or absolute positioning (see Chapter 21 for details on both).

Of course, there are endless variations on two-column layouts in terms of page components, measurements, backgrounds, and so forth. The examples in this section represent just a few very basic possibilities. They reveal the general strategy for approaching two-column designs and should serve as a good head start toward implementing your own layouts. It should be noted, however, that they are based on the assumption that the main content column will be longer than the side columns. If your side columns are longer, it may be necessary to make adjustments to the code examples shown here.

Using Floats

The markup and styles in this example produce a page with a header area, a main column of content, a sidebar of links, and a footer for copyright information, as shown in Figure 24-2.

This markup provides the necessary elements for the two-column layout. The masthead and footer are optional and could be omitted for a minimal two-column structure.

```
<div class="masthead">
Masthead and headline
</div>

<div class="main">
Main article
</div>

<div class="sidebar">
list of links
```

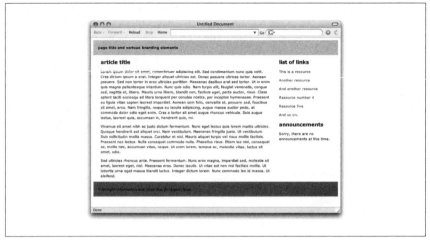

Figure 24-2. Two-column layout

```
</div>

<div class="footer">
copyright information
</div>
```

The source document has been divided into four divs, one each for the masthead, content, sidebar, and footer. The content has been placed before the sidebar in the source document so that it is accessed first by users with non-graphical browsers. That means that we can't float the sidebar because it will not float above the preceding block element to the top of the page. Instead, the main content div is floated to the left and set to 70% of the page width, and the sidebar div flows around it. The style rules that take care of the floating are provided here:

```
.masthead {
    background: #CCC;
    padding: 15px;}

.main {
    float: left;
    width: 70%;
    margin-right: 3%; /* adds space between columns */
    margin-left: 3%; }

.footer {
    clear: left; /* starts the footer below the floated content */
    padding: 15px;
    background: #666;
}
```

A right margin is applied to the main content div to add some space between the columns. Padding and a border could be added as well to clarify the division between columns. Of course, this is just the minimal styling to set up the column framework. Additional styles would likely be added to format the content on the page.

Using Absolute Positioning

You can also use absolute positioning to create a multicolumn page. This method absolutely positions the sidebar div element in its place on the right side of the page and gives the main content div a right margin wide enough to make a space for the newly positioned box. With absolute positioning, the order of the source document is not as critical as it was in the float method, because boxes can be picked up and placed anywhere. However, absolutely positioned elements can overlap one another, which isn't an issue with floating.

This example starts with the same markup as before, but places the sidebar on the right using absolute positioning. The resulting layout is shown in Figure 24-3. Again, the masthead and footer elements could be omitted for a simple two-column format. This example uses percentage width values to create a fluid design that resizes with the browser window.

```
<div class="masthead">
Masthead and headline
</div>

<div class="main">
Main article...
</div>>

<div class="sidebar">
list of links
</div>

<div class="footer">
copyright information
</div>
```

Figure 24-3. Two-column layout with absolute positioning

This is the style sheet that positions the elements as shown in Figure 24-3. Comments throughout explain the effects of significant rules.

```
body {margin: 0; padding: 0;}  /* clears default spacing around the page */

.masthead {
    height: 70px;
    background: #CCC;}

.main {margin-right: 30%; /* makes room for the positioned sidebar */
    margin-left: 5%; }

.sidebar {
    position: absolute;
    top: 70px;    /* places the sidebar below the masthead */
    right: 0px;   /* places it against the right edge of the window */
    width: 25%;
    background: #EEE;}

.footer {
    padding: 15px;
    background: #666;
    margin-right: 30%; /* keeps the footer aligned with content */
    margin-left: 5%; }
```

Notice that in this example, the margins applied to the main content were also applied to the footer element. That is to prevent the footer from being overlapped by a long sidebar.

More Two-Column Layouts

These examples demonstrate the basics of formatting columns with CSS. For additional information, I recommend these online resources:

From Table Hacks to CSS Layout: A Web Designer's Journey, by Jeffrey Zeldman (*www.alistapart.com/articles/journey*)
Join Jeffrey Zeldman through the trials and tribulations of converting a table-based layout into a CSS-based design.

Creating Liquid Layouts with Negative Margins, by Ryan Brill (*www.alistapart. com/articles/negativemargins*)
In this demonstration, Ryan creates a two-column layout using negative margins to make way for the sidebar element. It is testament to the fact that CSS design problems come with many solutions.

Three-Column Layouts

Three-column layouts are fundamentally the same as the previous two-column examples; they just require some extra planning for the third column. These examples use length values instead of percentages to create fixed layouts. In addition, padding, borders, and margins are added in one of the examples, requiring a fix for a well-known browser bug. Browser bugs and fixes are briefly addressed here but are covered in detail in Chapter 25. Again, these examples assume that the main content column will be longer than the side columns, which of course, is not always the case in the real world. It may be necessary to make adjustments to these examples to make them work for your content, but they are a good push in the right direction.

Floating Three Columns

This example uses floated elements to create a three-column layout (a main content column flanked by left and right sidebars) with optional header and footer (Figure 24-4). The advantage of floating is that you can set the footer to start below the longest column without knowing its height ahead of time (usually not possible). Remember that with floating, the order that the elements appear in the source document is significant. To keep this example straightforward, the content div has been moved between the sidebar divs in the source.

Figure 24-4. Three-column layout using floats

The basic structure of the markup for the layout is shown here. In this example, all of the elements have been placed in a container div so the width of the entire layout can be specified. A border has been added to the container to reveal its edges.

```
<div id="container">

<div id="masthead">
Masthead and headline
</div>

<div id="links">
list of links
</div>

<div id="main">
```

```
Main article...
</div>>

<div id="news">
Announcements...
</div>

<div id="footer">
copyright information
</div>

</div>
```

The style sheet floats the links, main, and news div elements to the left. The result is that they accumulate against the left edge of the containing block, thus creating three columns. The clear:both property has been added to the footer to make sure it starts below all of the floated elements. Because there are no padding, border, or margin settings for each floated element, the sum of their widths is equal to the width of the outer container. Space within each content div could be added with margins or padding on the content elements (h1, p, etc.). Without further ado, the style sheet...

```
h1, p {margin: 6px 12px; }    /* adds space between columns */

#container {width: 700px; border: solid 1px; }

#masthead {
    background: #CCC;
    padding: 15px; }

#links {
    width: 150px;
    float: left;
    background: #EEE; }

#main {
    float: left;
    width: 400px; }

#news {
    float: left;
    width: 150px;
    background: #EEE; }

#footer {
    clear: both;    /* starts the footer below the floated content */
    padding: 15px;
    background: #666; }
```

Absolute Three-Column Positioning

Finally, this section demonstrates how to create a three-column layout with absolute positioning. The examples in this section start with the same markup used in

---

the previous examples, unless otherwise noted. Several variations will be demonstrated.

Positioning the sidebars

In this example, only the left and right sidebars are positioned. Margins are used on the remaining main content and footer elements to make room for the resulting column (Figure 24-5). The advantage here is that it is possible to keep the footer information below the content, although the footer still does not run across the whole bottom of the page as in the float example.

It should be noted that if the main content element were also positioned, it too would be removed from the document flow. This would cause the footer to float up to the top of the page. There are JavaScript workarounds for positioning a footer element below absolutely positioned elements, but they are beyond the scope of this chapter.

Figure 24-5. Positioning the sidebars only

The style sheet that makes this layout happen is provided here. Comments have been inserted to point out key style rule functions. The first thing to notice is that the container div has been relatively positioned (but not moved) to establish it as the containing block for its positioned descendant elements.

```
body {margin: 10px; padding: 10px; }

#container {
    position: relative;   /* establishes containing block */
    width: 700px;
    border: solid 1px; }   /* border added to show container edges */

#masthead {
    height: 70px;
    background: #CCC; }
```

```
#main {
    margin: 0 160px; }  /* makes space left and right for the sidebars */

#links {
    position: absolute;
    top: 70px;
    left: 0px;            /* positioned on left edge of container */
    width: 150px;
    background: #EEE; }

#news {
    position: absolute;
    top: 70px;
    right: 0px;           /* positioned on right edge of container */
    width: 150px;
    background: #EEE; }

#footer {
    margin: 0 160px;         /* same as content to make room left & right */
    padding: 15px;
    background: #666; }
```

Positioning three columns

In this example, all three columns are absolutely positioned. Background colors are included for the sidebars to indicate their size and position. The resulting layout (Figure 24-6) is slightly different from the previous example.

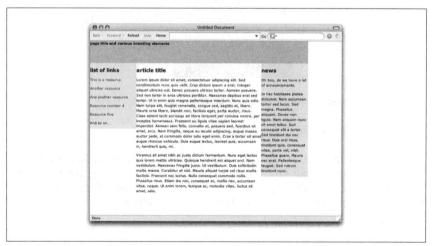

Figure 24-6. Absolutely positioning all three columns

You may notice that the footer and the rule around the page have been omitted. That is because when all three elements between the masthead and footer are absolutely positioned, they are removed from the document flow. That causes the footer to rise up to just below the masthead. Similarly, the rule around the container would only enclose the masthead and the footer at the top of the page, which is not the intended effect. To avoid complications that would require Java-Script and other complicated hacks, the footer and rule have been removed from this example.

This is the style sheet used to make this very basic three-column layout. Comments have been added to point out significant style rules and their functions.

```
body: {margin: 0; padding: 0; }

#container {
    position: relative; /* establishes the containing block */
    width: 700px; }

#masthead {
    height: 70px;
    background: #CCC; }

#main {
    position: absolute;
    top: 70px;
    left: 150px;       /* fixed design allows pixel length values */
    width: 400px; }

#links {
    position: absolute;
    top: 70px;
    left: 0px;       /* positioned against left edge of container */
    width: 150px;
    background: #EEE;
}

#news {
    position: absolute;
    top: 70px;
    left: 550px;     /* third column starts 550 pixels from left */
    width: 150px;
    background: #EEE;
}
```

Centering with borders and margins

The final three-column example improves on the previous absolute positioning example. First, padding, borders, and margins are added to the center column in a way that works for Internet Explorer 5 for Windows as well as current browsers. Then the entire layout is centered in the browser window using one of the techniques covered at the beginning of this chapter. The resulting layout is shown in Figure 24-7. Background colors have been added to the sidebar elements to reveal their size and position.

The source document hasn't changed, but there are three basic changes to the style sheet as pointed out in the comments and discussed in more detail following the example.

Figure 24-7. Adding padding, borders, and margins

```css
body {
    margin: 0px;
    padding: 0px;
    text-align: center; } /* to allow centering in IE */

#container {
    position: relative;  /* makes "container" the containing block */
    margin: 0 auto;        /* the proper CSS way to center */
    width: 700px;
    text-align: left; /* overrides text-align rule on body */
}

#masthead {
    height: 70px;
    background: #CCC; }

#main {
    position: absolute;
    top: 70px;
    left: 150px;
    width: 400px;
    border-left: solid 1px black;
    border-right: solid 1px black;
    margin: 0 10px;
    padding: 0 10px;
/* This is the box-model hack for IE 5 */
    voice-family: "\"}\"";
    voice-family:inherit;
    width:358px; }    /* provides the correct width value */

/* This is the "Be Nice to Opera" hack */
body>#main {width:358px; }
```

```
#links {
    position: absolute;
    top: 70px;
    left: 0px;
    width: 150px;
    background: #EEE; }

#news {
    position: absolute;
    top: 70px;
    left: 550px;
    width: 150px;
    background: #EEE; }
```

The changes are as follows:

Adding padding, borders, and margins to the "main" column

The sum of the widths of the three positioned column elements must equal 700 pixels (the width of the container in this example). Given that the sidebars take up 300 pixels of width (150 + 150), that allots 400 pixels to the center column.

Keep in mind that the width property is applied to the content area only. All padding, margins, and border amounts are added onto it according to the CSS box model (see Chapter 19). In this example, there is a total of 20 pixels of padding (10 pixels left and right), 20 pixels of margin, and 2 pixels of border. That means that we need to reduce the width of the element by 42 pixels to 358 (as specified in the final line of the #main style rule). There's more going on here related to element width, as explained next.

Setting a width for Internet Explorer 5 for Windows

IE 5/Windows incorrectly implements the box model and applies the width property to the outer edges of the element. To make the page display correctly in IE 5/Windows and all current browsers, we've added the well-known "Box Model Hack" to the style sheet. It works by supplying a width just for IE 5/Windows and then tricking IE 5/Windows into thinking the rule is over with a } value in the non-understood voice-family property. Then, when IE 5/Windows has stopped listening, the correct width value is provided for all compliant browsers. Because some older versions of Opera are also fooled by the Box Model Hack, the body>#main rule gets Opera back on track. These hacks are commonly used together.

 The Box Model Hack is discussed in more detail in Chapter 25.

Centering the layout in the window

The final adjustment made to the style sheet is to center the container element by setting its side margins to auto and including the text-align workaround for Internet Explorer. This centering technique is discussed at the beginning of the chapter.

Faux Columns

In the previous column examples, the background color ends at the bottom of the element box and does not extend to the bottom of the page. Unfortunately, there is no supported way of setting the height of an element to 100% of the height of the longest column without the use of JavaScript workarounds (which is beyond the scope of this book).

To get column backgrounds that fill the height of the page (or the containing element), you have to do a little trickery using a background graphic. The column shading in the example shown here was accomplished by setting a horizontal graphic with bands of color as a background image that is tiled vertically only. The result is stripes over which a multicolumn layout may be positioned. Of course, this works only with fixed-width layouts.

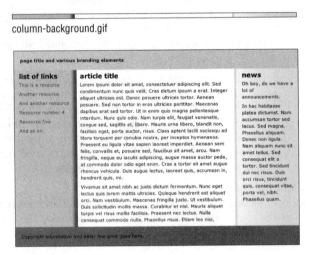

column-background.gif

This column background trick is courtesy of Dan Cederholm who documented it at *A List Apart* and in his book, *Web Standards Solutions* (Friends of Ed).

Boxes with Rounded Corners

Rounded corners are *de rigeur* in contemporary graphic design. Due to the rectangular nature of web design, there's no getting around using graphics for the rounded corners. But prior to CSS, the only option for creating an expanding box with rounded corners was to set up a nine-celled table. The same effect can be achieved using CSS styles and logical markup (and no tables, of course). As for most web design problems, there are many related solutions, the most simple of which are presented here. Other resources are listed at the end of this section.

Simple Rounded Box

The box in the first example creates a simple expandable rounded box filled with a solid color, as shown in Figure 24-8.

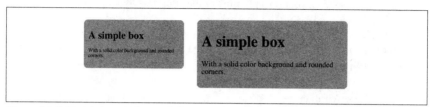

Figure 24-8. Simple box with rounded corners

 These separate images could be combined into a single image file and applied in varying positions to each corner of the box. The advantage is the need to load or preload only one image, as opposed to four. This technique is discussed in more detail in the upcoming "CSS Rollovers" section.

This technique takes four image files (one for each corner) and applies them as background images to four elements in the markup. Figure 24-9 shows each image file used in the example.

Figure 24-9. The corner graphics for the simple box

The trick is making sure that the markup has four available elements for background image placement. This is what CSS designers commonly refer to as finding *hooks* in the markup to which styles can be applied. If your document structure has fewer than four elements, it may be necessary to add a div or two to get the necessary number of hooks (see note below). This generic, all-purpose example is created entirely out of divs, but it is preferable to use actual elements that have been marked up semantically.

```
<div class="box">
    <div class="top">
        <div></div>
    </div>

    <div class="content">
            <h1>Header</h1>
            <p>The content goes here</p>
    </div>

    <div class="bottom">
        <div></div>
    </div>
</div>
```

Adding meaningless empty elements damages the semantic integrity of the source document and is generally frowned upon. Still, it may be necessary to achieve certain visual effects. As a designer and developer, you need to consider the trade-offs and implement a solution based on your own priorities or the priorities of your project.

The style sheet shown here applies background images to each of the top and bottom divs and the divs they contain. The background of the whole box is set to a matching RGB value in this example, but it could also be a small tiling image to ensure the color matches exactly.

```
/* set background images for corners */
.box { background: #CCC; }  /* could also use a repeating image */
.top div { background: url(top_left.gif) no-repeat top left; }
.top     { background: url(top_right.gif) no-repeat top right; }
.bottom div  { background: url(bottom_left.gif) no-repeat bottom left; }
.bottom      { background: url(bottom_right.gif) no-repeat bottom right; }

/* height and width details */
/* each image-holding div is set to the full width of the container */
.top div, .top, .bottom div, .bottom {
    width: 100%;
    height: 14px; /* match the width of your corner graphic */
    font-size: 1px;
}
.content  { margin: 0 14px; } /* match the width of your corner graphic */
.box { width: 20em; }        /* the box can be any width */
```

This markup and style sheet was adapted with permission from an article by Douglas Livingstone. See the original tutorial and additional CSS tests at *www.redmelon.net.*

The Future of Background Images

The CSS Level 3 specification allows multiple background images to be applied to different locations within a single element. This would greatly simplify the markup required to create the expanding box in the previous example, because the images could be applied to a single containing element. As of this writing, multiple background images are supported only in the Macintosh Safari browser, but one day, it will be a useful tool that offers to greatly reduce the amount of non-semantic markup required for visual effects.

Fancier Boxes

If your design calls for more graphical embellishments on the edges of the box, yet you still need the box to be expandable, then a slightly different approach is in order. This example produces the expanding box style shown in Figure 24-10.

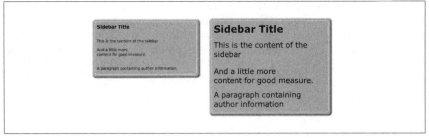

Figure 24-10. Fancier box edges

To achieve graphic effects on all four sides of the box, we start with the set of images shown in Figure 24-11.

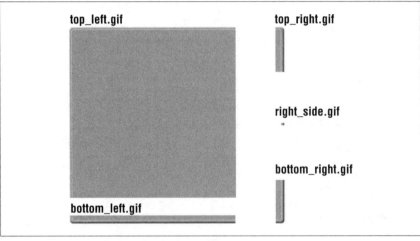

Figure 24-11. Image elements for the fancier box

In this example, the markup must provide five hooks for background image styles. Instead of all divs, this time, we'll take advantage of the existing h2 and p elements in the markup and add divs only as needed. This is the markup used in the example.

```
<div class="sidebar">
  <h2>Sidebar Title</h2>

  <div class="content">
    <p>This is the content of the sidebar</p>

    <p>And a little more<br />content for good measure.</p>
  </div>

  <div class="footer">
    <p>A paragraph containing author information</p>
  </div>
</div>
```

The style sheet that pulls it all together applies images to the divs, the h2, and the paragraph (p) in the article footer. The style sheet also includes 2 em vertical margin shifts to compensate for a gap inserted by carriage returns in paragraphs. This measurement may need to change based on the font size and line height in your content, so be sure to test in several browsers, especially Internet Explorer. Note that this method is not supported by Netscape 4.

```
div.sidebar {
    background: url(top_left.gif) top left no-repeat;
    width:35%; }

div.sidebar h2 {
    background: url(top_right.gif) top right no-repeat;
    font-size:1.3em;
    padding:20px;
    margin:0; }

div.content {
    background: url(right_side.gif) top right repeat-y;
    margin:0;
    margin-top:-2em;
    padding:20px; }

div.footer {
    background: url(bottom_left.gif) bottom left no-repeat; }

div.footer p {
    background: url(bottom_right.gif) bottom right no-repeat;
    display: block;
    padding: 20px;
    padding-bottom: 30px;
    margin:-2em 0 0 0; }
```

 This example appears in the article "CSS Design: Creating Custom Corners & Borders" by Søren Madsen, published in *A List Apart*. It is included here by permission. I recommend reading the original text, which includes step-by-step explanations of how the styles were written, at *www.alistapart.com/articles/customcorners/*. While at *A List Apart*, see also Dan Cederholm's article related to expanding rounded boxes entitled "Mountaintop Corners" (*www.alistapart.com/articles/mountaintop/*).

Image Replacement

Web designers frustrated with typography limitations on the Web have been replacing text with inline images for more than a decade. The problem with swapping out real text, such as an h1 element, for an img is that the text is removed from the source document entirely. Providing alternative text improves accessibility, but it does not repair the damage to the semantic structure of the document. Not only that, in terms of site maintenance, it's preferable to control matters of presentation from the style sheet and leave the source free of purely decorative elements.

The year 2003 saw the dawn of CSS image replacement techniques that replace a text element with a background image specified in a style sheet. The text element itself is still present in the source document, but is prevented from displaying via some CSS sleight of hand. It should be noted that, as of this writing, there is no ideal solution for CSS image replacement, just different approaches and trade-offs. Most techniques rely on users being able to read the content in images when the text is hidden, which means users who have CSS turned on but images turned off (or who are simply waiting for images to load over a slow connection) are not well served. This problem remains to be solved.

This section introduces the most popular image replacement techniques as of the end of 2005, along with the advantages and disadvantages of each. To check in with the state of image replacement, see David Shea's (of Zen Garden fame) list and articles at *www.mezzoblue.com/tests/revised-image-replacement/*.

The Future of Image Replacement

In CSS Level 3, image replacement may be accomplished using the expanded capabilities of generated content. To replace an h1 element with an image in CSS 3, the rule would look like this;

```
h1 { content: url(headline.gif); }
```

Unfortunately, current browsers do not support this use of generated content well enough for it to be a viable option as of this writing. Hopefully, one day that will change and the image replacement trickery in this chapter will be a quaint blip in web design's past.

The Original (FIR)

The image replacement technique that started it all is the Fahrner Image Replacement (FIR) technique created by Todd Fahrner and popularized by Doug Bowman. (See the original article at *www.stopdesign.com/articles/replace_text/*.) It is now discouraged from use due to serious drawbacks (noted later), but it is included here both for historical purposes and because it so clearly illustrates the basic concepts of image replacement.

In FIR, the content of an element is wrapped in a span that is used to hide the text, while a background image is applied to the element and appears in its place. The markup goes like this:

```
<h1 id="header"><span>This is the headline.</span></h1>
```

The styles that hide the text and replace it with a background image are extremely straightforward.

```
#header {
    background: url(headline.gif) top left no-repeat;
```

```
        width: 240;
        height: 20; }
#header span { display: none; }
```

The fatal flaw of FIR is that, although the content of the h1 element is preserved in the source document, presumably ensuring its accessibility to all users and devices, it turns out that some screen readers will honor the display: none property and simply not read the element. So FIR fails the accessibility test (as tested and documented by accessibility specialist Joe Clark).

The other aspect of FIR that is generally frowned upon is that it requires the insertion of a meaningless span element into the source, which is considered to be "bad" markup.

Like most other IR techniques, this one won't work if for some reason a user can't see the images but has CSS support turned on in his browser (the "CSS-on/Images-off" scenario).

Leahy/Langridge Image Replacement (LIR)

This technique developed simultaneously by Seamus Leahy and Stuart Langridge hides the text by setting the height of the element to 0 (zero) and setting its text overflow to hidden. The background image is applied to the padding area, which has been set to the height of the image.

```
<h1 id="header">This is the headline.</h1>

#header {
/* background image shows through top padding, set to image height */
    padding: 20px 0 0 0;
    overflow: hidden;
    background-image: url(headline.gif);
    background-repeat: no-repeat;
    height: 0px !important;
/* this is the IE Explorer hack */
    height /**/: 20px;
}
```

This method offers the following advantages:

- No extra span element
- Screen reader–accessible

Disadvantages include the following:

- It requires a hack to overcome box model problems in Internet Explorer 5 for Windows. Internet Explorer ignores the !important rule (because it doesn't support !important) and overrides it with the second height declaration. Compliant browsers recognize and enforce the first height declaration and ignore the second.
- It won't work under the CSS-on/Images-off scenario.

The Rundle/Phark Technique

This technique was developed by Mike Rundle for use on his Phark site. It hides the element text by setting an extremely large negative text-indent that pushes the text off the screen to the left where it can't be seen.

```
<h1 id="header">This is the headline.</h1>

#header {
    height: 20px;
    text-indent: -5000px;
    background: url(headline.gif) no-repeat;
}
```

This method offers the following advantages:

- No extra span element.
- Screen reader–accessible.
- It doesn't use any hacks.

Disadvantages include the following:

- It causes problems in Internet Explorer 5.0 for Windows (the background may be moved with the text).
- It won't work under the CSS-on/Images-off scenario.
- Some search engines look down upon pages that use large negative text-indent values.

The Gilder/Levin Method

This technique, named after Tom Gilder and Levin Alexander, is a bit different than the others in that it displays the text but immediately covers it up with an opaque image placed in an empty span. This is the only image replacement technique that does not suffer from the CSS-on/Images-off accessibility issue.

```
<h1 id="header">
    <span></span>This is the Headline
</h1>

#header {
    width: 240px;
    height: 20px;
    position: relative; }  */ makes this the containing block */

#header span {
    background: url(headline.gif) no-repeat;
    position: absolute;
    width: 100%;
    height: 100%; }
```

This method offers the following advantages:

- Screen reader–accessible.
- The text displays if the image doesn't, solving the CSS-on/Images-off dilemma.

Disadvantages include the following:

- It uses a non-semantic empty span.
- Transparent images allow the text behind them to show through.
- Resizing text very large may allow the text to show around the image edges.

Which Should You Use?

Which image replacement technique you use (or whether you use one at all) depends upon your personal priorities and the priorities of your project or client. It might be that one method is appropriate for one site while a different method is appropriate for another.

If you require 100% accessibility, including for users without images, then the Gilder/Levin "cover-up" method is the only option. You'll have to sacrifice semantic purity of the document and allow an empty span. You'll have to stick with opaque images as well.

If you can live with the CSS-on/Images-off scenario, the Rundle/Phark method is the most popular among the standards-conscious designers as of this writing and works well in all browsers. The original FIR method is obsolete and should not be used due to fundamental accessibility issues.

CSS Rollovers

A *rollover* is a visual effect in which an item on the page changes when the pointer is placed over it. It has proven to be an effective interface device for indicating that a button or link is interactive and is ready to be clicked. Previously, it was necessary to use JavaScript to create rollover effects, but the same thing can be accomplished with CSS alone using the :hover pseudoclass selector.

It should be noted that Internet Explorer 6 (and earlier) does not support :hover on elements other than links (a), so this section focuses on text and image link rollovers. The good news is that IE 7 expands the use of :hover to apply to all elements.

Text Rollovers

A rollover can be used to change any aspect of an element's appearance. You can change the size or color of the text, its background color, its decoration, or virtually any property that can be used to style text. Figure 24-12 shows just a few examples. Styles are applied to the a element, and an alternate style is specified with the a:hover selector for the rollover state.

Remember, to work correctly, the pseudoclass selectors must appear in the style sheet in the following order: :link, :visited, :hover, :active (think LVHA, or "Love, Ha!").

In all three examples, the default link is set in gray text with its underline turned off using this rule.

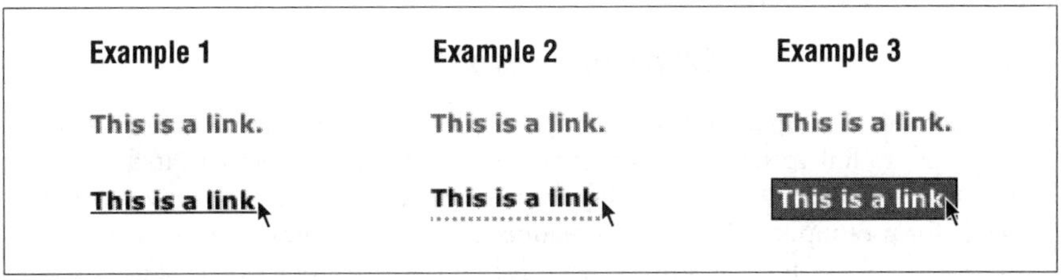

Example 1	Example 2	Example 3
This is a link.	This is a link.	This is a link.
This is a link.	This is a link.	This is a link.

Figure 24-12. Examples of text rollover effects on links

```
a:link {
    text-decoration: none;
    color: #666;
    }
```

In Example 1, the rollover changes the link to black and makes the underline appear.

```
a:hover {
    text-decoration: underline;
    color: #000; }
```

Example 2 demonstrates a popular technique of using a fancy bottom border instead of the generic underline. A little padding is added to give the link enough space.

```
a:hover {
    text-decoration: none;
    color: #000;
    padding-bottom: 2px;
    border-bottom: dotted 2px #999; }
```

In Example 3, both the foreground and background colors change on rollover. A border is thrown in for good measure.

```
a:hover {
    text-decoration: none;
    color: #FFF;
    padding: 2px;
    background-color: #666;
    border: solid 1px black; }
```

Image Rollovers

Image rollovers work on the same principle as described in the previous examples, only the value of background-image is changed for the hover state. Again, because Internet Explorer 6 and earlier support :hover on the a element only, a link is used in this example.

This example style sheet applies a background image (*button.gif*) to all links in a document. The a element is set to display as a block so that width and height values (matching the image dimensions) can be applied to it. The a:hover rule specifies a different background image (*button_over.gif*) to display when the mouse is over the link (Figure 24-13).

```
a {
    display: block;    /* allows width and height to be specified */
    width: 150px;
    height: 30px;
    background: url(button.gif) no-repeat #666;
    color: #FFF;
/* the next properties center the text horizontally and vertically*/
    text-align: center;
    text-decoration: none;
    line-height: 30px;
    vertical-align: middle;
    }

a:hover {
    background: url(button_over.gif) no-repeat #eee;
    color: #333; }
```

Figure 24-13. Simple image rollover

In some instances, such as graphical navigation bars, it is desirable for each link to have its own background and rollover images. In this case, it is necessary to give the containing elements unique identifiers.

```
<li id="info"><a href="#">more info</a></li>
<li id="contact"><a href="#">contact us</a></li>

a {display: block; width: 150px; height: 30px; }

#info a {background url(info.gif) no-repeat #666; }
```

```
#info a:hover {background url(info_over.gif) no-repeat #666; }

#contact a {background url(contact.gif) no-repeat #eee; }
#contact a:hover {background url(contact_over.gif) no-repeat #eee; }
```

Rollovers without preloading

Another popular method for handling image rollovers is known as the "Pixy No-Preload Rollover" technique introduced by Petr Staníček (aka "Pixy") in his article "Fast Rollovers without Preload" (*wellstyled.com/css-nopreload-rollovers. html*). In this method, all the rollover states are placed in one image, and only the background-position is changed for each link state. This avoids the need to load or preload multiple images for each rollover and can speed up display.

Figure 24-14 shows the image that contains both the default background image and the hover state. The style rule shifts the position of the initial background image down by the height of the element, revealing the appropriate portion of the image.

```
a { display: block;
    width: 150px;
    height: 30px;
    background: url(allbuttons.gif) top left no-repeat #666; }

a:hover {
    background url(allbuttons.gif) 30px left no-repeat #eee; }
```

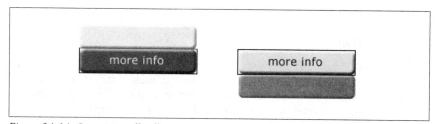

Figure 24-14. Containing all rollover states in one image

Applying background images and rollovers can cause a flickering effect in Internet Explorer on Windows. One solution is to apply the background image to both the link (a) and its containing element. For an in-depth look at this problem and possible solutions, see the article, "Minimize Flickering CSS Background Images in IE6" by Ryan Carver at *www.fivesevensix.com/studies/ie6flicker/*.

List-Based Navigation Bars

Horizontal navigation toolbars are a staple of web interface design. Traditionally, they were created with some number of adjacent text links or a line-up of images. Either way, there wasn't much meaning to their markup in the document source. When you think about it, it makes sense for a list of navigational options to be marked up as a list in the source. With CSS, it is possible to give it the appropriate semantic markup while visually presenting the options as a familiar horizontal bar.

There are two methods for changing a bulleted list into a horizontal navigation bar. The first makes the list items display inline instead of stacked (the default display mode for block elements). The second uses floats to line up the list items and links. Both examples below use this markup for an ordinary unordered (bulleted) list with five list items. Figure 24-15 shows how it looks using the default browser styles.

```
<ul id="nav">
    <li><a href="/">Water</a></li>
    <li><a href="/">Fire</a></li>
    <li><a href="/">Air</a></li>
    <li><a href="/">Earth</a></li>
    <li><a href="/">Beyond</a></li>
</ul>
```

- Water
- Fire
- Air
- Earth
- Beyond

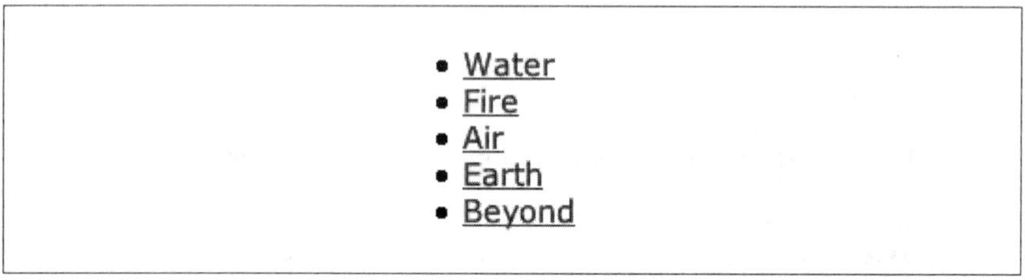

Figure 24-15. The unstyled list

Inline List Items

We'll start with the minimum style rules for removing the bullets (list-style-type: none) and making the list items appear next to each other instead of in a list (display: inline). The margins and padding are set to 0 to prepare for anchor (a) element styling. The results of the styles thus far are shown in Figure 24-16.

```
ul#nav {
    list-style-type: none;
    margin: 0px;
    padding: 0px; }

ul#nav li {
    display: inline; }
```

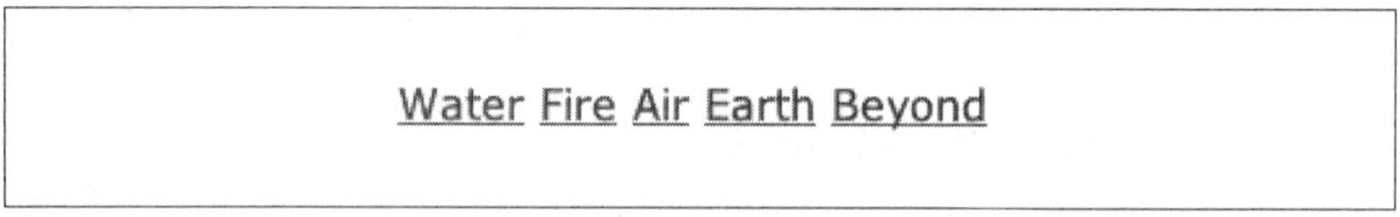

Water Fire Air Earth Beyond

Figure 24-16. Making a list display horizontally

With the pieces in place, you can then apply any style to the anchor (a) elements. In this example, the link underlines have been removed and a border, a background color, and padding have been added. An alternate style has been specified for the rollover state as demonstrated in the previous section. The resulting navigation list in Figure 24-17 is just one simple example of what can be done.

```
ul#nav li a {
    padding: 5px 20px;
    margin: 0px 2px;
    border: 1px solid #666;
    background-color: #CCC;
    text-decoration: none;
    text-align: center; }

ul#nav li a:hover {
    background-color: #333;
    color: #FFF;
```

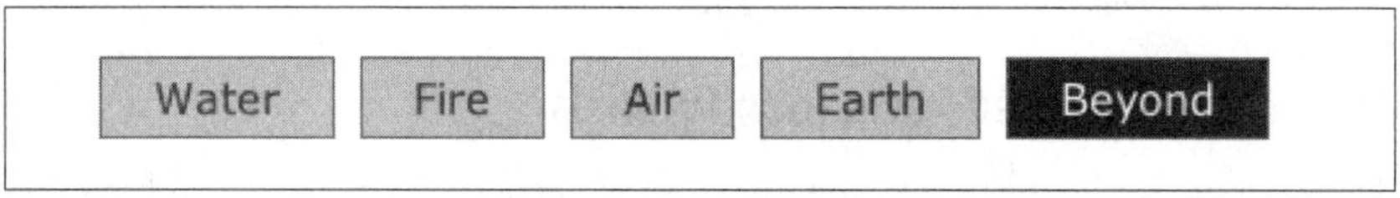

Figure 24-17. Adding styles to the inline list

Floated List Items

The other method for creating horizontal lists uses the `float` property to cause the list items to line up next to one another. When using `float`, it is important to set the following element in the source to `clear: both` to ensure that no page content wraps around the list.

This is just one of many variations on formatting navigation with floated list items. The primary steps are turning off the bullets (`list-style: none`), floating each list item (`float: left`), and then applying styles to the links (a) as block elements.

```
ul#nav {
    list-style: none;
    margin: 0;
    padding: 0; }

ul#nav li {
    float: left;
    margin: 0 2px;
    padding: 0; }

ul#nav li a {
    display: block;      /* allows width and height settings on a element  */
    float: left;         /* provided only to fix display in IE-Mac  */
    width: 100px;
    height: 28px;
    line-height: 28px;
    background: url(tab.gif) #CCC no-repeat;
    text-decoration: none;
    text-align: center; }

/* Commented backslash hack hides rule from IE5-Mac \*/
```

```
ul#nav li a { float: none; }
/* End IE5-Mac hack */

ul#nav li a:hover {
    background: url(tab_over.gif) #333 no-repeat;
    color: #FFF; }
```

This time instead of a solid background color, each link is styled with a background image that changes for rollovers, as shown in Figure 24-18.

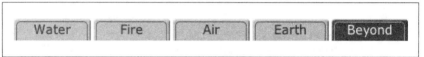

Figure 24-18. Tabbed navigation created with floated list items

More List and Tabbed Navigation Tutorials

The example in this section is only the most elementary introduction to how CSS can be used to create tabbed navigation from semantically logical list markup. For more sophisticated techniques and in-depth tutorials, these are just a few of the numerous resources online.

*"Sliding Doors of CSS (Parts I and II)," by Douglas Bowman (www.alistapart.com/
articles/slidingdoors and www.alistapart.com/articles/slidingdoors2)*
A problem with the floated list example above is that if a user resizes the text, it will bust out of the tab graphic. In this article, Doug Bowman introduces his ingenious technique for graphical tabs that resize larger with the text.

*"Accessible Image-Tab Rollovers," by David Shea (www.simplebits.com/notebook/
2003/09/30/accessible_imagetab_rollovers.html)*
This tutorial combines list-based tabbed navigation with image-replacement techniques.

*"CSS Design: Taming Lists" by Mark Newhouse (www.alistapart.com/stories/
taminglists)*
This article demonstrates a number of CSS tricks for controlling the presentation of lists, including various inline list item applications.

CSS Techniques Resources

With CSS (and a little know-how), you can make your page as hip, pretty, gothic, mod, or corporate as you like. It's limited only by your imagination. To see just how sophisticated CSS-based web design can be, I enthusiastically refer you to the CSS Zen Garden site at *www.csszengarden.com*. It is a showcase of stunningly varied designs, all based on the same marked-up XHTML document. The spin-off book, *The Zen of CSS Design: Visual Enlightenment for the Web* by Dave Shea and Molly E. Holzschlag (Peachpit Press) dissects design elements in 36 designs and demonstrates the CSS techniques behind them.

For more detailed demonstrations of what you can do with CSS, I recommend *Eric Meyer on CSS* and *More Eric Meyer on CSS*, written by (surprise) Eric Meyer (New Riders).

Another book that has served as a reference and inspiration for this chapter is *Web Standards Solutions: The Markup and Style Handbook* by Dan Cederholm (Friends of Ed).

There are also a number of online resources that offer CSS tips, techniques, and tutorials.

A List Apart (www.alistapart.com)
> *A List Apart* is the go-to source for articles on CSS and other web design matters. Their all-star contributing writers are authorities in all matters of web design.

Stopdesign (www.stopdesign.com)
> Doug Bowman is one of the top dogs in standards-based web design. His site offers useful tutorials and commentary on designing with CSS.

Mezzoblue (www.mezzoblue.com)
> This is the personal site of Dave Shea, the creator and cultivator of the CSS Zen Garden.

Meyerweb (www.meyerweb.com)
> The reigning king of CSS, Eric Meyer, publishes his tests, tricks, and tutorials here.

SimpleBits (www.simplebits.com)
> This is the personal and professional site of Dan Cederholm, a prominent web designer and the author of *Web Standards Solutions*.

css-discuss wiki (css-discuss.incutio.com)
> A "wiki" is a type of collaborative web site. This wiki is the companion to the popular *css-discuss* mailing list (*www.css-discuss.org*) and serves as a repository of CSS techniques and ideas generated by the *css-discuss* community.

25

Managing Browser Bugs: Workarounds, Hacks, and Filters

—by Aaron Gustafson

In an ideal world, software would be flawless, W3C Recommendations would be clear, and this chapter would never have to be written. Welcome to reality.

This chapter will address most of the common browser bugs you will encounter when designing with CSS and will help you quickly and easily wrangle those bugs into submission by using each browser's own misinterpretation or ignorance of the specs against them (in the form of *hacks* and *filters*). First, the chapter will tackle the buggy browsers on a per-browser basis and then, it will wrap with a hack management strategy that will make your life much easier, today and in the future.

Working with "Troubled" Browsers

Before getting into listing all of the problems that we, as CSS designers, have to deal with when it comes to browsers, it is important to take a step back and realize *why* we have browser bugs in the first place.

As anyone who has tried reading them can attest, the W3C specifications aren't exactly clear in many areas and they certainly are not a roadmap to implementation for browser manufacturers. In many cases, browser developers have to interpret what they read in the specs and try to make them work while simultaneously trying to get the browser out the door on time. In other cases, decisions have been made to deviate from the specs to make life "easier" for the designer or developer (see Internet Explorer's box model problem, later in this chapter).

We could spend countless hours discussing the problems with any one browser, but it's really best to take a step back and realize that no browser is perfect. Making yourself aware of each browser's inadequacies and figuring out what can be done (if anything) to overcome these problems is far more constructive. And this chapter will help you do exactly that.

The Browsers

This section will address the most common browsers and the hacks and filters that can be used to make sure they get the CSS rules they need (or don't get the ones they don't understand) to render pages appropriately. We'll start with some of the older browsers that are still kicking around and work toward modernity.

Netscape Navigator 4.x

Thankfully, this archaic browser is finally on its way out with less than 0.3% market share according to most statistics, and probably even lower by the time you read this. Originally launched in 1997, Netscape Navigator 4 (NN4.x) was an impressive browser. Needless to say, it hasn't aged all that well.

NN4.x's CSS support is pretty basic and, although some people still spend time designing for it, most sites do not get the kind of traffic that would warrant spending much time discussing its numerous issues. In fact, most CSS designers and web standards advocates have, instead, embraced the idea of "graceful degradation" and provide only the most rudimentary styling (mostly fonts and colors) to this outdated browser.

Be sure to consult your own site's browser statistics to decide when, and if, you need to degrade your design for a particular browser. Remember that percentages can be misleading: 0.3% of users who visit your personal photo gallery is likely to be a far cry from the same percentage visiting eBay. To make a design degrade gracefully for NN4.x, you need to serve it a simple style sheet and hide the stuff it doesn't understand. This is easily accomplished by using NN4.x's basic understanding of CSS against it in one of two ways. The first involves use of the @import rule, which is not understood by NN4.x:

```
<link rel="stylesheet" type="text/css" href="my_basic.css" />
<style type="text/css">@import(my_advanced.css)</style>
```

In the above example, NN4.x applies the first style sheet because it understands how to "link" a style sheet. The second style sheet it ignores, because Netscape has no idea what @import is.

For years, this was the preferred method of degrading designs for NN4.x, but it has the side effect of causing a flash of unstyled content (FOUC) in Internet Explorer on Windows if the head of the document does not contain any link or script elements. (For more information on the FOUC, visit *www.bluerobot.com/web/css/fouc.asp*.)

A new method has emerged for leaving NN4.x out in the cold involving media type assignment. NN4.x only understands the screen media type, so by adding additional media types to the link tag:

```
<link rel="stylesheet" type="text/css" media="screen,projection"
   href="my_advanced.css" />
```

you can easily avoid NN4.x, and get the added benefits of hiding your more advanced styles from many handheld devices, sidestepping the FOUC altogether.

Internet Explorer 5.x on Windows

When it comes to CSS hacks, Internet Explorer 5.x on Windows (IE 5.x/Win) really started it all. This browser version has caused many problems for CSS designers, and perhaps the worst was its flawed implementation of the *box model*, which led to the first CSS hack. We'll get to that hack in a moment, but first you should examine why it was created.

The W3C box model is perhaps best explained as *additive*. For example, the overall width of an element's "box" is the sum total of its border-left-width, padding-left, width, padding-right, and border-right-width. In contrast, the box model implemented by IE 5.x/Win, sometimes called the *border* box model, is *subtractive*. In this incorrect interpretation, the overall width of an element is the value set as its width, while the padding and border widths are subtracted from that.

Take a look at a simple example:

```
div {
    border: 5px;
    margin: 20px;
    padding: 20px;
    width: 200px;
}
```

To illustrate the vast ocean of difference between the two box models, consider Figure 25-1.

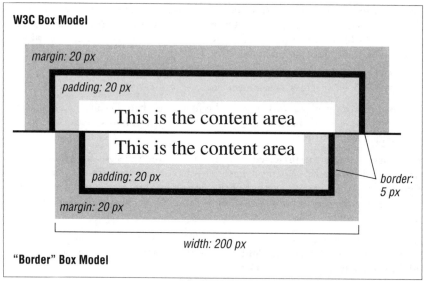

Figure 25-1. A comparison of the W3C and border box models

Clearly, this might present a problem, particularly with column-based layouts. In browsers that render according to the spec, the total width of the element's box is 250 pixels, or the following:

5px + 20px + 200px + 20px + 5px

The border box model would keep the overall width of the box at 200 pixels, squeezing the content—within the border and padding—into a mere 150 pixels, or:

200px – 5px – 20px – 20px – 5px

To get IE 5.x/Win to play well, Tantek Çelik, a Microsoft employee working on the Macintosh version of IE, invented something he dubbed the *Box Model Hack*. The hack uses the voice-family property (which is not supported by the browsers) along with some CSS-escaped quotes to trick IE 5.x/Win into thinking the declaration block has been closed. The following example demonstrates its use on a problem div:

```
div {
    border: 5px;
    margin: 20px;
    padding: 20px;
    width: 240px;          /* <-- 1 bad width fed to WinIE5.x     */
    voice-family: "\"}\""; /* <-- 2 WinIE5.x sees the end of the rule */
    voice-family: inherit; /* <-- 3 proper parsing browers reset here */
    width: 200px;          /* <-- 4 the real width                */
}
```

This hack caused a little problem in the Opera version available at the time (which, likewise, did not understand the voice-family property), newer versions of Opera do not have the problem, so you can safely ignore the old workaround.

More recently, Tantek devised an even better way to target these two problem browsers using what are called *filters*. Similar to how you hide styles from NN4.x, you can now *show* a particular style sheet to either of these two browsers. For example, to feed a specific style sheet to IE 5/Win, you would use the following @import within a style element in the head of your document or (better yet) within a linked or imported style sheet:

```
@media tty {
    i{content:"\";/*" "*/}}; @import 'hacks.pc.ie5.css'; {;}/*";}
}/* */
```

To do the same for IE 5.5/Win, you would use:

```
@media tty {
    i{content:"\";/*" "*/}}@m; @import 'hacks.pc.ie55.css'; /*";}
}/* */
```

In a volume such as this, we can't discuss the hows and whys of these filters, but, if you want to know more, visit Tantek's site at *www.tantek.com/CSS/Examples*.

Using filters such as these, you can keep your hacks separated from your proper CSS, which is the best way to manage CSS hacks over the long term, but more on that later.

Many of the browser issues encountered when dealing with IE 5.x/Win are also present in Internet Explorer 6, so the discussion can be found in that section. Also, if you are having trouble tracking down a computer old enough to still be running these browsers, you can download standalone versions from *browsers. evolt.org/?ie/32bit/standalone*. Now it's time to leave the Windows environment for a brief moment and check in with Internet Explorer's wiser (yet still buggy) counterpart on the Mac.

Internet Explorer 5.x on Macintosh

At the time, Internet Explorer 5 for Macintosh (IE 5.x/Mac) was tops for CSS-based design. IE 5/Mac's rendering code, dubbed The Tasman layout engine (which Tantek Çelik led the development of), was the first to offer complete support for CSS Level 1, HTML 4.01, PNG 1.0, as well as child and adjacent sibling selectors—pretty advanced stuff for 2000. That said, IE 5.x/Mac has its share of problems, too.

Many of IE 5.x/Mac's issues revolve around positioned elements and floats, resulting in unnecessary scrollbars, elements that are too wide, incorrect wrapping, and phantom margins. Though there are fairly straightforward workarounds for these bugs, some CSS designers have started to degrade their designs for IE 5.x/Mac as well. That said, there are many who continue to support IE 5.x/Mac to serve the numerous folks (often in public schools) using Macs that can only run Mac OS 9.x, where IE 5.1/Mac is the best browser they can use. Again, consulting your server logs is a good idea before dropping complete support for any browser.

 You can find a compendium of many IE 5.x/Mac bugs (as well as fixes for them) at *www.macedition.com/cb/ie5macbugs/index.html*.

There are a few different ways to hide CSS rules from IE 5.x/Mac. The first is known as the *Commented Backslash Hack* (*www.sam-i-am.com/work/sandbox/css/mac_ie5_hack.html*):

```
div {
    color: red;   /* <-- shown to IE5.x/Mac    backslash --> \*/
    color: green; /* <-- hidden from IE5.x/Mac    reset --> */
}
```

IE 5.x/Mac sees the backslash (\) and escapes the asterisk (*) in order to read it as a literal character, making it miss the close of the first comment. The browser assumes that everything that follows is still part of the comment and does not apply the rules. When it reaches the next comment, it sees the comment close normally and it assumes that to be the close of the original comment. Figure 25-2 gives a little better idea of how IE 5.x/Mac parses the above rule (minus the comments' contents) and how normal browsers parse it.

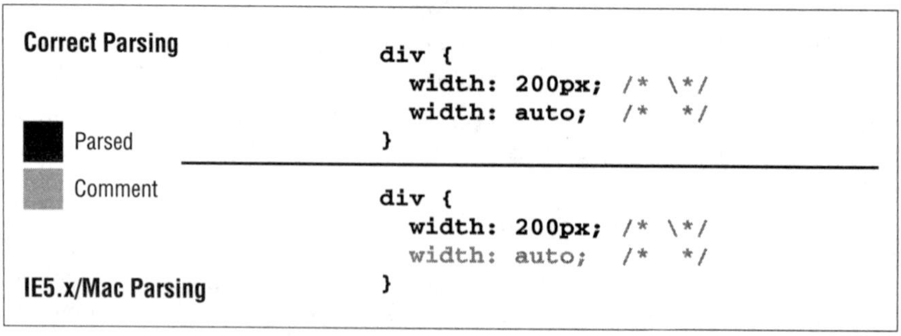

Correct Parsing

```
div {
    width: 200px;  /* \*/
    width: auto;   /* */
}
```

■ Parsed

▨ Comment

```
div {
    width: 200px;  /* \*/
    width: auto;   /* */
}
```

IE5.x/Mac Parsing

Figure 25-2. The correct interpretation of the Commented Backslash rule and the IE5.x/Mac interpretation

---

You also can exploit this particular bug in the IE 5.x/Mac parser to *show* certain styles (or an entire stylesheet) to that browser, as is the case with the IE 5/Mac *Band Pass Filter* developed by Tantek Çelik and documented by Douglas Bowman (*www.stopdesign.com/examples/ie5mac-bpf*):

```
/*\*//*/
  @import "hacks.mac.ie5.css";
/**/
```

This filter inverts the Commented Backslash Hack, showing the imported style sheet to IE 5.x/Mac and hiding it from every other browser. If your site needs to support IE 5.x/Mac, this is a very useful tool, allowing you to quarantine all the fixes this browser needs (see Table 25-1). Similarly, if you can get away with degrading your design in that browser, you can import the style sheet you want to hide from IE 5.x/Mac into the style sheet you want to show it.

 The W3C spec allows for an @import rule to receive a string or a URL as an argument. As the W3C recognizes strings as any value between either single or double quotes, it is perfectly legit to use any of the following three means of importing a style sheet:

```
@import "my.css";
@import 'test2.css';
@import url(my.css);
```

For example, in your document, you could add a linked style sheet:

```
<link rel="stylesheet" type="text/css" media="screen"
  href="simple.css" />
```

and then inside that linked style sheet, import another, more advanced style sheet, being careful to use single instead of double quotes:

```
@import 'test2.css'; /* <-- import for all other browsers */

/* The rules for IE5.x/Mac go here */
```

This particular filter does double duty, as it works to serve only the basic styles to NN4.x as well, so you can ensure consistency in your degraded site design.

Table 25-1. IE5.x/Mac bugs and fixes at a glance

Bug	Fix

Elements absolutely positioned to the right/bottom edge of the screen cause horizontal/vertical scrollbars:
<pre>div {
    position: absolute;
    bottom: 0;
    right: 0;
}</pre>
	Negate the hidden 15px margins:
	<pre>div {
	    right: 15px;
	    margin-right: -15px;
	    bottom: 15px;
	    margin-bottom: 15px;
	}</pre>

Shorthand margins will not center a table:
<pre>table {
    margin: 0 auto;
}</pre>
	Use longhand properties for setting the margins:
	<pre>table {
	    margin-left: auto;
	    margin-right: auto;
	}</pre>

Table 25-1. IE5.x/Mac bugs and fixes at a glance (continued)

Bug	Fix
An applied background-image is always positioned underneath the border of an element.	Use another element for the border if the border must be outside the background-image.
Use of overflow: auto can cause the page to expand to fit the entire contents of the element—even though part of it is hidden—creating scrollbars.	Always set width and height properties on any element on which you set overflow: auto.
clear is inherited into floated elements when the parent element has a clear value, even when the floated element is styled to clear: none.	No fix available.

Internet Explorer 6

This Windows-only browser is the bane of many a CSS designer's existence, mostly because its CSS parser and layout engine (Trident) has not seen an upgrade since the browser was released in late 2001. The major differences between Internet Explorer 6 (IE 6) and the IE 5 series for the PC (first introduced in 1999) were the inclusion of the DOCTYPE switch and the fixing of numerous CSS 1 bugs in "Standards mode."

Because IE 6/Windows's rendering engine has remained largely unchanged since its release, its bugs (see Table 25-2) are fairly well-documented and there are several ways to show/hide particular styles. You can find information about these bugs and more at *www.positioniseverything.net/explorer.html*.

To show a particular declaration block to IE 5+, you can use the *Tan Hack* (*www. info.com.ph/~etan/w3pantheon/style/starhtmlbug.html*) or as it is sometimes known, the * html (*Star HTML*) *Hack*:

```
div {
  color: green;
}
* html div { /* <-- will target IE5+ */
  color: red;
}
```

In any (X)HTML document, html is the root element (it has no parent). What the Tan Hack is essentially selecting is an element (in the example, a div) that is a descendant of html, which is a descendant of anything (using the universal selector: *). Theoretically, that is impossible to do, but IE 5+ apparently has an implied parent of the html element in its internal model, and that implied parent matches the initial *, making it a means for targeting particular rules to overcome its bugs.

It is possible to hide style rules from IE 5+/Win by using selectors that are not understood by the browser. A few examples are:

```
body>div#content {
  color: green;
}
div+div#content {
  color: green;
}
```

```
div[id='content'] {
  color: green;
}
```

All of the rules above use CSS 2 selectors (child, adjacent sibling, and attribute, respectively) that IE 5+/Win does not understand. In the interest of being forgiving (and somewhat forward compatible), when browsers encounter something they don't understand, they ignore it, so IE 5+/Win ignores all of the above rules.

Warning: whenever you use more advanced selectors (from CSS 2 or CSS 3) to hide rules from older browsers that don't support those selectors, make sure that the style rules you are writing are valid CSS (which you should always do anyway), and that the results you are expecting from those rules are in line with the specs. Don't use advanced selectors to send "fix up" style rules to non-compliant browsers.

When considering CSS hacks and filters, if at all possible, use them only for targeting older/obsolete/abandoned browsers. Avoid using hacks for current versions of browsers, as such code will likely break when those browsers are updated. With that in mind, Table 25-2 lists some IE 5+/Windows bugs and workarounds to consider.

Table 25-2. IE5+/Windows bugs and fixes at a glance

Bug	Fix
Content appearing alongside a floated element inside a box with `width: 100%;` will disappear (Peek-a-boo Bug; IE 6 only).	Apply `height: 1%` to the containing box (but hide it from IE 5.x/Mac): ```/**/ * html div {` ` height: 1%;` `}/**/``` This is known as the *Holly Hack*. It works by setting the height of a block to a small value (1% works almost universally). IE 5+/Win will make a box taller to fit the content (treating `height` like `min-height`) *and* trigger IE 5+/Win to behave as it should in many situations.
Disappearing backgrounds on lists (`dl`, `ol`, and `ul`) inside a block that is positioned relatively and floated.	Relatively position the offending list (but hide it from IE 5.x/Mac, which does not have this bug): ```/**/ * html ul {` ` position: relative;` `}/**/``` Although not technically a hack, using `position: relative;` can get you out of a lot of sticky situations with IE 5+/Win. There are many cases when you would not want to apply this rule, as it would create a new containing block where you might not want one, so use it sparingly.
The bottoms of floated elements are chopped off when certain links are hovered in the containing block (Guillotine Bug).	Apply the Holly Hack to the containing box.
An absolutely positioned element within a relatively positioned element has content that overflows off the bottom of the page without triggering scrollbars (Unscrollable Content Bug).	Apply the Holly Hack to the containing box.

Table 25-2. IE5+/Windows bugs and fixes at a glance (continued)

Bug	Fix
When multiple elements are floated alongside one another, text from the final float is occasionally duplicated below it. (See *www.positioniseverything. net/explorer/dup-characters.html*.)	Drop the width of the floated elements so they do not reach the edge of the container or make the `margin-right` on the final floated element in the row −3px or less.

Margins on the same side of a floated element as the direction it is floated are doubled:
 	
`div {`
`    float: left;`
`    margin-left: 100px;`
`}`
	Set the `display: inline;` on the floated element. According to the W3C, `display` should be ignored on floated elements unless its value is none (*www.w3. org/TR/CSS2/visuren.html#floats*).

There is a 3px gap between text in a block-level element and a floated element around which it flows (3 Pixel Jog Bug).	Apply the Holly Hack to the block-level element.
A block-level element that clears a float will have its `padding-top` doubled if the content flowing around the float does not go beyond the bottom of it (affects IE 5.5/6 for Windows).	Apply the Holly Hack to the block-level element that clears the float.
Anchors inside a relatively positioned container will lose their applied `background-image`.	Relatively position the anchors.
When a box with a `margin` is nested in a box with `padding`, the `margin-top` of the inner box and `padding-top` of the outer box are not added.	Double the `margin-top` on the inner box.
`class` or `id` names that begin with an underscore (_) are ignored.	Avoid using `class` or `id` names that begin with an underscore.
The `left` value of an absolutely positioned element is calculated with regard to the left edge of the first element in the containing block, not the left edge of the containing block itself (IE 5.5 and 6 for Windows).	Adjust the `left` value accordingly or position the containing block absolutely.
Margins applied to a table are ignored (IE 6 ignores margin altogether, IE 5.x/Win ignores only `margin-top` and `margin-bottom`).	Put the `table` inside a `div` and apply the margins to the `div` instead.

The Mozilla Family (Mozilla, Firefox, and Netscape)

Mozilla has always been a popular browser among Linux programmers, and while its latest incarnation, Firefox, was still in alpha, it began causing quite a stir in the CSS world due to advancements made to its layout engine, Gecko. At the time of Firefox 1.0's launch, Gecko was the layout engine rendering closest to the W3C specs and supported enough CSS 3 to make the hardcore CSS designers salivate. All browsers in the Mozilla family (Camino, Firefox, Mozilla, and Netscape) use Gecko.

 Netscape 8 (currently only available for Windows) allows the user to switch between the standard Gecko layout engine and the Trident layout engine from Internet Explorer. Also, America Online (AOL), the former parent of Mozilla, has released its own browser that sits on top of Internet Explorer 6.

Despite its best efforts, the Gecko engine still has a few quirks that need to be worked out (see Table 25-3), but, thankfully, they don't get in the way all that often. At the time of this writing, the Mozilla Foundation has released a beta of Firefox 1.5, and there have yet to be any new bugs discovered.

Table 25-3. Gecko bugs and fixes at a glance

Bug	Fix
`position: relative;` is not supported on `table` elements.	Wrap the `table` in another block-level element that can be positioned relatively, such as a `div`.
Any floated element following a heading (`h1`, `h2`, etc.) will be overlayed by the first line of text that should flow around it.	No fix available.

Safari

Safari is the Apple-built browser that began shipping with OS X 10.3 (Panther) in late 2003 and is now the default browser for Macintosh. It uses the WebCore layout engine, which is based on Konqueror's KHTML layout engine. Safari 2.0 (also known as Safari RSS) was released in 2005 along with OS X 10.4 (Tiger), just two days after David Hyatt, the lead developer on Safari, and his team managed to make Safari the first browser to pass the Web Standards Project's Acid2 test. Until Safari 2.0.2, which is just getting disseminated, no significant improvements to CSS handling or support had been made since Version 1.1, so that is what we will address here.

> The Acid2 test (*www.webstandards.org/act/acid2/*) was released in mid-April 2005 by the Web Standards Project as a way for makers of web browsers and web design tools to test their adherence to mature web standards. As of this writing, development versions of iCab and Konqueror have passed the test, and Opera should pass by the time this book publishes. On October 31, 2005, Safari 2.0.2 became the first publicly released, non-beta, non-preview browser to pass Acid2.
>
> Konqueror is the web browser and file manager/viewer part of the K Desktop Environment (KDE) and is quite popular on Linux/Unix operating systems. Currently, its market share is too small for it to be discussed here, but the developers are working to integrate much of the work on Safari's WebCore layout engine back into KHTML.

At this point in time, there are no reliable Safari filters or hacks and, with the release of the revised WebCore layout engine, the market share of the older Safari versions may drop off before any are invented. Likewise, although initial (1.x) versions of Safari had numerous bugs and quirks, as of Version 2.0+ there are relatively few layout bugs remaining in the Safari browser (see Table 25-4).

Table 25-4. Safari bugs and fixes at a glance

Bug	Fix

Setting the `display` property of a `fieldset` to `inline` will make form controls unclickable.
`fieldset {`
`    display: inline;`
`}`
	Position the `fieldset`:
	`fieldset {`
	`    display: inline;`
	`    position: relative;`
	`}`

Combining the `:hover` pseudoclass with an adjacent sibling in a selector causes erratic behavior.
`dt:hover+dd {`
`    color: green;`
`}`
	No fix available.

When the font size is enlarged, generated content can cause text to be pushed outside of its bounding box.	No fix available.

Opera

Historically, Opera has had a few CSS quirks, but the last few versions have been relatively stable. Market share for this browser has been low, yet steady. As of September 2005, with the release of Opera 8.5, the browser became free to the public (and free of ads), meaning its market share will likely increase. That same year, Opera made major inroads in the mobile market with Opera 8 and Opera Mini, making this a browser to watch closely.

As of this writing, Opera is readying Version 9 of its browser, which uses the Presto layout engine and is close to passing the Acid2 test. Versions 8 and 8.5 have very few bugs to speak of (see Table 25-5), making this browser very easy to support, and making filters and hacks unnecessary.

Table 25-5. Opera bugs and fixes at a glance

Bug	Fix

Using the `border-width` property on a block absolutely positioned to the bottom of its container will result in a `padding-bottom` equal to the `border-top` value (affects Opera 7.5–8.5).
`div {`
`    position: absolute;`
`    bottom: 0;`
`    border: solid #000;`
`    border-width: 20px 10px 10px 5px;`
`}`
	Set different border widths via the individual `border-width-*` properties:
	`div {`
	`    position: absolute;`
	`    bottom: 0;`
	`    border: 10px solid #000;`
	`    border-top-width: 20px;`
	`    border-left-width: 5px;`
	`}`

Combining the `:hover` pseudoclass with an adjacent sibling in a selector doesn't work.
`dt:hover+dd {`
`    color: green;`
`}`
	No fix available.

When inside a containing block that is positioned on a page by `text-align: center` or `text-align: right`, an absolutely positioned element will be positioned based on where the containing block *would have been* if it were not affected by the text alignment.	No fix available.

Hack and Workaround Management 101

Now that your head is spinning with all of the browser hacks and workarounds needed to make most of the modern browsers fall in line, it's time to bring some order to the chaos. In the browser world, change is steady, if not rapid. You need to plan for the future and for the eventuality of "retiring" certain browsers. You need to craft a strategy for long-term hack management.

Molly E. Holzschlag wrote an excellent article on long-term hack management for *InformIT* called "Integrated Web Design: Strategies for Long-Term CSS Hack Management," which you can find at *www.informit.com/articles/article. asp?p=170511&rl=1.* As her article outlines, you can manage the use of browser hacks and workarounds by making deliberate and thoughtful choices about what hacks you use and how you integrate them with the rest of your CSS. How might you organize your screen media CSS for a site that has the following requirements?

- Full support for IE 5.5+/Win, Netscape 7.1+, Firefox, Safari, and Opera
- Degraded support for NN4.x (typography) and IE 5.x/Mac (typography and color)
- Easy-to-add/change the color information for the site

Sometimes drawing the page out on paper gives the clearest picture. Figure 25-3 outlines one way you might address the requirements.

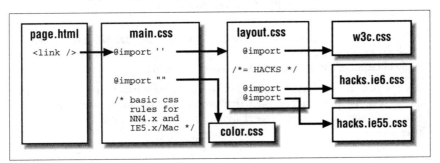

Figure 25-3. A basic outline of CSS file and rule management

If you start on the left with the (X)HTML page, you see this link to a single CSS file (*main.css*)

```
<link rel="stylesheet" type="text/css" media="screen" href="main.css" />
```

That file includes the basic rules you want to show NN4.x and IE 5.x/Mac as well as two @import rules. The first @import uses single quotes (') to hide the import of *layout.css* from IE 5.x/Mac; the second uses double quotes (") to allow IE 5.x/Mac to see the *color.css* file.

```
/*--------------------------------------------
Main CSS for MySite.com
----------------------------------------*/

/* =LAYOUT (HIDDEN FROM IE5.x/MAC USING ') */
```

```
@import 'layout.css';

/* =COLOR */
@import "color.css";

/* =START CSS FOR TYPOGRAPHY */
```

Continuing along the outline brings you to the *layout.css* file, which contains a series of @import rules but little else. Here is how that file might look:

```
/*----------------------------------------------
Layout CSS for MySite.com
Notes: This file links to the other files
       we need for layout
---------------------------------------------*/

/* =W3C COMPLIANT BROWSERS */
@import "/css/w3c.css";

/*----------------------------------------------
                HACKS & WORKAROUNDS
---------------------------------------------*/
/* =IE 6 (ALL RULES BEGIN * html) */
@import "hacks.ie6.css";
/* =IE 5.5 (FILTER) */
@media tty {
   i{content:"\";/*" "*/}}@m; @import 'hacks.ie55.css'; /*";}
}/* */
```

Notice how much commenting there is.* This ensures that whoever views this file—be it a colleague, client, or a new developer on the project—sees and immediately understands what is going on at any given point.

Now imagine the site has launched and you see a large influx of users on IE 5.x/ Mac, so a decision is made to offer that browser full layout support. Adding it in becomes a snap: you change @import for the *layout.css* file to use double instead of single quotes:

```
/* =LAYOUT */
@import "layout.css";
```

and add the IE 5.x/Mac Band Pass filter under the "Hacks & Workarounds" heading:

```
/*----------------------------------------------
                HACKS & WORKAROUNDS
---------------------------------------------*/
/* =IE6 (ALL RULES BEGIN * html) */
@import "hacks.ie6.css";
/* =IE5.5 (FILTER) */
@media tty {
   i{content:"\";/*" "*/}}@m; @import 'hacks.ie55.css'; /*";}
```

---

* These code samples also make use of Douglas Bowman's CSS comment flags (*www.stopdesign. com/log/2005/05/03/css-tip-flags.html*).

```
}/* */
/* =IE5.x/Mac (FILTER) */
/*\*//*/
  @import "hacks.mac.ie5.css";
/**/
```

Similarly, if the stats showed IE 5.5/Win was not being used and, therefore, not worth supporting anymore, you might simply drop the IE 5.5 filter block altogether.

By organizing your files using this technique (a technique Tantek Çelik dubbed *surgical correction*), you can save yourself some grief later. You won't need to hunt through hundreds of lines of CSS looking for a hack you used for a particular problem browser when you no longer need to support it. With your CSS neatly organized and prepared, you can easily remove hacks once they become obsolete, leaving behind clean, hack-free CSS, which is ideal.

IV

The Behavioral Layer: JavaScript and the DOM

26

Introduction to JavaScript

—by Aaron Gustafson

A web page that is semantically marked up and beautifully designed (with CSS, of course) is wonderful, but to really make it an *experience*, it needs some interactivity. This is what we call the "behavior layer" and, in most cases, it is made possible through use of a technology called JavaScript. This chapter will walk you through a little history of the JavaScript language and then discuss the basic building blocks of modern JavaScript.

A Little Background

JavaScript is an object- and prototype-based programming language that got its start in 1995 as the creation of Brendan Eich at Netscape. It was originally named "Mocha" and then "LiveScript" before being confusingly re-christened JavaScript in conjunction with its release in Netscape Navigator 2.0 Beta 3 in December of 1995.

It is important to note that JavaScript is not Java. Both are similar to the C programming language and share a similar syntax, but that is pretty much where their similarity ends. The Java programming language was creating quite a stir in the computer world when Netscape was readying LiveScript for release, and, somehow, the decision was made to rename the language JavaScript to cash in on some of the buzz. Unfortunately, it did more to confuse the programming world than it did to improve the popularity of JavaScript.

JavaScript was standardized in 1996 when it was turned over to the European Computer Manufacturer's Association (ECMA) for maintenance and further development. The latest version, JavaScript 1.5, arrived in 1999 and corresponds to ECMA-262 Edition 3. Consequently, JavaScript is sometimes referred to as ECMAScript.

Microsoft offers a competing language, VBScript, based on Visual Basic, but as it is only supported in Internet Explorer, it is a poor choice for the Web. It should also be noted that Microsoft offered its own port of JavaScript, JScript, which supports most of the standard JavaScript functions (albeit in sometimes peculiar ways) and extends some functionality, but, again, only for Internet Explorer.

JavaScript does have uses beyond the browser as well. It is available in PDF documents, is a primary driver in the Mozilla platform, and even powers the Dashboard Widgets in Apple's Mac OS X 10.4 (Tiger). Using JavaScript outside of a web context is beyond the scope of this chapter, but there are many resources online if you are interested in exploring.

One thing to keep in mind about JavaScript is that it is a *client-side* scripting language, which means it runs on the client's machine and not on the server. This is an important distinction as it means its implementation depends on the capabilities and settings of the browser viewing the page. That is why, before we get into the nuts and bolts of *writing* JavaScript, we should talk about the best ways to *use* JavaScript.

Using JavaScript

Like many tools, JavaScript can be used for good or evil. The evil uses of JavaScript are all around: rapid-fire pop-ups that open faster than you can close them, sites that automatically set themselves as your home page, the list goes on and on. If that's what you're interested in doing, please stop reading now.

JavaScript Dos and Don'ts

As web professionals, we have a duty to make the user experience as positive as possible and make our sites both usable and accessible. We always need to consider how our choices as programmers impact our users. Not only should we not wield JavaScript maliciously, but we should take care to use it in such a way that a page or site can be used without it.

What? No JavaScript?!

There are many situations in which users may not have JavaScript turned on, even if their browser supports it. In many corporate environments, security concerns around web browsers have led to JavaScript being disabled. Also, several accessibility experts have advocated for users of assistive devices (such as screen readers) to disable JavaScript because of the massive amount of *obtrusive* JavaScript in use that makes it difficult for them to easily navigate and use the Web.

As with CSS, JavaScript should "degrade gracefully," in other words, your scripts should be written in such a way that they know if they will be able to run or not and quietly fail if methods they make use of are not supported. It is also important, for many reasons, including accessibility, that your scripts be unobtrusive.

This is easily tested by turning off JavaScript support entirely in your browser to make sure the page can still be used.

This is a topic that will be touched on several times throughout this chapter and the next, but we'll begin by discussing how to use JavaScript in your pages.

Implementation Methods

JavaScript can be implemented on a single page or on an entire site. As with CSS, it can be embedded in a document, or externalized from that document. Both methods are accomplished using the script element.

We'll start with an embedded example:

```
<script type="text/javascript">
// <![CDATA[
... JavaScript code goes here ...
// ]]>
</script>
```

As you can see, the script element establishes the block as being a script and the MIME-type is set (using the type attribute) to be text/javascript (text/ecmascript would also be acceptable).

The // <![CDATA[and //]]> may be unfamiliar to you, but you can find out more about CDATA in Chapter 7. As for the //, which you see in front of each part of the CDATA designation, those are one of the ways of designating comments in Java-Script, and we are telling the script above to ignore the remainder of each of those lines.

Externalizing your JavaScript is the preferred method of implementation, as it affords you the opportunity to include the same functions or functionality on multiple pages (and you can avoid declaring the content as CDATA). Here is how you would externalize a script:

```
<script type="text/javascript" src="my_script.js"></script>
```

In this example, we have moved our JavaScript into a separate file and simply included it in our document by calling its filename as the source (src) of the script element. You can include as many scripts as you like in this way and even combine this approach with embedded script calls, as in this example from Google Analytics (*www.google.com/analytics/*):

```
<script src="http://www.google-analytics.com/urchin.js"
  type="text/javascript"></script>
<script type="text/javascript">
// <![CDATA[
_uacct = "UA-XXXXXX-X";
urchinTracker();
// ]]>
</script>
```

The external script resides on the Google server and is the same for everyone using Google Analytics. The embedded script establishes the user account (the _uacct variable) and then triggers the urchinTracker function to run.

It is recommended that you keep `script` elements in a common area in the head of your (X)HTML pages. This is more out of convention and maintainability than anything else. After all, who wants to have to hunt for a `script` within a several hundred- or thousand-line document? That said, `script` is perfectly valid within the body as well.

JavaScript Syntax

Once you get the hang of it, JavaScript can be a very easy language to write. In fact, it is very similar to other common web languages, including ActionScript (which is itself an ECMA scripting language and is the underlying language of Flash) and PHP (which is a server-side scripting language). We'll begin with the basics of syntax.

Statements

Each script we write consists of a series of statements. Statements can be terminated with a line break

```
first statement
second statement
```

or with a semicolon (;)

```
first statement; second statement;
```

For readability, and to avoid potential statement termination problems, it is recommended that you use both:

```
first statement;
second statement;
```

File Size Versus Readability

Using whitespace to improve readability does have one drawback: increased file size. Each whitespace character (tab, space, carriage return, or newline) is still a character in the document. With lots of whitespace (and comments, for that matter), a script file can get quite large.

To balance the need for whitespace and comments for legibility and the desire for fast downloads, many JavaScript developers keep two copies of every script they work on: a "working" copy with whitespace intact and a production version, which is "compressed" by stripping out all unnecessary whitespace and comments.

Comments

Sometimes it is helpful to make notes for yourself to keep track of what is going on in a script. As in HTML, JavaScript allows you to make comments in your code but offers a few different ways to do it. The first style of comment uses two forward slashes:

```
// this is a comment
```

This type of comment makes the interpreter ignore the remainder of the line. The second method allows you to comment out multiple lines:

```
/* this is a multi-line
   or block comment */
```

Apart from using comments to make notes to yourself, they are also quite useful in the debugging process: if you can't seem to figure out where an error is coming from, you can comment out a line or section of the code to see if it is the culprit.

Variables

Though not a strictly typed language, in JavaScript, you still need to declare variables before you begin using them. That said, you have a lot of flexibility in how you name and declare your variables.

Variables are declared using the reserved keyword var. Variable names can be any length and contain numbers, letters, and certain non-alphanumerics. Arithmetic operators (+, -, *, /) and quotes (' and ") need to be avoided in variable names. You also need to watch that your variable names do not conflict with JavaScript's reserved keywords (this, for, function, etc.). A text editor with a good syntax highlighter should help you avoid those pitfalls.

Variable names can be written in numerous cases and styles. And as JavaScript is case-sensitive, each of the following would be a unique variable:

```
var MYVAR;  // uppercase
var myvar;  // lowercase
var myVar;  // camel case
var MyVar;  // initial caps
var MyVaR;  // mixed case
```

It is common practice to separate words in multiword variable (or function) names with an underscore or to write them in "camelCase":

```
var my_cat;
var myCat;
```

You may consider writing all variables using one convention and all function names using the other to make it easier to distinguish them at a glance:

```
var my_variable;
function myFunction(){ ... }
```

Variables can also have their values assigned when they are declared:

```
var cat = 'Sabine';
```

or not:

```
var cat;
```

You can also declare multiple variables (again with or without value assignment) simultaneously:

```
var girl_cat = 'Sabine', boy_cat = 'Dakota', tortoise;
```

Data Types

JavaScript variables can be one of several different data types. Those data types fall into two different categories: scalars and arrays. *Scalar* variables have one value at a time. That value can be a string, a number, or a Boolean. *Arrays* can contain multiple values. We will discuss each type in turn.

Strings

Strings are enclosed by either single (') or double (") quotes and can contain zero or more characters:

```
var empty    = '';
var girl_cat = 'Sabine';
var boy_cat  = "Dakota";
var zip_code = '06517';
```

Your string can also contain quotes, but you need to be careful to escape any quotes that match the quotes you are using to enclose your string:

```
var my_string = 'This "quoted text" is fine';
    my_string = "This 'quoted text' is fine";
    my_string = 'This string\'s "quote" is escaped';
    my_string = "This string's \"quotes\" are escaped";
```

It can get a little confusing if you don't maintain some form of consistency. Most JavaScript developers tend to use single quotes to wrap strings. This is likely a holdover from other languages where double-quoted strings are processed differently than single-quoted ones.

Numbers

Numeric values are pretty self-explanatory, but here are a few examples

```
var my_age    = 28;
var birth_year = 1977;
var negNum    = -1.9304;
```

Booleans

Booleans are true/false values. They can be represented by the keywords `true` or `false` (without quotes around them) or the numbers 1 and 0, respectively:

```
var bald    = false; // I am not bald (yet -- fingers crossed)
var bearded = 1;     // I do have a beard
```

Arrays

Arrays allow you to group multiple values (called *members*) in a single variable. Standard array values are numerically indexed beginning with 0 and counting upward. They can be declared in a few different ways as well:

```
var array_1 = new Array( );  // empty array
var array_2 = new Array(2); // array with two undefined members
var array_3 = [];            // shorthand empty array
```

As with scalars, an array's values can be set when it is declared:

```
var cats  = new Array( 'Sabine', 'Dakota' );
var names = [ 'Aaron', 'Kelly' ];
```

or the values can be assigned afterward:

```
var cats  = new Array( );
cats[0]   = 'Sabine';
cats[1]   = 'Dakota';
```

An array can contain any sort of data in its members:

```
var sabine  = [ 'cat', 'female', 9, true ];
// Sabine is a 9-year-old female cat that is spayed
```

even other arrays:

```
var cats = new Array( 2 );
cats[0]  = [ 'Sabine', 'cat', 'female', 9, true ];
cats[1]  = [ 'Dakota', 'cat', 'male',   8, true ];
```

An array member can also have its value assigned by a variable:

```
var cats   = new Array( 2 );
var sabine = [ 'cat', 'female', 9, true ];
var dakota = [ 'cat', 'male',   8, true ];
cats[0] = sabine;
cats[1] = dakota;
```

Associative arrays are a specialized form of array (sometimes referred to as a "hash") that use keywords as their indexes. The following example uses a few different forms of arrays and scalars:

```
var cats = new Array( 2 );
cats['sabine'] = [ 'cat', 'female', 9, true ];
cats['dakota'] = [ 'cat', 'male',   8, true ];
var reps = [];
reps['sheldon'] = [ 'tortoise', 'male', 5, false ]
var animals = [];
animals['cats'] = cats;
animals['reptiles'] = reps;
```

Got all that? If not, here's a little translation:

- We establish the variable cats as an array with two members.
- The first member is indexed as sabine and is, itself, an array of mixed data about her.
- The second member is indexed as dakota and is an array of mixed data about him.

- We then declare a new array (using shorthand) called reps and create a member indexed as sheldon containing mixed data about him.
- Finally, we declare an array called animals and assign the variables cats and reps to be members of that array, indexed as cats and reptiles, respectively.

Operators

There are two categories of operators in JavaScript, arithmetic (or mathematical) and comparison.

Arithmetic operators

As you can probably guess, arithmetic operators are used to perform mathematical functions:

```
var add      = 1 + 1;   // 2
var subtract = 7 - 3;   // 4
var multiply = 2.5 * 2; // 5
var divide   = 4 / 2;   // 2
```

These arithmetic operators can also be applied to variables with numeric values:

```
var my_num  = 1 + 1;                 // 2
var new_num = my_num * 5;            // 10
var my_arr  = Array( 2, new_num );   // an array of numeric values
var big_num = my_arr[0] * my_arr[1]; // 20
```

In addition to *addition*, the + operator has another purpose: concatenation. Concatenation is the combining of two or more values into a new value. It is usually applied to strings:

```
var sentence = 'This is one phrase' + ' ' +
               'and this is another' + '.';
```

but also applies to combining numbers and strings:

```
var new_str = 10 + '20'; // '1020'
```

 When concatenating numbers with strings, the result is *always a string*.

There are also a few shorthand arithmetic operators you can use in specific cases, such as having a string or number add to itself:

```
var str  = 'Hello there';
    str += ', pilgrim.';  // 'Hello there, pilgrim.'
var num  = 2;
    num += 2;             // 4
```

There is a shorthand for incrementing or decrementing a number by one:

```
var num = 2;
    num++;  // 3
    num--;  // 2
```

Comparison operators

The other type of operators available in JavaScript are comparison operators. They are used to make assertions about the equality of two values (see Table 26-1).

Table 26-1. Comparison operators for equality

Operator	Meaning
>	Greater than
<	Less than
==	Equal to
!=	Not equal to
>=	Greater than or equal to
<=	Less than or equal to

There are also comparison operators that are used to assert identity (see Table 26-2).

Table 26-2. Comparison operators for identity

Operator	Meaning
===	Identical to
!==	Not identical to

To understand what identity is, take a look at two variables:

```
var bool = true;
var num  = 1;
```

bool is true, which is a Boolean value, and num is 1, a numeric value. If you recall back to the discussion of Booleans, however, you may recall that 1 and 0 are aliases for true and false, respectively. Therefore:

```
bool == num;  /* bool is equal to num -or-
                 true and 1 are equal */
```

An identity-check, however, allows you to tell the two apart:

```
bool !== num; /* bool is not identical to num -or-
                 true is not identical to 1 */
```

and that is why identity comparison operators are nice to have in your toolbox.

Control Structures

There are numerous control structures available to you in JavaScript. They are broken up into a few broad categories: *conditionals*, *loops*, *switches*, and *functions*.

On alert

alert is a helpful tool for alerting you to certain events occurring in your code. It creates a little dialog box with whatever statement you passed, along with an "OK" button that you can use to close it.

```
alert( 'send this message' );
```

For times when you only want a little information, this can be very helpful, but if you are calling alert many times throughout a large script, it can get a little frustrating to have to close each of the dialog boxes as they appear. Several tools have been developed to aid in JavaScript debugging that assist you in outputting information to the screen without using alert(). On the simple end, there is jsTrace (*www.easy-designs.net/code/jsTrace/*), a port of the ActionScript trace window, and for more robust debugging, there is fvLogger (*www.alistapart.com/articles/jslogging*), which is very similar to the JavaScript Console that comes with most Mozilla-based browsers and Opera.

Conditional statements

There are a few different ways to handle conditional statements. The first is the simple if statement. It tests a condition and then, if the condition is met, it executes:

```
if( 2 < 1 ){ alert( 'Something is wrong' ); }
```

This same statement could also be written in shorthand (without the curly braces):

```
if( 2 < 1 ) alert( 'Something is wrong' );
```

If you wanted to know the outcome either way, you would use an if...else statement:

```
if( 2 < 1 ){
  alert( 'Something is wrong' );
} else {
  alert( 'Everything is fine' );
}
```

You can also write this in shorthand, using what is called the *ternary operator*:

```
( 2 < 1 ) ? alert( 'Something is wrong' )
         : alert( 'Everything is fine' );
```

The ternary operator functions like this:

```
( test condition ) ? statement if true : statement if false;
```

and can even be used for value assignment to variables:

```
var total = ( money > 1000000 ) ? 'over $1Million'
                                : 'less than $1Million';
```

Now, suppose you wanted to know if one or more conditions were met. You could use an if...else if statement:

```
if( height > 6 ){
  alert( 'You\'re tall' );
} else if( height > 5.5 ){
  alert( 'You\'re average height' );
} else {
  alert( 'You\'re shorter than average' );
}
```

or a switch statement:

```
switch( true ){
  case ( height > 6 ):
    alert( 'You\'re tall' );
    break;
  case ( height > 5.5 ){
    alert( 'You\'re average height' );
    break;
  default:
    alert( 'You\'re shorter than average' );
    break;
}
```

In each of these instances, a comparison is performed, and if the condition is not met, the next comparison is tried.

A switch statement is a little different than a traditional conditional statement, and it acts almost like a hybrid of a conditional and a loop (which we will discuss momentarily). In a switch statement, each case is tested against the argument of the switch and if they are equal, the statements in that case are evaluated and the switch is exited (using break). In the above example, the argument is true, so the first case to test true will be evaluated (in this case, triggering an alert). We will examine more switch statements below.

There are a few operators we have not discussed yet as they come more into play when you are working with control structures. They are called *logical operators* and there are three of them: and, or, and not (see Table 26-3).

Table 26-3. Logical operators

Operator	Meaning
&&	and
||	or
!	not

"Not" should already be somewhat familiar to you from the comparison operators "not equal to" and "not identical to." It is used to negate a statement or condition or group of either:

```
if( !(num < 10) ){ alert( 'num is greater than 10' ); }
```

"And" and "or" are used to group conditions together so you can ensure they are either both met or at least one is:

```
if( (num > 10) && (num < 20) ){
  alert( 'num is between 11 and 19' );
```

```
  }
  if( (num <= 10) || (num >= 20) ){
    alert('num is not between 11 and 19' );
  }
```

The second example above could also be rewritten using the logical operator "not" in combination with "and":

```
  if( !(num > 10) && !(num < 20) ){
    alert( 'num is not between 11 and 19' );
  }
```

Or, we could use some additional parentheses to group the conditionals, negating them both at once:

```
  if( !( (num > 10) && (num < 20) ) ){
    alert( 'num is not between 11 and 19' );
  }
```

As you can see, there's more than one way to test the same condition.

Loops

Loops are another group of control structures, normally used to keep your code smaller by evaluating a statement or collection of statements a specified number of times.

Let's say we want to alert a countdown from 10 to 0. Without loops, we'd have to write:

```
  var i = 10;
  alert( i );
    i--;    // 9
  alert( i );
    i--;    // 8
  alert( i );
    i--;    // 7
  alert( i );
    i--;    // 6
  alert( i );
    i--;    // 5
  alert( i );
    i--;    // 4
  alert( i );
    i--;    // 3
  alert( i );
    i--;    // 2
  alert( i );
    i--;    // 1
  alert( i );
    i--;    // 0
  alert( i );
```

That's 22 lines of code and a lot of repetition. Using loops we can perform the same task. First let's see how we'd do it with a simple while loop:

```
var i = 10;
while ( i >= 0 ){
  alert( i );
  i--;
}
```

Using while, we were able to compress the whole thing down to five lines, which is pretty cool. What while does is test the condition set in the argument and then perform the statements within its curly braces over and over until the condition is no longer met. In pseudocode, that looks like this:

```
initialize;
while( condition ){
  statement;
  alter condition;
}
```

It is important to remember, when dealing with loops, that you need to pay attention to both your condition and how you alter your condition to make sure you loop will not execute *ad infinitum*. For example:

```
var i = 11;
while( i > 10 ){
  i++;
}
alert( i );        /* this statement is never reached because the
                      while loop's condition is always met */
```

A similar loop type is do...while. The difference between do...while and while is that a do...while loop is executed at least once, whereas a while loop may never execute at all:

```
var i = 10;
while( i > 10 ){
  i--;
}
alert( i );        // 10, the while loop never executed
do{
  i--;
}while( i > 10 )
alert( i );        // 9, because the do...while loop executed once
```

Here's the pseudocode for a do...while loop:

```
initialize;
do{
  statement;
  alter condition;
}while( condition )
```

A do...while loop won't really shorten our countdown, but another loop type will. It is the for loop and is perhaps the most common of all loop types. To rewrite our countdown requires only three lines of code:

```
for( var i = 10; i >= 0; i-- ){
  alert( i );
}
```

That may seem a little odd, but it is really quite simple. Take a look at the pseudocode:

```
for( initialize; test condition; alter ){
  statement;
}
```

To glance back at our example, what we did was initialize the for loop by declaring the variable i to be equal to 10. We then say we want the loop to run as long as i is greater than or equal to 0. Finally, we say that we want i to be decremented each time an iteration of the loop completes.

You will use for loops quite often when working with arrays, as they are useful for iterating through its members, usually in the form

```
for( var i=0; i < some_array.length; i++ ){
  // do something
}
```

This example also serves as a good introduction to object properties, which will be discussed in a moment. length is a property of arrays that tells you how many members an array has.

There is a slight variant of the for loop called a for...in loop. This is very similar to the for loop, but it loops through all of the members of an array without the need for initialization, condition, or alteration. The pseudocode for a for...in loop is as follows:

```
for( member in array ){
  statement involving array[member];
}
```

There are several nice things about for...in loops: they work well for iterating through both normal arrays *and* associative arrays, and you don't need to know the length of the array you are iterating through.

switch

Now that you understand a few more control structures, it's time to revisit the switch statement. As you saw in the previous switch example, each case within a switch is tried and, if it matches the argument of the switch, its statements are evaluated and the switch is exited (via break). There is also normally a default case (simply called default) that can act as a fallback (or an error alert) if none of the other cases are met.

To demonstrate the power of the switch, let's spice up the countdown loop a bit:

```
for( var i=10; i >=0; i-- ){
  switch( i ){
    case 2:
      alert( 'Almost...' );
      break;
    case 1:
      alert( 'There...' );
      break;
    case 0:
```

```
         alert( 'BOOM!' );
         break;
      default:
         alert( i );
         break;
   }
}
```

This code would initiate a countdown from 10 to 0, alert-ing each number, but replacing 2 with Almost..., 1 with There..., and 0 with BOOM!.

Functions

Now things get a little more interesting. *Functions* allow you to create discrete bits of reusable code, which you can call at any given time. These will make up the bulk of what you write in JavaScript.

Creating a function is easy. Here's the pseudocode for making one:

```
function functionName( arguments ){
   statements;
}
```

The function keyword designates the block as a function, and the arguments can be either a single variable or a comma-separated list of variables. Let's make a basic one and then put it to use:

```
function addThese( a, b ){
  var combination = a + b;
  return combination;
}
var my_var = addThese( 2, 10 );          // 12
var my_str = addThese( 'A', ' string' ); // 'A string'
```

The function we created adds/concatenates the two supplied arguments and then returns that new value using the return keyword.

 Functions do not need to return a value.

Functions can also be unnamed. These functions, called *anonymous* functions, are usually either assigned to a variable for use as objects or are used in event handling, both of which we will discuss shortly.

Before we move on, it is important to touch on the concept of variable scope. In JavaScript there are two kinds of variables: global and local. *Global* variables are initialized *outside* of any functions and are available for any function to use. *Local* variables are those variables that are declared *within* a function. No other functions will have access to those variables. The var keyword plays an important role in determining variable scope. Let's take a look at a quick example:

```
function square( num ){
  total = num * num;
  return total;
```

```
}
var total = 50;
var number = square( 20 );
alert( total );
```

In this instance, the alert-ed value will be 400. The reason for that is that the square function sets the variable total equal to the argument^2 (squared). total is initialized outside of the function, so it's value is changed from 50 to 400 when the square() runs. To keep the value of the global total from changing, we need to make the total variable used in the function a *local* variable:

```
function square( num ){
  var total = num * num;
  return total;
}
var total = 50;
var number = square( 20 );
alert( total );
```

Objects

JavaScript is an object-based language and as such, many of its components are themselves objects. Some of the native objects in JavaScript we've already discussed: Array and Function. Some others are Element, Math, and Date. You can also create custom objects, which we'll get to in a moment.

An object is essentially a self-contained collection of data. There are two data types available to it: *properties* and *methods*. Properties are values, while methods are functions. What makes objects useful is that they share access to their properties and methods.

Let's look at two examples of the built-in JavaScript objects in action:

```
var num = 1.76543;
    num = Math.round(num); // 2
var now  = new Date( );
var days = [ 'Sunday', 'Monday', 'Tuesday', 'Wednesday',
             'Thursday', 'Friday', 'Saturday'];
var day  = days[ now.getDay( ) ];
alert( 'Today is ' + day );
```

In the first example, we used a method of the Math object to round our variable up. In the second example, we created a new instance of the Date object and then used its getDay( ) method to tell us what today is by selecting the day name from an array of day names (the getDay( ) method returns the index number of the weekday, 0 through 6 starting with Sunday, which is why that worked). Table 26-4 has a listing of a few native JavaScript objects and their most commonly used properties and methods.

What Is this?

this is a reserved keyword in JavaScript that has many uses but is often poorly understood.

In the scope of an object, this is used to make the object reference itself. It is the owner of the property or method. Such is the case with:

```
function Cat( name, age ){
  this.name = name;
  this.age  = age;
}
```

What this code does is set the name property of the Cat object (Cat.name) equal to the argument passed the Cat object as name. The same goes for age. this can also be used to assign methods to an object that are external to it. Take this example:

```
function Cat(){
  this.purr = purr;
}
function purr(){
  alert('purrrrrrrrr');
}
```

this can also be used to refer to the owner of a function. This usually occurs when handling events, but it is where things can get really confusing.

The default owner (or this) of any function is the window, but there are ways of attaching a function to an event (onclick, for example) that can make this reference the element whose action it is associated with. Take the following code:

```
function change(){
  this.style.color = '#ff0000';
}
element.onclick = change;
```

By assigning a function to an event in this way, we are copying the entire contents of change( ) to the onclick of element. Whereas, if we were to assign it like this:

```
function change(){
  this.style.color = '#ff0000';
}
element.onclick = function( )(
  change( );
};
```

we would only be referencing the function, and this would still reference the owner of change( ): window. When it was triggered, the function would likely not produce the desired effect.

—Continued—

To ensure that event-driven functions always target the intended element, it is recommended that you pass a reference to it:

```
function change( obj ){
  obj.style.color = '#ff0000';
}
element.onlick = function( )(
  change( this );
};
```

By adding this simple fix, we can rest assured that our functions will behave as we intend them to and limit any possible confusion with this.

Table 26-4. Native objects and their commonly accessed methods

Object	Property or method	Use
Array	length	Sets or returns the number of members in an array
	concat( )	Joins two or more arrays and returns the result
	join( )	Puts all the members into a string, separated by the specified delimiter
	pop( )	Removes and returns the last element of an array
	push( )	Adds one or more members to the end of an array and returns the new length
	reverse( )	Reverses the order of the members in an array
	shift( )	Removes and returns the first member of an array
	slice( )	Returns selected members from an existing array
	sort( )	Sorts the members of an array
	splice( )	Removes and adds new members to an array
	unshift( )	Adds one or more members to the beginning of an array and returns the new length
Date	Date( )	Today's date and time
	getDate( )	The day of the month
	getDay( )	The day of the week
	getFullYear( )	The year, as a four-digit number
Math	abs(x)	Returns the absolute value of a number
	ceil(x)	Returns the value of a number rounded up to the nearest integer
	floor(x)	Returns the value of a number rounded down to the nearest integer
	max(x,y)	Returns the number with the highest value of x and y
	min(x,y)	Returns the number with the lowest value of x and y
	random( )	Returns a random number between 0 and 1
	round(x)	Rounds a number to the nearest integer

Object	Property or method	Use
String	`length`	Returns the number of characters in a string
	`concat( )`	Joins two or more strings
	`indexOf( )`	Returns the position of the first occurrence of a specified string value in a string
	`lastIndexOf( )`	Returns the position of the last occurrence of a specified string value, searching backward from the specified position in a string
	`match( )`	Searches for a specified string value in a string
	`replace( )`	Replaces some characters with others in a string
	`slice( )`	Extracts a part of a string and returns the extracted part in a new string
	`split( )`	Splits a string into an array of strings
	`substring( )`	Extracts the characters in a string between two specified indexes
	`toLowerCase( )`	Displays a string in lowercase letters
	`toUpperCase( )`	Displays a string in uppercase letters

Now let's make a custom object, Cat, and provide two properties to it: name and age. We can also define two methods for it: purr( ) and hiss( ). Let's take a look at the construction of that object:

```
function Cat( name, age ){
    this.name = name;
    this.age  = age;
    this.purr = function(){
                alert( 'purrrrrrrrr' );
             };
    this.hiss = function(){
                alert( 'hissssssss!' );
             };
}
```

Now we can access the properties and methods of any Cats we create:

```
var sabine = new Cat( 'Sabine', 9 );
var dakota = new Cat( 'Dakota', 8 );
alert( 'I should give Dakota ' + sabine.age +
       dakota.age + 'treats, because he is soooo good.' );
       // that's 17 treats, by the way
sabine.hiss( );
```

There are numerous ways to create objects. One, which has become quite common lately, is called an *object literal*. Here is the Cat object defined in that way:

```
var Cat = {
  name: false,
  age:  false,
  purr: function(){
          alert( 'purrrrrrrrr' );
        },
  hiss: function(){
```

```
          alert( 'hisssssss!' );
      }
};
```

As you can probably guess, this method is not nearly as flexible, as you can't create multiple instances of the Cat object. It can also be referred to as a *singleton object* as there can only be one instance of that object type. This approach is usually reserved for creating discrete objects that will not be replicated. Beyond that, however, the object's use is pretty much the same:

```
Cat.name = 'Sabine';
Cat.age  = 9;
Cat.hiss( );
```

Event Handling

With HTML 4.0, we were given the ability to tie scripts to certain events triggered on a web page. The most famous use of events is still probably JavaScript rollovers on links, triggered by the onmouseover and onmouseout events. Of course, CSS can handle that much easier now, but it doesn't render events useless, as there are many we can tap into (see Table 26-5) and put to good use.

Table 26-5. Common events

Event handler	Event
onblur	An element loses focus (note: buggy).
onchange	The content of a field changes.
onclick	The mouse clicks an object.
onerror	An error occurs when loading a document or an image.
onfocus	An element gets focus.
onkeydown	A keyboard key is pressed.
onkeypress	A keyboard key is pressed or held down.
onkeyup	A keyboard key is released.
onload	A page or an image is finished loading.
onmousedown	A mouse button is pressed.
onmousemove	The mouse is moved.
onmouseout	The mouse is moved off an element.
onmouseover	The mouse is moved over an element.
onmouseup	A mouse button is released.
onsubmit	The submit button is clicked on a form.

Tapping into events is not all that difficult to do. That said, there are good ways and bad ways. The old way to tap into an event was to place it inline as an attribute of the element you wanted the event handled on:

```
<a href="http://www.oreilly.com"
   onmouseover="window.status='Go to the O\'Reilly website';
   return true;" onmouseout="window.status='';
   return true;">O&#8217;Reilly</a>
```

In this example, we are updating the status bar of the browser window with the text "Go to the O'Reilly website" when the mouse passes over the O'Reilly link and resetting it when the mouse moves off of it. This example also goes against the central tenet of web standards: separation of content from presentation and behavior.

This particular means of event handling is just poor form, but there are plenty of examples on the Web of event handling actually decreasing the accessibility and usability of the page. Take this hypothetical example:

```
<a href="#"
   onclick="popup('http://www.oreilly.com');">O&#8217;Reilly</a>
```

Apart from the use of what we can only imagine is a pop-up function (which has its own accessibility and usability issues), what is wrong with this picture? What happens to that link if a user doesn't have JavaScript enabled in her browser? It doesn't work, plain and simple.

When we work with events, we need to be considerate of our users and conscious of any potential limitations they may have. After all, if they can't use your site, it is unlikely they will stay, let alone return.

There are better ways to write this link. This example still keeps the behavior and the content tied together, but at least it degrades gracefully:

```
<a href="http://www.oreilly.com"
   onclick="popup(this.href); return false;">O&#8217;Reilly</a>
```

The onclick event handler is now using the DOM (discussed in Chapter 27) to access the href of the anchor element and pass that to the pop-up function. If JavaScript were not available or disabled, the link would function as links normally do, opening the target in the current window.

An even better way to handle events is outside of the (X)HTML altogether. Using methods discussed in Chapter 27, you can identify elements on the page and tie events to them. Here's a little sneak peek at how:

```
function setPopups( ){
  var links = document.getElementsByTagName( 'a' );
  for( var i=0; i < links.length; i++ ){
    if( links[i].href.indexOf( 'http://' ) != -1 ){
      links[i].onclick = function( ){
                           popup( this.href );
                           return false;
                         };
    }
  }
}
window.onload = function( ){
                  setPopups( );
                };
```

This is by no means a production-quality script, it is simply a demonstration of how to assign a function to an event. In this example, we set two event handlers, one to the onclick event of all links on the page (provided http:// is found in the href) and another to the onload of the window.

There are other methods of assigning event handlers as well. In fact, a search has been underway to find the best means of adding and removing events. Dean Edwards recently offered the most robust solution (see *http://dean.edwards.name/my/events.js*). Using his addEvent( ) function, we could rewrite our little pop-up script to read:

```
function setPopups( ){
  var links = document.getElementsByTagName( 'a' );
  for( var i=0; i < links.length; i++ ){
    if( links[i].href.indexOf( 'http://' ) != -1 ){
      addEvent( links[i], 'click', function( ){
                              popup( this.href );
                              return false;
                            } );
    }
  }
}
addEvent( window, 'load', setPopups );
```

and, like the previous example, we would not need any inline event handlers. The other benefit to Dean's function is the ability to add multiple events to a single event handler.

The Browser Object

Finally, you should at least briefly consider the Browser Object Model or Browser Object. Using JavaScript, you can not only read and control the page and its contents, but also read and adjust properties of the browser displaying it. This can be in the form of resizing the window, or simply getting the value of the URI displayed in the address bar. Table 26-6 summarizes a few of the common properties and methods available to you in the Browser Object, which is accessed programmatically as window.

Table 26-6. Browser Object properties and methods

Property/method	Description
event	Represents the state of an event
history	Contains the URLs the user has visited within a browser window
location	Gives read/write access to the URI in the address bar
opener	Sets or returns a reference to the window that created the window
parent	Returns the parent window
screenLeft	Returns the x-coordinate of the upper-left corner of the browser relative to the upper-left corner of the screen
screenTop	Returns the y-coordinate of the top corner of the browser relative to the top corner of the screen
status	Sets or returns the text in the status bar of the window
alert( )	Displays an alert box with a specified message and an OK button
close( )	Closes the current window
confirm( )	Displays a dialog box with a specified message and an OK and a Cancel button
focus( )	Sets focus on the current window

Table 26-6. Browser Object properties and methods (continued)

Property/method	Description
open( )	Opens a new browser window
print( )	Prints the contents of the current window
setTimeout( )	Calls a function or evaluates an expression after a specified number of milliseconds

Where to Learn More

For a more in-depth discussion of JavaScript and access to a lot more properties and methods of native objects, be sure to check out *JavaScript: The Definitive Guide* by David Flanagan and *JavaScript and DHTML Cookbook* by Danny Goodman, both of which are published by O'Reilly.

27

DOM Scripting

—by Aaron Gustafson

The Document Object Model (DOM) is an Application Programming Interface (API) for working with structured documents or, in layman's terms, a means of accessing and manipulating the content of an HTML (or XML) file. The DOM is language agnostic and can be accessed by numerous languages, including C++, Java, Perl, PHP, Python, and Ruby. This chapter, however, will focus solely on how JavaScript interfaces with the DOM. Though our main focus will be working with (X)HTML documents, many of these same techniques will work equally well on XML documents.

A Sordid Past

During the Browser Wars of the late '90s, the two major players in the web browser world, Netscape and Microsoft, enabled developers to manipulate a web page to create what marketing folks termed *Dynamic HTML* (DHTML). DHTML was essentially a combination of HTML for markup, CSS for style, and JavaScript for manipulating both of those (mostly in the forms of mouseovers and form validation).

DHTML was good in theory, but the two companies pushing the technology each developed distinct ways of coding the same behavior and accessing the same parts of a document. This led many developers down the dark path to "code forking"—that is, writing code to do the same thing in at least two different ways, in order to supply each browser with code only it understands through an intricate (and often fragile) system of browser-detection scripts.

For instance, Netscape enabled you to interact with its proprietary label elements when you gave them a unique ID:

```
document.layers['myLayer'];
```

Microsoft enabled similar access, but through a slightly different method:

```
document.all['myLayer'];
```

And the differences didn't end there.

Programming in DHTML was time-consuming both in initial development as well as maintenance. Scripts, which should have been short and sweet, sprawled out over hundreds of lines of code. It was incredibly inefficient and frustrating for many. Eventually, DHTML became something of a black art, and the topic wasn't often discussed in polite web design circles. You will sometimes hear the collective access methods of this period in the history of the DOM referred to as "DOM Level 0."

Out of the Dark Ages

October 1998 saw the release of DOM Level 1 by the web standards body, the World Wide Web Consortium (W3C). A collective effort on the part of Microsoft, Netscape, and many other W3C members, the standardized DOM finally enabled DHTML to deliver on its promise of bringing interactivity to the web page through JavaScript. Moreover, it provided a means to manipulate any structured document using any programming language (as discussed above). The W3C defines the DOM as a "platform- and language-neutral interface that will allow programs and scripts to dynamically access and update the content, structure, and style of documents."

Thanks in a large part to the lobbying efforts of the Web Standards Project (WaSP), the newly standardized DOM found a home in Internet Explorer 5 and Netscape 6, making life easier for web developers everywhere. Unfortunately, this change went largely unnoticed in the web community, and many developers continued to ignore DHTML because of the stigma it gained early on.

With the arrival of 2003 came a resurgence of interest in the DOM and a shift in language away from the term DHTML to the new term: DOM Scripting. The shift in nomenclature is a conscious attempt to distance standards-based DOM manipulation from its checkered past. DOM Scripting encourages feature sniffing, browser independence, and graceful degradation. Sounds like a tall order, but in reality, more than 95% of the browsers on the market support at least DOM Level 1, with many even supporting the current standard, DOM Level 2.

The DOM

Perhaps the easiest way to think of the DOM is to think of the document tree. Let's take the following XHTML document as an example:

```
<!DOCTYPE html PUBLIC "-//W3C//DTD XHTML 1.0 Strict//EN"
  "http://www.w3.org/TR/xhtml1/DTD/xhtml1-strict.dtd">
<html xmlns="http://www.w3.org/1999/xhtml" xml:lang="en" lang="en">
<head>
  <title>Sample XHTML</title>
  <meta http-equiv="content-type"
    content="text/html; charset=iso-8859-1" />
  <meta http-equiv="Content-Language" content="en-us" />
</head>
<body>
  <h1>This is a heading, level 1</h1>
  <p>This is a paragraph of text with a
```

```
    <a href="/path/to/another/page.html">link</a>.</p>
  <ul>
    <li>This is a list item</li>
    <li>This is another</li>
    <li>And another</li>
  </ul>
</body>
</html>
```

This is a pretty basic web page, making use of a few different elements. If we were to visualize this as a document tree, it would look something like Figure 27-1.

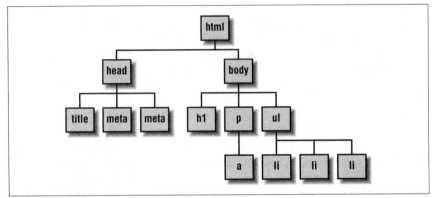

Figure 27-1. A sample document tree

A document tree like this is roughly akin to a very high level view of the DOM's *node tree*.

Essentially, the DOM is a collection of *nodes*. These nodes usually take one of three forms:

- Element nodes
- Attribute nodes
- Text nodes

These nodes are arranged in a hierarchy that we sometimes refer to using a familial model. In (X)HTML, the hierarchy begins with the html element, which is the *root element*, meaning it has no *ancestors*. In the above example, html has two *child nodes* (head and body). The head element has three child nodes of its own (a title and two meta elements), as does body (h1, p, and ul). The relationship goes in the other direction as well, with each child having a *parent node*. Similarly, elements that share a parent are referred to as *sibling nodes*.

If you are familiar with using selectors in Cascading Style Sheets (CSS), referring to element nodes in a familial structure should make perfect sense. There are, however, a few differences between the document tree used in CSS and node tree of the DOM, which bear further discussion.

Figure 27-1 is a very high-level view of the DOM because it is only showing the element nodes. Using the DOM, we can dig deeper. Figure 27-2 examines the paragraph element of the example above.

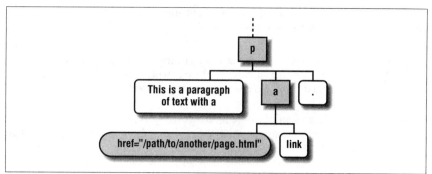

Figure 27-2. An examination of the p element in Figure 27-1

As you can see, the paragraph contains three child nodes of its own: two text nodes (the rounded white boxes) and an anchor element (a). The a, itself, has a child node that is a text node and it also has an attribute node: its href (the gray rounded box).

Using the DOM, we can leverage these relationships to do all sorts of things to our documents.

Manipulating Documents with the DOM

The majority of your DOM Scripting work will likely center around reading from and writing to the document. But before you can do that, you need to understand how to traverse the node tree.

Finding Your Way Around

The DOM offers many ways to move around and find what you want. As any HTML or XML document is essentially a collection of elements arranged in a particular hierarchy, we traverse the DOM using the elements as markers. In fact, a lot of what we do in the DOM is akin to wayfinding: using elements (especially uniquely id-ed ones) as signposts, which let us know where we are in our documents and help us get deeper and deeper into our documents without losing our way.

Let's take the following snippet of (X)HTML, for example:

```
<div id="content">
  <h1>This is a heading</h1>
  <p>This is a paragraph.</p>
  <h2>This is another heading</h2>
  <p>This is another paragraph.</p>
  <p>Yet another paragraph.</p>
</div>
```

If you wanted to find the h2 in this snippet, you would need to use two of JavaScript's interfaces to the DOM, getElementById( ) and getElementsByTagName( ):

```
var the_div = document.getElementById( 'content' );
var h2s     = the_div.getElementsByTagName( 'h2' )
var the_h2  = h2s[0];
```

In the first line, you use the DOM to find an element on the page with an id equal to content and assign it to the variable the_div.

 If you don't already have an element reference to begin with, default to the document object, which refers to the page. getElementById( ) is always used with document.

Once you have your container div assigned to the_div, you can proceed to find the h2 you want, using getElementsByTagName( ) (line 2). That method returns an array of elements (h2s), referred to as a *collection*. Finally, you know that the desired h2 is the first one in that collection and, as Chapter 26 showed, the first element in an array has an index of 0, therefore, the h2 we want is h2s[0]. There's a shorter way to write all of this, too:

```
var the_h2 = document.getElementById(
             'content' ).getElementsByTagName( 'h2' )[0];
```

On a side note, if you ever want a collection of all of the elements in a given document, you can use the universal selector (*) in combination with the getElementsByTagName( ) method:

```
var everything = document.getElementsByTagName( '*' );
```

Although not a horribly efficient means of collecting information from a page, this approach can be useful in certain instances.

The methods getElementById( ) and getElementsByTagName( ) are both quite useful, but sometimes you need to be able to move around without knowing the id, or even the type of the element you are accessing. For this reason, there are numerous properties available to move about the document easily: parentNode, firstChild, lastChild, nextSibling, and previousSibling. Each does exactly what you would expect: allows you to access any element filling the specified role. To access the first paragraph after the h2, for instance, you could write:

```
var the_el = document.getElementById(
             'content' ).getElementsByTagName( 'h2' )[0].nextSibling;
```

Another property available to you is childNodes, which is a collection of the element's children (element *and* text nodes). In certain instances, it may also be useful to test for child nodes before attempting to access them programmatically, using the hasChildNodes( ) method.

If you are moving around in the DOM using parentNode, nextSibling, and the like and want to know more information about the element you are targeting, there are a few properties available to you to provide more information. The first is nodeType, which, as you would expect, returns the type of node you are targeting. There are three commonly used nodeTypes, which are numbered:

1   Element node

2   Attribute node

3   Text node

The Empty Text Node Problem

It is important to keep in mind how much your (X)HTML source affects the DOM. Browsers with a strict interpretation of the DOM, such as the Mozilla family, will include whitespace used to indent your elements as text nodes. This behavior, although correct, can wreak havoc on your scripts if you are looking to use such properties as firstChild, lastChild, nextSibling, and so on. Take the following code snippet for example:

```
<ul>
  <li>This is a list item</li>
  <li>This is another list item</li>
</ul>
```

In the code, the DOM sees a ul with five children:

- A text node with a carriage return and two spaces
- A list item (li)
- Another text node with a carriage return and two spaces
- Another list item
- A final carriage return

If you're not paying attention to this and hope to grab the first list item with firstChild, you are likely to be surprised when an element is not returned.

To avoid this problem, you can either eliminate all unnecessary whitespace from your document or you could use a little script on those elements that you want to access the children of, by using this method:

```
function stripWS( el ){
  for(var i = 0; i < el.childNodes.length; i++){
    var node = el.childNodes[i];
    if( node.nodeType == 3 &&
        !/\S/.test(node.nodeValue) )
      node.parentNode.removeChild(node);
  }
}
```

A similar function called cleanWhitespace( ) is available as an Element method in the Prototype library (*prototype.conio.net*), which also includes several other helpful functions and methods.

You can also find the name of the node using the property nodeName. In the case of element and attribute nodes, nodeName is the element name or attribute name, respectively. Even if you are using XHTML, which requires lowercase tag and attribute names, the value returned by nodeName may be in uppercase, so it is considered a best practice to consistently convert the returned value to either upper- or lowercase when using it in a comparison. Using the (X)HTML example from earlier:

```
<div id="content">
  <h1>This is a heading</h1>
```

```
    <p>This is a paragraph.</p>
    <h2>This is another heading</h2>
    <p>This is another paragraph.</p>
    <p>Yet another paragraph.</p>
</div>
```

we could trigger an `alert( )` using `nodeType` and `nodeName` whenever an element node is encountered, letting us know what it is:

```
var the_div, children, node, name;
the_div = document.getElementById( 'content' );
if( the_div.hasChildNodes( ) ){
  children = the_div.childNodes;
  for( node in children ){
    if( children[node].nodeType == 1 ){
      name = children[node].nodeName.toLowerCase( );
      alert( 'Found an element named "'+name+'"' );
    }
  }
} else {
  return;
}
```

As you can see, there are many ways to "walk" the DOM: the direct route of `getElementById( )`, the meandering path of `getElementsByTagName( )`, and the step-by-step method of parent, child, sibling traversal. There are also numerous tools at your disposal to aid in orienting yourself, such as `id` attributes, but also node types and names.

Reading and Manipulating Document Structure

Once you can find your way around the DOM, it is easy to collect and alter the content of elements on the page. The content you collect can be in the form of other elements, attribute values, and even text content. The primary means of doing this is by using what are sometimes referred to as the "getters and setters" of the DOM: `innerHTML`, `nodeValue`, `getAttribute( )`, and `setAttribute( )`.

innerHTML

When compared to the surgical precision of other DOM methods and properties, `innerHTML` has all the subtlety of a sledgehammer. Originally part of the Internet Explorer DOM (i.e., not part of the W3C DOM), but now widely supported, this element property can be used to get and set all of the markup and content within the targeted element. The main problem with using `innerHTML` to get content is that the collected content is treated as though it is a string, so it's pretty much only good for moving large amounts of content from one place to another.

Using the example above, you could collect all of the contents of the content div by writing:

```
var contents = document.getElementById( 'content' ).innerHTML;
```

Similarly, you could replace contents of the div by setting its innerHTML equal to a string of text that includes HTML:

```
var contents = 'This is a <em>new</em> sentence.';
document.getElementById( 'content' ).innerHTML = contents;
```

It is also possible to append content to an element using innerHTML:

```
var div = document.getElementById( 'content' ).innerHTML;
div.innerHTML += '<p>This is a paragraph added using innerHTML.</p>';
```

nodeValue

Another property you can use to get and set the content of your document is nodeValue. The nodeValue property is just what it sounds like: the value of an attribute or text node. Assuming the following (X)HTML snippet:

```
<a id="easy" href="http://www.easy-designs.net">Easy Designs</a>
```

you could use nodeValue to get the value of the text node in the link and assign it to a variable named text:

```
var text = document.getElementById( 'easy' ).firstChild.nodeValue;
```

This property works in the other direction as well:

```
document.getElementById(
    'easy' ).firstChild.nodeValue = 'Easy Designs, LLC';
```

In the above example, we set the text of the link equal to Easy Designs, LLC, but we could just as easily have used concatenation to add the , LLC to the text:

```
document.getElementById( 'easy' ).firstChild.nodeValue += ', LLC';
```

getAttribute()/setAttribute( )

You can collect the value of an element's attributes using the getAttribute( ) method. Assuming the same (X)HTML as the example above, you could use getAttribute( ) to collect the value of the anchor's href attribute and place it in a variable called href:

```
var href = document.getElementById( 'easy' ).getAttribute( 'href' );
```

The value returned by getAttribute( ) is the nodeValue of the attribute named as the argument.

Similarly, you can add new attribute values or change existing ones using the setAttribute( ) method. If you want to set the href value of a specific page on *easy-designs.net*, you could do so using setAttribute( ):

```
var link = document.getElementById( 'easy' );
link.setAttribute( 'href', 'http://www.easy-designs.net/index.php' );
```

You could also add a title to the link using setAttribute( ):

```
link.setAttribute( 'title', 'The Easy Designs, LLC homepage' );
```

This brings us to our next topic: creating document structure using the DOM.

HTML Versus XML

There are a few differences between the HTML DOM and the XML DOM that can cause some confusion. Both are equally valid approaches, although the XML DOM is preferred for its forward compatibility.

Using the HTML DOM, you have quick access to element attributes, with each available as a property of that element:

```
link.href
```

To read the same attribute using the XML DOM, you would need to use the getAttribute( ) method:

```
link.getAttribute( 'href' );
```

Not only that, but accessing attributes as properties in the HTML DOM gives you the ability to both get and set the value of the attribute:

```
var old_href = link.href;
link.href = '/new/file.html';
```

There are also a few instances when you *must* use the HTML DOM method for cross-browser compatibility. Internet Explorer, for instance, does not allow read/write access to the class attribute using getAttribute( ) or setAttribute( ). Instead, you must use the className property of an element. Luckily, this property is well supported on other browsers.

When accessing the for attribute (used to associate label elements with form controls), you are in a similar situation. IE does not understand label. getAttribute('for'), but, instead, forces you to use label.htmlFor.

You can use both the HTML DOM and the XML DOM approach in (X)HTML documents. If you plan on serving your XHTML files as XML, however, HTML DOM properties (which also include innerHTML) will not work.

Creating Document Structure

JavaScript has a host of methods available for creating markup on the fly. We've already seen that setAttribute( ) can be used to add new attributes, in addition to modifying existing ones, but by using createElement( ) and createTextNode( ) methods, we can do so much more.

createElement( )

As you'd expect, the createElement( ) method (which is used on the document object) creates and returns new element. To build a div for example, do the following:

```
var new_div = document.createElement( 'div' );
```

This assigns your newly created element to the variable new_div. To actually see the newly created div on the page, we should probably put some content in it.

name and Element Creation in IE

Internet Explorer has a few DOM-related peculiarities, some of which we've already discussed. This one is particularly odd, however. In IE, elements that are generated through the DOM are incapable of being assigned a name attribute in any standard way. The following example *should* work (it does in all other browsers):

```
var input = document.createElement( 'input' );
input.setAttribute( 'name', 'fname' );
```

You might think that this is another special case like that of class or for, but the following HTML DOM method doesn't work either:

```
input.name = 'fname';
```

This is not normally a problem unless you are working with forms. If you are planning to use a generated form field to collect a response that will be used only by JavaScript, you should be fine as you can address a field by giving it an id. On the other hand, if you are planning on the form being submitted to the server, the value for the generated field will not go with it as it has no name to associate with the value.

The solution? A bastardization of the createElement( ) method that *only* works in IE:

```
var input = document.createElement( '<input name="fname">' );
```

In a standards-compliant browser, this fails because it tries to generate an element named <input name="fname">, which is not valid. So what do we do? We work around it.

The createNamedElement( ) method, when added to the document object as seen here, will allow you to generate named elements with the DOM that will work everywhere:

```
document.createNamedElement = function( type,
                                        name ){
  var element;
  try {
    element = document.createElement(
      '<' + type + ' name="' + name + '">');
  } catch( e ){}
  if( !element || !element.name ){
    element = document.createElement( type );
    element.name = name;
  }
  return element;
}
```

—Continued—

DOM Scripting

Here's a quick breakdown of what the script does:

1. Creates the variable `element`.
2. Tries `createElement( )` the IE way (using `try...catch` to trap any errors).
3. If `element` or `element.name` is `false` when the script reaches the conditional, the script generates the element the correct way.
4. Returns `element`.

To use it, simply call `document.createNamedElement( )`, passing it the element you want to generate and the name you want to give it:

```
input = document.createNamedElement( 'input',
                                      'fname' );
```

For more information, view the discussion at *easy-reader.net/archives/2005/09/ 02/death-to-bad-dom-implementations*.

createTextNode( )

Using the `createTextNode( )` method (also on the `document` object), we can generate a text node to attach to our newly created `div`. Let's assign the new text node to the variable `text`:

```
var text = document.createTextNode( 'This is a new div' );
```

We now have two newly created nodes, but they aren't connected. To do that, we need to use the DOM to make the text node a child of the `div`. We can accomplish this in a number of ways.

appendChild( )

The most common means of making one node a child of another is to use the `appendChild( )` method.

```
new_div.appendChild( text );
```

`appendChild( )` is a method available to any element node, and it takes only a single argument: the node you want to insert. With `appendChild( )`, you can also skip the intermediate step of assigning the text node to a variable, and directly append the new text node to the `div`:

```
new_div.appendChild( document.createTextNode( 'This is a new div' ) );
```

Of course, this only puts those two nodes together, so we still need to put our `div` into the body of the document to have it show up in the browser. Using `appendChild( )`, we can add the `div` to the body of the page, but `appendChild( )` simply does what it says: appends the argument to the target element. The `div` would become the last element in the body. What if we wanted our new `div` to be the first element in the body?

Scalpel Versus Sledgehammer

As we discussed earlier, innerHTML originated from the Internet Explorer DOM, but now enjoys widespread (though occasionally begrudging) acceptance. When compared to the surgical precision of the W3C's node-based content insertion and manipulation methods, innerHTML just feels, well, imprecise.

That said, there are some times where innerHTML can make your life a little easier. Take the insertion of special characters, for instance. Let's say we wanted to insert grammatically correct curly quotes into the content of a paragraph. Using a node-based approach would look like this:

```
var p, text;
p = document.createElement( 'p' );
text = 'Here we have some \u201Cquotes.\u201D.';
p.appendChild( document.createTextNode( text ) );
```

Chances are, you know the HTML entities a lot better than you know the Unicode character codes, so having to look them up each time you want to use a special character is a bit of an annoyance. Using innerHTML, you could simply set the content of the p using a more comfortable syntax:

```
p.innerHTML = 'Here we have some &#8220;quotes.&#8221;';
```

Similarly, adding numerous text nodes and inline elements as content within an element, such as a paragraph, can be an arduous process. Even something as simple as creating a sentence with an emphasis can be annoyingly convoluted:

```
p.appendChild( document.createTextNode( 'This content is ' ) );
var em = document.createElement( 'em' );
em.appendChild( document.createTextNode( 'emphasized' ) );
p.appendChild( em );
p.appendChild( document.createTextNode( '.' ) );
```

The above example uses a lot of shortcuts, but it is still a ton of steps. Using innerHTML would make the process a whole lot easier:

```
p.innerHTML += ' This content is <em>emphasized</em>.';
```

Of course, one benefit of using the DOM method is that the inserted nodes, if assigned to a variable, remain accessible through that variable even after being inserted into the document. So if we used the node-based example above, we could quickly swap out that em element (assigned to the em variable) for another text node:

```
em.parentNode.replaceChild(
document.createTextNode( 'not emphasized' ), em );
```

The choice of approach is ultimately up to you. There certainly are benefits to each though, again, it should be stressed that documents served as XML *must* use the DOM node method.

insertBefore( )

Well, in that case, we can use the insertBefore( ) method.

```
var body = document.getElementsByTagName( 'body' )[0];
body.insertBefore( new_div, body.firstChild );
```

insertBefore( ) takes two arguments: the first is the node you want to insert, and the second is the node you want to insert it in front of. In our example, we are inserting the new div in front of the firstChild of the body element.

replaceChild( )

Let's suppose that instead of inserting our new div before the firstChild of the body element, we wanted it to replace the firstChild.

To do so, we could use the replaceChild( ) method:

```
body.replaceChild( new_div, body.firstChild );
```

Like insertBefore( ), replaceChild( ) takes two arguments: The first argument is the node you want inserted in the place of the node that is the second argument.

removeChild( )

Because we're on the topic of node manipulation, we should take a look at the removeChild( ) method as well.

Using removeChild( ), we can remove a single node or an entire node tree from the document. This method takes a single argument: the node you want to remove. Suppose we wanted to remove the text node from our div. We could accomplish that easily using removeChild( ):

```
div.removeChild( div.firstChild );
```

We could even use removeChild( ) to delete the entire body from the page, which would not be a good thing, but demonstrates its power:

```
body.parentNode.removeChild( body );
```

cloneNode( )

One final method available to you when working with DOM nodes is cloneNode( ). Using this powerful method, you can replicate an individual node (by supplying the method with an argument of false) or the node and all of its descendant nodes (by supplying it with an argument of true). Here is an example of cloneNode( ) in use:

```
var ul = document.createElement( 'ul' );
var li = document.createElement( 'li' );
li.className = 'check';
for( var i=0; i < 5; i++ ){
  var new_li = li.cloneNode( true );
  new_li.appendChild( document.createTextNode( 'list item ' + ( i + 1 ) ) );
  ul.appendChild( new_li );
}
```

The benefits may not seem immediately apparent by looking at this example, but there is a major benefit in performance: cloning a node is a much faster process than building a new one from scratch.

Working with Style

Once you've mastered the art of structural manipulation with the DOM, you should turn your focus to working with Cascading Style Sheets. The DOM allows access to add, modify, and remove CSS styles. DOM-based CSS manipulation works just like applying inline style using the style attribute.

It is possible, in most modern browsers, to use the setAttribute( ) method to assign a value to the style attribute of an element:

```
var div = document.getElementById( 'content' );
div.setAttribute( 'style', 'color: #f00; font-weight: bold;' );
```

Unfortunately, Internet Explorer (at least through Version 6) does not support this method of style application. Thankfully, there is an HTML DOM convention that is available consistently in all browsers: the style property.

```
div.style.color = '#f00';
div.style.fontWeight = 'bold';
```

Although not nearly as efficient as using setAttribute( ), this convention does allow granular control of styles.

The style property can be used to get or set style values.

```
var old_color  = div.style.color; // red
div.style.color = '#f90';          // orange
```

Individual CSS properties are available as properties of the style property. Hyphenated property names are shortened to camel case to avoid conflict with the subtraction operator (-) in JavaScript. For example, font-weight becomes fontWeight, border-left-width becomes borderLeftWidth, and so on.

The DOM also gives you the ability to disable and enable entire style sheets. To do this, you simply tap into the link elements within the head of the page and then use getAttribute( ) to find the style sheet you want to disable/enable. Setting the disabled property of a style sheet's link element to true will disable it. Setting it to false will enable it again.

Resources

Before we dive into some real-world examples, here are a few great resources to help you on your way:

- WaSP DOM Scripting Task Force (*domscripting.webstandards.org*)
- *DOM Scripting: Web Design with JavaScript and the Document Object Model* by Jeremy Keith (Friends of Ed)
- *DHTML Utopia: Modern Web Design Using JavaScript & DOM* by Stuart Langridge (SitePoint)

DOM Scripting in Action

To better appreciate the power of DOM Scripting, take a look at two relatively simple examples. Instead of breaking down the JavaScript into chunks, helpful JavaScript comments have been added that discuss what the script is doing at each step in the process. The reasoning for this is twofold: it lets you see the script as a whole and it gets you used to seeing comments in code (a habit which is worth picking up to ease long-term maintenance).

Example 1: Style Sheet Switcher

This function is an extreme simplification of the technique employed in *Invasion of the Body Switchers* (*alistapart.com/articles/bodyswitchers*) by Andy Clarke and James Edwards. It also makes use of John Resig's addEvent( ) function (*quirksmode.org/blog/archives/2005/10/_and_the_winner_1.html*) for simple event management. It uses a single external CSS file to handle three different font sizes for the browser. We are going to change the font size of the page by changing a class on the body element.

We start with the external style sheet (*switcher.css*):

```css
body.normal {
  font-size: 80%;
}
body.large {
  font-size: 100%;
}
body.huge {
  font-size: 150%;
}
h1 {
  font-size: 2em;
}
p {
  font-size: 1em;
}
```

Then we have our XHTML page, with a link to our CSS file, and a placeholder script referring to our JavaScript file (*switcher.js*):

```html
<!DOCTYPE html PUBLIC "-//W3C//DTD XHTML 1.0 Strict//EN"
  "http://www.w3.org/TR/xhtml1/DTD/xhtml1-strict.dtd">
<html xmlns="http://www.w3.org/1999/xhtml" xml:lang="en" lang="en">
<head>
  <title>Switcher Example</title>
  <meta http-equiv="content-type" content="text/html;
    charset=iso-8859-1" />
  <meta http-equiv="Content-Language" content="en-us" />
  <link rel="stylesheet" type="text/css" media="screen"
    href="switcher.css" />
  <script type="text/javascript" src="switcher.js"></script>
</head>
<body class="normal">
  <div id="content">
    <h1>Title</h1>
```

```
      <p>This is a paragraph.</p>
      <p>This is another paragraph.</p>
    </div>
    <div>
      <form id="switcher_form" action="switch.php">
        <fieldset>
          <legend>Please choose a font size</legend>
          <select name="size">
            <option value="normal" selected="selected">Normal</option>
            <option value="large">Large</option>
            <option value="huge">Huge</option>
          </select>
          <input type="submit" value="Apply It" />
        </fieldset>
      </form>
    </div>
  </body>
</html>
```

Before we get to the JavaScript, let's take a quick look at the XHTML being used. Notice that the switcher form has an action (*switcher.php*). Even though we will be taking control of this form with JavaScript, we've provided a server-side alternative for non–JavaScript-enabled browsers. This is a prime example of graceful degradation.

All right, now on to the JavaScript. As this script will have only one use per page, I am going to create it as an *object literal* (see Chapter 26):

```
var switcher = {
    body:       false, // the body element of the page
    form:       false, // the switcher form
    controller: false, // the controlling form element
    init:       function(){ // the initialization function
      /* check for method availability,
         return if used methods are unsupported
         or id-ed elements used are not available */
      if( !document.getElementById ||
          !document.getElementsByTagName ||
          !document.getElementById( 'switcher_form' ) ) return;
      // assign the body
      switcher.body = document.getElementsByTagName( 'body' )[0];
      // assign the form
      switcher.form = document.getElementById( 'switcher_form' );
      // assign the select element to the controller
      switcher.controller = switcher.form.getElementsByTagName(
                            'select' )[0];
      // add an event
      switcher.addEvent( switcher.controller, // to the controller
                        'change',            /* trigger with the
                                                 onchange event */
                        function(){          // run this function
                          /* set the body's class equal to
                             the value of the controller */
                          switcher.body.className = this.value;
                        } );
```

```
      // get the submit button
      var input = switcher.form.getElementsByTagName( 'input' )[0];
      // delete it as our onchange event has made it redundant
      input.parentNode.removeChild( input );
    },
    addEvent:   function( obj, type, fn ){  // the add event function
      if (obj.addEventListener)
        obj.addEventListener( type, fn, false );
      else if (obj.attachEvent) {
        obj["e"+type+fn] = fn;
        obj[type+fn] = function() {
          obj["e"+type+fn]( window.event );
        };
        obj.attachEvent( "on"+type, obj[type+fn] );
      }
    }
  };
  /* using the object's built-in addEvent function,
     trigger this object's init() method on page load */
  switcher.addEvent( window, 'load', switcher.init );
```

Example 2: Page Glossary

This script is pageGlossary from Easy Designs (*easy-designs.net/code/pageGlossary/*).
It traverses a specified portion of the document (identified by an id), collecting all of
the abbreviation, acronym, and definition elements, and writes them out to the
designated portion of the page (also identified by an id) as a formal page glossary.
The script also removes duplicate entries and sorts the contents alphabetically. Here
it is:

```
var pageGlossary = {
  getFrom:   false, // where to collect terms from
  buildIn:   false, // where to place the glossary
  glossArr:  [],    // the working glossary as an array
  usedArr:   [],    // terms we've used ( to track duplicates )
  init:      function( fromId, toId ){ /* init() takes two arguments:
                                        * id of the collection area
                                        * id of the destination */
    // make sure the required methods and elements are available
    if( !document.getElementById ||
        !document.getElementsByTagName ||
        !document.getElementById( fromId ) ||
        !document.getElementById( toId ) ) return;
    // set the collection area
    pageGlossary.getFrom = document.getElementById( fromId );
    // set the destination area
    pageGlossary.buildIn = document.getElementById( toId );
    // run the collection method (below)
    pageGlossary.collect();
    // if the glossary array has no members, quit now
    if( pageGlossary.usedArr.length < 1 ) return;
    // resort the array in alphabetical order using ksort (below)
    pageGlossary.glossArr = pageGlossary.ksort(
                              pageGlossary.glossArr );
```

```
      // run the build method (below)
      pageGlossary.build();
    },
    collect:  function(){                      // the collection method
      /* get all the abbr, acronym and dfn elements
         inside the collection area */
      var dfns  = pageGlossary.getFrom.getElementsByTagName('dfn');
      var abbrs = pageGlossary.getFrom.getElementsByTagName('abbr');
      var acros = pageGlossary.getFrom.getElementsByTagName('acronym');
      var arr = [];            // a temp array to hold the collections
      // populate the temp array
      arr = arr.concat( dfns, abbrs, acros );
      // quit if nothing was collected
      if( ( arr[0].length == 0 ) &&
          ( arr[1].length == 0 ) &&
          ( arr[2].length == 0 ) ) return;
      // save processing time by storing the length of the raw array
      var arrLength = arr.length;
      // interate through the raw array
      for( var i=0; i < arrLength; i++ ){
        // store the nested array length
        var nestedLength = arr[i].length;
        // skip this array if it has no members
        if( nestedLength < 1 ) continue;
        // iterate through the array
        for( var j=0; j < nestedLength; j++ ){
          // make sure the element has some children
          if( !arr[i][j].hasChildNodes() ) continue;
          // collect the term
          var trm = arr[i][j].firstChild.nodeValue;
          // collect the definition
          var dfn = arr[i][j].getAttribute( 'title' );
          // if this term is not in the used array
          if( !pageGlossary.inArray( trm, pageGlossary.usedArr ) ){
            // push it to the used array
            pageGlossary.usedArr.push( trm );
            /* and store its definition in the glossary array,
               using the term as its key value */
            pageGlossary.glossArr[trm] = dfn;
          }
        }
      }
    },
    build:    function(){                      // the builder method
      // create a level heading
      var h2 = document.createElement('h2');
      // have it read "Page Glossary"
      h2.appendChild( document.createTextNode( 'Page Glossary' ) );
      // create the definition list
      var dl = document.createElement('dl');
      // give it a class of pageGlossary
      dl.className = 'pageGlossary';
      // iterate through the glossary array
      for( key in pageGlossary.glossArr ){
```

```
        // create a definition term element
        var dt = document.createElement( 'dt' );
        // make its text the term
        dt.appendChild( document.createTextNode( key ) );
        // append it to the list
        dl.appendChild( dt );
        // create the definition data element
        var dd = document.createElement('dd');
        // make its text the definition
        dd.appendChild( document.createTextNode(
                        pageGlossary.glossArr[key] ) );
        // append it to the list
        dl.appendChild( dd );
      }
      // append the h2 to the target element
      pageGlossary.buildIn.appendChild( h2 );
      // append the dl to the target element
      pageGlossary.buildIn.appendChild( dl );
    },
    addEvent: function( obj, type, fn ){  // the add event function
      if (obj.addEventListener) obj.addEventListener( type, fn, false );
      else if (obj.attachEvent) {
        obj["e"+type+fn] = fn;
        obj[type+fn] = function() {
          obj["e"+type+fn]( window.event );
        };
        obj.attachEvent( "on"+type, obj[type+fn] );
      }
    },
    ksort:    function( arr ){              // the key sorting function
      var rArr = [], tArr = [], n=0, i=0, el;
      for( el in arr ) tArr[n++] = el + '|' + arr[el];
      tArr = tArr.sort();
      var arrLength = tArr.length;
      for( var i=0; i < arrLength; i++ ){
        var x = tArr[i].split( '|' );
        rArr[x[0]] = x[1];
      }
      return rArr;
    },
    inArray:  function( n, h ){            // the inArray test
      var l = h.length;
      for( var i=0; i < l; i++ ){
        if( h[i] === n ) return true;
      }
      return false;
    }
};
// add pageGlossary.init() method to the page's onload event
pageGlossary.addEvent( window, 'load', function(){
                                        pageGlossary.init( 'content',
                                                'extras' );
                          } );
```

Supplement: Getting Started with Ajax

The start of 2005 saw the rise of a relatively new technology, dubbed "Ajax" by Jesse James Garrett of Adaptive Path. Ajax stands for Asynchronous JavaScript and XML. In a nutshell, it is the use of the nonstandard XMLHttpRequest( ) object to communicate with server-side scripts. It can send as well as receive information in a variety of formats, including XML, HTML, and even text files. Ajax's most appealing characteristic, however, is its "asynchronous" nature, which means it can do all of this without having to refresh the page. This allows you to update portions of a page based upon user events and provides one of the cornerstones of Rich Internet Applications (RIA) referred to in discussions of "Web 2.0."

The DOM plays into Ajax in a number of ways. How you use the DOM depends a good deal on how you handle the content returned from the server. You can treat the content as simple text using the responseText property of the server response, or you can treat it as XML using responseXML. Assuming the content you pull back from the server is an (X)HTML snippet and you've gotten it as responseText, you could drop that content into a particular spot on the page using innerHTML. On the flip side, if the content you pull back is XML and you've gotten it as responseXML, you can traverse its DOM, cherry-picking or performing functions on the elements, attributes, and text nodes.

This probably sounds very confusing, but it is pretty easy once we go over a few simple examples. For these examples, we are using the XHConn library for simplifying our interaction with XMLHttpRequest( ). The XHConn library is freely available at *xkr.us/code/javascript/XHConn/* and allows simple access to XMLHttpRequest( ) by creating a new XHConn object and then initiating its connect( ) method as you will soon see.

As with the DOM Scripting examples (above), for a blow-by-blow of what the script is doing, read the JavaScript comments.

Example 1: Ajax with innerHTML

For a simple innerHTML-based Ajax example, we'll create a quasi-functional address book application. We'll start with the XHTML page:

```
<!DOCTYPE html PUBLIC "-//W3C//DTD XHTML 1.0 Strict//EN"
  "http://www.w3.org/TR/xhtml1/DTD/xhtml1-strict.dtd">
<html xmlns="http://www.w3.org/1999/xhtml" xml:lang="en" lang="en">
<head>
  <title>Ajax Address Book</title>
  <meta http-equiv="content-type" content="text/html;
    charset=iso-8859-1" />
  <meta http-equiv="Content-Language" content="en-us" />
  <script type="text/javascript" src="XHConn.js"></script>
  <script type="text/javascript" src="addressBook.js"></script>
</head>
<body>
  <h1>Simple Ajax Address Book</h1>
  <form action="getAddress.php" method="POST">
    <fieldset>
      <legend>Please Choose a Person</legend>
```

```
          <select id="person" name="person">
            <option value="">Choose Someone</option>
            <option value="1">Bob Smith</option>
            <option value="2">Janet Jones</option>
          </select>
          <input type="submit" id="submit" name="submit"
            value="Get the Address" />
        </fieldset>
      </form>
      <pre id="address"></pre>
    </body>
  </html>
```

As you can see, we have a simple form with a select, from which to choose a person. Again, we are providing a fallback action for the form, in case our Java-Script cannot run. Below the form, we have a simple pre element that will be displaying the address information from the database.

And now for the JavaScript. Basically, we will be commandeering the select and using its onchange event handler to trigger an XMLHttpRequest( ) call to obtain the address information for the selected individual. The server will be returning this information as a string like this:

```
Bob Smith
123 School Street
Anytown, NY 12345
```

We will take this return as a string and dump it into the pre element using innerHTML. Take a look at the code:

```
var addressBook = {
  myConn:     false, // the XMLHttpRequest
  body:       false, // the body element
  target:     false, // the target container
  loader:     false, // the loader
  init:       function( controlId, sbmtBtnId, targetId ){
    /* init( ) takes three arguments:
       * the id of the controller (select)
       * the id of the submit button
       * the id of the target container */
    // test for methods & elements
    if( !document.getElementById ||
        !document.getElementsByTagName ||
        !document.getElementById( controlId ) ||
        !document.getElementById( sbmtBtnId ) ||
        !document.getElementById( targetId ) ) return;
    // set and test XHConn, quitting silently if it fails
    addressBook.myConn = new XHConn( );
    if( !addressBook.myConn ) return;
    // get the body
    addressBook.body = document.getElementsByTagName( 'body' )[0];
    // get the controller
    var control = document.getElementById( controlId );
```

```
        // get the submit button
        var sbmtBtn = document.getElementById( sbmtBtnId );
        // remove the submit button
        sbmtBtn.parentNode.removeChild( sbmtBtn );
        // get the target
        addressBook.target  = document.getElementById( targetId );
        // add the onchange event to the controller,
        addressBook.addEvent( control,
                              'change',
                              function( ){
                                  if( this.value != '' ){ /* if there's a
                                                             value, trigger
                                                             getAddress */
                                      addressBook.getAddress( this.value );
                                  } else { // otherwise empty the target
                                      addressBook.target.innerHTML = '';
                                  }
                              } );
    },
    getAddress:  function( id ){ // the Ajax call
      // let's let the user know something is happening (see below)
      addressBook.buildLoader( );
      // this is the function that is run once the Ajax call completes
      var fnWhenDone = function(oXML) {
        // get rid of the loader
        addressBook.killLoader( );
        // insert the returned address information into the target
        addressBook.target.innerHTML = oXML.responseText;
      };
      // use XHConn's connect method
      addressBook.myConn.connect( 'index.php', 'POST',
                                  'id='+id, fnWhenDone );
    },
    buildLoader: function( ){     // builds a loader
      // create a new div
      addressBook.loader = document.createElement( 'div' );
      // give it some style
      addressBook.loader.style.position   = 'absolute';
      addressBook.loader.style.top        = '50%';
      addressBook.loader.style.left       = '50%';
      addressBook.loader.style.width      = '300px';
      addressBook.loader.style.lineHeight = '100px';
      addressBook.loader.style.margin     = '-50px 0 0 -150px';
      addressBook.loader.style.textAlign  = 'center';
      addressBook.loader.style.border     = '1px solid #870108';
      addressBook.loader.style.background = '#fff';
      // give it some text
      addressBook.loader.appendChild(
        document.createTextNode( 'Loading Data, please wait\u2026' ) );
      // append it to the body
      addressBook.body.appendChild( addressBook.loader );
```

```
    },
    killLoader: function( ){      // kills the loader
      // remove the loader form the body
      addressBook.body.removeChild( addressBook.loader );
    },
    addEvent: function( obj, type, fn ){  // the add event function
      if (obj.addEventListener) obj.addEventListener( type, fn, false );
      else if (obj.attachEvent) {
        obj["e"+type+fn] = fn;
        obj[type+fn] = function( ) {
          obj["e"+type+fn]( window.event );
        };
        obj.attachEvent( "on"+type, obj[type+fn] );
      }
    }
  };
  /* run the init( ) method on page load, passing it
     the required arguments */
  addressBook.addEvent( window, 'load', function( ){
                                    addressBook.init( 'person',
                                                      'submit',
                                                      'address' );
                        } );
```

To see this script in action, visit *easy-designs.net/books/WDN3/27/Ajax1/index.php*.

Example 2: Ajax with Nodes

Let's alter the example, and instead of returning a string from the server, this time, make it XML:

```
<file>
  <name>
    <first>Bob</first>
    <last>Smith</last>
  </name>
  <address>
    <street>123 School Street</street>
    <city>Anytown</city>
    <state>NY</state>
    <zip>12345</zip>
  </address>
</file>
```

The XHTML page remains the same, but we need to make some minor adjustments to the JavaScript. To highlight the differences, I will touch on each change individually.

The first change, to the onchange event handler of the select, is pretty simple:

```
  ...
      addressBook.addEvent( addressBook.control,
                            'change',
                            function( ){
```

```
                          if( this.value != '' ){
                            addressBook.getAddress( this.value );
                          } else {
                            addressBook.target.removeChild(
                              addressBook.target.firstChild );
                          }
                        } );
      ...
```

Instead of setting the content of the target to empty using innerHTML, the DOM is removing the node that is the target's first child.

Next up is the getAddress( ) method:

```
    ...
  getAddress: function( id ){
    addressBook.buildLoader( );
    var fnWhenDone = function(oXML) {
      addressBook.killLoader( );
      if( addressBook.target.hasChildNodes( ) ){
        addressBook.target.removeChild( addressBook.target.firstChild );
      }
      xml = oXML.responseXML;
      var name    = addressBook.getNodeValue( xml, 'first' ) + ' ' +
                    addressBook.getNodeValue( xml, 'last' );
      var address = addressBook.getNodeValue( xml, 'street' );
      var csz     = addressBook.getNodeValue( xml, 'city' )  + ', ' +
                    addressBook.getNodeValue( xml, 'state' ) + ' ' +
                    addressBook.getNodeValue( xml, 'zip' );
      var txt = document.createTextNode( name+"\n"+address+"\n"+csz );
      addressBook.target.appendChild( txt );
    };
    addressBook.myConn.connect( 'getAddress.php', 'POST',
                                'id=' + id, fnWhenDone);
  },
  ...
```

As we are working with XML, we can use the responseXML property to get the return from the server as a node tree. Then we can traverse that tree, collecting the tidbits of information we need. In this example, we added a new method (getNodeValue( )) that makes working with XML returns easier:

```
  ...
  getNodeValue: function( tree, el ){
    return tree.getElementsByTagName( el )[0].firstChild.nodeValue;
  },
  ...
```

This method takes two arguments: the node tree (tree) and the element (el) whose content is wanted. It returns the nodeValue of the firstChild of the first el within tree or, in other words, the text value of the node requested from the node tree.

Once we have collected all of the requested contents from the XML, the text string is rebuilt and generated with the DOM before being appended to the target. The end result can be seen at *easy-designs.net/books/WDN3/27/Ajax2/index.php*.

DOM Scripting

You may be wondering, why do both examples do the exact same thing? It shows how you can work with two completely different backend systems and still get the results you want. In Ajax, as in many things, flexibility is important to get the job done.

Ajax Resources

For more information on Ajax, consult:

- *Foundations of Ajax* by Ryan Asleson and Nathaniel T. Schutta (Apress)
- Fiftyfoureleven's XMLHttpRequest Examples (see *www.fiftyfoureleven.com/ resources/programming/xmlhttprequest/examples*)
- The Ajaxian Blog (*ajaxian.com*)
- AHAH, a microformat for dealing with `XMLHttpRequest( )` and `innerHTML` (*microformats.org/wiki/rest/ahah*)

V

Web Graphics

28

Web Graphics Overview

Simply put, web graphics must be low-resolution, bitmapped images saved in GIF, JPEG, or PNG format. That statement may be loaded with new terms and acronyms, but rest assured, this chapter provides an explanation of each component. It also takes a look at how color works on monitors and in web browsers, and how that may impact your design decisions. Finally, it provides tips on finding and producing web graphics.

Web Graphic File Formats

Although there are dozens of graphic file formats out there in the world, only three are supported by web browsers for use on web pages: GIF (pronounced "jif"), JPEG ("jay-peg"), and PNG ("ping"). These formats were selected for use on the Web by browser creators because they are easily ported from platform to platform over a network.

What follows is a brief introduction to each of these online graphic formats. More detailed descriptions are provided in the upcoming chapters dedicated to each format.

GIF (Graphic Interchange Format)

The GIF (Graphic Interchange Format) file format is the traditional darling of the Web. It was the first file format to be supported by web browsers, and it continues to be the format for the vast majority of graphics on the Web today.

GIFs are indexed color files with a maximum 8-bit palette capacity, which means that a GIF can contain a maximum of 256 pixel colors. Because they compress color information by rows of pixels, GIF files are most appropriate for graphics that contain areas of flat color, such as logos, cartoon-like illustrations, icons, and line art. GIFs are not efficient at saving photographic images.

GIFs have other advantages. You can make parts of a GIF file transparent, allowing your background image or color to show through. They can also contain multiple images, allowing for simple, self-contained animations. The vast majority of animated ad banners you see on the Web are animated GIFs.

See Chapter 29 for complete information on the GIF file format. Animated GIFs are discussed in Chapter 32.

JPEG (Joint Photographic Experts Group)

JPEG (Joint Photographic Experts Group) files contain 24-bit color information—that's millions of colors, as opposed to a GIF file's 256. They use what is called a *lossy* compression scheme, which means that some image information is thrown out in the compression process, but in most cases, the degradation of the image is not detrimental or even noticeable. You can control the amount of compression when you save an image as a JPEG, so you can prioritize smaller file sizes or better image quality, based on your needs. JPEG offers excellent image quality packed into smaller files.

Photographic images, or any images with subtle gradations of color, are best saved as JPEG files, because JPEG compression is most efficient on continuous tones of color. JPEGs, however, are not a good solution for flat, graphical images, because the compression scheme may blur sharp edges, mottle colors, and result in a file that will generally be a lot larger than the same image saved as a GIF.

See Chapter 30 for complete information on the JPEG file format.

PNG (Portable Network Graphic)

Unlike GIF and JPEG, PNG (Portable Network Graphic) was developed specifically with the Web in mind. PNGs can support 8-bit indexed color, 16-bit grayscale, or 24-bit true color images with a *lossless* compression scheme, which means higher image quality and, in some cases, file sizes even smaller than their GIF counterparts. Not only that, but PNG files also have some nifty features such as built-in gamma control and variable transparency levels (which means you can have a background pattern show through a soft drop shadow).

Despite PNG being a robust file format, browsers and graphics tools were slow to fully support the format (variable transparency levels weren't supported in Internet Explorer until Version 7). For that reason, it lags significantly behind GIF and JPEG in popularity.

See Chapter 31 for complete information on the PNG file format.

Choosing the Right Format

Part of the trick to making quality web graphics that download quickly is choosing the appropriate file format for the job. Table 28-1 provides a good starting point.

 If you use Adobe Photoshop/ImageReady or Macromedia Fireworks, you can preview your image and resulting file size in various file formats to help make choosing a format easier; you can even do side-by-side comparisons.

Table 28-1. Choosing the right file format

If your image...	Use...	Because...
Is graphical, with flat colors	GIF or 8-bit PNG	It excels at compressing flat color.
Is a photograph or contains graduated color (such as a watercolor painting)	JPEG	JPEG compression works best on images with blended color, and the format can display millions of colors, resulting in better image quality at smaller sizes.
Is a combination of flat and photographic art	GIF or 8-bit PNG	In most cases, it is preferable to prevent dithering in the flat colors and to tolerate some dithering in the photographic areas. JPEG is notoriously inefficient at compressing flat colors and may blur text and fine details.
Requires transparency	GIF or PNG	Only GIF and PNG allow transparent areas within the graphic.
Requires animation	GIF	GIF is the only file format that can contain animation frames.

Image Resolution

GIFs, JPEGs, and PNGs are pixel-based, or *bitmapped* (also called *raster*), images. When you zoom in, you can see the image is like a mosaic made up of many pixels (tiny, single-colored squares). These are different from vector graphics that are made up of smooth lines and filled areas, all based on mathematical formulas (Figure 28-1).

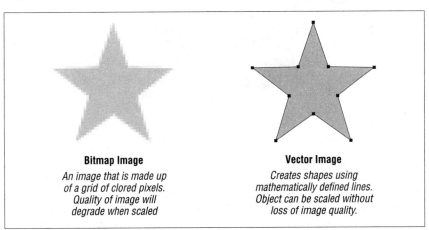

Bitmap Image
An image that is made up of a grid of clored pixels. Quality of image will degrade when scaled

Vector Image
Creates shapes using mathematically defined lines. Object can be scaled without loss of image quality.

Figure 28-1. Bitmapped versus vector graphics

When dealing with bitmapped images, you must be aware of the resolution, usually measured in the number of pixels per inch (*ppi*) of the image. On the Web, graphics are always displayed on low-resolution monitors, so high resolutions typical of print are unnecessary. Web designers typically create graphics at a resolution of 72 ppi as compared to 266 ppi, 600 ppi, or even higher resolutions common to print design.

Working at a low resolution may be an adjustment for a designer accustomed to handling the hi-res images appropriate for print. Most notably, the image quality is lower because there is not as much image information in a given space. This tends to make the image look more grainy or pixelated, and unfortunately, that's just the nature of images on the Web.

Image Size

When a graphic is displayed on a web page, the pixels in the image map one to one with the display resolution of the monitor. Monitors with a higher display resolution use smaller pixels. Therefore, a graphic that appears to be about one inch square on your 72 ppi monitor may actually appear to be quite a bit smaller on a monitor with a resolution closer to 100. See Figure 28-2.

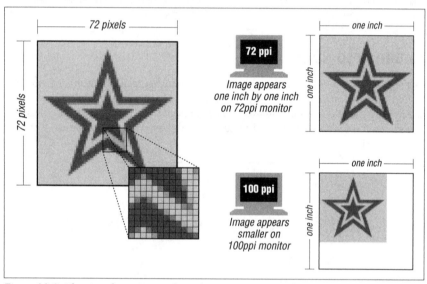

Figure 28-2. The size of an image is dependent on monitor resolution

Good Bye Inches, Hello Pixels

Because the final dimensions of a graphic are dependent on the resolution of the monitor, the whole notion of "inches" and even "pixels per inch" becomes irrelevant in the web environment. So while 72 ppi has become the *de facto* standard, in the end, the only meaningful measurement of a web graphic is its actual number of pixels.

After a while, thinking in pixels comes quite naturally. What's important is the size of the graphic relative to other graphics on that page and to the overall size of the browser window. For instance, if I want a header graphic to fit in an 800 × 600 monitor, I would make sure that it measures 760 pixels wide or less (to allow for the margins and scrollbar). Other graphics on the page will be measured in pixels relative to that image.

After this example, it should be fairly clear why graphics scanned in or shot on a digital camera at high resolutions (such as 300 dpi) are inappropriate for the Web. At higher resolutions, it's typical for images to be several thousand pixels across. With browser windows as small as 750 pixels wide, all those pixels are unnecessary and result in graphics that extend well beyond the browser window.

Color on the Web

It is an inescapable fact of web design that there is no guarantee that users will see the colors on your page the way you do. For some, they will look brighter; for others, darker. Some may see a dither pattern where you see smooth color. This is the nature of designing for a medium that is dependent on computer monitors for final display.

Although you can't absolutely control the end display of colors on your page, you can understand the ways monitors handle color. This understanding may influence the decisions you make when designing.

RGB Color

Computer monitors use the *RGB color model* to display colors. RGB color combines red, green, and blue light (thus, RGB) in various amounts to create a range of colors between black and white. The model is *additive*, which means the more light you add, the closer the resulting color is to white.

Although all monitors use the RGB color model, the actual hues of red, green, and blue light vary from monitor to monitor. This means that even specific RGB colors that are identified numerically may look quite different on different machines. As a web designer, you need to allow for a certain amount of variation in the way your chosen colors will look to your site's visitors.

Color Depth

The number of colors from the RGB color space a monitor can display at one time is known as its *color depth*. More specifically, color depth is the number of bits of data used to represent the color of a single pixel on the screen (also called *bits per pixel* or *bpp*).

The vast majority of monitors fall into one of three color depth categories: *Truecolor* (millions of colors), *Highcolor* (also called HiColor; thousands of colors), or *Indexed color* (256 colors or fewer). How these systems work has a direct impact on the quality of your colors and tasks such as matching colors in graphics and backgrounds.

Truecolor (24- or 32-bit)

Truecolor uses 24 bits of information per pixel, with 8 bits devoted to each color channel (red, green, and blue). Now we're going to do a little math. Eight bits of data can describe 256 colors ($2^8 = 256$), so that's 256 shades of red, 256 shades of green, and 256 shades of blue. The total possible number of combined colors is calculated by multiplying 256 × 256 × 256 for a total of 16,777,216 (usually referred to as "millions of colors").

Specific colors from the Truecolor space are identified by their numerical RGB values. Each value is an integer from 0 to 255. For instance, the RGB values for a particular dark orange color are R:198, G:83, B:52.

32-bit monitors also display Truecolor (16.7 million colors) but they include 8 bits of empty space that may be used to represent an alpha channel. 32-bit monitors have become popular because many modern computer systems work in units of 32, allowing for better optimization in graphics display.

Professional quality image editing programs, such as Photoshop, use 48-bit color (that's 16 bits, or 65,536 tones per channel) to track colors in images internally. Although the extra colors do not display on the monitor, the finer level of mathematical granularity is useful for Photoshop to handle subtle and repetitive image adjustments without rounding errors.

 As of August 2005, approximately 80% of users viewed the Web with 24- or 32-bit monitors (statistics from TheCounter.com).

Highcolor (15- or 16-bit)

Highcolor systems are capable of displaying thousands of colors. The most popular variation of Highcolor monitor is 16 bit, which assigns 5 bits of data to the red channel, 6 bits to green (because the human eye can discern more shades of green), and 5 bits to blue. This is often referred to as the *565 model*. If you do the math, that's 32 × 32 × 64 for a total of 65,536, or "thousands of colors."

15-bit monitors use a 555 model, with 5 bits of data assigned to each color channel, resulting in 32,768 colors. 15-bit monitors are extremely rare these days, so this section focuses on Highcolor in 16-bit monitors.

It is important to understand that the 16-bit high color spectrum is fundamentally different from 24-bit color. It is *not* merely a subset of the colors in the Truecolor space. It is an entirely different set of colors. To better understand, consider just the red color channel. In 24-bit color, the range of shades from 0% (black) to 100% (white) is divided into 256 increments. In 16-bit Highcolor, the range of shades from black to white is divided into 32 increments. Aside from black and white, the shades on the two scales do not coincide; they are always slightly different. Apply this across all three color channels and it should be clear how you get a completely different set of colors (at least mathematically) on 16-bit monitors.

What this means for web designers is that whatever color you specify by RGB color values on a scale from 1 to 255 (as is the case in image-editing programs and in HTML), that color will *always* be slightly shifted to the nearest available color on 16-bit monitors. Whether it gets bumped a shade lighter or darker often depends on the platform, the browser, and whether the color is in HTML, an inline graphic, or a background graphic. The upcoming "Matching Web Colors" section addresses these issues in more detail.

As of August 2005, approximately 20% of users viewed the Web with 16-bit monitors (statistics from TheCounter.com).

Indexed color (8-bit)

In 8-bit color systems, there are 8 bits of data to handle all the color in the monitor, which means that the monitor can display only 256 ($2^8 = 256$) colors at one time. There are also monitors with lower color depths, such as 1-bit (two colors: black and white) and 2-bit color (four colors), but they are fading out of use by the general public.

Indexed color is fundamentally different from the previous two models. Rather than assigning bits per channel, an indexed color system keeps a set of colors (called a *palette* or *color map*) that are available to be displayed at any one time. In 8-bit displays, each color in the palette is assigned a number, or an *index*, from 0 to 255. The color of each pixel in the display is represented by its index number, which then corresponds to the respective color in the palette.

Indexed color palettes consist of colors from the full RGB color space (in other words, 8-bit color is a subset of Truecolor). The 8 bits of data merely limit the number of colors that can be displayed *at one time*.

 Understanding indexed color in monitors is useful for understanding how color works in graphics in the GIF format, which also use 8-bit, indexed color.

For system-level operations, computers use a specific set of 256 colors called the *system palette*. Macs and PCs use slightly different sets of 256 colors in their system palettes. Specific applications may use their own palettes; for instance, browsers have a built-in palette, known as the *web palette*, discussed in the following section.

When an 8-bit system or application encounters a color that is not in its current palette, it does its best to approximate it. This can happen in two ways: *shifting* and *dithering*. Sometimes colors are simply replaced by, or shifted to, the nearest available palette color. Alternately, the monitor may try to approximate a color by dithering, mixing pixels of similar colors available in the palette, resulting in a random dot pattern.

Either method can result in large discrepancies between how color graphics and pages are rendered on a 24-bit display versus an 8-bit display.

 As of August 2005, fewer than 1% of consumers used 8-bit monitors (according to TheCounter.com). The percentage of 8-bit monitors has been steadily declining as computers become faster and more powerful.

The Web Palette

Web browsers running on 8-bit monitors reduce and remap colors to their own built-in palette known as the *web palette*. It is also known as the web-safe palette, browser-safe palette, non-dithering palette, the Netscape palette, and the 6 × 6 × 6 cube.

The web palette consists of the 216 colors shared by the Macintosh and Windows system palettes; therefore, theoretically, colors chosen from the web palette render accurately on Mac or Windows displays. The web palette was optimized for Macs and Windows; Unix machines use a different color model for their system palette, so "web-safe" colors may still shift or dither when viewed on Unix systems.

The remaining 40 colors that make up the difference between the 216 browser colors and the maximum 256 palette colors are taken from the system palette.

 You can see samples of all 216 colors online at *www. learningwebdesign.com/webpalette.html*.

The web palette growing obsolete

It is important to note that the web palette gets called into play on 8-bit monitors only. As mentioned earlier, 24- and 16-bit monitors do not use palettes and are capable of displaying colors without dithering.

Back in the mid-1990s, the majority of users had 8-bit monitors, making it necessary to ensure web pages would look more or less the same on all 8-bit systems.

As of this writing, 8-bit monitors account for less than 3% of traffic on the Web (or less than 1% percent, depending on whose statistics you use), and that share is continuing to shrink as old systems are retired. Many handheld devices still use 8-bit displays, but at the tiny size, there are more pressing graphic concerns than minor color shifts. As 8-bit displays vanish, so does the usefulness of the web palette.

 For an excellent and in-depth technical explanation of monitor color and how the web-safe palette fails to be web safe, I highly recommend "Death of the Websafe Color Palette?" by David Lehn and Hadley Stern on Webmonkey (*hotwired.lycos.com/webmonkey/00/ 37/index2a.html*). Although they wrote it in 2000, their findings still hold true.

Despite the fact that the web palette is on its way out, it is common to hear the name bandied about by clients and to find it handy in web authoring tools. For that reason, you may find it useful to have some level of familiarity with the palette and how to use it.

The web palette in numbers

In web production, we most often manipulate colors in the web palette by their numerical values. The web palette recognizes 6 shades of red, 6 shades of green, and 6 shades of blue, resulting in 216 possible color values (6 × 6 × 6 = 216). This is sometimes referred to as the 6 × 6 × 6 color cube.

In image editing programs, colors are specified by their decimal RGB values on a scale from 0 to 255. Web-safe colors use the following six values: 0, 51, 102, 153, 204, and 255 (ranging from black to white) for each color channel.

In HTML and CSS, colors are identified by the hexadecimal (base-16) equivalents of the same RGB values: 00, 33, 66, 99, CC, and FF. See Appendix D for a more thorough explanation of hexadecimal notation.

Table 28-2 shows the decimal, hexadecimal, and percentage values for each of the six component values in the web palette.

Table 28-2. Numerical values for web palette colors

Decimal	Hexadecimal	Percentage
0 (darkest)	00	0%
51	33	20%
102	66	40%
153	99	60%
204	CC	80%
255 (lightest)	FF	100%

Designing with the web palette

The primary advantage to designing with the web palette is that you know that the colors in your graphics (and HTML web page elements) will not dither or shift on 8-bit monitors. If that audience is still a concern, you can select colors from the web palette when you are creating your graphics and web page elements. The web palette is available in all web authoring tools via a handy pop-up palette usually located right near where you need to enter a color value. In Photoshop, you can load the web-safe palette into the swatches for easy access.

Gamma (Monitor Brightness)

Gamma refers to the overall brightness of a computer monitor's display. In more technical terms, it is a numerical adjustment for the nonlinear relationship of voltage to light intensity—but feel free to think of it as brightness. The default gamma setting varies from platform to platform. Images and pages created on a Macintosh generally look a lot darker when viewed on a Windows or Unix/Linux system. Images created on a Windows machine generally look washed out when seen on a Mac. The higher the gamma value, the darker the display. Table 28-3 shows the standard gamma settings for the major platforms.

Table 28-3. Common default gamma settings

Platform	Gamma
Macintosh	1.8
PC	2.2
Unix	2.3–2.5

Because the vast majority of users are viewing the Web from the Windows environment, gamma differences are of particular concern to developers who are designing pages and graphics on a Macintosh. However, if you are designing under Windows and anticipate a large percentage of Mac traffic to your site (such as a site for graphic designers), be sure to test your pages under Macintosh gamma conditions.

Both Adobe Photoshop and Macromedia Fireworks have controls for simulating the gamma of alternate platforms. In Photoshop, select View → Proof Setup → Windows RGB or Macintosh RGB. In Fireworks, select View → Windows Gamma if you are on a Mac or vice versa. These adjustments affect only how the image appears on your monitor; they do not in any way affect the actual brightness of the image. If you find that your image is too dark or too light under the alternative gamma settings, you need to make manual adjustments to the image brightness to fix it.

Web Graphics Production Tips

The nature of the Web and web browsers requires some special considerations when producing graphics. The unique limitations and techniques may take some getting used to, especially if you are more familiar with creating graphics for print.

This section presents a number of production tips that apply to web graphics in general. Additional format-specific techniques can be found in the respective GIF, JPEG, and PNG chapters.

Use Web Graphics Tools

Nearly all commercial graphics programs—both bitmap image editors and vector drawing programs—include some function for saving or exporting graphics in GIF and JPEG format. But if you are serious about creating high-quality images at small file sizes, it is highly recommended that you invest in a tool with web-specific features, such as Adobe Photoshop and ImageReady or Macromedia Fireworks. If you work on a PC and are on a budget, you might want to try out Corel Paint Shop Pro, which has many of the same features as Photoshop, but at a much lower cost.

Without a doubt, the *de facto* standard for creating web graphics is Adobe Photoshop and its web-specific sidekick, ImageReady. Since Version 5.5, Photoshop has included many web-specific features such as a Save to Web option that shows previews of your graphic in different file formats and at different compression rates.

The other major contender is Macromedia Fireworks, which has similar web graphics features as ImageReady with the addition of vector drawing tools. As this book goes to print, the fate of Fireworks is unclear as a result of Macromedia's acquisition by Adobe.

One of the greatest benefits of using these tools is that they offer previews of your optimization settings (even providing side-by-side comparisons), so you can make adjustments to the settings while keeping an eye on the resulting file size and overall image quality. Both offer very similar controls for file format, color depth, palette dithering, loss, and color palette editing.

Keep File Sizes Small

Here is the single most important guideline a web designer can follow:

Keep the file sizes of your graphics as small as possible!

The nature of publishing over a network creates a new responsibility for designers to be sensitive to the issue of download times. In fact, many corporate clients will set a kilobyte limit (sometimes referred to as the *K-limit*) that the sum of all the files on a page cannot exceed. Even if keeping files small is not a priority for you, it may be for your clients.

Detailed strategies for minimizing graphic file size for each file format appear in the format-specific chapters. Here are a few general strategies that help graphics load more quickly:

Limit dimensions
Though fairly obvious, the easiest way to keep file size down is to limit the dimensions of the graphic itself. There aren't any magic numbers; just don't make graphics any larger than they need to be.

Design for the compression scheme
One of the key ways to make your files as small as possible is to take full advantage of their compression schemes. For instance, because you know that GIF compression likes flat colors, don't design GIF images with gradient color blends when a flat color will suffice. And Because JPEGs like soft transitions and no hard edges, you can try strategically blurring images that will be saved in JPEG format. These techniques are discussed further in the "Optimizing" sections of the GIF and JPEG chapters.

Reuse and recycle
A browser temporarily stores files it has displayed in a cache, making them immediately available if that page is called up again. You can take advantage of the browser's cache by reusing graphics whenever possible on your site. That way, each graphic will need to download only once, speeding up the display of subsequent pages.

The only trick is that each instance of the graphic must have the exact same URL in its <img> element; that is, it must be a single graphic in a single directory. If you make copies of a graphic and put them in different directories, even though the file has the same name, the browser will do a fresh download when it sees the new pathname.

Work in RGB Mode

When you are creating graphics for the Web, it is important to work in the RGB color mode. CMYK mode, although common to the print world, is not appropriate for web graphics. JPEGs in CMYK mode may not display at all in some browsers.

If you work in Adobe Photoshop/ImageReady or Fireworks, it is easy to create and save an RGB original while merely exporting compressed JPEGs and indexed color GIFs or PNGs using the Save to Web or Export feature.

If you need to make an adjustment to an existing GIF, you should convert the color mode back to RGB before editing. This allows colors to be added from the full RGB spectrum to create blends and smooth text edges. If you work in index color mode, you will be limited to the colors in that GIF's index color palette (which may only be a handful of pixel colors).

The only exceptions to this rule are black and white images, which you can edit in grayscale mode.

Resize Images with Care

Although you know to limit your graphics' dimensions, take care when resizing them. Here are some useful tips:

Convert to RGB before resizing
> To resize an image, Photoshop (or any bitmap image editing tool) needs to create new transitions between areas of color in the image. Indexed color images (such as GIFs) are limited to the colors in the image's color table, which does not give Photoshop enough colors to create convincing "in-between" colors for these transitions.

Don't resize larger
> As a general rule, it is a bad idea to increase the dimensions of a low-resolution image (such as 72 ppi images typically used on the Web). Image editing tools cannot add image information to the file—they can only stretch out what's already there. This results in a pixelated and blotchy image.

Resize smaller in increments
> Images can be made slightly smaller without much degradation in image quality; however, drastic resizing (making a snapshot-sized image postage-stamp size) usually results in an unacceptably blurry image. When acquiring an image (whether by scanning or from a CD-ROM), it is best to choose an image that is slightly larger than final size. That way, you don't need to make it larger, and you won't have to scale it down too much. If you must make a very large image very small, try doing it in a number of steps, fixing quality or sharpening at each stage.

Keep an original
> Be sure to keep a clean copy of the original image in case you make something too small. Starting over is better than enlarging the image or resizing repeatedly.

Use Anti-Aliased Text

In general, to create professional-looking graphics for the Web, you should use anti-aliased text. Anti-aliasing is the slight blur used on curved edges to make smoother transitions between colors. Aliased edges, by contrast, are blocky and stair-stepped. Figure 28-3 shows the effect of aliasing (left) and anti-aliasing (right).

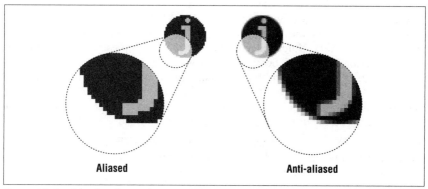

Aliased   **Anti-aliased**

Figure 28-3. Aliased and anti-aliased edges

One case in which anti-aliasing is not the best option is when using very small text (10 to 12 points or smaller, depending on the font design), for which anti-aliased edges blur the characters to the point of illegibility. Text at small sizes may fare better when anti-aliasing is turned off or set to None. You need to experiment on your own.

The trade-off for better-looking graphics is file size—anti-aliasing adds to the number of colors in the image and may result in a slightly larger file size. In this case, the improved quality is usually worth a couple of extra bytes.

Matching Web Colors

In the course of designing web pages, it is common to need to match the color of a graphic to an adjoining graphic, a background graphic, or an HTML color. Unfortunately, matching colors on web pages is not always possible due to the way monitors and graphic formats tend to slightly shift RGB colors. Even graphics and HTML elements with identical numeric RGB values will not necessarily match perfectly, as explained in the following scenarios.

Inline and background colors on 16-bit monitors

Often, you'll want a graphic in the foreground to blend seamlessly with the background HTML color or a background graphic. As mentioned earlier, this is problematic on 16-bit monitors, because all RGB colors need to be remapped to the available 16-bit color space. Unfortunately, the same RGB value may be shifted in different directions depending on whether it appears as an inline graphic or a background graphic. The result is that you can see the rectangular edges of the graphic standing out against the background color. This is possible even if the same image file is used in the foreground and background. The outlines may be subtle, or they may be glaring. It's unpredictable and unavoidable.

The solution for avoiding mismatched colors is to make the inline graphic a transparent GIF or PNG. That way, the background color merely shows through the edges of the graphic, and the rectangle is gone.

Adjacent GIFs and JPEGs

There are times when you want abutting GIF and JPEG graphics to blend seamlessly together, as in the case of an image that has been sliced up and held together with a table. Unfortunately, there is no way to preserve specific numerical RGB settings in a JPEG because of its lossy compression scheme. So although the images may start out with the exact same RGB color in the abutting edges, in the JPEG, that color has the potential to get blotchy and shift, while in the GIF, it is preserved in an index color table. The severity of this effect is dependent on the type of image and the degree of JPEG compression.

The only true solution is to make all adjacent graphics GIFs or 8-bit PNGs so the RGB values can be maintained. Otherwise, play around with higher quality JPEG compressions to minimize the difference.

For Further Reference

For more information on graphic production principles as they apply to the Web, see Lynda Weinman's very popular books, *Designing Web Graphics.4*, Fourth Edition (New Riders) or *Photoshop CS2 for the Web: Hands On Training* (Peachpit Press).

One of the best online resources for designers is Joe Gillespie's site, Web Page Design for Designers (*www.wpdfd.com*). It is packed with very detailed explanations of how type and graphics work on the Web.

29

GIF Format

GIF (Graphic Interchange Format) was the first graphic file type to be displayed by early web browsers, and it remains one of the most popular and versatile formats for distributing color images on the Web to this day. The GIF format was originally developed by CompuServe in 1987 to distribute images over their network to a variety of platforms (this is why you sometimes see GIFs referred to as "CompuServe GIF").

GIF files have the following characteristics:

- They are indexed color images with a maximum of 8-bit color information (256 colors).
- They use LZW compression, which is a lossless compression algorithm.
- They may be interlaced, displaying in a number of passes on download.
- They may contain transparent areas.
- They may contain multiple images, allowing for simple animations.

Any image can be saved as a GIF, but the format is most appropriate for images with areas of flat, solid color, such as logos, icons, charts, and so on (see Figure 29-1). Even if the image contains some photographic elements, if the majority of the image is flat color, GIF is your best bet. GIF is also a good option if you want portions of your image to be transparent, and it's your only option if you want the graphic to contain animation.

The GIF format is not particularly good for photographic images, because quality suffers as a result of the reduction to 256 colors and its compression scheme cannot work efficiently, resulting in larger files. Use JPEG for photos instead.

This chapter begins with further explanation of each of the features listed at the beginning of this chapter (with the exception of animation, which is covered in detail in Chapter 32). The second half of the chapter provides tips for creating GIFs, minimizing file size, and working with the web palette.

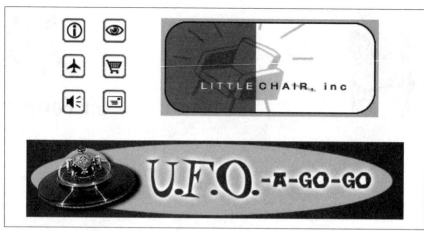

Figure 29-1. Examples of images well suited for GIF format

GIF History

CompuServe developed the GIF format to distribute color images over its network. The first version, GIF87a, was introduced in 1987 and featured LZW compression and the option of being interlaced. CompuServe released the improved GIF89a in 1989, which added transparency and animation capabilities. Both formats use the suffix *.gif* and are supported by all graphical browsers, however, the later GIF89a has become the standard because of its improved capabilities.

LZW Patent Controversy

When CompuServe based GIF on the LZW compression algorithm, they were not aware that it was covered by a U.S. patent held by Unisys corporation. In 1994, Unisys caused quite a stir when they decided to enforce their patent and charge royalties to all software developers that supported the GIF format. In the face of fees and legal hassles, the Internet population rushed to find nonproprietary alternatives to the GIF format, leading to the development of PNG. The U.S. patent on LZW compression ended in 2003, and will end worldwide by mid-2006.

8-Bit Indexed Color

GIF files are indexed color images that can contain a maximum of 8-bit color information (they can also be saved at lower bit rates). This means they can contain up to 256 colors—the maximum number that 8 bits of information can define ($2^8 = 256$). GIFs may be saved at lower bit depths as well. Lower bit depths result in fewer colors and also reduce file size. This is discussed in the section "Minimizing GIF File Sizes" later in this chapter.

Indexed color means that the set of colors in the image, its *palette*, is stored in a color table (also called a *color map*). Each pixel in the image contains a reference (or "index") to a position in the color table. Figure 29-2 illustrates how a 2-bit indexed color image references its color table for display. In Adobe Photoshop, you can view the table for an indexed color image by selecting Image → Mode → Color Table. The color table is also displayed when you choose GIF in the Save for Web window in Photoshop and the Optimize panel in Adobe ImageReady and Macromedia Fireworks.

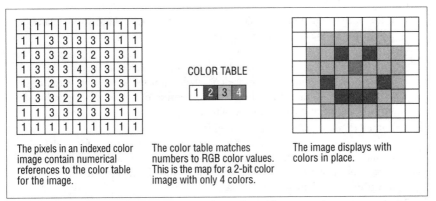

The pixels in an indexed color image contain numerical references to the color table for the image.

The color table matches numbers to RGB color values. This is the map for a 2-bit color image with only 4 colors.

The image displays with colors in place.

Figure 29-2. A 2-bit indexed color image and its color table

When you convert a 24-bit (millions of colors) image to GIF, the colors in the image must be reduced to a palette of 256 colors or fewer. In Photoshop and Fireworks, the conversion to indexed color happens as part of the Save to Web or Export function. Other image editing programs may require you to convert the image to indexed color manually prior to export. In either case, you are usually asked to choose a palette for the resulting image. The sidebar "Common Palettes" outlines the various options available in the most popular image tools.

LZW Compression

The GIF format uses LZW (Lempel-Zev-Welch) compression, which takes advantage of repetition in data streams. Translated into graphic terms, this means that LZW compression is extremely efficient at condensing strings of pixels of identical color. To use an extremely simplified example, when the compression scheme encounters a row of 15 identical blue pixels, it makes up a shorthand notation that means "15 blue pixels." The next time it encounters 15 blue pixels, it uses only the code shorthand. By contrast, when it encounters a row that has a gentle gradation from blue to black, it needs to store a description for every pixel along the way, requiring more data. This is why GIFs are efficient at storing simple graphical images; the areas of flat color take advantage of the LZW compression.

One of the advantages of LZW compression is that it is "lossless," meaning no image information is lost in the compression process, and the decompressed image is identical to the original. While some information may be lost in the

Common Palettes

All indexed color images (such as GIF or PNG-8) use a palette of colors to define the colors in the image. The standard available palettes along with explanations are listed here. Some, like Adaptive, are methods for producing a custom palette based on the colors in the image. Others, like Grayscale or Web216 apply a preexisting palette to the image.

Exact
> If the image contains fewer than 256 colors, the Exact palette option makes a palette out of the actual colors that are found in the image.

Adaptive
> This is a custom palette generated with the most commonly used pixel colors in the image. It allows for color-depth reduction while preserving the original character of the image. Because the number of colors is being reduced, some dithering and color shifting will occur.

Perceptual (Photoshop/ImageReady only)
> This creates a custom palette by giving priority to colors for which the human eye has greater sensitivity. Unlike Adaptive, it is based on algorithms, not just a pixel count. It generally results in images with better color integrity than Adaptive palette images.

Selective (Photoshop/ImageReady only)
> This is similar to Perceptual, but it gives preference to areas of broad color and the preservation of web-safe colors. It is the preferred palette for web graphics created with Photoshop/ImageReady.

Web Adaptive (Fireworks only)
> This is an adaptive palette in which colors that are near in value to web palette colors are converted to the closest web palette color.

Restrictive (Photoshop/ImageReady) or Web216 (Fireworks)
> This remaps the colors in the image to the 216 colors in the web-safe palette.

Mac OS or Windows
> Choosing either system palette converts the image to the palette of 256 colors as defined by each operating system.

Uniform
> This contains an evenly stepped sampling of colors from the RGB spectrum.

Custom
> This allows you to load a palette that was previously saved and apply it to the current image. Otherwise, it preserves the current colors in the palette.

Optimized Median Cut (Paint Shop Pro only)
> This reduces the image to a few colors using something similar to an Adaptive palette.

Optimized Octree (Paint Shop Pro only)
> Use this palette if the original image has just a few colors and you want to keep those exact colors.

conversion process from RGB to indexed color format, once it is converted, the compression itself is lossless.

Interlacing

Normal GIFs are either displayed one row of pixels at a time, from top to bottom, or all at once when the entire file has downloaded. On slow connections, this can mean potentially long waits with empty space and generic graphic icons on the screen.

As an alternative, you can save a GIF87a or 89a with interlacing. An interlaced GIF is displayed in a series of four passes, with the first hint of the upcoming image appearing after only 1/8th (12.5%) of the file has downloaded. The first pass has the appearance of a blurry mosaic; as more data flows in, the blurred areas are filled in with real image information, and the image becomes more defined (Figure 29-3). The three subsequent passes fill in 25%, 50%, and 100% of the image information, respectively.

Graphics programs that support the GIF format provide an interlacing option (usually a checkbox) in the Save As or Export dialog box. Simply turn the interlacing on or off when you save the GIF.

Figure 29-3. Interlaced GIFs display in a series of passes

The advantage to using interlacing is that it quickly gives the viewer some idea of the graphic to come. This peek may be enough to make some important decisions. For instance, if the graphic is a familiar image map, the user can use the link to go to another page before the entire image has downloaded. In some cases, the partially downloaded image might be enough for the viewer to decide that he doesn't want to wait for the rest. Now that broadband has become the norm, interlacing is less relevant than it used to be.

The main trade-off in choosing to make a GIF interlaced is that it slightly increases the file size of the resulting graphic. There are also aesthetic considerations involved that come down to a matter of personal taste. Some viewers would rather see nothing at all than look at the temporary visual chaos an interlaced GIF creates. For these reasons, you may choose to limit interlacing to instances when it makes sense, such as for large image maps, instead of using it for every graphic on a page.

Transparency

The GIF89a format introduced the ability to make portions of graphics transparent. Whatever is behind the transparent area (most likely the background color or pattern of the page) will show through. With transparency, graphics can appear to be shapes other than rectangles (Figure 29-4).

Figure 29-4. The same GIF image with transparency (left) and without (right)

GIF offers only binary transparency, meaning an area is 100% transparent, or it is 100% opaque (PNG one-ups GIF by offering variable levels of transparency). To understand how transparency works, you need to start with the color table (the table that contains the palette) for the indexed color image. In transparent GIFs, one position in the color table is designated as "transparent," and whatever pixel color fills that position is known as the Transparency Index Color (usually gray by default). All pixels in the image that are painted with that color will be transparent when viewed in a browser.

Creating Transparent GIFs

In image editing tools that use layers, such as Photoshop and Fireworks, you can choose to preserve transparent areas in your layered file when you save or export the GIF. In other graphics tools, the transparent area is specified by selecting a specific pixel color in the image with a special transparency pointer or eyedropper tool.

Preventing "Halos"

Occasionally, you see transparent graphics on the Web with light-colored fringe around the edges (called a "halo") that doesn't blend into the background color (see Figure 29-5).

Figure 29-5. A "halo" effect created by anti-aliased edges in a transparent graphic

This effect is the result of *anti-aliasing*, the slight blur used on curved edges to make smoother transitions between colors (like the image on the right in Figure 29-6). *Aliased* edges, by contrast, are blocky and stair-stepped (like the image on the left). The images below have been enlarged to make pixel-level detail more prominent.

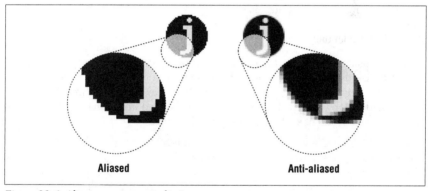

Figure 29-6. Aliasing versus anti-aliasing

When the color around an anti-aliased edge is made transparent, the blur along the edge remains intact, and you can see all those shades of gray between the graphic and the darker background. Halos make graphics look messy and unprofessional.

Unfortunately, once an image is saved as a GIF, the only way to fix a halo is to get in there and erase the anti-aliased edge, pixel by pixel. Even if you get rid of all the edges, you'll be left with blocky edges, and the quality of the image will suffer.

However, halos are very easy to prevent. Following are a few techniques to avoid that unwanted fringe in transparent graphics.

Use aliased edges

One way to avoid halos is to keep your image and text edges aliased (as shown in Figure 29-7). That way there are no stray pixels between your image and the background color.

Figure 29-7. Transparent graphic with aliased edges (no halo effect)

In Photoshop, the Marquee, Lasso, and Magic Wand selection tools all have the option of turning off anti-aliasing in their respective Option palettes. You can also choose to turn off anti-aliasing when creating text.

The advantages to aliased edges are that they are halo-proof and require fewer pixel colors (which potentially means smaller file sizes). The disadvantage is that the blocky edges often look just as bad.

Use the Matte color tool

If you are using Photoshop/ImageReady or Fireworks, the best way to prevent a halo is to use the Matte color tool. The tool requires that you start with a layered file that already contains transparent areas. In other words, the image must not have already been "flattened." The parts of the layered image that are transparent will remain transparent when exported to GIF format.

In the tool's optimization palette, simply set the Matte color to the same color as the background of the page on which the GIF will appear (Figure 29-8). When the GIF is exported with Transparency selected, the anti-aliased edges of the image blend with the selected Matte color. That blend ensures there will be no halo.

Minimizing GIF File Sizes

When you are designing and producing graphics for the Web, it is of utmost importance to keep your file sizes as small as possible. The standard "lowest common denominator" guideline for estimating download time over a modem is one second per kilobyte. Of course, actual download times will vary widely, but this gives you a ballpark number to use for comparisons.

Following are a few simple strategies you can follow to minimize the size of your GIF files while keeping an eye on image quality.

Design Strategically

You can help keep file size under control by the design decisions you make. After a while, designing graphics for the Web becomes second nature.

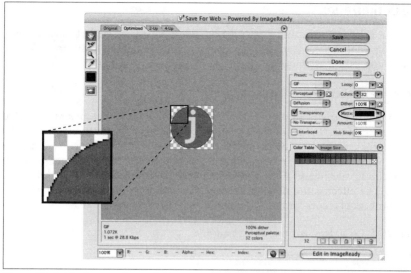

Figure 29-8. The Matte color tool (shown in Photoshop CS)

Limit dimensions

Though it may seem obvious, the easiest way to keep file size down is to limit the dimensions of your graphic. There aren't any numerical guidelines here; just don't make graphics larger than they need to be.

- Scale down large images.
- Crop out any extra space around the important areas of your image.
- Avoid large graphics if they are not absolutely necessary.

Design with flat color

If you design your graphics with flat color from the beginning, you are basically giving the LZW compression the kind of file it likes—rows of repetitive pixel colors.

- Fill areas with solid colors rather than gradients (fades from one color to another).
- Limit the amount of photographic material in your GIFs. Use JPEGs for photographic images.
- Favor horizontal fields of color in your designs when applicable; for example, horizontal stripes condense better than vertical stripes.
- Turn off anti-aliasing when it isn't necessary. The blur that makes smooth, not stair-stepped contours also adds to the number of colors in the image.

Use Optimization Tools

Photoshop/ImageReady and Fireworks provide a similar arsenal of tools for fine-tuning the optimization of GIF files. Most of these methods work to make the LZW compression as efficient as it can be.

Reduce the number of colors (bit depth)

Although GIF format can support 8-bit color information with a maximum of 256 colors, you don't necessarily have to use all of them. In fact, you can reduce the size of a file considerably by saving it at a lower bit depth, which corresponds to fewer colors. Photoshop and Fireworks allow you to select the number of colors you'd like in the image. Other tools may ask you to choose from a list of bit depths. The effect is the same; it's just useful to know how bit depth translates into numbers of colors for the latter (see Table 29-1 for translations).

Table 29-1. Color depth equivalents for bit depths

Bit depth	Number of colors
1-bit	2 (black and white)
2-bit	4
3-bit	8
4-bit	16
5-bit	32
6-bit	64
7-bit	128
8-bit	256

The goal is to find the minimum number of colors (smallest bit depth) that still maintains the integrity and overall character of the image. You may be surprised to find how many images survive a reduction to just 32 colors. Of course, the bit depth at which the image quality becomes unacceptable depends on the specific image and your personal preferences. I personally look at most images at 32 colors first, and add colors from there if I can't live with the results.

Reducing the number of colors decreases the file size in two ways. First, lower bit depths include less data in the file. In addition, clusters of similarly colored pixels become the same color, creating more pockets of repeating pixels for LZW compression to work on. For that reason, fewer image colors take better advantage of GIF's compression scheme, resulting in smaller files. The real file size savings kicks in when there are large areas of flat color. Even if an image has only eight pixel colors, if it has a lot of blends and gradients, you won't see the kind of file size savings you might expect with that kind of severe color reduction.

Limit dithering

Dithering is the random dot pattern that results when colors are approximated by mixing similar colors from a limited palette. Dithering is relevant to GIF file size because it interrupts the clean areas of flat color that are conducive to efficient LZW compression, and can make the file size larger than it needs to be.

Nearly all image editing tools allow you to turn dithering on and off. Current web graphics tools (Fireworks and Photoshop/ImageReady) go one step further by allowing the amount of dithering to be selected on a sliding scale from 0 to 100. You can preview the results of various settings, making it easy to select the best balance of file size and image quality.

Bear in mind, however, that dithering is usually beneficial to image quality in photographic or continuous tone areas, as it prevents "banding" of colors in the image. Dithering may even permit the image to be saved at a lower bit depth, which generally results in smaller file sizes, so it is not appropriate to simply set dithering to zero. The optimal setting will depend on the image.

Play with the "Loss" setting

As explained earlier in this chapter, GIF compression is "lossless," meaning every pixel in the image is preserved during compression. The current web graphics tools allow you to force some pixels out during the conversion process using the "Loss" or "Lossy" setting. Throwing out stray pixels is all in the name of maximizing repeated strings of pixel colors, thus allowing the LZW compression to work more efficiently. Depending on the image, a loss value of 5 to 30% will maintain the integrity of the image while reducing file sizes significantly. This technique works best on images with areas of continuous tone (blended colors) and photographic content.

Weighted optimization (Photoshop/ImageReady)

Photoshop and ImageReady offer yet another advance in graphic optimization. Their weighted optimization feature allows you to apply varying amounts of optimization to different parts of the image. This preserves the integrity of the most important areas while maximizing file size savings for the remainder.

Weighted optimization uses an alpha channel (called a mask) to select areas of the image for various optimization levels. The white areas of the mask correspond to the highest level of image quality, while black areas describe the lowest (gray areas are on a linear scale in between). Channels can be used to control color reduction, dithering, and lossiness in a GIF image.

To access the Modify dialog box (Figure 29-9), click the Channel button next to each of these controls on the Optimization palette. In the dialog box, use the sliders to set the maximum (white tab on the left) and minimum (black tab on the right) levels of optimization.

In Photoshop, create the alpha channel by saving a selection and giving the channel a name (the channel can then be accessed from the Modify dialog boxes). In ImageReady, you can create a new channel based on a selected image area on the fly when you click the Channel button.

Weighted color reduction

When you use the alpha channel to reduce colors in parts of an image, the white areas of the mask determine what areas of the image are most impor-

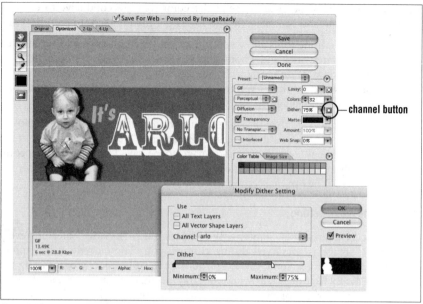

Figure 29-9. Weighted Optimization dialog box in ImageReady

tant. Colors in those areas will be weighted more heavily when calculating the color table for the image.

Weighted dithering
When using the alpha channel with dithering, the white areas of the mask correspond to the areas that receive the most dithering. Black areas yield the least dithering. Set the percentage amounts for each using the black and white tabs on the slider. With weighted dithering, you can allow photographic areas of an image to dither and keep flat colors flat.

Weighted lossiness
Similarly, when using the alpha channel with lossiness, the white areas of the mask correspond to the highest image quality. However, because more lossiness results in less quality, the settings are reversed. To set the highest level of quality drag the white tab or enter a value in the Minimum text box. For lowest level of quality, drag the right (black) tab or enter a value in the Maximum text box.

Optimize to a File Size function (Photoshop/ImageReady)

In some cases, you may know ahead of time what you'd like the file size of your GIF file to be, for example, when designing an ad banner with a specific file size limitation.

Photoshop offers an Optimize to File Size function that automatically optimizes an image to meet a target file size. This enables you to achieve your desired file size without having to test a variety of file size settings. The Optimize to File Size function is accessible from the Save for Web dialog box as shown in Figure 29-10.

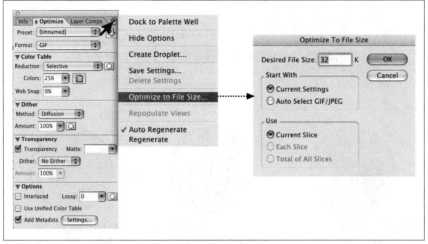

Figure 29-10. Optimize to File Size shown in Photoshop

Designing GIFs with the Web Palette

When your GIF is viewed in a browser on an 8-bit monitor, the colors in the image get remapped to the browser's built-in web-safe palette. This often results in unwanted dithering in areas of flat color. You can prevent dithering on 8-bit monitors by designing with colors from the web palette in the first place. It requires a little extra effort and an adjustment to a limited color choice, but the payoff is that you, not the browser, control whether and how the image dithers. Figure 29-11 shows how dithering can be avoided by using a web-safe color in the design.

Should You Worry About the Web Palette?

Remember that the web palette comes into play only on 8-bit monitors. 24-bit and 16-bit monitors do not use palettes and are capable of rendering your colors without dithering (although, there may be some slight color shifting on 16-bit monitors). For general web traffic, a mere 1 to 3% of users view web pages on 8-bit monitors, and those web users are probably used to reduced image quality by nature of the limited color display.

For a general consumer site, sacrificing color choice for 8-bit performance may not be worth it. However, if you know that a significant share of your audience may be using older systems with 8-bit monitors (such as schools), you may want to continue using the web palette in your designs to avoid unwanted dithering in flat color areas.

There are two opportunities to apply the web palette in the image creation process. The first is to choose web-safe colors when designing the image. As an alternative, you can apply the web palette to the image when reducing it to indexed color before saving or exporting a GIF or 8-bit PNG.

This GIF is designed with non-web-safe colors, resulting in dithering on 8-bit monitors.

On a 24-bit monitor, the solid colors are smooth and accurate.

On an 8-bit monitor, the colors are approximated by dithering colors from the web palette.

If the flat areas are filled with web-safe colors, the photograph still dithers, but the flat colors stay flat.

Figure 29-11. Designing with the web-safe palette prevents dithering

Selecting Web-Safe Colors

If you are making graphics from scratch, especially graphics such as logos or simple illustrations that contain areas of flat color, you can use web palette colors right from the start. The major drawback is that with only 216 colors to choose from (a good 30 of which you wouldn't be caught dead using for anything), the selection is extremely limited. The trick is to have the web palette colors loaded into the Swatches palette or in whatever device your graphics program uses for making colors handy. You should be aware, however, that even if you select web colors for fills, any shades of colors created by soft drop shadows or anti-aliased edges between areas of color probably will not be web-safe.

Converting to the Web Palette

Designing with web colors is one option. The other opportunity is to add (or preserve) web-safe colors in the conversion process from RGB to Indexed Color. As part of this process you will be asked to select a palette for the GIF.

To make all the colors in the image web-safe in Photoshop/ImageReady, apply the Restrictive (Web) palette when you choose Save for Web. In Fireworks, select the Web216 palette. This ensures that every pixel in your resulting GIF will be web-safe.

A better alternative is to make sure the colors in flat areas are web-safe to prevent dithering, but to allow colors in photographic or blended areas to dither as necessary to preserve image quality.

To do this in Photoshop/ImageReady, choose the Selective palette, which creates a custom palette while preserving web colors and broad areas of color. You can also use the Web Snap slider tool to control how many colors shift to their nearest web-safe neighbor. You can view the results of your choices immediately in the Optimized view when you choose Save for Web.

In Fireworks, the Web Adaptive palette creates a custom palette for the image but snaps colors to web-safe if they are close to a web palette color.

Web Palette Strategies

There are no hard and fast rules, since every image has its own requirements. The following are some basic guidelines for using—and resisting—the web palette if you are concerned about performance on 8-bit monitors.

Flat graphical images

To keep flat color areas from dithering while maintaining smoothness in the anti-aliased edges, use colors from the web palette to fill flat color areas when you are designing the image. Do not apply the strict web palette option when saving or exporting because you'll lose the gradations of color in the anti-aliasing. It is better to choose an Adaptive palette with a Web Snap option, if it is available. In Photoshop, set the amount of web snap with the slider scale. In Fireworks, apply the Web Adaptive palette. This will maintain the web colors in your flat areas but allow some non–web-safe colors in the anti-aliasing and other blends to remain.

Photographic images

To maintain clarity and color fidelity for the maximum number of users, first, if it is an entirely photographic image, consider saving it in JPEG format. Otherwise, choose the Selective or Adaptive palette to preserve the original color range in the image. That way, the image will look the best it possibly can for users with 16- and 24-bit monitors (the vast majority). For users with 8-bit monitors, the image will map again to the web palette, but dithering is usually not detrimental in photographic images. The only advantage to applying the web palette to a contin-uous-tone image in the saving process is that you know it will look equally bad to everyone.

Combination images (flat and photographic areas)

To keep the flat areas from dithering while allowing the continuous tone areas to dither with an Adaptive palette, use web-safe colors in the flat areas when you are designing the image. When it's time to save or export to GIF format, choose an Adaptive palette with a Web Snap option if it is available. Using the Adaptive or Selective palette preserves the color fidelity in the photographic areas, while the Web Snap option preserves the web-safe colors in the flat areas.

30

JPEG Format

Developed by and taking its name from the Joint Photographic Experts Group, JPEG is a compression algorithm used by files in the JFIF format, commonly referred to as "JPEG files." JPEGs use either the *.jpg* or *.jpeg* suffix. Like any graphics file format in widespread use on the Web, JPEGs are platform-independent.

JPEG files have the following characteristics:

- They are 24-bit color images.
- They use JPEG's "lossy" compression scheme.
- They may be "progressive" (interlaced), displaying in a number of passes on download.

Any image can be saved in JPEG format, but due to its true color capacity and the way JPEG compression works, the format is ideal for photographic and other continuous tone images, such as paintings, watercolor illustrations, and grayscale images with the 256 shades of gray (see Figure 30-1). JPEGs do not support transparency or animation.

JPEGs are notably *not* good at compressing graphical images with large areas of solid color, such as logos, line art, type, and cartoon-like illustrations. Not only could the image end up blotchy, but the file usually will be quite a bit larger than a GIF file of the same image. JPEG compression is also not good at sharp edges or typography because it tends to leave artifacts that "ripple" the edges.

This chapter begins with further explanations of the JPEG features listed earlier. It also discusses strategies for keeping JPEG file sizes at a minimum.

24-Bit Color

JPEG images contain 24-bit RGB color information, which means they are composed of colors from the Truecolor space of millions of colors (see Chapter 28

Figure 30-1. Examples of images appropriate for JPEG format

for a description of 24-bit color). JPEG files can also carry grayscale images. 24-bit color allows for higher image quality and richer and more subtle color variations. Unlike GIF files, JPEGs do not use palettes for referencing color information.

Be aware that specific RGB color values may not be maintained after an image is compressed as a JPEG. So although you may fill an area with a color using its numeric RGB values, the way the JPEG compression scheme samples and compresses the image may result in blotchy color or overall color shifting. The effect is lessened at higher image quality levels (using less JPEG compression), but there is still no guarantee a specified color will remain numerically exact. If you need to match a graphic to a specific RGB color (such as the background color of a page), use a GIF with its fixed color table.

The color in a JPEG may also be altered (or more accurately, approximated) when the image is viewed on an 8-bit monitor. On 8-bit monitors, the browser will remap the colors in the JPEG to its built-in web palette. This dithering is generally acceptable in photographic image areas.

JPEG Compression

JPEG uses what is known as a "lossy" compression scheme, meaning that some image information is actually thrown out in the compression process. Fortunately, for photographic images at most compression levels, this loss is not discernible to the human eye, particularly when the image is displayed on a monitor at screen resolution (and even less so for images saved at print resolutions).

Using "lossy" compression algorithms, JPEG is able to achieve 10:1 to 20:1 data-compression ratios without visible loss in quality. Of course, the savings in file size at any given compression depends on the content of the specific image, and results vary. If maintaining high image quality is not a priority, these ratios can go even higher.

The efficiency of JPEG compression is based on the spatial frequency, or concentration of detail, of the image. Image areas with low frequency (smooth gradients, like a blue sky) are compressed much further than areas with higher frequency (lots of detail, like blades of grass). Even a single sharp color boundary, although not giving "lots of detail," represents a surge in spatial frequency and therefore poses problems for JPEG compression.

The compression algorithm samples the image in 8 × 8–pixel squares and then translates the relative color and brightness information into mathematical formulas. These sampling squares may become visible when images are compressed with the highest compression ratios (lowest quality settings).

It is perhaps most meaningful to compare JPEG and GIF compression on photographic images. A detail-rich photographic image that takes up 85K of disk space as a GIF image may require only 35K as a JPEG. Again, the rate of compression depends on the specific image, but in general, a JPEG compresses a photographic image two to three times smaller than GIF. For flat-color graphics, however, GIF is far more efficient than JPEG.

Image Loss

Once image quality is lost in JPEG compression, you can never get it back again. Loss in image quality is also cumulative, meaning you lose a little bit more information each time you decompress and compress an image. Each time you open a JPEG and resave it, you degrade the image further. Not only that, you may introduce new artifacts to the image that prevent the second compression from working as efficiently as the first, resulting in higher file sizes.

It is a good idea to hang on to one copy of the original digital image if you anticipate having to make changes, so your final image only goes through the compression process once. You should also start from an original image each time to experiment with different compression levels. Current web graphics tools (Adobe Photoshop/ImageReady and Macromedia Fireworks) make this easy because they always retain the original and allow you to export graphics with your chosen settings.

Variable Compression Levels

One advantage to JPEGs is that you can control the degree to which the image is compressed. The higher the quality, the larger the file. The goal is to find the smallest file size that still maintains acceptable image quality.

The quality of a JPEG image is denoted by its "Q" setting, usually on a scale from 0 to 100. In nearly all programs, the lower numbers represent lower image quality but better compression rates (and smaller files). The higher numbers result in better image quality and larger files.

For the most part, the Q setting is an arbitrary value with no specific mathematical significance. It is just a way to specify the image quality level you'd like to maintain. When JPEG compression goes to work, it compresses as much as it can while maintaining the targeted Q setting. The actual compression ratio depends on the content of the individual image.

The scales for specifying Q-settings (or "Quality") vary among tools that create JPEGs. Most current web tools use a scale from 0 to 100; however, you will still find some that use a scale from 0 to 10 or 0 to 12. The numbers themselves are not significant (a 30 in one program may be radically different than a 30 in another); what matters is the way the image looks and its resulting file size.

JPEG Decompression

JPEGs need to be decompressed before they can be displayed; therefore, it takes a browser longer to decode and assemble a JPEG than a GIF of the same file size. Bear in mind that a small portion of the download time-savings gained by using a JPEG instead of a GIF is lost to the added time it takes to display. (Not much though, so don't sweat it.)

JPEGs in AOL Browsers

America Online members generally use some flavor of Internet Explorer for viewing the Web; however, the pages they see have passed through the AOL proxy servers before they reach their browser window.

En route to AOL users, all web page graphics are run through Johnson & Grace compression software for faster downloads. The J&G compression can wreak havoc on image quality and has some particularly sticky issues with JPEGs. Although users can turn off the Use Compressed Graphics option in their Preferences, you can't count on them to do so. Unfortunately, there's nothing you can do about it as a developer.

Progressive JPEGs

Progressive JPEGs are just like ordinary JPEGs except they display in a series of passes (like interlacing in the GIF format). Each pass contains more detailed information, until the whole image is rendered clearly. Graphics programs allow you to specify the number of passes it takes to fill in the final image (3, 4, or 5 scans). Bear in mind that over a fast Internet connection, the image may load and render so quickly the user may not see any passes at all.

The advantage to using Pro-JPEGs is that like interlaced GIFs, they provide some indication of the full image for the reader to look at without having to wait for the entire image to download. Progressive JPEG files are also generally slightly smaller than standard JPEG files.

One disadvantage to Progressive JPEGs is that they require more processing power to display. The higher the specified number of passes, the more power it takes the user's machine to render the image. The other disadvantage is that this feature of JPEG is not supported by Internet Explorer, so it will be lost on the vast majority of your audience.

Creating JPEGs

Because JPEG is a standard file format, it is supported by all the popular graphics tools. Adobe Photoshop/ImageReady, JASC Paint Shop Pro, and Macromedia Fireworks all provide similar options for saving JPEGs. All of these products allow you to set the quality/compression level and save images in Progressive JPEG format.

Make sure your file is in RGB or grayscale format. You can apply JPEG compression to CMYK files in some applications, but these files are not compatible with web browsers. Be sure to name your file with the suffix *.jpg* or *.jpeg*. This is necessary for the browser to recognize it as a readable JPEG file type.

Minimizing JPEG File Size

As for all files intended for web delivery, it is important to optimize JPEGs to make the file size as small as possible. Because JPEGs are always 24-bit by nature, reducing bit-depth is not an option. For the most part, all you have to play with is the Quality setting, but it is possible to prepare an image prior to compression. There are a number of strategies and tools available for making JPEGs as small as they can be while letting you make decisions about image quality.

Aggressive Compression Ratios

The most direct way of optimizing a JPEG is to adjust its Quality setting. If your image has a lot of continuous tone or gradient colors, you can be pretty aggressive with the compression level and not worry too much about loss of quality in the resulting JPEG. Even at some of the lowest quality settings, the image quality is still suitable for viewing on web pages. Of course, this depends on the individual image. A low quality setting (for example, below 30 in Photoshop) usually results in a blocky or blotchy image, which may be unacceptable to you.

Each tool provides sliders for controlling quality/compression ratios, although they use different numbering systems. Fireworks uses a percentage value from 1 to 100%. Paint Shop Pro uses a scale from 1 to 100, but it works as the inverse of the standard scale: lower numbers correspond to higher image quality and less compression.

Photoshop uses a scale of 0 to 12 when you select JPEG from the Save As dialog box. When you choose Save for Web in Photoshop or Save Optimized in Image-Ready, the quality rating is on a scale from 0 to 100. It should be noted that Photoshop is much less aggressive with its numbering; 0 on the Photoshop scale corresponds to about 30 on the standard scale.

The easiest way to get the balance of compression and image quality just right is to watch the effects of your settings in the image preview available in Photoshop/ImageReady and Fireworks.

"Optimized" JPEGs

Standard JPEGs use a precalculated, general purpose compression table (called the Huffman table) for compressing an image. Some tools offer the ability to create an "optimized" compression table that is customized for the particular image. This results in better color fidelity and slightly smaller file sizes. To optimize a JPEG in Photoshop/ImageReady, simply put a check next to "Optimize" in the Save for Web or Optimize palettes.

Softening the Image for Better Compression

JPEG compression does an admirable job of condensing photographic images without requiring much extra attention. However, if you are serious about making your JPEGs as compact as possible, you may want to maximize JPEG compression's strengths by feeding it the kind of image it likes—an image with subtle gradations, fewer details, and no hard edges. By applying a slight blur to all or part of the image, you allow the compression scheme to do its work more efficiently.

If you are using Photoshop/ImageReady or Fireworks, you will find a setting with the optimization options that softens the image. In Photoshop, the tool is called Blur; in Fireworks, it's Smoothing. If you apply a soft blur, the JPEG compression works better, resulting in a smaller file. If you don't have these tools, you can soften the whole image manually by applying a slight blur to the image with the Gaussian Blur filter (or similar). Compare the file sizes of the original image (left) and the slightly blurred image (center) in Figure 30-2.

A more sophisticated approach is to apply aggressive blurs to areas of the image that are not important and leave areas of detail alone. For instance, if you are working with a portrait, you could apply a blur to the background while maintaining detail in the face, as shown in the example on the right in Figure 30-2.

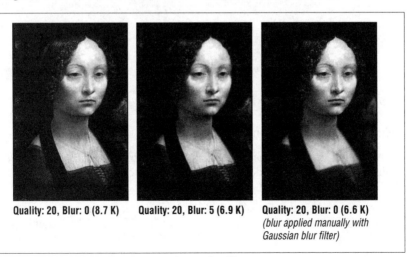

Quality: 20, Blur: 0 (8.7 K) Quality: 20, Blur: 5 (6.9 K) Quality: 20, Blur: 0 (6.6 K)
(blur applied manually with Gaussian blur filter)

Figure 30-2. Blur all or part of an image for smaller file sizes

Weighted Optimization (Photoshop/ImageReady)

Photoshop and ImageReady offer a Weighted Optimization function that lets you smoothly vary the optimization settings across an image using an alpha channel (also called a mask). This allows you to let Photoshop know in which areas of the image quality should be preserved, and where quality may be sacrificed to achieve a smaller file size.

To save a JPEG with Weighted Optimization in Photoshop, first select the portion of the image that you want to retain the highest quality. Save the selection (using the Select menu) and give it a name. This creates the alpha channel that will be referenced when optimizing the image.

From the Save for Web dialog box, select the channel button to the right of the Quality text box (see Figure 30-3). In the Modify Quality Setting dialog that appears, select your named channel from the pop-up menu. Use the sliders to set the minimum (applied to black areas of the mask) and maximum (applied to white areas of the mask) quality levels. The results of your settings can be seen in the Optimized Preview.

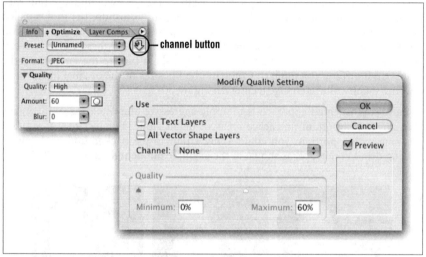

Figure 30-3. Weighted Optimization for JPEGs using ImageReady

Selective Quality (Fireworks)

Fireworks has a function called Selective Quality that works similarly to Photoshop's Weighted Optimization by allowing you to compress different areas of a JPEG at different levels.

To compress selected areas of a JPEG, select an area of the image and choose Modify → Selective JPEG → Save Selection as JPEG Mask. In the Optimize panel, click the edit icon next to Selective Quality and enter the compression value in the box. Entering a low value compresses the Selective JPEG area more than the rest of the image. Entering a high value compresses the Selective JPEG area less than the rest of the image. You can also elect to preserve quality of text items and/or button quality, automatically exporting them at a higher quality level.

Optimize to File Size (Photoshop/ImageReady)

If you know ahead of time the size you'd like your JPEG to be, try using the Optimize to File Size feature in Photoshop/ImageReady. Optimize to File Size (accessible via the Save for Web dialog box) allows you to achieve your target file size automatically without trying out lots of different optimization settings. The Optimize to File Size function as it applies to GIFs is discussed in Chapter 29 (see Figure 29-10).

JPEG

31

PNG Format

The Portable Network Graphic format (PNG for short—pronounced "ping") is a versatile and full-featured graphics file format. Despite some attractive features and the fact that it was created with web use specifically in mind, the PNG has been slow to catch on in the web development world. This is due in part to initial poor browser support and the lack of tools capable of making PNG files as small as they ought to be. But all that is changing, and PNG is poised to live up to its full potential.

PNGs offer an impressive lineup of features:

- They can store 24- or 48-bit color, 16-bit grayscale, or 8-bit indexed color images.
- They use a lossless compression scheme that offers better compression than GIF for indexed color images and no cumulative degradation like JPEG.
- They offer 8- or 16-bit alpha-channel transparency information, which means pixels can have 256 or up to 65,000 shades of transparency. They also offer binary (on/off) transparency like GIFs.
- They may use progressive display (similar to, yet more sophisticated than GIF interlacing).
- They may contain gamma adjustment and color correction information.
- They may contain embedded text for information like author, copyright, and so on.

This chapter introduces these impressive features and provides basic guidelines for creating and optimizing PNG graphics.

When to Use PNGs

PNG is capable of supporting both indexed and Truecolor image types, so there's no bitmapped graphic it can't handle. Virtually all browsers in use today support

PNGs as inline images, although they may not support all the bells and whistles, as you'll see in the "Platform/Browser Support" section later in this chapter.

For web design purposes, there are a few criteria to consider for choosing PNG over another format for an image.

Potential GIF Substitute

For images with sharp edges and areas of flat color that would typically be saved as GIFs, the 8-bit PNG is a viable option. It can even handle transparency. You may find that a PNG version of an image has a smaller file size than the GIF version of the same image, but that depends on whether your image editing tool handles PNG compression properly and efficiently. Adobe Photoshop/ImageReady and Macromedia Fireworks now do an impressive job of creating PNGs. Using the Preview function in both tools, it's easy to compare the file sizes of each format. If the PNG is smaller, use it with confidence.

Not a JPEG Substitute

Although PNG does support 24-bit color and higher, its lossless compression scheme nearly always results in larger files than JPEG's lossy compression when applied to the same image. The high bit depth support was developed so PNGs could take the place of TIFF files for saving highly detailed images where loss of image information is unacceptable (such as medical images). For web purposes where every byte counts, photographic and continuous tone images are still best saved as JPEGs.

For Multiple Levels of Transparency

If you want a background pattern to show through a soft drop shadow, PNG is the only graphic file format to offer multiple levels of transparency, and is thus your only choice. Unfortunately, not all browsers (Internet Explorer 6 and earlier being the most notable) support this type of transparency. PNG's transparency features are discussed in detail later in this chapter.

PNG Features

PNG is like a superhero of the graphics format world. This section takes a more detailed look at PNG's capabilities.

8-bit Palette, Grayscale, and Truecolor

PNG was designed to replace GIF for online purposes and the inconsistently implemented TIFF format for image storage and printing. As a result, there are three types of PNG files: indexed color (palette images), grayscale, and Truecolor.

8-bit palette images

Like GIFs, PNGs can be saved as 8-bit indexed color, containing up to 256 colors, the maximum number that 8 bits of information can define. Indexed color is discussed in detail in Chapter 29.

Although 8-bit is the maximum, PNGs may be saved at 1-, 2-, and 4-bit depths as well, thus reducing the maximum number of colors in the image (and the file size).

Grayscale

PNGs can also support 16-bit grayscale images—that's as many as 65,536 shades of gray (2^{16}), enabling black-and-white photographs and illustrations to be stored with enormous subtlety of detail. This is useful for medical imaging and other types of imaging where detail must be maintained, but it is not much of an advantage for images intended for web delivery due to the inherent limitations of low-resolution images. Grayscale images are supported at 1-, 2-, 4-, and 8-bit depths as well.

Truecolor

PNG can support 24- and 48-bit Truecolor images. The term "Truecolor" refers to the full color range (millions of colors) that can be defined by combinations of red, green, and blue (RGB) light on a computer monitor (see Chapter 28 for more information). Truecolor images do not use color tables and are limited only by the number of bits available to describe values for each color channel. In PNG format, each channel can be defined by 8- or 16-bit information. It should be noted that 48-bit images are useless for the Web. Even 24-bit should be used with care (JPEG usually offers smaller file sizes with acceptable image quality).

PNG Compression

The most notable aspect of PNG compression is that it is "lossless," meaning no information is lost in the compression process. A decompressed PNG image is identical to the original.

PNGs use a "deflate" compression scheme (the same engine used to "zip" files with gzip, WinZip, and similar programs). Like GIFs, PNG's compression works on rows of pixels, taking advantage of repetition in bytes of information. By use of internal filters, it can take advantage of some vertical patterns as well. PNG's compression engine typically compresses images 5 to 25% better than GIF (and up to 39% better under optimal conditions). Not all tools implement PNG compression to its full potential. See "Creating PNG Files" later in this chapter.

Filters

Before PNG compresses an image, it first runs the image data, row by row, through one of five filters (Sub, Up, Average, Paeth, or Adaptive). The filters use different methods for finding patterns in the image information that can then be condensed more efficiently. The process is similar to how LZW compression takes advantage of horizontal repetition in GIFs, but PNG can look for vertical repetition as well.

In most applications, the filters are applied internally and are hidden from the end user (as they should be). If your tool provides filter options, there are only two you need to remember:

- Use None for all indexed color images (or grayscale images with fewer than 16 shades).
- Use Adaptive for all other image types.

Transparency

Both 24- and 8-bit indexed color PNGs can have variable levels of transparency. This sophisticated transparency function allows for smooth transitions between foreground and background elements (Figure 31-1). Transparency works for grayscale images as well. PNGs also support simple binary transparency (like transparent GIFs), in which a pixel is either totally transparent or totally opaque.

PNGs use two methods for handling variable levels of transparency. The first uses an *alpha channel* (think of it as a separate layer) that keeps track of the transparent areas of the image. The other method works for 8-bit indexed images and uses the index color table to store transparency information.

Alpha channel transparency

In addition to the standard channels for RGB color values for Truecolor images, PNGs may contain another alpha channel used for transparency information. Each pixel is then defined by its RGBA values. For 24-bit images, the alpha channel can contain up to 8 bits of information for 256 levels of transparency for every pixel in the image (resulting in a 32-bit image). The alpha channel may also contain simple binary transparency information, like GIFs. Keep in mind,

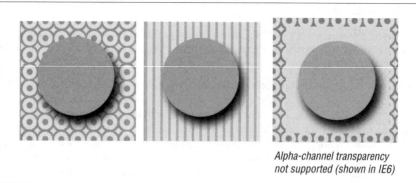

Alpha-channel transparency
not supported (shown in IE6)

*Figure 31-1. A PNG with variable transparency and how it looks in a browser (IE 6)
without alpha channel support (right)*

however, that an RGB PNG file with alpha channels will be about 20% larger than one without.

Not all browsers have native support alpha-channel transparency, most notably Internet Explorer 6 and earlier (see the sidebar "Alpha Transparency in Internet Explorer" for workarounds). Figure 31-1 shows what happens when transparency is not supported. It is interesting to know that 48-bit PNGs may contain an alpha channel with 16 bits of information—that's over 65,000 levels of transparency. 48-bit images, however, are inappropriate for the Web and are poorly supported elsewhere.

Alpha Transparency in Internet Explorer

Although IE 6 and earlier do not have native support for multiple levels of transparency, there are solutions using Microsoft's proprietary AlphaImageLoader filter and a bit of JavaScript. The details of the process are beyond the scope of this chapter, but these resources are good places to start if you want to ensure cross-browser support for your transparent PNGS.

Start with the AlphaImageLoader filter documentation on the MSDN (Microsoft Developers Network) site at *msdn.microsoft.com/workshop/author/filter/reference/ filters/alphaimageloader.asp*.

These articles introduce variations and alternative techniques:

- "PNG Behavior," *webfx.eae.net/dhtml/pngbehavior/pngbehavior.html*
- "Cross-Browser Variable Opacity with PNG: A Real Solution," *www.alistapart. com/articles/pngopacity*
- "Cross-browser semi-transparent backgrounds," *www.daltonlp.com/daltonlp. cgi?item_type=1&item_id=217*

8-bit transparency

Indexed color PNGs can also contain variable levels of transparency (up to 256 levels); however, this information is not handled in a distinct alpha channel as for 24-bit images. Instead, each transparency level occupies a position in the index color table. So, if you have a red area that fades out using eight levels of transparency, that red would be present in eight slots in the color table, each with its own transparency setting. In other words, each slot in the color table can store RGBA information. So while it is alpha channel–like (because it has variable levels), it's not true alpha-channel transparency.

Other than adding to the number of pixel colors in the color table, adding transparency to an 8-bit PNG does not significantly increase its file size, making it the preferable of the two methods for web use. Unfortunately, it faces the obstacle of poor tool and browser support. PNGs with palette transparency may display as binary (on/off) transparency by browsers that don't support them.

 Saving transparent PNGs in Fireworks and Photoshop is discussed in the upcoming "Creating PNG Files" section.

Progressive Display (Interlacing)

Like GIFs, PNGs can be encoded for interlaced display. When this option is selected, the image displays in a series of passes; the first pass displays after only a portion of the file has been downloaded, and each subsequent pass increases in detail and clarity until the whole image is rendered.

Interlaced PNGs display over a series of seven passes (using a method known as Adam7, named for its creator, Adam Costello). The first rendering of the image appears after only 1/64 of the file has downloaded (that's eight times faster than GIF). Unlike GIF, which fills in horizontal rows of information, PNGs fill in both horizontally and vertically. Interlacing can add to the file size of PNGs, especially on small images (which don't really need to be interlaced anyway). To keep file sizes as small as possible, turn interlacing off.

Gamma Correction

Gamma refers to the brightness setting of a monitor (for more information on gamma, see Chapter 28). Because gamma settings vary by platform (and even by manufacturer), the graphics you create may not look the way you intend. In general, graphics created on Macs look dark on PCs and graphics created on PCs look washed out on Macs.

PNGs can be tagged with information regarding the gamma setting of the platform on which they were created. This information can then be interpreted by software on the user's end (the browser) to make appropriate gamma compensations. When this is implemented on both the creator and end user's side, the PNG retains its intended brightness and color intensity. Unfortunately, as of this writing, this feature is poorly supported.

Embedded Text

PNGs also have the ability to store strings of text. This is useful in permanently attaching text to an image, such as copyright information or a description of what is in the image. The only tools that allow text annotations to PNG graphics are Corel Paint Shop Pro and the GIMP (a free image editor for the X Window System on Unix). Fireworks will preserve embedded text information in PNGs. Ideally, the meta-information in the PNG could be accessible via right-clicking on the graphic in a browser window, but this feature is not implemented in current browsers.

PNGs in Motion

One of the only features PNG is missing is the ability to store multiple images for animation. The first effort to add motion to PNGs was the MNG format (Multiple-image Network Graphic). It gained some browser support, but its popularity suffered from the fact that MNGs were not backward compatible with PNGs. If a browser didn't support MNG, it would display a broken graphic.

More recently, there has been a proposed extension to PNG called APNG (Animated Portable Network Graphic) that addresses the issue of backward compatibility. If a browser does not support an APNG, it displays the first frame as a static image PNG instead.

Both of these formats are in development and are not well supported as of this writing.

Platform/Browser Support

PNG was designed to be network-friendly, so naturally it is recognized and supported on all platforms. Fortunately, as of this writing, PNGs can be displayed as inline images in virtually all browsers (initially, PNGs required plug-ins such as PNG Live). However, not all of the advanced features, such as progressive display and embedded text, are supported. In fact, Internet Explorer didn't start natively supporting alpha-channel transparency until its Version 7 release.

Table 31-1 lists the more popular browsers capable of displaying PNGs and the features they support. Note that there are myriad lesser-known browsers out there that also support PNG in all its glory. Some older browsers are included in the table for historical interest. For a complete list of PNG behavior on all browsers, see the browser support page on the official PNG web site at *www.libpng.org/pub/ png/pngapbr.html*.

Table 31-1. Browser support for PNG

Browser	Progressive display	Binary transparency	Alpha channel transparency	Gamma correction
Windows				
IE 7 (beta)	Yes	Yes	Yes	Yes
IE 6	Yes	Partial	—	Yes
IE 5.5	Yes	Partial	—	Yes
IE 4.0	Yes	Partial	—	—
Mozilla/Firefox	Yes	Yes	Yes	Yes
NN 6	Yes	Yes	Yes	Yes
NN 4.x	Yes	—	—	—
Opera 5	Yes	Broken	—	Yes
Macintosh				
Mozilla/Firefox	Yes	Yes	Yes	Yes
Safari	Yes	Yes	Yes	Yes
IE 5	Yes	Yes	Yes	Yes
NN 6	Yes	Yes	Yes	Yes
NN 4.x	Yes	—	—	—
iCab	—	Yes	Yes	—
Unix				
Mozilla/Firefox	Yes	Yes	Yes	Yes
IE 6 beta	Yes	Partial	—	Yes
NN 6	Yes	Yes	Yes	Yes

Creating PNG Files

While browser support played a part in PNG's slow adoption, the other side of the coin was the lack of image tools that could do the PNG format justice. For a while, decent PNGs could be created only with fairly obscure command-line utilities (see the sidebar "For PNG Geeks Only"). Fortunately, decent (albeit often incomplete) PNG support is now available in most professional graphics programs. This section outlines the ins and outs of creating PNGs in the two most popular professional web graphics tools, Photoshop/ImageReady and Fireworks.

 For a comprehensive list of image editing tools and graphics file converters that support PNG compression (as well as their known bugs), see the official PNG site at *www.libpng.org/pub/png/pngaped.html*.

Adobe Photoshop/ImageReady

Adobe Photoshop introduced read/write PNG support in Version 4, but due to poor support for the PNG compression engine, the resulting PNG file sizes couldn't compete with their GIF counterparts, thus knocking PNGs temporarily out of the race. Compression support has since improved, and the later versions of Photoshop (CS2 is the latest as of this writing) are able to squeeze an 8-bit image smaller in PNG format than GIF at the same settings.

Saving as PNG

To save an image as a PNG in Photoshop, simply select PNG-8 or PNG-24 from the file format pop-up menu in the Save for Web dialog box. In ImageReady, select PNG-8 or PNG-24 in the Optimize panel. Creating a PNG-8 is essentially the same as making a GIF, and the same optimization tools and guidelines apply. 24-bit PNGs may be interlaced or contain transparency, but there are no settings for optimization.

PNG transparency in Photoshop/ImageReady

File size aside, the "killer feature" that PNG has over GIF is the ability to contain multiple levels of transparency (commonly referred to as "alpha-channel transparency"). Unfortunately, Photoshop CS2 and earlier allows you to apply true alpha-channel transparency to 24-bit PNGs only. For 8-bit GIFs, binary (GIF-style) transparency is the only option.

To save a PNG with transparency in Photoshop or ImageReady, start with a layered image that has transparent areas you'd like to preserve. For alpha-channel transparency, select PNG-24 from the file format pop-up window, and click Transparency. For PNG-8, the interface for working with transparency and matte colors works the same as for GIFs.

Figure 31-2 shows the available transparency options and resulting images for 24- and 8-bit PNGs in ImageReady.

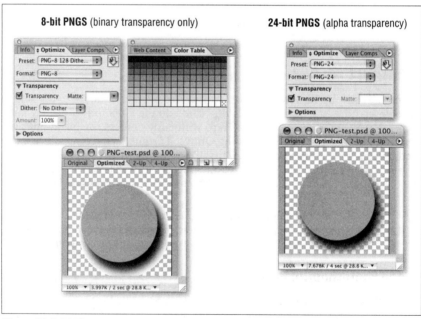

Figure 31-2. PNG transparency options in ImageReady

Macromedia Fireworks

Macromedia Fireworks is currently the best commercial software for creating PNG graphics. Not only does it have the most efficient PNG compression among its competitors, it also supports all varieties of PNG transparency, including the coveted multilevel 8-bit palette transparency. Fireworks also uses PNG as its native source file format because of its lossless compression.

Exporting PNG files

When creating a PNG in Fireworks, it is important to use the Export function rather than just saving the file (resulting in a Fireworks-native PNG file with loads of extra data). The Export Preview dialog box allows you to choose 8-, 24-, or 32-bit PNG format. The 8-bit PNG option gives you the same controls used for GIF compression: palette selection, color reduction, dither control, and transparency.

PNG transparency in Fireworks

Start with a layered image that has transparent areas (the checkerboard pattern shows through). To apply true alpha-channel transparency to a 24-bit PNG, choose 32-bit PNG in the Optimize palette. To save variable levels of transparency in an 8-bit PNG, check Transparency, and then select Alpha Transparency from the pull-down menu. If you view the color table for the image, you will see that it is full of colors that are marked with transparent areas. Choosing Index Transparency results in on/off binary transparency, similar to GIF transparency.

PNG

The GIMP

The GIMP (GNU Image Manipulation Program) is a free, Photoshop-like image-editing tool that runs on the X Window System under Unix. There is also a Microsoft Windows port available. The GIMP is virtually unknown by most professional graphic designers, but it bears mention here due to its superior implementation of the PNG format.

The GIMP offers excellent compression, full transparency support, gamma correction, and embedded text entry. You can apply compression incrementally using the deflate compression level knob (a sophisticated tool that no other image program offers). For more information, see *www.gimp.org*.

Figure 31-3 shows the available transparency options and resulting images for 32- and 8-bit PNGs in Fireworks. Notice that the cells in the 8-bit indexed color table give an indication that they contain transparency information.

PNG Optimization Strategies

The following are a few strategies for keeping PNG file sizes small and for using PNGs wisely.

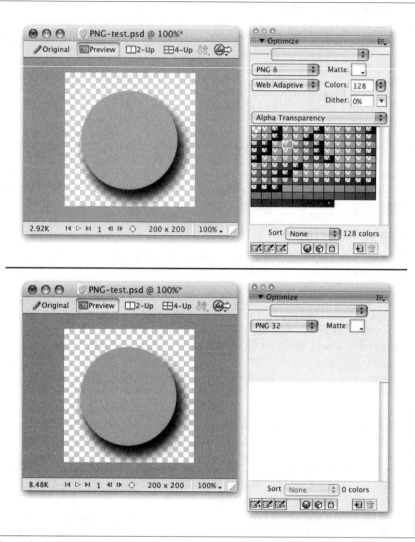

Figure 31-3. PNG transparency options in Fireworks

Use 8-bit (or smaller) PNGs.   Index color PNGs are always smaller than their 24-bit RGB counterparts.

Use JPEGs instead of RGB (24-bit) PNGs.   Photographic images are best saved in JPEG format for use online. The resulting file sizes are smaller (with only minimal image quality loss) and more appropriate for web delivery.

Use GIF optimization techniques.   8-bit PNGs benefit from all the same tactics used to minimize GIFs, including limiting dithering and reducing the number of colors and bit depth. See Chapter 29 for more information on optimization methods.

Avoid interlacing. Interlacing always adds to the size of a PNG. It is usually unnecessary anyway for small graphics or any graphic accessed via a high-bandwidth connection or locally (as from disk or CD-ROM).

Use maximum compression (if available) for final images. If your image tool offers control over compression, use level 9 (or "max" or "slowest") for the final version of your image. Use lower compression (3 or 6) for intermediate saves. Most commercial programs (such as Fireworks and Photoshop) handle compression and filter application internally, so you may not have control over specific levels.

For PNG Geeks Only

If you are serious about optimizing PNGs, you should download Glenn Randers-Pehrson's *pngcrush* application (freeware, available at *pmt.sourceforge.net/pngcrush/*). It is a command-line DOS application, but it can run in batch mode. *pngcrush* takes existing PNGs and makes them smaller, losslessly.

To convert RGB alpha-channel transparency (32-bit) into 8-bit palette transparency, try the *pngquant* command-line utility (written by Greg Roelofs, one of the creators of the PNG format). The resulting PNG will be significantly smaller and more suitable for web use.

For Further Reading

If you are interested in learning more about the PNG format, definitely check out *PNG: The Definitive Guide* by Greg Roelofs (O'Reilly). There are also a few good resources available online:

PNG home page (www.libpng.org/pub/png/)
This site is written and maintained by Greg Roelofs. It contains a complete history of PNG's birth, descriptions of its features, and up-to-date lists of applications that support the new format. It also includes a copy of the PNG Specification and the official PNG extensions documents (as well as the draft MNG Spec). It is written with so much enthusiasm that you can't help but become a PNG fan.

PNG Specification (www.w3.org/TR/png.html)
This is the complete PNG specification (Version 1.0) as published by the W3C. For a technical document, it is very user-friendly to nonprogrammers and offers detailed information on how PNGs work, as well as some useful background information and tutorials. The updated Version 1.2 of the specification is available at the PNG web site at *www.libpng.org/pub/png/spec/*.

32

Animated GIFs

It's just about impossible to browse the Web without seeing the flashing, bouncing, and wiggling of GIF animation. The animated GIF is ubiquitous, and there are many reasons for its popularity.

Users need no special software or plug-in. All they need is a browser that supports GIF animation, which is true of nearly all graphical browsers available today.

GIF is the standard file format for the Web. Animated GIFs are not a unique file format in themselves, but merely take advantage of the full capabilities of the original GIF89a specification. Even if a browser cannot display all of its frames, the GIF will still be visible as a static image.

They're easy to create. There are scores of GIF animation tools available (some are built into larger web graphics applications), and they're simple to learn and use.

They require no server configuration. Because they are standard GIF files, you do not need to define a new file type on the server.

They use streaming technology. Users don't need to wait for the entire file to download to see something. Each frame displays as soon as it downloads.

The only drawback to animated GIFs is that they may cause some extra work for the user's hard disk to keep refreshing the images. And they can be annoying, but more on that later.

How They Work

Animated GIFs work a lot like traditional cell animation. The file contains a number of frames layered on top of each other. In simple animations, each frame is a complete scene. In more sophisticated animations, the first frame provides the background and subsequent frames just provide the changing portion of the image.

A GIF animation file consists of a number of images and a set of instructions that specify the length of delay between frames, as well as other attributes like transparency and palettes.

Using Animated GIFs

Nowhere has GIF animation made a larger impact than in banner advertising. Ad agencies aren't stupid; they know that adding motion and flashing lights to a web page is a sure-fire way to attract attention. And it's true—adding animation is a powerful way to catch a reader's eye.

But beware that this can also work against you. Many users complain that animation is *too* distracting, making it difficult to concentrate on the content of the page. Although it adds a little "pizzazz" to the page, overall, too much animation can quickly spoil the user's enjoyment of your page.

Use animated GIFs wisely. A few recommendations:

- Avoid more than one animation on a page.
- Use the animation to communicate something in a clever way (not just as gratuitous flashing lights).
- Avoid animation on text-heavy pages that might require concentration to read.
- Consider whether the extra bandwidth to make a graphic "spin" is actually adding value to your page.
- Decide whether your animation needs to loop continuously.
- Experiment with timing. Sometimes a long pause between loops can make an animation less distracting.

Tools

You don't need to search very far to find a GIF animation tool—there seem to be scores of them available. Regardless of the tool you choose, the interface is basically the same. Tools tend to differ somewhat in the degree to which they are able to optimize (shrink the file size of) the resulting graphic. The following sections provide an overview of the most popular and/or recommended tools.

Applications That Include GIF Animation Tools

GIF animation tools are built in or bundled with many popular graphics applications, eliminating the need to jump between different software packages.

Adobe ImageReady (Mac and Windows)
Adobe ImageReady is a tool (bundled with Photoshop 5.5 and higher) especially for preparing and optimizing web graphics. It includes a GIF animation tool that converts layers into frames and allows easy layer editing. ImageReady offers advanced optimization methods for making the smallest possible animations. For more information, see Adobe's site at *www.adobe.com*.

Macromedia Fireworks (Mac and Windows)
Macromedia Fireworks was designed specifically for the creation of web graphics. It supports multiple layers that can be converted to multiple animation frames. Among other features are automatic super-palette optimization and the ability to perform LZW optimization. For more information, see Macromedia's site at *www.macromedia.com/software/fireworks/*. As of this writing, Fireworks' fate is unknown, as Macromedia has been acquired by Adobe.

Animation Shop (Windows only)
Animation Shop is a tool that complements Paint Shop Pro, an inexpensive and powerful graphics creation application from Corel (it was originally developed by JASC Software, Inc.). For more information, see Corel's web site at *www.corel.com*.

GIF Animation Utilities

The following are just a few dedicated tools for creating animated GIF files. For a complete list, see the article "Optimizing Animated GIFs" by Andrew King, *www.webreference.com/dev/gifanim/index.html*.

GIFmation (Mac and Windows)
This is commercial software from BoxTop Software that comes highly recommended by web developers. It features sophisticated palette-handling options and a bandwidth simulator. It also uses the efficient "frame differencing" method (discussed later in this chapter) for optimizing animations significantly better than its competition. GIFmation costs $49.95 and is available at *www.boxtopsoft.com*.

Ulead GIF Animator 5.0 (Windows only)
Ulead's GIF Animator features wizards for quickly and easily constructing animations, 200 levels of undo, pixel-level optimization, built-in transition and animation effects, a plug-in architecture for adding new animation modules, and support for AVI and QuickTime videos and layered Photoshop files. GIF Animator is $44.95. You can download a preview copy from *www.ulead.com*.

Creating Animated GIFs

Regardless of the tool you choose, the process of creating an animated GIF is about the same and involves making decisions about a standard set of features and options. The exact terminology may vary from tool to tool, but the concepts and settings are consistent.

Frame Delay

Also called "interframe delay," this setting specifies the amount of time between frames. Frame delays are measured in 1/100ths of a second. You can apply a different delay time to each frame in the animation to create pauses and other timing effects. This differs from digital video formats, in which the delay between all frames is consistent.

Transparency

You can set transparency for each frame within an animation. Previous frames will show through the transparent area of a later frame if disposal methods are set correctly.

If the background frame is made transparent, the browser background color or pattern will show through.

Don't be surprised if the transparent areas you specified in your original graphics are ignored when you import them into a GIF animation utility. You may need to set transparency in the animation package. Some standard transparency options include:

None
> No transparency.

White
> All the white pixels in the image will become transparent.

Based on first pixel
> The color of the "first pixel"—that is, the top-left pixel, the one at coordinates 0,0—is transparent. This is a handy option, because you'll often have an image in the center, and the four corners will be transparent.

Other
> This option lets you select one of the palette colors as transparent.

Disposal Methods

The disposal method gives instructions on what to do with the previous frame once a new frame is displayed.

Most GIF animation utilities offer "optimization," a file size–reducing process that takes advantage of the fact that previous frames will "show through" transparent areas of a later frame. In order for this process to work, the disposal method must be set to Do Not Dispose (or Leave Alone, Leave As Is, and the like). With this method, areas of previous frames continue to display unless covered up by an area in a succeeding frame.

The most common disposal method choices are listed here, but not all of these are available in all animation tools.

Unspecified (Nothing)
> Use this option to replace one full-size, nontransparent frame with another.

Do Not Dispose (Leave As Is)
> In this option, any pixels not covered by the next frame continue to display. Use this when you want a frame to continue to show throughout the animation.

Restore to Background
> The background color or background tile shows through the transparent pixels of the new frame (replacing the image areas of the previous frame).

Restore to Previous

This option restores to the state of the previous, undisposed frame. For example, if you have a static background that is set to Do Not Dispose, that image will reappear in the areas left by a replaced frame.

This disposal method is not correctly supported in Netscape Navigator (it is treated like Do Not Dispose), leading to all the frames being visible and stacking up. Although it can produce better optimized animation files, it is safest not to use it.

Automatic (ImageReady)

This selects the disposal method automatically based on whether there are transparent areas in the frames.

The effects of each of these disposal methods are compared in Figure 32-1.

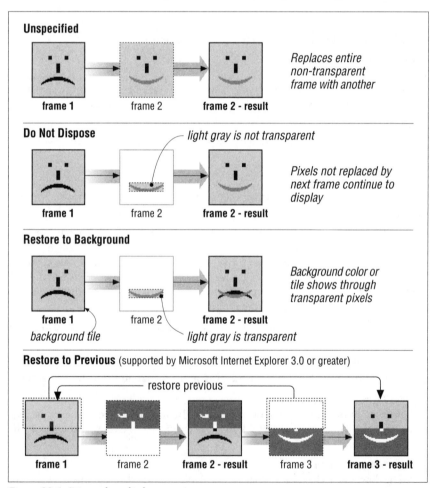

Figure 32-1. Disposal method comparison

In ImageReady, you access the disposal method by right-clicking (Windows) or Control-clicking (Mac) to reveal the disposal options (Automatic, Do Not Dispose, and Restore to Background). In Fireworks, you access the disposal settings via a trash can icon on the Animation panel of the Export Preview. Select the frame and then choose from Unspecified, None, Restore to Background, or Restore to Previous.

Color Palette

Animated GIFs, like static GIF files, use a list of up to 256 colors that can be used in the image. They can have multiple palettes (one for each frame) or one global palette. The palette choice affects how well the images appear on the inevitable variety of systems and monitor setups.

One problem with using multiple, frame-specific palettes is that they can cause a flashing effect on some early versions of Navigator (it cannot load the frames and their respective palettes in sync). In any case, multiple palettes dramatically increase file size. It is recommended you use one global palette for the whole animation. GIFMation and Ulead GIF Animator allow you to create a customized global palette. In fact, any image editor can be used to create a global palette. Just place all images to be used in one document, and then index the document. The resulting palette will be a global palette for the entire animation.

Other Options

The following are descriptions of other aspects of animated GIF files that can be set within most animation programs.

Loop

You can specify the number of times an animation repeats—none, forever, or a specific number. As noted earlier, not all browsers support a specific number of loops (the animation either loops or does not). One workaround to this problem is to build looping right into a file by repeating the frame sequence a number of times; of course, this increases the file size and download time.

Interlaced

Like ordinary GIF89a graphics, you can set animated GIFs to interlace, which causes them to display in a series of passes (starting blocky, finishing clear). It is recommended that you leave the interlacing option set to No or Off, because each frame is on the screen for only a short amount of time.

Color depth

This option allows you to limit the bit depth of the image to some number less than 8 (the default for GIF). Bit depth and its effect on file size is discussed in detail in Chapter 28. Note that if you select the web (6 × 6 × 6) palette, you will need to keep the bit depth set to 8.

Dithering
Dithering is a way to simulate intermediate color shades. It should be used with continuous-tone images.

Background color
Regardless of what color you select in the background color option, Navigator and Internet Explorer display the background color or image you specify in your HTML page. So, this option doesn't affect the display of the GIF in a browser, only within the tool itself.

Starting Points

These settings are a good starting point for creating full-frame animations:

Color Palette: Global, adaptive palette

Interlacing: Off

Dithering: On for photographic images; Off for drawings with few colors

Image Size: Minimum Size

Background Color: Black

Looping: None or Forever

Transparency: Off

Disposal Method: Do Not Dispose

Optimizing Animated GIFs

As with any file served over the Web, it is important to keep animated GIFs as small as possible. I highly recommend reading "Optimizing Animated GIFs," an article and tutorial by Andrew King in WebReference.com, from which many of the following tips were summarized (with permission). You can find it at *www. webreference.com/dev/gifanim/index.html*. It is a little dated, but it is still an excellent starting point for understanding how GIF animations work and the tools available for optimizing them.

Image Compression

Start by applying the same file size–reduction tactics used on regular, static GIF files to the images in your animation frames. For more information, see "Minimizing GIF File Sizes" in Chapter 29. These measures include:

- Reducing the number of colors/bit depth.
- Eliminating unnecessary dithering.
- Applying the "loss" feature available in Adobe ImageReady and Macromedia Fireworks. ImageReady allows you to do weighted optimization where loss can be applied more aggressively to selected areas of the image. If your tool does not include a loss function, you can manually remove stray pixels from otherwise solid areas.

Optimizing Methods

In addition to the standard image-compressing methods, GIF animation tools optimize animations by eliminating the repetition of pixels in unchanging image areas. Only the pixels that change are recorded for each frame. Different tools use different optimizing methods, which are not equally efficient. These methods, in order from least to most compression, include:

Bounding box (also called "minimum bounding rectangle")
> In this method, the changed portion of the image is saved, but it is always saved in the smallest rectangular area necessary to contain the changed pixels.

Redundant pixel removal (or frame differencing)
> In frame differencing, *only* the individual pixels that change are stored for each frame. This is a more efficient method than minimum bounding rectangle, which includes a lot of unnecessary pixel information to make up the rectangle.

LZW interframe optimization
> This optimization method uses the LZW compression scheme to minimize the frequency of changes in pixel patterns between frames. This compression method, when used in conjunction with frame difference, is capable of producing the smallest possible file sizes. Macromedia Fireworks, SuperGIF 1.0, and WebPainter 3 all take advantage of LZW compression for animations.

VI

Media

Audio on the Web

Simple audio files found their way onto the Web in its earliest days when they could be linked to and downloaded like any other file. The drawback to this technique is that traditional audio files are generally quite large and may take a prohibitively long time to download. As the Web evolved, some major breakthroughs have been made in web audio. First, streaming audio (files that play as they download) made long-playing audio and even live broadcasts possible. Then the MP3 format exploded into popularity around 1999. MP3's ability to crunch audio files to one-tenth their original size while maintaining very good quality made it a perfect solution for sharing music over the Internet.

Obviously, audio, even specialized for the Web, is a rich and complex topic that cannot be thoroughly treated in a single chapter of a Nutshell reference book. This chapter introduces general audio concepts and a number of popular web audio file formats, including MP3, QuickTime, RealAudio, Windows Media, Flash audio, MIDI, and AAC. It also discusses the many options for adding audio to a web site. It begins with an introduction to basic audio terminology that will be useful to know when it comes time to create and optimize sound files.

Basic Digital Audio Concepts

To distribute recorded speech or music over the Internet, an analog signal must be converted to digital information (described by bits and bytes). This process is called *encoding*. It is analogous to scanning a photograph to a digital bitmap format, and many of the same concepts regarding quality and file size apply. Some audio file formats (such as MPEG) are compressed in size during encoding using a specialized audio compression algorithm to save disk space. In the encoding process, you may be asked to provide settings for the following aspects of the audio file.

Sampling rate

To convert an analog sound wave into a digital description of that wave, samples of the wave are taken at timed intervals (see Figure 33-1). The number of samples taken per second is called the *sampling rate*. The more samples taken per second, the more accurately the digital description can recreate the original shape of the sound wave, and therefore the better the quality of the digital audio. In this respect, sampling rate is similar to image resolution for digital images.

Sample rates are typically measured in kilohertz (kHz). On the high end, CD-quality audio has a sampling rate of 44.1 kHz (or 44,100 samples per second). On the low end, 8 kHz produces a grainy sound quality that is equivalent to a transistor radio. Standard sampling rates include 8 kHz, 11. 025 kHz, 11.127 kHz, 22.05 kHz, 44.1 kHz, and 48 kHz. The high-end standard is 96K, which may be seen in DVD audio but is not applicable to the Web. The higher the sampling rate, the more information is contained in the file, and therefore the larger the file size.

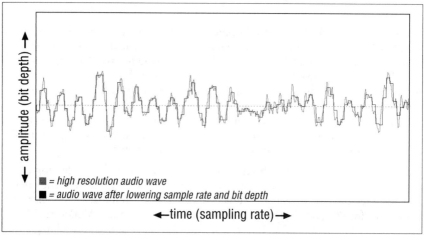

Figure 33-1. Audio wave after lowering sample rate and bit depth

Bit depth

Like images, audio files are measured in terms of their bit depth (also called sampling resolution or word length). The *bit depth* corresponds to the resolution of the amplitude (or volume) of the sound file. The more bits, the better the quality of the audio, and of course, the larger the resulting audio file. This is similar to bit depth in images—the more bits, the more colors the image can contain.

Some common bit depths are 8-bit (which can sound thin or tinny, like a telephone signal) and 16-bit, which is required to describe music of CD quality. High-end digital audio is now capable of 20-, 24-, 32-, and 48-bit depths. The higher the bit depth, the larger the file.

Channels

Audio files may contain one or more channels of audio information. The most familiar channel configurations are mono (one channel) and stereo (two channels), but some file formats can support multichannel surround sound such as 5.1, 6.1, and 7.1. Most file formats support only mono and stereo, but we will be seeing a lot more support for multichannel surround formats in the coming years. Here again, more channels translates to more data, which makes for a larger file.

Bit rate

All of the above come together to determine the overall *bit rate*, the number of bits per second devoted to storing audio data. Bit rate is a function of the file's bit depth, sampling rate, and channel count, so you reduce the bit rate by reducing a combination of those settings. Bit rate is measured in kilobits per second (Kbps) and can be calculated by dividing the file size by the length of the audio clip in seconds. In general, it is advisable for the bit rate of streaming audio files to be lower than the bit rate of the user's connection to the Internet to ensure smooth playback. Conveniently, most Internet connections are also measured in Kbps, so it is easy to figure out how to target audio files for a 56 Kbps dial-up modem or a 256 Kbps DSL line.

It stands to reason that before you can put your own audio files on the Web, you first need to create them. Your options are to find existing audio resources (such as from a royalty-free CD) or to record them yourself.

Using Existing Audio

The simplest way to add audio to a site is to use found music, sound effects, or other resources. But before you start featuring music and sound effects from your personal CD collection, it is important to be aware of copyright issues.

Copyright Restrictions

With few exceptions, it is illegal to reproduce, distribute, or broadcast a sound recording without the permission of the copyright owner. Copyright issues have been brought to the forefront with the growing popularity of MP3 distribution through peer-to-peer networks, but they apply to all audio published on the Internet. To get permission, you usually need to pay licensing fees.

Be aware that simply posting somebody else's music or recordings from a CD without her expressed written permission is a copyright violation. Record companies, entertainment corporations, and the RIAA (Recording Industry Association of America) are taking measures to crack down on the illegal use of copyrighted material. So be smart and be sure that you have the rights to the sound you use on your site.

Royalty-Free Audio Resources

Fortunately, collections of prerecorded sound effects and music are available for multimedia and Internet use. Many are royalty-free, meaning once you've purchased the package of sounds, you can use them however you wish and pay no licensing fees. Search Google for "royalty-free audio" for a list of vendors.

Preparing Your Own Audio

Recording and producing your own audio can require a significant investment in hardware, software, and time spent learning. If you need to put professional-quality audio on your site but aren't likely to make the investment in time and equipment yourself, consider outsourcing the work to professionals.

The final product may be anything from a simple personal greeting to a live concert broadcast. The preparation of original audio requires a number of standard steps: recording, basic sound editing, and then optimization for web delivery.

Recording

The first step is to make a recording of the music, spoken word, or sound effects for your site. As for most things, when it comes to sound quality, you get what you pay for. It is possible to capture sound using available resources (such as the microphone that came with your computer), but the quality will not be appropriate for a professional site. The cost of recording equipment escalates quickly for each level of sound quality. An investment of $800 to $4,000 in equipment (not counting the computer) is enough to get started on creating a home or small business studio. Getting a studio up and running also requires investments of time, effort, and education.

Although this may be a good choice for a business, it may be too expensive for many hobbyists and garage bands. It may be more cost-effective for an individual or organization on a strict budget or tight deadline to hire the services of a professional studio. Depending on how well the studio is equipped, it can cost from $30 to $250 per hour, and up.

Basic Sound Editing and Effects

Once you've recorded raw audio, the next step is to clean up the recording. This can involve removing unwanted sounds, setting the beginning and end of the file, and/or making a loop. You may want to apply effects to the sound, such as reverb or a delay.

Consider also using mastering processing techniques such as normalization or compression that can balance out the level of your audio such that no part is too loud or too quiet.

There is a huge selection of software for audio editing and format conversion. The software ranges from single-purpose utilities available via free download to professional digital-audio editing suites costing thousands of dollars. Some popular professional-level tools are listed in the following sections.

Cross-platform audio tools

These tools are available for multiple operating systems:

Audacity (audacity.sourceforge.net/)
> Audacity is an open source audio recording and editing application for Windows, Mac, and Linux. With many built-in effects and editing tools, it can't be beat for the price (free).

Cubase (Steinberg, www.steinberg.net)
> This multitrack recording environment offers both MIDI and audio editing with lots of effects plug-ins, virtual instruments, and recording tools for creating an entire virtual studio inside your computer. Cubase is available for Windows and Mac. Street price is around $600, while a more limited entry-level "SE" version is available for around $100 as of this writing.

ProTools (Digidesign, www.digidesign.com)
> Long the industry standard for multitrack computer recording, ProTools offers everything you'd ever need for a professional-quality recording studio in your computer. The company's high-end "Mix" systems, including both software and custom hardware, start at $7,000 and go up from there, but Digidesign has recently started making consumer-level solutions such as the Digi001 and the MBox which offer ProTools software and a hardware input/ output box for around $900 and $400, respectively.

Windows audio tools

The following tools are available for use on Windows:

Sound Forge (Sony, www.sonicfoundry.com)
> Sound Forge is limited to editing stereo files, but it includes many plug-ins for effects such as chorus, delay, distortion, reverb, and compression. Street price is about $250.

Audition (Adobe, www.adobe.com/products/audition/)
> In 2003, Adobe purchased Syntrillium Software and turned Cool Edit into Adobe Audition, a full-fledged multitrack recording and mixing environment with many included effects, processors, and tools for everything from audio restoration to surround sound encoding and CD burning. Adobe Audition sells for about $300.

Mac audio tools

These tools can be used on Mac systems:

Peak (Bias, www.bias-inc.com)
> With built-in batch processing and a street price of less than $400, this application has been the Mac standard when it comes to stereo editing. Bias also offers the more streamlined Peak LE for $99. This "Light Edition" may be sufficient for most entry-level users.

Audio

Garage Band (Apple, www.apple.com/ilife/garageband/)
Apple offers several levels of audio editing software and Garage Band is their entry-level multitrack audio application. It comes free with most Macs or as part of Apple's $60 iLife bundle. Garage Band comes bundled with several virtual instruments and effects including a guitar amp emulator. For the price, it can't be beat.

Digital Performer (MOTU, www.motu.com)
Performer software has evolved from a MIDI sequencing application into a full-fledged digital recording studio environment offering top-quality effects plug-ins and audio editing. Musicians can make entire recordings with this software, but it is also just as capable at adding audio to video or mixing radio programs. Street price is around $550.

Logic (Apple, www.apple.com/logicpro/)
Apple's high-end audio application is Logic. It offers most of the features that you'll find in ProTools or Digital Performer and comes bundled with a huge assortment of digital effects and virtual instruments. Logic sells for about $1,000.

Optimizing for the Web

After the sound files have been recorded and edited, it is time to convert them to their target web audio format and make them as small as possible for web delivery. The tool you use may depend on the file format. There are also several tools specialized for the creation of MP3s. Tools are discussed with their respective file formats later in this chapter.

One great all-purpose tool is Autodesk's Cleaner, which is available for the Mac and Windows systems. This program is designed to get the best quality files at the smallest size in whatever format you choose. Cleaner can compress a number of file formats, including QuickTime and RealMedia. It can also do batch processing. The program sells for about $500 as of this writing. Regardless of the tool you use, there are standard ways to reduce the size of an audio file so it is appropriate for downloading via a web page. Not surprisingly, this usually requires sacrificing quality. The aspects of the audio file you can control are:

Length of the audio clip
It might seem obvious, but you should keep the audio sample as short as possible. For example, consider providing just part of a song rather than the whole thing. If you are recording a greeting, make it short and sweet.

Number of channels
A mono audio file requires half the disk space of a stereo file and may be adequate for some audio uses.

Bit depth
Audio files for the Web are often saved at 8 bits, which will result in a file that is half the size of a 16-bit file. MP3s can handle 16-bit due to their efficient compression.

Sampling rate

    Cutting the sampling rate in half cuts the file size in half (e.g., a sampling rate of 22.05 kHz requires half the data than one of 44.1 kHz). As a general guideline, audio files that are voice-only can be reduced to 8 kHz. Sound effects work at 8 kHz or 11.025 kHz. Music sounds acceptable at 22 kHz.

Using these guidelines, if you start with a one-minute music sample at CD quality (10 MB) and change it to a mono, 8-bit, 22 kHz WAV file, its size is reduced to 1.25 MB, which is much more reasonable for downloading. Using MP3 compression, you can keep the quality of that one-minute sample at 16-bit, 44.1 kHz stereo (similar to CD quality) with a resulting file size of less than 1 MB. Combining these methods (a mono, 8-bit, 22 kHz MP3), you can offer one-minute clips at acceptable audio quality at only a few hundred K.

Obviously, just how stingy you can be with your settings while retaining acceptable quality depends on the individual audio file. You should certainly do some testing to see how small you can make the file without sacrificing essential audio detail.

Streaming Audio

Once upon a time, the only way to play audio from a web page was to link to it and wait for it to download to the hard drive so it could be played. With this method, once the file finishes downloading, the browser either launches an external player or uses a plug-in (or ActiveX control in Internet Explorer on Windows) to play the audio. The most common players are QuickTime, Windows Media Player, and RealPlayer, all of which are available on Mac and Windows.

Downloaded audio has a few distinct disadvantages. First, because the file needs to download to the hard disk in its entirety before it can begin playing, users may be faced with a very long wait before they hear any sound. In addition, because the audio file is copied to the hard drive, it is more difficult for artists and publishers to limit distribution and protect copyrights.

Although it is still possible and common to deliver static audio files in this manner, it is far more effective to use one of several streaming media technologies. Streaming media (be it audio or video) begins playing almost immediately after the request is made and continues playing as the audio data is being transferred. Streaming audio technology was developed to address the problem of unacceptable download times. It can even be used to broadcast live programs, such as concerts or baseball games.

The advantages to streaming audio are:

- Audio begins playing soon after the stream begins.
- Using new technologies and formats, sound quality doesn't need to be as severely sacrificed.
- Artists and publishers can better control distribution and protect copyright because the user never gets a copy of the audio file.

Consider also these disadvantages:

- The potentially high cost of server software may be prohibitive.
- Some formats require a dedicated or preconfigured server, which may be problematic with some hosting services.
- Sound quality and stream may be adversely affected by low speed or inconsistent Internet connections.

 For more information on streaming audio, consult *Streaming Audio: The FezGuys' Guide*, by Jon Luini and Allen Whitman (New Riders).

Streaming File Formats

It used to be that if you wanted audio to stream, you had to use RealAudio technology. Not so anymore. As it became obvious that streaming was the best way to deliver sound to the Web, we've seen the development of a number of competing proprietary technologies, as well as solutions for streaming standard file formats such as MP3 and QuickTime. The following formats have streaming functionality:

- RealNetwork's RealMedia and RealAudio
- Apple's QuickTime
- Microsoft's Windows Media
- Streaming MP3s (using a streaming MP3 server like SHOUTcast)
- Macromedia Flash

These file formats are discussed in more detail later in the chapter.

Server Software and Protocols

True streaming relies on special server software that permits the uninterrupted flow of data. The information in the song is broken up into little "packets" and sent out in order over the lines. These packets are then reassembled on the user's end. The audio player collects a number of packets before playback begins (a process called *buffering*) to increase the likelihood of smooth playback.

Streaming media takes advantage of UDP (User Datagram Protocol), RTSP (Real-Time Streaming Protocol), or RTP (RealTime Transfer Protocol) for the transmission of data. What makes these protocols effective at streaming is that if a packet of information is dropped or missing, the data transmission continues without it. This is in contrast to HTTP, the traditional protocol of the Web, which stops and tries to resend lost packets, potentially halting the stream.

UDP was the first protocol used for streaming media because of its improvements over HTTP. The newer RTSP is more efficient than UDP. RTSP is a two-way streaming protocol, allowing the user to send messages back to the server (such as rewinding the tape). By contrast, RTP (used by Apple QuickTime) is a one-way stream (similar to HTTP in this regard), only the file never downloads completely to the user's hard drive as it does in HTTP or FTP transfers.

Commercial streaming server software such as Windows Media and Helix Server can handle thousands of simultaneous streams. It provides robust administrative tools and offers advanced functions such as bandwidth negotiation (where the proper bit rate version is delivered based on the connection speed). The software and hardware to set up a dedicated streaming server can be quite costly. On top of that, some services charge licensing fees based on number of streams.

Pseudostreaming

Some media formats are designed to begin playing before they've completely downloaded, producing a streaming effect even when the files are served from an HTTP server. This is known as *pseudostreaming* or HTTP-streaming.

The advantage to pseudostreaming is that it requires no special (and costly) server software. You just put the files on your server as you would a GIF or JPEG. This is a good solution for broadcasting relatively short audio tracks to just a few simultaneous listeners.

There are a number of key limitations to serving streaming media from a web server. It cannot handle heavy server loads and multiple simultaneous connections. You also sacrifice the advanced administration tools and bandwidth negotiation (users have to choose the appropriate file for themselves). This method also makes it impossible to do live broadcasts since the whole file needs to be available for download.

With the proper player on the user's end, Windows Media, RealMedia, Quick-Time, MP3, and Flash files will pseudostream from an HTTP server.

 There are legal copyright differences between streaming and pseudostreaming formats. The issue involves whether the media becomes "affixed" to your hard drive or not. In this sense, the download and pseudostreaming methods are seen as giving away a recording of the audio, while streaming is seen more like broadcast and is subject to different copyright terms.

Audio Formats

At last, we get to the heart of web audio—the various file formats. This section provides an introduction to some of the most common formats for web audio.

WAV/AIFF (.wav, .aif, .aiff)

The WAV and AIFF audio formats are very similar in performance and these days are probably ill suited for most web audio. However, these formats remain the standard for high-quality uncompressed audio before it gets converted for use on the Web. The Waveform Audio File Format (*.wav*) was originally developed as the standard audio format for the Microsoft Windows operating system, but it is now supported on the Macintosh as well. WAV files can support arbitrary sampling rates and bit depths, although 8 kHz and 11.025 kHz at 8 or 16 bits are most common for Web use.

The Audio Interchange File Format (.aif or .aiff) was developed as the standard audio format for the Macintosh platform, but it is now supported by Windows and other platforms. It can support up to six channels and arbitrary sampling rates and bit depths, with 8 kHz and 11.127 kHz at 8 and 16 bits being the most common online.

WAV and AIFF files are less commonly used on the Web than they once were, now that we have audio formats that are better suited for web delivery (MP3) or designed specifically for the Web (streaming formats). They sound good when uncompressed, but they suffer drastic loss of quality when compressed to small file sizes. For this reason they are useful for very short, downloadable audio clips, such as short greetings. They are usually added to web pages via a link for download.

The following summarizes the WAV and AIFF formats:

Good for...	Storing high-quality source audio before converting to web formats, delivering short clips where pristine sound quality is not important, reaching the lowest common denominator (because everyone can play them).
Delivery	Download.
Creation tools	The majority of sound editing tools can save files in WAV and AIFF format.
Player	WAVs and AIFFs generally play using the browser's default function for sound handling (such as Windows Media Player or the QuickTime plug-in).

MP3 (.mp3)

MP3's explosion in popularity is nothing short of a phenomenon and has changed the way we use and view the Internet. The key to its success is MP3's ability to maintain excellent sound fidelity at very small file sizes. In fact, its compression scheme can reduce an audio source to just one-tenth of its original size. For instance, four minutes of high-quality music in WAV format requires 40 MB of disk space; as an MP3, the same file weighs in at just 3.5 MB! With the discovery of MP3, it was suddenly feasible to transfer songs over the Internet without prohibitive download times. The rest is history.

MPEG compression

The MP3s that we've grown to love are technically MPEG-1, Layer-III files. MPEG is actually a family of multimedia standards created by the Moving Picture Experts Group. It supports three types of information: video, audio, and streaming (which, in the context of MPEG compression, is synchronized video and audio).

MPEG uses a lossy compression scheme that is based on human auditory perception. Sounds that are not discernible to the human ear are thrown out in the compression process. The resulting file sounds nearly the same, but contains much less data than the original.

There are a number of MPEG standards: MPEG-1 was originally developed for video transfer at VHS quality and is the format used for MP3s; MPEG-2 is a higher-quality standard that was developed for television broadcast; other MPEG specs that address other needs (such as MPEG-7) are currently in development.

MPEGs can be compressed using one of three schemes: Layer-I, -II, or -III (the "3" in MP3 refers to its compression scheme layer). To learn more about MPEG, visit the MPEG web site (*www.mpeg.org*).

Creating MP3s

Any audio source file (usually a WAV or AIFF file) can be turned into an MP3 using an MP3 encoder such as Xing AudioCatalyst, iTunes (Mac), or Music-Match Jukebox. For a complete list of MP3 creation tools, see MP3-Converter. com (*www.mp3-converter.com*).

To make an MP3, begin with raw audio saved in WAV or AIFF format. If the audio is coming from a CD, it will need to be "ripped" first (extracted from the CD format and saved in a format a computer can understand). The next step is to encode the raw audio into the MP3 format. Many MP3 tools rip and encode audio tracks in one step.

When encoding, you'll be asked to set the quality level, or bit rate. The standard quality setting for putting music on the Internet is 128 Kbps (which is near-CD quality sound) at 44.1 kHz. For personal use (to play from your computer or portable MP3 player), you can use the next higher levels (160 or 192 Kbps). To keep file sizes extra small, choose 112 Kbps or lower, but expect a loss in audio quality. To stream MP3s at rates acceptable for 28.8 modem users, many MP3 online "radio" stations use 22.05 K mono files compressed at a mere 24 Kbps.

When encoding, you'll also need to decide whether you want to make *CBR* (constant bit rate) or *VBR* (variable bit rate) files. Variable bit rate MP3s adjust their bit rate based on the complexity of the current audio passage. Variable bit rate MP3s can provide an enormous increase in quality at similar bit rates, but because VBR is inconsistently supported, the most reliable choice is CBR. Most of the new MP3 players support VBR, so keep an eye out for VBR to gain more support in the coming years.

Serving MP3s

MP3s can be served from a traditional FTP or HTTP server. MP3s can also be streamed using server solutions such as SHOUTcast (discussed later in this section). Along with the main advantages of streaming, this means that the MP3 file is not actually downloaded to the user's computer, providing better copyright protection.

And speaking of copyright, remember that although there is no problem creating MP3s for your own personal use, it is illegal to upload and distribute audio if you do not hold the copyright for it.

One of the most popular software packages used for streaming MP3s is SHOUT-cast from Nullsoft. It makes it possible for people to broadcast audio from their PCs with a minimum amount of hardware and knowledge, over any speed Internet connection (although more bandwidth certainly helps). You can broad-cast MP3s to individual users or to many users at once by redirecting your stream to a high-bandwidth server. To listen to a SHOUTcast server stream, open Winamp, iTunes, or any other stream-capable MP3 player and bring up the Open

Location dialog box. Enter the URL of the server you want to listen to and hit Enter. For a list of SHOUTcast servers (and for more information), visit *www. shoutcast.com*. SHOUTcast server licenses are free.

The following summarizes the MP3 format:

Good for...	Distribution and sale of high-quality audio (like music tracks), radio broadcast-style transmissions at lower bit rates.
Delivery	Streaming, download.
Creation tools	One of dozens of MP3 encoding programs. See *www.mp3-converter.com* for a complete list.
Player	One of dozens of free MP3 players, such as WinAmp (Windows) or iTunes; browsers may support MPEG audio via the QuickTime or Windows Media players. You can select a program for MP3 playback in the browser's application preferences.

Apple QuickTime Audio (.mov)

Although QuickTime is best known as a video technology, it is also possible to create audio-only QuickTime Movies (*.mov*). QuickTime is a container format, meaning it can contain a wide variety of media. In fact, the QuickTime format can store still images (JPEG, BMP, PICT, PNG, and GIF), a number of movie formats including MPEG-1, 360-degree panoramic images, Flash movies, MP3 audio, and other audio formats. Once you package up media in a QuickTime *.mov* file, you can take advantage of QuickTime features such as dependable cross-platform performance, excellent compression, and true streaming.

Although the QuickTime system extension is needed to play a *.mov* file, it is widely distributed and available for both Windows and Macintosh systems. In addition, with the QuickTime plug-in, a QuickTime audio player can be embedded right on the page. And QuickTime has proven itself as a reliable format since you can assume most users have the appropriate plug-in or player.

QuickTime is discussed further in Chapter 34. For more information on Quick-Time, see *www.apple.com/quicktime/*.

The following summarizes the QuickTime format:

Good for...	Continuous-play audio (music, narration).
Delivery	True streaming via RTP or RTSP (using QuickTime Server on Mac OS X Server or the open source Darwin Streaming Server on Unix and NT), pseudostreaming on HTTP servers, download.
Creation tools	QuickTime Pro for $29.95.
Player	QuickTime plug-in for viewing within a web browser or QuickTime Player (standalone utility).

MIDI (.mid)

MIDI (which stands for Musical Instrument Digital Interface) is a different breed of audio file format. It was originally developed in the early 1980s as a standard way for electronic musical instruments to communicate with each other.

A MIDI file contains no actual audio information (the digital representation of analog sound), but rather numeric commands that trigger a series of notes (with instructions on each note's length and volume). These notes are played by a MIDI player using the available "instrument" sounds in the computer. The function is similar to the way a player piano roll creates a song when run through on the player piano.

As a result, MIDI files are incredibly compact and ideal for low-bandwidth delivery. They are capable of packing a minute of music into just 10K, which is 1,000 times smaller than a one-minute uncompressed WAV file (approximately 10 MB).

QuickTime and most other MIDI file handlers install a General MIDI (GM) soundset with instruments like piano, drums, bass, orchestral strings, and even vocal "oohs" and "aahs" in standardized MIDI locations. Although these sounds may vary in quality and timbre from player to player, General MIDI files can depend on getting a piano sound when they send to Program 1, Channel 1 of the GM Player (built into QuickTime, etc.). These sound sets can be surprisingly good, but they still can't compete with recordings created in a studio. In general, MIDI files will always sound "computery."

Despite this limitation, MIDIs are an extremely attractive alternative for adding instrumental music to your web site with very little download time.

 Because of the incredibly small download size and the availability of inexpensive tiny GM sound chips, MIDI has become a very popular format for mobile phone rings.

The following summarizes the MIDI format:

Good for...	Background music and loops. Mobile phone rings.
Delivery	Download.
Creation tools	Requires special MIDI sequencer software, such as Vision, Cakewalk, and Digital Performer. Creating and editing MIDI files can be complicated. Consider using an existing MIDI file if you are inexperienced with music composition and digital audio.
Player	QuickTime plug-in or Windows Media Player. MIDI sound engines are built into most of the current web browsers.

RealMedia/RealAudio (.rm, .ra)

RealNetworks was a pioneer in producing a viable technology for bringing streaming audio to the Web. Despite heavy competition, it continues to lead the pack in terms of widespread use and popularity, and it has grown to be the standard for streaming audio, including live broadcasts.

RealAudio is a server-based streaming audio solution. Real's Helix server offers advanced features for streaming audio delivery, including bandwidth negotiation (the proper bit rate version is delivered based on the speed of the connection), RTSP transmission for smooth playback, and administrative tools for tracking usage and minimizing server load. Using the SureStream feature, the bandwidth can be adjusted on the fly (while the file is streaming) to accommodate bit rate fluctuations.

A robust Helix system can allow thousands of simultaneous listeners. The server software requires a large investment, and RealNetworks charges licensing fees for the number of streams. There is, however, a free version that allows five simultaneous listeners. For more information, see the RealNetworks site at *www.realnetworks.com*.

If you aren't ready to commit to Helix, RealMedia and RealAudio files can be pseudostreamed from an ordinary HTTP server for sites with a limited amount of traffic.

To listen to RealAudio files, users must have RealPlayer, which is available for Windows, Mac, and Unix systems. The RealPlayer plug-in comes installed with most systems and makes it possible to embed a RealMedia player right in the web page.

RealNetworks also offers tools for creating RealAudio and RealMedia files. The latest version (as of this writing) is RealProducer Plus, which provides complete tools for converting audio and video to streaming format. Audio can be saved in either the current and preferred RealMedia format (*.rm*) or the RealAudio format (*.ra*) for support in older versions of RealPlayer.

The process for adding RealAudio to a web page is covered in detail later in this chapter. For more information, visit the RealNetworks site at *www.realnetworks.com*. For consumer-oriented information and downloads, see *www.real.com*.

The following summarizes the RealAudio format:

Good for...	Continuous-play audio and live broadcasts to large numbers of people.
Delivery	Streaming (via RTSP), pseudostreaming (via HTTP).
Creation tools	One of the RealNetworks encoders (such as RealProducer Plus) or a third-party tool such as Cleaner from Autodesk.
Player	Freely available RealPlayer, Commercial RealPlayer Plus (with added features), RealPlayer plug-in.

Windows Media (.wma, .asf)

Microsoft's Windows Media is a streaming media system similar to RealMedia. Like RealMedia, it comes with the standard components for creating, playing, and serving Windows Media files. Windows Media wraps all media elements into one Active Streaming File (*.asf*), Microsoft's proprietary streaming media format. Audio may also be saved as nonstreaming Windows Media Audio format (*.wma*). Because Media Player is part of the Windows operating system, it is widely distributed and stable on the Windows platform. A version of Media Player is available for the Mac as well, but it generally lags behind the Windows release and may not support the latest Windows Media codec standards.

Windows Media Audio files are encoded using the special Windows Media Audio codec (currently in Version 9), which is ideal for all types of audio at bit rates from 16 Kbps to 192 Kbps. For voice-only audio at low bit rates (8 Kbps), use the alternative ACELP codec.

The Windows Media system has its advantages and disadvantages. On the good side, the server software comes free with Windows NT Server 4.0 and later, and there are no charges for streams as there are with RealMedia. Administration tools make it easy to track performance and bill per view or per minute. The disadvantages to Windows Media are that the server only runs on Windows NT and it doesn't support Flash or SMIL (Synchronized Multimedia Integration Language) like RealMedia.

For more information on Windows Media, see *www.microsoft.com/windows/windowsmedia/default.mspx*. The FAQ is a good starting point.

The following summarizes the Windows Media format:

Good for...	Continuous-play audio and live broadcasts.
Delivery	Streaming, download.
Creation tools	Windows Media Encoder for converting to Windows Media format, Windows Media Author for creating synchronized multimedia presentations. See the Windows Media site for a complete list of creation tools at *www.microsoft.com/windows/windowsmedia/forpros/AudioProd.aspx*.

Flash (*.swf*), developed by Macromedia, is an ideal format for adding high-impact interactivity and animation to web sites. Audio (from short clips to long-playing audio) can be embedded in a Flash movie and triggered instantly by user actions. Recent versions of Flash can also embed streaming and pseudostreaming MP3 audio (and video). The popularity and power of the Flash browser plug-in and standalone Flash Player have quickly made Flash a viable alternative for custom players and interactive audio. Creating Flash audio players can be a challenge, but the payoff can be very impressive custom audio players only limited by imagination. Flash is covered in more detail in Chapter 35. For more information, see Macromedia's site, *www.macromedia.com*.

The following summarizes the Flash formats:

Good for...	Interactive sound effects, specialized web applications with embedded long-playing sound.
Delivery	Streaming (via QuickTime 8 or RealServer), pseudostreaming (via HTTP), download.
Creation tools	Macromedia Flash, Adobe LiveMotion.

AAC (.m4a, .m4p, .mp4)

The Advanced Audio Coding (AAC) format was developed by the MPEG group as an improvement on MP3 and other previous MPEG audio formats. It is the audio format at the core of the new MPEG-4 standard and offers several considerable improvements over MP3. Probably the most notable is that it offers higher sound quality at lesser bit rates than MP3s. The format supports multichannel surround sound capability and takes less computing power to decode. In 2003, Apple added AAC support to the iPod and since that time has used copy-protected AAC (*.m4p*) as the format for distribution of audio from the iTunes Store. Look for this format to take over for MP3 in the coming years.

Choosing an Audio Format

Which audio format or system you choose depends on your communication goals, the scale of your site, and your budget. Table 33-1 provides suggestions for some common scenarios. Consider them only as starting points for researching the solution that best meets your needs.

Table 33-1. Suggested audio formats

Audio needs	Suggested formats
Short voice greetings	QuickTime (via regular HTTP server), MP3, AAC
Narration (news broadcasts, interviews, and other voice-only content)	Streaming solutions such as RealAudio, Windows Media, or QuickTime for large audiences; RealAudio or QuickTime via HTTP server for limited traffic and few simultaneous listeners
Background music (ambient sound loops)	MIDI, WAV
Short interactive sound effects (such as button rollover and transition sounds)	Flash
Music samples for a limited audience	MP3, AAC, RealMedia, or QuickTime via HTTP server
Music samples for a large-scale site with heavy traffic	Complete streaming solution, such as Real Helix or Windows Streaming Media
Radio-style music broadcasting	Real Helix, streaming MP3s (via a streaming server such as SHOUTcast), Windows Media System
Distribution and sale of CD-quality audio	MP3, AAC
Live broadcasting	Real Helix, QuickTime, Windows Media System
Musical e-greeting card	Flash, MIDI or WAV background sound
Specialized audio applications (such as virtual CD players, mixers, etc.)	Flash, QuickTime

Adding Audio to a Web Page

There are a number of ways to add audio to a web page. This section covers the most common techniques.

A Simple Link

You can link to an audio file from a web page using a simple anchor (a) element, as follows:

```
<a href="audio/song.mp3">Play the song (3.5 MB)</a>
<a href="groovy.mp3"><img src="buttons/playme.gif"></a>
```

When the reader clicks on the linked text or image, the browser retrieves the audio file from the server and launches a helper application (or plug-in, if the browser is so configured) to play the file. Files accessed in this manner are typically downloaded to the user's hard drive (stored in cache).

If the browser uses an external player, a new small window from the helper application opens with the controls for playing the audio. If the browser is configured to use a plug-in player (such as the popular QuickTime plug-in), a control panel may load right in the browser window, replacing the original web page.

It is good web etiquette to warn readers of the size of an audio file so they can make an informed decision as to whether they want to spend the time downloading the file.

Background Sound

Although it is possible to embed an audio file on a web page so that it starts playing automatically when the page loads, this technique is not recommended. The problem with background sounds is that users have no way of turning the sound off if they do not like it. Also, if the audio file is large, you are forcing a potentially lengthy download on the user. Furthermore, background music on a web page is almost always unnecessary.

If you do need to add a background sound to a page, you can do it with this nonstandard markup. Be aware that this element will cause your document not to validate.

```
<embed src="audio/song.mid" autostart="true" hidden="true"></embed>
```

Adding RealMedia

RealMedia (including RealAudio) files can be added to a web page via two methods. The first and most straightforward triggers the browser to launch RealPlayer as an external application (what Real calls the "three-pane environment"). The second plays the media file in a player embedded directly in the browser window using the RealPlayer plug-in.

RealNetworks provides extensive tutorials for producing, managing, and serving RealMedia. Start with these online guides:

- *service.real.com/help/library/guides/realone/IntroGuide/HTML/ prodintro.htm*
- *service.real.com/help/library/guides/realone/ProductionGuide/ HTML/realpgd.htm*

Real recommends displaying RealMedia content in the RealPlayer three-panel environment, because it enables you to take advantage of the full range of features and doesn't require potentially complicated markup and scripting that cross-browser embedding can entail.

In either case, you do not create a link directly to the RealMedia file itself, but rather to a special reference file, called a *metafile*. The metafile is a simple text document that contains the URL of the RealMedia file. These reference files are generally kept in the same directories as the HTML documents, although that is not a requirement.

There is a three-step process from click to playback. First, clicking the HTML link downloads the metafile from the server to the browser. Once it arrives at the browser, the metafile tells the browser to launch the RealPlayer and provides the player with URL information. Finally, the player uses the URL to request the actual media file from the server and begins playing the stream.

Metafiles are useful for maintenance and control purposes. To change the audio, all you have to do is change the tiny metafile, rather than having to dig through HTML source code. You can also do things like call multiple streaming media files from one metafile. One link to the metafile plays all the files.

This indirect linking process is demonstrated in the following two examples.

Linking to RealMedia (external player)

When the user accesses RealMedia via a link (using the a element), the browser launches the external RealPlayer application.

In the HTML document, make a link to the metafile that points to the RealMedia file as follows:

```
<a href="song.ram">Link to the song</a>
```

When linking to RealMedia, the metafile uses the *.ram* suffix. The metafile is a small text-only file that contains only the URL that points to the RealAudio file (suffix *.rm* or *.ra*):

```
rtsp://domainname.com/song.rm
```

Embedding RealPlayer on the page

The most common method for embedding RealPlayer on a web page is to use a combination of the standards-compliant object element that works for Internet Explorer 5+ on Windows and the embed element for browsers that use the Netscape plug-in architecture.

It should be noted that the audio stops playing when the user leaves the page. Also, it is more difficult to get consistent cross-browser performance when the player is embedded. For these reasons, it is generally preferable to link to the audio and use the external player.

 The example in this section uses the nonstandard embed element that will prevent (X)HTML documents from validating. In an ideal world, only the standards-compliant object element would be necessary to embed media objects on a web page, but as of this writing, the embed element is still required for full cross-platform functionality. You are encouraged to explore whether the object element alone may be sufficient for your needs.

The following sample code uses both the object (with parameters) and embed elements to embed the player on the page. When RealMedia is embedded, the suffix of the metafile should be *.rpm*. This tells the browser to start playing the media in the browser window.

```
<object
    classid="clsid:CFCDAA03-8BE4-11cf-B84B-0020AFBBCCFA"
    height="150" width="250" border="0">
<param name="SRC" value="realmedia/oakshoes.rpm">
```

```
<param name="CONTROLS" value="all">
<param name="AUTOSTART" value="true">

    <embed src="realmedia/oakshoes.rpm" height="150" width="250"
    autostart="false" controls="all" border="0">
    <noembed>You need the RealPlayer plugin to play this song.</noembed>
    </embed>
</object>
```

The embed element contains attributes for pointing to the metafile (src), specifying the size of the embedded player (width, height), whether the file starts playing automatically (autostart), whether it displays control buttons (control), and a border (border).

These same settings are made in the object tag using attributes and additional parameters (indicated by param elements). It is important that the classid attribute be specified *exactly* as it is shown in the example, as it is the unique identifier of the RealAudio plug-in. This may not be changed.

The easiest way to create the HTML code for handling RealAudio is to use the RealProducer or RealPublisher tool and allow it to do the work for you. The process for naming and accessing RealAudio has changed several times over the last few years, so be sure to refer to current documentation for up-to-date instructions.

Adding Windows Media

Before linking to Windows Media files (*.asf* or *.wma*), be sure they are saved in the *ASFROOT* directory on the NT Server running the Windows Media Administrator.

To link to a downloadable (nonstreaming) Windows Media Audio file (*.wma*), use a simple link directly to the audio file:

```
<a href="song.wma">Link to the song</a>
```

Linking to streaming Windows Media works much like the process described for RealAudio above. Streaming Windows Media uses a go-between reference file called an "active stream redirector" file (*.asx*), similar to RealAudio's metafile. The ASX file contains the URL information that points the player to the actual media file. This method of providing a single stream to a single user on demand is called *unicasting*. In the HTML document, create a link to the redirector file as shown in this example:

```
<a href="streamingsong.asx">Stream the song</a>
```

The content of the *.asx* file looks like this:

```
<ASX version="3">
    <Entry>
        <ref href="path/streamingsong.asf" />
    </Entry>
</ASX>
```

Change the path in the ref so that it points to your Windows Media file. The *.asx* file should be saved in the same directory as the Windows Media file.

Another method for delivering Windows Media is *multicasting*, in which a single media stream is delivered (at a time determined by the publisher) and multiple users share the stream. You can multicast prerecorded or live content. To add a multicast to your site, it is recommended that you use the tools and wizards provided by the Windows Media Services program. For more information, see the MSDN Library located at *msdn.microsoft.com/library/default.asp*.

Video on the Web

Like audio, video clips were linked to web pages in the Web's earliest days. Delivering video via the Web is especially problematic because video files require huge amounts of data to describe the video and audio components, making for extremely large files.

Many of the same technologies that have improved the experience of receiving audio over the Web have been applied to video as well. As with audio, you have the option of simply linking a video to your web page for download and playback, or you can choose from a number of streaming solutions. *Streaming* means the file begins playing almost immediately after the request is made and continues playing as the data is transferred; however, the file is never downloaded to the user's machine. For a more complete description of streaming versus nonstreaming media, see Chapter 33.

Many of the principles for developing and delivering video content for the Web are the same as those for audio. In fact, some of the file formats are the same as well. This chapter introduces you to basic video technology and concepts, including the video file formats QuickTime, Windows Media, RealMedia, AVI, and MPEG. If you are interested in learning how to produce video files for the Web, the books listed at the end of this chapter are a good start.

Basic Digital Video Concepts

The following is a list of aspects of digital video that can be manipulated with standard video-editing software. It is important to be familiar with these terms so you can create video optimized for web delivery.

Movie length

It's a simple principle: limiting the length of your video clip limits its file size. Videos longer than a minute or two may cause prohibitively long download times. If you must serve longer videos, consider one of the streaming video solutions.

Frame size

Obviously, the size of the frame has an impact on the size of the file. "Full-screen" video is 640 × 480 pixels. The amount of data required to deliver an image of that size would be prohibitive for most web applications. The most common frame size for web video is 320 × 240 pixels. Some producers go as small as 160 × 120 pixels.

Frame rate

The frame rate is measured in number of frames per second (fps). Standard TV-quality video uses a frame rate of approximately 30 frames per second to create the effect of smooth movement. For the Web, a frame rate of 15 or even 10 fps is more appropriate and still capable of producing fairly smooth video playback. For "talking head" and other low-motion subjects, even lower frame rates may be satisfactory. Commercial Internet broadcasts are routinely done as low as 0.5, 0.25, or even 0.05 frames per second (resulting in a slideshow effect rather than moving video).

Quality

Many video-editing applications allow you to set the overall quality of the video image. The degree to which the compression algorithms crunch and discard data is determined by the target quality setting. A setting of Low or Medium results in fairly high compression and is appropriate for web delivery. Frame rate, frame size, and quality are often traded off in different degrees in relation to each other, depending on the application, to reduce bandwidth requirements.

Color bit depth

The size of the video is affected by the number of pixel colors in each frame. Reducing the number of colors from 24- to 8-bit color will drastically reduce the file size of your video, just as it does for still images. Of course, you also sacrifice image quality.

Data rate (bit rate)

This is the rate at which data must be transferred for the video to play smoothly without interruption. The data rate (also called "bit rate") for a movie is measured in kilobytes per second (K/sec or Kbps). It can be calculated by dividing the size of the file (in K) by the length of the movie (in seconds). So, for example, a highly compressed movie that is 1900K (1.9 MB) and 40 seconds long has a data rate of 47.5K/sec.

For streaming media in particular, a file's data rate is more important than its total size. This is because the total bandwidth available for delivery may be severely limited, particularly over a dial-up connection. For example, even an ISDN line at 128 Kbps offers a capacity to deliver only about 16K of data per second.

Compression

Digital video wouldn't be possible without methods for compressing the vast amounts of data necessary to describe sound and frame images. Video files can be compressed in a number of ways. This section looks at a variety of compression

---

schemes and introduces the methods they use for achieving compression rates. Understanding your options can help you make better decisions for optimizing your video files.

Lossless Versus Lossy Compression

Compression can be *lossless*, which means no information is lost and the final file is identical to the original.

Most compression schemes use forms of lossy compression. *Lossy* compression sacrifices some data from the file to achieve much higher compression rates. Lossy compression schemes, such as MPEG, use complicated algorithms that toss out data for sound and image detail that is not discernible to the human ear or eye. The decompressed file is extremely similar in character to the original, yet is not identical. This is similar to the way JPEG handles still images.

Spatial Versus Temporal Compression

Spatial (or intraframe) compression takes place on each individual frame of the video, compressing the pixel information as though it were a still image.

Temporal (or interframe) compression happens over a series of frames and takes advantage of areas of the image that remain unchanged from frame to frame, throwing out data for repeated pixels.

Temporal compression relies on the placement of key frames interspersed throughout the frames sequence. The key frames are used as masters against which the following frames (called delta frames) are compared. It is recommended that a key frame be placed once every 3 to 10 seconds. Videos without a lot of motion, such as talking head clips, take the best advantage of temporal compression. Videos with pans and other motion are compressed less efficiently.

Video Codecs

There are a number of *codecs* (compression/decompression algorithms) that can be used to compress video files for the Web. Many of these codecs can be applied to several different file formats (discussed in the next section of this chapter).

Video-editing software packages often offer a long list of codecs in their compressor list options. This list focuses on just those that are relevant to video intended for web delivery.

Sorenson
>   The Sorenson Video codec was designed for low-bandwidth applications and is capable of producing files with lower data rates (if you select the Limit Data Rate option) than Cinepak while maintaining excellent quality. Because it uses complicated compression algorithms, it requires a lot of processing power and may not run smoothly on older machines.

H.264/AVC
>   This codec (also known as MPEG-4, Part 10) was designed to provide good video quality at drastically reduced bit rates, making it an exciting new codec for web video. It was created by ITU-T in collaboration with the group that

developed MPEG (together known as the Joint Video Team). The H.264 standard and MPEG-4, Part 10 standard are technically identical, and the technology is also known as AVC, for Advanced Video Coding. In addition to being useful for Internet transmission, it may accommodate higher bit rates for broadcast, DVD, and telephony.

Apple Computer integrated support for H.264 compression into its OS X 10. 4 (Tiger) operating system as well as QuickTime 7, both released in 2005.

Windows Media Video Codec
Microsoft uses its own proprietary video and audio codecs for use with the Windows Media System (in Version 9 as of this writing). It serves as the basis for the video codec VC-1, which is in the process of being standardized. For more information on Windows Media video codecs, see *www.microsoft.com/ windows/windowsmedia/howto/articles/codecs.aspx*.

MPEG
The MPEG codec can be used only when the final video file will be in MPEG format (it is not compatible with other file types). It uses a lossy compression scheme (although it may be lossless at high-quality settings) and spatial and temporal compression. Some other codecs (H.264 and Windows Media Video) are based on MPEG compression.

Intel Indeo
The Indeo codec provides compression rates similar to Cinepak by the use of spatial and temporal compression, with lossy compression at low quality levels. Its drawbacks are that it does not maintain quality at data rates as low as Cinepak, and it requires high-end machines to perform at its best.

Radius Cinepak
Cinepak provides decent compression/decompression rates. It employs both spatial and temporal compression and a lossy compression scheme at lower quality levels. Cinepak is well supported, but due to grainy video quality and the availability of alternative compression schemes, it is outdated and seldom used.

Animation
If your video clip is all computer-generated graphical imagery (i.e., not sourced from videotape), you may want to try the Animation compressor.

Video File Formats

As with audio, in the early days of the Web, adding video to a web page meant using one of the currently available video formats (such as QuickTime or AVI) and linking it to a page for download. The evolution of streaming media has changed that, and now adding video content like movie trailers, news broadcasts, even live programming to a web site is much more practical and widespread.

This section looks at the video formats that are most common for web delivery.

Windows Media (.wmv or .asf)

Windows Media is a new standard for audio and video, created by Microsoft and therefore very closely integrated with the Windows OS. The Windows Media Player is capable of playing Microsoft's proprietary Windows Media Video (*.wmv*) and Advanced Streaming Format (*.asf*), as well as a number of other formats such as AVI, MPEG, MP3, and QuickTime.

Windows Media movies are encoded using the proprietary Windows Media Video codec designed especially for the Windows Media system. They may also feature DRM (digital rights management) capabilities.

In addition to the player, the Windows Media 9 Series platform includes Windows Media Encoder, Windows Media Rights Manager 9 Series SDK, Windows Media Services, and a collection of audio and video codecs.

For more general information about Window Media, visit Microsoft's site at *www.microsoft.com/windows/windowsmedia/*. Resources related specifically to codecs (video and audio) are available at *www.microsoft.com/windows/windowsmedia/mp10/codecs.aspx*. If you want to create and stream Windows media, the book *Microsoft Windows Media Resource Kit*, by Tricia Gill, Bill Birney, and the Microsoft Windows Media Team (Microsoft Press) offers a comprehensive overview.

The following summarizes the Windows Media format:

Good for...	Delivering video to a wide audience (very good support).
Delivery	Streaming or download.
Creation tools	Windows Media Encoder for converting to Windows Media format, Windows Movie Maker for making simple movies on a PC. A growing number of third-party video editors support Windows Media, including Avid, Adobe Premiere, Autodesk Cleaner XL, and Sorenson Squeeze.
Player	Windows Media Player (shipped with Windows OS), also available as a download for the Mac as well as a variety of handheld devices.

QuickTime Movie (.mov)

QuickTime is a highly versatile and well-supported media format. While originally developed as a video format, it has evolved into a container format capable of storing all sorts of media (still images, audio, video, Flash, and SMIL presentations).

QuickTime, a system extension that makes it possible to view audio/video information on a computer, was introduced by Apple Computer in 1991. Although developed for the Macintosh, it is also supported on PCs via QuickTime for Windows. QuickTime has grown to be an industry standard for multimedia development, and most hardware and software offer QuickTime support.

Streaming

QuickTime movies may be downloaded (via HTTP) or streamed using a number of streaming server packages, including Apple's QuickTime Streaming Server for Mac OS X or its open source Darwin Streaming Server for Unix, Linux, and

Windows. To give the illusion of streaming from an HTTP server (pseudo-streaming), create FastStart QuickTime movies that begin playing right away and continue playing as the file downloads.

Creating QuickTime movies

You can take care of rudimentary video editing, such as deleting and rearranging, right in Apple's free QuickTime Player. The QuickTime Pro version ($29.95) offers more features and is sufficient for most basic tasks.

For advanced video editing, use a professional video editing tool such as Apple Final Cut Pro, Adobe Premiere or Adobe After Effects (most video editors support QuickTime). You may also use a file converter, such as Cleaner from Autodesk (*www.autodesk.com*) or Sorenson Squeeze from Sorenson Communications (*www.sorenson.com*), to convert existing files to QuickTime format.

An important step to remember when saving a movie is to make it self-contained. This process resolves all data references and prepares the file to go out on the Internet on its own. You will also be asked to pick a codec. QuickTime supports several codecs including the advanced H.264 codec (see earlier description) introduced in QuickTime 7.

Reference movies

Another interesting feature of QuickTime is its support for reference movies. Reference movies are used as pointers to alternate versions (or "tracks") of a movie, each optimized for a different connection speed. When a user downloads the reference movie, the plug-in ensures that the best track for the current connection speed is played.

For more information

The process for adding QuickTime to a web page is discussed later in this chapter. For general information on QuickTime, see Apple's site at *www.apple.com/quicktime/*. For complete information on all aspects of QuickTime creation and delivery, I recommend the book *QuickTime for the Web for Windows and Macintosh* by Steven Gulie (Morgan Kaufmann).

The following summarizes the QuickTime format:

Good for...	Delivering video to a wide audience (very good support).
Delivery	True streaming via RTP or RTSP (using QuickTime Server on Mac OS X Server or the open source Darwin Streaming Server on Unix and Windows), pseudostreaming on HTTP servers, download.
Creation tools	Most video editing and conversion tools support QuickTime, or use Apple's basic editing tool, QuickTime Pro, for $29.95.
Player	QuickTime plug-in (part of Netscape Navigator and Internet Explorer) for viewing within a web browser or QuickTime Player (standalone utility).

RealMedia (.rm)

RealNetworks (which used to be Progressive Networks) first launched its streaming video capabilities in Version 3.0 of its RealMedia line of products (of which RealAudio is the star component). RealMedia files (.rm) are viewed using RealPlayer. The wide distribution of RealPlayer makes RealMedia a popular choice for adding streaming media to a web site.

The components of the RealMedia system (RealPlayer for playback, Helix Server for serving simultaneous streams, and RealProducer and RealProducerPlus for creating .rm files) are the same as for RealAudio. RealMedia movies are encoded using a proprietary codec built into RealProducer and RealPlayer.

For more information, visit the RealNetworks site at *www.realnetworks.com*. For consumer-oriented information and downloads, see *http://www.real.com*.

The following summarizes the RealAudio format:

Good for...	Long-playing video clips and live broadcasts to large numbers of people.
Delivery	Streaming (via RTSP), pseudostreaming (via HTTP).
Creation tools	One of the RealNetworks encoders (such as RealProducer Plus or Basic) or a third-party tool such as Autodesk Cleaner. A plug-in is available for Final Cut Pro, Adobe After Effects, and Avid Xpress for exporting to RealMedia format.
Player	Freely available RealPlayer and commercial RealPlayer Enterprise.

AVI (.avi)

AVI (which stands for Audio/Video Interleaved) was introduced by Microsoft in 1992 as the standard movie format to work with its Video for Windows (VFW) multimedia architecture for Windows 95. In AVI files, the audio and video information is interleaved in every frame, which in theory produces smoother playback. The AVI format has been replaced by the more robust Windows Media as the standard media format for Windows. Macintosh users can view AVI files using the QuickTime player.

With the growing (and well-deserved) popularity of streaming media systems, AVI movies are becoming scarce for web distribution. More often, they serve as the high-quality video source file that is converted into a more web-friendly format.

The following summarizes the AVI format:

Good for...	Short web video clips, high-quality video source files.
Delivery	Download.
Creation tools	Most video editing tools support AVI.
Player	Windows Media Player, QuickTime Player.

MPEG (.mpg or .mpeg)

MPEG is a set of multimedia standards created by the Moving Picture Experts Group. It supports three types of information: video, audio, and streaming (which, in the context of MPEG compression, is synchronized video and audio).

MPEG was initially popular as a web format because it was the only format that could be produced on the Unix system.

MPEG files offer extremely high compression rates with little loss of quality. They accomplish this using a lossy compression technique that strips out data that is not discernible to the human ear or eye.

There are a number of MPEG standards. MPEG-1 was originally developed for video transfer at VHS quality. MPEG-2 is a higher-quality standard that was developed for television broadcast and DVD authoring. The most recent released standard is MPEG-4, made popular by its support by QuickTime (though MPEG-4 support is not limited to QuickTime).

MPEGs can be compressed using one of three schemes, Layer-I, -II, or -III. The complexity of the coding (and therefore the processor power needed to encode and decode) increases at each level. Due to this complexity, you need special encoding tools to produce MPEG videos.

MPEG-1 (which uses the *.mpg* or *.mpeg* suffix) is the most appropriate format for web purposes. MPEG-2 files are rare except in broadcast studios and on DVDs and are not well suited for web delivery. MPEG-4 is proving to be an attractive option for web video.

To learn more about MPEG, visit the MPEG web site (*http://www.mpeg.org*).

The following summarizes the MPEG movie format:

Good for...	High-quality video.
Delivery	Streaming, download.
Creation tools	QuickTime 7 Pro, professional video editing software such as Adobe Premiere and After Effects, Apple Final Cut Pro.
Player	Windows Media Player, QuickTime Player.

Which Format to Choose

To deliver long-playing video (like a full movie trailer) or live video broadcasts, you should definitely use one of the streaming media solutions (Windows Media, streaming QuickTime, or RealMedia). Which you choose will come down to the individual requirements of your site. If you expect heavy traffic and many simultaneous streams, definitely invest in a dedicated true streaming system.

If you have just a few short clips to share with a limited number of visitors, you may be able to get away with pseudostreaming RealMedia or FastStart QuickTime movies on your regular web server.

Because all streaming video formats are capable of supporting multiple file formats, are fairly stable, and feature well but not universally distributed players and plug-ins, the decision will likely come down to which server matches your budget or expertise.

For articles and news related to all matters of streaming media, see *StreamingMedia.com*.

Adding Video to an HTML Document

This section looks at the ways video files can be linked to or embedded within an HTML document.

A Simple Link

Like audio, downloadable video files (AVI, MPEG, Windows Media, and Quick-Time) can be linked to HTML documents using the standard anchor (a) element:

```
<a href="video.mov">Check out the video (1.3MB)</a>
```

When the user clicks on the link, the browser looks at the file type (as defined in the filename suffix) and launches an external player application or uses a plug-in to play the movie right in the browser window. Which player it uses depends on the file format and how that user has the browser configured, so it is out of the control of the web page designer.

When linking to media, it is good form to provide an indication of the file size so users with slower connections can make the decision whether to click.

Streaming Video

As in audio, streaming media in the RealMedia (*.rm*) and streaming Windows Media (*.asf*) formats are added to web pages via linked or embedded reference files (also called metafiles). The process, covered in detail at the end of Chapter 33, is exactly the same for video as for audio.

Windows Media

To link to a Windows Media Video file for download and playback, create a link directly to the video file:

```
<a href="movie.wmv">See the movie</a>
```

To link to a streaming Windows Media file for *unicasting* (a single stream triggered by a user request), make a link to an active stream redirector file (*.asx*).

```
<a href="streamingmovie.asx">See a streaming movie</a>
```

The content of the *.asx* file is the location (URL) of the actual movie and looks like this:

```
<ASX version="3">
    <Entry>
        <ref href="path/streamingmovie.asf" />
    </Entry>
</ASX>
```

For *multicasting* (a publisher-controlled broadcast of a single stream that is viewed by many users simultaneously), it is recommended that you generate code using the tools and wizards provided by the Windows Media Services program.

RealMedia

In brief, to link to a RealMedia movie, create a link to a RealMedia metafile (*.ram*) as shown in this example:

```
<a href="movie.ram">Link to the streaming movie</a>
```

The metafile is a small text-only file that contains only the URL for the RealMedia file (suffix *.rm*). When the user clicks the link, the browser accesses the metafile, which launches the player and passes it the URL of the actual media file:

```
pnm://domainname.com/movie.rm
```

Embedded QuickTime Movies

In addition to simply linking to a QuickTime movie, you can place the player right in the web page like an image. The QuickTime plug-in is required to play *.mov* files inline, but it is bundled with Internet Explorer, Netscape, and Safari and is supported Firefox, Opera, and most other browsers, making it a relatively safe and cross-platform method for putting a video right on a page.

To place a QuickTime movie on a web page so that it will be supported by all browsers (including IE), it is necessary to use both the object and embed elements. Be aware that embed is a nonstandard element, and will cause your document not to validate. Unfortunately, at this time, to take advantage of the full functionality of the QuickTime plug-in player, the embed element is the only option, because there is no method for passing parameters to the player using object alone.

 If you only require default play settings, there is a standards-compliant method for embedding QuickTime movies using nested object elements and a bit of CSS. The process is beyond the scope of this chapter, but you can read a tutorial at *realdev1.realise.com/rossa/rendertest/quicktime.html*.

This is the markup used in common practice for placing a *.mov* file that is 240 × 180 pixels on a web page for cross-browser compatibility. One day, there will be a standards-compliant embedding method that works with the QuickTime plug-in player, but for the time being, the embed element is required for all but the default player settings. By default, the movie is displayed with a small controller on its bottom edge for controlling playback. The movie will start playing automatically unless autoplay is set to false, as is shown in this example. The required markup is in bold.

```
<object classid="clsid:02BF25D5-8C17-4B23-BC80-D3488ABDDC6B" width="240"
height="196" codebase="http://www.apple.com/qtactivex/qtplugin.cab">
<param name="SRC" value="movies/vacation.mov" />
<param name="AUTOPLAY" value="false" />
```

```
<embed src="movies/vacation.mov" width="240" height="196" autoplay="false"
pluginspage="http://www.apple.com/quicktime/download/">
</embed>

</object>
```

The classid attribute in the object element calls in an ActiveX control in Internet
Explorer that plays QuickTime movies. The codebase and pluginspage attributes
function similarly in pointing to the location where the QuickTime plug-in is
available.

 It is important to add 16 pixels to the actual height of the movie in
the height attribute to accommodate the controller.

Attributes and parameters

The embed element has a number of attributes for controlling various aspects of
playback and display. These attributes are recognized by every browser that
supports the embed element and are supported by the QuickTime plug-in as well.

These attributes and their values are provided to the object element using name/
value pairs in the param elements. Notice in the example that the false value of the
autoplay attribute in embed is repeated as a param element where name="autoplay"
and value="false".

The attributes that are part of the definition of the embed element are listed here.
The attributes are described as they apply to QuickTime movies. They may have
other functions for other media.

src="url"
  Required. This attribute points to the video file you want to play.

width="number of pixels" height="number of pixels"
  Required. These attributes set the width and height in number of pixels for
  the video frame. It is important that the values of width and height be at least
  2, even when the player is set to be hidden. A value of less than 2 results in
  crashes in some browsers. Add 16 pixels to the height of your movie if you
  have also set the controller tag to true, so that the QuickTime controller
  strip has room to display.

hidden="true|false"
  When set to true, the plug-in player is not displayed. Be sure that the height
  and width are set to at least 2 even if the player is hidden to prevent crashes.
  This attribute is listed here for thoroughness' sake, but it is more appropriate
  for QuickTime audio (used as a background sound) than for video.

pluginspage="http://www.apple.com/quicktime/download/"
  This provides a link to a source from which to acquire the QuickTime plug-in
  if the browser can't find it on the system.

```
loop="true|false|palindrome"
```
true causes the video to loop continuously. false (the default) causes the video to play through once. palindrome makes the video play through, then play in reverse, then play through, continuously.

```
href="url"
```
This attribute makes your movie a link to another page.

```
type="MIME type"
```
Specifies the MIME type of the file (such as video/quicktime or image/x-quicktime) if you aren't sure the web server will provide it (it usually does).

Special QuickTime attributes

There are dozens of specialized attributes that are recognized by the QuickTime plug-in. The list below includes only a few of the most common. A complete list is available online at *www.apple.com/quicktime/tutorials/embed.html.*

```
autoplay="true|false"
```
The video will start playing automatically if this attribute is set to true. The default depends on the user's settings, but it is generally false (meaning the user will have to start the video with the Play button).

```
controller="true|false"
```
A control bar for the video will be visible when this is set to true (or by default). Although it is possible to turn off the controls, it is usually advisable to leave them visible and available for use.

```
volume="percent" (%0 to %300)
```
By default, audio is played at full volume (100%). You can set it lower to compensate for an especially loud audio track. Setting it higher than 100% is discouraged because it causes distortion and lessens audio quality.

```
playeveryframe="true|false"
```
When set to false (the default), you allow the video to skip frames in order to ensure smooth playback. Do not set this attribute to true if you have audio with your movie as it will be muted during playback.

Embedding Windows Media

Windows Media movies may also be embedded on a web page. The minimal markup for embedding Windows Media is quite simple, but it can get complicated quickly when taking advantage of scripting features, custom buttons, and so on. This section covers just the basics.

Embedded movies are played in Internet Explorer (Windows) using an ActiveX control and in other browsers using the Windows Media Player plug-in. Recently released Gecko-based browsers (Netscape Navigator 7.1 and Firefox 1.0) also now support the ActiveX control. The basic markup for embedding Windows Media is shown here.

```
<object id="Player" height="280" width="320"
        classid="clsid:6BF52A52-394A-11d3-B153-00C04F79FAA6">
    <param name="URL" value="movies/europe.wmv" />
```

```
        <param name="autoStart" value="false" />
        <param name="UIMode" value="full" />
    </object>
```

The classid attribute in the object element specifies the ActiveX control by its identifying number. The value beginning with clsid:6BF... is used with Windows Media Player Version 9 and 7. It is incompatible with earlier versions that use a different clsid.

This example uses these three common parameters:

URL (value="*url*")
  Specifies the location of the movie file. This parameter replaces "Filename" used in earlier versions.

autoStart (value="true|false")
  Specifies whether the movie begins playing automatically. The default is true.

UIMode (value="invisible|none|mini|full|custom")
  Specifies whether (or which version) of the controls are displayed. The default is full.

> For a complete list of Windows Media Player parameters, go to the MSDN Library (*msdn.microsoft.com/library*) and do a search for "PARAM Tags."

Browser support

The downside to embedding Windows Media is that you have to jump through a lot of hoops to get it to work on all browsers and platforms. Some solutions involve browser-sniffing and scripting—even Java applets—that are beyond the scope of this chapter.

> As of this writing, the existing Windows Media Player plug-in for Macintosh does not support the very latest Windows Media codecs.

Most sites that provide embedded WM movies as of this writing use that old fallback, the embed element, to provide play parameters to the Windows Media Player plug-in. It's not standards-compliant, and it will prevent your page from validating. You are encouraged to experiment with using the standard object element (or nested object elements) alone to see if it meets your needs.

The embed element is nested inside the object element as shown in this example:

```
<object id="Player" height="280" width="320"
        classid="clsid:6BF52A52-394A-11d3-B153-00C04F79FAA6"
        type="application/x-oleobject"                    codebase="HTTP://
ACTIVEX.MICROSOFT.COM/ACTIVEX/CONTROLS/MPLAYER/EN/NSMP2INF.
CAB#VERSION=6,4,7,1112">
    <param name="URL" value="movies/europe.wmv" />

    <embed type="application/x-mplayer2" name="MediaPlayer" width="320"
    height="280" src="movies/europe.wmv">
```

```
    <noembed><a href="streamingmovie.asx">See a streaming movie</a></
noembed>
      </embed>

    </object>
```

Browsers that can use the ActiveX control will get their instructions from the object and param elements. Browsers that don't understand the outer object element will look inside that object for alternative content (the embed element). Browsers that don't support the embed element will display the content of the noembed element, which is a link to play the movie in the external Windows Media Player.

The Flash Platform

—by Todd Marks

Flash has come a long way since its infancy as FutureSplash in the late 1990s. "Flash" started as means of adding animation and interaction to a web page, but has since evolved into a robust platform. Flash has seen significant improvements in not only its content delivery capabilities, including the addition of video and an object-oriented programming language, but also in its ability to allow for live communications and Rich Internet Applications (RIA) development. At the core of these features is the real hero of it all, the *Flash Player*.

The Flash Player allowed Flash to take off on the Web due to its small plug-in size and use of vector graphics and reusable shapes. Vector graphics were a big improvement over traditional raster graphics, because they were typically much smaller in file size and allowed users to animate graphics easier. The Flash Player's and Flash files' biggest contribution, however, was that they brought reusable graphical shapes to the Web. Flash allows graphics, buttons, and code objects to be duplicated over and over in a Flash file, but without adding additional file size to the page. This shift allowed designers and developers to start creating worlds to explore over the Web, during the pre-broadband era.

The name "Flash" traditionally has referred to the Macromedia Flash authoring environment, which produces *.swf* files, and the Macromedia Flash Player, which plays those files on the Web. Now, the name "Flash" refers to a platform, with the Flash Player at the center and several applications leveraging the power of that player.

The Flash authoring environment is still the primary application that uses the Flash Player. Flash includes tools for illustration, animation, interaction sequencing, sound editing, video, and working with its procedural language, ActionScript. *Macromedia Flash 8*, the latest version as of this writing, offers an improved interface, new templates for handheld and mobile devices, a new video codec and encoder, as well as several new "components," which are packaged as customizable code objects that can be used to add robust functionality to a web page or application. These features make Flash one of the most versatile and powerful formats for web multimedia.

This chapter focuses mostly on using and implementing Flash via the authoring environment and the web-based Flash Player, but also touches on several other applications that leverage the Flash Player to give you a better picture of all pieces that now contribute to the *Flash Platform*.

Using Flash on Web Pages

Flash movies can be placed *on* a web page, or they can be used *as* a web page. Moreover, with the advanced scripting present since Flash 5, and the inclusion of server-side applications such as Flash Media Server 2, Breeze, and Flex, the uses for Flash movies are limited only by imagination. Some possibilities include:

- Art and motion graphics
- Animation and cartooning
- Splash pages, intros, and ad banners
- Interaction and navigation
- Multimedia web sites
- Video and audio players
- E-commerce
- Rich media applications
- Data and statistical applications
- Web-based training
- Distance learning
- Live communication

While Flash introduces a number of significant improvements over what can be accomplished using just HTML and scripting in the browser, there are a few drawbacks to using Flash as well. Let's look at the pros and cons of using Flash on a site.

Advantages

Many aspects of the Flash file format make it ideal for adding interactive content to web pages:

File sizes are small. Flash allows for reusable graphics, buttons, and code objects without adding additional bytes for every instance used. Flash movies also use vector graphics, which rely on math to designate lines and color as opposed to storing the colors of individual pixels, such as with raster graphics. This saves a lot of file size.

It is scalable. Flash images and animations can be resized with no loss of detail, making it easy to fill the whole browser window with a Flash interface without adding to the file size. Flash can be used to create static images, such as maps, where zooming in to view the image in finer detail is desirable.

Image quality is high. Real-time anti-aliasing smoothes the edges of graphics and text, regardless of the display size. Users can zoom in on vector graphics with no loss of image quality.

It uses streaming technology. Flash files start playing quickly and continue to play as they download, so they can be pseudostreamed from an HTTP server. The Flash Player itself can stream video and audio, including MPEG and Flash video files.

Integrated audio and video. Flash is a good way to bring background sound and user-triggered sound effects to a web site. With the advent of Flash MX you can also import files of type *.mov* (QuickTime), AVI, and *.mpg* (MPEG), and with the professional version of Flash MX 2004, you can edit and crop the video before adding it to the timeline. With Flash 8, you can employ VP6 codec for very high-resolution video.

The Flash format is well supported. The Flash Player, which is required to play Flash (*.swf*) files, is available for Windows, Mac OS, Linux, and Sun Solaris platforms. As of this writing, the current version is the Flash 8 Player. Over 98% of all browsers currently support Flash, with the newest player being shipped with new computers.

It is scriptable. Flash uses the ActionScript scripting language for controlling Flash behaviors. (ActionScript is discussed in detail later in this chapter.) In addition, you can use JavaScript commands from the HTML file to control a Flash element on a page. The reverse is true as well; by using FSCommands in the Flash movie, you can activate JavaScript commands from within the Flash file to control web page elements.

It has an open format. Macromedia has made the Flash file format publicly available, which means that other software developers can build Flash support into their applications.

Font sets are transferable. Any font used in a Flash *.swf* file can be read on any system, whether or not it has that font in its system.

Consistency. Although different types of browsers have different implementations of JavaScript and even HTML and CSS, Flash Players provide a cross-browser consistency.

Disadvantages

Of course, you must also consider the downside to Flash.

A plug-in player is required. Standard Flash files require the Flash Player to be installed on the user's machine, though all major browsers come standard with some version of the Flash Player. The words "plug-in required," however, are enough to make many clients say "no way" without a second thought. Although Flash reaches over 98% of all browsers, your client might have an older player that doesn't support newer features you are attempting to use, so double-check with them before beginning development.

Resisting Plug-In Resistance

How do you respond when clients say no upon hearing a plug-in is required? To its credit, Macromedia has anticipated such resistance and has responded with some strategies. For example, the Publish feature in Flash 4 and higher (previously the Aftershock utility) makes it easy to generate code that detects the specific player version. Flash 8 has made it even easier for both detection and update, which can now occur seamlessly behind the scenes.

Additionally, there are alternatives. Flash Player Java Edition enables Flash files to play on any Java-enabled browser. The Flash authoring tool also allows you to export your animation as an animated GIF, although you may need to optimize it in a dedicated GIF animation utility.

Older Flash Players and .swf files are not 508 compliant. Using Flash movies for document headlines and navigation introduces the same problems as using static graphics in place of text for nongraphical browsers and screen readers. The contents of the Flash movie are a black box to these users. alt text helps, but is limited. Fortunately with the advent of the Flash 6 Player (the current version is now the Flash 8 Player), screen readers such as JAWS and Windows-eyes can access the content in the Flash movie.

It always starts on the initial page of the movie. Other web sites cannot link to a certain page or scene within a Flash movie on another site.

Unix support is limited. Although there is a Netscape plug-in available for Linux Red Hat 6 and higher as well as Solaris, other Unix users are out of luck when it comes to viewing Flash files. The Flash Player Java Edition is one solution to this problem. There is no Unix version of the Flash authoring tool.

Authoring software is required. Flash MX costs $499 ($199 to upgrade from a previous version), and the professional version costs $699 ($299 to upgrade from a previous version). Several third-party tools, such as *Swish* (*SWISHzone.com*) and *Wildform*, let you produce Flash (*.swf*) files at a fraction of the cost of Macromedia Flash, but, of course, they have only a fraction of the functionality of Flash.

 Educators and students can purchase Flash at a much reduced charge of $99, though even this cost is subsidized by many schools and universities when purchased on campus.

Creating Flash Movies

Although it is beyond the scope of this book to teach the myriad information about Flash authoring, this section will give you a high-level overview of creating Flash movies, by reviewing file formats, interface basics, optimization, server configuration, action scripting, and adding Flash movies to a web page. Full-featured Flash movies are best created using Macromedia's Flash software, but I will also show you several third-party software products that allow you to create specific types of *.swf* files and still use the Flash player. For a more hands-on look at creating movies, I recommend using the tutorials that come with the software as well as support documents provided by Macromedia (*www.macromedia.com/ support/flash/*). For an incredibly thorough book of tutorials and reference material, check out *Flash 8 Bible* by Robert Reinhardt and Snow Dowd (Visual).

File Formats

The Flash authoring tool saves information about a movie in a *.fla* source file (also called a "Flash document" or "Flash editor document"). The *.fla* file contains all the separate elements that make up the movie and its timeline information in a fully editable format.

When the movie is ready to go on the Web, it must be exported to *.swf* format. The suffix originally stood for Shockwave Flash, but in the face of confusion with Macromedia's Shockwave for Director format, the meaning is more accurately understood as simply a compiled Flash application.

Flash Interface Basics

To better understand the way Flash handles multimedia content, it is useful to be generally acquainted with the Flash authoring environment. Figure 35-1 shows the core features of the Flash interface as seen on Windows XP.

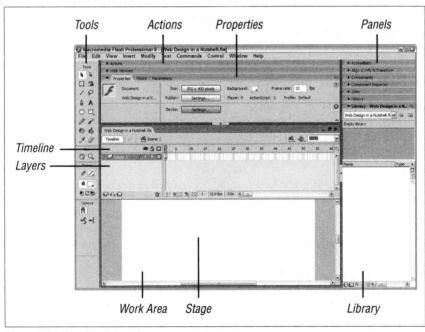

Figure 35-1. The Flash interface

Tools
The Toolbox contains all the tools for drawing, painting, selecting, viewing, and modifying artwork.

Stage
The Stage is the area where you compose and preview the movie.

Layers
The elements on a Timeline may be stored on separate layers (similar to layers in image editing tools). Layers in Flash control the arrangement of objects from background to foreground, support masking, enable motion and shape tweening, and contain guide elements, frame labels, and actions.

Timeline
The Timeline is where you control the timing of the animation and assemble the elements from separate layers.

Frames
Like film, Flash movies divide lengths of time into individual frames. A keyframe is a frame in which you define a change in the animation. Static frames reflect no change and merely repeat the content of the prior frame. Animation effects are added by changing content over a series of frames.

Library
The Library is where you store all imported items (such as images and audio), native symbols (Flash objects that you want to use repeatedly in the same movie, such as a button), and components (Flash objects that you can use repeatedly across movies). When you place an object on the Stage, you create an instance of that object.

Properties
The Properties inspector is where you access and modify all of the attributes of the given object selected on the Stage.

Actions
The Actions panel allows you to create new objects via code and to manipulate the objects on the stage or within the Library during runtime by means of the native scripting language, ActionScript.

Panels
There are several other panels in addition to the Library that appear in the same area of the application interface. These panels include the Accessibility panel, which allows you to make a Flash movie section 508 compliant, and the Components panel, which allows you to reuse Flash objects between movies, among others.

Optimizing Flash Movies

There are several measures you can take up front to make your *.swf* compress as small as it can. The following are just a few tips:

- Keep your artwork as simple as possible.
- Remove unnecessary points in vector drawings (choose Optimize from the Modify menu).

- Limit the number of gradients (choose flat color fills instead).
- Limit the number of fonts and amount of text.
- Use "tweens" and motion guide layers for animation rather than extra keyframes.
- Minimize bitmap usage and avoid setting bitmap images in motion.
- Use symbols and nested symbols whenever possible. However, do not allow symbols to be too large as they can slow down streaming playback.
- Optimize imported media (images, audio) prior to placement in Flash.
- Use MP3 compression for audio whenever possible. You can select MP3 compression in the library for each asset, or select it in the Publish settings for all audio assets.

It is a good idea to use Flash's Test Movie functionality to check your movie's performance. The Bandwidth Profiler simulates various connection speeds. You can also generate size reports to check the size of media components within the movie (it may reveal elements that could be optimized better).

Configuring the Server

Although no special server software is necessary to serve standard Flash files, you will need to configure your server to recognize a new MIME type. The following information will suit the needs of most servers:

- Type/subtype: `application/x-shockwave-flash`
- File extension for Flash: *.swf*

The specific syntax for configuration varies for different servers, so coordinate with your system administrator and see Macromedia's site for further support information.

ActionScript

Flash uses the robust ActionScript scripting language for adding behaviors and advanced interactivity to Flash movies. ActionScript is an object-oriented language based on a version of ECMAScript (the ECMA-262 Edition 4 spec, for those who need to know), so although it shares characteristics with the JavaScript we know and love, the two are not 100% compatible.

ActionScript, which was introduced in Flash 4, evolved into a much more powerful and useful tool in Flash 5, and later again with ActionScript 2.0 in Flash MX 2004 and Flash 8 to adhere more closely to ECMAScript standards. Not only is it responsible for controlling basic playback and user-triggered behaviors, it also enables Flash to integrate with JavaScript, XML, web services, and other server technology. If you are set on becoming a Flash power-user, you will definitely want to learn ActionScript 2.0. For a robust overview of ActionScript, check out Macromedia's learning guides, *www.macromedia.com/devnet/flash/actionscript/actionscript.html*. The following gives a quick overview of their different features.

ActionScript 1.0

ActionScript started out with simple commands to control the Timeline, such as play and stop. Additionally you could control the Timelines of objects within the Flash environment, called Movie Clips, as well as control their x and y placement, and width and height. You could also set and return variables, use loops, and communicate with databases using PHP, ASP, ColdFusion, and so on, and that was about all that was required to make Flash explode. Developers were soon adding code to create spinning DNA helixes, complex animations, games, and web applications such as shopping carts and multimedia galleries.

ActionScript 1.0, with the release of Flash MX, evolved to include several more objects and available methods, and would allow for object oriented programming, but it was limited with regards to its implementation of classes. It wasn't long after, however, that ActionScript 2.0 was released with the next version of Flash, Flash MX 2004, although ActionScript 1.0 remained to provide easy scripting for nonprogrammers. Flash 8 once again includes a Script Assistant to help nonprogrammers with object scripting, which was in previous versions of Flash, but omitted with the last version, Flash MX 2004.

ActionScript 2.0

ActionScript 2.0 was released with Flash MX 2004, to account mostly for some shortcomings with class structures. A majority of the language still mirrors the syntax of ActionScript 1.0, but for the power users, there are a few notable differences.

The ActionScript 2.0 class structure now supports public, private, and static class members, as well as inheritance and interfaces. ActionScript 2.0 also allows for Strong Typing and Function Return typing.

For more detailed information and further description of all the new features of ActionScript 2.0, check out this ActionScript 2.0 primer at *www.flash-mx.com/flash/ actionscript_lott.cfm*. Also, for more information on ActionScript, read *ActionScript for Flash MX: The Definitive Guide* and *Essential ActionScript 2.0,* both by Colin Moock and published by O'Reilly. Macromedia also posts the ActionScript Dictionary, which lists all available objects and their methods, including code examples, at *www.macromedia.com/support/flash/action_scripts/actionscript_dictionary/*.

Adding Flash to a Web Page

Flash movies are exported by the Flash authoring environment using a combination of the object and embed elements with parameters and attributes for controlling display and playback. Both elements are used in order to accommodate the incompatibilities of the various web browsers while still providing as many player attribute settings as possible.

Internet Explorer on Windows uses the object element, which also enables it to automatically download the ActiveX controls for playing Flash media. Netscape on PC and Mac, and Internet Explorer and Safari on Mac, do not support ActiveX, so they use embedding information provided by the embed element. Note, the embed element is not standards-compliant and doubles much, if not all, of the information found in the object element.

You can generate the HTML using Flash's Publish feature, write it out by hand, or add a Flash element to a page using a What You See Is What You Get (WYSIWYG) editor such as Macromedia Dreamweaver MX 2004. The following sections take a look at the first two methods.

Using Flash Publish Settings

The easiest way to get your SWF files on the Web is to let the Flash authoring tool do the work for you. Flash 4 introduced the Publish feature for exporting movies along with automatically generated HTML for placing the Flash (.swf) file in an HTML document.

The Publish Settings dialog box also allows you to select the export format of the movie (whether it's to be a Flash movie, Standalone Projector, static graphic format, and so on) and control the variables of the export. For now, I'll focus on the HTML settings that are relevant to placing an SWF movie on a page.

The most welcomed feature of the HTML Publish Settings is the collection of preformatted templates that generate object and embed elements tailored to specific uses. The Flash Only (Default) template generates bare minimum code. Other templates generate HTML code with extra functionality, including:

- Flash for Pocket PC 2003
- Flash HTTPS
- Flash Only
- Flash with AICC Tracking
- Flash with FSCommand
- Flash with Named Anchors
- Flash with SCORM 1.2 Tracking
- Flash with SCORM 2004 Tracking
- Image Map
- QuickTime

The HTML Publish Settings also allow you to fine-tune various parameters and attributes in the code with simple checkbox and menu options. Upon export, the resulting HTML file can be brought into an HTML editor or authoring tool for integration with the rest of the page or for additional manual tweaking.

Using object and embed

To mark up your page so it is accessible to the maximum number of users, use a combination of the object and embed elements. The attributes for both elements are described below. Note that the embed element duplicates much of the parameters of the parent object element. Both tags are included for browsers that are unable to read the object element successfully (for more detail about which browsers, read the "Adding Flash to a Web Page" section). The embed element itself is not standards compliant, but is still the norm for Flash objects so I included it next.

Flash

Flash's Templates now use XHTML-compliant code. Note that technologies change quickly and Macromedia revises their markup instructions from time to time. Consult the Macromedia support pages (*www.macromedia.com/support/ flash/*) for updates.

The object element

The object element tells Internet Explorer (3.0 and later) to download and install the particular ActiveX player for Flash files and allows you to set many of the attributes for the Flash movie. The following is an example of the basic object element:

```
<object classid="clsid:d27cdb6e-ae6d-11cf-96b8-444553540000"
codebase="http://fpdownload.macromedia.com/pub/shockwave/cabs/flash/swflash.
cab#version=8,0,0,0" width="550" height="400" id="file" align="middle">
    <param name="allowScriptAccess" value="sameDomain" />
    <param name="movie" value="path/file.swf" />
    <param name="quality" value="high" />
    <param name="bgcolor" value="#ffffff" />
</object>
```

The classid parameter identifies the Flash ActiveX control, and codebase provides the browser with its location for downloading. The value of the classid attribute should appear in your HTML file exactly as it is shown above and applies to all Flash versions. Notice that the codebase attribute points to the Version 8 player. Other player versions and subreleases can be targeted with this method by adjusting the version number.

The width and height attributes are required. Note that you can also specify the dimensions in percentages (corresponding to the percentage of the browser window the movie fills).

By default, standard id and align attributes are exported as well from the authoring tool (for more information about publishing with Flash, see the earlier section "Using Flash Publish Settings").

There are a number of parameters (param), which can be added as child nodes to the object element.

param name="allowScriptAccess" value="always|never|sameDomain"
This attribute controls the Flash movie's ability to access JavaScript or VBScript on the HTML page containing the Flash movie. Flash can call JavaScript or VBScript using functions using fscommand( ) or getURL( ) calls within the Flash movie. A value of sameDomain allows the Flash movie to access any script on the page as long as the HTML and *.swf* files reside on the same domain. A value of always allows the Flash movie to access any script on the page regardless of the domain, and a value of never prevents the Flash movie from accessing any scripts.

param name="movie" value="path/file.swf"
The movie parameter is probably the most significant attribute in that you need this to tell the Flash Player what file to play. Otherwise, you'll get nothing but a colored rectangle on the screen.

```
param name="quality" value="low|autolow|autohigh|high|medium|best"
```
This attribute controls the anti-aliasing quality. autolow starts the animation at low quality (aliased) and switches to high quality (anti-aliased) if the user's computer is fast enough. Conversely, autohigh starts the animation in high-quality mode and reverts to normal quality if the computer is too slow. high anti-aliases the animation regardless of computer speed. medium (new starting with Flash 5) displays more smoothly than low, but not as well as high. best goes further than high by also anti-aliasing all bitmaps. It is the most processor-intensive option.

```
param name="bgcolor" value="#rrggbb"
```
Use this setting to override the background color of the Flash movie frame, for instance, to make it match the background color of a web page. The value is a hexadecimal RGB value. (See Appendix D for an explanation of specifying RGB colors in HTML.)

```
param name="play" value="true|false"
```
If play is set to true, the movie will begin playing automatically. A setting of false requires the user to initiate the movie. The default is true.

```
param name="loop" value="true|false"
```
Specifies whether the movie plays in a continuous loop. The default is true.

```
param name="menu" value="true|false"
```
Right-clicking in Windows or Control-clicking on a Mac on a Flash movie brings up a pop-up menu of playback controls. Setting menu to false reduces the choices in the pop-up right-click menu to "About Flash Player," eliminating the playback settings of zoom, quality, play, loop, rewind, forward, back, and print.

```
param name="scale" value="showall|noborder|exactfit"
```
This is used in conjunction with percentage width and height values for defining how the animation fits in the player frame. showall (the default) fits the movie into the frame while maintaining the image proportion (the frame background may be visible along one or two edges of the movie). noborder scales the movie to fill the frame while maintaining the aspect ratio of the movie (one or two edges might get cut off). exactfit fits the image into the frame exactly but may result in image distortion if the scale described and the scale of the movie are inconsistent.

```
param name="salign" value="l|t|r|b"
```
This attribute positions the movie within the frame and is used in conjunction with the scale attribute. The letters l, r, t, and b correspond to left, right, top, and bottom, respectively. You can use any combination of l or r with t or b; for example, lt aligns the movie to the top-left corner of the browser window. If the showall attribute is selected, the leftover space appears below and to the right of the movie.

```
param name="wmode" value="window|opaque|transparent"
```
This attribute allows you to set the transparency of the background color layer of the Flash movie. The default value of window will have a solid color background the color of the Stage in the Flash movie or the value of the bgcolor parameter. The value of opaque allows you to have DHTML layers

Flash

ride over the Flash movie without it covering that layer, and transparent allows you to hide the background so that you can see other HTML content beneath your animations. Note, this feature works only in IE 3 or higher for all Flash Players, but works in most other browsers with the 6.045 or higher Flash Player.

param name="devicefont" value="true|false"
This attribute specifies whether or not to use device fonts for all embedded text in the Flash movie. Note, embedded fonts cannot have some effects applied to them in the Flash authoring environment, and this feature works only with Windows machines. The default is false.

param name="flashvars" value="name=value"
This attribute allows you to pass variables into the Flash movie. Similar to passing variables on a URL string, you can pass name/value pairs here, which will be available on the root Timeline of the Flash movie.

The same additional controls as outlined for the object tag (quality, loop, play, etc.) can be used with the embed tag as well. Again, the embed tag is not standards compliant but still recommended to provide the most functionality to the widest offering of browsers. If you want to try to deliver a Flash movie that is entirely standards compliant by excluding the embed tag, it is recommended that you read this article: *http://alistapart.com/articles/flashsatay/*, which describes the success and difficulties of eliminating the embed tag for Flash movie playback.

The embed element

The basic embed tag is as follows:

```
<embed src="path/file.swf" quality="high" bgcolor="#ffffff" width="550"
height="400" name="file" align="middle" allowScriptAccess="sameDomain"
type="application/x-shockwave-flash" pluginspage="http://www.macromedia.com/
go/getflashplayer" />
```

The src attribute tells the Flash Player where the file to load is located, similar to the movie parameter of the object tag. The width and height tags again specify the dimensions of the image or movie in pixels. The pluginspage attribute provides a URL to the page where the user can download the Flash Player if it is not found on the user's computer (use the exact URL shown in the example code). It is a recommended attribute, but not mandatory.

There are a number of attributes (some Flash-specific) in total that can be added within the embed tag. The following list details all the attributes available. Note, many of these attributes are duplicates of the parameters found in the object tag. If no explanation for the attribute is given here, please refer to its counterpart for the object tag written previous to this text:

src="path/file.swf" quality="low|autolow|autohigh|high|medium|best"
id="text" *or* name="*text*"
The name attribute assigns a name to the movie, which is necessary if it is going to be called from a JavaScript or within a form. It is general practice to use the same name as the *.swf* file with the suffix omitted.

```
bgcolor="#rrggbb"
width="(number of pixels)"
height="(number of pixels)"
align ="left|right|top|bottom|middle"
```
The align attribute lets you determine where to position the Flash Player within its boundaries. The default is middle and it's generally considered better to allow a td tag to determine this setting.

```
allowScriptAccess="always|never|sameDomain"
type="application/x-shockwave-flash"
pluginspage="http://www.macromedia.com/go/getflashplayer"
loop="true|false"
play="true|false"
menu="true|false"
align="left|right|top|bottom"
scale="showall|noborder|exactfit"
salign="l|r|t|b"
base = "url"
```
base sets the base URL and directory that is used for relative pathnames within the Flash movie.

```
swLiveConnect="true|false"
```
This tag enables Netscape's LiveConnect feature, which allows plug-ins and Java applets to communicate with JavaScript. Set this attribute to true when you have FSCommands in your movie; otherwise, it is best set to false (the default), because it can cause a delay in display.

```
scale="showall|noborder|exactfit"
wmode="window|opaque|transparent"
devicefont="true|false"
```

Putting it together for all browsers

To make your Flash content available to the maximum number of users, it is recommended that you use both the object and embed elements. It is important to keep the embed element within the object elements so Internet Explorer users don't get two copies of your movie.

To place an anti-aliased Flash 8 animation on the page with a width of 550 and a height of 400, that plays and loops automatically, you could use code like this:

```
<object classid="clsid:d27cdb6e-ae6d-11cf-96b8-444553540000"
codebase="http://fpdownload.macromedia.com/pub/shockwave/cabs/flash/swflash.
cab#version=8,0,0,0" width="550" height="400" id="animation" align="middle">
<param name="allowScriptAccess" value="sameDomain" />
<param name="movie" value="animation.swf" />
<param name="quality" value="autohigh" />
<param name="play" value="true" />
<param name="loop" value="true" />
<param name="bgcolor" value="#ffffff" />
```

Flash

```
<embed src="test.swf" quality="autohigh" bgcolor="#ffffff" width="550"
height="400" name="test" align="middle" play="true" loop="true"
allowScriptAccess="sameDomain" type="application/x-shockwave-flash"
pluginspage="http://www.macromedia.com/go/getflashplayer" />
</object>
```

Integrating Flash with Other Technologies

Flash has proven to be such a popular multimedia format for the Web that it can now be integrated with the other web media staples such as QuickTime and Real-Media. Additionally, Flash files can be used within both Macromedia Director and Macromedia Dreamweaver.

Flash and QuickTime

QuickTime is a multitrack container format. Traditionally, this meant tracks for audio and video. In the evolution of QuickTime, support has been added for other tracks such as text, timecode, and (starting with QuickTime 4) Flash content.

To add a Flash track to a QuickTime movie, use the Flash authoring tool and export the file to the QuickTime format (*.mov*). The resulting file is a QuickTime movie that can simultaneously play video, audio, and Flash media elements.

The QuickTime 4 Player or higher is required to view QuickTime Flash. Quick-Time 5 supports most of the functions of Flash 4. QuickTime 6 supports ActionScript and most Flash 5 player features.

As an alternative to using the Flash authoring tool, you can also import an existing *.swf* file into QuickTime Player (or Player Pro) and save it as a Quick-Time movie. Plus, as mentioned in the "Advantages" section previously, you can import and trim QuickTime movies in the Flash 8 Professional authoring environment and output them as FLV files using the new On2 VP6 codec.

Flash and Director

Macromedia Director is capable of importing Flash files into its Cast and having those Flash elements play in its Timeline. When including Flash elements in Director, the Flash Assets Xtra plug-in is automatically included in the list of dependent plug-ins added to the movie.

Although there is a Shockwave Player for Director movies published for the Web, Director has increasingly become a product for developing interactive and robust CD-ROM presentations. For more information about Flash and Director, see Macromedia's web site:

www.macromedia.com/software/director/resources/integration/

Flash and Dreamweaver

Macromedia Dreamweaver allows you to add Flash elements to a web page using a graphical interface. Dreamweaver has a Properties Inspector that allows you to edit the properties of the Flash movie.

Starting with Dreamweaver MX, you can also link to the source file that was used to produce a Flash movie so you can launch the Flash authoring environment to edit that object directly from Dreamweaver. Dreamweaver additionally has some built-in Flash objects, which you can edit without requiring the Flash authoring environment.

The Flash Player

Several applications now leverage the Flash Player, such as Macromedia Flash Media Server 2 for real-time audio and video communications, Macromedia Breeze for web conferencing and distance learning, Macromedia Captivate for software simulation creation, the Macromedia Flex Builder and Macromedia Zorn for web application development, as well as several third-party applications, such as Swift 3D (Electric Rain) and 3ds Max (Autodesk) for three-dimensional art, and Swish and Wildform for producing text effects and animations at a lower price point than Flash 8.

The Flash Player, in addition, has now completely broken away from its roots as a web browser plug-in with several flavors to choose from. The Stand-Alone Flash Player has recently taken a big step with Macromedia Central harnessing it to combine the power of the Web with desktop applications.

The Flash Player has also crossed over well into the world of handheld and mobile devices. There now exists not only the Flash Player for Pocket PCs, but the new Flash Lite and Macromedia FlashCast client-server solution for delivering rich data services to mobile phones. Flash is also available in a wide array of other consumer electronics, including set-top boxes, home control systems, toys, refrigerators, electronic keyboards, and many others. The best part is that all of these platforms can still be developed for, using the Flash authoring environment.

To keep abreast of all these innovations, check Macromedia's web site at *www. macromedia.com*. You can search for any of the applications or players mentioned, and the site will direct you to several resources including forums, developer centers, download locations, and training.

Flash Player Versions

Just as web browsing has moved from PCs to handhelds and now mobile phones, the Flash Player has morphed into new versions to support each of the different platforms. The Flash Players available currently are:

The Flash Player
> The standard player used with a web browser. At the time of this writing, the Flash 8 Player was the most current, supported by Internet Explorer, Safari, Netscape, Firefox, Mozilla, and Opera for PC, Mac, and Linux operating systems. For a closer look at the specific browser and player versions that are supported, check Macromedia's web site, *www.macromedia.com/shockwave/ download/alternates/*.

The Stand-Alone Flash Player
> The player used for standalone Flash content. This player can interact with the computer's filesystem, though interaction is limited. This player does not require a web browser to view Flash content.

The Flash Player for Pocket PC
> The player used with Pocket PC 2002 and 2003. This player is supported by most current personal data assistants (PDAs) running Pocket Windows Explorer; it currently supports Flash 6.

Flash Lite
> The player used for mobile devices. The Flash Lite 1.0 player currently supports Flash 5 objects and Flash 4 ActionScript. Flash Lite 2.0 supports Flash Player 7 and ActionScript 2.0. For more information about Flash for mobile devices, see Macromedia's web site: *www.macromedia.com/devnet/devices/*.

Flash Power Tools

The following is a brief overview of the different Power Tools that leverage the Flash Player as part of their solution. Each of these tools can be developed for using Flash MX 2004 or Flash MX Professional 2004.

Macromedia Flash Media Server 2 (www.macromedia.com/software/flashmediaserver/productinfo/features/)
> The Flash Media Server 2 allows Flash movies to have real-time streaming audio and video for collaboration, video on demand, and distance learning.

Macromedia Breeze (www.macromedia.com/software/flashcom/)
> Breeze harnesses the Flash Media Server 2 and Microsoft Power Point taking online training, marketing, sales, and web conferencing to a whole new level. After installing an add-on to the Flash 6 or 7 Players, users can share desktop applications and control the shared applications of other users over the Web.

Macromedia Flex (www.macromedia.com/software/flex/)
> Flex is a presentation server and a graphical user interface (known as the Flex Builder) for creating Rich Internet Applications following a standards-based programming methodology. The Flex Builder creates MXML, which can be read and displayed by a Flash movie. For example, an airport's arrival and departure system could benefit from Flex. The system itself could have a Flash frontend to allow for video advertisements and rich animations, but would require a robust backend with a lot of data communication with the frontend to handle the display of the flight information.

Macromedia Flash Central (www.macromedia.com/software/central/)
> Flash Central takes the power of web applications to the desktop by harnessing the Flash Player in its desktop client. Flash Central leverages AOL AIM and ICQ services for messaging and presence to create robust, cross-platform desktop applications.

Macromedia FlashCast (www.macromedia.com/software/flashcast/)
FlashCast is a client-server solution that allows mobile devices to display rich data. FlashCast leverages the Flash Lite player and can be developed against using Flash MX Professional 2004.

Flash Resources

If you need a book about Flash, again try *Flash 8 Bible* by Robert Reinhardt and Snow Dowd (Visual). For information on ActionScript, see *ActionScript for Flash MX: The Definitive Guide*, and *Essential ActionScript 2.0*, both by Colin Moock and published by O'Reilly. In addition to the many shelves full of other Flash books in your local bookstore, there are a number of resources for Flash online.

- Macromedia's Flash Page: *www.macromedia.com/software/flash*
- Macromedia's Developer Center: *www.macromedia.com/desdev/mx/flash/*
- Flash Kit: *www.flashkit.com*
- ChattyFig listserver Search: *chattyfig.figleaf.com*
- Ultrashock: *www.ultrashock.com/*
- Flash Magazine: *www.flashmagazine.com/*
- ActionScripts.Org: *www.actionscripts.org/*

36

Printing from the Web

The Web is undeniably an amazing resource for information, but it's not the most comfortable or portable of reading environments. For this reason, many people print web pages to read away from their desks or to file for later use.

The ability to print the contents of the window has been built into browsers from the beginning. The real breakthrough in controlling printed versions of web pages is the use of Cascading Style Sheets to customize the presentation of the document for the printed page. This alleviates the need for separate HTML documents or templates that provide "printer-friendly" versions of every page on a site.

The Web has proven to be an effective delivery device for printed documents in the form of PDF (Portable Document Format) files. Flash movies also offer some interesting possibilities for printing. This chapter explores all of these methods for bringing content from the Web to the printed page.

Browser Print Mechanisms

All graphical browsers have basic print and page setup controls that interface with the printer the same as any other application. In the Page Setup dialog box, users can generally select whether the page should print in portrait (vertical) or landscape (horizontal) format and specify how many copies to print.

In addition, most browsers have a Print Preview that shows how the page will look when it is printed. The Preview may also provide the ability to add headers and footers with URL and other page information, whether images print, and whether background and text colors should be preserved.

In most cases, browsers do a reasonably good job of printing web pages by default. They generally try to shrink the contents to fit the print area, and they may also be sophisticated enough to preserve background and text colors (for printing light text on a dark background). But if you want to be absolutely sure your pages print in a predictable way, you may choose to take measures into your own hands.

Cascading Style Sheets for Print

In the past, to provide a version of a web page that was appropriate for printing, it was common to create an alternate, "printer-friendly" version of each page on a site. In general, printer-friendly pages were stripped-down versions of the document, containing just the necessary content and presented in a single column with minimal markup (see the sidebar, "Still Need a Printer-Friendly Version?").

 Your client may have specific ideas of what a printout of their site should look like. Some clients may want the printout to match the way it looks on the screen. Be sure to have a conversation about print version expectations before launching into the print style sheet production.

Now that Cascading Style Sheets (CSS) are widely supported, it is possible to create a version of the document that is customized for print without having to create a separate document. One well-structured and semantically marked up (X)HTML document provides the content (yet another reason to start with good markup), and CSS does all the rest. The method involves creating two style sheets —one appropriate for screen display and one appropriate for print—and using the media attribute or @media rule to match the style sheet to its intended medium. A more detailed explanation follows.

Still Need a Printer-Friendly Version?

There may be some cases in which you may choose to create an alternate (X)HTML source document just for print. For example, if your story has been broken up into pieces that appear in separate HTML documents, you will need to put the pieces back together in HTML to make the whole story available for print.

If you do find yourself creating a "printer-friendly" version, many of the considerations listed for CSS print style sheets also apply to alternate HTML pages, such as customizing content, using black text on white backgrounds, and removing background images. If the page is set to a fixed size, make sure that it is under 750 pixels to be sure the right edge is not clipped off when printing.

Creating the Style Sheets

The simplified example in this section demonstrates the basics of creating an all-purpose source document and targeted style sheets. In the real world, the documents and style sheets would no doubt be longer and more complex, but the core concepts are the same.

This simple, yet properly marked up, XHTML document (*sample.html*) is the source for both the screen version and the printed page, shown in Figure 36-1. The html and head elements have been omitted to save space, but they are implied.

```
<body>
<div id="printonly">
  <p><strong>LITTLECHAIR, Inc.</strong> | For more information, visit us at
  www.littlechair.com</p>
</div>

<div id="masthead">
    <img src="masthead.png">
</div>

<h1>Style Guides and Documentation</h1>
<p>I have found ... </p>
<!-- content continues -->
</body>
```

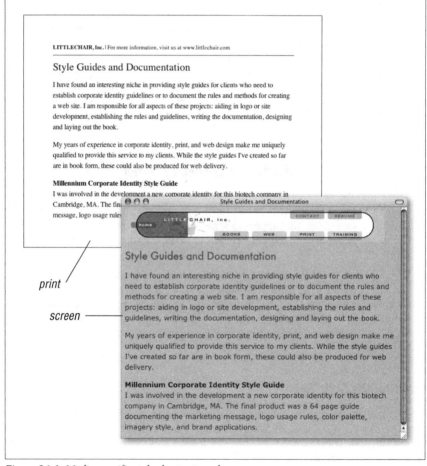

Figure 36-1. Media-specific style sheets at work

The style sheet used for the screen adds a background color to the page and formats the text in a way that is appropriate for web browsers, using relative measurements (ems and percentages). It also uses the display property to hide the div labeled printonly that contains identifying header information that is not needed on the web page. This style information is saved in an external style sheet called *screen.css*.

```
#printonly {display: none;}
body {background: #CCC; color: #333; font: 95%;}
h1 {font: 1.5em Futura, Verdana, sans-serif; color: #C03;}
p {font: 1em/1.5em Verdana }
```

A second style sheet (*print.css*) includes style information just for printouts. There are a couple of points of interest here. First, the display property is used to hide the masthead, and the printonly header gets a bottom border to set it apart from the content. The content is set to appear in black, serif text on a white background, which is appropriate for laser printing (print versions don't necessarily need to be black and white, however). Finally, the text has been resized in points. Points, you say? Yes, although point measurements should be avoided for screen presentation, they are the most appropriate choice for printouts. Fonts specified in pixels may print way too small.

```
#masthead {display: none; }
#printonly {
    padding-bottom: 10px;
    border-bottom: 1px solid;
    font-size: 10pt;}
body {background: white; color: black;
    width: auto; }
h1 {font: 18pt Times bold;}
p {font: 12pt/18pt Times; }
```

We're not done yet—we still need to link the style sheets to the XHTML document.

Targeting Media with Style Sheets

The various methods for attaching style sheets to (X)HTML documents are discussed in detail in Chapter 16. This section looks at the mechanisms for applying style sheets to specific media.

The target medium can be one of nine different media types defined in the CSS 2. 1 specification: all, screen, print, projection, braille, embossed, aural, tv, and tty. These media values are defined in Chapter 16. Here, we'll focus on the values relevant to printouts: all (the default), screen, and print, which incidentally, are values current browsers support most reliably.

The target medium is specified using the media attribute in the link or style elements or by using the @media or @import at-rules in a style sheet. Each of these methods is demonstrated here.

Linking to media-dependent style sheets

When an external style sheet is linked to a document using the link element, the media attribute provides the name of the medium. In this example, the two linked style sheets are differentiated by the values of their media attributes.

```
<head>
<link rel="stylesheet" type="text/css"
    href="screen.css" media="screen" />
<link rel="stylesheet" type="text/css"
    href="print.css" media="print" />
</head>
```

By specifying that *print.css* has a media of print, it is called into use only when the document is printed.

Using two embedded style sheets

A document may contain two embedded style sheets targeted at different media. The styles are differentiated using the media attribute in the style element.

```
<head>
<style type="text/css" media="screen">
    #printonly {display: none;}
    body {background: #CCC; color: #333; font: 95%;}
    h1 {font: 1.5em Futura, Verdana, sans-serif; color: #C03;}
    p {font: 1em/1.5em Verdana }
</style>
<style type="text/css" media="print">
    #masthead {display: none; }
    #printonly {padding-bottom: 10px; border-bottom: 1px solid;
        font-size: 10pt; }
    body {background: white; color: black; width: auto; }
    h1 {font: 18pt Times bold;}
    p {font: 12pt/18pt Times; }
</style>
</head>
```

@import rule

An external style sheet can be imported based on the display medium using the @import rule in a style sheet. Simply add the target medium value at the end of the rule as shown in this example:

```
<style>
<!--
@import url(screen.css) screen;
@import url(print.css) print;
-->
</style>
```

@media rule

The @media rule enables style instructions for a number of media to be placed within one style sheet. Each @media rule can be interpreted as, "If the medium is going to be this, use these style instructions." Using the same style sheet information from the original example, the style sheet would look like this:

```
<style>
@media screen {
    #printonly {display: none;}
    body {background: #CCC; color: #333; font: 95%;}
    h1 {font: 1.5em Futura, Verdana, sans-serif; color: #C03;}
    p {font: 1em/1.5em Verdana }
}
@media print {
    #masthead {display: none; }
    #printonly {padding-bottom: 10px; border-bottom: 1px solid;
        font-size: 10pt; }
    body {background: white; color: black; width: auto; }
    h1 {font: 18pt Times bold;}
    p {font: 12pt/18pt Times; }
}
</style>
```

Screen Versus All

The first style sheet in this example targets screen display specifically. If the media had been left unspecified for that style sheet, it would apply to all media (because all is the default).

A style sheet that targets all media may be used strategically if there is a lot of redundant information between the screen and print versions. The print style sheet would then contain only styles that override the general settings.

When using this approach, be careful that unwanted styles that apply to "all" don't leak through into the print version. It may be necessary to increase the specificity of the selectors in the print style sheet or use the !important qualifier to ensure that critical styles are properly overridden.

It may be easier to keep screen and print style sheets completely separate so these problems are not an issue.

Considerations for Print Style Sheets

The previous section provides only the most rudimentary example of what can be done to customize a page for print using media-specific style sheets. There are many aspects of the printed document to keep in mind when crafting the print style sheet.

Many of the concepts here are inspired by these highly recommended articles on print style sheets by Eric Meyer, published by *A List Apart*. The articles document the details of building a print style sheet for *A List Apart*, and then building it again.

- "CSS Design: Going to Print" (*www.alistapart.com/articles/goingtoprint/*)
- "ALA's New Print Styles" (*www.alistapart.com/articles/ala-printstyles/*)

Think about content

As shown in the earlier example, CSS allows you to hide and reveal page elements, which means you have an opportunity not only to change the style of your web page for print, but also to tailor the content to be appropriate to the medium. Chances are, people just want the content of the page for later reading or filing. To save on ink, consider hiding such elements as navigation, search boxes, decorative mastheads, and so on. Whether you show ads may be more of a marketing mandate than a design decision, but in general, they should be left out, too.

You may also want to include information on the print version that does not show up in the browser. In the instance that the printout is passed along to a friend, or rediscovered in a file months later, it may be useful to include the URL of the page. It may include a marketing message or other call to action.

Upgrade Your Images

Page content isn't the only thing that can be hidden and revealed with CSS print styles. A similar technique may be used to serve an appropriately low-resolution image for the screen and a high-resolution image that will look sharper when it is printed. This technique is introduced by Ross Howard in his article "High-Resolution Image Printing" in *A List Apart* (*www.alistapart.com/articles/hiresprinting*).

Text and backgrounds

When styling text for print, it is best to specify dark type on a light background. Not only is it more legible, but it saves on toner. Most browsers don't print background images by default, but it doesn't hurt to turn them off with a style rule explicitly to make sure nothing hinders the readability of the text.

Also, as mentioned in the example, font size is best specified in points for print, as they will be handled more predictably than pixels.

Background images don't print out by default (although users may change that in the browser preferences). This means that any text replaced by background images according to CSS image replacement techniques (see Chapter 24) may cause content to be lost. If you do use image replacement, make sure those styles are targeted to screen only and not all by default (see the earlier "Screen Versus All" sidebar). The other option is to rewrite styles in order to override the techniques in the print style sheet.

Width and margins

Although not strictly necessary, you may want to get rid of multicolumn formatting (if there is any) and display the content in one column that fills the available width of the page. Changing the position of positioned elements to static and changing the float for floated elements to none should take care of undoing the columns. Setting the width of all elements to auto is the best approach for making sure they'll occupy the full width of the page after margins are applied (either by the browser or in the style sheet).

If your web page uses floats for long elements, make sure that the print style sheet resets the float to none. There is a bug in Gecko-based browsers that causes long floats to get clipped after the second or third page. Setting float: none for long elements fixes this problem. For more information, see the *A List Apart* article, "Going to Print," referenced earlier.

Handle your hypertext

An obvious difference between the web and print versions of your document is that hypertext links lose their usefulness in print. Whether you make linked text stand out more in the print version (for example, by making it bold and/or a different color than the surrounding text) or remove all styles so links blend in completely depends on your preferences and the requirements of the content. Whatever you do, make sure that it is a thoughtful and conscious decision.

You may also want to take advantage of the generated text capabilities of CSS 2 to write out the URL for each link. That way, if visitors want to follow up on links from a printout later, they'll know where to go.

URLs can be included by using the :after or :before selectors and the content property that grabs the value of the href attribute in each a element. In this example, the URLs for links and visited links in a section labeled maincontent will be written out in parentheses after the linked text.

```
#maincontent a:link:after, #maincontent a:visited:after {
    content: " (" attr(href) ") ";
}
```

Generated content is discussed in more detail in Chapter 23, including examples and screenshots of URLs written out after links in this manner.

Printing from the Web

Unfortunately, generated text is not supported by Internet Explorer, so this won't work for everyone. The good news is, it will be ignored by browsers that don't support it, so it won't do any harm to better serve a portion of your audience.

 If you have a document with lots of links, displaying all those URLs could make your document cumbersome to read. Aaron Gustafson describes a method for turning those URLs into endnotes using JavaScript in his article, "Improving Link Display for Print," on *A List Apart* (*www.alistapart.com/articles/improvingprint/*). Aaron also contributed Chapters 24, 25, and 26 to this edition.

Portable Document Format (PDF)

PDF (Portable Document Format) is a technology developed by Adobe for sharing electronic documents. The remarkable thing about PDF files is that they preserve the fonts, colors, formatting, and graphics of the original source document. Ideally, a PDF document looks exactly the way it was designed, regardless of the platform, hardware, and software environment of the end user. It can be viewed on the screen or printed out to a high-quality hardcopy.

PDF existed before the Web, but the two make great partners—PDF is the ideal file format for sharing documents, and the Web provides a highly accessible network for distributing them. You can make any document into a PDF file and make it available from a web page. The advantage, of course, is that you have precise control over fonts and layout.

Forms, documentation, and any other materials that rely on specific formatting are good candidates for PDF files. For example, the IRS makes tax forms available for download in PDF format so taxpayers can print them out at home.

PDF files are not necessarily static. They can contain links to online material and other PDF files. With Adobe Acrobat, authors can even create interactive PDF forms that can be filled out, automatically updated, and submitted online. PDFs can also be dynamically generated based on user input.

With the control PDF offers over presentation, it's tempting to want to use it for all online material. It's important to understand that PDF is not a substitute for HTML and CSS, nor is it likely ever to be. But it is a powerful tool for sharing any sort of document electronically. It's like sending a piece of paper through the lines.

Viewing PDF Files

PDFs are viewed and printed via the freely available and widely distributed Acrobat Reader. Acrobat Reader is also available as a plug-in (called PDFViewer) or ActiveX control and is supported by all the popular browsers (Internet Explorer, Netscape, Firefox/Mozilla, Safari, Opera) on a variety of platforms including Windows, Mac, and Unix.

When a user clicks on a link to a PDF file from a web page, what happens depends on how the browser is configured. If the browser has the PDFViewer plug-in, the document displays right in the browser window; the plug-in adds a toolbar to the browser window for navigating through the PDF document. If the browser is configured to use Acrobat Reader as a helper application, the browser automatically launches the reader, and the PDF displays in the separate application window.

Without the Reader or plug-in, when a browser encounters a PDF file, it issues a prompt to install the plug-in, choose a helper application, or save the file to disk.

Creating PDF Files

Creating PDFs is easy. Because it is open source, support for PDF has been built into many document creation tools. For example, Microsoft Word allows authors to save as PDF from the Print dialog box. Macintosh OS X includes native support for PDF, so any document may be saved as a PDF from the Print dialog box. When you save the PDF, be sure that you give it the proper *.pdf* suffix.

Adobe Acrobat

The commercial application for creating PDF files is Adobe Acrobat, which is in Version 7 as of this writing. Acrobat gives publishers the greatest control over PDF creation, including the ability to make interactive PDFs, a single PDF from multiple documents, electronic signatures, and other advanced features that you don't get when simply printing to PDF.

When Acrobat is installed on a computer, PDFs can be created from within Adobe, Microsoft Office, and selected other applications at the click of a button. In non-Adobe applications, such as QuarkXPress, the document is printed to a PostScript file (choose File instead of Printer in the Print dialog box) and then converted to PDF using Acrobat Distiller, part of the Acrobat package.

Once the PDF file has been created, it can be opened in Acrobat for further fine-tuning and advanced settings. See the Adobe web site (*www.adobe.com/products/acrobat/main.html*) or the Acrobat documentation for more information on creating and fine-tuning PDF files.

Fast Web view

You may also choose to optimize the PDF for Fast Web view. This enables page-at-a-time delivery of long PDF documents. When PDFs are not optimized, the entire document needs to be downloaded before it can be viewed. Check with your server administrator to be sure that your server supports page-at-a-time downloading.

Alternatives to Acrobat

Acrobat is not your only option for creating PDFs. Because PDF is an open source technology, Adobe has opened the door to third-party developers who want to support the ability to save documents as PDFs.

The best place to look for PDF-related tools is PlanetPDF (*www.planetpdf.com*), the "home of the PDF community." They maintain the most comprehensive and up-to-date listing of PDF tools and services.

Printing from the Web

Online PDF Converters

There are online PDF conversion services that convert uploaded documents to PDF for a small fee or subscription. Adobe has its own conversion service called Create Adobe PDF Online that charges a monthly fee, but your first five conversions are free. It is available at *createpdf.adobe.com*. Even better, check out PDF Online (*www.gohtm.com*), where they convert many file formats to PDF for free.

These services may be a good alternative if you only need to create PDFs occasionally. If you plan to make PDFs part of your publishing process, Acrobat is a good investment because of the advanced features it offers.

Adding PDF Files to Web Pages

There are two basic ways of accessing a PDF file from a web page: linking to the file (or a specific page within it) and embedding it in the page like an image.

Linking to a PDF file

Creating a link to a PDF file is the same as linking to any other document. Just include the filename in the URL, as shown in this example:

```
<a href="documentation.pdf">Link to documentation (PDF)</a>
```

The PDF file resides on the server like any other media file. Most modern server software is preconfigured to recognize the PDF MIME type (type `application/pdf`, extension *.pdf*).

Tips for linking to PDF files

As for any large media file, it is good web design etiquette to provide some indication of what users will get when they click on a link to a PDF file. The file format itself can be shown with a small PDF icon, by writing out the name of the file with its *.pdf* suffix, or by identifying the file type next to the link in parentheses, e.g., "link (PDF)."

As a courtesy to your users, consider also including a link to the Acrobat Reader download site. As of this writing, the URL is *www.adobe.com/products/acrobat/readermain.html*.

Embedding a PDF file

PDF files may also be embedded in a web page like an image. The standards-compliant markup for embedding a PDF is:

```
<object type="application/pdf" data="directions.pdf" width="450"
height="600">
</object>
```

Browsers that use the Netscape plug-in architecture may require the nonstandard embed element to display the PDF inline. The href attribute is added so multipage PDF files will open in the reader if the image is clicked. (In Internet Explorer, multipage PDFs are accessible inline using the embedded Acrobat Reader controls for paging through the file.)

It is common for web authors to combine object and embed elements to cover all the bases like this:

```
<object type="application/pdf" data="directions.pdf" width="450"
height="600">
  <embed src="directions.pdf" width="450" height="400" href="directions.
pdf">
    <noembed><a href="directions.pdf">Link to documentation (PDF)</a></
noembed>
  </embed>
</object>
```

Be aware that embed is a nonstandard element that will prevent an (X)HTML document from validating. We are moving toward a standards-compliant Web in which the object element alone will be sufficient, but for the time being, the embed element is still being used to ensure cross-browser support of embedded media.

Flash Printing

Another interface between the browser and printer comes from the folks at Macromedia. Flash 4.0 introduced a new feature to give developers control over printing Flash content. Prior to Version 4, when a Flash movie was printed from a browser, the printout contained only the first frame (probably not the most useful frame) or nothing at all. To fix this, Flash Player can print any content specified by the designer.

This feature can be used to print out a more meaningful frame from the movie, but why stop there? Because any content can be cued to print, the Flash movie can serve as an interactive interface to all sorts of documents. A banner ad can spit out a coupon that shoppers can take to the store. A children's drawing program could print out the finished artwork or other coloring book–like pages. A small diagram could print pages of detailed specifications. Flash printing offers powerful possibilities for enhancing online interactivity with print components.

Users print Flash content via a context-sensitive menu accessed when clicking (Option-click for Windows; Control-click for Mac) on the Flash content, or by using a button designed into the Flash movie itself. The print function in the browser does not print the alternative Flash content.

The Flash print command triggers an ActionScript (the scripting language used in Flash) that detects the plug-in version; if it finds the compatible plug-in, it prints the specified Flash content. The content it prints is stored in a separate file in the

Flash (SWF) format. This could be an image chosen from the current Flash movie, or any document created in Macromedia Flash, Freehand, Adobe Illustrator, or any program that supports Flash (SWF) files.

Because there is no print preview available for Flash content, it is recommended that you label your Flash print button very clearly with what happens if it is clicked. This is especially true if there is a large discrepancy between what you see on the screen and what will come out of the printer (such as a banner ad that prints a 12-page brochure).

VII

Appendixes

HTML Elements and Attributes

This appendix contains an alphabetical listing of all elements and attributes in the HTML 4.01 and XHTML Recommendations, as well as a few nonstandard elements that are well-supported by current browsers. Elements and attributes marked as "Deprecated" have been removed from the (X)HTML Strict DTDs and are discouraged from use, usually in favor of Cascading Style Sheets. Attributes marked as "Required" must be included in the element for the markup to be valid.

Common Attributes and Events

A number of attributes in the HTML 4.01 and XHTML Recommendations are shared by nearly all elements. To save space, they have been abbreviated in this appendix as they are in the Recommendations. This section explains each attribute's shorthand and serves as a reference for the remainder of the appendix.

When *Core* is listed under Attributes, it refers to the set of core attributes that may be applied to the majority of elements (as noted in each element listing).

id
    Assigns a unique identifying name to the element

class
    Assigns one or more classification names to the element

style
    Associated style information

title
    Advisory title/amplification

When *Internationalization* appears in the attribute list, it means the element accepts the set of attributes used to specify language and reading direction.

`lang`

Specifies the language for the element by its language code.

`xml:lang`

XHTML only. This is the attribute for specifying language for elements in XHTML documents.

`dir`

Specifies the direction of the element (left to right, or right to left).

When *Events* is listed for the element, it indicates that the core events used by scripting languages are applicable to the element. Additional events that apply to the element that are not part of the core events are listed separately for that element.

`onclick`

Occurs when the pointing device button is clicked over an element.

`ondblclick`

Occurs when the pointing device button is double-clicked over an element.

`onmousedown`

Occurs when the pointing device button is pressed over an element.

`onmouseup`

Occurs when the pointing device button is released over an element.

`onmouseover`

Occurs when the pointing device is moved onto an element.

`onmousemove`

Occurs when the pointing device is moved while it is over an element.

`onmouseout`

Occurs when the pointing device is moved away from an element.

`onkeypress`

Occurs when a key is pressed and released over an element.

`onkeydown`

Occurs when a key is pressed down over an element.

`onkeyup`

Occurs when a key is released over an element.

a

`<a>...</a>`

Defines an anchor within the document. An anchor is used to create a hyperlink to another document or Internet resource. It can also serve to label a fragment within a document (also called a named anchor), which serves as a destination anchor for linking to a specific point in a document.

Attributes

Core (id, class, style, title), *Internationalization*, *Events* (plus onfocus, onblur)

`accesskey="`*`character`*`"`
Assigns an access key (shortcut key command) to the link. Access keys are also used for form fields. The value is a single character. Users may access the element by hitting Alt-*key* (PC) or Ctrl-*key* (Mac).

`charset="`*`charset`*`"`
Specifies the character encoding of the target document. See Chapter 6 for information on character sets.

`coords="`*`x,y coordinates`*`"`
Specifies the x,y coordinates for a clickable area in an image map. The HTML 4.01 Recommendation proposes that client-side image maps be replaced by an object element containing the image and a set of anchor elements defining the "hot" areas (with shapes and coordinate attributes). This system has not yet been implemented by browsers.

`href="`*`URL`*`"`
Specifies the URL of the destination document or web resource (such as an image, audio, PDF, or other media file).

`id="`*`text`*`"`
Gives the link a unique name (similar to the `name` attribute) so it can be referenced from a link, script, or style sheet. It is more versatile than `name`, but it is not as universally supported. In XHTML, the `id` attribute is required for document fragments.

`hreflang="`*`language code`*`"`
Specifies the base language of the target document. See Chapter 6 for a list of two-letter language codes.

`name="`*`text`*`"`
HTML only; XHTML documents use `id` for document fragments. Places a fragment identifier within an HTML document.

`rel="`*`relationships`*`"`
Establishes one or more relationships between the current document and the target document. Common relationships include `stylesheet`, `next`, `prev`, `copyright`, `index`, and `glossary`.

`rev="`*`relationships`*`"`
Specifies one or more relationships from the target back to the source (the opposite of the `rel` attribute).

`shape="rect|circle|poly|default"`
Defines the shape of a clickable area in an image map. This is only used in the a element as part of HTML 4.01's proposal to replace client-side image maps with a combination of object and a elements. This system has not yet been implemented by browsers.

`tabindex="`*`number`*`"`
Specifies the position of the current element in the tabbing order for the current document. The value must be between 0 and 32767. It is used for tabbing through the links on a page (or fields in a form).

`target="`*`text`*`"`
Specifies the name of the window or frame in which the target document should be displayed.

type="*media type*"

Specifies the media or content type (MIME type) of the defined content, for example, text/html.

Link examples

To a local file:

```
<a href="filename.html">...</a>
```

To an external file:

```
<a href="http://server/path/file.html">...</a>
```

To a named anchor:

```
<a href="http://server/path/file.html#fragment">...</a>
```

To a named anchor in the current file:

```
<a href="#fragment">...</a>
```

To send an email message:

```
<a href="mailto:username@domain">...</a>
```

To a file on an FTP server:

```
<a href="ftp://server/path/filename">...</a>
```

abbr

```
<abbr>...</abbr>
```

Identifies the enclosed text as an abbreviation.

Attributes

Core (id, class, style, title), *Internationalization, Events*

title="*text*"

Provides the full expression for the abbreviation. This may be useful for nonvisual browsers, speech synthesizers, translation systems, and search engines.

Example

```
<abbr title="Massachusetts">Mass.</abbr>
```

acronym

```
<acronym>...</acronym>
```

Indicates an acronym.

Attributes

Core (id, class, style, title), *Internationalization, Events*

title="*text*"

Provides the full expression for the acronym. This may be useful for nonvisual browsers, speech synthesizers, translation systems, and search engines.

Example

```
<acroynym title="World Wide Web">WWW</acronym>
```

address

`<address>...</address>`

Supplies the author's contact information, typically at the beginning or end of a document.

Attributes

Core (id, class, style, title), *Internationalization, Events*

applet

`<applet>...</applet>`

Deprecated. This element (first introduced in Netscape Navigator 2.0) is used to place a Java applet on the web page. The `applet` element has been deprecated in favor of the object element, but it is still supported and commonly used. Some applets require the use of applet. Furthermore, Navigator 4 and earlier and Internet Explorer 4 do not support Java applets via the `object` element.

Attributes

Core (id, class, style, title)

`align="left|right|top|middle|bottom"`
Aligns the applet and allows text to wrap around it (same as image alignment).

`alt="text"`
Provides alternate text if the applet cannot be displayed.

`archive="URLs"`
Provides a space-separated list of URLs with classes to be preloaded.

`code="class"`
Required. Specifies the class name of the code to be executed.

`codebase="URL"`
URL from which the applet code is retrieved.

`height="number"`
Height of the initial applet display area in pixels.

`hspace="number"`
Holds *number* pixels of space clear to the left and right of the applet window.

`name="text"`
Deprecated in XHTML 1.0. Names the applet for reference from elsewhere on the page.

`object="text"`
This attribute names a resource containing a serialized representation of an applet's state. Use either code or object in an `applet` element, but not both.

`vspace="number"`
Holds *number* pixels of space clear above and below the applet window.

`width="number"`
Width of the initial applet display area in pixels.

area

`<area />`

The area element is used within the map element of a client-side image map to define a specific "hot" (clickable) area.

Attributes

Core (id, class, style, title), *Internationalization, Events, Focus*

alt="*text*"
> *Required.* Specifies a short description of the image that is displayed when the image file is not available.

coords="*values*"
> Specifies a list of comma-separated pixel coordinates that define a "hot" area of an image map.

href="*url*"
> Specifies the URL of the document or file that is accessed by clicking on the defined area.

nohref
> Defines a "mouse-sensitive" area in an image map for which there is no action when the user clicks in the area.

shape="rect|circle|poly|default"
> Defines the shape of the clickable area.

target="*text*"
> Specifies the name of the window or frame in which the target document should be displayed.

b

`<b>...</b>`

Enclosed text is rendered in bold. This is one of the few presentational elements preserved in the XHTML 1.0 Strict and XHTML 1.1 DTDs.

Attributes

Core (id, class, style, title), *Internationalization, Events*

base

`<base />`

Specifies the base pathname for all relative URLs in the document. Place this element within the head of the document.

Attributes

href="*url*"
> *Required.* Specifies the URL to be used.

target="*name*"
> Defines the default target window for all links in the document. Often used to target frames.

basefont

`<basefont />`

Deprecated. Specifies certain font attributes for the content that follows it. It can be used within the head element to apply to the entire document or within the body of the document to apply to the subsequent text.

Attributes

`id="text"`
This attribute assigns a name to an element. This name must be unique in a document.

`color="#rrggbb" or "color name"`
Deprecated. Sets the color of the following text using hexadecimal RGB values.

`face="typeface" (or list of typefaces)`
Deprecated. Sets the font for the following text.

`size="number"`
Deprecated. Sets the base font size using the HTML size values from 1 to 7 (or relative values based on the default value of 3). Subsequent relative size settings are based on this value.

bdo

`<bdo>...</bdo>`

Stands for "bi-directional override" and is used to indicate a selection of text that reads in the opposite direction than the surrounding text. For instance, in a left-to-right reading document, the bdo element may be used to indicate a selection of Hebrew text that reads right-to-left (rtl).

Attributes

Core (id, class, style, title)
Events (XHTML only)
`dir="ltr|rtl"`
Required. Indicates whether the selection should read left to right (ltr) or right to left (rtl).

`lang="language code"`
This attribute specifies the language of the element using a language code abbreviation. (See Chapter 6 for a list of language codes.)

`xml:lang="text"`
XHTML only. This is the method for specifying languages in XML documents using a language code abbreviation. (See Chapter 6 for a list of language codes.)

big

`<big>...</big>`

By default, big sets the type one font size increment larger than the surrounding text. This is an example of presentational HTML that should be avoided in favor of semantic markup and style sheets for presentation.

Attributes

Core (id, class, style, title), *Internationalization, Events*

blockquote

```
<blockquote>...</blockquote>
```

Enclosed text is a quote block consisting of one or more paragraphs.

Attributes

Core (id, class, style, title), *Internationalization, Events*

cite="*URL*"
Provides information about the source from which the quotation was borrowed.

body

```
<body>...</body>
```

The body of a document contains the document's content. Content may be presented visually (as in a graphical browser window) or aurally (as by a screen reader).

Attributes

Core (id, class, style, title), *Internationalization, Events* (plus onload, onunload)

alink="*#rrggbb*" *or* "*color name*"
Deprecated. Sets the color of active links (the color while the mouse button is held down during a click). Color is specified in hexadecimal RGB values or by standard web color name.

background="*URL*"
Deprecated. Provides the location of a graphic file to be used as a tiling graphic in the background of the document.

bgcolor="*#rrggbb*" *or* "*color name*"
Deprecated. Sets the color of the background for the document. Color is specified in hexadecimal RGB values or by standard web color name.

link="*#rrggbb*" *or* "*color name*"
Deprecated. Sets the default color for all the links in the document. Color is specified in hexadecimal RGB values or by standard web color name.

text="*#rrggbb*" *or* "*color name*"
Deprecated. Sets the default color for all the non-hyperlink and unstyled text in the document. Color is specified in hexadecimal RGB values or by standard web color name.

vlink="*#rrggbb*" *or* "*color name*"
Deprecated. Sets the color of the visited links (links that have already been followed) for the document. Color is specified in hexadecimal RGB values or by standard web color name.

br

```
<br />
```

Inserts a line break in the content. This is one of the few presentational elements preserved in the XHTML 1.0 Strict and XHTML 1.1 DTDs.

Attributes

Core (id, class, style, title)

clear="none|left|right|all"
> *Deprecated.* Specifies where the next line should appear after the line break in relation to floated elements (such as an image that has been floated to the left or right margin). The default, none, causes the next line to start where it would normally. The value left starts the next line below any floated objects on the left margin. Similarly, right starts the next line below floated objects on the right margin. The value all starts the next line below floats on both margins.

button

<button>...</button>

Defines a "button" that functions similarly to buttons created with the input element but allows for richer rendering possibilities. Buttons can contain content such as text and images (but not image maps).

Attributes

Core (id, class, style, title), *Internationalization, Events, Focus* (accesskey, tabindex, onfocus, onblur)

disabled="disabled"
> Indicates that the form button is initially nonfunctional.

name="*text*"
> *Required.* Assigns the control name for the element.

value="*text*"
> Assigns the value to the button control. The behavior of the button is determined by the type attribute.

type="submit|reset|button"
> Identifies the type of button: submit button (the default type), reset button, or custom button (used with JavaScript), respectively.

caption

<caption>...</caption>

Provides a brief summary of the table's contents or purpose. The caption must immediately follow the table start tag and precede all other table elements. The width of the caption is determined by the width of the table. The caption's position as displayed in the browser can be controlled with the align attribute.

Attributes

Core (id, class, style, title), *Internationalization, Events*

align="top|bottom|left|right"
> *Deprecated.* Positions the caption relative to the table. The default is top.

center

...

Deprecated. Centers its contents horizontally in the available width of the page or the containing element. It has been deprecated in favor of style sheets for alignment.

Attributes

Core (id, class, style, title), *Internationalization, Events*

cite

<cite>...</cite>

Denotes a citation—a reference to another document, especially books, magazines, articles, and so on.

Attributes

Core (id, class, style, title), *Internationalization, Events*

code

<code>...</code>

Denotes a program code sample. By default, code is rendered in the browser's specified monospace font (usually Courier).

Attributes

Core (id, class, style, title), *Internationalization, Events*

col

<col />

Specifies properties for a column (or group of columns) within a column group (colgroup). Columns can share attributes (such as text alignment) without being part of a formal structural grouping.

Attributes

Core (id, class, style, title), *Internationalization, Events*

span="*number*"
> Specifies the number of columns "spanned" by the col element. The default value is 1. All columns indicated in the span are formatted according to the attribute settings in col.

width="*pixels, percentage, n**"
> Specifies the width of each column spanned by the col element. Width can be measured in pixels or percentages, or defined as a relative size (*). For example, 2* sets the column two times wider than the other columns; 0* sets the column width at the minimum necessary to hold the column's contents. The width attribute in the col element overrides the width settings of the containing colgroup element.

colgroup

<colgroup>...</colgroup>

Creates a column group: a structural division within a table. A table may include more than one column group. The number of columns in a group is specified either by the value of the span attribute or by a tally of columns (col) within the group.

Column groups may be useful in speeding table display (for example, the columns can be displayed incrementally without waiting for the entire contents of the table) and provide a system for display on nonvisual display agents such as speech- and Braille-based browsers.

Attributes

Core (id, class, style, title), *Internationalization, Events*

span="*number*"
> Specifies the number of columns in a column group. If span is not specified, the default is 1.

width="*pixels, percentage, n**"
> Specifies a default width for each column in the current column group. Width can be measured in pixels, percentages, or defined as a relative size (*). 0* sets the column width at the minimum necessary to hold the column's contents.

dd

<dd>...</dd>

Denotes the definition portion of an item within a definition list.

Attributes

Core (id, class, style, title), *Internationalization, Events*

del

<del>...</del>

Indicates deleted text. It may be useful for legal documents and any instance where edits need to be tracked. Its counterpart is inserted text (<ins>). Both can be used to indicate either inline or block-level elements.

Attributes

Core (id, class, style, title), *Internationalization, Events*

cite="*URL*"
> Can be set to point to a source document that explains why the document was changed.

datetime="*YYYY-MM-DDThh:mm:ssTZD*"
> Specifies the date and time the change was made. Dates and times follow the format listed above where YYYY is the four-digit year, MM is the two-digit month, DD is the day, hh is the hour (00 through 23), mm is the minute (00 through 59), and ss is the seconds (00 through 59). The TZD stands for Time Zone Designator and its value can be Z (to indicate UTC, Coordinated Universal Time), an indication of the number of hours and minutes ahead of UTC (such as +03:00), or an indication of the number of hours and minutes behind UTC (such as –02:20).

> This is the standard format for date and time values in HTML. For more information, see *www.w3.org/TR/1998/NOTE-datetime-19980827*.

dfn

`<dfn>...</dfn>`

Indicates the defining instance of the enclosed term. It can be used to call attention to the introduction of special terms and phrases.

Attributes

Core (id, class, style, title), *Internationalization, Events*

dir

`<dir>...</dir>`

Deprecated. Creates a directory list consisting of list items (li). Directory lists were originally designed to display lists of files with short names, but they have been deprecated with the recommendation that unordered lists (ul) be used instead. Most browsers render directory lists as they do unordered lists (with bullets), although some use a multicolumn format.

Attributes

Core (id, class, style, title), *Internationalization, Events*

compact
> *Deprecated.* Makes the list as small as possible. Few browsers support the compact attribute.

div

`<div>...</div>`

Denotes a generic "division" within the document. This element is used to add a customizable block element to the document. The content within the div element is typically given a name via a class or id attribute and then formatted with style sheets.

Attributes

Core (id, class, style, title), *Internationalization, Events*

align="center|left|right"
> *Deprecated.* Aligns the text within the element to the left, right, or center of the page.

Example

    <div id="sidebar">Content of sidebar...</div>

dl

`<dl>...</dl>`

Indicates a definition list, consisting of terms (dt) and definitions (dd).

Attributes

Core (id, class, style, title), *Internationalization, Events*

compact
>   *Deprecated.* Makes the list as small as possible. Few browsers support the compact attribute.

dt

`<dt>...</dt>`

Denotes the term portion of an item within a definition list.

Attributes

Core (id, class, style, title), *Internationalization*, *Events*

em

`<em>...</em>`

Indicates emphasized text. User agents generally render emphasized text in italic by default.

Attributes

Core (id, class, style, title), *Internationalization*, *Events*

embed

`<embed>...</embed>` or `<embed />`

Nonstandard. Embeds an object into the web page. Embedded objects are most often multimedia files that require special plug-ins to display (for example, Flash movies, QuickTime movies, and the like). In addition to the attributes listed below, certain media types and their respective plug-ins may have proprietary attributes for controlling the playback of the file. The closing tag is not always required, but is recommended.

The W3C recommends the object element for embedding media objects, but embed is still in common use for backward compatibility. If you want the browser to prompt for a missing plug-in, you might need to break conformance and use embed. Many developers use both object and embed for a single media object.

Attributes

`align="left|right|top|bottom"`
>   *NN 4.0+ and MSIE 4.0+ only.* Controls the alignment of the media object relative to the surrounding text. The default is bottom. While top and bottom are vertical alignments, left and right position the object on the left or right margin and allow text to wrap around it.

`height="number"`
>   Specifies the height of the object in number of pixels. Some media types require this attribute.

`hidden="yes|no"`
>   Hides the media file or player from view when set to yes. The default is no.

`name="text"`
>   Specifies a name for the embedded object. This is particularly useful for referencing the object from a script.

`palette="foreground|background"`

NN 4.0+ and MSIE 4.0+ only. This attribute applies to the Windows platform only. A value of `foreground` makes the plug-in's palette the foreground palette. Conversely, a value of `background` makes the plug-in use the background palette; this is the default.

`pluginspage="URL"`

NN 4.0+ and MSIE 4.0+ only. Specifies the URL for information on installing the appropriate plug-in.

`src="URL"`

Required. Provides the URL to the file or object to be placed on the page.

`width="number"`

Specifies the width of the object in number of pixels. Some media types require this attribute.

Internet Explorer only

`alt="text"`

Provides alternative text when the media object cannot be displayed (same as for the img element).

`code="filename"`

Specifies the class name of the Java code to be executed.

`codebase="URL"`

Specifies the base URL for the application.

`units="pixels|en"`

Defines the measurement units used by height and width. The default is pixels. En units are half the point size of the body text.

Netscape Navigator only

`border="number"`

Specifies the width of the border (in pixels) around the media object.

`frameborder="yes|no"`

Turns the border on or off.

`hspace="number"`

Used in conjunction with the align attribute, the horizontal space attribute specifies (in pixels) the amount of space to leave clear to the left and right of the media object.

`pluginurl="URL"`

Specifies a source for installing the appropriate plug-in for the media file. Netscape recommends that you use pluginurl instead of pluginspage.

`type="media (MIME) type"`

Specifies the MIME type of the media in order to load the appropriate plug-in. Navigator uses either the value of the type attribute or the suffix of the filename given as the source to determine which plug-in to use.

`vspace="number"`

Used in conjunction with the align attribute, the vertical space attribute specifies (in pixels) the amount of space to leave clear above and below the media object.

fieldset

`<fieldset>...</fieldset>`

Groups related form controls and labels. Fieldset elements are placed within the form element. It is similar to div but is specifically for grouping fields. It was introduced to improve form accessibility to users with alternative browsing devices.

Attributes

Core (id, class, style, title), *Internationalization, Events*

font

`<font>...</font>`

Deprecated. Used to affect the style (color, typeface, and size) of the enclosed text.

Attributes

Core (id, class, style, title), *Internationalization*

`color="#RRGGBB" or "color name"`
Deprecated. Specifies the color of the enclosed text. For information on how to specify color, see Appendix D.

`face="typeface" (or list of typefaces)`
Deprecated. Specifies a typeface for the text. The specified typeface is used only if it is found on the user's machine. You may provide a list of fonts (separated by commas), and the browser uses the first available in the string.

`size="value"`
Deprecated. Sets the size of the type to an absolute value on a scale from 1 to 7 (3 is the default), or by using a relative value *+n* or *-n* (based on the default or basefont setting).

form

`<form>...</form>`

Indicates an interactive form that contains controls for collecting user input and other page content. There can be more than one form in an HTML document, but forms cannot be nested inside one another, and it is important that they do not overlap.

Attributes

Core (id, class, style, title), *Internationalization, Events*, (plus onsubmit, onblur)

`accept="content-type-list"`
Specifies a comma-separated list of file types (MIME types) that the server will accept and is able to process. Browsers may one day be able to filter out unacceptable files when prompting a user to upload files to the server, but this attribute is not yet widely supported.

`accept-charset="charset list"`
Specifies the list of character encodings for input data that must be accepted by the server to process the current form. The value is a space- and/or comma-delimited list of ISO character set names. The default value is unknown. This attribute is not widely supported.

action="*URL*"

Required. Specifies the URL of the application that will process the form. The default is the current URL.

enctype="*content type*"

Specifies how the values for the form controls are encoded when they are submitted to the server when the method is post. The default is the Internet Media Type (application/x-www-form-urlencoded). The value multipart/form-data should be used in combination with the file input element.

method="get|post"

Specifies which HTTP method will be used to submit the form data. With get (the default), the information is appended to and sent along with the URL itself.

name="*text*"

Deprecated in XHTML 1.0; use id instead. Assigns a name to the form.

target="*name*"

Specifies a target for the results of the form submission to be loaded so results of a form can be displayed in another window or frame. The special target values _bottom, _top, _parent, and _self may be used.

frame

<frame />

Defines a single frame within a frameset.

Attributes

Core (id, class, style, title)

bordercolor="#rrggbb" or "*color name*"

Nonstandard. Sets the color for a frame's borders (if the border is turned on). Support for this attribute is limited to Netscape 3.0+ and Internet Explorer 4.0+.

frameborder="1|0" (IE 3+ and W3C Rec.); "yes|no" (NN 3+)

Determines whether there is a 3D separator drawn between the current frame and surrounding frames. A value of 1 turns the border on. A value of 0 turns the border off. The default value is 1 (border on). Netscape also accepts the values 1 and 0.

longdesc="*URL*"

Specifies a link to a document containing a long description of the frame and its contents. Although longdesc is included in the HTML 4.01 and XHTML 4.0 Recommendations, no browsers currently support it.

marginwidth="*number*"

Specifies the amount of space (in pixels) between the left and right edges of the frame and its contents. The minimum value according to the HTML specification is 1 pixel. Setting the value to 0 to place objects flush against the edge of the frame works in some browsers but may yield inconsistent results.

marginheight="*number*"

Specifies the amount of space (in pixels) between the top and bottom edges of the frame and its contents. The minimum value according to the HTML specification is 1 pixel. Setting the value to 0 to place objects flush against the edge of the frame works in some browsers but may yield inconsistent results.

name="*text*"

> *Deprecated in XHTML 1.0; use* id *instead.* Assigns a name to the frame. This name may be referenced by targets within links to make the target document load within the named frame.

noresize="noresize"

> Prevents users from resizing the frame. By default, despite specific frame size settings, users can resize a frame by clicking and dragging its borders.

scrolling="yes|no|auto"

> Specifies whether scrollbars appear in the frame. A value of yes means scrollbars always appear; a value of no means scrollbars never appear; a value of auto (the default) means scrollbars appear automatically when the contents do not fit within the frame.

src="*URL*"

> Specifies the location of the initial HTML file to be displayed by the frame.

frameset

<frameset>...</frameset>

Defines a collection of frames or other framesets.

Attributes

Core (id, class, style, title), onload, onunload

border="*number*"

> *Nonstandard.* Sets frame border thickness (in pixels) between all the frames in a frameset (when the frame border is turned on). Mozilla browsers do not support border.

bordercolor="*#rrggbb*" *or* "*color name*"

> *Nonstandard.* Sets a border color for all the borders in a frameset. Mozilla and Opera browsers do not support bordercolor.

cols="*list of lengths*" *(number, percentage, or *)*

> Establishes the number and sizes of columns (vertical frames) in a frameset. The number of columns is determined by the number of values in the list. Size specifications can be in absolute pixel values, percentage values, or relative values (*) based on available space.

frameborder="1|0"; "yes|no"

> *Nonstandard.* Determines whether 3D separators are drawn between frames in the frameset. A value of 1 (or yes) turns the borders on; 0 (or no) turns the borders off. Netscape also supports values of 1 and 0. The Frameset DTD does not include the frameborder attribute for the frameset element.

rows="*list of lengths*" *(number, percentage, or *)*

> Establishes the number and size of rows (horizontal frames) in the frameset. The value is a comma-separated list of measurements. The number of rows is determined by the number of values in the list. Size specifications can be in absolute pixel values, percentage values, or relative values (*) based on available space.

h1, h2, h3, h4, h5, h6

`<hn>...</hn>`

Specifies a heading that briefly describes the section it introduces. There are six levels of headings, from h1 (most important) to h6 (least important).

Attributes

Core (id, class, style, title), *Internationalization, Events*

`align="center|left|right"`
> *Deprecated.* Used to align the header left, right, or centered on the page. Microsoft Internet Explorer 3.0 and earlier does not support right alignment.

head

`<head>...</head>`

Defines the head (also called the "header") portion of the document that contains information about the document that is not considered document content. The head element serves as a container for the other header elements, such as title, base, link, and meta.

Attributes

Internationalization (lang, xml:lang, dir)

`profile="URLs"`
> Provides the location of one or more predefined metadata profiles separated by whitespace that are used to define properties and values that can be referenced by meta elements in the head of the document, rel and rev attributes, and class names. This attribute is not yet implemented by browsers.

hr

`<hr />`

Adds a horizontal rule to the page that can be used as a divider between sections of content. This is an example of a presentational HTML element. A rule between sections of a document may be better handled using a border on the top or bottom edge of a block element.

Attributes

Core (id, class, style, title), *Internationalization, Events*

`align="center|left|right"`
> *Deprecated.* If the rule is shorter than the width of the window, this attribute controls horizontal alignment of the rule. The default is center.

`noshade="noshade"`
> *Deprecated.* This displays the rule as a solid bar with no shading.

`size="number"`
> *Deprecated.* Specifies the thickness of the rule in pixels.

`width="number" or "number%"`
> *Deprecated.* Specifies the length of the rule in pixels or as a percentage of the page width. By default, rules are the full width of the browser window.

html

```
<html>...</html>
```

This is the root element of an HTML document, meaning all other elements are contained within it. The html element has no ancestors. Placed at the beginning and end of the document, this element indicates that the entire document is HTML or XHTML.

Attributes

Internationalization (lang, xml:lang, dir)

```
xmlns="http://www.w3.org/1999/xhtml"
```
    Required; XHTML only. In an XHTML document, this declares the XML namespace for the document.

```
version="-//W3C//DTD HTML 4.01//EN"
```
    Deprecated in HTML 4.01. In HTML, the value of version is a Formal Public Identifier (FPI) that specifies the version of HTML the document uses (the value above specifies 4.01). In HTML 4.01, the version attribute is deprecated because it is redundant with information provided in the DOCTYPE declaration. In XHTML 1.0, the value of version has not been defined.

i

```
<i>...</i>
```

Enclosed text is displayed in italic. It is discouraged from use in favor of the more semantic em (emphasized) element. This is one of the few presentational elements preserved in the XHTML 1.0 Strict and XHTML 1.1 DTDs.

Attributes

Core (id, class, style, title), *Internationalization, Events*

iframe

```
<iframe>...</iframe>
```

Defines an inline (floating) frame within a document. An iframe displays the content of an external document and may display scrolling devices if the content doesn't fit in the specified window area. Inline frames are positioned similarly to images.

Attributes

Core (id, class, style, title)

```
align="top|middle|bottom|left|right"
```
    Deprecated. Aligns the inline frame on the page within the flow of the text. Left and right alignment allows text to flow around the inline frame.

```
frameborder="1|0"
```
    Turns on or off the display of a 3D border for the inline frame. The default is 1, which displays the border.

```
height="number"
```
    Specifies the height of the inline frame in pixels or as a percentage of the window size. Internet Explorer and Navigator use a default height of 150 pixels.

`hspace="number"`

Nonstandard. Used in conjunction with left and right alignment, this attribute specifies the amount of space (in pixels) to hold clear to the left and right of the inline frame.

`longdesc="URL"`

Specifies a link to a document containing a long description of the inline frame and its contents. This addition to the HTML 4.01 specification may be useful for nonvisual web browsers.

`marginheight="number"`

Specifies the amount of space (in pixels) between the top and bottom edges of the inline frame and its contents.

`marginwidth="number"`

Specifies the amount of space (in pixels) between the left and right edges of the inline frame and its contents.

`name="text"`

Deprecated in XHTML 1.0. Assigns a name to the inline frame to be referenced by targeted links.

`scrolling="yes|no|auto"`

Specifies whether scrollbars appear in the frame. A value of yes means scrollbars always appear; a value of no means scrollbars never appear; a value of auto (the default) means scrollbars appear automatically when the contents do not fit within the frame.

`src="URL"`

Specifies the URL of the HTML document to display initially in the inline frame.

`vspace="number"`

Nonstandard. Used in conjunction with left and right alignment, this attribute specifies the amount of space (in pixels) to hold clear above and below the inline frame.

`width="number"`

Specifies the width of the inline frame in pixels or as a percentage of the window size. Internet Explorer and Navigator use a default width of 300 pixels.

img

`<img />`

Places an image on the page.

Attributes

Core (id, class, style, title), Internationalization, Events

`align="type"`

Deprecated. Specifies the alignment of an image using one of the following values:

Type	Resulting alignment
bottom	Aligns the bottom of the image with the text baseline. This is the default vertical alignment.
left	Aligns the image on the left margin and allows subsequent text to wrap around it.

Type	Resulting alignment
middle	Aligns the text baseline with the middle of the image.
right	Aligns the image on the right margin and allows subsequent text to wrap around it.
top	Aligns the top of the image with the top of the tallest object on that line.

alt="*text*"

Required. Provides a string of alternative text that appears when the image is not displayed. Internet Explorer 4.0+ and Netscape 6 on Windows display this text as a "tool tip" when the mouse rests on the image.

border="*number*"

Deprecated. Specifies the width (in pixels) of the border that surrounds a linked image.

height="*number*"

Specifies the height of the image in pixels. It is not required, but is recommended to speed up the rendering of the web page.

hspace="*number*"

Deprecated. Specifies (in number of pixels) the amount of space to leave clear to the left and right of the image.

ismap

Indicates that the graphic is used as the basis for a server-side image map (an image containing multiple hypertext links).

longdesc="*URL*"

Specifies a link to a long description of the image or an image map's contents. This may be used to make information about the image accessible to nonvisual browsers. It is supported only by Netscape 6 as of this writing.

lowsrc="*URL*"

Nonstandard. Specifies an image (usually of a smaller file size) that will download first, followed by the final image specified by the src attribute.

name="*text*"

Deprecated in XHTML 1.0; use id instead. Assigns the image element a name so it can be referred to by a script or style sheet.

src="*URL*"

Required. Provides the location of the graphic file to be displayed.

usemap="*URL*"

Specifies the map containing coordinates and links for a client-side image map (an image containing multiple hypertext links).

vspace="*number*"

Deprecated. Specifies (in number of pixels) the amount of space to leave clear above and below the image.

width="*number*"

Specifies the width of the image in pixels. It is not required, but is recommended to speed up the rendering of the web page.

input

```
<input />
```

The input element is used to create a variety of form input controls. The type of control is defined by the type attribute. Following is a complete list of attributes (with descriptions) that can be used with the input element. Not all attributes can be used with all control types. The attributes associated with each control type are also provided.

Attributes

Core (id, class, style, title), *Internationalization*, *Events* (onfocus, onblur, onselect, onchange

alt="*text*"
Specifies alternative text for an image used as a button.

accept="*MIME type*"
Specifies a comma-separated list of content types that a server processing the form will handle correctly. It can be used to filter out nonconforming files when prompting a user to select files to send to the server.

accesskey="*character*"
Assigns an access key (keyboard shortcut) to an element for quicker access.

checked="checked"
When this attribute is added, a checkbox will be checked by default.

disabled="disabled"
Disables the control for user input. It can only be altered via a script. Browsers may display disabled controls differently (grayed out, for example), which could be useful for dimming certain controls until required info is supplied.

maxlength="*number*"
Specifies the maximum number of characters the user can input for this element.

name="*text*"
Required by all input types except submit *and* reset. Assigns a name to the control. A script program uses this name to reference the control.

readonly="readonly"
Indicates that the form input may not be modified.

size="*number*"
Specifies the size of a text-entry box (measured in number of characters). Users can type entries that are longer than the space provided, causing the field to scroll to the right.

src="*URL*"
Provides the URL of an image used as a push button.

tabindex="*number*"
Specifies position in the tabbing order. Tabbing navigation allows the user to cycle through the active fields using the Tab key.

type="text|password|checkbox|radio|submit|reset|file|hidden|image|button"
Specifies type of form control.

value="*text*"
Specifies the value for this control.

`<input type="button" />`

Creates a customizable "push" button. Customizable buttons have no specific
behavior but can be used to trigger functions created with JavaScript controls. Data
from type="button" controls is never sent with a form when a form is submitted to the
server; these button controls are only for use with script programs on the browser.

Attributes

Core (id, class, style, title), *Internationalization*, *Events*, *Focus* (accesskey, tabindex,
onfocus, onblur)

align="left|middle|right|top|bottom" (*Deprecated*)

disabled="disabled"

name="*text*" (*Required*)

value="*text*"

`<input type="checkbox" />`

Creates a checkbox input element within a form. Checkboxes are like on/off switches
that can be toggled by the user. Several checkboxes in a group may be selected at one
time. When a form is submitted, only the "on" checkboxes submit values to the server.

Attributes

Core (id, class, style, title), *Internationalization*, *Events*, *Focus* (accesskey, tabindex,
onfocus, onblur)

align="left|middle|right|top|bottom" (*Deprecated*)

checked="checked"

disabled="disabled"

name="*text*" (*Required*)

readonly="readonly"

value="*text*" (*Required*)

`<input type="file" />`

Allows users to submit external files with their form submissions by providing a
browsing mechanism in the form.

Attributes

Core (id, class, style, title), *Internationalization*, *Events*, *Focus* (accesskey, tabindex,
onfocus, onblur)

accept="*MIME type*"

disabled="disabled"

maxlength="*number*"

name="*text*" (*Required*)

readonly="readonly"

size="*number*"

value="*text*"

<input type="hidden" />

Creates a control that does not display in the browser. Hidden controls can be used to pass special form-processing information to the server that the user cannot see or alter.

Attributes

accesskey="*character*"

tabindex="*number*"

name="*text*" *(Required)*

value="*text*" *(Required)*

<input type="image" />

Allows an image to be used as a substitute for a submit button. If a type="image" button is pressed, the form is submitted.

Attributes

Core (id, class, style, title), *Internationalization*, *Events*, *Focus* (accesskey, tabindex, onfocus, onblur)

align="left|middle|right|top|bottom" *(Deprecated)*

alt="*text*"

disabled="disabled"

name="*text*" *(Required)*

src="*URL*"

<input type="password" />

Creates a text-input element (like <input type="text">), but the input text is rendered in a way that hides the characters, such as by displaying a string of asterisks (*) or bullets (•). Note that this does *not* encrypt the information entered and should not be considered to be a real security measure.

Attributes

Core (id, class, style, title), *Internationalization*, *Events*, *Focus* (accesskey, tabindex, onfocus, onblur)

disabled="disabled"

maxlength="*number*"

name="*text*" *(Required)*

readonly="readonly"

size="*number*"

value="*text*" *(Required)*

<input type="radio" />

Creates a radio button that can be turned on and off. When a group of radio buttons share the same control name, only one button within the group can be "on" at one time, and all the others are "off." This makes them different from checkboxes, which allow multiple choices to be selected within a group. Only data from the "on" radio button is sent when the form is submitted.

Attributes

Core (id, class, style, title), *Internationalization*, *Events*, *Focus* (accesskey, tabindex, onfocus, onblur)

checked="checked"

disabled="disabled"

name="*text*" *(Required)*

readonly="readonly"

value="*text*" *(Required)*

<input type="reset" />

Creates a reset button that clears the contents of the elements in a form (or sets them to their default values).

Attributes

Core (id, class, style, title), *Internationalization*, *Events*, *Focus* (accesskey, tabindex, onfocus, onblur)

disabled="disabled"

name="*text*"

value="*text*"

<input type="submit" />

Creates a submit button control; pressing the button immediately sends the information in the form to the server for processing.

Attributes

Core (id, class, style, title), *Internationalization*, *Events*, *Focus* (accesskey, tabindex, onfocus, onblur)

disabled="disabled"

name="*text*"

value="*text*"

<input type="text" />

Creates a text input element. This is the default input type, as well as the most useful and common.

Attributes

Core (id, class, style, title), *Internationalization*, *Events*, *Focus* (accesskey, tabindex, onfocus, onblur)

disabled="disabled"

maxlength="*number*"

name="*text*" *(Required)*

readonly="readonly"

size="*number*"

value="*text*"

ins

`<ins>...</ins>`

Indicates text that has been inserted into the document. It may be useful for legal documents and any instance in which edits need to be tracked. Its counterpart is deleted text (del). Both can be used to indicate either inline or block-level elements.

Attributes

Core (id, class, style, title), *Internationalization, Events*

`cite="URL"`
    Can be set to point to a source document that explains why the document was changed.

`datetime="YYYY-MM-DDThh:mm:ssTZD"`
    Specifies the date and time the change was made. See del for an explanation of the date/time format.

isindex

`<isindex />`

Deprecated. Marks the document as searchable. The server on which the document is located must have a search engine that supports this searching. The browser displays a text entry field and a generic line that says, "This is a searchable index. Enter search keywords." This method is outdated; more sophisticated searches can be handled with form elements and CGI scripting.

The isindex element is not part of the form system and does not need to be contained within a form element.

Attributes

Core (id, class, style, title), *Internationalization*

`prompt="text"`
    Provides alternate text (not the default) to be used as a query by the user.

kbd

`<kbd>...</kbd>`

Stands for "keyboard" and indicates text entered by the user.

Attributes

Core (id, class, style, title), *Internationalization, Events*

label

`<label>...</label>`

Used to attach information to controls. Each label element is associated with exactly one form control.

Attributes

Core (id, class, style, title), *Internationalization, Events*, onfocus, onblur

accesskey="*character*"
Assigns an access key (keyboard shortcut) to an element for quicker access.

for="*text*"
Explicitly associates the label with the control by matching the value of the for attribute with the value of the id attribute within the control element.

Example

```
<label for="lastname">Last Name: </label>
<input type="text" id="lastname" size="32" />
```

legend

```
<legend>...</legend>
```

Assigns a caption to a fieldset (it must be contained within a fieldset element). This improves accessibility when the fieldset is rendered nonvisually.

Attributes

Core (id, class, style, title), *Internationalization*, *Events*

accesskey="*character*"
Assigns an access key (keyboard shortcut) to an element for quicker access.

align="top|bottom|left|right"
Deprecated. Aligns the text relative to the fieldset.

li

```
<li>...</li>
```

Defines an item in a list. It is used within the ol, ul, menu (deprecated), and dir (deprecated) list elements.

Attributes

Core (id, class, style, title), *Internationalization*, *Events*

type="*format*"
Deprecated. Changes the format of the automatically generated numbers or bullets for list items.

Within unordered lists (ul), the type attribute can be used to specify the bullet style (disc, circle, or square) for a particular list item.

Within ordered lists (ol), the type attribute specifies the numbering style (see options under the ol listing) for a particular list item.

start="*number*"
Nonstandard. Within ordered lists, you can specify the first number in the number sequence.

value="*number*"
Deprecated. Within ordered lists, you can specify the number of an item. Following list items increase from the specified number.

link

`<link />`

Defines the relationship between the current document and another document. Although it can signify such relationships as index, next, and previous, it is most often used to link a document to an external style sheet.

Attributes

Core (id, class, style, title), *Internationalization*, *Events*

charset="*charset*"
Specifies the character encoding of the target document. See Chapter 6 for information on character sets.

href="*URL*"
Identifies the target document.

hreflang="*language code*"
HTML 4.01. Specifies the base language of the target document. See Chapter 6 for a list of two-letter language codes.

media="all|screen|print|handheld|projection|tty|tv|projection|braille|aural"
Identifies the target medium for the linked document so an alternate style sheet can be accessed. The media attribute is explained in more detail in Chapters 16 and 36.

rel="*relationships*"
Describes one or more relationships from the current source document to the target. Common relationship types include stylesheet, next, prev, copyright, index, and glossary.

rev="*relationships*"
Specifies one or more relationships of the target document back to the source (the opposite of the rel attribute).

target="*name*"
Defines the default target window for all links in the document. Often used to target frames.

type="*resource*"
Shows the media or content type of an outside link. The value text/css indicates that the linked document is an external Cascading Style Sheet.

map

`<map>...</map>`

Specifies a client-side image map. It contains some number of area elements that establish clickable regions within the image map. The map must be named using the name attribute in HTML documents, the id attribute in XHTML documents, or both for backwards-compatibility.

Attributes

Core (id, class, style, title), *Internationalization*, *Events*

id="*text*"

> *Required.* Gives the map a unique name so it can be referenced from a link, script, or style sheet. This attribute is required in the XHTML 1.0 & 1.1 Recommendations.

name="*text*"

> *Deprecated in XHTML 1.0 only; use* id *instead.* Gives the image map a name that is then referenced within the img element. This attribute is required in HTML.

menu

<menu>...</menu>

Deprecated. This indicates a menu list, which consists of list items li. Menus are intended to be used for a list of short choices, such as a menu of links to other documents. It is little used and has been deprecated in favor of ul.

Attributes

Core (id, class, style, title), *Internationalization, Events*

compact

> *Deprecated.* Displays the list as small as possible (not many browsers do anything with this attribute).

meta

<meta />

Provides additional information about the document. It should be placed within the head of the document. It is commonly used to identify the media type and character set for a document. It can also provide keywords, author information, descriptions, and other metadata.

Attributes

Internationalization (lang, xml:lang, dir)

content="*text*"

> *Required.* Specifies the value of the meta element property and is always used in conjunction with name or http-equiv.

http-equiv="*text*"

> The specified information is treated as though it were included in the HTTP header that the server sends ahead of the document. It is used in conjunction with the content attribute (in place of the name attribute).

name="*text*"

> Specifies a name for the meta information property.

scheme="*text*"

> Provides additional information for the interpretation of metadata.

noembed

<noembed>...</noembed>

Nonstandard. The text or object specified by noembed appears when an embedded object cannot be displayed (such as when the appropriate plug-in is not available). This element is used within or beside the embed element.

noframes

`<noframes>...</noframes>`

Defines content to be displayed by browsers that cannot display frames. Browsers that do support frames ignore the content in the `noframes` element.

Attributes

Core (id, class, style, title), *Internationalization, Events*

noscript

`<noscript>...</noscript>`

Provides alternate content when a script cannot be executed. The content of this element may be rendered if the user agent doesn't support scripting, if scripting support is turned off, or if the browser doesn't recognize the scripting language.

Attributes

Core (id, class, style, title), *Internationalization, Events*

object

`<object>...</object>`

A generic element used for placing an `object` (such as an image, applet, or media file) on a web page. The attributes required for the `object` element vary with the type of content it is placing. The `object` element may also contain a number of `param` elements that pass important information to the object when it displays or plays. Not all objects require additional parameters. The `declare`, `standby`, and `tabindex` attributes are not universally supported. Browsers vary in support of some media types placed with the `object` element.

Attributes

Core (id, class, style, title), *Internationalization, Events*

`align="baseline|center|left|middle|right|textbottom|textmiddle|texttop"`
> *Deprecated.* Aligns object with respect to surrounding text. See the `img` element for explanations of the `align` values.

`archive="URLs"`
> Specifies a space-separated list of URLs for resources that are related to the object.

`border="number"`
> *Deprecated.* Sets the width of the border in pixels if the object is a link.

`classid="URL"`
> Identifies the location of an object's implementation. It is used with or in place of the `data` attribute. The syntax depends on the object type. Not supported by Gecko browsers.

`codebase="URL"`
> Identifies the base URL used to resolve relative URLs in the object (similar to `base`). By default, `codebase` is the base URL of the current document.

`codetype="codetype"`
> Specifies the media type of the code. It is required only if the browser cannot determine an applet's MIME type from the `classid` attribute or if the server does not deliver the correct MIME type when downloading the object.

data="*URL*"

> Specifies the URL of the data used for the object. The syntax depends on the object.

declare="declare"

> Declares an object but restrains the browser from downloading and processing it. Used in conjunction with the name attribute, this facility is similar to a forward declaration in a more conventional programming language, letting you defer the download until the object actually gets used.

height="*number*"

> Specifies the height of the object in pixels.

hspace="*number*"

> *Deprecated.* Holds *number* pixels of space clear to the left and right of the object.

name="*text*"

> Specifies the name of the object to be referenced by scripts on the page. Removed from the XHTML 1.1 Recommendation in favor of the id attribute.

standby="*message*"

> Specifies the message to display during object loading.

tabindex="*number*"

> Specifies the position of the current element in the tabbing order for the current document. The value must be between 0 and 32767. It is used for tabbing through the links on a page (or fields in a form).

type="*type*"

> Specifies the media type for the data.

usemap="*URL*"

> Specifies the image map to use with the object.

vspace="*number*"

> *Deprecated.* Holds *number* pixels of space clear above and below the object.

width="*number*"

> Specifies the object width in pixels.

ol

<ol>...</ol>

Defines an ordered (numbered) list, which consists of list items (li). The browser inserts item numbers automatically.

Attributes

Core (id, class, style, title), *Internationalization, Events*

compact

> *Deprecated.* Displays the list as small as possible (not many browsers do anything with this attribute).

start="*number*"

> *Deprecated.* Starts the numbering of the list at *number* instead of at 1.

type="1|A|a|I|i"

> *Deprecated.* Defines the numbering system for the list shown next.

Type value	Generated style	Sample sequence
1	Arabic numerals (default)	1, 2, 3, 4
A	Uppercase letters	A, B, C, D
a	Lowercase letters	a, b, c, d
I	Uppercase Roman numerals	I, II, III, IV
i	Lowercase Roman numerals	i, ii, iii, iv

optgroup

`<optgroup>...</optgroup>`

Defines a logical group of options elements. This could be used by browsers to display hierarchical cascading menus. An `optgroup` element cannot contain other `optgroup` elements (they cannot be nested).

Attributes

Core (id, class, style, title), *Internationalization*, *Events*

`disabled="disabled"`
Indicates that the group of options is nonfunctional. It can be reactivated with a script.

`label="text"`
Required. Specifies the label for the option group.

option

`<option>...</option>`

Defines an option within a select element (a multiple-choice menu or scrolling list). The content of the `option` element is the value that is sent to the form processing application (unless an alternative value is specified using the value attribute).

Attributes

Core (id, class, style, title), *Internationalization*, *Events*

`disabled="disabled"`
Indicates that the selection is initially nonfunctional. It can be reactivated with a script.

`label="text"`
Allows the author to provide a shorter label than the content of the option. This attribute is not supported.

`selected="selected"`
Makes this item selected when the form is initially displayed.

`value="text"`
Defines a value to assign to the option item within the select control, to use in place of option contents.

p

`<p>...</p>`

Denotes a paragraph. Browsers are instructed to ignore multiple empty p elements.

Attributes

Core (id, class, style, title), *Internationalization, Events*

`align="center|left|right"`
Deprecated. Aligns the text within the element to the left, right, or center of the page.

param

`<param />`

Supplies a parameter within an applet or object element.

Attributes

`id="text"`
Provides a name (similar to the name attribute) so it can be referenced from a link, script, or style sheet. It is more versatile than name, but it is not as universally supported.

`name="text"`
Required. Defines the name of the parameter.

`value="text"`
Defines the value of the parameter.

`valuetype="data|ref|object"`
Indicates the type of value: data indicates that the parameter's value is data (default); ref indicates that the parameter's value is a URL; object indicates that the value is the URL of another object in the document.

`type="content type"`
HTML 4.01. Specifies the media type of the resource only when the valuetype attribute is set to ref. It describes the types of values found at the referred location.

pre

`<pre>...</pre>`

Delimits preformatted text, meaning that lines are displayed exactly as they are typed in, honoring whitespace such as multiple character spaces and line breaks. By default, text within a pre element is displayed in a monospace font such as Courier.

Attributes

Core (id, class, style, title), *Internationalization, Events*

`width="number"`
Deprecated. This optional attribute determines how many characters to fit on a single line within the pre block.

q

`<q>...</q>`

Delimits a short quotation that can be included inline, such as "to be or not to be." It differs from `blockquote`, which is a block-level element used for longer quotations. Some browsers automatically insert quotation marks. When used with the `lang` (language) attribute, the browser may insert language-specific quotation marks.

Attributes

Core (id, class, style, title), *Internationalization*, *Events*

cite="*url*"
   Designates the source document from which the quotation was taken.

s

`<s>...</s>`

Deprecated. Enclosed text is displayed as strike-through text (same as `strike` but introduced by later browser versions).

Attributes

Core (id, class, style, title), *Internationalization*, *Events*

samp

`<samp>...</samp>`

Delimits sample output from programs, scripts, and so on. Sample text is generally displayed in a monospace font.

Attributes

Core (id, class, style, title), *Internationalization*, *Events*

script

`<script>...</script>`

Places a script in the document (usually JavaScript for web documents). It may appear any number of times in the head or body of the document. The script may be provided in the script element or in an external file (by providing the src attribute).

Attributes

charset="*character set*"
   Indicates the character encoding of an external script document (it is not relevant to the content of the `script` element)

defer="defer"
   Indicates to the user agent that the script will not generate document content, so the user agent may continue rendering.

language="*text*"
   Deprecated. Provides the name of the scripting language, but since it is not standardized, it has been deprecated in favor of the type attribute.

src="*url*"
Provides the location of an external script.

type="*content-type*"
Required. Specifies the scripting language used for the current script. This setting overrides any default script setting for the document. The value is a content type, most often text/javascript.

select

<select>...</select>

Defines a multiple-choice menu or a scrolling list. It is a container for one or more option elements. This element may also contain one or more optgroup elements.

Attributes

Core (id, class, style, title), *Internationalization*, *Events*, onfocus, onblur, onchange

disabled="disabled"
Indicates that the select element is initially nonfunctional. It can be reactivated with a script.

multiple="multiple"
This allows the user to select more than one option from the list. When this attribute is absent, only single selections are allowed.

name="*text*"
Required. Defines the name for select control; when the form is submitted to the form-processing application, this name is sent along with each selected option value.

size="*number*"
Specifies the number of rows that display in the list of options. For values higher than 1, the options are displayed as a scrolling list with the specified number of options visible. When size=1 is specified, the list is displayed as a pop-up menu.

The default value is 1 when multiple is *not* used. When multiple is specified, the value varies by browser (but a value of 4 is common).

tabindex="*number*"
Specifies position in the tabbing order. Tabbing navigation allows the user to cycle through the active fields by using the Tab key.

small

<small>...</small>

Renders the type smaller than the surrounding text.

Attributes

Core (id, class, style, title), *Internationalization*, *Events*

span

`<span>...</span>`

Identifies a generic inline element. It can be used in conjunction with the class and/or id attributes and formatted with Cascading Style Sheets.

Attributes

Core (id, class, style, title), *Internationalization, Events*

strike

`<strike>...</strike>`

Deprecated. Enclosed text is displayed as strikethrough text (crossed through with a horizontal line). It has been deprecated in favor of style sheet controls.

Attributes

Core (id, class, style, title), *Internationalization, Events*

strong

`<strong>...</strong>`

Enclosed text is strongly emphasized. User agents generally render strong elements in bold.

Attributes

Core (id, class, style, title), *Internationalization, Events*

style

`<style>...</style>`

Inserts style sheet rules into the head of a document. The minimum markup for embedding a Cascading Style Sheet is:

```
<style type="text/css">...</style>
```

Attributes

Internationalization (lang, dir, xml:lang)

`media="all|aural|braille|handheld|print|projection|screen|tty|tv"`
Specifies the intended destination medium for the style information. It may be a single keyword or a comma-separated list. The default is screen.

`title="text"`
Gives the embedded style sheet a title.

`type="content type"` (text/css)
Required. Specifies the style sheet language. For Cascading Style Sheets (currently the only style type option), the value is text/css.

sub

`<sub>...</sub>`

Formats enclosed text as subscript.

Attributes

Core (id, class, style, title), *Internationalization*, *Events*

sup

`<sup>...</sup>`

Formats enclosed text as superscript.

Attributes

Core (id, class, style, title), *Internationalization*, *Events*

table

`<table>...</table>`

Indicates a table. The end tag is required, and its omission may cause the table not to render in some browsers.

Attributes

Core (id, class, style, title), *Internationalization*, *Events*

`align="left|right|center"`

> *Deprecated.* Aligns the table within the text flow (same as align in the img element). The default alignment is left. The center value is not universally supported.

`bgcolor="#rrggbb" or "color name"`

> *Deprecated.* Specifies a background color for the entire table. Value is specified in hexadecimal RGB values or by color name. (See Appendix D for more information on specifying colors in HTML.)

`border="number"`

> Specifies the width (in pixels) of the border around the table and its cells. Setting its value to 0 (zero) turns the borders off completely. The default value is 1. Adding the word border without a value results in a 1-pixel border, although this is not valid in XHTML.

`cellpadding="number"`

> Sets the amount of space, in number of pixels, between the cell border and its contents. The default value is 1.

`cellspacing="number"`

> Sets the amount of space (in number of pixels) between table cells. The default value is 2.

`frame="void|above|below|hsides|lhs|rhs|vsides|box|border"`

> Tells the browser where to draw borders around the table. The values are as follows:

table | 677

Value	Description
void	The frame does not appear (default).
above	Top side only.
below	Bottom side only.
hsides	Top and bottom sides only.
vsides	Right and left sides only.
lhs	Left side only.
rhs	Right side only.
box	All four sides.
border	All four sides.

When the border attribute is set to a value greater than zero, the frame defaults to border unless otherwise specified.

height="*number, percentage*"

Nonstandard. Specifies the minimum height of the entire table. It can be specified in a specific number of pixels or by a percentage of the parent element.

rules="all|cols|groups|none|rows"

Tells the browser where to draw rules within the table. Its values are as follows:

Value	Description
none	No rules (default).
groups	Rules appear between row groups (thead, tfoot, and tbody) and column groups.
rows	Rules appear between rows only.
cols	Rules appear between columns only.
all	Rules appear between all rows and columns.

When the border attribute is set to a value greater than zero, rules defaults to all unless otherwise specified.

This attribute was introduced by Internet Explorer 3.0 and now appears in the HTML 4.01 specification. Netscape supports it in Version 6t only.

summary="*text*"

Provides a summary of the table contents for use with nonvisual browsers.

width="*number, percentage*"

Specifies the width of the entire table. It can be specified by number of pixels or by percentage of the parent element.

tbody

<tbody>...</tbody>

Defines a row or group of rows as the "body" of the table. It must contain at least one row element (tr). "Row group" elements (tbody, thead, and tfoot) could speed table display and provide a mechanism for scrolling the body of a table independently of its head and foot. Row groups could also be useful for printing long tables for which the head information could be printed on each page. The char and charoff attributes are not supported by current commercial browsers.

Attributes

Core (id, class, style, title), *Internationalization, Events*

align="left|right|center|justify|char"

Specifies the horizontal alignment of text in a cell or cells. The default value is left. The align attribute as it applies to table cell content has not been deprecated and appears in the Tables Module of the XHTML 1.1 Recommendation.

char="*character*"

Specifies a character along which the cell contents will be aligned when align is set to char. The default character is a decimal point (language-appropriate). This attribute is generally not supported by current browsers.

charoff="*length*"

Specifies the offset distance to the first alignment character on each line. If a line doesn't use an alignment character, it should be horizontally shifted to end at the alignment position. This attribute is generally not supported by current browsers.

valign="top|middle|bottom|baseline"

Specifies the vertical alignment of text in the cells of a column. The valign attribute as it applies to table cell content has not been deprecated and appears in the Tables Module of the XHTML 1.1 Recommendation.

td

<td>...</td>

Defines a table data cell. The end tag is not required in HTML markup but may prevent unpredictable table display, particularly if the cell contains images. The end tag is required in XHTML for the document to be valid. A table cell can contain any content, including another table.

Attributes

Core (id, class, style, title), *Internationalization, Events*

abbr="*text*"

Provides an abbreviated form of the cell's content.

align="left|right|center|justify|char"

Specifies the horizontal alignment of text in a cell or cells. The default value is left. The align attribute as it applies to table cell content has not been deprecated and appears in the Tables Module of the XHTML 1.1 Recommendation.

axis="*text*"

Places a cell into a conceptual category, which could then be used to organize or search the table in different ways.

background="*url*"

Nonstandard. Specifies a graphic image to be used as a tile within the cell.

bgcolor="*#rrggbb*" or "*color name*"

Deprecated. Specifies a color to be used in the table cell. A cell's background color overrides colors specified at the row or table levels.

char="*character*"

Specifies a character along which the cell contents will be aligned when align is set to char. The default character is a decimal point (language-appropriate). This attribute is generally not supported by current browsers.

`charoff="`*`length`*`"`

Specifies the offset distance to the first alignment character on each line. If a line doesn't use an alignment character, it should be horizontally shifted to end at the alignment position. This attribute is generally not supported by current browsers.

`colspan="`*`number`*`"`

Specifies the number of columns the current cell should span. The default value is 1. According to the HTML 4.01 specification, the value zero (0) means the current cell spans all columns from the current column to the last column in the table; in reality, however, this feature is not supported in current browsers.

`headers="`*`id reference`*`"`

Lists header cells (by *id*) that provide header information for the current data cell. This is intended to make tables more accessible to nonvisual browsers.

`height="`*`pixels, percentage`*`"`

Deprecated. Specifies the height of the cell in number of pixels or by a percentage value relative to the table height. The height specified in the first column will apply to the rest of the cells in the row. The height values need to be consistent for cells in a particular row. Pixel measurements are more reliable than percentages, which work only when the height of the table is specified in pixels.

`nowrap="nowrap"`

Deprecated. Disables automatic text wrapping for the current cell. Line breaks must be added with a `<br>` or by starting a new paragraph.

`rowspan="`*`number`*`"`

Specifies the number of rows spanned by the current cell. The default value is 1. According to the HTML 4.01 Recommendation, the value zero (0) means the current cell spans all rows from the current row to the last row; in reality, however, this feature is not supported by browsers.

`scope="row|col|rowgroup|colgroup"`

Specifies the table cells for which the current cell provides header information. A value of col indicates that the current cell is the header for all the cells that fall below. colgroup indicates the current cell is the header for the column group that contains it. A value of row means that the current cell is the header for the cells in the rest of the row. A value of rowgroup means the current cell is the header for the containing row group. This is intended to make tables more accessible to nonvisual browsers.

`valign="top|middle|bottom|baseline"`

Specifies the vertical alignment of text in the cells of a column. The valign attribute as it applies to table cell content has not been deprecated and appears in the Tables Module of the XHTML 1.1 Recommendation.

`width="`*`pixels, percentage`*`"`

Deprecated. Specifies the width of the cell in number of pixels or by a percentage value relative to the table width. The width specified in the first row will apply to the rest of the cells in the column, and the values need to be consistent for cells in the column.

textarea

`<textarea>...</textarea>`

Defines a multiline text-entry control. The content of the textarea element is displayed in the text-entry field when the form initially displays.

Core (id, class, style, title), *Internationalization, Events,* onselect, onchange, *Focus* (accesskey, tabindex, onfocus, onblur)

cols="*number*"

> *Required.* Specifies the visible width of the text-entry field, measured in number of characters. Users may enter text lines that are longer than the provided width, in which case the entry scrolls to the right (or wraps if the browser provides some mechanism for doing so).

disabled="disabled"

> Disables the control for user input. It can only be altered via a script. Browsers may display disabled controls differently (grayed out, for example), which could be useful for dimming certain controls until required info is supplied.

name="*text*"

> *Required.* Specifies a name for the text input control. This name will be sent along with the control content to the form-processing application.

readonly="readonly"

> Indicates that the form control may not be modified.

rows="*number*"

> *Required.* Specifies the height of the text-entry field in number of lines of text. If the user enters more lines than are visible, the text field scrolls down to accommodate the extra lines.

tfoot

<tfoot>...</tfoot>

Defines the foot of a table. It is one of the "row group" elements. A tfoot element must contain at least one row (tr).

Attributes

See tbody for more information and a list of supported attributes.

th

<th>...</th>

Defines a table header cell. Table header cells provide important information and context to the table cells in the row or column that they precede. They are a key tool for making the information in tables accessible. In terms of markup, they function the same as table data cells (td).

Attributes

The th element accepts the same attributes as the td element. See listing under td.

thead

<thead>...</thead>

Defines the head of the table and should contain information about a table. It is used to duplicate headers when the full table is broken over pages, or for a static header that appears with a scrolling table body. It must contain at least one row (tr). The thead element is one of the "row group" elements.

Attributes

See tbody for more information and a list of supported attributes.

title

`<title>...</title>`

Required. Specifies the title of the document. The title generally appears in the top bar of the browser window. According to the HTML 4.01 and XHTML specifications, all documents must contain a meaningful `title` within the head of the document.

Attributes

Internationalization (`lang`, `xml:lang`, `dir`)

tr

`<tr>...</tr>`

Defines a row of cells within a table. A table row element contains no content other than a collection of table cells (`td`). Settings made in the `tr` element apply to all the cells in that row, but individual cell settings override those made at the row level.

Attributes

Core (`id`, `class`, `style`, `title`), *Internationalization, Events*

`align="left|right|center|justify|char"`
> Specifies the horizontal alignment of text in a cell or cells. The default value is left. The `align` attribute as it applies to table content has not been deprecated and appears in the Tables Module of the XHTML 1.1 Recommendation.

`bgcolor="#rrggbb" or "color name"`
> *Deprecated.* Specifies a color to be used in the row. A row's background color overrides the color specified at the table level.

`char="character"`
> Specifies a character along which the cell contents will be aligned when `align` is set to char. The default character is a decimal point (language-appropriate). This attribute is generally not supported by current browsers.

`charoff="length"`
> Specifies the offset distance to the first alignment character on each line. If a line doesn't use an alignment character, it should be horizontally shifted to end at the alignment position. This attribute is generally not supported by current browsers.

`valign="top|middle|bottom|baseline"`
> Specifies the vertical alignment of text in the cells of a column. The `valign` attribute as it applies to table cell content has not been deprecated and appears in the Tables Module of the XHTML 1.1 Recommendation.

tt

`<tt>...</tt>`

Formats enclosed text as teletype text. The text enclosed in the `tt` element is generally displayed in a monospace font such as Courier.

Attributes

Core (id, class, style, title), *Internationalization*, *Events*

u

`<u>...</u>`

Deprecated. Enclosed text is underlined when displayed. The HTML 4.01 specification prefers style sheet controls for this effect.

Attributes

Core (id, class, style, title), *Internationalization*, *Events*

ul

`<ul>...</ul>`

Defines an unordered list, in which list items (li) have no sequence. By default, browsers insert bullets before each item in a bulleted list, lists may be formatted in any fashion (including as horizontal navigation elements) using Cascading Style Sheet properties.

Attributes

Core (id, class, style, title), *Internationalization*, *Events*

compact="compact"
> *Deprecated.* Displays the list block as small as possible. Not many browsers support this attribute.

type="disc|circle|square"
> *Deprecated.* Defines the shape of the bullets used for each list item.

var

`<var>...</var>`

Indicates an instance of a variable or program argument, usually rendered in italics.

Attributes

Core (id, class, style, title), *Internationalization*, *Events*

CSS 2.1 Properties

This Appendix provides an alphabetical listing of all the properties and values included in the Cascading Style Sheets 2.1 specification. It is organized into properties pertaining to visual, paged, and aural media. For updated information, see the World Wide Web Consortium (W3C) site at *www.w3.org/Style/CSS*.

Visual Media

background

Shorthand property for specifying all aspects of an element background.

Values:	[<'background-color'>||<'background-image'>|| <'background-repeat'>||<'background-attachment'>|| <'background-position'>]|inherit
Initial value:	See individual properties.
Applies to:	All elements.
Inherited:	No.
Percentages:	Allowed on background-position.
Computed value:	See individual properties.

background-attachment

Specifies whether the background image scrolls with the document or is fixed in the viewport (typically the browser window).

Values:	scroll	fixed	inherit
Initial value:	scroll
Applies to:	All elements.
Inherited:	No.
Computed value:	As specified.

background-color

Specifies a solid background color for the element that appears behind its content area, padding, and border.

Values:	<color>	transparent |i nherit
Initial value:	transparent
Applies to:	All elements.
Inherited:	No.
Computed value:	As specified.

background-image

Specifies an image to be used as the background for an element.

Values:	<uri>	none	inherit
Initial value:	none
Applies to:	All elements.
Inherited:	No.
Computed value:	Absolute URI.

background-position

Sets the position of the background origin image, relative to the element.

Values:	[[<percentage>	<length>	left	center	right] [<percentage> |<length>	top	center	bottom]?	[[left	center	right] || [top	center	bottom]]	inherit
Initial value:	0% 0% /* same as left top */
Applies to:	All elements.

Inherited:	No.
Percentages:	Refer to the size of the box itself.
Computed value:	Absolute length offsets or percentage values.

background-repeat

Controls the tiling pattern for the background image. Backgrounds can be set to tile in both directions, vertically, horizontally, or not at all. Images repeat in both directions starting with the origin image.

Values:	repeat	repeat-x	repeat-y	no-repeat	inherit
Initial value:	repeat
Applies to:	All elements.
Inherited:	No.
Computed value:	As specified.

border

Shorthand property for specifying the border style, width, and color to be applied to all sides of an element.

Values:	[<border-style> || <border-width> || <border-color>]	inherit
Initial value:	See individual properties.
Applies to:	All elements.
Inherited:	No.
Computed value:	As specified.

border-bottom

Shorthand property for specifying style, width, and color for the bottom edge of the element.

Values:	[<border-style> || <border-width> || <border-color>]	inherit
Initial value:	See individual properties.
Applies to:	All elements.
Inherited:	No.
Computed value:	See individual properties.

border-bottom-color

Specifies a color for the border on the bottom edge of an element.

Values: `<color>` | `transparent` | `inherit`

Initial value: The value of the color property for the element

Applies to: All elements.

Inherited: No.

Computed value: As specified (the foreground color is used if no border color is specified).

border-bottom-style

Specifies the style of the border on the bottom edge of the element. The value must be something other than none for the border to appear.

Values: `none` | `dotted` | `dashed` | `solid` | `double` | `groove` | `ridge` | `inset` | `outset`

Initial value: `none`

Applies to: All elements.

Inherited: No.

Computed value: As specified.

border-bottom-width

Specifies the width of the border on the bottom edge of an element.

Values: `thin` | `medium` | `thick` | `<length>` | `inherit`

Initial value: `medium`

Applies to: All elements.

Inherited: No.

Computed value: As specified.

border-collapse

Specifies the border rendering model for a table element.

Values: collapse | separate | inherit

Initial value: separate

Applies to: Table and inline-table elements.

Inherited: Yes.

Computed value: As specified.

border-color

Shorthand property for specifying the border color for each side of an element.

Values: [<color> | transparent]{1,4} | inherit

Initial value: See individual properties.

Applies to: All elements.

Inherited: No.

Computed value: See individual properties.

border-left

Shorthand property for specifying style, width, and color for the left edge of the element.

Values: [<border-style> || <border-width> || <border-color>] | inherit

Initial value: See individual properties.

Applies to: All elements.

Inherited: No.

Computed value: See individual properties.

border-left-color

Specifies a color for the border on the left edge of an element.

Values: <color> | transparent | inherit

Initial value: The value of the color property for the element.

Applies to:	All elements.
Inherited:	No.

Computed value: As specified (foreground color is used if no border color is specified).

border-left-style

Specifies the style of the border on the left edge of the element. The value must be something other than none for the border to appear.

Values:	none | dotted | dashed | solid | double | groove | ridge | inset | outset
Initial value:	none
Applies to:	All elements.
Inherited:	No.

Computed value: As specified.

border-left-width

Specifies the width of the border on the left edge of an element.

Values:	thin | medium | thick | <length> | inherit
Initial value:	medium
Applies to:	All elements.
Inherited:	No.

Computed value: Absolute length; 0 if the style is set to none or hidden.

border-right

Shorthand property for specifying style, width, and color for the right edge of the element.

Values:	[<border-style> || <border-width> || <border-color>] | inherit
Initial value:	See individual properties.
Applies to:	All elements.
Inherited:	No.

Computed value: See individual properties.

border-right-color

Specifies a color for the border on the right edge of an element.

Values: `<color>` | `transparent` | `inherit`

Initial value: The value of the `color` property for the element.

Applies to: All elements.

Inherited: No.

Computed value: As specified (the foreground color is used if no border color is specified).

border-right-style

Specifies the style of the border on the right edge of the element. The value must be something other than none for the border to appear.

Values: `none` | `dotted` | `dashed` | `solid` | `double` | `groove` | `ridge` | `inset` | `outset`

Initial value: `none`

Applies to: All elements.

Inherited: No.

Computed value: As specified.

border-right-width

Specifies the width of the border on the right edge of an element.

Values: `thin` | `medium` | `thick` | `<length>` | `inherit`

Initial value: `medium`

Applies to: All elements.

Inherited: No.

Computed value: Absolute length; 0 if the style of the border is none or hidden.

border-spacing

Specifies the amount of space to be held between table cell borders when the separate border model is selected.

Values:	<length> <length>?	inherit
Initial value:	0
Applies to:	Table and inline-table elements.
Inherited:	Yes.
Computed value:	As specified.

border-style

Shorthand property for specifying the border style for each side of an element. The value must be something other than none for the border to appear.

Values:
[none|dotted|dashed|solid|double|groove|ridge|inset|outset]{1,4}|inherit

Initial value:	See individual properties.
Applies to:	All elements.
Inherited:	No.
Computed value:	See individual properties.

border-top

Shorthand property for specifying style, width, and color for the top edge of the element.

Values:	[<border-style>		<border-width>		<border-color>]	inherit
Initial value:	See individual properties.
Applies to:	All elements.
Inherited:	No.
Computed value:	See individual properties.

border-top-color

Specifies a color for the border on the top edge of an element.

Values:	<color>	transparent	inherit
Initial value:	The value of the color property for the element.
Applies to:	All elements.

Inherited: No.

Computed value: As specified (the foreground color is used if no border color is specified).

border-top-style

Specifies the style of the border on the top edge of the element. The value must be something other than none for the border to appear.

Values: none | dotted | dashed | solid | double | groove | ridge | inset | outset

Initial value: none

Applies to: All elements.

Inherited: No.

Computed value: As specified.

border-top-width

Specifies the width of the border on the top edge of an element.

Values: thin | medium | thick | <length> | inherit

Initial value: medium

Applies to: All elements.

Inherited: No.

Computed value: Absolute length; 0 if the border style is none or hidden.

border-width

Shorthand property for specifying the width of the border for each side of the element.

Values: [thin | medium | thick | <length>]{1,4} | inherit

Initial value: See individual properties.

Applies to: All elements.

Inherited: No.

Computed value: See individual properties.

bottom

Specifies the offset between the bottom outer edge of a positioned element and the bottom edge of its containing block.

Values: `<length>` | `<percentage>` | `auto` | `inherit`

Initial value: `auto`

Applies to: Positioned elements (where position value is `relative`, `absolute`, or `fixed`).

Inherited: No.

Percentages: Refer to height of containing block.

Computed value: For static elements, `auto`. For length values, the absolute length. For percentage values, the specified value. For relatively positioned elements, if both `bottom` and `top` are auto, their computed values are both 0; if one of them is auto, it becomes the negative of the other; if neither is auto, `bottom` will become the negative of the top. Otherwise, auto.

caption-side

Specifies whether the table caption should appear above or below the table.

Values: `top` | `bottom` | `inherit`

Initial value: `top`

Applies to: Table-caption elements (`caption` in HTML).

Inherited: Yes.

Computed value: As specified.

clear

Specifies whether to allow floating elements on an element's sides (more accurately, the sides along which floating items are *not* accepted). none means floated elements are allowed (but not required) on both sides.

Values: `left` | `right` | `both` | `none` | `inherit`

Initial value: `none`

Applies to: Block-level elements.

Inherited: No.

Computed value: As specified.

clip

Specifies the dimensions of a clipping rectangle through which the contents of an absolutely positioned element are visible.

Values: rect(*top, right, bottom, left*) | auto | inherit

Initial value: auto

Applies to: Absolutely positioned elements.

Inherited: No.

Computed value: Four lengths representing the edges of the clipping area.

color

Used to describe the foreground (text color for HTML elements) color of an element.

Values: <color> | inherit

Initial value: Depends on user agent.

Applies to: All elements.

Inherited: Yes.

Computed value: As specified.

content

Defines the generated content to be placed before or after an element.

Values: normal | [<string> | <uri> | <counter> | attr(<identifier>) | open-quote | close-quote | no-open-quote | no-close-quote]+ | inherit

Initial value: normal

Applies to: :before and :after pseudoelements.

Inherited: No.

Computed value: As specified.

counter-increment

Specifies the increment amount for a counter (positive and negative values are accepted).

Values:	[<identifier> <integer>?]+	none	inherit
Initial value:	None.
Applies to:	All elements.
Inherited:	No.
Computed value:	As specified.

counter-reset

Resets a counter to any value (positive or negative).

Values:	[<identifier> <integer>?]+	none	inherit
Initial value:	Depends on user agent.
Applies to:	All elements.
Inherited:	No.
Computed value:	As specified.

cursor

Defines a cursor shape to be used when the mouse pointer is over the element.

Values:	[[<uri>,]* [auto	default	pointer	crosshair	move	e-resize	ne-resize	nw-resize	n-resize	se-resize	sw-resize	s-resize	w-resize	text	wait	help	progress]]	inherit
Initial value:	auto
Applies to:	All elements.
Inherited:	Yes.
Computed value:	For <uri> values, an absolute URI; otherwise, as specified.

direction

Specifies the writing direction for text in the document (right to left or left to right).

Values: ltr | rtl | inherit

Initial value: ltr

Applies to: All elements.

Inherited: Yes.

Computed value: As specified.

display

Defines the type of box the element generates during layout.

Values: inline | block | list-item | run-in | inline-block | table | inline-table | table-row-group | table-header-group | table-footer-group | table-row | table-column-group | table-column | table-cell | table-caption | none | inherit

Initial value: inline

Applies to: All elements.

Inherited: No.

Computed value: As specified (varies for floated, positioned, and root elements).

empty-cells

Specifies whether the background and borders of an empty table cell should be rendered when the separated border model is selected.

Values: show | hide | inherit

Initial value: show

Applies to: Table cell elements.

Inherited: Yes.

Computed value: As specified.

float

Defines the direction in which an element is floated (allowing the following document flow to wrap around it).

Values: left | right | none | inherit

Initial value: none

Applies to: All elements.

Inherited: No.

Computed value: As specified.

font

Shorthand property for specifying (at minimum) the font size and family, as well as style, variant, weight, and line height. Additional keywords pull in fonts from various operating system elements.

Values: [[<'font-style'> || <'font-variant'> || <'font-weight'>]? <'font-size'> [/<'line-height'>]? <'font-family'>] | caption | icon | menu | message-box | small-caption | status-bar | inherit

Initial value: Uses individual property default values.

Applies to: All elements.

Inherited: Yes.

Computed value: See individual properties.

font-family

Specifies any font (or list of fonts, separated by commas) for a text element. Bear in mind, however, that the font needs to be present on the user's machine to display.

Values: [[<family-name> | <generic-family>] [,<family-name> | <generic-family>]*] | inherit

Initial value: Depends on user agent (the default font in the browsing device).

Applies to: All elements.

Inherited: Yes.

Computed value: As specified.

font-size

Specifies the size of the font for a text element.

Values: xx-small | x-small | small | medium | **large** | x-large | xx-large | smaller | larger | <length> | <percentage> | inherit

Initial value: medium

Applies to: All elements.

Inherited: Yes.

Percentages: Refer to parent element's font size.

Computed value: Absolute length.

font-style

Specifies the "posture" of the font for a text element (normal, *italic*, or oblique).

Values: normal | italic | oblique | inherit

Initial value: normal

Applies to: All elements.

Inherited: Yes.

Computed value: As specified.

font-variant

Specifies the use of a small-caps font for the text element. **If no** true small-caps font is available, it is approximated using reduced uppercase letters **from** the current font.

Values: normal | small-caps | inherit

Initial value: normal

Applies to: All elements.

Inherited: Yes.

Computed value: As specified.

font-weight

Specifies the weight or "boldness" of the font for a text element.

Values:	normal | bold | bolder | lighter | 100 | 200 | 300 | 400 | 500 | 600 | 700 | 800 | 900 | inherit
Initial value:	normal
Applies to:	All elements.
Inherited:	Yes.
Computed value:	Numeric value or numeric value plus one of the relative values (bolder or lighter) if specified.

height

Specifies the height of an element's content area. Padding, borders, and margins are added to this value. Negative values are not permitted.

Values:	<length> | <percentage> | auto | inherit
Initial value:	auto
Applies to:	Block-level elements and replaced elements (such as images); it is ignored for inline text (nonreplaced) elements.
Inherited:	No.
Percentages:	Refer to the height of the generated box's containing block. If the height of the containing block is not specified explicitly, and this element is not absolutely positioned, the value computes to auto. A percentage height on the root element is relative to the initial containing block.
Computed value:	As specified (unless the property doesn't apply to the element, then auto).

left

Specifies the offset between the left outer edge of a positioned element and the left edge of its containing block.

Values:	<length> | <percentage> | auto | inherit
Initial value:	auto
Applies to:	Positioned elements (where position value is relative, absolute, or fixed).

Inherited:	No.
Percentages:	Refer to width of containing block.
Computed value:	For static elements, auto. For length values, the absolute length. For percentage values, the specified value. For relatively positioned elements, the computed value of left always equals right. Otherwise, auto.

letter-spacing

Specifies an amount of space to be added between the letters of a text element.

Values:	normal	<length>	inherit
Initial value:	normal
Applies to:	All elements.
Inherited:	Yes.
Computed value:	Absolute length as specified; otherwise, normal.

line-height

Specifies the minimum amount of space between baselines of adjacent text lines. Negative values are not permitted.

Values:	normal	<number>	<length>	<percentage>	inherit
Initial value:	normal
Applies to:	All elements.
Inherited:	Yes.
Percentages:	Relative to the font size of the element itself.
Computed value:	For length and percentage values, the absolute values; otherwise, as specified.

list-style

Shorthand property for specifying the type, image, and position of markers for a list.

Values:	[<list-style-type> || <list-style-image> || <list-style-position>]	inherit
Initial value:	See individual properties.

Applies to:	Elements whose display value is list-item (in HTML, the ul, ol, and li elements).
Inherited:	Yes.
Computed value:	See individual properties.

list-style-image

Specifies an image to be used as a marker for a list.

Values:	<uri>	none	inherit
Initial value:	none
Applies to:	Elements whose display value is list-item (in HTML, the ul, ol, and li elements).
Inherited:	Yes.
Computed value:	The absolute URI (when provided) or none.

list-style-position

Specifies the position of the marker relative to the content area of the list. By default, the marker is placed some distance outside the border edge. Setting it to inside makes the marker behave as an inline element at the beginning of the list item.

Values:	inside	outside	inherit
Initial value:	outside
Applies to:	Elements whose display value is list-item (in HTML, the li element by default).
Inherited:	Yes.
Computed value:	As specified.

list-style-type

Defines the type of marker or numbering system to be used for a list. A value of none suppresses the display of the marker, but does not prevent the item from being counted.

Values:	disc	circle	square	decimal	decimal-leading-zero	lower-roman	upper-roman	lower-greek	lower-latin	upper-latin	lower-alpha	upper-alpha	none	inherit
Initial value:	disc

Applies to:	Elements whose display value is `list-item` (in HTML, the `li` element by default).

Inherited:	Yes.

Computed value:	As specified.

margin

Shorthand property for specifying the amount of margin to appear on each side of an element. Negative values are permitted.

Values:	`[<length>	<percentage>	auto]{1,4}	inherit`

Initial value:	See individual properties.

Applies to:	All elements (except elements with table display types other than `table` and `inline-table`).

Inherited:	No.

Percentages:	Refer to width of containing block.

Computed value:	See individual properties.

margin-bottom

Specifies the width of the bottom margin for an element. Negative values are permitted.

Values:	`<length>	<percentage>	auto	inherit`

Initial value:	0

Applies to:	All elements (except elements with table display types other than `table` and `inline-table`).

Inherited:	No.

Percentages:	Refer to width of the containing block.

Computed value:	Percentage values or absolute length as specified.

margin-left

Specifies the width of the left margin for an element. Negative values are permitted.

Values:	`<length>	<percentage>	auto	inherit`

Initial value:	0

Applies to:	All elements (except elements with table display types other than table and inline-table).
Inherited:	No.
Percentages:	Refer to width of the containing block.
Computed value:	Percentage values or absolute length as specified.

margin-right

Specifies the width of the right margin for an element. Negative values are permitted.

Values:	`<length>`	`<percentage>`	`auto`	`inherit`
Initial value:	0
Applies to:	All elements (except elements with table display types other than table and inline-table).
Inherited:	No.
Percentages:	Refer to width of the containing block.
Computed value:	Percentage values or absolute length as specified.

margin-top

Specifies the width of the top margin for an element. Negative values are permitted.

Values:	`<length>`	`<percentage>`	`auto`	`inherit`
Initial value:	0
Applies to:	All elements (except elements with table display types other than table and inline-table).
Inherited:	No.
Percentages:	Refer to width of the containing block.
Computed value:	Percentage values or absolute length as specified.

max-height

Specifies the maximum height of an element. Negative values are not permitted.

Values:	`<length>`	`<percentage>`	`none`	`inherit`
Initial value:	none

Applies to: All elements except nonreplaced inline elements (i.e., inline text elements), table columns, and column groups.

Inherited: No.

Percentages: Refer to the height of the containing block; if the height of the containing block is not specified and the element is not absolutely positioned, the percentage value is treated as 0 (zero).

Computed value: Percentage values or absolute length as specified; otherwise, none.

max-width

Specifies the maximum width of an element. Negative values are not permitted.

Values: <length> | <percentage> | none | inherit

Initial value: none

Applies to: All elements except nonreplaced elements (i.e., inline text elements), table rows, and row groups.

Inherited: No.

Percentages: Refer to width of the containing block.

Computed value: Percentage values or absolute length as specified.

min-height

Specifies the minimum height of an element. Negative values are not permitted.

Values: <length> | <percentage> | none | inherit

Initial value: none

Applies to: All elements except nonreplaced elements (i.e., inline text elements), table columns, and column groups.

Inherited: No.

Percentages: Refer to the height of the containing block; if the height of the containing block is not specified and the element is not absolutely positioned, the percentage value is treated as 0 (zero).

Computed value: Percentage values or absolute length as specified.

min-width

Specifies the minimum width of an element. Negative values are not permitted.

Values: `<length>` | `<percentage>` | `none` | `inherit`

Initial value: none

Applies to: All elements except nonreplaced elements (i.e., inline text elements) and table elements.

Inherited: No.

Percentages: Refer to width of the containing block.

Computed value: Percentage values or absolute length as specified; otherwise, none.

outline

Shorthand property for specifying the outline for an element.

Values: `[<outline-color> || <outline-style> || <outline-width>]` | `inherit`

Initial value: See individual properties.

Applies to: All elements.

Inherited: No.

Computed value: See individual properties.

outline-color

Sets the color for the visible portions of the outline of an element.

Values: `<color>` | `invert` | `inherit`

Initial value: invert, or browser-specific for those that do not support invert.

Applies to: All elements.

Inherited: No.

Computed value: As specified.

outline-style

Sets the style for the overall outline of an element. The style must be set to something other than none for the outline to appear.

Values:	none | dotted | dashed | solid | double | groove | groove | ridge | inset | outset | inherit
Initial value:	none
Applies to:	All elements.
Inherited:	No.
Computed value:	As specified.

outline-width

Sets the width for the overall outline of an element. If the style is none, the width is effectively set to 0 (zero).

Values:	thin | medium | thick | <length> | inherit
Initial value:	medium
Applies to:	All elements.
Inherited:	No.
Computed value:	Absolute length; 0 if the style is none or hidden.

overflow

Specifies what happens to content that doesn't fit in the content area of an element.

Values:	visible | hidden | scroll | auto | inherit
Initial value:	visible
Applies to:	Block-level and replaced elements.
Inherited:	No.
Computed value:	As specified.

padding

Shorthand property for specifying the amount of padding to be applied to each side of an element. Negative values are not permitted.

Values: [<length> | <percentage>]{1,4} | inherit

Initial value: See individual properties.

Applies to: All elements.

Inherited: No.

Percentages: Refer to the width of the containing block.

Computed value: See individual properties.

padding-bottom

Specifies the amount of padding to be applied to the bottom of an element. Negative values are not permitted.

Values: <length> | <percentage> | inherit

Initial value: 0

Applies to: All elements, except elements with table display types other than table, inline-table, and table-cell.

Inherited: No.

Percentages: Refer to the width of the containing block.

Computed value: Percentage values or absolute length, as specified.

padding-left

Specifies the amount of padding to be applied to the left edge of an element. Negative values are not permitted.

Values: <length> | <percentage> | inherit

Initial value: 0

Applies to: All elements, except elements with table display types other than table, inline-table, and table-cell.

Inherited: No.

CSS 2.1
Properties

| Percentages: | Refer to the width of the containing block. |

| Computed value: | Percentage values or absolute length, as specified. |

padding-right

Specifies the amount of padding to be applied to the right edge of an element. Negative values are not permitted.

| Values: | `<length> | <percentage> | inherit` |

| Initial value: | 0 |

| Applies to: | All elements, except elements with table display types other than table, `inline-table`, and `table-cell`. |

| Inherited: | No. |

| Percentages: | Refer to the width of the containing block. |

| Computed value: | Percentage values or absolute length, as specified. |

padding-top

Specifies the amount of padding to be applied to the top of an element. Negative values are not permitted.

| Values: | `<length> | <percentage> | inherit` |

| Initial value: | 0 |

| Applies to: | All elements, except elements with table display types other than table, `inline-table`, and `table-cell`. |

| Inherited: | No. |

| Percentages: | Refer to the width of the containing block. |

| Computed value: | Percentage values or absolute length, as specified. |

position

Specifies the method for positioning an element.

| Values: | `static | relative | absolute | fixed | inherit` |

| Initial value: | `static` |

| Applies to: | All elements. |

Inherited: No.

Computed value: As specified.

quotes

Specifies the quotation marks for lists and nested lists. Quotation marks are inserted with the content property.

Values: [<string> <string>]+ | none | inherit

Initial value: Depends on user agent.

Applies to: All elements.

Inherited: Yes.

Computed value: As specified.

right

Specifies the offset between the right outer edge of a positioned element and the right edge of its containing block.

Values: <length> | <percentage> | auto | inherit

Initial value: auto

Applies to: Positioned elements (where position value is relative, absolute, or fixed).

Inherited: No.

Percentages: Refer to width of containing block.

Computed value: For static elements, auto. For length values, the absolute length. For percentage values, the specified value. For relatively positioned elements, the computed value of left always equals right.

table-layout

Selects the table layout algorithm used for laying out the table cells, rows, and columns.

Values: auto | fixed | inherit

Initial value: auto

Applies to: table and inline-table elements.

Inherited: No.

Computed value: As specified.

text-align

Specifies the horizontal alignment of text in block-level elements and table cells.

Values:
    left | right | center | justify | inherit

Initial values: left for languages that read left to right
                      right for languages that read right to left

Applies to: Block-level elements and table cells.

Inherited: Yes.

Computed value: As specified.

text-decoration

Specifies text effects that draw lines under, over, or through text.

Values: none | [underline || overline || line-through || blink] |
                  inherit

Initial value: none

Applies to: All elements.

Inherited: No, but a text decoration is "drawn through" any child elements.

Computed value: As specified.

text-indent

Specifies an amount of indent for the first line of text in a block-level element.

Values: <length> | <percentage> | inherit

Initial value: 0

Applies to: Block-level elements and table cells.

Inherited: Yes.

Percentages: Refer to the width of the containing block.

Computed value: Percentage values or absolute length, as specified.

text-transform

Specifies the capitalization scheme for a text element.

Values: none | capitalize | lowercase | uppercase | inherit

Initial value: none

Applies to: All elements.

Inherited: Yes.

Computed value: As specified.

CSS 2.1
Properties

top

Specifies the offset between the top outer edge of a positioned element and the top edge of its containing block.

Values: <length> | <percentage> | auto | inherit

Initial value: auto

Applies to: Positioned elements (where position value is relative, absolute, or fixed).

Inherited: No.

Percentages: Refer to height of containing block.

Computed value: For static elements, auto. For length values, the absolute length. For percentage values, the specified value. For relatively positioned elements, if both top and bottom are auto, their computed values are both 0; if one is auto, it becomes the negative of the other; if neither is auto, bottom will become the negative value of top.

unicode-bidi

Allows the author to generate levels of embedding within the Unicode embedding algorithm.

Values: normal | embed | bidi-override | inherit

Initial value: normal

Applies to: All elements.

Inherited: No.

Computed value: As specified.

vertical-align

Specifies the vertical alignment of an inline element's baseline relative to the baseline or line box of the line in which it resides. When used with table cells, only the values baseline, top, middle, and bottom apply.

Values: baseline | sub | super | top | text-top | middle | text-bottom | bottom | <percentage> | <length> | inherit

Initial value: baseline

Applies to: Inline elements and table cell elements.

Inherited: No.

Percentages: Refer to the line-height of the element itself.

Computed value: For percentage and length values, the absolute length; otherwise, as specified.

visibility

Specifies whether an element is rendered. Invisible boxes still affect layout.

Values: visible | hidden | collapse | inherit

Initial value: visible

Applies to: All elements.

Inherited: Yes.

Computed value: As specified.

white-space

Specifies how whitespace in the element source is handled in layout.

Values: normal | pre | nowrap | pre-wrap | pre-line | inherit

Initial value: normal

Applies to: All elements (as of CSS 2.1); block-level elements (CSS 1 and CSS 2).

Inherited: Yes.

Computed value: As specified.

width

Defines the width of an element's content area. Padding, borders, and margins are added to this value. Negative values are not permitted.

Values: <length> | <percentage> | auto | inherit

Initial value: auto

Applies to: Block-level elements and replaced elements (such as images).

Inherited: No.

Percentages: Refer to the width of the containing block.

Computed value: The percentage value or auto as specified or the absolute length; auto if the property does not apply.

word-spacing

Specifies an amount of space to be inserted between words in a text element. Negative values are permitted.

Values: normal | <length> | inherit

Initial value: normal

Applies to: All elements.

Inherited: Yes.

Computed value: For normal, the absolute length 0; otherwise, the absolute length.

z-index

Specifies the stacking level for a positioned element.

Values: <integer> | auto | inherit

Initial value: auto

Applies to: Positioned elements.

Inherited: No.

Computed value: As specified.

Paged Media

orphans

Specifies the minimum number of lines of a paragraph that must be left at the bottom of a page.

Values: `<integer> | inherit`

Initial value: 2

Applies to: Block-level elements.

Inherited: Yes.

Computed value: As specified.

page-break-after

Specifies whether page breaks should be placed after an element.

Values: `auto | always | avoid | left | right | inherit`

Initial value: `auto`

Applies to: Block-level elements.

Inherited: No.

Computed value: As specified.

page-break-before

Specifies whether page breaks should be placed before an element.

Values: `auto | always | avoid | left | right | inherit`

Initial value: `auto`

Applies to: Block-level elements.

Inherited: No.

Computed value: As specified.

page-break-inside

Specifies whether page breaks should be placed inside an element.

Values:	auto | always | avoid | left | right | inherit
Initial value:	auto
Applies to:	Block-level elements.
Inherited:	No.
Computed value:	As specified.

widows

Specifies the minimum number of lines of a paragraph that must be left at the top of a page.

Values:	<integer> | inherit
Initial value:	2
Applies to:	Block-level elements.
Inherited:	Yes.
Computed value:	As specified.

Aural Styles

Note that aural styles are only "informative" in CSS 2.1.

azimuth

Specifies the horizontal angle from which a sound should seem to emanate.

Values:	<angle> | [[left-side | far-left | left | center-left | center | center-right | right | far-right | right-side] || behind] | leftwards | rightwards | inherit
Initial value:	center
Applies to:	All elements.
Inherited:	Yes.
Computed value:	Normalized angle.

cue

Shorthand property for specifying cue-before and cue-after.

Values: [<'cue-before'> || <'cue-after'>] | inherit

Initial value: See individual properties.

Applies to: All elements.

Inherited: No.

Computed value: See individual properties.

cue-after

Specifies an auditory icon to play after the element content.

Values: <uri> | none | inherit

Initial value: none

Applies to: All elements.

Inherited: No.

Computed value: Absolute URI or none.

cue-before

Specifies an auditory icon to play before the element content.

Values: <uri> | none | inherit

Initial value: none

Applies to: All elements.

Inherited: No.

Computed value: Absolute URI or none.

elevation

Specifies the vertical angle from which a sound should seem to emanate.

Values: <angle> | below | level | above | higher | lower | inherit

Initial value: level

Applies to: All elements.

Inherited: Yes.

Computed value: Normalized angle.

pause

Specifies a pause to be observed before or after an element (or both).

Values: [[<time> | <percentage>]{1,2}] | inherit

Initial value: See individual properties.

Applies to: All elements.

Inherited: Yes.

Percentages: Refers to the inverse of the value of the speech-rate property.

Computed value: Time.

pause-after

Specifies a pause to be observed after an element.

Values: <time> | <percentage> | inherit

Initial value: 0

Applies to: All elements.

Inherited: No.

Percentages: Refers to the inverse of the value of the speech-rate property.

Computed value: Time.

pause-before

Specifies a pause to be observed before an element.

Values: <time> | <percentage> | inherit

Initial value: 0

Applies to: All elements.

Inherited: No.

Percentages: Refers to the inverse of the value of the speech-rate property.

Computed value: Time.

pitch

Specifies the average pitch (a frequency) of the speaking voice.

Values: `<frequency> | x-low | low | medium | high | x-high | inherit`

Initial value: `medium`

Applies to: All elements.

Inherited: Yes.

Computed value: Frequency.

pitch-range

Specifies variation in average pitch, i.e., how much the fundamental frequency may deviate from the average pitch.

Values: `<number> | inherit`

Initial value: `50`

Applies to: All elements.

Inherited: Yes.

Computed value: As specified.

play-during

Specifies a sound to be played as a background while an element's content is spoken.

Values: `<uri> [ mix || repeat ]? | auto | none | inherit`

Initial value: `auto`

Applies to: All elements.

Inherited: No.

Computed value: Absolute URI; rest as specified.

richness

Specifies the richness, or brightness, of the speaking voice. A rich voice will "carry" in a large room, a smooth voice will not.

Values:	`<number>` | `inherit`
Initial value:	50
Applies to:	All elements.
Inherited:	Yes.
Computed value:	As specified.

speak

Specifies how and whether an element's contents will be audibly rendered.

Values:	`normal` | `none` | `spell-out` | `inherit`
Initial value:	`normal`
Applies to:	All elements.
Inherited:	Yes.
Computed value:	As specified.

speak-header

Specifies whether the content of table headers is spoken before every cell or only when the header changes.

Values:	`once` | `always` | `inherit`
Initial value:	`once`
Applies to:	Elements containing table header information.
Inherited:	Yes.
Computed value:	As specified.

speak-numeral

Specifies how numbers are spoken.

Values: digits | continuous | inherit

Initial value: continuous

Applies to: All elements.

Inherited: Yes.

Computed value: As specified.

speak-punctuation

Specifies how punctuation is spoken.

Values: code | none | inherit

Initial value: none

Applies to: All elements.

Inherited: Yes.

Computed value: As specified.

speech-rate

Specifies the average rate at which words are spoken.

Values: <number> | x-slow | slow | medium | fast | x-fast | faster | slower | inherit

Initial value: medium

Applies to: All elements.

Inherited: Yes.

Computed value: An absolute number.

stress

Specifies the height of "local peaks" in the intonation contour of a voice.

Values: <number> | inherit

Initial value: 50

Applies to: All elements.

Inherited: Yes.

Computed value: As specified.

voice-family

Specifies a list of voice families that can be used in the audio rendering of an element's content (comparable to font-family). The generic voices are male, female, and child.

Values:
[[<specific-voice> | <generic-voice>],]* [<specific-voice> | <generic-voice>] | inherit

Initial value: Depends on user agent.

Applies to: All elements.

Inherited: Yes.

Computed value: As specified.

volume

Specifies the median volume level.

Values: <number> | <percentage> | silent | x-soft | soft | medium | loud | x-loud | inherit

Initial value: medium

Applies to: All elements.

Inherited: Yes.

Computed value: As specified.

C

Character Entities

This appendix lists the Numeric Character References (both decimal and hexadecimal) and predefined character entities as defined in the HTML 4.01 and XHTML Recommendations.

ASCII Character Set

HTML and XHTML documents use the standard 7-bit ASCII character set in their source. The first 31 characters in ASCII (not listed) are such device controls as backspace (&#08;) and carriage return () and are not appropriate for use in HTML documents.

HTML 4.01 defines only four entities in this character range: less than (<, <), greater than (<, >), ampersand (&, &), and quotation mark (", "), that are necessary for escaping characters that may be interpreted as markup. XHTML also includes the ' entity that is included in every XML language. In XHTML documents, the ampersand symbol (&) must always be escaped in attribute values. For better compatibility with XML parsers, authors should use numerical character references instead of named character references for all other character entities.

Decimal	Hex	Entity	Symbol	Description
 	 			Space
!	!		!	Exclamation point
"	"	"	"	Quotation mark
#	#		#	Octothorpe
$	$		$	Dollar symbol
%	%		%	Percent symbol
&	&	&	&	Ampersand

Decimal	Hex	Entity	Symbol	Description
&#039;	&#x27;	XML/XHTML only: '	'	Apostrophe (single quote)
&#040;	&#x28;		(	Left parenthesis
&#041;	&#x29;		)	Right parenthesis
&#042;	&#x2A;		*	Asterisk
&#043;	&#x2B;		+	Plus sign
&#044;	&#x2C;		,	Comma
&#045;	&#x2D;		-	Hyphen
&#046;	&#x2E;		.	Period
&#047;	&#x2F;		/	Slash
0-9	0-9		0–9	Digits 0–9
&#058;	&#x3A;		:	Colon
&#059;	&#x3B;		;	Semicolon
&#060;	&#x3C;	&lt;	<	Less than
&#061;	&#x3D;		=	Equals sign
&#062;	&#x3E;	&gt;	>	Greater than
&#063;	&#x3F;		?	Question mark
&#064;	&#x40;		@	Commercial at sign
A-Z	A-Z		A–Z	Letters A–Z
&#091;	&#x5B;		[	Left square bracket
&#092;	&#x5C;		\	Backslash
&#093;	&#x5D;		]	Right square bracket
&#094;	&#x5E;		^	Caret
&#095;	&#x5F;		_	Underscore
&#096;	&#x60;		`	Grave accent (no letter)
a-z	a-z		a–z	Letters a–z
&#123;	&#x7B;		{	Left curly brace
&#124;	&#x7C;		|	Vertical bar
&#125;	&#x7D;		}	Right curly brace
&#126;	&#x7E;		~	Tilde

Nonstandard Entities (‚–Ÿ)

The character references numbered 130 through 159 are not defined in HTML and therefore are invalid characters that should be avoided.

Some nonstandard numerical entities in this range are supported by browsers (such as — for an em dash), however, they all have standard equivalents listed in the "General Punctuation" section of this appendix. If you need an em dash, use — or — instead.

Latin-1 (ISO-8859-1)

Decimal	Hex	Entity	Symbol	Description
				Nonbreaking space
¡	¡	¡	¡	Inverted exclama-tion mark
¢	¢	¢	¢	Cent sign
£	£	£	£	Pound symbol
¤	¤	¤	¤	General currency symbol
¥	¥	¥	¥	Yen symbol
¦	¦	¦	¦	Broken vertical bar
§	§	§	§	Section sign
¨	¨	¨	¨	Umlaut
©	©	©	©	Copyright
ª	ª	ª	ª	Feminine ordinal
«	«	«	«	Left angle quote
¬	¬	¬	¬	Not sign
­	­	­	–	Soft hyphen
®	®	®	®	Registered trade-mark
¯	¯	¯	¯	Macron accent
°	°	°	°	Degree sign
±	±	±	±	Plus or minus
²	²	²	2	Superscript 2
³	³	³	3	Superscript 3
´	´	´	´	Acute accent (no letter)
µ	µ	µ	µ	Micron (Greek mu)
¶	¶	¶	¶	Paragraph sign
·	·	·	·	Middle dot
¸	¸	¸	¸	Cedilla
¹	¹	¹	1	Superscript 1
º	º	º	º	Masculine ordinal
»	»	»	»	Right angle quote
¼	¼	¼	1/4	Fraction one-fourth
½	½	½	1/2	Fraction one-half
¾	¾	¾	3/4	Fraction three-fourths
¿	¿	¿	¿	Inverted question mark
À	À	À	À	Capital A, grave accent
Á	Á	Á	Á	Capital A, acute accent

Decimal	Hex	Entity	Symbol	Description
&#194;	&#xC2;	&Acirc;	Â	Capital A, circumflex accent
&#195;	&#xC3;	&Atilde;	Ã	Capital A, tilde accent
&#196;	&#xC4;	&Auml;	Ä	Capital A, umlaut
&#197;	&#xC5;	&Aring;	Å	Capital A, ring
&#198;	&#xC6;	&AElig;	Æ	Capital AE ligature
&#199;	&#xC7;	&Ccedil;	Ç	Capital C, cedilla
&#200;	&#xC8;	&Egrave;	È	Capital E, grave accent
&#201;	&#xC9;	&Eacute;	É	Capital E, acute accent
&#202;	&#xCA;	&Ecirc;	Ê	Capital E, circum-flex accent
&#203;	&#xCB;	&Euml;	Ë	Capital E, umlaut
&#204;	&#xCC;	&Igrave;	Ì	Capital I, grave accent
&#205;	&#xCD;	&Iacute;	Í	Capital I, acute accent
&#206;	&#xCE;	&Icirc;	Î	Capital I, circumflex accent
&#207;	&#xCF;	&Iuml;	Ï	Capital I, umlaut
&#208;	&#xD0;	&ETH;	Ð	Capital eth, Icelandic
&#209;	&#xD1;	&Ntilde;	Ñ	Capital N, tilde
&#210;	&#xD2;	&Ograve;	Ò	Capital O, grave accent
&#211;	&#xD3;	&Oacute;	Ó	Capital O, acute accent
&#212;	&#xD4;	&Ocirc;	Ô	Capital O, circum-flex accent
&#213;	&#xD5;	&Otilde;	Õ	Capital O, tilde accent
&#214;	&#xD6;	&Ouml;	Ö	Capital O, umlaut
&#215;	&#xD7;	&times;	×	Multiplication sign
&#216;	&#xD8;	&Oslash;	Ø	Capital O, slash
&#217;	&#xD9;	&Ugrave;	Ù	Capital U, grave accent
&#218;	&#xDA;	&Uacute;	Ú	Capital U, acute accent
&#219;	&#xDB;	&Ucirc;	Û	Capital U, circum-flex accent
&#220;	&#xDC;	&Uuml;	Ü	Capital U, umlaut
&#221;	&#xDD;	&Yacute;	Ý	Capital Y, acute accent
&#222;	&#xDE;	&THORN;	Þ	Capital Thorn, Icelandic

Decimal	Hex	Entity	Symbol	Description
ß	ß	ß	ß	Small sz ligature, German
à	à	à	à	Small a, grave accent
á	á	á	á	Small a, acute accent
â	â	â	â	Small a, circumflex accent
ã	ã	ã	ã	Small a, tilde
ä	ä	ä	ä	Small a, umlaut
å	å	å	å	Small a, ring
æ	æ	æ	æ	Small ae ligature
ç	ç	ç	ç	Small c, cedilla
è	è	è	è	Small e, grave accent
é	é	é	é	Small e, acute accent
ê	ê	ê	ê	Small e, circumflex accent
ë	ë	ë	ë	Small e, umlaut
ì	ì	ì	ì	Small i, grave accent
í	í	í	í	Small i, acute accent
î	î	î	î	Small i, circumflex accent
ï	ï	ï	ï	Small i, umlaut
ð	ð	ð	∂	Small eth, Icelandic
ñ	ñ	ñ	ñ	Small n, tilde
ò	ò	ò	ò	Small o, grave accent
ó	ó	ó	ó	Small o, acute accent
ô	ô	ô	ô	Small o, circumflex accent
õ	õ	õ	õ	Small o, tilde
ö	ö	ö	ö	Small o, umlaut
÷	÷	÷	÷	Division sign
ø	ø	ø	ø	Small o, slash
ù	ù	ù	ù	Small u, grave accent
ú	ú	ú	ú	Small u, acute accent
û	û	û	û	Small u, circumflex accent
ü	ü	ü	ü	Small u, umlaut
ý	ý	ý	ý	Small y, acute accent

Decimal	Hex	Entity	Symbol	Description
þ	þ	þ	þ	Small thorn, Icelandic
ÿ	ÿ	ÿ	ÿ	Small y, umlaut

Latin Extended-A

Decimal	Hex	Entity	Symbol	Description
Œ	Œ	Œ	Œ	Capital ligature OE
œ	œ	œ	œ	Small ligature oe
Š	Š	Š	Š	Capital S, caron
š	š	š	š	Small s, caron
Ÿ	Ÿ	Ÿ	Ÿ	Capital Y, umlaut

Latin Extended-B

Decimal	Hex	Entity	Symbol	Description
ƒ	ƒ	ƒ	ƒ	Small f with hook

Spacing Modifier Letters

Decimal	Hex	Entity	Symbol	Description
ˆ	ˆ	ˆ	ˆ	Circumflex accent
˜	˜	˜	˜	Tilde

Greek

Decimal	Hex	Entity	Symbol	Description
Α	Α	Α	A	Greek capital alpha
Β	Β	Β	B	Greek capital beta
Γ	Γ	Γ	Γ	Greek capital gamma
Δ	Δ	Δ	Δ	Greek capital delta
Ε	Ε	Ε	E	Greek capital epsilon
Ζ	Ζ	Ζ	Z	Greek capital zeta
Η	Η	Η	H	Greek capital eta
Θ	Θ	Θ	Θ	Greek capital theta
Ι	Ι	Ι	I	Greek capital iota
Κ	Κ	Κ	K	Greek capital kappa
Λ	Λ	Λ	Λ	Greek capital lambda

Decimal	Hex	Entity	Symbol	Description
Μ	Μ	Μ	M	Greek capital mu
Ν	Ν	Ν	N	Greek capital nu
Ξ	Ξ	Ξ	Ξ	Greek capital xi
Ο	Ο	Ο	O	Greek capital omicron
Π	Π	Π	π	Greek capital pi
Ρ	Ρ	Ρ	P	Greek capital rho
Σ	Σ	Σ	Σ	Greek captial sigma
Τ	Τ	Τ	T	Greek capital tau
Υ	Υ	Υ	Y	Greek capital upsilon
Φ	Φ	Φ	Φ	Greek capital phi
Χ	Χ	Χ	X	Greek capital chi
Ψ	Ψ	Ψ	Ψ	Greek capital psi
Ω	Ω	Ω	Ω	Greek capital omega
α	α	α	α	Greek small alpha
β	β	β	β	Greek small beta
γ	γ	γ	γ	Greek small gamma
δ	δ	δ	δ	Greek small delta
ε	ε	ε	ε	Greek small epsilon
ζ	ζ	ζ	ζ	Greek small zeta
η	η	η	η	Greek small eta
θ	θ	θ	θ	Greek small theta
ι	ι	ι	ι	Greek small iota
κ	κ	κ	κ	Greek small kappa
λ	λ	λ	λ	Greek small lambda
μ	μ	μ	μ	Greek small mu
ν	ν	ν	ν	Greek small nu
ξ	ξ	ξ	ξ	Greek small xi
ο	ο	ο	o	Greek small omicron
π	π	π	π	Greek small pi
ρ	ρ	ρ	ρ	Greek small rho
ς	ς	ς	ς	Greek small letter final sigma
σ	σ	σ	σ	Greek small sigma
τ	τ	τ	τ	Greek small tau
υ	υ	υ	υ	Greek small upsilon
φ	φ	φ	φ	Greek small phi
χ	χ	χ	χ	Greek small chi
ψ	ψ	ψ	ψ	Greek small psi
ω	ω	ω	ω	Greek small omega

Decimal	Hex	Entity	Symbol	Description
ϑ	ϑ	ϑ	ϑ	Greek small theta symbol
ϒ	ϒ	ϒ	ϒ	Greek upsilon with hook
ϖ	ϖ	ϖ	ϖ	Greek pi symbol

General Punctuation

Decimal	Hex	Entity	Symbol	Description
				En space
				Em space
				Thin space
‌	‌	‌	Non-printing	Zero-width non-joiner
‍	‍	‍	Non-printing	Zero-width joiner
‎	‎	‎	Non-printing	Left-to-right mark
‏	‏	‏	Non-printing	Right-to-left mark
–	–	–	–	En-dash
—	—	—	—	Em-dash
‘	‘	‘	`	Left single quotation mark
’	’	’	'	Right single quotation mark
‚	‚	‚	‚	Single low-9 quotation mark
“	“	“	"	Left double quotation mark
”	”	”	"	Right double quotation mark
„	„	„	„	Double low-9 quotation mark
†	†	†	†	Dagger
‡	‡	‡	‡	Double dagger
•	•	•	•	Bullet
…	…	…	...	Ellipses
‰	‰	‰	‰	Per mille symbol (per thousand)
′	′	′	′	Prime, minutes, feet
″	″	″	″	Double prime, seconds, inches
‹	‹	‹	‹	Single left angle quotation (nonstandard)
›	›	›	›	Single right angle quotation (nonstandard)

Decimal	Hex	Entity	Symbol	Description
&#8254;	&#x203E;	&oline;	‾	Overline
&#8260;	&#x2044;	&frasl;	⁄	Fraction slash
&#8364;	&#x20AC;	&euro;	€	Euro symbol

Letter-like Symbols

Decimal	Hex	Entity	Symbol	Description
&#8465;	&#x2111;	&image;	ℑ	Blackletter capital I, imaginary part
&#8472;	&#x2118;	&weierp;	℘	Script capital P, power set
&#8476;	&#x211C;	&real;	ℜ	Blackletter capital R, real part
&#8482;	&#x2122;	&trade;	™	Trademark sign
&#8501;	&#x2135;	&alefsym;	ℵ	Alef symbol, or first transfinite cardinal

Arrows

Decimal	Hex	Entity	Symbol	Description
&#8592;	&#x2190;	&larr;	←	Left arrow
&#8593;	&#x2191;	&uarr;	↑	Up arrow
&#8594;	&#x2192;	&rarr;	→	Right arrow
&#8595;	&#x2193;	&darr;	↓	Down arrow
&#8596;	&#x2194;	&harr;	↔	Left-right arrow
&#8629;	&#x21B5;	&crarr;	↵	Down arrow with corner leftward
&#8656;	&#x21D0;	&lArr;	⇐	Leftward double arrow
&#8657;	&#x21D1;	&uArr;	⇑	Upward double arrow
&#8658;	&#x21D2;	&rArr;	⇒	Rightward double arrow
&#8659;	&#x21D3;	&dArr;	⇓	Downward double arrow
&#8660;	&#x21D4;	&hArr;	⇔	Left-right double arrow

Mathematical Operators

Decimal	Hex	Entity	Symbol	Description
&#8704;	&#x2200;	&forall;	∀	For all
&#8706;	&#x2202;	&part;	∂	Partial differential

Decimal	Hex	Entity	Symbol	Description
&#8707;	&#x2203;	&exist;	∃	There exists
&#8709;	&#x2205;	&empty;	∅	Empty set, null set, diameter
&#8711;	&#x2207;	&nabla;	∇	Nabla, backward difference
&#8712;	&#x2208;	&isin;	∈	Element of
&#8713;	&#x2209;	&notin;	∉	Not an element of
&#8715;	&#x220B;	&ni;	∋	Contains as a member
&#8719;	&#x220F;	&prod;	∏	N-ary product, product sign
&#8721;	&#x2211;	&sum;	Σ	N-ary summation
&#8722;	&#x2212;	&minus;	−	Minus sign
&#8727;	&#x2217;	&lowast;	*	Asterisk operator
&#8730;	&#x221A;	&radic;	√	Square root, radical sign
&#8733;	&#x221D;	&prop;	∝	Proportional
&#8734;	&#x221E;	&infin;	∞	Infinity symbol
&#8736;	&#x2220;	&ang;	∠	Angle
&#8743;	&#x2227;	&and;	∧	Logical and, wedge
&#8744;	&#x2228;	&or;	∨	Logical or, vee
&#8745;	&#x2229;	&cap;	∩	Intersection, cap
&#8746;	&#x222A;	&cup;	∪	Union, cup
&#8747;	&#x222B;	&int;	∫	Integral
&#8756;	&#x2234;	&there4;	∴	Therefore
&#8764;	&#x223C;	&sim;	~	Tilde operator, varies with, similar to
&#8773;	&#x2245;	&cong;	≅	Approximately equal to
&#8776;	&#x2248;	&ap;	≈	Almost equal to, asymptotic to
&#8800;	&#x2260;	&ne;	≠	Not equal to
&#8801;	&#x2261;	&equiv;	≡	Identical to
&#8804;	&#x2264;	&le;	≤	Less than or equal to
&#8805;	&#x2265;	&ge;	≥	Greater than or equal to
&#8834;	&#x2282;	&sub;	⊂	Subset of
&#8835;	&#x2283;	&sup;	⊃	Superset of
&#8836;	&#x2284;	&nsub;	⊄	Not a subset of
&#8838;	&#x2286;	&sube	⊆	Subset of or equal to
&#8839;	&#x2287;	&supe	⊇	Superset of or equal to

Decimal	Hex	Entity	Symbol	Description
⊕	⊕	⊕	⊕	Circled plus, direct sum
⊗	⊗	⊗	⊗	Circled times, vector product
⊥	⊥	⊥	⊥	Up tack, orthogonal to, perpendicular
⋅	⋅	⋅	·	Dot operator

Miscellaneous Technical Symbols

Decimal	Hex	Entity	Symbol	Description
⌈	⌈	⌈	⌈	Left ceiling
⌉	⌉	⌉	⌉	Right ceiling
⌊	⌊	⌊	⌊	Left floor
⌋	⌋	⌋	⌋	Right floor
〈	〈	⟨	⟨	Left-pointing angle bracket
〉	〉	⟩	⟩	Right-pointing angle bracket

Geometric Shapes

Decimal	Hex	Entity	Symbol	Description
◊	◊	◊	◊	Lozenge

Miscellaneous Symbols

Decimal	Hex	Entity	Symbol	Description
♠	♠	♠	♠	Black spade suit
♣	♣	♣	♣	Black club suit
♥	♥	♥	♥	Black heart suit
♦	♦	♦	♦	Black diamond suit

D

Specifying Color

This appendix contains background information regarding specifying color that applies to both CSS properties and HTML attributes.

There are two methods for specifying colors in web documents: numeric RGB values and color names.

Specifying Color by RGB Values

The most common and precise way to specify a color is by its numeric RGB (red, green, blue) values. Using RGB values, you can specify any color from the "true color" space (millions of colors). For an explanation of RGB color, see Chapter 28.

Using an image editing tool such as Adobe Photoshop, you can determine the RGB values (on a scale from 0 to 255) for a selected color. These are the RGB values for a particularly lovely spring green:

Red: 212
Green: 232
Blue: 119

Color values are most often provided in a two-digit hexadecimal (base-16) form, not decimal, although these values may be used as-is in one CSS color format. Hexadecimal numbering is discussed in more detail in the next section. The same RGB values for that spring green look like this when converted to hexadecimal:

Red: D4
Green: E8
Blue: 77

In the CSS and HTML document, the most common way of representing these values is in a six-character string, preceded by the # symbol:

    #D4E877

The underlying syntax is this:

    #RRGGBB

where *RR* stands for the hexadecimal red value, *GG* stands for the hexadecimal green value, and *BB* stands for the hexadecimal blue value. CSS has additional formats for RGB values, as listed in the upcoming "RGB Colors in CSS" section.

Fortunately, Adobe Photoshop makes the hexadecimal values for colors readily available at the bottom of the color picker next to the "#" symbol. The hex values can be copied from the color picker and pasted into a style sheet or HTML document.

If you are using an image tool that does not list hexadecimal values, you'll need to convert decimal to hexadecimal yourself. The next section tells you how.

The Hexadecimal System

The hexadecimal numbering system is base-16 (as compared to base-10 for decimal numbers). It uses the following 16 characters:

    0, 1, 2, 3, 4, 5, 6, 7, 8, 9, A, B, C, D, E, F

A through F represent the decimal values 10 through 15.

Converting decimal to hexadecimal

You can calculate hex values in the 0 to 255 range by dividing a number by 16 to get the first digit, then using the remainder for the second digit. For example, dividing the decimal number 203 by 16 yields 12 with a remainder of 11. The hexadecimal value of 12 is C; the hex value of 11 is B. Therefore, the hexadecimal equivalent of 203 is CB.

Fortunately, there are simpler methods for converting numbers to hexadecimal:

- Use a hexadecimal calculator. Windows users can find a hexadecimal calculator in the "Scientific" view of the Windows standard calculator. Mac users with OS X 10.4 (Tiger) can download the free Hex Calculator Widget at *www.apple.com/downloads/dashboard/calculate_convert/hexcalculatorwidget.html*.
- Use Table D-1, which translates decimal values from 0 to 255.

Table D-1. Decimal to hexadecimal equivalents

dec = hex	dec = hex	dec = hex	dec = hex	dec = hex	dec = hex
0 = 00	43 = 2B	86 = 56	129 = 81	172 = AC	215 = D7
1 = 01	44 = 2C	87 = 57	130 = 82	173 = AD	216 = D8
2 = 02	45 = 2D	88 = 58	131 = 83	174 = AE	217 = D9
3 = 03	46 = 2E	89 = 59	132 = 84	175 = AF	218 = DA
4 = 04	47 = 2F	90 = 5A	133 = 85	176 = B0	219 = DB
5 = 05	48 = 30	91 = 5B	134 = 86	177 = B1	220 = DC
6 = 06	49 = 31	92 = 5C	135 = 87	178 = B2	221 = DD
7 = 07	50 = 32	93 = 5D	136 = 88	179 = B3	222 = DE
8 = 08	51 = 33	94 = 5E	137 = 89	180 = B4	223 = DF
9 = 09	52 = 34	95 = 5F	138 = 8A	181 = B5	224 = E0
10 = 0A	53 = 35	96 = 60	139 = 8B	182 = B6	225 = E1
11 = 0B	54 = 36	97 = 61	140 = 8C	183 = B7	226 = E2
12 = 0C	55 = 37	98 = 62	141 = 8D	184 = B8	227 = E3
13 = 0D	56 = 38	99 = 63	142 = 8E	185 = B9	228 = E4
14 = 0E	57 = 39	100 = 64	143 = 8F	186 = BA	229 = E5
15 = 0F	58 = 3A	101 = 65	144 = 90	187 = BB	230 = E6
16 = 10	59 = 3B	102 = 66	145 = 91	188 = BC	231 = E7
17 = 11	60 = 3C	103 = 67	146 = 92	189 = BD	232 = E8
18 = 12	61 = 3D	104 = 68	147 = 93	190 = BE	233 = E9
19 = 13	62 = 3E	105 = 69	148 = 94	191 = BF	234 = EA
20 = 14	63 = 3F	106 = 6A	149 = 95	192 = C0	235 = EB
21 = 15	64 = 40	107 = 6B	150 = 96	193 = C1	236 = EC
22 = 16	65 = 41	108 = 6C	151 = 97	194 = C2	237 = ED
23 = 17	66 = 42	109 = 6D	152 = 98	195 = C3	238 = EE
24 = 18	67 = 43	110 = 6E	153 = 99	196 = C4	239 = EF
25 = 19	68 = 44	111 = 6F	154 = 9A	197 = C5	240 = F0
26 = 1A	69 = 45	112 = 70	155 = 9B	198 = C6	241 = F1
27 = 1B	70 = 46	113 = 71	156 = 9C	199 = C7	242 = F2
28 = 1C	71 = 47	114 = 72	157 = 9D	200 = C8	243 = F3
29 = 1D	72 = 48	115 = 73	158 = 9E	201 = C9	244 = F4
30 = 1E	73 = 49	116 = 74	159 = 9F	202 = CA	245 = F5
31 = 1F	74 = 4A	117 = 75	160 = A0	203 = CB	246 = F6
32 = 20	75 = 4B	118 = 76	161 = A1	204 = CC	247 = F7
33 = 21	76 = 4C	119 = 77	162 = A2	205 = CD	248 = F8
34 = 22	77 = 4D	120 = 78	163 = A3	206 = CE	249 = F9
35 = 23	78 = 4E	121 = 79	164 = A4	207 = CF	250 = FA
36 = 24	79 = 4F	122 = 7A	165 = A5	208 = D0	251 = FB
37 = 25	80 = 50	123 = 7B	166 = A6	209 = D1	252 = FC
38 = 26	81 = 51	124 = 7C	167 = A7	210 = D2	253 = FD
39 = 27	82 = 52	125 = 7D	168 = A8	211 = D3	254 = FE
40 = 28	83 = 53	126 = 7E	169 = A9	212 = D4	255 = FF
41 = 29	84 = 54	127 = 7F	170 = AA	213 = D5	
42 = 2A	85 = 55	128 = 80	171 = AB	214 = D6	

Hexadecimal values for web palette colors

The web palette is a set of 216 colors that will not shift or dither when rendered in browsers on 8-bit monitors. (For a thorough explanation of the web palette, see Chapter 29.) All colors in the web palette are made up of combinations of the following six hexadecimal values: 00, 33, 66, 99, CC, and FF.

RGB Colors in CSS

RGB colors can be specified in style rules by any of the methods listed in Table D-2.

Table D-2. Methods for specifying RGB colors

Method	Syntax	Example
Six-digit hexadecimal.	#RRGGBB	color: #0033FF
Three-digit RGB shorthand. This method may be used when each RGB value is double digits.	#RGB (interpreted as #RRGGBB)	color: #03F (interpreted as color: #0033FF)
Three decimal values.	rgb(n, n, n)	color: rgb(0,51,255)
Three percentage values (calculated as a percentage of 255).	rgb(%, %, %)	color: rgb(0%, 20%, 100%)

RGB Colors in HTML

Because color is presentational, it should always be specified using style sheets, but should you need to specify color in the HTML document, it is always done using the six-digit hexadecimal syntax:

    #RRGGBB

For example:

    <td bgcolor="#2D1F60">...</td>

Specifying Colors by Name

Colors may also be identified by predefined color names. This technique is less common in everyday practice. The syntax for using color names is extremely straightforward.

    color: green

    <body link="navy">

Standard Color Names

In HTML 4.01, XHTML, CSS 1, and CSS 2, there are only 16 valid color names. They are listed in Table D-3 with their equivalent RGB values.

Table D-3. Valid color names and equivalent RGB values

Color name	RGB value	Color name	RGB value
black	#000000	green	#008000
silver	#C0C0C0	lime	#00FF00
gray	#808080	olive	#808000
white	#FFFFFF	yellow	#FFFF00
maroon	#800000	navy	#000080
red	#FF0000	blue	#0000FF
purple	#800080	teal	#008080
fuchsia	#FF00FF	aqua	#00FFFF

CSS 2.1 adds orange (#FFA500) for a total of 17 supported colors.

CSS Extended Color Names

Many browsers have historically supported a set of 140 nonstandard color names originally developed for the X Window System. These color names have finally been standardized in the CSS 3 Color Module (*www.w3.org/TR/css3-color*). Be aware that not all browsers support all of these colors (or all spellings of gray versus grey), and thus you should use the equivalent numerical color values instead. They are included here in the interest of thoroughness and historical value.

The complete list appears in Table D-4, sorted alphabetically with their numerical values.

Table D-4. Nonstandard color names with their numeric values

Color name	RGB values	Hexadecimal
aliceblue	240 - 248 - 255	F0F8FF
antiquewhite	250 - 235 - 215	FAEBD7
aqua	0 - 255 - 255	00FFFF
aquamarine	127 - 255 - 212	7FFFD4
azure	240 - 255 - 255	F0FFFF
beige	245 - 245 - 220	F5F5DC
bisque	255 - 228 - 196	FFE4C4
black	0 - 0 - 0	000000
blanchedalmond	255 - 235 - 205	FFEBCD
blue	0 - 0 - 255	0000FF
blueviolet	138 - 43 - 226	8A2BE2
brown	165 - 42 - 42	A52A2A
burlywood	222 - 184 - 135	DEB887
cadetblue	95 - 158 - 160	5F9EA0
chartreuse	127 - 255 - 0	7FFF00
chocolate	210 - 105 - 30	D2691E

*Table D-4. Nonstandard color names **with their** numeric values (continued)*

Color name	RGB values	Hexadecimal
coral	255 - 127 - 80	FF7F50
cornflowerblue	100 - 149 - 237	6495ED
cornsilk	255 - 248 - 220	FFF8DC
crimson	220 - 20 - 60	DC143C
cyan	0 - 255 - 255	00FFFF
darkblue	0 - 0 - 139	00008B
darkcyan	0 - 139 - 139	008B8B
darkgoldenrod	184 - 134 - 11	B8860B
darkgray (darkgrey)	169 - 169 - 169	A9A9A9
darkgreen	0 - 100 - 0	006400
darkkhaki	189 - 183 - 107	BDB76B
darkmagenta	139 - 0 - 139	8B008B
darkolivegreen	85 - 107 - 47	556B2F
darkorange	255 - 140 - 0	FF8C00
darkorchid	153 - 50 - 204	9932CC
darkred	139 - 0 - 0	8B0000
darksalmon	233 - 150 - 122	E9967A
darkseagreen	143 - 188 - 143	8FBC8F
darkslateblue	72 - 61 - 139	483D8B
darkslategray (darkslate-grey)	47 - 79 - 79	2F4F4F
darkturquoise	0 - 206 - 209	00CED1
darkviolet	148 - 0 - 211	9400D3
deeppink	255 - 20 - 147	FF1493
deepskyblue	0 - 191 - 255	00BFFF
dimgray (dimgrey)	105 - 105 - 105	696969
dodgerblue	30 - 144 - 255	1E90FF
firebrick	178 - 34 - 34	B22222
floralwhite	255 - 250 - 240	FFFAF0
forestgreen	34 - 139 - 34	228B22
fuchsia	255 - 0 - 255	FF00FF
gainsboro	220 - 220 - 220	DCDCDC
ghostwhite	248 - 248 - 255	F8F8FF
gold	255 - 215 - 0	FFD700
goldenrod	218 - 165 - 32	DAA520
gray (grey)	128 - 128 - 128	808080
green	0 - 128 - 0	008000
greenyellow	173 - 255 - 47	ADFF2F
honeydew	240 - 255 - 240	F0FFF0
hotpink	255 - 105 - 180	FF69B4
indianred	205 - 92 - 92	CD5C5C

Table D-4. Nonstandard color names with their numeric values (continued)

Color name	RGB values	Hexadecimal
indigo	75 - 0 - 130	4B0082
ivory	255 - 255 - 240	FFFFF0
khaki	240 - 230 - 140	F0E68C
lavender	230 - 230 - 250	E6E6FA
lavenderblush	255 - 240 - 245	FFF0F5
lawngreen	124 - 252 - 0	7CFC00
lemonchiffon	255 - 250 - 205	FFFACD
lightblue	173 - 216 - 230	ADD8E6
lightcoral	240 - 128 - 128	F08080
lightcyan	224 - 255 - 255	E0FFFF
lightgoldenrodyellow	250 - 250 - 210	FAFAD2
lightgreen	144 - 238 - 144	90EE90
lightgray (lightgrey)	211 - 211 - 211	D3D3D3
lightpink	255 - 182 - 193	FFB6C1
lightsalmon	255 - 160 - 122	FFA07A
lightseagreen	32 - 178 - 170	20B2AA
lightskyblue	135 - 206 - 250	87CEFA
lightslategray (light-slategrey)	119 - 136 - 153	778899
lightsteelblue	176 - 196 - 222	B0C4DE
lightyellow	255 - 255 - 224	FFFFE0
lime	0 - 255 - 0	00FF00
limegreen	50 - 205 - 50	32CD32
linen	250 - 240 - 230	FAF0E6
magenta	255 - 0 - 255	FF00FF
maroon	128 - 0 - 0	800000
mediumaquamarine	102 - 205 - 170	66CDAA
mediumblue	0 - 0 - 205	0000CD
mediumorchid	186 - 85 - 211	BA55D3
mediumpurple	147 - 112 - 219	9370DB
mediumseagreen	60 - 179 - 113	3CB371
mediumslateblue	123 - 104 - 238	7B68EE
mediumspringgreen	0 - 250 - 154	00FA9A
mediumturquoise	72 - 209 - 204	48D1CC
mediumvioletred	199 - 21 - 133	C71585
midnightblue	25 - 25 - 112	191970
mintcream	245 - 255 - 250	F5FFFA
mistyrose	255 - 228 - 225	FFE4E1
moccasin	255 - 228 - 181	FFE4B5
navajowhite	255 - 222 - 173	FFDEAD
navy	0 - 0 - 128	000080

Specifying Color

Color name	RGB values	Hexadecimal
oldlace	253 - 245 - 230	FDF5E6
olive	128 - 128 - 0	808000
olivedrab	107 - 142 - 35	6B8E23
orange	255 - 165 - 0	FFA500
orangered	255 - 69 - 0	FF4500
orchid	218 - 112 - 214	DA70D6
palegoldenrod	238 - 232 - 170	EEE8AA
palegreen	152 - 251 - 152	98FB98
paleturquoise	175 - 238 - 238	AFEEEE
palevioletred	219 - 112 - 147	DB7093
papayawhip	255 - 239 - 213	FFEFD5
peachpuff	255 - 218 - 185	FFDAB9
peru	205 - 133 - 63	CD853F
pink	255 - 192 - 203	FFC0CB
plum	221 - 160 - 221	DDA0DD
powderblue	176 - 224 - 230	B0E0E6
purple	128 - 0 - 128	800080
red	255 - 0 - 0	FF0000
rosybrown	188 - 143 - 143	BC8F8F
royalblue	65 - 105 - 225	4169E1
saddlebrown	139 - 69 - 19	8B4513
salmon	250 - 128 - 114	FA8072
sandybrown	244 - 164 - 96	F4A460
seagreen	46 - 139 - 87	2E8B57
seashell	255 - 245 - 238	FFF5EE
sienna	160 - 82 - 45	A0522D
silver	192 - 192 - 192	C0C0C0
skyblue	135 - 206 - 235	87CEEB
slateblue	106 - 90 - 205	6A5ACD
slategray (slategrey)	112 - 128 - 144	708090
snow	255 - 250 - 250	FFFAFA
springgreen	0 - 255 - 127	00FF7F
steelblue	70 - 130 - 180	4682B4
tan	210 - 180 - 140	D2B48C
teal	0 - 128 - 128	008080
thistle	216 - 191 - 216	D8BFD8
tomato	253 - 99 - 71	FF6347
turquoise	64 - 224 - 208	40E0D0
violet	238 - 130 - 238	EE82EE
wheat	245 - 222 - 179	F5DEB3
white	255 - 255 - 255	FFFFFF

Table D-4. Nonstandard color names with their numeric values (continued)

Color name	RGB values	Hexadecimal
whitesmoke	245 - 245 - 245	F5F5F5
yellow	255 - 255 - 0	FFFF00
yellowgreen	154 - 205 - 50	9ACD32

E

Microformats: Extending (X)HTML

—by Tantek Çelik

XHTML stands for the Extensible HyperText Markup Language. HTML 4 was also designed to be extended, albeit much more subtly. In the past few years, there has been a resurging interest in extending HTML and XHTML. XHTML was originally designed to be extended with other XML elements, in other namespaces. In practice, such extensions have yet to meaningfully materialize on the Web.

Instead, using extension mechanisms introduced in HTML 4, such as the class, id, and rel attributes, web designers, developers, and technologists have been extending the semantics of their HTML and XHTML documents. In the past couple of years, common patterns and conventions have emerged for using these mechanisms. *Microformats* are an effort to standardize these conventions and are specifically designed for ease of use by web authors and to leverage existing interoperable standards. By doing so, microformats have enabled the simple sharing of even more semantic content on the Web without having to learn a new language or duplicate content (either in comments or separate files).

This appendix introduces a few of the open microformats standards being developed by the microformats community. To learn more, visit the *microformats.org* community site.

Extending HTML 4 and XHTML

By following many of the techniques recommended in this book, you may already be extending HTML for your own purposes without even knowing it. Chapter 10 discusses how to provide more semantic descriptions of your content using the class and id attributes. Every meaningful class name and ID extends the semantics expressed by your HTML documents.

HTML 4 has three built-in extension mechanisms. In addition to using semantic class and id attributes, web authors can create their own link relationships with the rel and rev attributes, and property names and values for use with the meta tag. Two of these mechanisms, class/id and rel/rev, are being leveraged into microformats. The third, meta, shows less promise, as is discussed in the sidebar "meta Names and Values."

---

meta Names and Values

The HTML 4 specification discusses how to extend the meta-information provided in a document by defining and using new meta property names and values. There have been various efforts to standardize such efforts (e.g., Dublin Core). Because the invisible meta-information in the head of a document is often disconnected from and out of sync with the visible content of a document, however, these methods have proved to be problematic in practice, especially as documents age or are maintained by multiple authors. Even meta keywords, once used by all search engines, are ignored by Google and others. In fact, most authors no longer waste time or bandwidth with meta keywords in web documents. Similarly, other techniques for embedding invisible metadata, such as using HTML comments or script tags to hide content or markup, should also be avoided, since they too are invisible to and thus ignored by both human users and search engines.

Semantic Class Names

HTML 4 has a limited set of built-in semantics. In 2004, a few web developers realized that by using carefully chosen sets of class names based on existing publishing behaviors and widely adopted Internet standards, they could extend HTML to meaningfully publish information about contacts, events, reviews, and other web data types. This section introduces microformats created for handling contact information and calendar events.

Publishing Contact Information with hCard

Most web sites publish contact information for the site's author or company, for example:

```
<div>
<div>O'Reilly</div>
<div>1005 Gravenstein Highway North</div>
<div>Sebastopol, CA 95472</div>
<div>USA</div>
<div>T: (707) 827-7000</div>
<div>F: (707) 829-0104</div>
<div><a href="http://www.oreilly.com">www.oreilly.com</a></div>
</div>
```

By marking it up with the hCard microformat (which is based on the widely support vCard Internet contact information standard, hence the vcard class name), visitors to the site can easily add the site's contact info to their address book application using an hCard-to-vCard proxy service.

```
<div class="vcard">
  <div class="fn org">O'Reilly</div>
  <div class="adr">
    <div class="street-address">1005 Gravenstein Highway North</div>
    <span class="locality">Sebastopol</span>, <span class="region">CA</span>
    <span class="postal-code">95472</span>
    <div class="country-name">USA</div>
  </div>
  <div class="tel"><abbr class="type" title="work">T:</abbr> (707) 827-7000</div>
  <div class="tel"><abbr class="type" title="fax">F:</abbr> (707) 829-0104</div>
  <div><a class="url" href="http://www.oreilly.com">www.oreilly.com</a></div>
</div>
```

This is an hCard because it uses specific class names established as part of the hCard microformat. The specific elements are not relevant with the exception of the use of the abbr element to abbreviate the type of each phone number, and the addition of a few spans and divs to mark up the distinct hCard properties. For a complete list of hCard class names, more about hCard, and hCard-to-vCard proxy services, see the hCard specification at *microformats.org/wiki/hcard*.

Publishing Events with hCalendar

Similar to hCard, the hCalendar (hCal for short) microformat is based on the iCalendar Internet calendaring standard, and can be used to publish event information in a manner that users can easily copy or subscribe to using an hCalendar-to-iCalendar proxy service:

```
<div class="vevent">
  <div class="summary">O'Reilly Emerging Technology Conference</div>
  <abbr class="dtstart" title="20050306">Mar 6</abbr>-
  <abbr class="dtend" title="20050310">9, 2006</abbr>
  <div class="location">Manchester Grand Hyatt, San Diego, CA</div>
  <a class="url" href="http://events.oreilly.com/pub/e/403">Permalink</a>
</div>
```

Note the use of the abbr element to present an abbreviated human-readable date and represent a precise machine-readable ISO 8601 date in the title attribute. For a complete list of hCalendar class names, more hCalendar details, and hCalendar proxy services, see the hCalendar specification at *microformats.org/wiki/hcalendar*.

Link Relationships

The most common use of link relationships in HTML is to link to a style sheet (as explained in Chapter 16). In doing so, the author uses the rel attribute to communicate that the resource "over there" (referenced by the href attribute) is a "style sheet" for the current document. HTML 4 specifically allows for web authors to create and use their own link relationship values, and suggests using a profile to define them. Several popular new link relationship values have emerged to describe, for example, social network relationships between people, licenses for documents, and "tags" for blog posts. Many of these are quickly becoming de facto standards and have been documented as microformats.

XHTML Friends Network

Since the previous edition of this book, blogs and the larger blogging phenomenon have taken the Web by storm. As of this writing, there were approximately 22.6 million blogs according to real-time search engine Technorati (*technorati. com*). Many of these bloggers publish lists of links to blogs they themselves read, called *blogrolls*. Some indicate the relationship to the people in their blogrolls using symbols, such as asterisks (*) next to people they have met. Typical blogrolls are published as a list of hyperlinks:

```
<ul>
<li><a href="http://molly.example.com">Molly*</a></li>
<li><a href="http://jeff.example.com">Jeff*</a></li>
</ul>
```

In 2003, a few web developers proposed a standard called the XHTML Friends Network (XFN) for explicitly indicating social relationships using new rel attribute values on blogroll links. In the above example, to indicate that Molly is a colleague you have met and Jeff is a friend you have also met, simply add XFN values to rel attributes:

```
<ul>
<li><a rel="colleague met" href="http://molly.example.com">Molly</a></li>
<li><a rel="friend met" href="http://jeff.example.com">Jeff</a></li>
</ul>
```

For a full list of XFN relationship values and more information on using XFN, see the XFN home page at *gmpg.org/xfn/*.

Other Link Relationships

XFN was the first such popular extension of the rel attribute, and others followed soon after. The Creative Commons is a non-profit organization that encourages authors and artists to share their digital works using a standard set of online licenses. Authors can indicate that a document is published under a Creative Commons license by linking from the document to the license and adding a rel attribute with value of license:

```
<a rel="license" href="http://creativecommons.org/licenses/by/2.5/">...</a>
```

Search engines, including both Yahoo! and Google, recognize such license links and offer the ability to search for content available under such licenses.

The practice of visibly "tagging" content on the Web—in particular, links and photos—inspired the creation of the tag relationship value to indicate that the destination of a link represents a "tag" for the current document or portion thereof. A blog post can be tagged as being about "CSS" by including the following visible tag link inside the contents of the post:

```
<a rel="tag" href="http://technorati.com/tag/css">CSS</a>
```

Newer search engines, such as Technorati and Ice Rocket, recognize such tag links and have incorporated tagged content into their search results and other services.

To help combat web spam, publishers and search engine companies developed the nofollow extension. Many automatic and third-party generated hyperlinks are published with rel="nofollow", which search engines use to afford less weight to those links.

XFN and new link relationships were the beginning of a larger movement by web authors to convey more semantic meaning, in a way that is easy to learn, write, and style with CSS. For example, links with relationships can be styled with CSS attribute selectors described in Chapter 17.

More Microformats

The *microformats.org* site has a comprehensive listing of well-established micro-formats that are broadly adopted, as well as nascent microformat efforts that are being designed. Table E-1 provides a summary of several types of content and the microformats that have been developed to represent them.

Table E-1. Examples of microformats

Microformat	Content
hCard	People, organizations, contacts
adr, geo	Address and latitude/longitude location
hCalendar	Calendars and events
hReview	Reviews, ratings
XOXO	Lists and outlines
XFN	Social network relationships
rel-license	Licenses
rel-tag	Tags, topics, categories
xFolk	Tagged links
rel-directory	Directory inclusion
rel-enclosure	Enclosures to be downloaded
VoteLinks	Votes
rel-nofollow, Robots Exclusion	Robot exclusion/filtering
hAtom	Syndicated content
hResume	Resumes
XMDP	(X)HTML metadata profiles

More than the microformats themselves, the *microformats.org* site is the center of an open community of web designers and developers with very active irc chan-nels, email lists, and wiki pages, and it is a great place to learn more about how to use microformats.

Glossary

accessibility

Refers to building web sites, applications, and pages so that there are as few barriers to use as possible for anyone, regardless of ability and the device used to access the information.

AIFF

Audio Interchange File Format. Standard audio format originally developed for the Macintosh, which is now supported on PCs as well. It is one of the formats commonly used for distributing audio on the Web.

Ajax

A web development technique for creating interactive web applications using a combination of (X)HTML, CSS, the DOM, and the nonstandard XMLHttpRequest object to exchange data asynchronously with the server. Because the page doesn't need to refresh with each user interaction, Ajax makes web applications feel more like desktop applications.

alpha channel

In graphics formats, an extra channel for storing information about an image. The alpha channel works like a mask that applies properties (such as transparency) to the pixels in the image. Other channels typically include color value information—as in the red, green, and blue channels of an RGB image.

alpha-channel transparency

The method of transparency used by 24-bit PNGs, which use an additional (alpha) channel to store variable levels of transparency (up to 256) for each pixel in the image.

animated GIF

A GIF89a that contains multiple frames and a "control block" for controlling the animation timing and display.

Apache

A popular open source (free) web server.

applet

A self-contained mini-executable program, such as one written in the Java programming language.

ASCII (American Standard Code for Information Interchange)

A coded character set that includes 128 characters mostly from the Roman alphabet used in modern English.

ASP

Active Server Pages. The part of Microsoft's Internet Information Server software that allows server-side scripting for the creation of dynamically generated web pages and database functions. Web pages created with ASP commonly have the suffix *.asp.*

attribute minimization

The SGML practice in which certain attributes can be reduced to just the attribute value. XML does not support minimization, so all the attributes have to be explicitly declared (for example, checked="checked").

audio bit depth

The number of bits used to define the resolution of the amplitude (or volume) of a digital audio waveform—the more bits, the more accurate the rendering of the original audio source and the larger the resulting audio file. Some common bit depths are 8-bit (which sounds thin or tinny, like a telephone signal) and 16-bit, which is required to describe music of CD quality.

AVI

Audio/Video Interleaved. A digital video format developed by Microsoft in which audio and video information are interleaved in every frame for smoother playback.

Basic Multilingual Plane (BMP)

The first 16 bits, or 65,536 positions in Unicode, which includes most of the common characters used in the languages of the world, such as character sets for Latin, Greek, Cyrillic, hirgana, katakana,

and others, as well as mathematical and other miscellaneous characters.

behavioral layer

A term used to refer to the interactivity added to a web page via scripting (usually in JavaScript). See also *structural layer* and *presentational layer.*

binary files

Files made up of compiled data (ones and zeros), such as executable programs, graphic images, movies, etc. Some programs refer to the binary mode as "raw data" or "image data."

block-level elements

Elements that start a new line and tend to stack up like blocks in the normal flow of the document. Block elements make up the main components of document structure.

cascade

In CSS, this refers to a hierarchical system for handling conflicting style sheets that assigns different weights to various sources of style information.

CGI

Common Gateway Interface. The mechanism for communication between the web server and other programs (CGI scripts) running on the server.

character encoding

The method used to transform the character stream in a document to a byte stream that is interpreted by user agents.

character entity

An abbreviated name for a character that is predefined in a DTD for use in a markup language. Character entities are provided as a convenience for authors because they may be easier to remember than the Numeric Character Reference for the character.

character set

Any collection of characters that are used together for a particular function. Many character sets are standardized, such as Latin-1 (ISO-8859-1) and Unicode.

client

A software application that extracts services from a server somewhere on the network. A web browser is a client that renders and displays documents on remote servers.

CMYK

A four-channel color model describing Cyan, Magenta, Yellow, and Black ink colors. Images in CMYK mode are not appropriate for web graphics, which must be RGB.

code point

The numeric position of a character in a coded character set such as Unicode.

codec

Compression/decompression algorithms applied to media files.

combinator

In CSS, a specific character used to signify the type of relationship between the elements in a rule selector.

CSS (Cascading Style Sheets)

A style sheet language used to describe the presentation of documents written in HTML, XHTML, and other XML languages.

data rate

In video, the rate at which data must be transferred for the video to play smoothly without interruption. The data rate (also called "bit rate") for a movie is measured in kilobytes per second (K/s or KB/s). It can be calculated by dividing the size of the file (in K) by the length of the movie (in seconds).

declaration

In CSS, the portion of a style rule that contains the property and value to be applied to an element or set of elements.

deprecated

In the HTML 4.0 and 4.01 Recommendations, a label identifying an HTML element or attribute as "outdated" and discouraged from use in favor of newer constructs (most often CSS properties).

DHTML

Short for "Dynamic HTML," a bit of marketing jargon used to describe the integration of JavaScript, Cascading Style Sheets, and the Document Object Model. The term "DHTML" is falling out of favor because of its associations with an era of browser-sniffing and obtrusive scripting. The preferred (and more standards-oriented) term is now "DOM Scripting."

dithering

The approximation of a color by mixing pixels of similar colors that are available in the image palette. The result of dithering is a random dot pattern or noise in the image.

DOCTYPE declaration

Specifies the DTD used in an HTML or XHTML document. The DOCTYPE declaration is required for validation.

document character set

In SGML documents, this is the base character set for interpreting character references.

Document Object Model (DOM)

A platform- and language-neutral interface that allows programs and scripts to dynamically access and update the content, structure, and style of HTML and XML documents.

document tree

The hierarchical structure of a document established by the markup of elements and their relationship to one another.

dpi

Dots per inch. In graphics, this is the measurement of the resolution of a printed image. It is commonly (although incorrectly) used to refer to the screen resolution of web graphics, which is technically measured in ppi (pixels per inch). See also *ppi*.

Document Type Definition (DTD)

A document that defines the elements, attributes, and entities as well as the rules of their use in a markup language. A document that conforms to its DTD is said to be valid. The syntax for DTD definitions follows the rules of SGML.

DTD

See *Document Type Definition*.

Ecma (European Association for Standardizing Information and Communication Systems)

The Ecma manages information-technology standards, including ECMAScript, the standardized version of JavaScript.

encoding (audio)

The process of converting an analog source (such as an analog audio signal) into digital format. An encoder is the software that does the converting.

escaped character (or escaping)

A character that is represented by its character reference. The character reference may be numerical or a predefined character entity. In XML, XHTML, and HTML documents, escaped characters are preceded by & and end with ; (for example, &). In CSS, escaped characters are indicated by a backslash (\) and are terminated with a space (for example, \C7).

frame rate

In video, frames per second; used as a measure of video quality.

FTP

File Transfer Protocol. A protocol for moving files over the Internet from one computer to another. FTP is a client/server system: one machine must be running an FTP server; the other, an FTP client.

gamma

Refers to the overall brightness of a computer monitor's display. In technical terms, it is a numerical adjustment for the nonlinear relationship of voltage to light intensity.

GIF

Graphic Interchange Format. Common file format of web graphic images. GIF is a palette-based, 8-bit format that compresses images with the lossless LZW compression scheme. GIF is most appropriate for images with areas of flat color and sharp contrast. See also *LZW compression*.

hexadecimal

A base-16 numbering system consisting of the characters 0, 1, 2, 3, 4, 5, 6, 7, 8, 9, A, B, C, D, E, and F, where A through F represent the decimal values 10 through 15. It is used in (X)HTML and XML to provide RGB color values and Numerical Character References that use hexadecimal Unicode code points.

HTML

Hypertext Markup Language. The markup language used for web documents.

HTTP

Hypertext Transfer Protocol. The protocol that defines how web pages and media are requested and transferred between servers and browsers.

HTTP header
Information about a document that the web server sends to the user agent along with the document when it is requested by a user agent.

i18n
The W3C abbreviation for "internationalization" ("i," 18 letters, then "n"), relating to efforts to ensure that the formats and protocols defined by the W3C are usable worldwide in all languages and writing systems.

IETF (The Internet Engineering Task Force)
An international community of network designers, operators, vendors, and researchers concerned with the evolution of the Internet as a whole. It publishes Request for Comments (RFCs) that define how things are done over the Internet, including FTP, TCP/IP, HTTP, and email.

image map
A single image that contains multiple hypertext links.

indexed color
In graphics, a system for rendering colors in 8-bit images. Indexed color files, such as GIFs, contain an index (also called a palette or color lookup table) of colors and associated index numbers, which is used to render color in the image.

inheritance
In CSS, the concept by which styles are passed down from an element to its descendants. A child element is said to *inherit* property values from its parent.

inline elements
Elements that occur in the flow of text and do not cause line breaks by default.

ISO (International Organization for Standardization)
The standards organization that manages more than 10,000 international standards for everything from information systems to manufacturing specifications. Their seal of approval helps keep commerce and information technologies compatible worldwide.

Java
A cross-platform, object-oriented programming language developed by Sun Microsystems. It can be used to create whole applications; however, its primary contribution to the Web has been in the form of Java applets: self-contained, mini-executable programs.

JavaScript
A client-side scripting language originally developed by Netscape and later standardized as ECMA-Script that adds interactivity and conditional behavior to web pages. It has little in common with Java.

JPEG
A lossy compression algorithm developed by the Joint Photographic Experts Group. It is used by files in the JFIF format, which are commonly referred to as "JPEG files." JPEG is most efficient at compressing images with gradations in tone and no sharp edge contrasts. Photographic images are typically best saved in JPEG format.

key frames
In video, master frames placed throughout a video against which the following frames are compared (for use with temporal, or interframe, compression).

Linux
A version of Unix designed to run on PCs.

lossy compression

A method for reducing file size in which some data (usually indiscernible to human perception) is deleted to achieve a higher compression rate.

lossless compression

A method for reducing the size of a file without loss of data; in lossless compression, redundant information is removed.

LZW compression

Short for Lempel-Zev-Welch, the names of the inventors. A lossless compression scheme that takes advantage of repetition in data streams (such as a row of pixels of identical color). It is the compression scheme used by graphic files in the GIF format.

MathML

Math Markup Language. An XML application for describing mathematical notation and capturing its structure and content.

MIDI

Musical Instrument Digital Interface. This audio format uses numerical commands to describe the pitch and endurance of notes that are "played" by available digital instrument sounds.

MIME types

Multimedia Internet Mail Extensions. A protocol that defines a number of content types and subtypes and allows programs like web browsers, news readers, and email clients to recognize different kinds of files and deal with them appropriately. The MIME type specifies what media a file is, such as an image, audio, or video, and the subtype identifies the precise file format.

MP3

Audio file format (MPEG I, Level-III) capable of high levels of compression with little discernible loss of quality. It has become the standard for sharing audio files over the Internet.

MPEG

A family of multimedia standards created by the Motion Picture Experts Group, commonly used to refer to audio and video files saved using one of the MPEG compression schemes.

namespace

A uniquely named group of element and attribute names. XML documents refer to namespaces in order to prevent confusion between competing element names.

nonreplaced element

In CSS, an element whose text content is included in the source document, such as a heading or paragraph.

normal flow

The default left-to-right, top-to-bottom rendering of content in (X)HTML documents in left-to-right reading languages. The only way to remove an element from the normal flow is to float or position it using style rules. The normal flow for right-to-left reading languages is from right-to-left, top-to-bottom.

palette

A table in an 8-bit indexed color file (such as GIF) that provides color information for the pixels in the image.

PDF

Portable Document Format. A file format developed by Adobe Systems used for capturing formatted page layouts for distribution. PDF documents are viewed with the required Adobe Acrobat Reader.

PHP

Hypertext Preprocessor. An open source, server-side tool for creating dynamically generated web pages (similar to Microsoft's ASP).

PNG

Portable Network Graphic. A versatile graphics file format that features support for both 8-bit (PNG8) indexed images and 24-bit images (PNG24). PNGs also feature variable transparency levels, automatic color correction controls, and a lossless yet highly efficient compression scheme.

ppi

Pixels per inch. The measurement of the resolution of a screen image.

presentation

The way a document is displayed or delivered to the user, whether it's on a computer monitor, a cell phone display, or read aloud by a screen reader

presentational layer

A term used to refer to style information applied to elements in a document. In web documents, presentation is controlled by Cascading Style Sheets. See also *structural layer* and *behavioral layer.*

QuickTime

A system extension that makes it possible to view audio and video information on a computer. It was originally developed for the Macintosh but is now available for Windows machines as well, and has been adopted as the video standard by the ISO in their development of MPEG-4. The term also refers to the file format.

RDF

Resource Description Framework. An XML application used to define the structure of metadata for documents, i.e., data that is useful for indexing, navigating, and searching a site.

replaced element

In the CSS, an element whose content is not provided in the source document, but rather acts as a placeholder for content brought in from an external source (such as an img) or rendered by the user agent (such as most form controls).

RGB color

A color system that describes colors based on combinations of red, green, and blue light.

rollover

The act of passing the mouse pointer over an element's space, or the events triggered by that action (such as a changing style, image, or pop-up message, sometimes called rollover events).

root element

The element that contains all other elements, called the root element because it has no ancestors. In HTML and XHTML documents, the root element is html.

sampling rate

In a digital audio file, the number of samples taken per second.

selector

In CSS, the portion of a style rule that targets an element or set of elements for the application of style properties

semantic

Of or related to meaning. In terms of web authoring, documents should be marked up semantically, that is, choosing (X)HTML elements that accurately describe the meaning of their contents.

server

Any networked computer running software that enables it to answer requests for documents and other data.

Server Side Includes (SSI)

Special placeholders in an HTML document that the server is to replace with actual data just before sending the final document to the browser. Extended SSI (XSSI) (part of Apache 1.2 and higher) provides more advanced command functions, including conditional behaviors.

SGML
Standard Generalized Markup Language. A meta-language that provides a comprehensive set of syntax rules for marking up the structure of documents and data. HTML is a subset of SGML.

sIFR
Scalable Inman Flash Replacement. A technique for replacing short text elements in a web document with small Flash movies in order to achieve rich typography on web pages without sacrificing accessibility, search engine friendliness, or markup semantics.

SMIL
Synchronized Multimedia Integration Language, an XML-based language for creating multimedia, time-based presentation. SMIL combines audio, video, text, animation, and graphics in a precise, synchronized fashion.

spatial compression
In video, spatial compression is applied to each individual frame of the video, using compression schemes commonly used on still images (also called "intraframe" compression).

spatial frequency
Refers to the concentration of detail in an image. For example, an image of a blue sky would be considered to have low frequency. A detailed image, such as a close-up of blades of grass, has high frequency.

structural layer
A term used to describe the marked up content of the source document

that provides structure of and serves as a foundation for presentation instructions (added with Cascading Style Sheets) and behaviors (added by a scripting language such as JavaScript). See also *presentational layer* and *behavioral layer*.

SVG
Standardized Vector Graphics. An XML language for defining two-dimensional vector graphics.

Telnet
An internet protocol for logging into and using a remote system on the Internet. Telnet is a client/server system that requires a Telnet server running on one computer and a Telnet client on the other.

temporal compression
In video, temporal compression takes place over a series of frames, deleting information that is repeated between frames (also called "interframe" compression).

Universal Character Set (UCS)
This is the document character set used by HTML, XHTML, and XML documents. It is defined by both the Unicode and ISO/IEC 10646 standards.

Unix
A multiuser, multitasking operating system developed by Bell Laboratories. It also provides programs for editing text, sending email, preparing tables, performing calculations, and many other specialized functions that normally require separate applications programs.

valid markup
In an XML application, markup that properly uses the elements and attributes as specified in a Document Type Definition (DTD).

validating parser
A parser that checks a document for conformance with its declared DTD.

W3C

The World Wide Web Consortium. A consortium of many companies and organizations that "exists to develop common standards for the evolution of the World Wide Web."

WAI

Web Accessibility Initiative. The committee at the World Wide Web Consortium (W3C) that ensures that web technologies are accessible to users with disabilities.

WAV

Waveform Audio File Format. This format was developed for the PC but is now supported on Macintosh as well.

web palette

The set of 216 colors that will not dither or shift when viewed with browsers on 8-bit monitors.

well-formed

Describes a marked up document that abides by the strict syntax rules of XML.

WML

Wireless Markup Language. An XML-based language for creating applications for wireless devices. It is part of the Wireless Application Protocol (WAP). WML is growing obsolete

XHTML

A reworking of the HTML 4.01 specification to abide by the rules and syntax of XML.

XML

Extensible Markup Language. A new standard for marking up documents and data. XML is based on SGML, but with a reduced feature set that is more appropriate for distribution via the Web. XML allows authors to create customized markup languages.

XML declaration

The first line in XML documents that specifies the version of XML used. The character encoding may also be specified. XML declarations are optional but recommended. For example, `<?xml version="1.0" encoding="UTF-8"?>`.

XML Schema

A method for defining the elements, attributes, and entities in an XML markup language. It is equivalent to a Document Type Definition (DTD), but it is written according to the syntax of XML (DTDs are based on SGML).

XSL

Extensible Style Language. A system for controlling the presentation of complex XML documents and structured data. It is more robust than Cascading Style Sheets.

XSLT (Extensible Stylesheet Language for Transformations)

A subset of XSL (Extensible Stylesheet Language), an XSLT style sheet is necessary when an XML document is "transformed" before final display, such as translating it from one XML language to another, or replacing certain content with other content.

Index

We'd like to hear your suggestions for improving our indexes. Send email to *index@oreilly.com*.

anti-aliasing
  Flash and, 611, 619
  preventing halos, 535
  text, 527
  turning off, 536
  web palette and, 543
AOL (see America Online browser)
Apache servers, 43, 46, 76
Apache Software Foundation, 45
API (Application Programming
    Interface), 488
APNG (Animated Portable Network
    Graphic), 558
' character entity, 80, 96, 167
apostrophe ('), 167
appendChild( ) method, 498
applet element, 193, 201, 645
applets
  alternative content and, 196
  defined, 45
  object element and, 195
  overview, 201–203
Application Programming Interface
    (API), 488
application/pdf type, 636
application/xhtml+xml media type, 139
application/xml media type, 139
archive attribute (object), 196
area element, 190, 646
arithmetic operators, 469, 472
Array object (JavaScript), 480, 482
arrays, 470, 471
arrows, 730
ASCII (American Standard Code for
    Information Interchange), 4,
    51, 53
ASCII character set
  character entities, 722–723
  character references and, 78
  FTP link and, 175
  markup and, 115
  quotation marks, 415
  Unicode encoding, 75
.asf file extension, 588, 589, 599
Asleson, Ryan, 512
ASP (Active Server Pages), 43, 45
assistive technology, 57–59
associative arrays, 471
asterisk (*)
  blogroll usage, 745
  frames and, 238

as universal selector, 298, 454
.asx file extension, 593
asynchronous communication, 507
Asynchronous JavaScript and XML
    (Ajax), 507–512
ATAG (Authoring Tool Accessibility
    Guidelines), 60
Atom publishing protocol, 109
attaching images, 364–365
attlist (attribute) declarations, 97, 99,
    101, 102
attribute minimization, 124
attribute nodes, 490, 492, 493
attribute selectors, 301, 302
attributes
  authoring practices, 128
  case sensitivity, 123
  common, 641, 642
  DTDs and, 97
  elements and, 90
  HTML DOM and, 496
  namespaces and, 103, 136
  overview, 117
  quotation marks, 123
  well-formed documents, 97
Audacity audio tool, 579
audience, knowing your, 25
audio
  adding to web pages, 590–594
  basic concepts, 575–577
  choosing formats, 590
  copyright restrictions, 577
  editing and format
      conversion, 578–580
  file formats, 583–589
  Flash integration, 611, 623
  overview, 575
  recording, 578
  royalty-free resources, 577
  streaming, 581–583, 593
Audio Interchange File Format
    (AIFF), 583, 585
Audio/Video Interleaved (AVI), 601
Audition audio tool, 579
auditory impairment, 57
aural browsers, 59
aural impairment, 60
aural media type, 282, 629
author meta name, 142
Authoring Tool Accessibility Guidelines
    (ATAG), 60

authoring tools
  browser variety and, 23
  "design-to-size", 36
  fixed-width designs, 33
  Flash and, 612, 613
  HTML/XHTML, 126–129
  standards recommendations, 23
  URL pathnames, 49
  web graphics, 522, 524
  WYSIWYG, 127–128
authors, style sheets and, 285
auto keyword, 344
autoplay attribute (embed), 200, 606
AVI (Audio/Video Interleaved), 601
.avi file extension, 601
azimuth property (CSS), 715

B

b element, 161, 646
background attribute (body), 143, 359
background color
  animated GIFs, 570
  borders and, 347
  columns, 432
  element boxes, 338
  halos and, 535
  margins and, 346
  overview, 357–358
  padding and, 354
  printing text, 632
  stacking order, 395
  tables and, 396
  transparency, 567
background images
  accessibility and, 68
  borders and, 347
  columns and, 432, 433, 434
  element boxes, 338
  expanding box style, 435, 436
  future of, 434
  margins and, 346
  matching colors, 527
  overview, 358–367
  padding and, 354
  rollovers, 441–443
  tables and, 396
background property (CSS)
  col/colgroup elements, 215
  overview, 366, 684
  recommendations, 220
  tables and, 396, 397

background sounds, 591
background-attachment property
  (CSS), 364–365, 684
background-color property
  (CSS), 357–359, 685
background-image property (CSS)
  browser bugs, 454, 456
  overview, 358–359, 685
background-position property
  (CSS), 361–364, 367, 443, 685
background-repeat property
  (CSS), 360–361, 364, 686
backslash (\), 80
backward compatibility, 126
Band Pass Filter, 453
bandwidth negotiation, 583
base attribute (embed), 621
base element
  content and, 116
  defined, 137
  frames and, 242
  overview, 171, 646
basefont element, 162, 299, 647
baseline, 325, 330
Basic Multilingual Plane (BMP), 75, 79
bdo element, 83, 84, 647
:before selector, 304, 306, 412, 633
behavioral layer, 6, 8, 114
Benkmann, Matthias, 188
Berners-Lee, Tim
  HTML language, 92
  W3C founded, 113
  World Wide Web and, 13, 276
bgcolor attribute
  body element, 143, 357
  deprecation of, 220
  embed element, 621
  object element, 619
big element, 161, 647
binary files, 51, 53
bit depth, 538, 576, 580, 596
bit rates, 577, 583, 596
bitmapped images, 517
bits per pixel (bpp), 519
Bitstream, 310
_blank target name, 242
blink element, 324
blinking effect, 323
block-level elements
  browser bugs, 456
  clear property, 375

block-level elements (*continued*)
  content edge, 377
  inline tables, 393
  listed, 144
  normal flow, 368
  overview, 146–149, 288–290
blockquote element, 147, 148, 151, 648
blogrolls, 745
blogs, 107
BMP (Basic Multilingual Plane), 75, 79
body, document, 130
body element
  background-image property, **359**
  centering pages, 420
  color property and, 357
  description, 130
  initial containing block, 377, **387**
  noframes element and, 236
  overview, 142, 143, 648
Boolean values, 470, 473
border attribute
  frameset element, 241
  img element, 170, 185
  table element, 219
border property (CSS)
  browser bugs, 450, 454
  col/colgroup elements, 215
  overview, 352, 686
  tables and, 396, 397
border-bottom property (CSS), **352, 686**
border-bottom-color property
  (CSS), 350, 687
border-bottom-style property
  (CSS), 348, 349, 687
border-bottom-width property
  (CSS), 349, 687
border-collapse property (CSS), **397,**
  398, 688
border-color property (CSS), 351, **352,**
  357, 688
border-left property (CSS), 352, **688**
border-left-color property (CSS), 350,
  688
border-left-style property (CSS), 348,
  349, 689
border-left-width property (CSS), **349,**
  450, 689
border-right property (CSS), 352, **689**
border-right-color property (CSS), 350,
  690

border-right-style property (CSS), 348,
  349, 690
border-right-width property (CSS), 349,
  450, 690
borders
  box model and, 338, 347–352
  element boxes and, 290, 291
  floated elements, 371
  frame, 240–241
  images and, 185
  internal elements and, 393
  margins and, 344
  padding and, 352
  tables and, 218, 396, 398–401
  three-column layouts, 429–431
  two-column layouts, 422
border-spacing property (CSS)
  cellspacing attribute and, 218, 397
  overview, 398, 399, 690
border-style property (CSS)
  border conflicts and, 401
  combining properties, 352
  overview, 348–349, 691
border-top property (CSS), 352, 691
border-top-color property (CSS), 350,
  691
border-top-style property (CSS), 348,
  349, 692
border-top-width property (CSS), 349,
  692
border-width property (CSS), 349–350,
  352, 458, 692
Bos, Bert, 276
Bosak, Jon, 92
bottom keyword, 362
bottom property (CSS)
  absolute positioning, 385
  fixed positioning, 389
  overview, 377, 693
  relative positioning, 391
  table captions, 395
Boutell, Thomas, 188, 553
Bowman, Doug, 30, 295, 437, 446, 453
box model
  borders, 338, 347–352
  Box Model Hack, 451
  browser bugs and, 450
  margins, 338, 344–347
  overview, 290–291
  padding and, 338, 352–354
  tables, 393

capitalization
 camel case, 501
 common methods, 483
 filenames and, 50
 nodeName property, 493
 overview, 322, 323
caption element
 caption-side property, 394
 overview, 211, 213, 649
 summary attribute, 221
caption keyword, 322
caption-side property (CSS), 213, 394,
 693
Carver, Ryan, 443
cascade, 284
Cascading Style Sheets (CSS)
 adding to documents, 278–283
 aligning form elements, 268
 benefits, 274, 275
 block and inline elements, 288–290
 browsers and, 23, 293
 DHTML and, 488
 div element, 154
 document tree, 490
 DOM and, 501
 escaping characters, 80
 extended color names, 737–741
 form controls, 267
 further reading, 294–296
 guiding concepts, 283–291
 lists, 406–411
 mobile devices, 40
 normal flow of documents, 368
 overview, 275
 PDF and, 634
 presentation and, 114, 161, 228
 presentation layer and, 6–7
 printing and, 627–634
 RGB colors in, 736
 rollovers, 440–443
 rule syntax, 275–278
 standards support, 5, 21
 tables and, 10, 218, 219, 392–395
 technique resources, 446
 text formatting, 307
 XML and, 93, 105
case sensitivity
 authoring practices, 129
 elements and, 90, 123
 HTML, 116
 JavaScript, 469

XHTML, 123
XML, 90
CBR (constant bit rate), 585
CDATA attribute type, 102
CDATA section, 96, 125, 467
Cederholm, Dan
 column background trick, 432
 expanding rounded boxes, 436
 informative personal sites, 296, 447
 web standards, 11, 294, 447
ceil( ) method, 482
Çelik, Tantek
 Band Pass Filter, 453
 Box Model Hack, 342, 451
 extending XHTML, 742–746
 informative personal sites, 296
 surgical correction, 461
 Tasman layout engine, 452
cellpadding attribute (table), 217, 397
cells (table)
 basic structure, 207–210
 collapsing border model, 400, 401
 content alignment, 219, 396
 padding, 217, 228
 rows and, 393
 separated borders model, 398–399
 spacing, 217, 397
 td element and, 209
 th element and, 221
cellspacing attribute (table), 217, 397
center element, 649
center keyword, 362, 363
center tag, 419
centering
 three-column layouts, 429–431
 web pages, 419–421
CGI (Common Gateway Interface), 44
CGI scripts, 44, 52, 192
cgi-bin directory, 45
channels, audio files, 577
char attribute (table), 219
character encoding
 character sets and, 73–78
 defined, 73
 directionality and, 83
 meta element, 136, 139, 140
 XML declaration and, 94
character entities
 arrows, 730
 ASCII character set, 722–723
 cursive joining behavior, 84

"code forking", 488
code points, 73, 74, 75, 79
code position, 73
codebase attribute
  adding video, 605
  applet element, 202
  object element, 196, 203, 618
codecs
  audio, 588
  video, 597, 598, 600
coded character sets, 73
codetype attribute (object), 195
cognitive impairment, 57
col element
  boxes and, 393
  cell content alignment, 219
  internal elements and, 393
  overview, 215–216, 650
colgroup element
  boxes and, 393
  cell content alignment, 219
  internal elements and, 393
  overview, 215–216, 650
collapsing border model, 400, 401
colon (:)
  automatic counters, 417
  namespaces, 104
  pseudoselectors and, 302
  style rules, 277
color
  accessibility and, 68
  assistive technology and, 60
  borders and, 347, 350–352
  GIF format and, 530
  graphics and, 519–524
  JPEG format and, 516, 544
  matching, 527, 528
  optimization tools, 538
  PNG format, 554
  specifying by name, 736–741
  specifying by RGB values, 733–736
  specifying in style sheets, 292, 293
  web-safe, 542
  (see also background color; color
      depth; foreground color)
color attribute (font), 163
color depth
  animated GIFs, 569
  overview, 519–521
  video files, 596
color maps, 521, 531

color property (CSS), 355–357, 694
cols attribute
  frameset element, 237–238
  textarea element, 259
colspan attribute (td), 210, 211
column groups, 214–216
columns
  data tables, 206
  framesets and, 234
  hiding, 383
  overview, 214–216
  spanning, 210, 211
  stacking order, 395
  tables and, 393, 397
  three-column layouts, 424–431
  two-column layouts, 421–424
combinator character, 298
Commented Backslash Hack, 453
comments
  authoring practices, 129
  browsers ignoring, 119
  hack management, 460
  HTML, 119
  JavaScript and, 467, 468
  metadata and, 743
  protecting scripts, 125
  well-formed documents, 97
  XML documents, 95
Common Gateway Interface (CGI), 44
comparison operators, 472, 473
Components panel (Flash), 614
compression
  animated GIFs, 570
  audio file formats and, 575, 580
  file sizes and, 525
  Flash movies, 614, 615
  GIF format and, 529
  J&G, 547
  JPEG format and, 544–551
  LZW, 553
  matching colors and, 528
  MPEG, 584
  PNG format, 559, 563
  video, 596–598
  video and, 602
  (see also lossless compression
      scheme; lossy compression
      scheme; LZW compression)
concat( ) method, 482, 483
conditional statements, 474–476
confirm( ) method, 486

constant bit rate (CBR), 585
contact information, 743, 744
containing blocks
    browser bugs, 456, 458
    defined, 371
    floated elements and, 373, 374
    overview, 377
    positioning and, 386, 391
content
    accessibility of, 265
    building blocks of, 146–149
    document body, 130
    DOM and, 494, 495
    DTDs and, 101
    element boxes and, 290, 291
    elements and, 116
    frameset element and, 234
    generated, 412–418, 437, 633
    internal elements and, 393
    normal flow and, 369
    object element and, 196
    styling tables, 396
    table cell alignment, 219
    tagging, 745
    WCAG, 64
    XML documents and, 91
content area
    borders and, 347
    box model, 338, 340, 341
    calculating positioning, 388
    floated elements, 371
    padding and, 352
content attribute (meta), 140
content edge, 377
content property (CSS), 412, 414, 417,
    694
content types (see MIME types)
contextual selectors, 298, 299
control structures, JavaScript, 473–480
controller attribute (embed), 606
controls
    buttons, 262, 263
    form, 248, 250–263, 298, 496
    input, 251–258
    menus and select element, 259–262
    multiline text areas, 259
    nesting, 264
copyright meta name, 142
copyrights
    audio files and, 577
    MP3 format and, 585

pseudostreaming and, 583
    streaming audio and, 581, 583
    symbol for, 168
Core Web Fonts collection
    (Microsoft), 312
Corel Paint Shop Pro, 524
The Counter, 19, 20, 35
counter( ) function, 417
counter-increment property
    (CSS), 417–418, 695
counter-reset property (CSS), 158, 416,
    695
counters
    automatic, 416–418
    content property and, 413
    generated content and, 412
counters( ) function, 417
country name codes, 81–83
createElement( ) method, 496, 497, 498
createNamedElement( ) method, 497,
    498
createTextNode( ) method, 498
The Creative Commons, 745
CSS (see Cascading Style Sheets)
CSS Zen Garden site, 446
Cubase audio tool, 579
cue property (CSS), 716
cue-after property (CSS), 716
cue-before property (CSS), 716
curly braces { }, 277
cursive fonts, 311
cursor property (CSS), 695
Custom color palette, 532

D

data
    accessible tables and, 220–225
    associating headers with, 223–225
    as text, 91
data attribute
    object element, 194, 196
    object/param elements, 195
    param element, 194
data cells (see cells)
data rate, 596
data tables, 206
data types, JavaScript, 470–472
Date( ) method, 482
Date object (JavaScript), 480, 482
datetime attribute (del/ins), 153
Davidson, Mike, 309

M

.m4a file extension, 589
.m4p file extension, 589
Macintosh environment
    audio tools, 579
    browser bugs, 452–454
    browser canvas dimensions, 29
    color palettes, 532
    favicons, 187
    FTP and, 50
    gamma settings, 523, 524
    JavaScript and, 466
    PNG format and, 559
    web palette, 522
Macromedia Breeze, 624
Macromedia Director, 622
Macromedia Dreamweaver
    authoring tools, 23, 33, 36
    description, 127
    Flash and, 622
    FTP functions, 50
    image map tools, 188
    URL pathnames, 49
Macromedia Fireworks
    animated GIFs, 566, 570
    color palettes, 532
    converting to web palette, 543
    embedded text, 558
    GIF format, 531, 536, 538
    JPEG format, 548–550
    PNG format, 561
    web graphics, 524, 526
Macromedia Flash Central, 624
Macromedia Flash (see Flash)
Macromedia FlashCast, 625
Macromedia Flex, 623, 624
Macromedia Zorn, 623
Madsen, Søren, 436
mailto: protocol, 174
map element, 190, 668
.map file extension, 192
margin property (CSS)
    border-style property and, 349
    browser bugs, 456
    centering pages, 420
    img element and, 369
    overview, 344, 345, 702
    tables and, 395, 396
margin-bottom property (CSS), 344, 456, 702
marginheight attribute (frame), 240

margin-left property (CSS), 344, 420, 702
margin-right property (CSS), 344, 420, 703
margins
    box model and, 338, 344–347
    browser bugs, 456
    centering pages and, 420
    direction property and, 335
    element boxes and, 290, 291
    expanding box style, 436
    floated elements, 371
    frame, 240
    internal elements and, 393
    negative, 374, 421
    printing and, 633
    tables and, 396
    three-column layouts, 427, 429–431
    two-column layouts, 424
margin-top property (CSS), 344, 456, 703
marginwidth attribute (frame), 240
markers, 406–408, 491
Marks, Todd, 609–625
markup
    DHTML and, 488
    DTD and, 103
    generated content and, 413
    HTML basics, 115–119
    math, 104
    semantic, 90, 91, 145
    SGML and, 92
    XML documents and, 92
masks, 539, 540
match( ) method, 483
Math object (JavaScript), 480, 482
mathematical equations, 91
Mathematical Markup Language (see MathML)
mathematical operators, 730–732
MathML (Mathematical Markup Language)
    CSS and, 277
    overview, 9, 111, 112
    XHTML and, 104, 120
    XML documents and, 91
Matte color tool, 536
max( ) method, 482
max-height property (CSS), 343, 703, 704
max-width property (CSS), 343, 704
Means, W. Scott, 112

monospace fonts, 311, 312
Moock, Colin, 625
Mosaic browser, 13
mouse, assistive technology, 58
.mov file extension, 586, 599, 611, 622
movie attribute (object), 618
Moving Picture Experts Group (see
    MPEG)
Mozilla browser, 14, 20, 456, 466
MP3 format, 582, 583, 584–586, 615
.mp4 file extension, 589
MPEG (Moving Picture Experts Group)
    MP3 and, 584
    overview, 601
    QuickTime player and, 586
    video codecs, 597, 598
.mpg file extension, 601, 611
MSN-TV Viewer, 41
multicasting, 594, 604
multichannel surround sound, 577
multiple attribute (select), 260
Multiple-image Network Graphic
    (MNG), 558
Multipurpose Internet Mail Extension
    (MIME), 53
Musical Instrument Digital Interface
    (MIDI), 586, 587
MySQL database server, 46

N

name attribute
    a element, 171
    DOM and, 497
    embed element, 620
    form controls, 250
    form element, 249, 264
    overview, 126, 139
namespaces, 103, 104, 108, 136
naming conventions
    authoring practices, 129
    JavaScript, 469
    servers, 50
    XML, 99
National Center for Supercomputing
    Applications (NCSA), 13
navigation
    design considerations, 37, 226
    floating and, 369
    frames and, 232, 233
    linking and, 171
    list based, 443–446

lists and, 407
modular style sheets, 282
tutorials, 446
WCAG, 63
NCSA (National Center for
    Supercomputing
    Applications), 13
negative margins, 374, 421
nesting
    controls, 264
    descendant selectors, 298
    elements, 118, 124, 288, 289
    frames, 238, 239
    lists, 160
    quotation marks and, 416
    table headers, 224
    tables, 226, 228
Netscape Navigator browser
    canvas dimensions, 29
    description, 15, 16
    frames and, 232
    history, 13, 20
    HTML and, 5
    managing bugs, 449, 456
    PNG format and, 559
    usage trends, 22
    XML support, 105
Newhouse, Mark, 446
news: protocol, 175
news readers, 107
nextSibling property (DOM), 492, 493
nntp:// protocol, 175
nobr element, 165
node tree (DOM), 490–494
nodeName property (DOM), 493, 494
nodes
    Ajax with, 510–512
    attribute, 490, 492, 493
    child, 490, 491, 492
    DOM and, 490
    parent, 490
    sibling, 490
    (see also element nodes)
nodeType property (DOM), 492, 494
nodeValue property (DOM), 495
noembed element, 200, 669
nofollow extension, 746
noframes element, 233, 235–237,
    245–246, 670
nonbreaking space, 167
non-replaced elements, 330, 340, 371
non-validating parsers, 97

output devices, 59
overflow property (CSS), 379, 380, 454, 706
overlap, 373, 374, 383
overlines, 323

P

p element
  cell content alignment, 219
  empty, 119
  overview, 146, 147, 673
  text wrapping, 184
packets, streaming audio and, 582
padding
  box model and, 338, 352–354
  cell, 217, 228
  element boxes and, 290, 291
  internal elements and, 393
  tables and, 397
  three-column layouts, 431
  two-column layouts, 422
padding edge, 377
padding property (CSS)
  browser bugs, 450, 456
  overview, 353, 707
  tables and, 397
  td element, 217
padding-bottom property (CSS), 353, 458, 707
padding-left property (CSS), 353, 450, 707, 708
padding-right property (CSS), 353, 450, 708
padding-top property (CSS), 353, 456, 708
page-break-after property (CSS), 714
page-break-before property (CSS), 714
page-break-inside property (CSS), 715
pages (see web pages)
Paint Shop Pro
  animated GIFs, 566
  common palettes, 532
  creating JPEGs, 548
  embedded text, 558
palette, color
  animated GIFs, 569
  common, 532
  Indexed color and, 531
  web graphics and, 521–524
Paoli, Jean, 92

paragraphs
  carriage returns, 436
  ignoring empty elements, 119
  quotation marks, 416
  text elements and, 146, 147
param element
  ActiveX controls and, 196
  applets and, 202
  browser support, 197
  class selectors and, 299
  embedding video, 608
  overview, 194, 673
parameter entities, 102
parent directory, 46, 48
parent nodes, 490
parent property (Browser Object), 486
_parent target name, 243
parent/child relationships
  child subdirectory, 46
  document structure, 91, 284
  nesting and, 118
  parent directory, 46, 48
  viewing XML in browsers, 105
parentNode property (DOM), 492
parsed character data (#PCDATA), 100
parsers
  defined, 93
  entity references, 96
  namespaces and, 104
  non-validating, 97
  validating, 93, 99
  XML declaration and, 94
passwords, 252
pathnames, 46–49
pause property (CSS), 717
pause-after property (CSS), 717
pause-before property (CSS), 717
pc unit of measurement, 316
#PCDATA, 100
PDF (Portable Document Format), 634–637
PDFViewer plug-in, 634
Peak audio tool, 579
Pederick, Chris, 17
percent sign (%)
  parameter entities, 102
  percentage values, 293
percentage values
  aligning text with, 332
  box model, 342
  color, 293

percentage values (*continued*)
fonts, 315
positioning images, 363
web palette and, 523
Perceptual color palette (Adobe), 532
period (.)
in CSS selectors, 299
XML names, 99
permissions, setting, 52
photographic images
JPEG format and, 529, 546, 549, 562
web palette strategies, 543
PHP language, 45, 46, 468
phrase elements, 149–152
Pilgrim, Mark, 108
pitch property (CSS), 718
pitch-range property (CSS), 718
pixels per inch (ppi), 517, 518
pixels (see px unit of measurement)
Pixy No-Preload Rollover
technique, 443
PlanetPDF web site, 635
Platz, Brian, 295
play attribute
embed element, 621
object element, 619
play-during property (CSS), 718
playeveryframe attribute (embed), 200,
606
pluginspage attribute
adding video, 605
embed element, 200, 605, 620, 621
pluginurl attribute (embed), 200
plus sign (+), 299
PNG (Portable Network Graphic)
format
choosing as format, 517
color, 554
compression, 555, 559, 563
creating files, 559–561
favicons, 187
further reading, 563
gamma settings, 557–559
GIF history and, 530
images and, 179, 517
interlacing, 557, 559, 563
matching colors, 528
optimization strategies, 561
overview, 516, 552
platform/browser support, 558, 559
production tips, 526

transparency and, 534, 554,
555–561
when to use, 552–554
point measurements, 629
pop( ) method, 482
pop-up windows, 34, 173
Portable Document Format
(PDF), 634–637
position property (CSS)
browser bugs, 455, 457
fixed elements, 389
frames, 232
overview, 376, 708
relative positioning, 391
table captions, 395
positioning
elements, 226, 368
fixed, 232, 377, 389
floating and, 369, 372, 373
images, 361–364
markers, 408, 409
normal flow, 369
overview, 375–385
relative, 376, 390, 391
sidebars, 427
tables, 395, 397
(see also absolute positioning)
post method, 249
PostScript files, 635
posture, font, 319
pound symbol (£), 167
Power Tools (Flash), 624
ppi (pixels per inch), 517, 518
pre element, 148, 673
presentation
CSS and, 114, 273
definition lists, 160
designing "above the fold", 37
document structure and, 115
fixed vs. liquid web pages, 30–36
img element, 180
mobile devices, 37–41
PDF files and, 634
SGML and, 114
style sheets for, 228
tables and, 206, 216–220, 392, 396
unknown monitor resolution, 28–29
unordered lists, 157
web standards and, 6
presentation layer
defined, 6
HTML and, 114

scripts/scripting
.asp files and, 45
behavioral layer, 8
comments in, 468
custom buttons, 256, 257
externalizing, 467
Flash support, 611
id attribute and, 300
protecting, 125
server-side, 281
statements and, 468
variables and, 469
(see also DOM; JavaScript)
scrolling attribute (frame), 239
scrolling/scrollbars
background images and, 358, 364
frames and, 239
menus and, 261
mobile devices, 39
overflow property and, 380
textarea element and, 259
search engines
frames and, 233, 245
Ice Rocket, 746
meta element and, 138, 141, 743
Technorati, 745, 746
Section 508 standard, 64, 65
security
FTP process and, 51
JavaScript and, 466
post method and, 250
select element
menus and, 259–262
overview, 675
size attribute, 261
selected attribute (option), 261
Selective color palette (Adobe), 532,
542, 543
selectors
attribute, 301, 302
class, 299–300
contextual, 298, 299
defined, 275, 297
element nodes and, 490
ID, 299–300
listed, 305–306
pseudoselectors, 302–304, 412, 440
type, 297, 298
_self target name, 243
semantic markup, 91, 115, 145

semicolon (;)
escaping the character, 79
as separator, 277
separated borders model, 398–399
sequences, multiple elements and, 100,
101
serif fonts, 311, 312
servers
basic functions, 43–44
character encoding, 76
configuring for Flash, 615
defined, 42
file naming conventions, 50
file types, 53–55
FTP and, 50–52
popular software, 43
Unix directory structures, 46–49
server-side image maps, 188, 189, 192
server-side processing
Ajax and, 507
defined, 42
programming, 44–46
streaming audio, 582
servlets, Java, 45
setAttribute( ) method, 495, 496, 501
setTimeout( ) method, 487
SGML (Standard Generalized Markup
Language)
attribute minimization, 124
DTDs and, 92, 97
overview, 92
presentation and, 114
Shea, Dave
centering a page, 421
CSS design, 294, 446
CSS Zen Garden site, 295
image replacement, 437
image-tab rollovers, 446
informative personal sites, 295, 447
min-height workaround, 343
shift( ) method, 482
shifting, color, 521
shorthand properties, 353, 367
SHOUTcast package (Nullsoft), 585
sibling nodes, 490
siblings, 284
sidebars, positioning, 427
sIFR (Scalable Inman Flash
Replacement), 309

single quote (')
  escaping the character, 79
  @import directive, 459
singleton objects, 484
size attribute
  font element, 163
  hr element, 166
  select element, 261
slash (/)
  JavaScript comments, 469
  opening/closing tags, 116
  Unix directory structures, 46
  URLs and, 44, 116, 250
slice( ) method, 482, 483
small caps font face, 320
small element, 161, 675
small keyword, 313
small-caption keyword, 322
smaller keyword, 315
SMIL (Synchronized Multimedia
    Integration Language)
  CSS and, 277
  overview, 9, 110, 111
  Windows Media and, 589
snooping, vulnerability to, 44
soft drop shadows, 554
"soft hyphen", 165
Sorenson Video codec, 597
sort( ) method, 482
Sound Forge audio tool, 579
sound (see audio)
Sowden, Paul, 281
space (see whitespace)
spacing
  cell, 217
  modifier letters, 727
  table layouts and, 226
  text, 332–335
span attribute (col), 216
span element
  FIR and, 437
  hCard microformat and, 744
  indicating emphasis, 151
  overview, 154, 676
spatial compression, 597
speak property (CSS), 719
speak-header property (CSS), 719
speak-numeral property (CSS), 720
speak-punctuation property (CSS), 720
special characters, inserting, 499
specificity, 287, 288
speech media type, 283

speech-rate property (CSS), 720
Sperberg-McQueen, Michael, 92
splice( ) method, 482
split( ) method, 483
src attribute (embed), 200, 605, 620
stacking order
  elements, 383–385
  tables, 395
Stage (Flash), 614
standalone attribute, 94, 98
Standard Generalized Markup Language
    (see SGML)
Standards mode
  box model and, 337, 338, 342
  centering pages, 420
  DOCTYPE switching, 134, 135
  positioning and, 389
  specifying DTDs, 122
standards (see web standards)
standby attribute (object), 195
Staníček, Petr, 443
start attribute (ol), 158
start tags, 116
state, focus, 67, 265, 266, 442
statements
  conditional, 474–476
  JavaScript, 468
statistics, usage, 19–22, 35–36
status property (Browser Object), 486
status-bar keyword, 322
stereo channel configuration, 577, 580
Stern, Hadley, 522
streaming audio, 581–583, 593, 611
streaming video
  data rate and, 596
  defined, 595
  Flash and, 611
  HTML documents and, 603, 604
  QuickTime movies and, 599
stress property (CSS), 719, 720
Strict DTD
  description, 122
  DOCTYPE switching, 135
  frames and, 235
  options, 132, 133
  XHTML, 98, 99, 119, 120, 121
strike element, 161, 676
strike-throughs, 323
String object (JavaScript), 483
strings, 470
  (see also text)

column groups, 214–216
columns and, 210, 211, 214–216
CSS and, 10, 392–395
data, 206
descriptive elements, 211–213
display values, 403–405
inline, 393
layout, 206, 207, 226–231, 268
nesting, 226, 228
presentation, 216–220
row groups, 213, 214
rows and, 207–211
style sheets and, 337
styling, 396–397
WCAG, 61
width and height, 401–403
tabs, 118
tags
    Browser Wars, 5
    case sensitivity, 90
    closing, 116
    language, 81
    link relationships and, 745
    meaningful markup, 90
    opening, 116
    semantic descriptions, 90
    well-formed documents, 97
Tan Hack, 454
target attribute (a), 173, 242
Tasman layout engine, 15, 452
tbody element
    cell content alignment, 219
    overview, 214, 678, 679
td element
    cell content alignment, 219
    headers and, 212, 221
    headers attribute, 224, 225
    internal elements and, 393
    overview, 209, 210, 226, 679, 680
    padding property, 217
    rowspan attribute, 211, 230
    scope attribute, 224
Technorati search engine, 745, 746
television, 41
telnet:// protocol, 175
temporal compression, 597
ternary operator, 474
testing
    accessibility, 68–71
    Acid2 test, 457
    automated tools, 70

browsers, 25
loops and, 477
text
    aligning, 327–332
    anti-aliased, 527
    browsers and, 308–310
    browsers ignoring in comments, 119
    capitalization, 322, 323
    as data, 91
    deleted and inserted, 152, 153
    direction, 335, 336
    embedded, 558
    float property, 370
    generated content, 412, 413
    image replacement, 309, 436–440
    img element and, 181
    indented, 148
    line-height property, 325–327
    preformatted, 148
    printing, 632
    rollovers, 440
    scaling, 67
    spacing, 332–335
    styling tables, 396
    SVG standard and, 110
    type attribute (input), 251
    wrapping, 184, 185
text attribute (body), 143
text editors
    character encoding, 78
    HTML, 90, 126
    XHTML, 126
text elements
    character entity references, 167, 168
    deleted and inserted text, 152, 153
    generic elements, 153–156
    inline elements, 149–152
    listed, 144, 145
    lists and, 156–161
    overview, 146–149
    presentational elements, 161–166
    selecting, 145
text nodes
    depicted, 491
    DOM and, 490
    nodeType property and, 492
    whitespace and, 493
text-align property (CSS)
    browser bugs, 458
    cell content and, 220, 396
    centering pages, 420

text-align property (CSS) (*continued*)
overview, 710
text horizontal alignment, 328
text wrap and, 184
textarea element, 259, 680, 681
text/css style type, 279
text-decoration property
(CSS), 323–325, 710
text/ecmascript type, 467
text/html media type, 139
text-indent property (CSS), 327, 439,
710
text-transform property (CSS), 322,
323, 711
text/xml media type, 139
tfoot element, 214, 219, 681
th element
abbr attribute, 222
cell content alignment, 219
data tables and, 221, 222
id attribute, 225
internal elements and, 393
overview, 211, 212, 681
scope attribute, 223
thead element, 214, 219, 681
this keyword, 469, 481, 482
three-column layouts, 424–431
"three-pane environment", 591
TIFF format, 553, 554
tiling images, 359, 360, 364
Timeline (Flash), 614, 616, 622
title attribute
abbr/acronym elements, 151
del/ins elements, 153
form controls, 266
frame element, 245
hCalendar microformat, 744
overview, 641
title element, 130, 137, 682
toLowerCase( ) method, 483
Toolbox (Flash), 614
top keyword, 362
top property (CSS)
absolute positioning, 385
calculating position, 389
fixed positioning, 389
overview, 377, 711
relative positioning, 391
table captions, 395
_top target name, 243
toUpperCase( ) method, 483

tr element
cell content alignment, 219
headers and, 212
internal elements and, 393
number of rows and, 211
overview, 208, 210, 226, 682
trademark symbol, 167
transforming, 93
Transitional DTD
body attribute, 143
deprecated elements and, 145
description, 122
DOCTYPE switching, 135
frames and, 235
iframe element, 204
options, 133
XHTML, 119, 120
transparency
animated GIFs, 567
GIF format and, 516, 528, 534–536
JPEG format and, 544
PNG format and, 516, 554, 555–561
Trident layout engine, 15, 16, 454
true keyword, 470
Truecolor color depth
JPEG format and, 544
overview, 519
PNG format and, 552, 554
TrueDoc Dynamic fonts, 310
try...catch block, 498
tt element, 162, 682
tty media type, 283, 629
tv media type, 283, 629
two-column layouts, 421–424
type attribute
embed element, 606, 621
embedding JavaScript, 467
input element, 252–258
lists, 158
type selectors, 297, 298
typefaces (see fonts)
typography, 307–310
(see also fonts; text)

U

u element, 162, 683
UAAG (User Agent Accessibility
Guidelines), 60
UCS (Universal Character Set), 74
UDP (User Datagram Protocol), 582

ul element
  browser bugs, 455
  nesting, 160
  overview, 156, 683
  positioning and, 387
Ulead GIF Animator utility, 566, 569
underlines, 323, 324
underscore (_)
  attributes, 117
  browser bugs, 456
  naming conventions, 50
  reserved target names, 242
  variable names, 469
  XML names, 99
unicasting, 603
Unicode character set
  code points, 73
  markup and, 115
  Numeric Character Reference, 79
  overview, 74–75
  quotation marks, 415
  standards body, 4
  World Wide Web and, 73
  XML and, 92
Unicode Consortium, 4, 74
unicode-bidi property (CSS), 84, 336, 711
Uniform color palette, 532
units of measurement, 291, 316
Universal Character Set (UCS), 74
universal element selector (*)
  assigning color globally, 357
  centering pages, 420
  descendants and, 454
  getElementsByTagName( ) method, 492
  wildcards and, 298
Unix environment
  directory structure, 46–49
  Flash and, 612
  gamma settings, 523
  PNG format and, 559
  web palette, 522
unordered lists, 156–157, 387
unshift( ) method, 482
uppercase (see capitalization)
URLs
  absolute, 170, 410
  encoding and, 250
  forms and, 249
  property values and, 277
  query strings and, 250

slashes in, 44, 116, 250
  (see also relative URLs)
usage statistics, 19–22, 35–36
usemap attribute (img), 190
User Agent Accessibility Guidelines (UAAG), 60
user agent string, 19
user agents
  character encoding, 76
  row groups and, 214
  style sheets and, 285
  th element, 221
User Datagram Protocol (UDP), 582
user interfaces, WCAG, 62, 64
user testing, 70
UTF-16 encoding, 75, 77
UTF-32 encoding, 75
UTF-8 encoding, 75, 76, 77, 94

V

valid documents, 92, 94, 99
validating parsers, 93, 99
validation, 10, 11, 637
valign attribute, 219, 220
value attribute (input), 252, 257
values, 277, 291–293
var element, 150, 683
var keyword, 469
variable bit rate (VBR), 585
variables
  arithmetic operators and, 469, 472
  arrays and, 471
  global, 479
  JavaScript, 469
  local, 479
  scalar, 470
VBR (variable bit rate), 585
VBScript, 465
vector graphics
  bitmapped images and, 517
  Flash and, 609, 611
  XML documents and, 91, 110
version attribute, 94
vertical alignment
  cell content, 220
  img element and, 183
  inline box and, 327
  text, 329–332
vertical bar (|)
  attribute selector, 302
  as separator, 101

About the Author

Jennifer Niederst Robbins was one of the first web designers. As the designer of O'Reilly's Global Network Navigator (GNN), the first commercial web site, she has been designing for the Web since mid-1993. Soon thereafter, she became Creative Director of Songline Studios (a subsidiary of O'Reilly) and went on to form her own design and consulting company, Littlechair, Inc., in 1996. In addition to this Nutshell book, Jennifer writes and maintains *Learning Web Design* and *(X)HTML Pocket Reference*, both published by O'Reilly Media. She has taught courses on web design at the Massachusetts College of Art in Boston, MA, and at Johnson & Wales University in Providence, RI. She has been a regular on the speaker circuit, presenting at South by Southwest Interactive, AIGA events, Seybold Seminars, and the GRAFILL conference in Norway. Jennifer combines her passions for cooking, indie rock music, and making stuff in her project, The Jenville Show (a.k.a. "Cooking with Rockstars") available at *www.thejenvilleshow.com*. Her latest production is a son named Arlo, who doesn't leave her much time for all of the above. You can visit Jennifer online at *littlechair.com* and *jenville.com*.

Colophon

The animal on the cover of *Web Design in a Nutshell* is a least weasel (*Mustela nivalis*). There are 67 species of weasel, including the mink, ermine, ferret, otter, and skunk. Weasels, which are characterized by long, slender bodies and short legs, are found on all continents except Antarctica and Australia, and in a vast variety of habitats.

The least weasel is the smallest of the 67 species of weasel. Weighing in at approximately two ounces and measuring less than 10 inches long, the least weasel is the smallest carnivore on Earth. It is found throughout the world in northern climates. In warm weather this weasel's coat is brown, with a white underside. In winter it turns completely white. Thanks to its camouflage abilities and its speed and agility, the least weasel is rarely caught.

The diet of the least weasel is made up primarily of voles and mice, which, because of the weasels' high metabolism, they hunt constantly. One family of these little weasels can consume thousands of rodents each year, making them important in controlling pest populations. Because it is so small, the least weasel can follow mice into their burrows and eat them there. Like other weasels, they will occasionally then make their victim's home their own, lining it with the fur of the former resident when preparing to nest. Least weasels can produce two litters a year, with three to five young per litter.

The cover image is an original illustration by Lorrie LeJeune. The cover font is Adobe ITC Garamond. The text font is Linotype Birka; the heading font is Adobe Myriad Condensed; and the code font is LucasFont's TheSans Mono Condensed.

Better than e-books

Buy *Web Design in a Nutshell*, 3rd Edition
and access the digital edition FREE on
Safari for 45 days.

Go to www.oreilly.com/go/safarienabled
and type in coupon code K1CW-J4RD-RI4Y-TMDX-1TW3

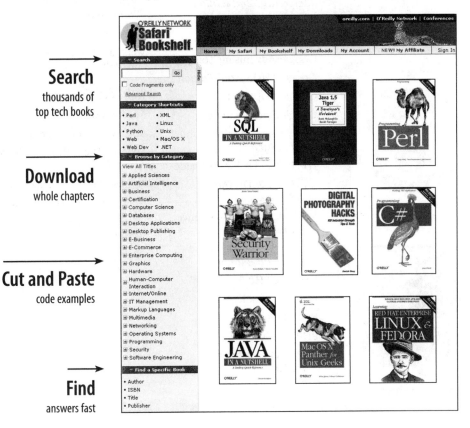

Related Titles from O'Reilly

Web Programming

ActionScript Cookbook

ActionScript for Flash MX: The Definitive Guide, *2nd Edition*

Ajax Hacks

Dynamic HTML: The Definitive Reference, *2nd Edition*

Flash Hacks

Essential PHP Security

Google Advertising Tools

Google Hacks, *2nd Edition*

Google Map Hacks

Google Pocket Guide

Google: The Missing Manual, *2nd Edition*

HTTP: The Definitive Guide

JavaScript & DHTML Cookbook

JavaScript Pocket Reference, *2nd Edition*

JavaScript: The Definitive Guide, *4th Edition*

Learning PHP 5

PHP Cookbook

PHP Hacks

PHP in a Nutshell

PHP Pocket Reference, *2nd Edition*

PHPUnit Pocket Guide

Programming ColdFusion **MX**, *2nd Edition*

Programming PHP

Upgrading to PHP 5

Web Database Applications with PHP and MySQL, *2nd Edition*

Web Site Cookbook

Webmaster in a Nutshell, *3rd Edition*

Web Administration

Apache Cookbook

Apache Pocket Reference

Apache: The Definitive Guide, *3rd Edition*

Perl for Web Site Management

Squid: The Definitive Guide

Web Performance Tuning, *2nd Edition*

O'REILLY®

Our books are available at most retail and online bookstores.

To order direct: 1-800-**998-9938** · *order@oreilly.com* · *www.oreilly.com*

Online editions of most **O'Reilly** titles are available by subscription at *safari.oreilly.com*